MANUAL ON INTERNATIONAL COURTS
AND TRIBUNALS

MANUAL ON INTERNATIONAL COURTS AND TRIBUNALS

Authors

RUTH MACKENZIE
Senior Lecturer in International Law, University of Westminster, London

CESARE P.R. ROMANO
Professor of Law, Loyola Law School, Los Angeles

YUVAL SHANY
Hersch Lauterpacht Chair in Public International Law, Hebrew University, Jerusalem

With

PHILIPPE SANDS
Professor of Law and Director of the Centre on International Courts and Tribunals, Faculty of Laws, University College London

OXFORD
UNIVERSITY PRESS

OXFORD
UNIVERSITY PRESS

Great Clarendon Street, Oxford, OX2 6DP,
United Kingdom

Oxford University Press is a department of the University of Oxford.
It furthers the University's objective of excellence in research, scholarship,
and education by publishing worldwide. Oxford is a registered trade mark of
Oxford University Press in the UK and in certain other countries

Published in the United States of America by Oxford University Press
198 Madison Avenue, New York, NY 10016, United States of America

British Library Cataloguing in Publication Data
Data available

Library of Congress Cataloging in Publication Data
Data available

ISBN 978-0-19-954527-8

CONTENTS

V HUMAN RIGHTS BODIES

VI INSPECTION, REVIEW, AND COMPLIANCE MECHANISMS IN INTERNATIONAL FINANCIAL INSTITUTIONS

VII COMPLIANCE PROCEDURES IN MULTILATERAL ENVIRONMENTAL AGREEMENTS

THE PROJECT ON INTERNATIONAL COURTS AND TRIBUNALS (PICT)

The Project on International Courts and Tribunals (PICT) addresses challenges and opportunities created by the growing number and role of international courts and tribunals and other dispute settlement bodies that has taken place since the early 1990s.

PICT was jointly established in 1997 by the Center on International Cooperation (CIC), at New York University, and the Foundation for International Environmental Law and Development (FIELD), at the School of Oriental and African Studies, University of London. Since the early years, PICT has undergone several changes. In 2002, the London home of PICT moved to University College London with the establishment at the Faculty of Laws of the Centre for International Courts and Tribunals. In 2007, PICT was transformed from a joint undertaking of two institutions to an ongoing project, a research agenda, and a set of related activities carried out by a network of institutions and individuals.

PICT's activities include research and policy dialogue, in particular through the organization of international conferences and symposia. For example, one current PICT project addresses the Impact of International Criminal Procedures on Domestic Criminal Procedures in Mass Atrocity Cases (DOMAC).[1] Another is examining the Process and Legitimacy in the Nomination, Election, and Appointment of International Judges.[2] A third is, in cooperation with the International Law Association, developing guidelines and principles on the conduct of counsel, advocates, and others appearing before international courts and tribunals, to supplement the Burgh House Principles on the Independence of the International Judiciary.[3] And a fourth project looks at the effectiveness of international courts.[4] The outcomes of research projects, symposia, and other activities are disseminated through various means, including PICT's website (<http://www.pict-pcti.org>), a dedicated series by Oxford University Press on

---

[1] <http://www.domac.is>.
[2] <http://www.ucl.ac.uk/laws/cict/index.shtml?judicial-selection>.
[3] <http://www.ucl.ac.uk/laws/cict/docs/burgh_final_21204.pdf>.
[4] <http://www.effective-intl-adjudication.org/>.

international courts and tribunals,[5] and a number of different law journals.[6] PICT couples academic research with concrete action aimed at facilitating the work of international courts and tribunals, and at developing the legal and policy skills of those involved in the life of international courts and tribunals. For instance, PICT's activities include also teaching and training on the law and procedure on international courts and tribunals.

PICT has four Directors, located at four different institutions: Ruth Mackenzie, of the University of Westminster and the Centre for International Courts and Tribunals; Cesare Romano, at Loyola Law School Los Angeles; Thordis Ingadottir, at Reykjavík University, and Yuval Shany, at Hebrew University. They work with PICT's Chairman, Philippe Sands, and a Steering Committee, comprising seventeen distinguished international legal scholars, practitioners, and judges that oversee PICT as a whole.

PICT's agenda is developed by the Directors with the support of the Chairman, in consultation with and endorsement by the Steering Committee. Each PICT Director works independently or together with other Directors or other researchers around the world, as opportunities arise, on a part of the overall research agenda.

The work undertaken by PICT has generated considerable interest, not only among academics, practitioners, governments, and international and non-governmental organizations, but also among the judges and secretariats of the various international courts and tribunals themselves. Each of these groups has been actively engaged and represented in work undertaken by PICT. PICT has contributed to the growing role of international courts and tribunals, in particular by generating greater public awareness on key issues. It has emerged as a primary source of information on the activities of international judicial bodies, and it has laid down the basis for the creation of a permanent forum for communication and learning between international courts and tribunals.

For further information on PICT, visit our website <http://www.pict-pcti.org> or contact one of the co-Directors.

---

[5] Y Shany, *The Competing Jurisdictions of International Courts and Tribunals* (2003); C P R Romano, A Nollkaemper, and J Kleffner (eds), *Internationalized Criminal Courts and Tribunals: Sierra Leone, East Timor, Kosovo, and Cambodia* (2004); C Schulte, *Compliance with Decisions of the International Court of Justice* (2004); S Rosenne, *Provisional Measures in International Courts and Tribunals* (2005); C Brown, *A Common Law of International Adjudication* (2007); D Terris, C Romano, and L Swigart, *The International Judge: An Introduction to the Men and Women who Decide the World's Cases* (2007) (published in the US by UPNE); Y Shany, *Regulating Jurisdictional Relations between National and International Courts* (2007); J Kleffner, *The Principle of Complementarity in the ICC Statute* (2008); L Bartels, *Applicable Law before International Courts and Tribunals* (2010).

[6] Other noteworthy recent PICT publications include C P R Romano (ed), *The Sword and the Scales: The United States and International Courts and Tribunals* (2009), and the special symposium issue of the Loyola of Los Angeles International and Comparative Law Review containing papers presented at PICT's 10th anniversary symposium 'International Courts and Tribunals in the 21st Century: The Future of International Justice'.

INTRODUCTION AND ACKNOWLEDGEMENTS

By Philippe Sands

Introduction

On 29 July 1899, a select group of 28 states adopted a Convention for the Pacific Settlement of International Disputes. By this Convention they undertook 'to use their best efforts to ensure the pacific settlement of international differences' and to organize a Permanent Court of Arbitration (PCA).[1] Although the PCA was neither permanent nor a court, its creation constituted a landmark decision to establish the world's first standing body charged with adjudicating international disputes. In embryonic form, it was the forerunner to the Permanent Court of International Justice and its successor, the International Court of Justice. The 1899 Convention marked a turning point in favour of international adjudication before standing bodies. In the intervening century an almost bewildering array of international courts, tribunals, and other adjudicatory bodies have been established providing fora for the pursuit of international claims. Such courts include a number of international criminal courts (the most notable of which is the International Criminal Court (ICC)),[2] a panoply of human rights committees, commissions, and courts established to receive claims from states and individuals alleging violations of human rights norms. Other mechanisms which have been put in place allow foreign investors to bring arbitral claims against 'expropriating' states or permit aggrieved persons to challenge lending decisions of multilateral development banks; special arrangements to address disputes over trade matters and in respect of maritime issues; and a large number of courts created within the context of regional economic and free trade arrangements to address a wide range of matters touching upon economic integration.

The transformation over the past two decades in particular has been a remarkable one. Alongside international organizations legislating standards there now exists an international 'judiciary', the powers of which seem to be ever more

---

[1] Convention for the Pacific Settlement of International Disputes, 29 July 1899, UKTS 9 (1901), Cd 798, arts 1 and 20; see *infra* at Chapter 4.

[2] See Rome Statute of the International Criminal Court, 17 July 1998, 2187 UNTS 90.

extensive and, consequentially, intrusive upon areas previously thought to lie exclusively within national sovereignty. It is a judiciary that increasingly relates to or impinges upon proceedings in domestic courts and to which litigants can turn in their efforts to assert rights and enforce obligations. Indeed, in many countries international litigation—that is to say litigation before international courts—is often front-page news. At the time of writing, issues before international courts include the legality of Kosovo's declaration of independence, allegations of ethnic cleansing in the Georgia–Russia conflict, an increasing number of WTO cases involving China, an ever-growing number of investment disputes before ICSID, and so on. National courts, too, are frequently presented with issues raised by decisions of international courts. This is evidenced in the most dramatic terms by the various proceedings before the House of Lords to consider whether Senator Pinochet should be extradited to Spain for acts carried out in Chile in the 1970s, and before the US Supreme Court concerning the effect of ICJ decisions on the execution of Mexican nationals held in the US. These and other proceedings have raised most starkly the question of the proper relationship between national courts and the International Criminal Court, and the principle of 'complementarity' that governs their relations. Relatedly, many international courts and tribunals refer to each other's judgments, creating a degree of cross-fertilization between courts, as well as occasional conflicts. On occasion, one tribunal may even defer to another in an expression of international judicial or arbitral comity, as happened in the *MOX Plant* case,[3] and there is increasing opportunity for litigants to choose between different fora.

In short, there has been a sharp increase in the number of international adjudicatory bodies, a greater willingness to resort to them, and a rise in the range of legal and procedural issues that arise. Nevertheless, despite the fact that most judicial bodies have been operating for more than a decade, knowledge about them—where they are, what they are, who sits on them, what they can do, how they relate to national proceedings—still remains limited even in well-informed legal circles. Many academics and practitioners in the field of international law are familiar with selected bodies, but few are informed about the range of international judicial and quasi-judicial bodies now available. And at the national level knowledge is opaque. In that sense, international courts—and their practice—remain a somewhat exotic subject, and perhaps more marginal than it should be. The main purpose of this Manual is to fill a gap by making information on a wide range of these international bodies more easily available.

It is appropriate to note that the development of international adjudication occurred in four phases. Prior to the establishment of the PCA, international disputes were adjudicated almost exclusively between states alone and before ad hoc

---

[3] *MOX Plant* (Ireland v UK), 42 ILM 1187 (2003).

bodies often established to deal with a particular dispute, although there were some exceptions to that arrangement. The decision in 1899 to organize the PCA marked a turning point and an entry into a second phase, with the recognition of the need to establish a standing body. A third phase began in the 1940s and 1950s with the establishment of the ICJ, the ECJ, and the European Commission and Court of Human Rights. This phase lasted up to the early 1980s, and encompassed also the establishment of the International Centre for the Settlement of Investment Disputes. The fourth phase begun with the creation of the International Tribunal for the Law of the Sea: this phase is characterized by compulsory jurisdiction and binding decision-making powers, as is now also reflected in the provisions of the WTO's Dispute Settlement Understanding (DSU).

What is clear is that by the early 1980s there were already in place a growing number of international adjudicatory bodies with permanent status. This reflected a movement away from the ad hoc arrangements which had dominated until the early years of this century,[4] and a trend towards 'judicialization' and recourse to third party adjudication. Far from comprehensive in their coverage these bodies nevertheless provided fora for international litigation, on general or specific matters, at the regional and global levels. Some had compulsory jurisdictions, others did not. At the global level the principal institutions were the PCA and the ICJ (established in 1945), both located in The Hague. In the field of human rights, regional courts or commissions had been established for Europe, the Americas, and Africa, and the UN Human Rights Committee fulfilled a more limited (or less judicial) function at the global level. In the international economic field, the panel system of the General Agreement on Tariffs and Trade (GATT) was dealing with a growing number of cases and attracting increased support, and the European Court of Justice in Luxembourg had established itself as an international tribunal with broad competence. At various international organizations—the World Bank, the ILO, the UN, and the OECD—administrative tribunals had been established to address employment disputes between the organizations and their employees.[5] Public and private arbitration mechanisms were made available for the resolution of foreign investment disputes between states and non-state actors respectively, particularly within the framework of the International Centre for Settlement of Investment Disputes (ICSID) and the International Chamber of Commerce, as well as by other arrangements, including ad hoc arbitration.[6] By the 1980s the network of

---

[4] P Sands and P Klein, *Bowett's Law of International Institutions* (6th edn, 2009).

[5] See eg C F Amerasinghe, *The Law of the International Civil Service* (2nd rev edn, 1994); K Papanikolaou (ed), *International Administrative Tribunals in a Changing World* (2008).

[6] See eg W L Craig, W W Park, and J Paulsson, *International Chamber of Commerce Arbitration* (3rd edn 2000); H M Holtzmann and E Kristjandottir (eds), *International Mass Claims Processes: Legal and Practical Perspectives* (2007).

institutions was already extensive, even if it was not comprehensive in terms of the jurisdiction it established, either in relation to the subject matters which could be addressed, or the persons entitled to bring (or defend) claims. Nevertheless, the network reflected a growing willingness of states to accept the role of adjudication in international political relations.[7] This trend is even more apparent if one takes into consideration the various ad hoc arrangements created to deal with particular situations (eg the Iran-US Claims Tribunal and the subsequent UN Compensation Commission).

Since the early 1980s many new international bodies have been created which present new opportunities for international litigation. Although the number may not seem significant in itself, it becomes so if one considers it on a relative basis by reference to what previously existed. The new developments have several features that distinguish them from the earlier arrangements, suggesting that international litigation is now in a new, fifth, phase. First, they reflect a trend in favour of compulsory jurisdiction for discrete areas of international law, such as the law of the sea and international trade law. Second, they point to the emergence of new types of 'non-contentious' proceedings designed to contribute towards greater compliance with specific treaty obligations, and to assist in the prevention of escalation of disputes an approach now reflected in multilateral agreements addressing a range of environmental issues.[8] Third, they reflect the growing role of individuals or groups of individuals, either as potential 'plaintiffs' or 'defendants', in cases involving states or international organizations. Examples of the latter include the Inspection Panels established by the World Bank and other multilateral development banks, and the International Criminal Tribunals for the former Yugoslavia and for Rwanda. And fourth, they present new opportunities for private lawyers to promote the interests of their clients—whether governmental or not—and become involved in international practice. These developments are amplified, particularly in the criminal field, by the emergence of mixed (or hybrid) courts which apply national and

---

[7] States may also become involved in arbitration with international organizations. For example, the General Conditions used for loan documentation by the IBRD and IDA provide that disputes which have not been settled amicably are to be submitted to binding ad hoc arbitration. However, as yet these provisions have not been used. See M Augenblick and D A Ridgway, 'Dispute Resolution in International Financial Institutions' (1993) 10 *Journal of International Arbitration* 73 at 74–5.

[8] On this trend, see M Koskenniemi, 'Breach of Treaty or Non-Compliance? Reflections on the Enforcement of the Montreal Protocol' (1992) 3 *Yearbook of International Environmental Law* 123; P Szell, 'The Development of Multilateral Mechanisms for Monitoring Compliance', in W Lang (ed), *Sustainable Development and International Law* (1995); M Ehrmann, 'Procedures of Compliance Control in International Environmental Treaties' (2002) 13 *Colo J Int'l Envtl L & Pol'y* 377; T Treves et al (eds), *Non-compliance Procedures and Mechanisms and the Effectiveness of International Environmental Agreements* (2009).

international norms, and which acknowledge the diminishing gap between national and international legal systems. Another notable development has been the gradual expansion upon the jurisdiction of specialized courts into areas of general international law—examples of this can be seen in the judgments of the ECJ on the effect of UN Security Council resolutions or the UN Convention on the Law of the Sea,[9] and the creation of the African Court of Justice and Human Rights which will meld economic and human rights matters into a single jurisdiction.[10]

The trend towards compulsory jurisdiction

Recent developments suggest a trend towards the establishment of dispute settlement arrangements having compulsory mandatory jurisdiction and binding decision-making powers, within particular treaty regimes.[11] This is most evident in the arrangements established under the 1982 UN Convention on the Law of the Sea and the 1994 World Trade Organization Dispute Settlement Understanding. It is also reflected in the non-compliance mechanism created in multilateral environmental agreements. Other developments reflecting this trend include the Inspection Panels established by the World Bank and other regional development banks, the International Criminal Tribunals for the former Yugoslavia and for Rwanda, and the International Criminal Court (the jurisdictional provisions of which cause concern to certain states).

The emergence of compulsory non-contentious proceedings

In some new areas of international law, states have been unwilling to introduce compulsory judicial or arbitral procedures, or even conciliation. The question of non-compliance with environmental agreements has received increased attention, and resulted in the creation of new approaches designed to enhance compliance with treaty obligations using non-contentious, non-judicial mechanisms. The non-compliance procedure established in 1990 under the 1987 Montreal

---

[9] See eg Joined Cases C-402/05P & C-415/05P, *Kadi v Council*, ECJ Judgment of 3 September 2008; Case C84/95, *Bosphorous Hava Yollari Turizm ve Ticaret AS v Minister for Transport, Energy and Communications, Ireland* [1996] ECR I-3953; Case C-124/95, *The Queen, ex parte Centro-Com Srl v HM Treasury and Bank of England* [1997] ECR I-81; Case C-177/95, *Ebony Maritime SA and Loten Navigation Co. Ltd v Prefetto della Provincia di Brindisi and others*, 1997 ECR I-1111; CFI Case T-184/95, *Dorsch Consult Ingenieurgesellschaft mbH v Council* of the *European Union*, 1998 ECR II-667; and Case C-308/06, *The Queen on the application of Intertanko and Others v Secretary of State for Transport*, ECJ Judgment of 3 June 2008.

[10] See *infra* Chapter 13.

[11] C Romano, 'The Shift from the Consensual to the Compulsory Paradigm in International Adjudication: Elements for a Theory of Consent' (2007) 39 *NYU J Int'l L P* 791.

Protocol on Substances that Deplete the Ozone Layer[12] was the first of its kind, and has been followed in the context of other environmental agreements.[13]

The increasing role of non-state actors

International adjudication is no longer a matter over which states have a monopoly, as is reflected by the steadily increasing number of international courts, tribunals, and other bodies being made available for use by individuals, associations, and corporations, as well as international organizations. A further factor acknowledging the strengthening role of non-state actors is the increase in international litigation that has occurred since the first edition of this Manual was published a decade ago. It is worth noting that the role of the private, non-state actor—whether as lawyer or litigant—is not without its controversial elements. A traditional approach to international law posits that it is a domain within which states have an exclusive competence, and that the system of international dispute settlement has a strong intergovernmental focus. The nature of the issues posed by the conflict between a traditional approach and more modern tendencies was highlighted in the context of the World Trade Organization, when St Lucia (an intervening third party in the proceedings) sought to participate in panel proceedings with the assistance of two lawyers from private law firms. Other WTO members objected, with the result that the private lawyers were prevented from participating by decision of the panel. The same point was taken in proceedings on appeal to the Appellate Body, where there was a similar objection made. The Appellate Body accepted that under customary international law states were generally entitled to choose whoever they wished to represent them. It found that there were no provisions in the Marrakech Agreement Establishing the World Trade Organization (the 'WTO Agreement'), in the Dispute Settlement Understanding or in the Working Procedures that specified who could represent a government in making its representations in an oral hearing of the Appellate Body. It noted that

> representation by counsel of a government's own choice may well be a matter of particular significance—especially for developing-country Members—to enable them to participate fully in dispute settlement proceedings. Moreover, given the Appellate Body's mandate to review only issues of law or legal interpretation in panel reports, it is particularly important that governments be represented by qualified counsel in Appellate Body proceedings.[14]

---

[12] *Montreal Protocol on Substances that Deplete the Ozone Layer*, 16 September 1987, in force 1 January 1989, 26 ILM (1987) 154.

[13] See *infra* Chapter 19.

[14] WTO Appellate Body Report, *European Communities—Regime for the Importation, Sale and Distribution of Bananas*, WT/DS27/AB/R, 9 September 1997, at paras 11 and 12.

Subsequent WTO panels have also allowed private lawyers to participate in proceedings, marking a change in what seems to have been the last vestige of governmental monopoly in legal practice. This has been followed by increased resort to *amicus curiae* interventions—for example in the foreign investment field—and the expansion of individual complaints mechanisms reflected in new protocols to UN human rights treaties such as CEDAW and the ICESCR.[15]

More international litigation

Of continuing notice is the almost universal increase in the number of cases being brought before the various international adjudicative bodies.[16] The ICJ appears to be busier than it has ever been, pushing through cases in a speedier and more efficient manner than was previously ever the case. ICSID continues to see a significant increase in the number of cases being filed, building on developments of the 1990s. The volume of cases led to the establishment of a Court of First Instance at the ECJ. The WTO Dispute Settlement Understanding has, in its 15 years of existence, received far more cases than in the 45-year existence of the GATT. Further, there is no indication that this trend is likely to change. The factors which contribute to international litigation—more rules, more actors, more bodies, the sense that international litigation is increasingly the norm rather than the exception, changing perceptions about the function of international adjudication, etc—all appear to be now well established. Further, and with the increased acceptance of international litigation, some major interconnected issues have been engendered. The ECHR, for example, has been increasingly overwhelmed with individual applications, which means that whilst it meets exceptionally high quotas in terms of applications dealt with per year, it will nevertheless remain hard pressed (at least in its current format) in terms of meeting public expectations.

Policy issues

The increase in the number of international courts and tribunals raises a host of policy issues. The birth of many of these new bodies has not occurred in the context of a considered structure of the function of international adjudication. Little, if any, thought has been given to the relationship between the international bodies themselves, although this subject is now receiving increased attention. The subject of *litis pendens,* for example, had barely been considered in relation to these bodies before the late 1990s.[17] Appreciation of international

---

[15] See *infra* at Part V.

[16] P Sands, 'Enhancing Participation in International Litigation' (1998) 24 *Commonwealth Law Bulletin* 540 at 548–550.

[17] See generally Y Shany, *The Competing Jurisdictions of International Courts and Tribunals* (2003).

decisions at the national level varies widely from jurisdiction to jurisdiction. In this regard, it is instructive to compare the approach of the US Supreme Court in the *Breard* and *LaGrand* cases[18] with that of the Privy Council of the House of Lords in *Thomas and Hilaire*.[19] The appointment of international judges remains an ad hoc matter, and the whole question of a truly international bar—including characteristics which we expect our international lawyers to display—has received remarkably little consideration.[20]

The great increase in the number of international courts and tribunals poses many issues, a factor which is reflected in a growing literature.[21] However, the literature has tended to focus on specific fora or on specific disputes, and is mostly concerned with procedural or substantive aspects. It is difficult to identify literature dealing with general trends in international litigation.[22] Even a manual summarizing the information on available international fora, which is up to date, comprehensive, and easily accessible on the number and types of cases, as well as the participation of different categories of states, appears not to be available (although the internet is certainly making matters easier).

The Manual

It is in the context of these developments and issues that the Project on International Courts and Tribunals has prepared this revised version of the Manual originally published in 1999, inspired in part by the most useful *Handbook of the United Nations* published annually by the Government of New Zealand. This Introduction indicates the extent to which the number of fora available for international litigation has increased, particularly in recent years. Whether or not this reflects a 'genuine "renaissance" of international justice',[23] it points to

---

[18] *Breard v Greene* (1998) 523 US 371; *Fed. Republic of Germany v United States*, (1999) 526 US 111. A sceptical view towards ICJ proceedings was also taken by the US Supreme Court in *Medellin v Texas* (2008) 128 S Ct 1346 and *Sanchez-Llamas v Oregon* (2006) 548 US 331.

[19] Privy Council Appeal No 60 of 1998, *Thomas and Hilaire v Baptiste*, judgment of 27 January 1998 (delivered on 17 March 1998).

[20] But see D Terris, C Romano, and L Swigart, *The International Judge: An Introduction to the Men and Women who Decide the World's Cases* (2007).

[21] For example, see the Oxford University Press International Courts and Tribunals Series featuring C Romano, A Nollkaemper, and J Kleffner (eds), *Internationalized Criminal Courts: Sierra Leone, East Timor, Kosovo, and Cambodia* (2004); S Rosenne, *Provisional Measures in International Law: The International Court of Justice and the International Tribunal for the Law of the Sea* (2004); C Schulte, *Compliance with Decisions of the International Court of Justice* (2004); Y Shany, *The Competing Jurisdictions of International Courts and Tribunals* (2003); C Brown, *A Common Law of International Adjudication* (2007); Y Shany, *Regulating Jurisdictional Relations between National and International Courts* (2007); J Kleffner, *Complementarity in the Rome Stature and National Criminal Jurisdictions* (2008).

[22] Some exceptions can be found however. See eg K Alter, *The New Terrain of International Law: International Courts in International Politics* (forthcoming).

[23] See G Guillaume, 'The Future of International Judicial Institutions' (1995) 44 *British Institute of Comparative Law Quarterly* 848.

conditions in which international litigation will proliferate. States, including developing countries and economies in transition, as well as other actors, are already finding themselves increasingly involved as litigants (whether as applicant/plaintiff, respondent/defendant, or intervenor) in disputes between states, between states and non-state actors, or in proceedings involving international organizations. Despite the general increase in international litigation it is also clear that a great many people, including academics, journalists, practitioners, and legal advisers, have little knowledge about many of these bodies: What are they? Where are they? What are their powers? Who sits on them? Who may initiate proceedings before them? Surprisingly, no single text provides in a readily accessible format the answers to these basic questions. It is therefore the purpose of this Manual to provide an updated reference guide to the principal international courts and tribunals that are now active.

In preparing the first edition of the Manual, the Project on International Courts and Tribunals was conscious of the need to provide a reliable source of basic information on the principal bodies—both global and regional. In deciding which bodies to include, and the degree of detail to enter into, we considered the activities of the bodies—past and present—and the amount of information a user might need to have. In deciding what material to include, it was considered appropriate to place oneself in the position of a potential user of the body, or someone who wanted to obtain the most basic information on the various bodies. In that regard, we have been especially conscious of the need to ensure that potential users who are most disadvantaged—developing states and non-state actors—are able to gain access to basic information. In relation to the principal bodies the manual therefore seeks to address the most commonly asked questions:

- What are the principal international courts and tribunals, where are they located, and how can they be contacted?
- What issues do they address?
- What rules and instruments govern their activities (constituent instrument, Statutes, Rules of Procedure, Regulations, etc), and where can you find them?
- How are they organized and who are the judges?
- What is their contentious or advisory jurisdiction, in terms of persons, subject matter, and time?
- How do you institute proceedings, and what procedures govern their activities?
- Can they order provisional or interim measures (injunctions, etc), and if so are they binding?
- How are written pleadings organized and oral arguments presented, and who is entitled to appear?

- Can you intervene as a third party?
- What powers do they have to take binding decisions and impose remedial measures?
- Are there any grounds of appeal?
- What are the likely costs of proceedings, and is financial assistance available?
- How can judgments or decisions be executed, including in the national courts?
- Where can more information be found, including reports of judgments, awards, and decisions?

Each chapter is arranged with subheadings to address these issues, together with footnote references to relevant instruments, indicative court decisions, and a selected bibliography. The Manual does not strive to be comprehensive. Certain bodies have not been addressed, either because they have fallen into desuetude, or because they were established but in practice have never become operational. Many new bodies have been established, as predicted in the first edition, including an individual complaints procedure in respect of the Convention on Elimination of Discrimination against Women[24] and a whole raft of hybrid criminal courts.[25] Nor is the Manual intended to replace the specialist texts which provide the indispensable detail which the litigator is bound to rely upon, texts such as Rosenne's *The Law and Practice of the International Court*,[26] Lasok's *The European Court of Justice: Practice and Procedure*,[27] Zimmermann's commentary on the Statute of the International Court of Justice,[28] Schabas's *The UN International Criminal Tribunals: The Former Yugoslavia, Rwanda and Sierra Leone*,[29] and Schreuer's ICSID commentary.[30] We welcome comments from readers on any errors that may have crept in, or suggestions as to other improvements that might be made in future editions.

Acknowledgements

The second edition of the Manual is the result of an extensive team effort, involving many individuals with busy schedules. We have received constant

---

[24] Optional Protocol to the Convention on the Elimination of All Forms of Discrimination against Women, 6 October 1999, art 2, GA Res 54/4, annex, 54 UN GAOR Supp (No 49) at 5, UN Doc A/54/49 (Vol I) (2000).

[25] See *infra* Chapter 8.

[26] S Rosenne, *The Law and Practice of the International Court, 1920–2005* (4th edn, 2006).

[27] K P E Lasok, *The European Court of Justice: Practice and Procedure* (2nd edn 1994).

[28] A Zimmerman, *The Statute of the International Court of Justice: A Commentary* (2006).

[29] W Schabas, *The UN International Criminal Tribunals: The Former Yugoslavia, Rwanda and Sierra Leone* (2006).

[30] C Schreuer, L Malintoppi, A Reinisch, and A Sinclair, *The ICSID Convention: A Commentary* (2nd edn 2009).

guidance and support from the members of the PICT Steering Committee. In relation to the individual chapters, we have received significant support and assistance from the following individuals, for which we are extremely grateful: Judge Bruno Simma of the ICJ, Judge Tullio Treves of the ITLOS, Mr Philippe Gautier of the ITLOS Registry, Mr Kaarlo Castren of the WTO Secretariat, Prof Joost Pauwelyn of the Graduate Institute of International and Development Studies, Mr Antonio Parra of the International Council for Commercial Arbitration, Judge Christine Van den Wyngaert of the ICC and Ms Olivia Swaak-Goldman of the ICC's Office of the Prosecutor, Judge Fausto Pocar and Ms Valeria Bolici of the ICTY, Judge Eric Møse of the ICTR, Mr Gregory Townsend of the Special Court for Sierra Leone, Mr Guido Acquaviva of the Special Tribunal for Lebanon, Dr Craig Etcheson of the Office of the Prosecutor of the Extraordinary Chambers in the Courts of Cambodia, Judge Alan Rosas of the ECJ, Judge Carl Baudenbacher of the EFTA Court, Judge Jacob Wit and Ms Radha Permanand of the Caribbean Court of Justice, Judge Jorge Ricardo Vigil Toledo and Ms Maria Angela Sasaki of the Andean Tribunal of Justice, Dr Alena F Douhan of Belarusian State University, Judge Nina Vajic of the ECtHR, Prof Monica Pinto of the University of Buenos Aires, Prof Frans Viljoen of the University of Pretoria, Judge Fatsah Ouguergouz of the African HR Court, Sir Nigel Rodley of the Human Rights Committee, Prof David Kretzmer of the Hebrew University (and formerly with the Human Rights Committee), Dr Markus Schmidt of the Office of the High Commissioner for Human Rights, Mr Thomas Mensah, former president of the ITLOS, Mr Brooks Daly and Ms Judith Levine of the Permanent Court of Arbitration, and Prof Laurence Boisson de Chazournes of the University of Geneva. All of the said individuals cooperated with the research process leading to the conclusion of this edition of the Manual in their personal, not institutional, capacity. Of course, responsibility for any mistakes or omissions in the Manual rests solely with the authors.

Thanks are also due to the very diligent research assistants who have helped the authors throughout the last two years in working on the Manual—Ms Natalie Rosen, Ms Erin Gray, Mr Eran Sthoeger, and Mr Evgeni Zagrebelny (who have all assisted Yuval Shany), Ms Melissa Keaney, Ms Jessica Kirshbraun, Ms Yuri Guardado, Ms Reema Radwan, Ms Mariya Furman, Ms Sri Panchalam, and Ms Jenna Gilbert (who have all assisted Cesare Romano), and Mr Gauthier Vannieuwenhuyse, Ms Sonalini Gunasekera, Mr Aleksandr Popov, and Ms Lemonia Tsaroucha (who have all assisted Ruth Mackenzie). Finally, we thank Kate Barber and Kimberlee Moran, administrators of the Centre for International Courts and Tribunals at University College London, for their wonderful assistance.

It is also appropriate to restate our thanks to all those who assisted in the preparation of the first edition of the Manual back in 1999. I can do no better than to reproduce parts of the original acknowledgements. In preparing the first edition, we received constant guidance and support from members of the PICT Steering Committee. In relation to the individual chapters, we received significant support and assistance from the following individuals, for which we remain extremely grateful: Mr Eduardo Valencia Ospina (in relation to the ICJ); Ambassador Hans Jonkman and Ms Bette Shifman (in relation to the PCA); Mr Gritakumar Chitty and Mr David Browne (in relation to the ITLOS); Ms Christa Allott and Prof Lucius Caflisch (in relation to the OSCE Court of Conciliation and Arbitration); Mr Jacob Werksman (in relation to the WTO dispute settlement system and the Implementation Committee of the Montreal Protocol); Ms Margrete Stevens and Mr Antonio Parra (in relation to ICSID); Mr Fabien Gélinas (in relation to the International Court of Arbitration of the International Chamber of Commerce); Mr Tom Kennedy and Mr Maurice Sheridan (in relation to the ECJ); Ms Diana Torrens (in relation to the EFTA Court); Ms Norma Allegra Cerrato (in relation to the Central American Court of Justice); Dr Mahnoush Arsanjani (in relation to the ICC); Mr Jon Cina (in relation to the ICTY); Mr Gregory Townsend (in relation to the ICTR); Prof Laurence Boisson de Chazournes (in relation to the inspection mechanisms of the World Bank, IDB and ADB); Mr Marc Paquin and Mr David Markell (in relation to NAFTA); Ms Leyla Kayacik-Tirmangil (in relation to the European Social Charter); and Ms Veronica Gomez (in relation to the IACHR). In relation to the chapters on the human rights bodies in the first edition, we are particularly grateful to Ms Natalia Schiffrin and her colleagues at Interights, Anselm Chidi Odinkalu, Ibrahima Kane, Sara Hossain and Borislav Petranov, and also to Ms Kelli Loftman, Mr Jeremy McBride and Ms Laura Cox, QC for taking responsibility for the final review. We also received great assistance from colleagues at the Foundation for International Environmental Law and Development, where Margaret Enstone and Ms Louise Rands Silva diligently contributed to the administrative and secretarial aspects with their usual huge commitment and attention to detail, and Jacob Werksman and Erasmo Lara Cabrera similarly contributed to the legal content. We had input from a number of interns, including, in particular, Gabor Baranyai, Kristina Leggett, Tom Tadoc, Charlotte Salpin and Silvia Francescon. From the New York University side of our Project (the Centre for International Cooperation), Shepard Forman provided his characteristic intellectual and strategic support, with the attendant enthusiasm which we have come to value so greatly. We would like to thank Judge Rosalyn Higgins for contributing the Foreword to the first edition, and for her support to the

Project. Thanks are also due to Butterworths, for their enthusiastic support for the publication of the first edition. For making the first edition of the Manual possible, we thank PICT's funders, in particular the William and Flora Hewlett Foundation and the Ford Foundation.

Last but not least, it is customary to conclude with a word of thanks for our publishers. In this case, warm thanks are especially due to OUP for their enthusiastic support of this revised edition of the Manual, John Louth, Rebecca Smith, Merel Alstein, and Emma Barber, in particular.

Philippe Sands
University College London
1 October 2009

LIST OF ABBREVIATIONS

AB	Appellate Body (of the WTO)
ACJHR	African Court of Justice and Human Rights
ADB	Asian Development Bank
AfDB	African Development Bank
AfDB IRM	Independent Review Mechanism of the African Development Bank
African Charter	African Charter on Human and Peoples' Rights
African HR Commission	African Commission on Human and Peoples' Rights
African HR Court	African Court on Human and Peoples' Rights
AHAT	Ad Hoc Arbitral Tribunals (of Mercosur)
AIS	Andean Integration System
ATJ	Andean Community Tribunal of Justice
ATJ Treaty	Treaty Creating the Andean Tribunal of Justice, 1979
AU	African Union
BIT	Bilateral Investment Treaty
CAO	Compliance Adviser/Ombudsman
CARICOM	Caribbean Community
CAT	UN Convention against Torture and other Cruel, Inhuman or Degrading Treatment or Punishment
CAT Committee	UN Committee against Torture
CCJ	Caribbean Court of Justice
CCJ Agreement	Agreement Establishing the Caribbean Court of Justice, 2001
CCO	Chief Compliance Officer (in relation to the EBRD)
CEDAW	UN Convention on the Elimination of All Forms of Discrimination against Women
CEDAW Committee	UN Committee on the Elimination of Discrimination against Women
CERD	Convention on the Elimination of All Forms of Racial Discrimination
CERD Committee	Committee on the Elimination of Racial Discrimination
CFCs	chlorofluorocarbons
CFI	Court of First Instance (of the ECJ)
CIS	Commonwealth of Independent States
CRMU	Compliance Review and Mediation Unit (in relation to the African Development Bank)

CRP	Compliance Review Panel (in relation to the Asian Development Bank)
CSME	CARICOM Single Market and Economy
DAC	Development Assistance Committee
DSB	Dispute Settlement Body (of the WTO)
DSU	Dispute Settlement Understanding (of the WTO)
EBRD	European Bank for Reconstruction and Development
EC	European Community
EC Treaty	Treaty Establishing the European Community
ECCC	Extraordinary Chambers in the Courts of Cambodia for the Prosecution of Crimes Committed during the Period of Democratic Kampuchea
ECCIS	Economic Court of the Commonwealth of Independent States
ECCIS Agreement	Agreement on the Status of the Economic Court, 1992
ECHR	European Convention on Human Rights
ECtHR	European Court of Human Rights
ECJ	European Court of Justice
ECSR	European Committee of Social Rights
EEA	European Economic Area
EFTA	European Free Trade Association
ESA/Court Agreement	Agreement between the EFTA States on the Establishment of a Surveillance Authority and Court of Justice
EU	European Union
EU Treaty	Treaty on European Union
EurAsEC	Eurasian Economic Community
GATT	General Agreement on Tariffs and Trade
GRULAC	Latin American and the Caribbean Group of States
HRC	Human Rights Committee
IAHR	Inter-American Court of Human Rights
IAHR Convention	American Convention on Human Rights, 1969
IBRD	International Bank for Reconstruction and Development
ICC	International Criminal Court
ICJ	International Court of Justice
ICCPR	International Covenant on Civil and Political Rights
ICESCR	International Covenant on Economic, Social and Cultural Rights
ICRC	International Committee of the Red Cross
ICSID	International Centre for Settlement of Investment Disputes
ICSID Convention	Convention on the Settlement of Investment Disputes between States and Nationals of Other States, 1965
ICTR	International Criminal Tribunal for Rwanda

ICTY	International Criminal Tribunal for the former Yugoslavia
IDA	International Development Association
IDB	Inter-American Development Bank
IFC	International Finance Corporation
IIM	Independent Investigation Mechanism (of the Inter-American Development Bank)
ILO	International Labour Organization
INTERPOL	International Criminal Police Organization
IRM	Independent Recourse Mechanism (in relation to the EBRD)
ITLOS	International Tribunal for the Law of the Sea
Mercosur	Common Market of the Southern Core (Mercado Común del Sur)
MIGA	Multilateral Investment Guarantee Agency
MWC	Convention on the Protection of the Rights of All Migrant Workers and Members of Their Families, 1990
NAAEC	North American Agreement on Environmental Cooperation
NAALC	North American Agreement on Labor Cooperation
NAFTA	North American Free Trade Agreement
NAO	National Administrative Offices (related to NAFTA)
NGO	Non Governmental Organization
OAS	Organization of American States
OAU	Organization of African Unity
OECD	Organization for Economic Cooperation and Development
OECS	Organization of Eastern Caribbean States
OHADA	Arbitration of the Organization for the Harmonization of Business Law in Africa
OSPAR Convention	The Convention for the Protection of the Marine Environment of the North East Atlantic
OTP	Office of the Prosecutor
PCA	Permanent Court of Arbitration
PCIJ	Permanent Court of International Justice
PCM	Project Complaints Mechanism (in relation to the EBRD)
PICT	Project on International Courts and Tribunals
PTR	Permanent Tribunal of Review (of Mercosur)
RJLSC	Regional Judicial and Legal Services Commission (in relation to the CCJ)
RTLM	Radio Télévision Libre des Mille Collines
RUF	Revolutionary United Front
SBDC	Seabed Disputes Chamber
SCSL	Special Court for Sierra Leone
SPF	Special Project Facilitator (in relation to the Asian Development Bank)

SPS Agreement	The WTO Agreement on the Application of Sanitary and Phytosanitary Measures
STL	Special Tribunal for Lebanon
UN	United Nations
UNCITRAL	United Nations Commission on International Trade Law
UNCLOS	United Nations Convention on the Law of the Sea
UNECE	United Nations Economic Commission for Europe
UNFCCC	United Nations Framework Convention on Climate Change
UN ICC Agreement	Negotiated Relationship Agreement between the International Criminal Court and the United Nations
WEOG	Western European and other Group of States
WHO	World Health Organization
WTO	World Trade Organization
WTO Agreement	Agreement Establishing the World Trade Organization, 1994

PART I

GLOBAL COURTS

,

Introduction

This Part of the Manual describes a diverse set of international courts. They have been grouped together here as they are either potentially available to all states and/or their subject-matter jurisdiction is potentially unlimited: the International Court of Justice has potentially unlimited subject-matter jurisdiction relating to disputes involving any state. For its part, the International Tribunal for the Law of the Sea is potentially available to all states which are parties to the 1982 UN Convention on the Law of the Sea, in respect of disputes relating to that Convention (although in practice a great majority have opted in principle for recourse to other fora). The WTO Appellate Body is available for the resolution of trade disputes between parties to the WTO—an organization with an increasingly global membership.

The first tribunal addressed is the International Court of Justice (ICJ). Established in 1945 as the successor to the Permanent Court of International Justice, the ICJ is the principal judicial organ of the United Nations, and currently 192 states are parties to its Statute. The Court has considered cases involving an enormous range of subject matters, including territorial disputes, maritime delimitation, use of force, transboundary watercourses, interpretation of treaties, consular protection, and genocide. The principal limitation to the contentious jurisdiction of the ICJ is that it is limited to *states*. Thus the Court is not empowered to hear disputes involving private parties or international organizations. In this respect at least, the jurisdiction *ratione personae* of many of the other dispute settlement bodies considered later in this Manual is broader than that of the International Court. The need to obtain the consent of all parties to litigation is another jurisdictional limit, which increasingly sets apart the ICJ from newer courts that tend nowadays to be entrusted with compulsory jurisdiction over the states parties to their constitutive instruments.

In addition to its contentious jurisdiction, the Court is also empowered to give advisory opinions on legal questions submitted to it by UN organs and authorized institutions.

After a period of relatively low use in the 1970s and 1980s, the ICJ's caseload increased in the 1990s and in the first decade of the 21st century. In fact, the Court is currently finding it more and more difficult to address its current caseload, which includes some of the more complicated and politically charged cases ever brought before to international adjudication. A key challenge for the Court in the next decades will be to continue the process of procedural reforms (on which it already embarked through the issuance of Practice Directions), that will render its procedures shorter and more effective. It will also need to find ways to continue and assert its intellectual and professional leadership as the only permanent court covering the entire field of international law in a world of dispute settlement increasingly dominated by regional and specialized courts.

The second mechanism considered in this Part is the International Tribunal for the Law of the Sea, a permanent court established under the 1982 UN Convention on the Law of the Sea (it only became operational in 1996). The ITLOS is notable for at least two reasons: first, under UNCLOS it exercises compulsory jurisdiction in relation to certain types of dispute; and second, in accordance with the relevant provisions of UNCLOS, its jurisdiction *ratione personae* potentially extends beyond states, to include private parties (at least in the context of disputes over the seabed).

Part XV of UNCLOS provides that certain disputes arising under the Convention are subject to compulsory binding dispute settlement and, upon ratification of UNCLOS, parties may select one or more of the dispute settlement mechanisms set out in article 287, which include the ITLOS, the ICJ, and recourse to arbitration in accordance with Annex VII of UNCLOS (and special arbitration under Annex VIII for certain types of dispute). By the end of July 2009, 25 parties to UNCLOS had made a declaration under article 287(1) selecting the ITLOS as a preferred means for settlement of disputes under UNCLOS. In addition to exercising jurisdiction in these circumstances, the ITLOS has compulsory jurisdiction vis-à-vis parties to UNCLOS in relation to certain specific causes of action enumerated in UNCLOS, notably prompt release of vessels.

The ITLOS also comprises a Seabed Disputes Chamber to decide disputes under Part XI of UNCLOS. The Seabed Disputes Chamber has compulsory jurisdiction over certain types of dispute relating to activities in the seabed area. The personal jurisdiction of the Seabed Disputes Chamber extends beyond states parties to UNCLOS, and includes the International Seabed Authority (established under LINCLOS) as well as private parties engaged in seabed activities.

At the time of writing, 15 sets of proceedings had been initiated before the ITLOS. In addition to its contentious jurisdiction, the ITLOS and the Seabed Disputes Chamber are authorized to give advisory opinions in certain circumstances. While the ITLOS has dealt expeditiously with the cases that have come before it, it remains underutilized. Its principal caseload has comprised applications for prompt release of vessels and applications for provisional measures pending the establishment of an Annex VII arbitral tribunal. The full potential of the ITLOS thus has yet to be realized.

The third and last mechanism covered in this Part is the dispute settlement system of the World Trade Organization, established under the Dispute Settlement Understanding (DSU), an annex to the 1994 Agreement establishing the WTO. The system established under the DSU comprises a Dispute Settlement Body (DSB), ad hoc panels, and a standing seven-member Appellate Body, as well as a provision for arbitration. The dispute settlement system provides for compulsory jurisdiction, in accordance with the provisions of the DSU, over disputes between WTO members arising under the 'covered agreements' listed in Appendix 1 to the DSU. Proceedings begin by way of a request for consultations, but if such consultations fail to resolve the dispute within 60 days, a member is entitled to request the establishment of a panel by the DSB. In contrast to the previous GATT dispute settlement procedures, panel and Appellate Body reports are adopted by the DSB, and thus become binding, on the basis of 'reverse consensus'—ie they are adopted unless all the members of the DSB (comprising the WTO membership) agree by consensus not to adopt the report.

In terms of caseload, the WTO dispute settlement system has been the busiest of the three mechanisms surveyed in this Part. Between January 1995 and July 2009, 397 requests for consultations were made to the DSB. While many of these disputes were resolved without recourse to a panel, more than 150 panel reports and 97 Appellate Body reports were issued. The WTO dispute settlement system is also notable for the system of surveillance of implementation of its recommendations and ruling by members, which incorporates further mechanisms for the resolution of implementation-related disputes.

While the WTO procedures are widely considered a success, there remain criticisms. A number of proposals have been put forward regarding possible improvements to the system. Controversy remains over concerns about the lack of transparency of WTO dispute settlement proceedings, particularly in cases which are considered to involve non-trade issues of wider public interest, such as health or the environment.

1

THE INTERNATIONAL COURT
OF JUSTICE

Introduction

Name and seat of the body

1.1 The International Court of Justice (ICJ) is a permanent international court, which is open for use by virtually all states. It has its seat in The Hague, at the following address:

> The Peace Palace
> Carnegieplein 2
> 2517 KJ The Hague
> The Netherlands
> Tel: 31 70 302 23 23
> Fax: 31 70 364 99 28
> Website: <http://www.icj-cij.org>

General overview

1.2 The ICJ is the principal judicial organ of the United Nations (UN), and its Statute forms an integral part of the UN Charter. It began its operation on 18 April 1946. The ICJ replaced the Permanent Court of International Justice (PCIJ), which functioned from 1922 until its dissolution after the Second World War. Although being a new institution, the powers and procedures of the ICJ were closely modelled on those of the PCIJ.

The court has two heads of jurisdiction. It may receive any legal dispute referred to it by states for settlement in accordance with international law; and it may render advisory opinions on legal questions presented to it by the General Assembly, Security Council, and other duly authorized UN organs and special agencies. All 192 members of the UN are party to the Statute of the ICJ and may bring cases before the Court. Provided they comply with specified conditions, states that are not members may join the Statute of the Court at any time, or subject to a distinct set of conditions being met, they may participate in cases before the Court on an ad hoc basis, without joining the Statute at all.

Since 1946 the Court has decided, or otherwise disposed of, 103 contentious cases and 24 Advisory Opinions. As of January 2009, 13 contentious cases and one request for an advisory opinion were pending before the ICJ.

Institutional Aspects

Governing texts

Procedural law

The two principal texts governing the structure, powers, and work of the Court **1.3**
are the UN Charter[1] and the Statute of the Court.[2] The Charter establishes the
Court and provides the general outline of its powers; whilst the Statute governs
the composition and organization of the Court, its jurisdiction, and the basic
rules of procedure applicable to cases before it. Other relevant texts are the Rules
of Court[3] (which provide detailed rules of procedure), the Practice Directions[4] (a
set of guidelines relating to the conduct of proceedings before the Court), a 1976
Resolution concerning the internal judicial practice of the court,[5] and a more
recent Note concerning the preparation of pleadings.[6]

---

[1] *The Charter of the United Nations*, 26 June 1945, XV UNCIO 335 ('UN Charter').

[2] *Statute of the International Court of Justice*, 26 June 1945, XV UNCIO 355 ('ICJ Statute').

[3] *Rules of Court*, 1 July 1978, ICJ Acts & Docs No 5 (1990) ('ICJ Rules'). The Rules were amended in 2001 and in April and September 2005.

[4] *Practice Directions*, 31 October 2001, ICJ Acts & Docs (last amended on 6 December 2006). Before resorting to Practice Directions, the Court issued some of its instructions in a Note presented to parties to new cases: see *Note Containing Recommendations to the Parties to New Cases*, Annexed to Press Communiqué 98/14 (6 April 1998, as amended on 12 January 2001) (Press Communiqué 2001/1). The Court modified the Note in December 2000 in order to expedite its preliminary objections proceedings, in October 2001 in order to take into account the adoption of Practice Directions (see 2000–2001 *ICJ Yearbook*, at 196), and again in July 2004 following the amendment of existing Practice Direction V and the promulgation of new Practice Directions X, XI, and XII.

[5] *Resolution Concerning the Internal Judicial Practice of the Court*, 12 April 1976, (1990) ICJ Acts & Docs No 5.

[6] *Note Concerning the Preparation of Pleadings* ICJ Acts & Docs, <http://www.icj-cij.org/documents/index.php?p1=4&p2=5&p3=1>.

Substantive law

1.4 The ICJ decides cases in accordance with international law. It applies international treaties to which the states before it are parties, international customary law, and general principles of the law.[7] The Court also uses judicial decisions, and the writings of prominent international jurists, as subsidiary means of determining the law. Unilateral Declarations and UN Resolutions have also been relied upon in several cases as binding sources of law, subsidiary means for determining the law, or as 'soft law'.[8]

The parties may also request the Court to apply rules and principles which do not constitute part of existing international law. Indeed, in the *Libya/Tunisia Continental Shelf* case, the parties authorized the Court to apply 'equitable principles' as well as 'new accepted trends in the Third Conference on the Law of the Sea', in addition to the standard rules of international law.[9] The Court accepted that the parties had the power to specifically direct it towards new rules and principles that could apply as *lex specialis* in their bilateral relations, but held that in the circumstances of the case the additional sources identified by the parties were mere interpretative aids that the Court had competence to invoke anyway.[10]

The parties may agree to authorize the Court to decide a case on the basis of equitable considerations (*ex aequo et bono*), although as yet such an authorization has never been granted.[11]

Organization

Composition, appointment, and disqualification

1.5 The court is composed of 15 independent judges, elected by the General Assembly and Security Council of the UN for a renewable term of nine years.[12]

---

[7] ICJ Statute, art 38(1).

[8] See *Nuclear Tests* (New Zealand v France) [1974] ICJ Rep 457 at 474; *Legal Consequences of the Construction of a Wall in the Occupied Palestinian Territory* [2004] ICJ Rep 136 at 176–177.

[9] *Continental Shelf (Tunisia/Libya)* [1982] ICJ Pleadings 26.

[10] Ibid at 37–38.

[11] ICJ Statute, art 38(2). This, however, does not imply that the Court may not apply equity in other cases, where international law calls for the application of such considerations. See eg *North Sea Continental Shelf (FRG/Denmark; FRG/Netherlands)* [1969] ICJ Rep 4 at 48; S Rosenne, 'The Position of the International Court of Justice on the Foundations of the Principle of Equity in International Law' in A Bloed and P Van Dijk (eds), *Forty Years of the International Court of Justice* (1988) at 85; T M Franck, *Fairness in International Law and Institutions* (1995) at 47–80; W Friedmann, 'The North Sea Continental Shelf Cases—A Critique' (1970) 64 *Am J Int'l Law* 229; T M Franck and D M Sughrue, 'The International Role of Equity-as-Fairness' (1993) 81 *Geo L J* 563.

[12] ICJ Statute, arts 3(1), 4(1), 13(1). The possibility of re-election has been criticized as not fully compatible with judicial independence. See L R Helfer and A-M Slaughter, 'Why States Create International Tribunals: A Response to Professors Posner and Yoo' (2005) 93 *Calif L Rev* 899 at 950; R Mackenzie and P Sands, 'International Courts and Tribunals and the Independence of the International Judge' (2003) 44 *Harv Int'l L J* 271 at 276–279.

Judges must be persons of high moral character and they should possess qualifications for appointment to the highest judicial office in their own countries, or be jurists of recognized competence in international law.[13] No two judges can have the nationality of the same state and the entire bench ought to represent the main forms of civilization and the principal legal systems.[14]

In practice, the court is comprised of judges from the five permanent members of the Security Council of the UN, and the remaining 10 seats are divided amongst the different regional groupings of the UN according to a predetermined ratio.[15] While some judges have served as national judges or university professors before their appointment to the bench, it has also been common practice to nominate former diplomats and legal advisers as judges.[16]

NOTE :
Nov 2017
= UK lost
Seat to
India

The Court elects its President and Vice-President for a renewable period of three years. As of July 2009, Judges Hisashi Owada and Peter Tomka serve as President and Vice-President, respectively.[17]

Ad hoc judges   If a party to a case before the court does not have a judge of its nationality on the bench, it may appoint an ad hoc judge to sit for the duration of that case.[18] Ad hoc judges must meet the same service requirements as the permanent judges, and they participate in the deliberations of the Court on terms of full equality with the other judges.[19] An ad hoc judge may be of a nationality other than that of the appointing party, but should preferably be chosen from those persons who were previously nominated as candidates to serve in the ICJ.[20]

1.6

---

[13] ICJ Statute, art 2.

[14] Ibid, arts 3(1), 9; ICJ Rules, art 7(2).

[15] One of the adverse effects of the existence of regional quotas for judicial appointments is that competition between prospective judges over 'regional seats' is limited and, like with other UN positions, seats are often distributed between states on a rotating basis. Such a system does not always ensure election of the best available candidates. See E A Posner and J C Yoo, 'Judicial Independence in International Tribunals' (2005) 93 *Calif L Rev* 1 at 35; D R Robinson, 'The Role of Politics in the Election and the Work of Judges of the International Court of Justice' (2003) 97 *Am Soc'y Int'l L Proc* 277 at 278.

[16] As of March 2009, the composition of the Court is: President: Hisashi Owada (Japan), Vice-President: Peter Tomka (Slovakia), Judges: Awn Shawkat Al-Khasawneh (Jordan), Antonio Cançado Trindade (Brazil), Shi Jiuyong (China), Abdul G Koroma (Sierra Leone), Abdulqawi Ahmed Yusuf (Somalia), Thomas Buergenthal (United States of America), Bruno Simma (Germany), Christopher Greenwood (United Kingdom), Ronny Abraham (France), Kenneth Keith (New Zealand), Bernardo Sepulveda-Amor (Mexico), Mohamed Bennouna (Morocco), Leonid Skotnikov (Russian Federation).

[17] ICJ Statute, art 21(1).

[18] Ibid, art 31(2), (3).

[19] Ibid, art 31(6).

[20] Ibid, art 31(2), (3); ICJ Rules, art 35(1). It is increasingly common for parties to appoint ad hoc judges of other nationalities than their own.

Moreover, ad hoc judges should not have acted as agent, counsel, or advocate before the ICJ in the three years preceding their appointment.[21]

A party that wishes to appoint an ad hoc judge should notify the Court of its intention as soon as possible, and must provide the Court with the name, nationality, and summary of biographical details of the person of its choice not later than two months before the date for submission of the Counter-Memorial.[22] If both states parties are entitled to appoint ad hoc judges, one of the parties may propose to the other that they both abstain from appointing them.[23] Indeed, in a few exceptional cases, the litigating parties have mutually agreed to dispense with the right to appoint ad hoc judges.[24]

The institution of ad hoc judges serves the important function of maintaining the confidence of the parties in the judicial process before the ICJ.[25] In particular, ad hoc judges may ensure that their appointing party's arguments are properly considered and fully understood by the Court during its deliberations. Still, the institution of ad hoc judges is in many ways anathema to notions of judicial independence and impartiality, and there is a body of opinion that it ought to be abolished (probably, together with a new rule imposing a duty on national judges to recuse themselves whenever their national state is a party to the proceedings).[26]

1.7 **Disqualification of judges** A judge may not participate in a case in which he or she was previously involved as a party representative, member of another dispute settlement body, or in any other capacity.[27] The Court will decide any doubts as to whether past involvement in a dispute, or any other special reason, precludes a judge from participation in a case.[28]

In a preliminary order issued during the *Wall* advisory proceedings, the Court considered the indirect involvement of one judge in that case. It was held

---

[21] Practice Direction VII, ICJ Act & Docs (as amended on 6 December 2006).

[22] ICJ Rules, art 35(1).

[23] Ibid, art 35(2).

[24] *Certain Phosphate Lands in Nauru* (Nauru v Australia) [1992] ICJ Rep 240; *Temple of Preah Vihear* (Cambodia v Thailand) [1961] ICJ Rep 17; *Sovereignty over Certain Frontier Land* (Belgium/Netherlands) [1959] ICJ Rep 209.

[25] See S Rosenne, *The Law and Practice of the International Court 1920–2005* (4th edn, vol III, 2006) at 1079–1081; G Fitzmaurice, 'The Law and Procedure of the International Court of Justice: General Principles and Substantive Law' (1950) 27 *Brit Y B Int'l L* at 1–2; S M Schwebel, 'National Judges and Judges Ad Hoc of the International Court of Justice' (1999) 48 *ICLQ* 889 at 892.

[26] See E Lauterpacht, *Aspects of the Administration of International Justice* (1991) at 77–82; S M Schwebel, *supra* note 25, at 892–893. Statistical analysis shows that ad hoc judges vote about 90 per cent of the time in favour of the positions of their appointing party. See A M Smith, ' "Judicial Nationalism" in International Law: National Identity and Judicial Autonomy at the ICJ' (2005) 40 *Tex Int'l LJ* 197 at 218; E A Posner & M F P de Figueiredo, 'Is the International Court of Justice Biased?' (2005) 34 *J Legal Stud* 599 at 615.

[27] ICJ Statute, art 17(2).

[28] Ibid, arts 17(3), 24.

that the judge's previous work in a diplomatic capacity, and public comments that he offered prior to his appointment to the ICJ, and which pertained to some background issues related to the case, did not amount to his having previously taken part in the case and should not result in disqualification. [29] This position may, however, be open to criticism for its excessive timidity.[30] Indeed, the dissenting judge in the *Wall* case—Judge Buergenthal—suggested that the Court has broad inherent powers to disqualify judges not only upon proof of past participation, but in any case in which their involvement or conduct raises an 'appearance of bias'. [31]

Any motion for disqualification will be brought to the Court by the President, acting on his or her own initiative, or upon the confidential request of a party to the case.[32] A party to a case may also file with the Court an objection to the appointment of an ad hoc judge by a party to the dispute (ie in circumstances where an ad hoc judge does not meet the service requirements).[33] Any objection must be presented within a time limit fixed by the Court, following the notification on the appointment of the ad hoc judge by the other party. The Court will then decide on the objection, or resolve any doubts of its own pertaining to the qualifications of the ad hoc judge, after hearing the parties if necessary.[34]

In the event that a judge ceases to fulfil the conditions for service, as required by the Statute, the other judges may, after hearing the judge in question, decide by way of a unanimous vote to remove that judge from office.[35] Such a decision is then to be communicated to the Secretary-General of the UN, who will declare the seat vacant.[36]

Plenary/chambers

The Court can hear cases in plenary (the quorum is nine judges) or in chambers.[37] The Statute provides for the establishment of permanent and ad hoc chambers. As in cases before the plenary court, parties in cases brought before chambers are entitled to have judges of their nationality on the bench (either ICJ judges or, in their absence, ad hoc judges).[38] The procedure before chambers is

1.8

---

[29] *Legal Consequences of the Construction of a Wall in the Occupied Palestinian Territory* (Order on composition of the bench) [2004] ICJ Rep 3.

[30] See Y Shany and S Horovitz, 'Judicial Independence in The Hague and Freetown: A Tale of Two Cities' (2007) 20 *Leiden J Int'l L* 113.

[31] *Construction of a Wall* [2004] ICJ Rep 3 at 7.

[32] ICJ Rules, art 34.

[33] Ibid, art 35(3).

[34] Ibid, art 35(4).

[35] ICJ Statute, art 18; ICJ Rules, art 6.

[36] ICJ Statute, art 18(3).

[37] Ibid, arts 25, 26.

[38] Ibid, art 31(4).

generally similar to the procedure before the full Court.[39] In the same vein, the effect of a chamber judgment is the same as the effect of a judgment issued by the plenary Court.[40]

1.9 **Chamber of Summary Procedure** The Court must annually form a Chamber of Summary Procedure.[41] The Chamber of Summary Procedure comprises five judges (three judges elected by the Court, plus the President and Vice-President), who may be re-elected.[42] A request for referral of a case to a Summary Procedure Chamber is to be made in the document instituting proceedings, and the agreement of the other party to the case is required.[43] So far, no case has been brought before this chamber.

[Handwritten margin note: NOTE: USED TWICE IN PCIJ = INTERPRETATION OF THE TREATY OF NEUILLY (1924) ② INTERPRETATION OF ①]

1.10 **Chambers for particular categories of cases** The Statute authorizes the Court to form chambers for dealing with particular categories of cases (such as labour or transit and communication cases).[44] If the Court decides to establish a permanent chamber, it will determine the category of cases to be referred to that chamber, the number of judges sitting in it, and the extent of their term of office.[45] When electing judges for a permanent chamber, the Court should take into consideration the particular knowledge, expertise, or past experience of the candidates.[46] A case will be referred to a chamber for a particular category of cases if the parties so agree (a request should be made at the initiation of proceedings).[47] So far, the ICJ has formed only one permanent chamber for a particular topic—the seven-member Chamber for Environmental Matters created in July 1993. This chamber has not yet been utilized, and as of 2006 the Court has ceased electing members thereto.[48]

1.11 **Ad hoc chambers** The ICJ may also hear cases in ad hoc chambers, formed to deal with particular cases.[49] Parties may request the Court to form such a chamber at any time before the end of the written stage of the proceedings.[50] According to the Statute, the parties must approve the number of judges sitting in the chamber (until now all ad hoc chambers have comprised five judges), but

---

[39] ICJ Rules, art 90. Specific procedures for written and oral pleadings for chamber proceedings are provided in art 92 of the Rules.

[40] ICJ Statute, art 27; S Oda, 'Further Thoughts on the Chambers Procedure of the International Court of Justice' (1988) 82 *Am J Int'l L* 556 at 559.

[41] ICJ Statute, art 29.

[42] Ibid, art 29; ICJ Rules, art 15(1), (2).

[43] ICJ Rules, art 91(1).

[44] ICJ Statute, art 26(1).

[45] ICJ Rules, art 16(1).

[46] Ibid, art 16(2).

[47] ICJ Statute, art 26(3); ICJ Rules, art 91(1).

[48] ICJ Report, 1 August 2007–31 July 2007, GAOR 62nd Sess, Supp No 4 (A/62/4) at 52.

[49] ICJ Statute, art 26(2).

[50] Ibid, art 26(3); ICJ Rules, art 17(1).

do not have the authority to determine the composition of the chamber. The election of judges for chambers is undertaken by the Court after ascertaining the views of the parties on the composition of the chamber.[51] In all six cases that have taken place before an ad hoc chamber to date,[52] the selection of judges by the Court conformed to the wishes of the parties.

Contrary to some expectations, the procedures before chambers are not significantly more expedient than before the full bench.[53] Still, by allowing parties to influence the choice of judges the chamber system appears to narrow the difference between ICJ adjudication and arbitration:[54] it appears that the main utility of ad hoc chambers is that it allows the parties to exclude judges whom they view as unsympathetic to their legal positions or national interests.[55] This, in turn, may increase the attractiveness of ICJ adjudication in the eyes of some parties.

Appellate structure

The ICJ has no appellate structure.   **1.12**

Scientific and technical experts

The parties to a case may introduce expert witnesses before the Court.[56] Under   **1.13**
the control of the President, the other party to a case may question the experts; and the judges may present questions to them also.[57] The Court may, on its own initiative, otherwise arrange to seek information from, or to invite expert

---

[51] ICJ Statute, art 26(2); ICJ Rules, art 17(2)–(3).

[52] *Delimitation of the Maritime Boundary in the Gulf of Maine Area* (Canada/United States) [1982] ICJ Rep 3; *Frontier Dispute* (Burkina Faso/Mali) [1985] ICJ 6; *Elettronica Sicula SpA (ELSI)* (United States v Italy) [1987] ICJ Rep 3; *Land, Island and Maritime Frontier Dispute* (El Salvador/Honduras; Nicaragua intervening) [1987] ICJ Rep 10; *Frontier Dispute* (Benin/Niger) [2002] ICJ Rep 613; *Application for Revision of the Judgment of 11 September 1992 in the Case concerning the Land, Island and Maritime Frontier Dispute* (El Salvador/Honduras; Nicaragua intervening) [2002] ICJ Rep 618.

[53] See S Rosenne, *Procedure in the International Court: A Commentary on the 1978 Rules of the International Court of Justice* (1983) at 42–45. But see also S M Schwebel, 'Ad Hoc Chambers of the International Court of Justice' (1987) 81 *Am J Int'l L* 831 at 846 (chamber cases can be processed more quickly).

[54] See *Frontier Dispute* (Benin/Niger) (Declaration of Judge Oda) [2002] ICJ Rep 616 where it was noted that 'in order for an *ad hoc* Chamber formed under Article 26 of the Statute—*an institution which is essentially an arbitral tribunal*—to be constituted, it must be clear beyond all doubt that the litigating parties have agreed, before the Court decides on the constitution, not only as to the number of Chamber members but also as to who they ought to be' (emphasis added); S Oda, 'Further Thoughts on the Chambers Procedure of the International Court of Justice' (1988) 82 *Am J Int'l L* 556 at 562; R Ostrihansky, 'Chambers of the International Court of Justice' (1988) 37 *ICLQ* 30 at 35, 42.

[55] Ostrihansky, *supra* note 54, at 41–45.

[56] ICJ Statute, art 43(5); ICJ Rules, art 63(1). For a recent discussion of the use of party experts by the Court, see R Higgins, 'Speech to the Sixth Committee of the General Assembly' (2 November 2007) at 2–4, <http://www.icj-cij.org/presscom/files/3/14123.pdf>.

[57] ICJ Statute, art 51; ICJ Rules, art 65.

witnesses, where necessary.[58] In addition, after hearing the parties the Court can order that an inquiry or expert opinion be sought.[59] In this event, the Court will determine the mandate of the experts, their number and method of appointment, and the procedure they should follow. The parties will then be given an opportunity to comment upon the findings of the inquiry, or on the expert opinion.[60]

Although the resort to Court-appointed experts has been meagre in practice,[61] the professional staff of the Court's registry are occasionally required to provide the Court with expert advice. This practice appears to invite criticism, however, for its lack of transparency to the parties.

In full Court or chamber cases, the Statute and Rules also authorize the Court to appoint assessors to sit on the bench without voting rights.[62] The appointment of assessors (which is made by way of election by the Court)[63] is intended to enable the Court to enjoy the benefit of experts having specialized knowledge in a given area, which could be valuable in disputes of a highly technical nature. The need for appointment of assessors is to be decided by the Court, acting on its own initiative, or upon the request of a party made not later than the end of the written proceedings.[64] In the history of the ICJ (or the PCIJ for that matter), no use has ever been made of the possibility to appoint assessors.

Registry

1.14 The Court appoints a Registrar and a Deputy Registrar (as of January 2009 Philippe Couvreur and Thérèse de Saint Phalle, respectively), for a renewable seven-year term.[65] The other members of the Registry are appointed by the Court, or by the Registrar (with the approval of the President).[66] The Registrar is responsible, *inter alia*, for the following functions: serving as the official channel of communications with the Court; maintaining the archives of the Court;

---

[58] ICJ Rules, art 62.

[59] ICJ Statute, art 50; ICJ Rules, art 67(1). See generally, G White, 'The Use of Experts by the International Court' in V Lowe and M Fitzmaurice (eds), *Fifty Years of the International Court of Justice* (1996) at 528.

[60] ICJ Rules, art 67(2).

[61] Experts were appointed in the very first ICJ case. *Corfu Channel* (United Kingdom v Albania) (Order for Expert Opinion) [1948] ICJ Rep 124. An expert has been appointed in only one subsequent case, at the request of both parties. *Delimitation of the Maritime Boundary in the Gulf of Maine Area* (Canada/United States) (Order on Appointment of Expert) [1984] ICJ Rep 165. During the life of the PCIJ, an expert committee was appointed in one case only. *Factory at Chorzów Indemnity* (Germany v Poland) [1928] PCIJ (ser A) No 17 (order of 13 September 1928).

[62] ICJ Statute, art 30(2); ICJ Rules, art 9(1), (4).

[63] ICJ Rules, art 9(3).

[64] Ibid, art 9(1).

[65] ICJ Statute, art 21(2); ICJ Rules, arts 22(1), 23.

[66] ICJ Rules, art 25(1).

preparing minutes of Court meetings; providing translation and interpretation services; publishing decisions of the Court and other publishable materials; supervising the administration of the Court—including financial management; and assisting in maintaining relations between the ICJ and other UN bodies and agencies.[67]

The Registry operates under instructions and Staff Regulations which are proposed by the Registrar and approved by the Court.[68] It is composed of a Department of Legal Matters, Department of Linguistic Matters, and Department of Information; and the following Divisions: Administrative and Personnel; Finance; Publications; Documents-Library; Information Technology; Archives, Indexing, and Distribution; Shorthand, Typewriting, and Reproduction; General Assistance. The registry is also responsible for the employment of the judges' secretaries.

Jurisdiction and access to the Court

Ratione personae

Only states may be parties to contentious cases before the Court.[69] The Court is open to use by all 192 states parties to the UN Charter, which are also *ipso facto* members of the Statute.[70] States not parties to the Charter may also ratify the Statute subject to conditions set by the UN General Assembly and Security Council being met.[71] Following the accession of Nauru and Switzerland to the UN in 1999 and 2002, respectively, there are no more states who, not being members of the UN, are parties only to the Statute. Furthermore, it is unlikely that such states would appear in the foreseeable future.

States who are neither members of the Charter nor the Statute may participate in cases before the ICJ subject to the 'special provisions contained in treaties in force', and provided that they deposited with the ICJ Registry a declaration that meets the requirements laid down by the Security Council.[72] The term 'treaties in force' was narrowly construed by the Court in the *NATO Bombings* case as referring to treaties in force in 1945 (being the time of drafting of the Statute).[73] This has proved to be a rather controversial interpretation which, in effect, bars

1.15

---

[67] Ibid, art 26(1).

[68] Ibid, art 28(3), (4).

[69] ICJ Statute, art 34(1).

[70] Ibid, art 35(1).

[71] UN Charter, art 93. The conditions for ratification include acceptance of the provisions of the Statute; an undertaking to comply with ICJ decisions; and an undertaking to make an annual contribution to the expenses of the Court.

[72] ICJ Statute, art 35(2). The conditions for participation of a state, which is not a party to the Statute, are, in essence, acceptance of the jurisdiction of the Court and an undertaking to comply in good faith with its decisions.

[73] *Legality of Use of Force* (Yugoslavia v Belgium) [2004] ICJ Rep 279 at 324.

in most cases the participation of states who are not party to the Statute from ICJ proceedings.[74]

The exercise of jurisdiction by the Court depends on consent being given by all parties to the case. Consent to the jurisdiction of the ICJ can be expressed in a number of ways, discussed in the following sections.

1.16 **Special agreements** The jurisdiction of the Court encompasses all cases which the parties to a dispute refer to it.[75] Such cases normally come before the Court by notification to the Registry of an agreement known as a special agreement (or *compromis),* concluded by the parties for the purpose of presenting a case to the ICJ. In a number of cases, brought before the Court unilaterally by one of the parties to an alleged special agreement, the Court had to decide whether a particular instrument presented before it can be qualified as a legal agreement, and whether it actually represents an intention to submit to the Court's jurisdiction.[76]

So far, 16 cases have been brought to the Court on the basis of special agreements.

Moreover, the Court has been willing to infer specific consent to its jurisdiction from the conduct of the parties to the dispute even in the absence of a special agreement (eg if, following a unilateral application, the respondent party appears before the Court without challenging its jurisdiction—a practice sometimes referred to as *forum prorogatum*).[77]

1.17 **Provisions in treaties and conventions in force** The jurisdiction of the Court also comprises all matters that the parties referred to it pursuant to treaties and conventions in force.[78] Such referrals are normally found in compromissory clauses referring to the ICJ disputes concerning the interpretation or application

---

[74] For criticism, see *Legality of Use of Force* (Joint Declaration of Vice-President Ranjeva, Judges Guillaume, Higgins, Kooijmans, Al Khasawneh, Buergenthal, and Elaraby) [2004] ICJ Rep at 330–334, ibid at 341 (Separate Opinion of Judge Higgins), ibid at 358–363 (Separate Opinion of Judge Elaraby); and J R Crook, 'Current Development: The 2004 Judicial Activity of the International Court of Justice' (2005) 99 *Am J Int'l L* 450 at 454–456.

[75] ICJ Statute, art 36(1).

[76] See *Maritime Delimitation and Territorial Questions between Qatar and Bahrain* (Qatar v Bahrain) [1994] ICJ Rep 1 126; *Aegean Sea Continental Shelf* (Greece v Turkey) [1978] ICJ Rep 3.

[77] See *Corfu Channel* [1948] ICJ Rep 15. In two recent cases, the respondent party accepted the Court's jurisdiction after proceedings were unilaterally brought by the applicant state. *Certain Criminal Proceedings in France* (Republic of the Congo v France), Letter from the Minister for Foreign Affairs of the French Republic (Consent to the Jurisdiction of the Court to Entertain the Application Pursuant to Article 38, paragraph 5, of the Rules of Court), 8 April 2003, <http://www.icj-cij.org/docket/files/129/13344.pdf>; *Certain Questions of Mutual Assistance in Criminal Matters* (Djibouti v France), Letter from the Minister for Foreign Affairs of the French Republic (Consent to the Jurisdiction of the Court to Entertain the Application Pursuant to Article 38, paragraph 5, of the Rules of Court), 25 July 2006, <http://www.icj-cij.org/docket/files/136/13916.pdf>.

[78] ICJ Statute, art 36(1).

of the treaty in question,[79] or general dispute settlement treaties providing for submission of all disputes, or some categories of disputes, once they arise, to the jurisdiction of the ICJ.[80] The Statute also explicitly states that the ICJ will have jurisdiction based on treaties and conventions in force, which refer disputes between the contracting parties to the PCIJ (or other tribunals established by the League of Nations).[81]

Until now, 83 cases have been brought before the Court, either wholly or partially on the basis of treaty clauses (11 of which cases were brought on the basis of general dispute settlement treaties). Note, however, that parties to compromissory clauses—which have sometimes been concluded long before the dispute has arisen—have on occasion been reluctant to appear before the Court, or to fully cooperate with the proceedings.[82]

Declarations under the optional clause   A state may submit to the Secretary-General of the UN a declaration under article 36(2) of the Statute, recognizing *ipso facto* the compulsory jurisdiction of the ICJ (optional clause declarations).[83] Optional clause declarations may be relied upon by any other state that has also made a declaration under article 36(2). Old declarations accepting the compulsory jurisdiction of the PCIJ, which are still in force, are deemed as declarations of acceptance of the ICJ's jurisdiction.[84] Hence, states who have submitted optional clause declarations are parties to a 'system within a system'—a system of compulsory jurisdiction applying between optional clause states, functioning within the broader system of non-compulsory jurisdiction governing relations between states who have not made optional clause declarations and between such states and optional clause states.   **1.18**

---

[79] See Convention on the Prevention and Punishment of the Crime of Genocide, 9 December 1948, art 9, 78 UNTS 278. For a comprehensive list of treaties investing the Court with jurisdiction (mostly, on the basis of compromissory clauses), see <http://www.icj-cij.org/jurisdiction/index.php?p1=5&p2=1&p3=4>.

[80] ICJ Statute, art 37.

[81] There is one universal dispute settlement treaty: the General Act for Pacific Settlement of Disputes, 26 September 1928, 93 LNTS 342, art 17 (revised on 28 April 1949, 71 UNTS 101). Six cases sought support for jurisdiction on this basis, but the Court has never directly applied the General Act. There are also two regional dispute settlement treaties: the American Treaty on Pacific Settlement (the Pact of Bogota), 30 April 1948, 30 UNTS 55 art XXXI (invoked in six cases; so far only one case has proceeded to judgment. *Territorial and Maritime Dispute between Nicaragua and Honduras in the Caribbean Sea* (Nicaragua v Honduras), Judgment of 8 October 2008); and the European Convention for the Peaceful Settlement of Disputes, 29 April 1957, 320 UNTS 243 art 1 (only two cases have sought jurisdiction on this basis: *Certain Property* (Liechtenstein v Germany) [2005] ICJ Rep 6 (jurisdiction declined) and *Proceedings instituted by the Federal Republic of Germany against the Italian Republic* (Germany v Italy) (submitted in 2008; still pending)).

[82] See *Fisheries Jurisdiction* (United Kingdom v Iceland) [1973] ICJ Rep 3; *United States Diplomatic and Consular Staff in Tehran* (United States v Iran) [1980] ICJ Rep 3.

[83] ICJ Statute, art 36(2), (4).

[84] Ibid, art 36(5).

At present there are 66 optional clause declarations in force. However, since the Statute permits the deposition of conditional declarations (ie declarations made for a certain time, or excluding certain categories of dispute),[85] many of the existing declarations contain far-reaching conditions and limitations on the acceptance of the jurisdiction of the Court. Moreover, the ICJ has held in *Certain Norwegian Loans* that the principle of reciprocity requires that jurisdiction is conferred upon the Court in cases brought on the basis of article 36(2) only to the extent to which the applicant's and respondent's declarations coincide in conferring it.[86] This means that the actual jurisdiction invested in the Court by the optional clause 'system within a system' is rather limited in its scope. In addition, the Court has held in *Canadian Fisheries Jurisdiction* that due weight should be given in the interpretation of reservations to declarations under the optional clause, to the intentions of the reserving states as deduced from the text, context, and surrounding circumstances.[87] This means that a subjective interpretation of the intentions of the reserving party may be preferred at times over an objective interpretation of the scope of the Court's jurisdiction.

So far 38 cases have been brought before the Court on the basis of optional clause declarations. Here too, respondent parties have sometimes challenged the jurisdiction of the Court pursuant to the declarations and refused to cooperate fully with procedure.[88]

Ratione materiae

1.19 Parties may refer to the Court any legal dispute arising between them. However, the instrument constituting the basis for jurisdiction may restrict the subject-matter competence of the ICJ. In cases brought in pursuance of declarations under the optional clause, the Court may deal (subject to conditions and limitations found in the declarations) with all legal disputes concerning: (i) the interpretation of a treaty; (ii) any question of international law; (iii) the existence of any fact which, if established, would constitute a breach of an international obligation; (iv) the nature or extent of the reparation to be made for the breach of an international obligation.[89] In a series of cases, the Court has defined what constitutes a legal dispute, and held that it must be shown that the claim of one

---

[85] Ibid, art 36(3).

[86] *Certain Norwegian Loans* (France v Norway) [1957] ICJ Rep 9 at 23–24.

[87] *Fisheries Jurisdiction* (Canada v Spain) [1998] ICJ Rep 432 at 454. See also *Aegean Sea* [1978] ICJ Rep 3 at 29; *Anglo-Iranian Oil Co.* (United Kingdom v Iran) [1952] ICJ Rep 93 at 107.

[88] *Military and Paramilitary Activities in and against Nicaragua* (Nicaragua v United States) [1984] ICJ Rep 393; *Nuclear Tests* (New Zealand v France) [1974] ICJ Rep 457; *Nuclear Tests* (Australia v France) [1974] ICJ Rep 253.

[89] ICJ Statute, art 36(2).

party is positively opposed by the other.[90] Hence, a matter definitely settled by an agreement concluded by the parties cannot be deemed as an existing legal dispute.[91]

Ratione temporis

In general, there are no time limits for reference of disputes to the ICJ. **1.20** Nonetheless, such restrictions may be found in the instruments constituting the basis of jurisdiction. Hence, in a number of cases the Court refused to accept jurisdiction, or—during provisional measures proceedings—to assert prima-facie jurisdiction over disputes which had arisen before the time covered by the jurisdiction-conferring instrument in question.[92]

Advisory jurisdiction

By virtue of article 65 of the Statute, the Court may give an advisory opinion on **1.21** any legal question at the request of a body authorized to request such an opinion under the UN Charter.[93] The UN Charter authorizes the General Assembly and the Security Council to refer any legal question to the ICJ, and permits other UN organs and specialized agencies, authorized by the General Assembly, to present requests for advisory opinions, but only on legal questions arising within the scope of their activities.[94] Indeed, in the *Legality of Nuclear Weapons in Armed Conflicts* case, the Court refused to accommodate a request by the WHO to issue

---

[90] See *South West Africa* (Ethiopia v South Africa; Liberia v South Africa) [1962] ICJ Rep 319 at 328. See also *Applicability of the Obligation to Arbitrate under Section 21 of the United Nations Headquarters Agreement of 26 June 1947* [1988] ICJ Rep 12 at 27; *Northern Cameroons* (Cameroon v United Kingdom) [1963] ICJ Rep 15 at 27; *Interpretation of Peace Treaties with Bulgaria, Hungary and Romania* [1950] ICJ Rep 65 at 74. An earlier formulation offered by the PCIJ, which defined a dispute as a 'disagreement on a point of law or fact, a conflict of legal views or interests between two persons', is excessively broad and fails to distinguish between legal disputes, other disputes, and between actual disputes and conflicts of interests. *Mavrommatis Palestine Concessions* (Greece v United Kingdom) [1923] PCIJ (Ser A), No 2, at 11.

[91] See *Territorial and Maritime Dispute Case* (Colombia v Nicaragua) Judgment of 13 December 2007, at 138.

[92] See eg *Certain Property* [2005] ICJ Rep 6; *Legality of Use of Force* [1999] ICJ Rep 124; *Phosphates in Morocco* [1938] PCIJ (Ser A/B), No 74 (1938).

[93] ICJ Statute, art 65(1).

[94] UN Charter, art 96. The following organs and agencies are at present authorized to request advisory opinions: General Assembly; Security Council; Economic and Social Council; Trusteeship Council; Interim Committee of the General Assembly; International Labour Organization; Food and Agriculture Organization of the United Nations; United Nations Educational, Scientific and Cultural Organization; World Health Organization; International Bank for Reconstruction and Development; International Finance Corporation; International Development Association; International Monetary Fund; International Civil Aviation Organization; International Telecommunications Union; International Fund for Agricultural Development; World Meteorological Organization; International Maritime Organization; World Intellectual Property Organization; United Nations Industrial Development Organization; International Atomic Energy Agency.

an advisory opinion on the legality of nuclear weapons[95] (although the Court agreed to provide an advisory opinion in the parallel proceedings on the legality of nuclear weapons that were initiated by the General Assembly, whose competence to request advisory opinions is essentially unlimited).[96] Even where the requesting organization is competent to request the opinion, the Court may decline to issue an opinion for 'compelling reasons'.[97] Still, the ICJ never used its discretionary power to decline to exercise its advisory competence (whereas the PCIJ had refused to issue an opinion in only one case—the *Eastern Carelia* case).[98]

Through its advisory competence, the Court is able to offer UN bodies legal guidance with regards to the proper conduct of their business[99] and to provide them with interpretations of international law instruments, and customary law that may assist the referring organizations in their work.[100] More controversial has been the use of the advisory procedure to refer disputes to the Court which could not be brought to it under its ordinary competence over contentious cases. This includes disputes involving international organizations and states[101] (or in some cases, international organizations and their employees),[102]

---

[95] *Legality of the Use by a State of Nuclear Weapons in Armed Conflict Case* [1996] ICJ Rep 66 at 81.

[96] *Legality of the Threat of Use of Nuclear Weapons Case* [1996] ICJ Rep 226.

[97] See eg *Construction of a Wall* [2004] ICJ Rep 136 at 156–157; *Western Sahara* [1975] ICJ Rep 12 at 21; *Legal Consequences for States of the Continued Presence of South Africa in Namibia (South West Africa) notwithstanding Security Council Resolution 276* [1971] ICJ Rep 16 at 27.

[98] *Status of Eastern Carelia* [1923] PCIJ (Ser B), No 5 (1923). The objection of Russia (who was not a member of the League of Nations or the PCIJ Statute at the time) to the Court's jurisdiction and the lack of sufficient evidence were deemed in that case suitable reasons for the Court to decline jurisdiction.

[99] See *Difference Relating to Immunity from Legal Process of a Special Rapporteur of the Commission on Human Rights* [1999] ICJ Rep 62; *Certain Expenses of the United Nations (Article 17, paragraph 2, of the Charter)* [1962] ICJ Rep 151; *Competence of Assembly regarding Admission to the United Nations* [1950] ICJ Rep 4; *Reparation for Injuries Suffered in the Service of the United Nations* [1949] ICJ Rep 174.

[100] See eg *Nuclear Weapons* [1996] ICJ Rep 226; *Reservations to the Convention on Genocide* [1951] ICJ Rep 15.

[101] See eg *Special Rapporteur Immunity* [1999] ICJ Rep 62; *Applicability of Article VI, Section 22, of the Convention on the Privileges and Immunities of the United Nations* [1989] ICJ 177; *Obligation to Arbitrate under UN Headquarters Agreement* [1988] ICJ Rep 12.

[102] See eg *Application for Review of Judgment No 333 of the United Nations Administrative Tribunal* [1987] ICJ Rep 18. According to UN GA Res 957 (X) of 8 November 1955, UN Doc A/Res/10/957(X) (1955), a special committee—the Committee on Applications for Review of Administrative Tribunal Judgments—was formed and entrusted with referring, where appropriate, appeals against findings of the UN administrative tribunal in cases relating to UN employees to the ICJ for an advisory opinion. Still, the wisdom of transforming the ICJ into a de facto supreme labour court has been questioned. See *UN Doc* A/C.6/48/SR.36 (1993); V Morris and M C Bourloyannis-Vrailas, 'Current Development: The Work of the Sixth Committee at the Fiftieth Session of the UN General Assembly' (1996) 90 *Am J Int'l L* 491 at 493–494; V Morris and M C Bourloyannis-Vrailas, 'Current Development: The Work of the Sixth Committee at the Forty-Eighth Session of the UN General Assembly' (1994) 88 *Am J Int'l L* 343 at 358–360. In 1995, the committee's authority to request advisory opinions was repealed. GA Res 54 of 11 December 1995, UN Doc A/Res/50/54 (1995).

and—even more controversially—inter-state disputes referred to the Court without the consent of all parties.[103] Although the latter use of the advisory procedure circumvents the need for obtaining consent to proceedings by the immediate parties to disputes by emphasizing the benefits accruing to the requesting organization from clarifying the legal issues underlying the dispute,[104] the legitimacy of this application of advisory jurisdiction remains open to challenge (especially in cases where the immediate parties withhold their cooperation from the process).[105]

A request for an advisory opinion is to be presented to the ICJ by the Secretary-General of the UN, or the chief administrative officer of the specialized agency making the request.[106] The request is made in written form and includes an exact statement of the question on which the opinion is sought and any relevant documents likely to throw light on the question. The Registrar will notify all states of the request, and will invite states and international organizations that (in the view of the Court) are likely to provide it with relevant information to submit written statements within fixed time limits.[107] These states and international organizations will also be given the opportunity to comment upon each others' written submissions, in accordance with the appropriate time limits and procedure as determined by the Court.[108] The Court may also, on request, decide to hold oral hearings in which the states and international organizations concerned are permitted to make oral statements.[109] In the *Wall* case, the Court decided to confer upon Palestine—a non-state entity with observer status before the UN General Assembly—the right to present the Court with written and oral statements. This allowance was made on account of Palestine's special status, and particular involvement in the UN proceedings which led to the request for the opinion.[110]

The procedure for advisory opinions generally conforms to the rules of procedure applicable in contentious cases.[111] In urgent cases, upon request of the body that referred the case to the Court, or on the Court's own motion, the procedure

---

[103] *Western Sahara* [1975] ICJ Rep 12 is the most obvious example of an advisory opinion relating to an inter-state dispute (but see also *Construction of a Wall* [2004] ICJ Rep 136; *Namibia* [1971] ICJ Rep 16; and *Interpretation of Peace Treaties* [1950] ICJ Rep 65.

[104] See eg *Western Sahara* [1975] ICJ Rep 12 at 24–25; *Construction of a Wall* [2004] ICJ Rep 136 at 157–159; *Namibia* [1971] ICJ Rep 16 at 24.

[105] See generally A Zimmermann, *The Statute of the International Court of Justice: A Commentary* (2006) at 1412.

[106] ICJ Statute, art 65(2); ICJ Rules, art 104.

[107] ICJ Statute, art 66(1), (2).

[108] Ibid, art 66(4); ICJ Rules, art 105.

[109] ICJ Statute, art 66(2); ICJ Rules, art 105(2)(b).

[110] *Legal Consequences of the Construction of a Wall* (Order on Time Limits and Statements) [2003] ICJ Rep 428 at 429. A comparable procedural right was conferred subsequently on the 'Authors of the Unilateral Declaration of Independence' of Kosovo. *Accordance with International Law of the Unilateral Declaration of Independence by the Provisional Institutions of Self-Government of Kosovo*, ICJ Order of 17 October 2008.

[111] ICJ Statute, art 68; ICJ Rules, art 102(2).

will be accelerated.[112] In the event that the ICJ finds that the request for an advisory opinion relates to a pending legal dispute between two or more states, it will enable these states to appoint ad hoc judges.[113]

The decision of the Court takes the form of an advisory opinion containing, *inter alia*, the following information: a summary of the proceedings, a statement of the facts, reasons in points of law for the opinion, and a reply to the question put before the Court.[114] Any judge may append to the opinion his or her separate or dissenting opinion.[115] The opinion is to be read in public and made publicly available.[116] In all events, advisory opinions are not formally binding—not even on the requesting organization.[117]

Procedural Aspects

Languages

1.22 The two official languages of the ICJ are English and French.[118] The parties may agree that the proceedings will be conducted in only one of the official languages, otherwise either of the two languages can be used.[119] Normally, all oral presentations made in one official language will be interpreted into the other.[120] The Court may authorize a party to use another language in its submissions; however, that party must provide for translation or interpretation into one of the official languages.[121]

Instituting proceedings

1.23 Cases may be initiated before the ICJ either by way of unilateral application or notification of a special agreement referring a case to the Court.[122]

---

[112] ICJ Rules, art 103.

[113] Ibid, art 102(3). Indeed, an ad hoc judge was appointed by Morocco in the *Western Sahara* case. See *Western Sahara* (Order on Judges Ad Hoc) [1965] ICJ Rep 6. In an earlier advisory opinion, the Court rejected the application of the South African government for leave to choose a judge ad hoc. See *Legal Consequences for States of the Continued Presence of South Africa in Namibia (South West Africa) notwithstanding Security Council Resolution 276 (1970)* (Order on Judges Ad Hoc) [1971] ICJ Rep 12.

[114] ICJ Rules, art 107(2).

[115] Ibid, art 107(3).

[116] ICJ Statute, art 67; ICJ Rules, art 107(1).

[117] See eg ICJ President Shi's speech before the General Assembly Sixth Committee, Press Release GA/L/3266 of 5 November 2004, <http://www.un.org/News/Press/docs/2004/gal3266.doc.htm>.

[118] ICJ Statute, art 39(1).

[119] Ibid, art 39(1), (2); ICJ Rules, art 51(1).

[120] ICJ Rules, art 70(1).

[121] ICJ Statute, art 39(3); ICJ Rules, arts 51(2), (3), 70(2), 71(2).

[122] ICJ Statute, art 40(1).

Application

An application should be made in writing and filed with the Registrar. It should   **1.24**
include the following information:

(a) the party making the application; the state against which the claim is
    brought;
(b) the subject of the dispute; the legal grounds upon which the jurisdiction of
    the Court is based; the precise nature of claim—including a succinct state-
    ment of facts and legal grounds; and the name of agent for applicant.[123]

Notification

A notification can be made by all of the parties to the special agreement,   **1.25**
or by one or more of them. It will be accompanied by a copy of the special
agreement, and will indicate the names of the parties and the subject matter
of the dispute unless as much is apparent from the agreement.[124] As soon as
a case is initiated, the Registrar will forward the application or notification
to the other parties to the case.[125] Additional copies will be sent to the UN
Secretary-General and to all states parties to the Statute.[126] After the initiation of proceedings, the President will summon the agents of the parties to
meet him, as soon as possible, in order to ascertain the views of the parties on
questions of procedure.[127]

Financial assistance

States that wish to present a case to the Court by special agreement, but that   **1.26**
need financial assistance to enable them to do so, may apply for assistance
from the Secretary-General's Trust Fund to Assist States in the Settlement of
Disputes through the International Court of Justice, established on 1 November
1989.[128]

---

[123] Ibid, art 40(1); ICJ Rules, arts 38(1), (2), 40(2). In cases brought by a state who is not party
to the Statute (either by way of application or notification), a declaration conforming to the condition set by the Security Council in accordance with Article 35(2) of the Statute must also be
appended, if not already submitted to the Court. ICJ Rules, art 41.
[124] ICJ Rules, art 39.
[125] ICJ Statute, art 40(2); ICJ Rules, arts 38(4), 39(1).
[126] ICJ Statute, art 40(3); ICJ Rules, art 42.
[127] ICJ Rules, art 31.
[128] See 28 ILM 1589 (1989). Until 2009, six states had availed themselves of the Trust
Fund and one of them ultimately decided not to use the funds because of the complexity of
the procedures it involved: J R Crook, 'Current Development: The 2002 Judicial Activity of
the International Court of Justice' (2003) 97 *Am J Int'l L* 352 at 358. See also Committee on
Transnational Dispute Resolution, International Law Association, American Branch, 'Study
and Evaluation of the UN Secretary-General's Trust Fund to Assist States in the Settlement
of Disputes through the International Court of Justice', reprinted in (2002) 1 *Chinese
J Int'l L* 234.

Provisional measures

1.27 The ICJ may indicate provisional measures where such measures are necessary to preserve the respective rights of the parties,[129] provided that the Court is of the view that it has prima-facie jurisdiction over the case[130] and that the measures are urgently needed to 'prevent irreparable prejudice to the rights that are the subject of the dispute before the Court has had an opportunity to render its decision'.[131] While the prima-facie jurisdiction condition has generally been applied in a liberal manner (the exception being the *NATO Bombing* case),[132] the standard set by the Court for establishing irreparable prejudice appears to be rather high. [133]

A party can bring a request for provisional measures at any time during the proceedings. The request is to be made in writing and should specify the measures requested and the anticipated consequences in the event that they are not granted.[134] The Court can also raise on its own initiative the question of whether it should indicate provisional measures.[135] Until the decision on whether to indicate provisional measures has been taken, the President may call on the parties to act in a way which would not frustrate possible measures that the ICJ may indicate.[136]

A request for provisional measures will be treated as a matter of urgency and will have priority over all other cases.[137] The parties are to be given the opportunity of participating in oral proceedings, and may submit to the Court their observations.[138] The measures indicated by the Court may be different from those requested,[139] and any of its decisions on provisional measures may be reviewed at a later date, if a change in the situation is demonstrated.[140] The

---

[129] ICJ Statute, art 41(1). Provisional measures have been requested so far in 38 ICJ cases.

[130] See eg *Application of the Convention on the Prevention and Punishment of the Crime of Genocide* (Bosnia-Herzegovina v Yugoslavia) [1993] ICJ Rep 3 at 11–12; *Vienna Convention on Consular Relations* (Paraguay v United States) [1998] ICJ Rep 248 at 255. The classic example where the Court issued provisional measures but ultimately held that it lacks jurisdiction over the case is the *Anglo-Iranian Co* case. *Anglo-Iranian Oil* [1951] ICJ Rep 89; [1952] ICJ Rep 93. A more recent example may be found in *Request for Interpretation of the Judgment of 31 March 2004 in the Case Concerning Avena and Other Mexican Nationals (Mexico v United States)* (Mexico v United States), Judgment of 19 January 2009.

[131] *Pulp Mills on the River Uruguay* (Argentina v Uruguay), Order of 13 July 2006 at 62. See also *Passage through the Great Belt* (Finland v Denmark) [1991] ICJ Rep 12 at 17; *Certain Criminal Proceedings in France* [2003] ICJ Rep 102 at 107.

[132] *Legality of Use of Force* (Yugoslavia v Belgium) [1999] ICJ Rep 124.

[133] *Pulp Mills, supra* note 131, at 73–78.

[134] ICJ Rules, art 73.

[135] Ibid, art 75(1). See *LaGrand* (Germany v United States) [1999] ICJ Rep 9 at 14.

[136] ICJ Rules, art 74(4).

[137] Ibid, art 74(1), (2).

[138] Ibid, art 74(3).

[139] Ibid, arts 75(2), (3), 76.

[140] Ibid, art 76. See eg *Application of the Genocide Convention on the Prevention and Punishment of the Crime of Genocide* (Bosnia and Herzegovina v Yugoslavia) [1993] ICJ Rep 325 at 337.

Court may also request information on the implementation of the provisional measures.[141]

In the *LaGrand* case, the Court held that provisional measures orders issued by the Court have 'binding effect' upon the parties to the case.[142] This decision had resolved a long-standing controversy over the precise legal effect of provisional measures orders.

Preliminary objections

A party that objects to the jurisdiction of the Court, the admissibility of the application, or to any other issue of a preliminary nature may file a preliminary objection with the Registry before the expiration of the time limit fixed for the submission of the counter-memorial (see para 1.30 *infra*).[143]

1.28

The following legal grounds were raised as objections to the Court's jurisdiction over the case or its admissibility[144] during the preliminary objections stage of the proceedings or, when objections to jurisdiction were joined to the merits phase, at the merits stage of the proceedings. These objections have led the Court to decline jurisdiction in some 20 cases (resulting in dismissal of the case) or to refuse to hear in many other cases part of the claim brought before it: lack of a valid jurisdiction-conferring instrument in force between the parties,[145] invalidity of optional clause declarations,[146] applicability of a reservation to the said agreements or declarations,[147] non-membership of the ICJ Statute,[148] lack of exhaustion of local remedies,[149] lack of right of standing or diplomatic protection,[150]

---

[141] ICJ Rules, art 78. According to Practice Direction XI (as amended on 30 July 2004), the parties 'should not enter into the merits of the case beyond what is strictly necessary' for the purpose of addressing the need for issuing provisional measures.

[142] *LaGrand* [2001] ICJ Rep 466 at 506.

[143] ICJ Rules, art 79(1). Preliminary objections have been filed in 25 cases so far, while questions of jurisdiction or admissibility have also been brought forward in some 13 other cases.

[144] For the distinction between jurisdiction and admissibility, see J Collier and V Lowe, *The Settlement of Disputes in International Law: Institutions and Procedures* (1999) at 155–156.

[145] See eg *Aegean Sea* [1978] ICJ Rep 3 at 44; *Maritime Delimitation between Qatar and Bahrain* [1994] ICJ Rep 112 at 122.

[146] See eg *Military and Paramilitary Activities* [1984] ICJ Rep 392 at 412–413; *Aerial Incident of July 27th 1955* (Israel v Bulgaria) [1959] ICJ Rep 127 at 145.

[147] See eg *Certain Norwegian Loans* [1957] ICJ Rep 9 at 27; *Fisheries Jurisdiction* [1998] ICJ Rep 432 at 454. The validity of the reservations themselves may also be at issue in such preliminary proceedings: see eg *Certain Norwegian Loans,* ibid at 55 (Separate Opinion of Judge Lauterpacht); and *Interhandel* (Switzerland v United States) [1959] ICJ Rep 6 at 76–78 (Dissenting Opinion of President Klaesad), as well as 101–102 (Dissenting Opinion of Judge Lauterpacht).

[148] *Legality of Use of Force* [2004] ICJ Rep 279 at 314–315.

[149] See *Interhandel* [1959] ICJ Rep at 27–29; *Avena* [2004] ICJ Rep at 34–36; *Ahmadou Sadio Diallo* (Guinea v Democratic Republic of the Congo), Judgment of 24 May 2007 at 41–48.

[150] See eg *Nottebohm* (Liechtenstein v Guatemala) [1955] ICJ Rep 4 at 26; *South West Africa* [1962] ICJ Rep 319 at 328; *Barcelona Traction, Light and Power Co. Ltd* (Belgium v Spain) [1970] ICJ Rep 3 at 51; *Diallo, supra* note 149, at 62.

infringement upon rights of third parties,[151] and lack or mootness of the dispute or lack of purpose to the proceedings.[152] It has also been suggested by the PCIJ in *obiter dicta* that it may dismiss a case if another court is clearly invested with exclusive jurisdiction over the same dispute.[153]

Some of the grounds for lack of jurisdiction and inadmissibility in contentious proceedings have also been raised in advisory proceedings, although to date the Court accommodated (except in one case)[154] all requests for advisory opinions referred to it. It may also be noted that all objections to jurisdiction—in both contentious and advisory cases—based on the alleged political nature of the proceedings had failed.[155]

Any objection to jurisdiction or admissibility must set out the arguments of fact and the law upon which it is based, indicate evidence relevant to the objection that the objecting party intends to present, and include copies of supporting documents.[156] Upon the filing of a preliminary objection the proceedings are suspended and the Court fixes a time limit for the other party to submit its written observations and submissions on the matter.[157] All other proceedings on the motion are normally oral.[158] After hearing the parties, the Court renders its decision as to the objection in the form of a judgment. The judgment may uphold or reject the objection, or defer the decision by joining jurisdictional issues to the merits stage.[159]

---

[151] See eg *Monetary Gold Removed from Rome in 1943* (Italy v France, United Kingdom, United States) [1954] ICJ Rep 19 at 33; *East Timor* (Portugal v Australia) [1995] ICJ Rep 90 at 101–104.
[152] *Northern Cameroons* (Cameroon v United Kingdom) [1963] ICJ Rep 15 at 38; *Nuclear Tests* (Australia v France) [1974] ICJ Rep 253 at 271–272; *Territorial and Maritime Dispute, supra* note 91, at 138.
[153] See *Factory at Chorzow* [1927] PCIJ (Ser A), No 9 at 30. At the same time, the Court rejected objections to jurisdiction and admissibility which were based on the supposed exclusive jurisdiction of the UN Security Council over matters relating to international peace and security. *Military and Paramilitary Activities* [1984] ICJ Rep at 431–436; *Diplomatic and Consular Staff in Tehran* [1980] ICJ Rep 3 at 20–24. See also *Certain Phosphate Lands* [1992] ICJ Rep 240 at 245–246 (Court rejecting Australia's argument that the UN Trusteeship Council and General Assembly had exclusive jurisdiction).
[154] *Legality of the Use by a State of Nuclear Weapons* [1996] ICJ Rep 66.
[155] See eg *Military and Paramilitary Activities* [1984] ICJ Rep at 431–436; *Construction of a Wall* [2004] ICJ Rep 136 at 162.
[156] ICJ Rules, art 79(1), (4).
[157] Ibid, art 79(5). Such time limit will generally not exceed four months. Practice Direction V, <http://www.icj-cij.org/documents/index.php?p1=4&p2=4&p3=0>.
[158] ICJ Rules, art 79(6).
[159] Ibid, art 79(9). The Court will join discussion of jurisdictional issues with the merits if the two aspects cannot be addressed separately or if deciding on jurisdiction would prejudge the merits of the case. See *Barcelona Traction* [1964] ICJ Rep 6 at 43. However, there is no bar against adjudicating jurisdictional issues which merely touch upon questions belonging to the merits stage. See *Territorial and Maritime Dispute, supra* note 91, at 51; *Certain German Interests in Polish Upper Silesia* [1925] PCIJ (Ser A), No 6 at 15. In addition, the Court will jointly decide the preliminary objection and the merits if the case, if the parties so agree. ICJ Rules, art 79(10).

Written phase

Proceedings before the ICJ are divided into two parts—written and oral.[160]   **1.29**

Written proceedings open with the filing of a memorial on behalf of the applicant and the subsequent filing of a counter-memorial by the respondent.[161] In cases brought by way of Special Agreement, the parties may agree on the number and order of written pleadings. Although the Rules of Court provide that, in the absence of an agreement to the contrary, the parties will file their memorial and counter-memorial within the same time limits,[162] the Court expressed displeasure with the simultaneous submission of written pleadings in Practice Direction I, and strongly urged the parties to agree on consecutive filings.[163]

In all cases the Court may authorize the submission of an applicant's Reply and a respondent's Rejoinder, if it finds such pleadings to be necessary (either upon the request of a party, or acting *proprio motu),* or if the parties so agree.[164] After the closure of the written proceedings, no documents may be submitted to the Court, except with the consent of the other party, or the authorization of the Court (in which case, the other party will be able to comment upon the submission and present additional supporting documents).[165]

A memorial is to include a clear and concise statement of the relevant facts and law and the submissions of the relevant party.[166] A counter-memorial will contain an admission or denial of the facts stated in the memorial, any additional facts, observations on the applicant's statement of law, a statement of law in answer thereto, and the respondent's submissions.[167] Relevant supporting documents must be attached to the pleadings.[168] Time limits for filing of all submissions are determined by the Court, after ascertaining the views of the parties.[169] Any agreement between the parties as to the schedule of the case will normally be given effect to (unless it results in unjustified delay).[170]

The respondent party may present a counter-claim, provided that it is directly connected to the subject matter of the original claim and falls under the

---

[160] ICJ Statute, art 43(1).
[161] Ibid, art 43(2); ICJ Rules, art 45(1).
[162] ICJ Rules, art 46.
[163] Practice Direction I, <http://www.icj-cij.org/documents/index.php?p1=4&p2=4&p3=0>.
[164] ICJ Statute, art 43(2); ICJ Rules, arts 45(2), 46(2).
[165] ICJ Rules, art 56.
[166] Ibid, art 49(1). See also Practice Directions II–III.
[167] ICJ Rules, art 49(2).
[168] Ibid, art 50(1). The parties should refrain from appending lengthy and irrelevant annexes. See Practice Direction III.
[169] ICJ Statute, art 43(3); ICJ Rules, art 44(1).
[170] ICJ Rules, art 44(2).

jurisdiction of the ICJ.[171] A counter-claim must be included in the counter-memorial, and it will constitute part of the submissions of the respondent state.[172] The applicant may challenge the admissibility of the counter-claim before the Court, which shall decide on the matter, after hearing the parties.[173]

Oral phase

1.30   After the end of the written stage of the proceedings, the Court fixes dates for holding of oral hearings.[174] It will also determine, after ascertaining the views of the parties, the order of the oral proceedings (including whether evidence or arguments will be presented first), the method of handling of evidence (including examination of witnesses), and the number of representatives to be heard on behalf of each party.[175]

The oral statements of the parties are to be as succinct as possible, and should focus on issues which still divide the parties (as opposed to a mere repetition of the written submissions).[176] The Court may indicate points or issues on which it would like the parties to elaborate or refrain from arguing.[177] The Court may also put questions and ask for explanations from the representatives of the parties (it may also call for the production of evidence necessary to elucidate matters at issue).[178] However, in actuality, the Court tends to apply its investigative powers in a sparse manner (presenting few questions, normally in writing, and allowing the parties ample time to respond)—an attitude which suggests a high degree of deference to the sovereignty of the states appearing before the Court.

During oral hearings the parties may call witnesses and experts on their behalf to testify before the Court.[179] A list of prospective witnesses must be communicated to the Registrar in sufficient time before the opening of the oral stage of the proceedings.[180] Witnesses not on the list can be summoned only

---

[171] Ibid, art 80(1). See eg *Application of the Genocide Convention on the Prevention and Punishment of the Crime of Genocide* (Bosnia and Herzegovina v Serbia and Montenegro) [1997] ICJ Rep 243 at 259 (counter-claims order); *Oil Platforms* (Islamic Republic of Iran v United States) [1998] ICJ Rep 190 at 205; *Land and Maritime Boundary between Cameroon and Nigeria* (Cameroon v Nigeria; Equatorial Guinea intervening) [1999] ICJ Rep 983 at 985–986; *Armed Activities on the Territory of the Congo* (Democratic Republic of the Congo v Uganda) [2001] ICJ Rep 660 at 678–681.

[172] ICJ Rules, art 80(2).

[173] Ibid, art 80(3).

[174] ICJ Statute, art 48; ICJ Rules, art 54(1).

[175] ICJ Rules, art 58.

[176] Ibid, art 60(1). See also Practice Direction VI.

[177] ICJ Rules, art 61(1).

[178] Ibid, arts 61(2)–(4), 62(1). If the Court receives answers or evidence after the end of oral proceedings, it will communicate the submission to the other party, and may reopen the proceedings if necessary. ICJ Rules, art 72. See also Zimmermann, *supra* note 105, at 1101.

[179] ICJ Statute, art 43(5); ICJ Rules, art 63(1).

[180] ICJ Rules, art 57.

if the other party does not object or with the authorization of the Court. The Court may also summon, on its own initiative, witnesses and experts to testify in the proceedings, although here again such powers are used sparingly.[181] The parties and the judges may question the witnesses and experts.[182]

Oral hearings before the ICJ are public, unless the Court decides otherwise, or unless the parties demand, at any time, that some or all sessions will be closed to the public.[183]

Third party intervention

A third state that has an interest of a legal nature, and which may be affected by the decision in a case, may request to intervene in proceedings before the ICJ.[184] In addition, in disputes relating to the interpretation of a convention to which states other than the states litigating before the Court are parties, those third states have the right to intervene in the proceedings.[185] **1.31**

Although initially there was some uncertainty over the question of whether the intervening party should establish an independent jurisdictional title for its own dispute with the parties to the proceedings, it is now well established that no additional jurisdictional title is needed and that the Statute can serve as a sufficient basis for intervention of parties thereto in pending cases.[186]

A request for intervention due to a legal interest is referred to as intervention under article 62 of the ICJ Statute, and must be filed with the Registry as soon as possible and (except in extraordinary circumstances) not later than the end of the written stage of the proceedings.[187] The application should specify, *inter alia*, the interest of a legal nature that might be affected by the decision in the case, the precise object of the intervention, and any basis of jurisdiction between the intervening state and the parties to the case (although, as noted above, the existence of such jurisdiction is not essential).[188]

---

[181] Ibid, art 62(2); Zimmermann, *supra* note 105, at 1101.

[182] ICJ Statute, art 51; ICJ Rules, art 65.

[183] ICJ Statute, art 46; ICJ Rules, art 59. The Court has held closed hearings in a few cases, including in the *Temple of Preah Vihear* and *Tunisia/Libya Continental Shelf* cases. See Rosenne, *supra* note 53, at 129. In 1971, an application by the South African government in the *Namibia* case was heard in closed session. The application was rejected and, at the conclusion of the proceedings, the closed hearings were made public.

[184] ICJ Statute, art 62. This rule constitutes a 'mirror-image' of the 'third party rights and interests' doctrine developed by the Court in *Monetary Gold* and other cases, which bars litigation of disputes, where the rights and interests of third parties form the very subject matter of the dispute, without participation in the proceedings of the affected third parties. *Monetary Gold* [1954] ICJ Rep 19 at 33; *East Timor* [1995] ICJ Rep 90 at 101–104.

[185] ICJ Statute, art 63.

[186] *Land, Island and Maritime Frontier Dispute* (El Salvador/Honduras) [1990] ICJ Rep 92 at 135.

[187] ICJ Rules, art 81(1).

[188] Ibid, art 81(2), (3).

A state that wishes to intervene in cases concerning interpretation of a treaty (referred to as intervention under article 63 of the ICJ Statute) must file a declaration to this effect with the Registry—whether or not it has received a notification from the Registry indicating that the construction of a treaty to which it is party is at issue.[189] The declaration should also be submitted as soon as possible and (unless there are exceptional circumstances) not later than on the date of closure of the written proceedings. It must include, *inter alia*, the basis on which the declaring state considers itself to be a party to the relevant convention, the particular provisions of the convention the construction of which it considers to be in question, and the construction of those provisions which the intervening party contends.[190]

The Registrar will communicate copies of article 62 or article 63 declarations to the parties to the case, which will be invited to provide written observations on the request within time limits fixed by the Court (or the President).[191] The Court will then decide, as a matter of priority, whether to accept the application for intervention, or whether the declaration of intent to intervene is admissible. In the event that an objection is filed by one of the original parties to the proceedings, the Court will decide the motion only after hearing the intervening state, and any party to the case that objects to the intervention.[192] If a request to intervene is granted, the intervening party will be entitled to participate in the written and oral pleadings.[193]

So far the Court has received requests for intervention on ten occasions (eight times under article 62 and three times under article 63—one occasion featuring a request under both articles), although intervention has been permitted in three cases only.[194] The disinclination of the Court to permit third party intervention can be explained, perhaps, by the need to refrain from excessively complicating the proceedings and its reluctance to upset the expectations of the original parties to litigation (who may wish the Court to focus on their mutual legal relations only). A lenient standard of intervention might lead potential parties to ICJ litigation to prefer arbitration, a process from which third parties can be excluded altogether.

Multiple proceedings

1.32   The Statute of the ICJ clearly envisages multi-party proceedings. For instance, it specifies that in the event that several parties to a case are of the same legal interest they will appoint one ad hoc judge only.[195] The Court may also direct

---

[189] ICJ Statute, art 63; ICJ Rules, art 82(1), (3).

[190] ICJ Rules, art 82(2).

[191] Ibid, art 83(1).

[192] ICJ Statute, art 62(2); ICJ Rules, art 84.

[193] ICJ Rules, arts 85, 86.

[194] *Haya de la Torre* (Peru/Columbia) [1951] ICJ Rep 71; *Land, Island and Maritime Frontier Dispute* [1990] ICJ Rep 92; *Land and Maritime Boundary between Cameroon and Nigeria* (Cameroon v Nigeria) (Order on Application to Intervene by Equatorial Guinea) [1999] ICJ Rep 1029.

[195] ICJ Statute, art 31(5); ICJ Rules, art 36.

that proceedings in two or more cases be formally joined or litigated together without formal joinder.[196]

The Court first formally joined proceedings in 1961 when two cases separately initiated by Ethiopia and Liberia were found to feature the same litigation interests.[197] Formal joinder has been utilized several times since then.[198] It should be noted, however, that whilst a decision to join proceedings will practically always lead to the conclusion that parties are of the same interest, the opposite is not true. The Court may decline to hear cases of common interest together for a number of reasons, so that the number of joined cases does not reflect the number of cases with the same interest that the Court actually hears.[199] As stated, however, a formal order is not required to join cases.[200]

Amicus curiae briefs

The ICJ Statute and Rules introduce, at present, only procedures for submission **1.33** of materials to the Court by international organizations (ie *intergovernmental* organizations), which may be conducive to the settlement of pending cases. In contentious proceedings, international organizations may file, on their own initiative, a memorial with the Registry in relation to any case before the ICJ. The memorial needs to be submitted before the closing of the written pleadings, and should include any information relevant to the case.[201] The Court may ask

---

[196] ICJ Rules, art 47.

[197] See *South West Africa* [1961] ICJ Rep 13.

[198] See *North Sea Continental Shelf* [1968] ICJ Rep 9 (separate cases initiated on the basis of two distinct special agreements were joined because their submissions were set out in almost identical terms). See also the *Nuclear Tests* [1973] ICJ Rep 99.

[199] See Zimmermann, *supra* note 105, at 501–503. In the *Lockerbie* cases, the United Kingdom and the United States presented identical claims, yet a conflict of interest was declared to exist (because one of the presiding judges held the nationality of one of the states parties), which ultimately prevented the cases from being joined. The Court gave no explanation of its decision: *Questions of Interpretation and Application of the 1971 Montreal Convention arising from the Aerial Incident at Lockerbie* (Libyan Arab Jamahiriya v United Kingdom) [1998] ICJ Rep 9. The same also occurred in the *NATO Bombing* cases, where conflicts of interest (also the result of nationality clashes) caused proceedings of exactly the same nature to be heard separately. The action of the Court and its subsequent result were criticized by Judge Kreca, who suggested that if several parties of the same interest have a judge of their nationality on the bench, then the other party should be entitled to appoint as many ad hoc judges as required, in order to reflect the basic principle of the sovereign equality of the Court. As limited reasons are given for decisions whether to join cases or not, the matter is unclear and inconsistent. See *Legality of Use of Force* [1999] ICJ Rep 124 at 130 and at <http://www.icj-cij.org>, at 18.

[200] See the *Fisheries Jurisdiction* and *Nuclear Tests* cases, where arrangements were adopted to facilitate their hearing without the formal making of any order: *Fisheries Jurisdiction* [1973] ICJ Rep 3 and 49; *Nuclear Tests* (Australia v France) (New Zealand v France), ICJ Rep 253 and 457. In the *Legality of the Use of Force Cases,* Yugoslavia brought separate proceedings against ten NATO member states. Requests for the implementation of provisional measures made in the ten applications were heard in common hearings without the Court making specific orders to that effect.

[201] ICJ Statute, art 34(2); ICJ Rules, art 69(2), (4).

the organization for further information to be presented either in writing or orally,[202] and the parties will be given the opportunity to comment (orally or in writing) on the information presented by the international organization. In addition, the Court may, acting *proprio motu,* or upon the request of one of the parties, ask for information from an international organization (even if the latter did not submit a memorial).[203] In the event that the constituent instrument of an international organization, or an international convention adopted under its auspices, is at issue, the Court must notify the concerned international organization accordingly, so as to facilitate its involvement in the case.[204]

In advisory proceedings, the Court's Statute provides for the participation of international organizations considered likely to be able to furnish information on the question at hand.[205] Such organizations may participate in the advisory proceedings on the same footing as member states.

Practice Direction XII (as amended on 20 July 2004) regulates, for the first time, the submission of information to the Court by non-governmental organizations (NGOs) in the course of advisory proceedings. While the Direction prescribes that written statements or documents submitted by NGOs would not constitute part of the case file, states and international organizations may rely upon them in their submissions (like other publicly available information). At present, no NGO involvement in contentious cases is possible.[206]

Representation of parties

1.34 Parties to disputes before the Court are to be represented by agents who must have an address for service at the seat of the Court. Parties may have the assistance of counsel or advocates before the Court.[207]

---

202 ICJ Statute, art 34(2); ICJ Rules, art 69(2).

203 ICJ Rules, art 69(1).

204 ICJ Statute, art 34(3); ICJ Rules, art 69(3).

205 ICJ Statute, art 66(2).

206 Art 34, para 2 of the ICJ Statute has been narrowly interpreted so that the terms 'public international organization' and 'international organization' are limited to intergovernmental organizations only; this means that NGOs are prevented from appearing before the Court. In the *Asylum* case, the Court had the opportunity to interpret art 34 with some degree of flexibility, but considered such a course of action to be impossible. As a result, there has been no real attempt by NGOs to participate in contentious cases since the *Asylum* case. It may be noted that in 1997, during the *Gabcikovo-Nagymaros* case, NGOs offered to assist Hungary with establishing their scientific argument; but eventually Hungary chose instead to set up a team of high-ranking international scientists for that purpose.

The Practice Note to Practice Direction XII (issued by the Court on 30 July 2004) states that 'a written statement or information submitted on its initiative by an NGO to the court is not to be considered as part of the case at file'. Hence, every *amicus* appearance before the Court to date has been espoused by states or intergovernmental bodies. Requests from individuals to act as *amicus* have been refused until now for fear of opening the floodgates: see *The Registrar to Professor Reisman* (6 November 1970) (Correspondence) ICJ Acts & Docs (1970).

207 ICJ Statute, art 42; ICJ Rules, art 40.

According to Practice Direction VIII, past members of the Court (judges—including ad hoc judges—and other court officials) should not serve as party representatives in the first three years following their departure from the Court.

Decision

Final decisions of the ICJ on jurisdiction and the merits of the dispute are issued **1.35** in the form of a judgment containing, *inter alia*, a summary of the proceedings, the submissions of parties, a statement of the facts, legal motivations for the decision, operative provisions, and, where relevant, allocation of costs.[208] All questions before the ICJ are decided by a majority of the judges.[209] Still, any judge may append to the judgment his or her separate or dissenting opinions, or a declaration.[210]

In the event that one of the parties withdraws from the proceedings, or does not appear in them from the beginning, the Court may decide the case in favour of the other party, provided that it finds that it has jurisdiction over the claim and that the claim is well founded in fact and law.[211]

The judgment is read in public, and becomes binding on the parties on the day of the reading.[212]

Appeal

The judgments of the Court are final and binding, and are not subject to **1.36** appeal.[213]

Interpretation and revision of judgment

In the event that a dispute arises between the parties as to the meaning or scope **1.37** of the judgment (including a judgment of preliminary objections to jurisdiction), each party may request the ICJ to interpret it.[214] Still, the Court has held that its powers of interpretation should be applied cautiously, in ways which

---

[208] ICJ Statute, art 56; ICJ Rules, art 95(1).
[209] ICJ Statute, art 55. If the votes are even, the President will cast a decisive vote. In the work of the ICJ, the presidential vote has been decisive in only two cases: *South West Africa* [1966] ICJ Rep 6; *Legality of the Threat of Use of Nuclear Weapons Case* [1996] ICJ Rep 226. In the history of the PCIJ, a decisive presidential vote was cast in *Lotus* (France v Turkey) [1927] PCIJ (Ser A), No 10.
[210] ICJ Statute, art 57; ICJ Rules, art 95(2).
[211] ICJ Statute, art 53.
[212] ICJ Statute, art 58; ICJ Rules, art 94(2). On the *res judicata* nature of ICJ judgments (including judgments on jurisdiction), see *Application of the Genocide Convention on the Prevention and Punishment of the Crime of Genocide* (Bosnia and Herzegovina v Serbia and Montenegro), Judgment of 26 February 2007 at 114–120.
[213] ICJ Statute, art 60.
[214] ICJ Statute, art 60; ICJ Rules, art 98(1).

respect the *res judicata* nature of the judgment in question. Hence, in the *Asylum (Interpretation)* case, the Court stated that only requests whose real and sole purpose is to obtain clarification of binding parts of the judgment should be accommodated.[215] As a result, the request must 'relate to the operative part of the judgment and cannot concern the reasons for the judgment except in so far as these are inseparable from the operative part'.[216] To date, four applications for interpretation have been submitted to the Court, although only in one case (*Tunisia/Libyan Continental Shelf (Revision and Interpretation)*) did the Court find such an application to be admissible. In one case, which the Court eventually found to be inadmissible, provisional measures were issued.[217]

As far as the procedure of applying for judgment interpretation goes, a request for interpretation can be made by way of a unilateral application, or joint notification of a special agreement between the parties referring to the Court a question for interpretation. In any case, the request must specify the precise points in dispute between the parties.[218] If the request was made through a unilateral application, the Court will enable the other party to file its observations within a fixed time limit.[219]

An application for revision of a judgment can be made only on the basis of discovery of a new fact of such a nature as to be a decisive factor in the outcome of the case. This fact must have been unknown to the Court and to the party requesting a revision when the judgment was rendered, and the ignorance of the party must not have been due to negligence.[220] In *Bosnian Genocide (Revision)*, it was held that an application for revision cannot be based on new facts that occurred after the judgment was issued, even if such facts conferred new legal meaning on the facts which had been before the Court at the time.[221] Hence, the readmission of Yugoslavia to the UN in 2000 could not affect the validity of the 1996 judgment (which was premised on the view that Yugoslavia should be regarded, at least for jurisdictional purposes, as bound by the UN Charter

---

[215] *Request for Interpretation of the Judgment of 20 November 1950 in the Asylum Case* (Colombia/Peru) [1950] ICJ Rep 395 at 402. See also *Application for Revision und Interpretation of the Judgment of 24 February 1982 in the Case concerning the Continental Shelf (Tunisia/Libyan Arab Jamahiriya)* (Tunisia v Libya) [1985] ICJ Rep 192 at 223.

[216] *Request for Interpretation of the Judgment of 11 June 1998 in the Case concerning the Land and Maritime Boundary between Cameroon and Nigeria (Cameroon v Nigeria)* (Nigeria v Cameroon) [1999] ICJ Rep 31 at 35.

[217] *Request for Interpretation of the Judgment of 31 March 2004 in the Case concerning Avena and Other Mexican Nationals (Mexico v United States)* (Mexico v United States), Order of 16 July 2008.

[218] ICJ Rules, art 98(2).

[219] Ibid, art 98(3). In all cases the ICJ may request the parties to provide additional written or oral explanations. Ibid, art 98(4).

[220] ICJ Statute, art 61(1).

[221] *Application for Revision of the Judgment of 11 July 1996 in the Case concerning Application of the Convention on the Prevention and Punishment of the Crime of Genocide (Bosnia-Herzegovina v Yugoslavia)* (Bosnia-Herzegovina v Yugoslavia) [2003] ICJ Rep 7 at 30.

and ICJ Statute). So far the Court has been asked to revise its judgments in three cases[222]—although all these applications were found to be inadmissible.

In terms of the procedure governing revision motions, the application for revision must be filed within six months from the date of discovery of the new fact, and in no case after ten years from the date of judgment.[223] The application should include all particulars necessary to show that the conditions for revision have been met, and should be supported by relevant documents.[224] The other party will be given the opportunity to submit written observations on the admissibility of the application within a time limit fixed by the Court.[225] The Court then decides on the admissibility of the application, after providing the parties with an additional opportunity, if necessary, of presenting their views.[226] If the Court finds the application admissible, it will fix time limits for proceedings on the merits of the application (after ascertaining the views of the parties where necessary).[227]

The decision of the Court, with regards to motions for both interpretation and revision, is made in the form of a judgment.[228] In cases relating to judgments rendered by a chamber of the ICJ, any requests for interpretation or revision will be dealt with by the same chamber.[229]

Costs

The expenses of the ICJ are borne by the states parties to the Statute.[230] In the **1.38** event that a state not party to the ICJ Statute appears before the Court, the Court will fix the amount it must pay towards the expenses of the Court.[231] Each of the parties to any case before the Court bears its own expenses, unless the Court decides otherwise.[232]

Execution of decision, recognition, and enforcement

The judgments of the Court are final and binding, and must be complied **1.39** with.[233] In the event that a party to a case fails to perform the obligations

---

[222] Ibid; *Application for Revision of the Judgment of 11 September 1992 concerning the Land, Island and Maritime Frontier Dispute* (El Salvador/Honduras; Nicaragua Intervening) [2003] ICJ Rep 392; *Tunisia/Libyan Continental Shelf (Revision and Interpretation)*, [1985] ICJ Rep 192.
[223] ICJ Statute, art 61(4), (5).
[224] ICJ Rules, art 99(1).
[225] Ibid, art 99(2).
[226] ICJ Statute, art 61(2).
[227] ICJ Rules, art 99(4).
[228] Ibid, art 100(2).
[229] Ibid, art 100(1).
[230] ICJ Statute, art 33. That article provides that the UN will bear the expenses of the Court. Non-UN members that are parties to the Court's Statute have also been required to pay their share of the Court's expenses.
[231] Ibid, art 35(3).
[232] Ibid, art 64; ICJ Rules, art 97.
[233] UN Charter, art 94(1).

incumbent upon it under a judgment, the other party may have recourse to the Security Council, which may adopt recommendations or binding decisions pertaining to the enforcement of judgment.[234] To date, the Security Council's judgment-enforcement powers have never been used.[235] Still, states have normally complied with the Court's judgments (although there have been some conspicuous cases of non-compliance or significant delay in compliance).[236]

Evaluation

Although the ICJ constitutes the 'principal judicial organ' of the United Nations,[237] the Charter drafters' expectations that the Court would assume a central place in the post-war world order and enjoy a greater success in this field than the PCIJ have not been fully realized. In fact, the caseload of the ICJ (some 120 contentious cases in 63 years—that is, on average, less than two cases per year) has been lighter than the comparable caseload of the PCIJ, although the latter served a much smaller community of states.[238] In the same vein, the actual number of advisory opinions referred to the Court by the UN principal organs and other international agencies has been lower than the comparable figure for the PCIJ (25 cases were presented to the ICJ in 63 years; whereas 27 cases

---

[234] Ibid, art 94(2). See generally Zimmermann, *supra* note 105, at 1246. This paragraph constitutes a special basis for seizing the jurisdiction of the UN Security Council, and does not presuppose that non-compliance with a judgment 'might lead to international friction or give rise to a dispute which is likely to endanger the maintenance of international peace and security'—as required per art 34 of the UN Charter.

[235] Recourse to the Security Council for judgment-enforcement has been attempted in only one case—*Military and Paramilitary Activities*. Nicaragua twice brought the matter before the Security Council in reliance on art 94(2). On each occasion, the draft resolution of the Security Council was defeated by the negative vote of the United States—a permanent member of the Council. The United States refused to acknowledge the jurisdiction of the Court in this matter, and refused to accept the Court's decisions with regard to it. From this precedent it can be assumed that the involvement of the Security Council in enforcing a judgment of the ICJ in accordance with art 94(2) will be meaningless if directed against a permanent member of the Security Council or its interests. See generally Zimmermann, *supra* note 105, at 120: the question whether decisions *other than judgments* of the ICJ could be enforced by means of art 94(2) was first raised in the *Anglo-Iranian Oil* case of 1951. The answer to this question first requires a definitive answer as to whether provisional measures ordered by the ICJ have the same binding quality as judgments. Since the ICJ eventually held that it has no jurisdiction over the cases, the question became moot.

[236] See C Paulson, 'Compliance with Final Judgments of the International Court of Justice since 1987' (2004) 98 *Am J Int'l L* 434; C Schulte, *Compliance with Decisions of the International Court of Justice* (2004); D J Harris, *Cases and Materials on International Law* (1998) at 1004; J M Trolldalen, *International Environmental Conflict Resolution, The Role of United Nations* (1992) at 19–20.

[237] UN Charter, art 92.

[238] The PCIJ addressed 29 contentious cases in less than 20 years of existence.

were presented to the PCIJ in less than 20 years of actual operation). A relative comparison of the numbers of states accepting the compulsory jurisdiction of the PCIJ and ICJ (59 out of 65 parties to the PCIJ Statute,[239] as opposed to 66 out of 192 parties to the ICJ Statute) is also unflattering to the ICJ, although one should note that the ICJ's jurisdiction is supported by many more multilateral conventions than the jurisdiction of the PCIJ.

While the limited business of the ICJ can be partly explained by the emergence of new international courts discussed elsewhere in this Manual (such as the World Trade Organization's dispute settlement bodies, or the European Court of Human Rights), it still attests to the less-than-central role that the ICJ plays in international life. (In fact, the establishment of new courts could be viewed as a vote of no-confidence in the ICJ's ability to handle many international disputes.)[240] Indeed, many of the major international conflicts of the post-Second World War era (ie Korea, Vietnam, the Israel-Arab Wars, and the Falklands) were hardly ever referred to the Court; and even when the Court addressed some peripheral aspects of major international conflicts—usually on the basis of unilateral applications or requests for advisory opinion (ie the *Tehran Hostages*, *Western Sahara*, or *Wall in Occupied Territories* cases)[241]—its actual contribution to resolution of the issues underlying the referred dispute or question has been modest.[242] The fact that only one of the permanent members of the Security Council (the UK) accepts the compulsory jurisdiction of the Court under the optional clause is also perhaps indicative of limited political acceptance of the Court's role in matters of 'high politics', which appertain to the interests of the 'big powers' (this being despite the fact that judges carrying the nationality of all five permanent members have, in effect, permanent seats in the Court).

The limited success of the Court in asserting itself as a dominant player in international life does not mean, however, that the Court's contribution to international dispute settlement has been negligible. On the contrary, it appears that the Court has been very effective in settling disputes of 'mid-level' importance, and in maintaining friendly relations between states. For example, the Court

---

[239] There were 65 states to which the Protocol of Signatures was opened for signature. Of those states invited to participate, six declined to sign and eight signatories declined to ratify.

[240] For a discussion, see Y Shany, *The Competing Jurisdictions of International Courts and Tribunals* (2003).

[241] *Construction of a Wall* [2004] ICJ Rep 136; *Diplomatic and Consular Staff in Tehran* [1980] ICJ Rep 3; *Western Sahara* [1975] ICJ Rep 12.

[242] The reluctance of the Court to issue provisional measures in the *NATO Bombing* and *Lockerbie* cases ((*Legality of Use of Force*) [1999] ICJ Rep 124; *Lockerbie* [1992] ICJ Rep 3) and its refusal to interfere with the Security Council's embargo challenged by Bosnia in the *Application of the Genocide Convention* case ([1993] ICJ Rep 3) are perhaps indicative of the Court's own understanding of the limits it faces in handling sensitive 'peace and security' matters.

successfully resolved numerous border delimitation disputes,[243] disputes over use and allocation of shared natural resources,[244] and diplomatic protection cases relating to the treatment of alien nationals.[245] This service should not be trivialized. Without the Court's involvement many such conflicts might have deteriorated into situations that posed a threat to international peace and security (and thus entered into the realm of 'high politics'). The frequent acceptance of the jurisdiction of the Court over border disputes and matters of comparable significance by states from all regions of the world, and the positive record of compliance with the Court's decisions over such matters, are clear indications of the Court's reputation for effectiveness in providing methods for resolving some conflicts and preventing the escalation of others. In addition, the recent growth in the Court's workload and the growing diversity of the cases and parties appearing before it is perhaps indicative of the increasing appeal of the Court and the potential of exerting its influence into new areas of international relations.

In addition, one should note that the Court has played throughout the years an extremely important role in developing international law, and adapting its substantive norms (including international law's 'constitutional components', which encompass, *inter alia*, its sources, law-changing procedures, and hierarchical features) to a changing international reality. Thus, over time, the Court has, for example, developed innovative concepts such as *erga omnes* norms,[246] facilitated the development of new rules on reservations from treaties,[247] integrated equitable considerations into international law,[248] contributed to the emergence of self-determination as a central principle of international law,[249] and clarified key elements in *jus in bello* and *jus ad bellum*.[250]

At the same time, one may identify some lingering problems that detract from the Court's overall standing: (a) politicization—throughout the 'Cold War' and in the post-Cold War era, the Court has come to be perceived by some states as a tool for political gain that can be employed for public relations pur-

---

[243] See eg *Frontier Dispute* [2005] ICJ Rep 90; *Land and Maritime Boundary* [2002] ICJ Rep 303; *Sovereignty over Pulau Ligitan and Pulau Sipadan* (Indonesia/Malaysia) [2002] ICJ Rep 625; *Maritime Delimitation between Qatar and Bahrain* [2001] ICJ Rep 40; *Kasikili/Sedudu Island* (Botswana/Namibia) [1999] ICJ Rep 1045; *Land, Island and Maritime Frontier Dispute* [1992] ICJ Rep 351.

[244] See eg *Gabcikovo-Nagymaros Project* (Hungary/Slovakia) [1997] ICJ Rep 7; *Continental Shelf* [1982] ICJ Rep 18; *North Sea Continental Shelf* [1969] ICJ Rep 3.

[245] See eg *Diallo, supra* note 149; *Avena* [2004] ICJ Rep 12; *Diplomatic and Consular Staff in Tehran* [1980] ICJ Rep 3.

[246] *Barcelona Traction* [1970] ICJ Rep 3 at 32.

[247] *Reservations to the Genocide Convention* [1951] ICJ Rep 15.

[248] *North Sea Continental Shelf* [1969] ICJ Rep at 48–49.

[249] *East Timor* [1995] ICJ Rep 90; *Western Sahara* [1975] ICJ Rep at 21–29.

[250] *Military and Paramilitary Activities* [1984] ICJ Rep 392; *Legality of Nuclear Weapons* [1996] ICJ Rep 226; *Construction of a Wall* [2004] ICJ Rep 136; *Armed Activities on the Territory of the Congo* [2001] ICJ Rep 660.

poses even in circumstances where judicial intervention is likely to be futile. The Court, anxious to broaden its caseload and influence, has cooperated, perhaps unwittingly, with these political agendas and accepted jurisdiction in highly politicized and contentious advisory cases. This development has tainted the image of the Court in the eyes of some and put it on a collision course with some member states; (b) quality of judgments—some of the Court's decisions, especially those related to jurisdictional issues, appear to be based on relatively weak reasoning.[251] While such decisions have helped the Court accommodate some short-term political pressures, they may harm the credibility of the Court, in the long term; (c) anachronistic structure and procedures—the Court's power to resolve disputes only between states renders it less relevant to today's world, in which non-state actors (such as international governmental organizations and NGOs) are becoming more dominant in international life.[252] In addition, the Court's procedures are often lengthy and cumbersome.[253] Although this can be sometimes attributed to the exceptional complexity of some of the cases brought before the Court, it may also be related to the excessive deference traditionally granted by the Court to the 'sovereign' states appearing before it. In particular, the Court's reluctance to engage in assertive cross-examination of agents and witnesses restricts its fact-finding capabilities, and detracts from the persuasive strength of some of its decisions.[254]

REFERENCE

SOURCES OF PREVIOUS CASE LAW, INCLUDING CASE REPORTS

Judgments and orders of court are published in a series titled 'Reports of Judgments, Advisory Opinions and Orders' (in short, ICJ Reports). Since 1949 an ICJ Reports

---

[251] See eg *Military and Paramilitary Activities* case, where the Court accepted jurisdiction even though Nicaragua had a weak basis on which to bring the claim. The resulting decision fuelled more controversy than any other judicial announcement of the ICJ to date and led to the United States withdrawing their acceptance of the Court's compulsory jurisdiction on 7 October 1985. Consider also the Court's contradictory decisions on jurisdiction in *Legality of Use of Force* [2004] ICJ Rep 279; and in *Application of the Genocide Convention* [1995] ICJ Rep 595.

[252] See C P R Romano, 'The Proliferation of International Judicial Bodies: The Pieces of the Puzzle' (1999) *31 NYU J Int'l L & Pol* 709 at 738–748.

[253] E Petersmann, 'Justice as Conflict Resolution: Proliferation, Fragmentation, and Decentralization of Dispute Settlement in International Trade' (2006) *27 U Pa J Int'l Econ* 273 at 301; G Griffith, 'International Dispute Resolution: The Role of the International Court of Justice at the Cusp of the Millennium' in T L H McCormack et al (eds), *A Century of War and Peace: Asia-Pacific Perspectives on the Centenary of the 1899 Hague Peace Conference* (2001) at 59–73.

[254] R B Lillich (ed), *Fact-Finding before International Tribunals* (1992) vii–x; J R Crook, 'Current Development: The 2003 Judicial Activity of the International Court of Justice' (2004) 98 *Am J Int'l L* 309–311.

volume is published each year (before that, a biannual volume covered 1947–48). All decisions of the Court can also be accessed at the Court's website. It is now the practice of the Registry to make judgments available on the Court's website as soon as they have been handed down.

SELECT BIBLIOGRAPHY

Official publications

ICJ Yearbooks published annually.

Summaries of Judgments, Advisory Opinions and Orders of the International Court of Justice, 1948–1991, United Nations, New York (1992) (ST/LEG/SER. F/l); Idem, 1992–1996, United Nations, New York (1998) (ST/LEG/SER. F/l/ Add 1). (Also available in other official languages of the United Nations.)

Books

S Rosenne, *The Law and Practice of the International Court 1920–2005* (4th edn, 2006).

A Zimmermann, *The Statute of the International Court of Justice: A Commentary* (2006).

C Schulte, *Compliance with Decisions of the International Court of Justice* (2004).

J Collier and V Lowe, *The Settlement of Disputes in International Law: Institutions and Procedures* (1999).

D Bowett, *The International Court of Justice: Process, Practice and Procedure* (1997).

A S Muller (eds), *The World Court at the Turn of the Century* (1997).

C Peck and R S Lee, *Increasing the Effectiveness of the International Court of Justice, Proceedings of the ICJ/UNILTAR Colloquium to Celebrate the 50th Anniversary of the Court* (1997).

A Eyffinger, *The International Court of Justice, 1946–1996* (1996).

V Lowe and M Fitzmaurice (eds), *The International Court of Justice as a World Court: Fifty Years of the International Court of Justice* (1996).

T J Bodie, *Politics and the Emergence of an Activist International Court of Justice* (1995).

S Rosenne, *The World Court: What it is and How it Works* (5th edn, 1995).

R Szafarz, *The Compulsory Jurisdiction of the International Court of Justice* (1994).

B M Yarnold, *International Fugitives: A New Role for the International Court of Justice* (1991).

A Bloed and P van Dijk (eds), *Forty Years of the International Court of Justice: Jurisdiction, Equity and Equality* (1988).

L F Damrosch (ed), *The International Court of Justice at a Crossroads* (1987).

G Fitzmaurice, *The Law and Procedure of the International Court of Justice*, 2 vols (1986).

ANNEX

States recognizing the compulsory jurisdiction of the Court (as of September 2009) [with or without reservations]

Australia, Austria, Barbados, Belgium, Botswana, Bulgaria, Cambodia, Cameroon, Canada, Côte d'Ivoire, Costa Rica, Cyprus, Democratic Republic of Congo, Denmark, Djibouti, Dominica, Dominican Republic, Egypt, Estonia, Finland, Gambia, Georgia, Germany,

Greece, Guinea, Guinea-Bissau, Haiti, Honduras, Hungary, India, Japan, Kenya, Lesotho, Liberia, Liechtenstein, Luxembourg, Madagascar, Malawi, Malta, Mauritius, Mexico, Netherlands, New Zealand, Nicaragua, Nigeria, Norway, Pakistan, Panama, Paraguay, Peru, Philippines, Poland, Portugal, Senegal, Slovakia, Somalia, Spain, Sudan, Suriname, Swaziland, Sweden, Switzerland, Togo, Uganda, United Kingdom, Uruguay.

2

THE INTERNATIONAL TRIBUNAL
FOR THE LAW OF THE SEA

Introduction	40	Procedural Aspects	52
Institutional Aspects	42	Evaluation	67

Introduction

Name and seat of the body

2.1 The International Tribunal for the Law of the Sea ('the ITLOS' or 'the Tribunal') is a permanent court established to adjudicate disputes concerning the interpretation or application of the United Nations Convention on the Law of the Sea (UNCLOS).[1] It has its seat in the Free and Hanseatic City of Hamburg in the Federal Republic of Germany. The contact details of the ITLOS are:

> International Tribunal for the Law of the Sea
> Am Internationalen Seegerichtshof 1
> 22609 Hamburg, Germany
> Tel: 49 (40) 35607-0
> Fax: 49 (40) 35607-245
> Email: itlos@itlos.org
> Website: <http://www.itlos.org>

General description

2.2 The ITLOS is an independent international judicial body, established by the 1982 United Nations Convention on the Law of the Sea (UNCLOS). It forms part of the regime established under Part XV of UNCLOS for the peaceful

---

[1] United Nations Convention on the Law of the Sea, 10 December 1982, art 284, UN Doc A/ CONF 62/122 (1982), 21 ILM 1261 (1982) ('UNCLOS').

settlement of disputes concerning the interpretation or application of the Convention and other agreements related to the purposes of the Convention.[2] The Tribunal is governed by its Statute (Annex VI to the Convention), Part XV and relevant provisions in Part XI section 5 of the Convention. The Tribunal is open to states parties and, in specific circumstances, to other states, international organizations, and entities other than states, including private persons and corporations. By July 2009, there were 159 parties to UNCLOS.

With the exception of certain specified categories of dispute, all disputes arising under UNCLOS between states parties are subject to compulsory binding third party settlement. The states parties may select, upon ratification of UNCLOS or at any time thereafter, one or more dispute settlement mechanisms from a menu of four procedures enumerated in article 287 of UNCLOS—the 'choice of procedure' clause. The four alternatives are—the ITLOS, the International Court of Justice, arbitration (under Annex VII to UNCLOS), or special arbitration (under Annex VIII to the Convention). In the event that two states have accepted the same procedure, that procedure will be used in disputes between them. If they have made no choice under article 287, or have selected different procedures, the dispute may only be submitted to arbitration under Annex VII unless the parties to the dispute otherwise agree.

Additionally, the ITLOS enjoys mandatory jurisdiction over all states parties to UNCLOS in relation to some specific causes of action. These are: applications for prompt release of detained vessels and crews;[3] requests for provisional measures, even when the dispute is submitted to arbitration in certain circumstances;[4] and disputes relating to activities in the seabed area.[5] The Tribunal may also receive cases on the basis of international agreements other than UNCLOS.[6]

The Tribunal was established on 1 August 1996. The first 21 judges of the Tribunal took the oath of office on 18 October 1996. The first application instituting a case before ITLOS was received on 13 November 1997, seeking the prompt release of a vessel (the *M/V 'Saiga'*) and its crew under article 292 of UNCLOS, and the first judgment of the Tribunal was delivered on 4 December 1997.[7] By July 2009, 15 cases had been instituted before the Tribunal. The bulk of the Tribunal's docket[8] has comprised applications for prompt release of vessels

---

[2] On the dispute settlement regime in UNCLOS, see generally N Klein, *Dispute Settlement in the UN Convention on the Law of the Sea* (2005).

[3] UNCLOS, art 292.

[4] Ibid, art 290.

[5] Ibid, art 187.

[6] Ibid, art 288(2).

[7] *The M/V 'Saiga'* (St Vincent and the Grenadines v Guinea), judgment of 4 December 1997, available at <http://www.itlos.org/start2_en.html>.

[8] By July 2009, there had been: nine applications relating to prompt release of vessels and crew (one discontinued by agreement of the parties); and four requests for provisional measures submitted under art 290(5) of UNCLOS.

under article 292 of UNCLOS, and applications for provisional measures orders in respect of disputes which have been submitted to an arbitral tribunal under Annex VII of UNCLOS.[9]

Institutional Aspects

Governing texts

Procedural law

2.3 The provisions of the legal instruments that govern the functions of the ITLOS are:

(a) Part XV of UNCLOS;

(b) section 5 of Part XI of UNCLOS, relating to disputes concerning the international seabed area and advisory opinions requested by the International Seabed Authority heard by the Seabed Disputes Chamber of the Tribunal (SBDC);

(c) the Statute of the Tribunal,[10] contained in Annex VI to UNCLOS, which regulates the organization of the ITLOS, its competence and procedure, and the SBDC (ITLOS Statute);

(d) the Rules of the Tribunal,[11] which provide detailed rules of procedure (Rules of the Tribunal);

(e) the Guidelines concerning the Preparation and Presentation of Cases before the Tribunal,[12] which provide potential parties with practical information concerning the preparation and presentation of their cases; and

(f) the Resolution on the Internal Judicial Practice of the Tribunal,[13] which outlines the procedures by which the Tribunal deliberates and drafts its judgments.

Substantive law

2.4 The ITLOS is to decide the cases before it in accordance with the substantive provisions of UNCLOS and other rules of international law not incompatible with the Convention.[14] If the parties agree, the Tribunal can decide a case

---

[9] UNCLOS, art 290(5).

[10] UNCLOS, Annex VI—Statute of the International Tribunal for the Law of the Sea, ('ITLOS Statute').

[11] Rules of the Tribunal, 28 October 1997 (as amended on 15 March and 21 September 2001, and on 17 March 2009), Doc ITLOS/8, 17 March 2009 ('ITLOS Rules').

[12] Guidelines concerning the Preparation and Presentation of Cases before the Tribunal (issued on 28 October 1997), Doc ITLOS/9, 14 November 2006.

[13] Resolution on the Internal Judicial Practice of the Tribunal (adopted on 31 October 1997), Doc ITLOS/10, 27 April 2005.

[14] UNCLOS, art 293(1); ITLOS Statute, art 23.

ex aequo et bono.[15] The SBDC, as well as applying the Convention and rules of international law, shall apply the rules, regulations, and procedures of the International Seabed Authority and the terms of contracts concerning activities in the area in matters relating to those contracts.[16]

Organization

Composition, appointment, and qualifications

The Tribunal is composed of 21 independent judges, elected by the states parties to UNCLOS from among persons enjoying the highest reputation for fairness and integrity and of recognized competence in the field of the law of the sea.[17] The representation of the principal legal systems of the world and equitable geographical distribution is to be assured, and no two judges may be nationals of the same state.[18] Under article 3(2) of the Tribunal's Statute, there should be no fewer than three judges from each of the five regional groups.[19] Judges are elected for a nine-year term and may be re-elected. The Tribunal elects a President and a Vice-President for a three-year term.[20]

2.5

Every party to a dispute before the ITLOS (or an ITLOS Chamber) is entitled to have a judge of its nationality on the bench. If there is no such judge, the party concerned may appoint a judge ad hoc (not necessarily of its nationality).[21] Judges ad hoc will participate in a case on equal footing to the other judges.[22]

---

[15] UNCLOS, art 293(2).

[16] ITLOS Statute, art 38.

[17] Ibid, art 2(1). As at 31 July 2009, the judges were: José Luis Jesus (Cape Verde) (President); Helmut Tuerk (Austria) (Vice-President); Hugo Caminos (Argentina); Vicente Marotta Rangel (Brazil); Alexander Yankov (Bulgaria); L Dolliver M Nelson (Grenada); P Chandrasekhara Rao (India); Joseph Akl (Lebanon); Rüdiger Wolfrum (Germany); Tullio Treves (Italy); Tafsir Malik Ndiaye (Senegal); Jean-Pierre Cot (France); Anthony Amos Lucky (Trinidad and Tobago); Stanislav Pawlak (Poland); Shunji Yanai (Japan); James Kateka (United Republic of Tanzania); Albert Hoffmann (South Africa); Zhiguo Gao (China); Boualem Bouguetaia (Algeria); Vladimir Vladimirovich Golitsyn (Russian Federation); and Jin-Hyun Paik (Republic of Korea).

[18] ITLOS Statute, arts 2(2), 3(1).

[19] In 2009 the states parties to UNCLOS decided upon a new arrangement for the allocation of seats on the Tribunal as follows: five members each from the Group of African States and Group of Asian States, four members from the Group of Latin American and Caribbean States, three members each from the Group of East European States and Group of Western European and other States (WEOG), and the one remaining seat elected from among the African and Asian Groups and WEOG. Press Release, SEA/1920, UN Department of Public Information, 29 June 2009. Doc SPLOS/203, 24 July 2009, para 101.

[20] ITLOS Statute, art 12(1).

[21] Ibid, art 17; ITLOS Rules, art 19(1). Two or more parties in the same cause are considered as one party only for the purposes of the appointment of a judge ad hoc, with the matter resolved by decision of the Tribunal where there is doubt, ITLOS Statute, art 17(5). In the *Southern Bluefin Tuna* cases, as parties in the same interest, Australia and New Zealand jointly nominated a single judge ad hoc, in two cases in which proceedings had been joined.

[22] ITLOS Rules, art 8(1).

No judge may participate in a case in which he or she was previously involved as a lawyer, member of another dispute settlement body, or in any other capacity.[23] The President may bring doubts pertaining to the previous involvement of a judge before the Tribunal, which shall decide the issue by a majority of the other judges.[24] The President may act in this manner on his or her own initiative or following information communicated to him or her by a party to the case in confidentiality.

Furthermore, if a judge ceases to fulfil the conditions for service, as required by the ITLOS Statute, the other judges may decide unanimously to remove him or her from office.[25]

Plenary/chambers

2.6 The ITLOS normally hears cases in plenary (a quorum of 11 judges is required).[26] However, the Tribunal may form special chambers, composed of three or more judges, for dealing with particular categories of dispute.[27] The Tribunal has established three such chambers: for Fisheries Disputes, for Marine Environment Disputes, and for Maritime Delimitation Disputes. Furthermore, the ITLOS annually forms a five-member Chamber of Summary Procedure (composed of the President and Vice-President as ex officio members and three elected judges) which may hear and determine disputes by summary procedure.[28]

The Seabed Disputes Chamber of the Tribunal has exclusive and compulsory jurisdiction over disputes with respect to activities in the international seabed area (within the scope of Part XI of UNCLOS).[29] Its jurisdiction, powers, and functions are provided in section 5 of Part XI of UNCLOS, section 4 of the ITLOS Statute, and section B of Part II of the Rules of the Tribunal. The SBDC consists of 11 judges, elected by a majority of judges of the Tribunal from among them. The SBDC members serve for three years and are eligible for re-election.[30] The composition of the SBDC must reflect the principal legal systems and equitable geographical distribution.[31] The members of the SBDC elect their President.

At the request of all parties to any case, a special ad hoc chamber of the ITLOS can be formed to deal with that particular dispute. The Tribunal, with

---

[23] ITLOS Statute, art 8(1).
[24] Ibid, art 8(4); ITLOS Rules, art 18.
[25] ITLOS Statute, art 9; ITLOS Rules, art 7.
[26] ITLOS Statute, art 13(1), (3).
[27] Ibid, art 15(1); ITLOS Rules, art 29. As far as possible, special chambers should be composed of judges having special expertise in the subject matter entrusted to the chamber.
[28] ITLOS Statute, art 15(3); ITLOS Rules, art 28.
[29] UNCLOS, art 186; ITLOS Statute, art 14.
[30] ITLOS Statute, art 35(3); ITLOS Rules, art 23.
[31] ITLOS Statute, art 35(2).

the approval of the parties, will determine the composition of such an ad hoc chamber.[32] Such a request is to be submitted to the Tribunal within two months from the date of initiation of proceedings. At the request of the parties to the dispute, the European Communities and Chile, such a chamber was formed for the *Case Concerning the Conservation and Sustainable Exploitation of Swordfish Stocks in the South-Eastern Pacific Ocean*.[33] The chamber comprised four sitting judges of the Tribunal and a judge ad hoc nominated by Chile in accordance with article 17 of the ITLOS Statute. It has been suggested that the availability of ad hoc chambers of the ITLOS potentially offers an attractive alternative to arbitration. In effect, it would allow the parties to a dispute to determine the composition of the chamber (subject to the relevant provisions of the Statute), but would free them from the additional costs associated with the establishment of an arbitral tribunal.[34]

Any party to an inter-state dispute before the SBDC may request the establishment of a three-judge ad hoc chamber of the SBDC.[35] The composition of the chamber is to be determined by the SBDC with the agreement of the parties. However, if the parties fail to agree, each party will nominate an SBDC judge and the third judge will be agreed upon or nominated by the President of the SBDC. In no case can a member of an ad hoc SBDC chamber be a national (or in the service) of one of the parties to the dispute.[36] The request for an ad hoc SBDC chamber should be made within three months from the date of initiation of proceedings.[37]

Appellate structure

The ITLOS has no appellate structure.   **2.7**

Scientific and technical experts

The Tribunal may on its own initiative, or in accordance with a request made by   **2.8**
a party to a case, select, in consultation with the parties, two or more scientific or technical experts.[38] The experts are to be chosen, preferably, from a list of experts maintained, in accordance with the provisions of Annex VIII to UNCLOS, by

---

[32] ITLOS Statute, art 15(2); ITLOS Rules, art 30.

[33] This case remained on the Tribunal's docket in 2009, with proceedings effectively suspended pending efforts by the parties to secure approval of a bilateral understanding on the conservation of swordfish stocks in the South Eastern Pacific Ocean. In December 2009, the case was removed from the Tribunal's list by Order 2009/1 of 16 December 2009.

[34] See, for example, Statement by Mr Rüdiger Wolfrum, President of the ITLOS, at the Sixty-Second Session of the General Assembly, 10 December 2007, para 20, available at <http://www.itlos.org/start2_en.html>.

[35] UNCLOS, art 188(1)(b); ITLOS Statute, art 36.

[36] ITLOS Statute, art 36(3).

[37] ITLOS Rules, art 27(1).

[38] UNCLOS, art 289; ITLOS Rules, art 15.

a variety of international organizations.[39] Experts should be independent and enjoy the highest reputation for fairness, competence, and integrity.[40] A request by a party for appointment of experts is to be presented not later than at the closure of written proceedings, but in appropriate cases the Tribunal may receive subsequent requests (in any case, before the end of the oral proceedings).[41] Once appointed, the experts will sit on the bench during the proceedings, but will not be able to vote. The same provision will apply *mutatis mutandis* to any chamber of the ITLOS.[42]

In addition, if the ITLOS considers it necessary, it can, after hearing the parties, arrange for an inquiry or an expert opinion.[43] In such case, the Tribunal will issue an order defining the subject of inquiry or opinion; the number and method of appointment of suitable persons; and the procedure to be followed. The report or opinion will be communicated to the parties and they will be given the opportunity to comment upon it.[44]

The parties may also present expert testimony before the Tribunal as part of the oral proceedings.[45] The parties and the judges may, under the control of the President, question expert witnesses.[46]

Registry

2.9 The Tribunal elects its Registrar and Deputy Registrar for a renewable term of five years from among candidates nominated by the judges.[47] The rest of the staff of the Registry is appointed by the Tribunal on proposals submitted by the Registrar, or by the Registrar with the approval of the President.[48]

The Registrar is the chief executive officer of the Tribunal. He or she is in charge of the Registry, which serves as the secretariat for the Tribunal. In this capacity, the Registrar, *inter alia*, is the channel for all communications with parties; provides the range of substantive and procedural legal services; executes budgetary, financial, and treasury functions; records all relevant documents; arranges translation and interpretation services; and is responsible for the administration and financial management of the ITLOS.[49]

---

[39] UNCLOS, Annex VIII, art 2.
[40] ITLOS Rules, art 15(3).
[41] Ibid, art 15(1).
[42] Ibid, art 15(4).
[43] ITLOS Rules, art 82(1).
[44] Ibid, art 82(2).
[45] Ibid, art 78. For example, in the *Southern Bluefin Tuna* cases, Australia and New Zealand called an expert, who was examined first on the *voir dire* on behalf of Japan, *Southern Bluefin Tuna* (New Zealand and Australia v Japan), Order of 27 August 1999, para 25.
[46] Ibid, art 80.
[47] ITLOS Statute, art 12(2); ITLOS Rules, arts 32(1), 33, as amended 21 September 2001.
[48] ITLOS Rules, art 35(1).
[49] Ibid, art 36.

Jurisdiction and access to the Tribunal

Ratione personae

ITLOS The jurisdiction *ratione personae* of the ITLOS encompasses the states **2.10** parties to UNCLOS,[50] as well as other states and entities other than states in certain circumstances.[51] Disputes may be submitted to the ITLOS by agreement between the parties.[52] Disputes concerning the interpretation and application of UNCLOS may also be referred to the ITLOS where both states parties to the dispute have accepted the jurisdiction of the ITLOS under article 287(1) UNCLOS.[53] By July 2009, 25 states parties had made a declaration under article 287(1) selecting the ITLOS as their preferred procedure for settlement of disputes under UNCLOS.[54]

In addition, the ITLOS has compulsory jurisdiction over all states parties to UNCLOS with respect to certain matters. In cases involving requests for prompt release of vessels and crews, the ITLOS will exercise jurisdiction over any two states parties or entities authorized by a state party, if the parties to the dispute fail to agree upon an alternative forum and one of the parties submits the dispute to the Tribunal.[55] An application for prompt release of a vessel can be made by the flag state of the detained vessel, or on its behalf.[56] The Tribunal has made clear that it has power to examine *proprio motu* the basis of its jurisdiction, even if that issue is not raised by the parties. In particular, it has insisted on satisfying itself that the applications have been made by or on behalf of a flag state.[57]

The ITLOS is also open to state and non-state entities, which are parties to agreements other than UNCLOS (but related to the purposes of that Convention), which confer jurisdiction on the Tribunal:[58] an agreement can explicitly provide for settlement of disputes arising under it before the ITLOS or in accordance with provisions of Part XV of UNCLOS.[59] In the case of an agreement which was adopted prior to UNCLOS, the ITLOS will have jurisdiction in disputes over its interpretation or application, upon the consent of all parties to that agreement.[60]

---

[50] ITLOS Statute, art 20(1).

[51] Ibid, art 20(2).

[52] For example, the *Saiga (No 2)* case was transferred to the ITLOS by agreement between Guinea and St Vincent and the Grenadines, after an initial application by the latter for the institution of arbitral proceedings under Annex VII UNCLOS. *The M/V 'Saiga' (No 2) Case* (Saint Vincent and the Grenadines v Guinea), Order of 11 March 1998, paras 12–15.

[53] UNCLOS, art 287(1), (4).

[54] See *infra* Annex.

[55] ITLOS Statute, art 292(1).

[56] Ibid, art 292(2).

[57] *'Grand Prince'* (Belize v France), Judgment of 20 April 2001, para 76ff.

[58] UNCLOS, art 288(2); ITLOS Statute, arts 20(2) and 21.

[59] See note 73 below.

[60] ITLOS Statute, art 22.

2.11 **Seabed Disputes Chamber**   The jurisdiction *ratione personae* of the SBDC includes:

(a)   disputes between states parties to UNCLOS;

(b)   disputes between a state party and the International Seabed Authority established to administer the seabed area;

(c)   disputes between parties to a contract governing activities in the seabed area (states parties, the Authority, state enterprises, or natural or juridical persons sponsored by a state party);

(d)   disputes between the Authority and prospective contractors (which are state enterprises or natural or juridical persons sponsored by a state party).[61] It should be noted that each party to a contractual dispute over the interpretation or application of a contract or plan of works may request that the dispute be referred to commercial arbitration.[62] However, such arbitral tribunal must refer to SBDC for a ruling on any question of interpretation of Part XI of UNCLOS (regulating the seabed area) and the Annexes relating to it.

Ratione materiae

2.12 **ITLOS**   The jurisdiction *ratione materiae* of the ITLOS includes any dispute concerning the interpretation and application of UNCLOS which is submitted to it in accordance with the Convention.[63] While section 1 of Part XV UNCLOS sets out general provisions relating to the obligations of states parties to the Convention to settle disputes by peaceful means, section 2 sets out compulsory procedures entailing binding decisions, which apply where no settlement has been reached by recourse to the means outlined in section 1. However, section 3 of Part XV provides for limitations and exceptions to the applicability of the compulsory procedures: article 297 sets out general limitations on the applicability of section 2, thus excluding certain types of dispute from compulsory procedures entailing binding settlement; and article 298 provides for optional exceptions to the applicability of section 2. A state party to UNCLOS has the right to submit a declaration indicating that it does not accept compulsory procedures in respect of one or more categories of dispute referred to in article 298.[64]

Although certain categories of dispute may be excluded from *compulsory* dispute settlement under Part XV of UNCLOS (and consequently from

---

[61]   UNCLOS, art 187.

[62]   Ibid, art 188(2).

[63]   UNCLOS, art 288(1); ITLOS Statute, art 21.

[64]   By July 2009, of 159 parties to UNCLOS, 29 had made declarations indicating that they do not accept compulsory binding dispute settlement procedures in respect of one or more of the categories of dispute set out in article 298. The updated list of such declarations is available at <http://www.un.org/Depts/los/settlement_of_disputes/choice_procedure.htm>.

the jurisdiction of the ITLOS), such disputes may nonetheless be submitted to the ITLOS through the special agreement of the parties to the dispute.[65] Furthermore, some of the disputes exempted from binding third party settlement may be subject to mandatory conciliation procedures under UNCLOS.[66]

As indicated above, the ITLOS also has compulsory jurisdiction over all states parties to UNCLOS in relation to certain cases.

First, the Tribunal has compulsory jurisdiction in certain circumstances with respect to the applications for the prompt release of a vessel and its crew.[67] Where a vessel flying the flag of a state party has been detained by another state party and it is alleged that the detaining state has not complied with the provisions of UNCLOS for the prompt release of the vessel or its crew upon the posting of a reasonable bond or other financial security, the question of release from detention may be submitted to any court or tribunal agreed upon by the parties or, failing such agreement within ten days from the time of detention, to a court or tribunal accepted by the detaining state under article 287 or to the ITLOS.[68]

Second, the Tribunal has compulsory jurisdiction in certain cases where a party to a dispute wishes to request provisional measures. There are two situations in which the ITLOS may be called upon to consider a request for provisional measures. First, where proceedings have been initiated before the ITLOS, article 290(1) UNCLOS empowers the ITLOS, if it considers prima facie that it has jurisdiction to decide the dispute, to prescribe any provisional measures that it considers appropriate pending the final decision.[69] Second, where a dispute is submitted to an arbitral tribunal under section 2 of Part XV of UNCLOS, then, pending the constitution of the arbitral tribunal, a request for provisional measures may be submitted to any court or tribunal agreed upon by the parties. Failing such agreement within two weeks from the date of the request for provisional measures, the request to prescribe provisional measures may be submitted to the ITLOS, which will then have jurisdiction to deal with the request.[70] Parties must comply with provisional measures prescribed by the ITLOS.[71]

---

[65] UNCLOS, art 299.

[66] Ibid, arts 297(2), (3), 298(1)(a). The procedure for compulsory conciliation is set out in UNCLOS, Annex V, section 2.

[67] UNCLOS, art 292.

[68] UNCLOS, art 292(1).

[69] See *The M/V 'Saiga' (No 2) Case* (Saint Vincent and the Grenadines v Guinea), Order of 11 March 1998.

[70] UNCLOS, art 290(5). Similar authorities were granted to the SBDC. By July 2009, the ITLOS had been called upon to consider requests for provisional measures under art 290(5) in four cases: *Southern Bluefin Tuna (Cases Nos 3 and 4), supra* note 45; *MOX Plant case* (Ireland v United Kingdom), Order of 3 December 2001; and *Land Reclamation by Singapore in and around the Straits of Johor* (Malaysia v Singapore), Order of 8 October 2003.

[71] UNCLOS, art 290(6).

The ITLOS can also exercise jurisdiction over disputes concerning the interpretation and application of international agreements, other than UNCLOS, which confer jurisdiction on the ITLOS, if such agreements relate to the purposes of UNCLOS.[72] A number of such agreements have now entered into force, but they have not yet given rise to the institution of proceedings before the ITLOS.[73]

2.13   **Seabed Disputes Chamber**   The SBDC has exclusive jurisdiction over the following categories of dispute pertaining to activities in the seabed area:

(a)   inter-state disputes over the interpretation or application of Part XI of UNCLOS and related Annexes, subject to the possibility of the parties to a dispute submitting the dispute to a special chamber of ITLOS;[74]

(b)   disputes between a state party and the Authority over acts or omissions of either party which are allegedly in contravention of Part XI of UNCLOS, related Annexes, or rules, regulations or procedures adopted by the Authority;[75]

(c)   disputes between a state party and the Authority over acts of the Authority which are allegedly in excess of jurisdiction, or misuse of power;[76]

(d)   disputes between parties to a contract over the interpretation or application of a contract or a plan of work, subject to the possibility of a dispute being submitted to commercial arbitration;[77]

(e)   contractual disputes over acts or omissions of a party to a contract relating to activities in the seabed area and directed to the other party or directly affecting its legitimate interests;[78]

---

[72] Ibid, art 288(2); ITLOS Statute, art 21.

[73] For example, 1995 UN Agreement for the Implementation of the Provisions of the UN Convention on the Law of the Sea of 10 December 1982 Relating to the Conservation and Management of Straddling Fish Stocks and Highly Migratory Fish Stocks, art 30, 4 August 1995, 34 ILM 1542 (1995); 1993 Agreement to Promote Compliance with International Conservation Measures by Vessels on the High Seas, art 9, 24 November 1993, 33 ILM 968 (1994); Protocol to the Convention on the Prevention of Marine Pollution by Dumping of Wastes and Other Matter, 1972, art 16, 7 November 1996, 36 ILM 7 (1997); Convention on the Conservation and Management of Highly Migratory Fish Stocks in the Western and Central Pacific Ocean, art 31, 5 September 2000, 40 ILM 278 (2001); Convention on the Conservation and Management of Fishery Resources in the South-East Atlantic Ocean, art 24, 20 April 2001, 41 ILM 257 (2002); Convention on the Protection of the Underwater Cultural Heritage, art 25, 2 November 2001, 41 ILM 40 (2002); Framework Agreement for the Conservation of the Living Marine Resources of the High Seas of the South-Eastern Pacific, art 14, 14 August 2000, <http://www.jus.uio.no/treaties/08/8-02/living-marine-resources. xml>; Convention on Future Multilateral Cooperation in North-East Atlantic Fisheries, art 18 *bis*, 11 November 2004, <http://www.jus.uio.no/treaties/08/8-02/northeast-atlantic-fisheries.xml>; Southern Indian Ocean Fisheries Agreement, art 20, 7 July 2006, <http://www.ecolex.org/server2. php/libcat/docs/multilateral/en/TRE144077.pdf>; International Convention on the Removal of Wrecks, art 15, 18 May 2007, <http://www.aidim.org/pdf/6Conv_Wreck_Removal07.pdf>.

[74] UNCLOS, arts 187(a), 188(1)(a).

[75] Ibid, art 187(b)(i).

[76] Ibid, arts 187(b)(ii), 189.

[77] Ibid, arts 187(c)(i), 188(2).

[78] Ibid, art 187(c)(ii).

(f) disputes between the Authority and a prospective contractor over refusal of a contract or a legal issue arising during negotiation of the contract;[79]

(g) disputes over the liability of the Authority vis-à-vis the other party to a contract for any damage arising out of wrongful acts in the exercise of its powers and functions.[80]

Ratione temporis

In general, there are no time limits for the referral of disputes to the ITLOS or the SBDC. There are, however, some temporal restrictions in relation to requests for prompt release of vessels and crews and for provisional measures. **2.14**

A request for prompt release can be submitted by the flag state of the detained vessel to the ITLOS only if the parties failed to agree on an alternative forum within ten days from the date of detention.[81]

A request for provisional measures pending the constitution of an arbitral tribunal may be submitted to the ITLOS only if the parties failed to agree on an alternative forum within two weeks from the date on which the requesting party notified the other party of the request.[82]

Advisory jurisdiction

ITLOS The ITLOS may render advisory opinions on a legal question if an international agreement related to the purposes of UNCLOS specifically provides for the submission to the ITLOS of a request for such an opinion.[83] The procedure governing such a request for an advisory opinion will be as prescribed in the said agreement and, *mutatis mutandis*, in the rules of procedure on SBDC advisory proceedings.[84] **2.15**

Seabed Disputes Chamber Under UNCLOS, the SBDC is authorized to render advisory opinions at the request of the Assembly or Council of the International Seabed Authority on legal questions arising within the scope of their activities.[85] **2.16**

Opinions are to be given as a matter of urgency.[86] All states parties to UNCLOS and international organizations that are likely to be able to furnish information should be notified of the request and given time to prepare and

---

[79] Ibid, art 187(d).

[80] Ibid, art 187(e); Annex III, art 22.

[81] UNCLOS, art 292(1).

[82] Ibid, art 290(5); ITLOS Rules, art 89(2).

[83] Ibid, art 138(1).

[84] Ibid, art 138(2), (3). It is interesting to note that the possibility of the ITLOS rendering advisory opinions in this manner is not expressly contemplated in the Statute of the Tribunal or in UNCLOS, but rather is provided in the Rules of the Tribunal.

[85] UNCLOS, arts 159(10), 191.

[86] Ibid, art 191; ITLOS Rules, art 132.

submit a statement.[87] The chamber may hold oral proceedings and invite states and international organizations to participate in them. At the end of the proceedings the SBDC issues an opinion.[88]

Separate or dissenting opinions may be attached to the opinion of the chamber.

By July 2009, the advisory jurisdiction of the SBDC or the ITLOS had not been invoked.

[handwritten note: NOTE: TWO ADVISORY OPINIONS HAVE NOW BEEN GIVEN TO THE INTERNATIONAL SEABED AUTHORITY & SUB REGIONAL FISHERIES COMMISSION]

Procedural Aspects

Languages

2.17 The official languages of ITLOS are English and French.[89] All pleadings ought to be submitted in one or both of the official languages.[90] A party may plead or introduce evidence in a language other than one of the official languages, but in the case of written submissions or documents it must produce a certified translation into an official language, and in the case of oral pleadings and testimony it must make arrangements for interpretation.[91] Where a language other than one of the official languages is chosen by the parties and that language is an official language of the United Nations, at the request of any party to the dispute the decision of the ITLOS shall be translated into that language at no cost for the parties.[92]

Instituting proceedings

2.18 Disputes are submitted to the Tribunal either by written application or by notification of a special agreement, addressed to the Registrar.[93] An application must include the following information: the identity of the claiming party; the identity of the party against which the claim is brought; the subject of the dispute; the legal grounds upon which the jurisdiction of the Tribunal is based; the precise nature of the claim; and a brief statement of the facts and grounds on which the claim is based.[94]

---

[87] ITLOS Rules, art 133.

[88] Ibid, art 135.

[89] Ibid, art 43.

[90] Ibid, art 64(1).

[91] Ibid, arts 64(2), (3), 85.

[92] Ibid, art 64(4). The applicant sought to avail itself of this provision in *The 'Camouco'* (Panama v France), and requested that the ITLOS provide a Spanish translation of its judgment. However, the Tribunal declined, noting that art 64(4) of the Rules dealt only with the situation where the parties chose a language other than English or French for their written pleadings, which had not been the case in the *'Camouco'* proceedings. *The 'Camouco' Case*, Judgment of 7 February 2000, para 77.

[93] ITLOS Statute, art 24(1).

[94] ITLOS Rules, art 54(1), (2).

If proceedings are initiated by way of special agreement, one or both of the parties will notify the Registrar accordingly and append to the notification a certified copy of the special agreement.[95] The notification must indicate the precise subject of the dispute and identify the parties to it, unless such information is apparent from the agreement. The Registrar is required to notify all states parties to UNCLOS whenever proceedings are instituted.[96]

In cases before the SBDC which are not exclusively between states parties or between states parties and the International Seabed Authority, the application must also include details pertaining to the permanent residence, address, or registered office of any natural or legal person; the identity of the state sponsoring the non-state party; address for service at the seat of the Tribunal; the subject of the dispute and the legal grounds on which jurisdiction is said to be based; the precise nature of the claim, together with a statement of the facts and the legal grounds on which the claim is based; the decision or measure sought; and the evidence on which the application is founded.[97]

The Registrar then transmits a certified copy of the application to the respondent and transmits a copy of the application to the state sponsoring the activities of the non-state entity.[98] That state may join proceedings in cases involving natural and juridical persons of its own initiative or, following a request by the other state to the dispute, appear in the proceedings on behalf of that person.[99] The respondent should lodge a defence within two months from the date of service of the application.[100]

Where proceedings are brought before the SBDC by notification of a special agreement, the notification should indicate the parties and any sponsoring state; the subject of the dispute; the precise nature of the claims of the parties; facts and legal arguments on which the claims are founded; decisions or measures sought by the parties; and the evidence on which the claims are founded.[101]

Financial assistance

A Trust Fund was established by the United Nations Secretary-General in 2000, **2.19** pursuant to General Assembly Resolution 55/7. The Fund is to provide financial

---

[95] Ibid, art 55.

[96] ITLOS Statute, art 24(3).

[97] ITLOS Rules, art 117.

[98] Ibid, arts 54(4), 118(1).

[99] UNCLOS, art 190; ITLOS Rules, art 119. According to UNCLOS, a state may join proceedings involving a natural or juridical person sponsored by it. In cases where a private party is the claimant and a state a respondent, that state may require the sponsoring state to appear in the proceedings on behalf of the sponsored person. Failing such appearance, the respondent state may arrange to be represented by a juridical person of its own nationality.

[100] ITLOS Rules, art 118.

[101] Ibid, art 120.

assistance to states parties to the Convention for expenses incurred in cases submitted, or to be submitted, to the ITLOS (including chambers of the ITLOS). The terms of reference of the Fund are annexed to GA Resolution 55/7. It is notable that, in relation to the other dispute settlement procedures available under the choice of procedure in article 287 UNCLOS, certain financial assistance mechanisms were already in existence. For example, the Secretary-General administers a Trust Fund for the International Court of Justice, and the Permanent Court of Arbitration (under the auspices of which a number of UNCLOS Annex VII arbitrations have been administered) has a Financial Assistance Fund. Thus the rationale for establishing the ITLOS Trust Fund was so that the burden of costs should not be a factor in the choice of procedure under UNCLOS.[102]

Preliminary proceedings/objections

Preliminary proceedings

2.20 Where an application is made in respect of a dispute referred to in article 297 (ie disputes excluded from compulsory procedures entailing binding decisions) the ITLOS may decide by way of preliminary proceedings to take no further action in the case.[103] Before reaching such a decision, the Tribunal must determine, acting either on a request by a party, or *proprio motu* (within two months from the initiation of proceedings),[104] that the claim constitutes an abuse of legal process or is prima facie unfounded. A request by a party for such a preliminary dismissal is to be presented within a time limit fixed by the President.[105] Upon service of an application, the respondent must be notified of the date until which it is entitled to request preliminary proceedings. The request must be made in writing and allege the two following grounds for dismissal: first, that the application is made in respect to a dispute covered by article 297 of the Convention; second, that the claim is an abuse of legal process or prima facie unfounded.[106]

Upon the receipt of such a request, or acting upon its own initiative, the ITLOS (or the President) will fix a time period not exceeding 60 days for the parties to lodge written observations and submissions.[107] Further proceedings, in which the Tribunal may request parties to present their legal and factual arguments and introduce evidence, will be oral, unless the Tribunal decides otherwise.[108]

---

[102] General Assembly Resolution 55/7, Annex I, para 2. The first request for assistance from the Trust Fund was made in 2004. *Annual Report of the International Tribunal for the Law of the Sea for 2004*, SPLOS/122, 30 March 2005, para 83; (2006) 21 *International Journal of Marine and Coastal Law* 382.
[103] UNCLOS, art 294; ITLOS Rules, art 96(1).
[104] ITLOS Rules, art 96(3).
[105] Ibid, art 96(2).
[106] Ibid, art 96(4).
[107] Ibid, art 96(5).
[108] Ibid, art 96(6), (7).

At the end of the preliminary proceedings, during which the proceedings on the merits will be suspended, the ITLOS will issue a judgment.[109]

It should be noted that institution of preliminary proceedings does not affect the right of any party to a dispute to raise preliminary objections.[110]

Preliminary objections

Preliminary objections to the jurisdiction of the Tribunal or to the admissibility **2.21**
of the application, or other objections of a preliminary nature, are to be made in writing within 90 days from the date of institution of proceedings.[111] The request should set out the facts and legal arguments on which it is based and include the submissions of the requesting party.[112] Upon receipt of a preliminary objection, the proceedings on the merits shall be suspended and the Tribunal (or President) will fix a time limit (not exceeding 60 days) for the other party to present its observations and submissions on the request.[113] The requesting party may be allocated additional time (not exceeding 60 days) to reply. Further proceedings, in which the Tribunal may request parties to present their legal and factual arguments and introduce evidence, will be oral, unless the Tribunal decides otherwise.[114] The Tribunal must give its decision in the form of a judgment, by which it shall uphold or reject the objection or declare that the objection does not possess an exclusively preliminary character.[115] The parties may agree that an objection be heard and determined in the merits stage.[116]

Provisional measures

The ITLOS and its SBDC have the power to prescribe provisional measures in **2.22**
order to preserve the respective rights of the parties to a case or prevent serious harm to the marine environment pending the final outcome of the claim.[117]

---

[109] Ibid, art 96(5), (8).
[110] UNCLOS, art 294(3).
[111] ITLOS Rules, art 97(1).
[112] Ibid, art 97(2).
[113] Ibid, art 97(3).
[114] Ibid, art 97(4), (5).
[115] Ibid, art 97(6).   [116] Ibid, art 97(7).
[117] UNCLOS, art 290(1); ITLOS Statute, art 25(1); ITLOS Rules, art 89(1). The explicit provision for the prescription of provisional measures specifically for the purpose of preventing serious environmental harm is an innovation in international law. The 1995 Straddling Fish Stocks Agreement, in art 30, provides that the dispute settlement provisions in Part XV UNCLOS apply *mutatis mutandis* to disputes between states parties to that Agreement, whether or not they are also parties to UNCLOS. Art 31 provides that, without prejudice to art 290 of UNCLOS, the court or tribunal to which the dispute has been submitted (which may include the ITLOS) may prescribe any provisional measures which it considers appropriate under the circumstances to preserve the respective rights of the parties to the dispute or to prevent damage to the fish stocks in question, as well as in certain other circumstances. Agreement for the Implementation of the Provisions of the United Nations Convention on the Law of the Sea of 10 December 1982 relating to the Conservation and Management of Straddling Fish Stocks and Highly Migratory Fish Stocks, arts 30, 31, 34 ILM 1547 (1995).

The Tribunal (or chamber) must, however, be satisfied that it has prima-facie jurisdiction over the dispute and that the measures requested are appropriate under the circumstances. As indicated above, the ITLOS and the SBDC may, in certain circumstances, also have jurisdiction to issue provisional measures in a case that is being submitted to an arbitral tribunal pending the constitution of an arbitral tribunal.[118] In such cases, the ITLOS must also be satisfied, first, that the arbitral tribunal to be constituted will have prima-facie jurisdiction over the dispute and, second, that the urgency of the situation justifies the prescription of provisional measures at that stage.[119]

A request for provisional measures in a case to be adjudicated before the ITLOS or SBDC can be submitted at any time during the course of the proceedings.[120] Requests for provisional measures, in cases being submitted on the merits to an arbitral tribunal, can be presented to the ITLOS (or SBDC) at any time if the parties so agree, or at any time after two weeks from the notification of a request for provisional measures if the parties fail to agree to submit the request to another court or tribunal.[121]

A request for provisional measures is to be made in writing and must indicate: the measures requested; the reasons for the request; and the possible consequences for the preservation of the respective rights of the parties or the prevention of serious harm to the marine environment, if the request is not granted.[122] Requests made pending the constitution of an arbitral tribunal, under article 290(5) of UNCLOS, must also specify: the legal grounds for jurisdiction of the arbitral tribunal which is to be constituted; and the urgency of the situation.[123]

Proceedings on the request for provisional measures will take precedence over all other proceedings before the Tribunal (with the possible exception of requests for prompt release of vessels and crews),[124] and hearings will be set for the earliest possible date before the Tribunal, SBDC, or Chamber for Summary Procedure.[125]

---

[118] UNCLOS, art 290(5).

[119] UNCLOS, art 290(5); ITLOS Rules, art 89(4). The arbitral tribunal, once constituted, can modify, revoke, or affirm the provisional measures prescribed by the ITLOS. The finding of prima-facie jurisdiction by the ITLOS does not affect the power of the arbitral tribunal to decide upon its jurisdiction. In the *Southern Bluefin Tuna* cases, ITLOS prescribed certain provisional measures under art 290(5) in its Order of 27 August 1999, having found that the arbitral tribunal would prima facie have jurisdiction over the dispute. The arbitral tribunal, once constituted, decided that it lacked jurisdiction. *Southern Bluefin Tuna* (Australia and New Zealand v Japan), Award on Jurisdiction and Admissibility, 4 August 2000.

[120] ITLOS Rules, art 89(1).

[121] UNCLOS, art 290(5); ITLOS Rules, art 89(2).

[122] ITLOS Rules, art 89(3).

[123] Ibid, art 89(4).

[124] Ibid, arts 90(1), 112(1). Art 112(1) states that if the Tribunal has to deal with both an application for the release of a vessel or crew and a request for the prescription of provisional measures, it shall take the necessary measures to ensure that both the application and the request are dealt with without delay.

[125] ITLOS Rules, arts 90(2), 91, 115.

The Tribunal may accept or reject the request, or prescribe measures different in whole or in part from those requested.[126] Rejection of a request for provisional measures will not prevent the party which made it from making a new request in the same case based on new facts.[127] Furthermore, a party can request the modification or revocation of provisional measures.[128] The parties to a dispute must comply promptly with any provisional measures prescribed by the ITLOS or one of its chambers.[129] Under article 95 of the Rules of the Tribunal, parties to cases are to submit reports on steps taken or proposed to be taken to ensure prompt compliance, and the Tribunal may request further information on any matter connected with the implementation of provisional measures it has prescribed. In each of the three provisional measures orders prescribed to date, the Tribunal has fixed dates by which the initial reports referred to in article 95 must be submitted. In three of these orders, the Tribunal has authorized the President to request such further reports or information as he may consider appropriate thereafter.[130]

Prompt release of vessels and crews

Where the authorities of a state party to UNCLOS have detained a vessel flying   **2.23**
the flag of another state party, and it is alleged that the detaining state has not complied with the provisions of UNCLOS for the prompt release of the vessel and crew upon the posting of a reasonable bond or other financial security,[131] the question of release from detention may be submitted to the ITLOS.[132] The issue can be submitted to any court or tribunal agreed upon by the parties. If there is no such agreement within ten days from the time of detention, the issue may be referred to a court or tribunal accepted by the detaining state under article 287 of UNCLOS. Failing such an agreement, an application for the release of the ship and crew may be submitted to the ITLOS unless the parties agree otherwise.[133] An application for release can be made only by, or on behalf of, the flag state of the vessel.[134]

An application to the ITLOS for prompt release must include a statement of facts on which the application is based, including: the time and place of detention

---

[126] Ibid, art 89(5). For example, in the *MOX Plant Case* the provisional measures prescribed by ITLOS were different from those requested by the applicant, Ireland. See *MOX Plant* (Ireland v UK) Order of 3 December 2001.
[127] Ibid, art 92.
[128] UNCLOS, art 290(2), (3); ITLOS Rules, art 93.
[129] UNCLOS, art 290(6).
[130] See *supra* note 70.
[131] See UNCLOS, art 73.
[132] UNCLOS, art 292(1). An analysis of the way in which the ITLOS has addressed issues arising in prompt release cases submitted to it by 2007 is contained in T Mensah, 'The Tribunal and the Prompt Release of Vessels' (2007) 22 *International Journal of Marine and Coastal Law* 425.
[133] UNCLOS, art 292(1).
[134] Ibid, art 292(2); ITLOS Rules, art 110(1).

of the vessel and the present location of the vessel and crew (if known); relevant information on the vessel and crew including, where appropriate, name, flag, port or place of registration of vessel, tonnage, cargo capacity, data relevant to the determination of its value, the name and address of the vessel owner, and operator and particulars of the crew. It must also indicate the amount, nature, and terms of bond or other financial security imposed by the detaining state and the extent to which these conditions have been met, and include further information relevant to the determination of the amount of a reasonable bond or other financial security and to any other issue in the proceedings.[135]

An application submitted on behalf of a state must also include an authorization from the flag state, and certification that a copy of the application has been delivered to that state.[136]

The application will be forwarded by the Registrar to the detaining state, which is entitled to submit a statement in reply (with supporting documents) not later than 96 hours before the date set for hearings.[137] Although the Tribunal is entitled to request supplementary statements, the rest of the proceedings are to be, as a rule, oral.[138] The application is to be heard before the plenary Tribunal or, upon request of the parties, before the Chamber of Summary Procedure.[139]

Upon receiving an application for prompt release, the Tribunal will deal without delay with the question of release exclusively (without prejudice to other aspects of the dispute before the appropriate domestic forum against the vessel, its owner, or crew).[140] It will give priority to applications for release of vessels or crews over all other proceedings before the Tribunal (with the possible exception of requests for provisional measures), and hearings will be set for the earliest date possible (within 15 days after the application was filed).[141] Normally, unless otherwise decided, each party will be given one day during the hearings to present its evidence and arguments.[142]

The ITLOS shall issue its decision on the application in the form of a judgment, not later than 14 days from the last day of hearings.[143] If the

---

[135] ITLOS Rules, art 111.

[136] Ibid, art 110(2), (3). The authorization should contain information on the competent authorizing state authority; the name and address of the person authorized; the office designated to receive notice of an application and the most expedient method of delivery of notices thereto; and any further clarifications, modifications, or withdrawal of authorization.

[137] ITLOS Rules, art 111(4).

[138] Ibid, art 111(5), (6).

[139] Ibid, art 112(2). Two requests have been made by applicants to have a prompt release application dealt with by the Chamber of Summary Procedure, the *M/V 'Saiga'* and the *'Chaisiri Reefer 2'*, but in each case the respondent did not concur. P C Rao and P Gautier (eds), *The Rules of the International Tribunal for the Law of the Sea: A Commentary* (2006) at 67.

[140] UNCLOS, art 292(3).

[141] ITLOS Rules, art 112(1), (3).

[142] Ibid, art 112(3).

[143] Ibid, art 112(4).

Tribunal finds that the allegation made by the applicant that the detaining state has not complied with a provision of UNCLOS for the prompt release of the vessel or the crew upon the posting of a reasonable bond or other financial security is well founded, it shall determine the amount, nature, and form of the bond or financial security to be posted for the release of the vessel or the crew.[144] Upon the posting of the bond or other financial security determined by the Tribunal, the authorities of the detaining state are to comply promptly with the decision of the ITLOS and release the vessel and/or its crew.[145]

While prompt release proceedings are intended to take place expeditiously, the time limits applicable in such proceedings created some problems in the early prompt release proceedings both for the parties and for the Tribunal itself. In light of these problems, the time limits were revised in 2001 by way of amendment to the ITLOS Rules.[146]

Written and oral proceedings on the merits

Proceedings in cases before the ITLOS consist of two parts—written and oral proceedings. The procedure in contentious cases before the ITLOS and the SBDC is as prescribed in UNCLOS, the ITLOS Statute, and the ITLOS Rules. The procedure in all cases is generally similar and is always subject to the relevant provisions of UNCLOS.[147] The Rules of the Tribunal provide that proceedings shall be conducted without unnecessary delay or expense.[148] They further provide that in every case submitted to the Tribunal, the President shall ascertain the views of the parties on questions of procedure.[149] **2.24**

In addition to the Statute and the Rules of the Tribunal, the Guidelines Concerning the Preparation and Presentation of Cases before the Tribunal, issued by the ITLOS pursuant to article 50 of the Rules, provide further guidance on the content and form of written and oral pleadings.

---

[144] Ibid, art 113(2). Much of the early ITLOS jurisprudence in prompt release cases has focused on the factors to be taken into consideration in determination of a reasonable bond. See, for example, *The 'Camouco' Case, supra* note 92, para 67; *'Volga'* (Russia v Australia), Judgment of 23 December 2002, para 65; *'Juno Trader'* (St Vincent and the Grenadines v Guinea-Bissau), Judgment of 18 December 2004, para 81ff; *'Monte Confurco'* (Seychelles v France), Judgment of 18 December 2000, para 76; *'Hoshinmaru'* (Japan v Russia), Judgment of 6 August 2007, paras 83–92.

[145] UNCLOS, art 292(4).

[146] The time limits referred to in this section are those provided in the amended ITLOS Rules. See P C Rao and P Gautier (eds), *The Rules of the International Tribunal for the Law of the Sea: A Commentary* (2006) at 318–319.

[147] ITLOS Rules, art 115.

[148] Ibid, art 49.

[149] Ibid, art 45.

Written phase

2.25 In a case begun by means of an application, the pleadings will consist of a memorial by the applicant and a counter-memorial by the respondent.[150] The memorial is to contain a statement of the relevant facts, a statement of law, and the submissions of the applicant.[151] A counter-memorial is to contain an admission or denial of the facts stated in the memorial; any additional facts, if necessary; observations concerning the statement of law in the memorial; a statement of law in answer thereto; and the submissions of the respondent.[152] The parties must append to their submissions supporting documents.[153] All submissions must be filed in a number of copies required by the Registrar; however, further copies may be requested at a later date.[154] A certified copy of every written submission and any document annexed thereto is to be communicated by the Registrar to the other party.[155]

The Tribunal may authorize or direct the parties to file a reply (on behalf of the applicant) and a rejoinder (on behalf of the respondent), if the parties agree to such procedure, or if the Tribunal decides that such additional submissions are necessary. The Tribunal may reach this decision following a request by one of the parties, or on its own initiative.[156] No further documents may be submitted to the Tribunal after the closure of the written proceedings, except with the consent of the other party or by authorization of the Tribunal.[157]

The number and order of filing of pleadings and the time limits for every submission are to be determined by the Tribunal, after the President has ascertained the view of the parties.[158] In any case, the time limit for each stage of pleading will not exceed six months unless extended by the Tribunal (but only on account of adequate justifications held valid by the Tribunal).[159]

In cases brought to ITLOS on the basis of a special agreement between the parties to the dispute, the number and order of the pleadings are to be governed by the provisions of the agreement, unless the Tribunal, after ascertaining the views of the parties, decides otherwise.[160] If the terms for filing written submissions

---

[150] Ibid, art 60(1).
[151] Ibid, art 62(1).
[152] Ibid, art 62(2).
[153] Ibid, arts 44(2), 63.
[154] Ibid, art 65(1).
[155] Ibid, art 66.
[156] Ibid, art 60(2).
[157] Ibid, art 71(1), (2). Further documents have been filed between the closure of written proceedings and the opening of oral proceedings, or during the oral proceedings, in a number of cases before the ITLOS. P C Rao and P Gautier (eds), *The Rules of the International Tribunal for the Law of the Sea: A Commentary* (2006) at 207–208.
[158] ITLOS Statute, art 27; ITLOS Rules, art 59(1).
[159] ITLOS Rules, art 59.
[160] Ibid, art 61(1).

were not agreed upon, both parties shall file a memorial and counter-memorial within the same time limit, and replies and rejoinder will not be admissible, unless the Tribunal finds them necessary.[161]

A respondent party may present a counter-claim, provided that it is directly connected to the principal claim and falls under the jurisdiction of the Tribunal.[162] Such a counter-claim should be presented in the counter-memorial, as part of the submissions of the respondent.[163]

Requests for ruling presented to the SBDC by a commercial arbitral **2.26** **tribunal**   Where a question of interpretation of Part XI of UNCLOS or the Annexes related thereto arises before a commercial arbitral tribunal established in pursuance of article 188(2) of UNCLOS, the question will be referred for ruling by the SBDC. In such a case, the President of the Chamber, upon receipt of the question, will fix time limits (not exceeding three months) for the parties to the proceedings and the states parties to submit written observations on the question.[164]

Oral phase

After the closure of the written proceedings and the initial deliberations (the **2.27** exchange of views of the ITLOS judges over the written proceedings), the Tribunal fixes a date for the opening of the oral proceedings. These are to be held without delay and within six months of the closure of the written proceedings, unless the Tribunal is satisfied that further delay is justified.[165] The date of the oral hearings will be determined with regard to the need to proceed without undue delay, the urgency of the case, the workload of the Tribunal, and the views expressed by the parties.[166] The Tribunal also determines, after ascertaining the views of the parties, the order in which the parties will be heard; the number of representatives to be heard on behalf of each party; the method of introducing evidence and examination of witnesses and experts; and whether arguments are to be made before or after introduction of evidence.[167]

The oral statements of the parties are to be as succinct as possible, within the limits necessary for adequate presentation of the contentions, and should focus on issues which are still in dispute between the parties after the written pleadings.[168] During the proceedings, the Tribunal can indicate any points or

---

[161] Ibid, art 61(2), (3).
[162] Ibid, art 98(1).
[163] Ibid, art 98(2).
[164] Ibid, art 123. In addition, each of the parties may request oral hearings, provided that the request is presented within one month from the expiration of the time period fixed for presentation of written submissions: Ibid, art 123(3).
[165] Ibid, arts 68, 69(1).
[166] Ibid, art 69(2).
[167] Ibid, art 73.
[168] Ibid, art 75(1).

issues that it would like the parties to address, or that it considers have been sufficiently argued already.[169] The Guidelines indicate that prior to the opening of oral proceedings, each party should submit to the Tribunal: (a) a brief note on the points which in its opinion constitute the issues that divide the parties; (b) a brief outline of the arguments it wishes to make in its oral arguments; and (c) a list of authorities, and relevant extracts, on which it intends to rely in its oral statement.[170] The Tribunal may put questions and ask for explanations from the representatives of the parties;[171] and it may call upon the parties to produce evidence or explanations necessary for the elucidation of any aspect of the matters in issue.[172] The Tribunal can also seek on its own initiative other information for this purpose, and arrange for the attendance of witnesses or experts.[173]

During the oral proceedings, a party may call any witnesses or experts, provided that they appear on a list communicated to the Registrar in good time before the start of the oral hearings.[174] Further witnesses or experts can also be called, but only with the consent of the other party, or if the Tribunal so authorizes. Witnesses and experts can be examined by the representatives of the parties, under the control of the President. They may also be questioned by the judges.[175]

At the conclusion of the last statement made by each of the parties, a representative of that party will read the final submission of the party. A copy of this text must be filed with the Tribunal and transmitted to the other party.[176]

Hearings are to be open to the public unless the Tribunal decides otherwise or the parties request that the public not be admitted.[177]

Third party intervention

2.28 A state party may submit a request to the Tribunal for permission to intervene in a case, if it considers that it has an interest of a legal nature, which may be affected by the decision of the Tribunal in the dispute.[178] There is no requirement for an intervening state to have accepted the jurisdiction of the ITLOS under the 'choice of procedure' clause (article 287 of UNCLOS).[179]

---

[169] Ibid, art 76(1).
[170] Guidelines concerning the Preparation and Presentation of Cases before the Tribunal, para 14.
[171] ITLOS Rules, art 76(2).
[172] Ibid, art 77(1).
[173] Ibid, art 77.
[174] Ibid, arts 72, 78(1). The list should include the name, nationality, description, and place of residence of each witness or expert and the points on which their evidence will be directed.
[175] Ibid, art 80.
[176] Ibid, art 75(2).
[177] ITLOS Statute, art 26(2); ITLOS Rules, art 74.
[178] ITLOS Statute, art 31(1).
[179] ITLOS Rules, art 99(3).

An application for permission to intervene shall be filed within 30 days of the Counter-Memorial being made available in accordance with the ITLOS Rules to the intervening state (or following a request on behalf of that state to receive a copy of that document). In exceptional circumstances, applications may also be admitted at a later stage.[180] The application to intervene must specify, *inter alia*, the interest of a legal nature which the state party applying to intervene considers may be affected by the Tribunal's decision, and the precise object of the intervention.[181]

An additional basis for intervention is provided in article 32 of the ITLOS Statute. This relates to cases that raise general questions of treaty interpretation or application. States parties to UNCLOS or parties to any other international agreement which confers jurisdiction on the ITLOS may join proceedings in which the interpretation and application of the instrument to which they are parties is in question. States which join proceedings in this way shall be bound by the interpretation given by the ITLOS.[182] The Registrar must notify all states parties to UNCLOS, or all parties to any other agreement, of any proceedings in which a question of the interpretation or application of the relevant instrument has arisen.[183] Any party wishing to intervene is to file a declaration to that effect within 30 days from the date of the Counter-Memorial becoming available to it (although, again, in exceptional circumstances a time extension may be allowed).[184] The declaration must state the particular provisions of UNCLOS or another international agreement the interpretation or application of which the declaring party considers to be in question, as well as the interpretation or application of those provisions for which the declaring party contends.[185]

Certified copies of application or declaration of intent to intervene (under either article 31 or 32 of the ITLOS Statute) are to be communicated to the parties to the case and they will be invited to furnish their written observations on the request within a time limit fixed by the Tribunal (or President).[186] The Tribunal shall decide whether the request to intervene should be granted (or declared admissible).[187] However, if within the time limit fixed by the Tribunal an objection is filed to the request for intervention, the Tribunal will hear the party seeking to intervene and the parties to the case before deciding.[188]

---

[180] Ibid, arts 67(1), 99(1).
[181] Ibid, art 99(2), (4).
[182] ITLOS Statute, art 32.
[183] Ibid, art 32(1), (2).
[184] ITLOS Rules, arts 67(1), 100(1).
[185] Ibid, art 100(2).
[186] Ibid, art 101(1).
[187] Ibid, art 102(1).
[188] Ibid, art 102(2).

If the request to intervene is granted, the intervening state party will receive copies of pleadings and documents and will be entitled to participate in the written and oral pleadings.[189] However, the intervening state party is not entitled to appoint a judge ad hoc.[190]

Multiple proceedings

2.29 The Statute of the ITLOS also envisages disputes between more than two parties. Thus, for example, as noted above, where several parties share the same legal interest, they will be considered as a single party for the purpose of appointment of an ad hoc judge.[191] Furthermore, even in cases filed separately, the Tribunal may order the joining of proceedings.[192] Thus, for example, in the *Southern Bluefin Tuna* cases, the Tribunal joined the proceedings on the requests for provisional measures by New Zealand and Australia against Japan, where the requests submitted by New Zealand and Australia had stated that they appeared as parties in the same interest.[193]

Amicus curiae briefs

2.30 Any international organization (ie intergovernmental organization) which is not a party to a case before the Tribunal may submit to the Registry information relevant to the case before the ITLOS, before the end of written pleadings.[194] The Tribunal may also, on its own initiative, request information or further clarifications on information already supplied by the international organization, by way of written and/or oral submissions. The ITLOS will invite an international organization to submit written observations and/or participate in oral proceedings in all cases where the construction of the organization's constituent instrument, or an international convention adopted under its auspices, is in question before the Tribunal.

The members of the Tribunal in plenary, and the Tribunal's Committee on Rules and Judicial Practice, have considered whether it was necessary to develop guidelines on *amicus curiae* submissions, but decided that it was premature to do so and that the matter could be reassessed in light of future practice before the Tribunal.[195]

---

[189] Ibid, arts 103, 104.
[190] Ibid, arts 103(4), 104(3).
[191] ITLOS Statute, art 17(5).
[192] ITLOS Rules, art 47.
[193] *Southern Bluefin Tuna* (Australia and New Zealand v Japan), Order of 16 August 1999.
[194] ITLOS Rules, art 84.
[195] *Annual Report of the International Tribunal for the Law of the Sea for 2004*, SPLOS/122, 30 March 2005, para 41.

Representation of parties

Parties to disputes before the ITLOS are to be represented by agents and may **2.31** have the assistance of counsel or advocates before the Tribunal.[196]

Decision

The final decision of the ITLOS on the dispute before it will be in the form of a **2.32** judgment. The judgment will contain, *inter alia*: the names of judges participating in it; the names of experts, if any, appointed under article 289 of UNCLOS; a summary of the proceedings; the submissions of parties; a statement of the facts; the reasons of law on which the judgment is based; the operative provisions of the judgment; a decision on costs; and the number and names of the judges constituting the majority and those constituting the minority, on each operative provision.[197]

All questions are decided by a majority of the judges.[198] Separate or dissenting opinions, or declarations, may be appended to judgments or orders.[199] The judgment shall be read at a public sitting of the Tribunal and becomes binding on the parties on the day of the reading.[200]

The decision of the Tribunal is final and is to be complied with by all the parties to the dispute. However, any decision has binding force only between the parties to the case and with respect to the dispute to which it relates.[201]

Interpretation and revision of judgment

In the event of dispute as to the meaning or scope of a judgment, any party **2.33** to the case may make a request for the interpretation of the judgment.[202] The request may be submitted by a unilateral application, or through agreement of the parties. In any case, the precise point (or points) in dispute should be indicated.[203] In cases brought by application, the Tribunal will allow the other party to file its observations within a time limit fixed by the Tribunal (or President).[204] In all cases, ITLOS may request the parties to present further written or oral explanations.[205]

---

[196] ITLOS Rules, art 53.
[197] ITLOS Statute, art 30(1), (2); ITLOS Rules, art 125(1).
[198] ITLOS Statute, art 29(1).
[199] Ibid, art 30(3); ITLOS Rules, art 125(2).
[200] ITLOS Rules, art 124(2).
[201] UNCLOS, art 296; ITLOS Statute, art 33(1), (2).
[202] ITLOS Statute, art 33(3); ITLOS Rules, art 126(1).
[203] ITLOS Rules, art 126(2).
[204] Ibid, art 126(3).
[205] Ibid, art 126(4).

A request for revision of a judgment can be made only when it is based upon the discovery of a fact of such a nature as to be a decisive factor, which was unknown to the Tribunal and to the party requesting a revision when the judgment was given; and provided that such ignorance was not due to negligence.[206] The request is to be presented within six months from the discovery of the new fact, and in no case after ten years from the date of judgment. The request should include all particulars necessary to show that conditions for revision have been met, and will have attached to it supporting documents.[207] The Tribunal will fix a time limit for the other party to submit observations on the admissibility of the request; and may afford the parties additional opportunity to present their views on the question of admissibility.[208] If the Tribunal finds that the request is admissible, it will fix time limits for such further proceedings on the merits of the application as, after ascertaining the views of the parties, it considers necessary.[209]

The decision on the request for interpretation or revision will be given in the form of a judgment, normally by the Tribunal or the chamber which rendered the original judgment.[210]

Appeal

2.34 A decision of the Tribunal is final and is not subject to appeal.[211]

Costs

2.35 The expenses of the Tribunal are borne by the states parties to UNCLOS and by the International Seabed Authority.[212] However, when an entity other than a state party or the International Seabed Authority is a party to a case submitted to the Tribunal, the Tribunal will fix the amount which that party is to contribute towards the expenses of the Tribunal.[213]

As to the legal costs and other expenses of the parties, each party will bear its own costs, unless otherwise decided by the Tribunal.[214]

Execution of decision, recognition, and enforcement

2.36 Judgments of the ITLOS are binding upon the parties and must be complied with.[215] However, the Convention and other instruments do not explicitly

---

[206] Ibid, art 127(1).
[207] Ibid, art 128(1).
[208] Ibid, art 128(2), (3).
[209] Ibid, art 128(5).
[210] Ibid, art 129.
[211] UNCLOS, art 296(1); ITLOS Statute, art 33(1).
[212] ITLOS Statute, art 19(1).
[213] Ibid, art 19(2).
[214] Ibid, art 34.
[215] UNCLOS, art 296(1); ITLOS Statute, art 33(1).

provide for an enforcement mechanism. On the other hand, decisions of the SBDC are to be enforceable in the territories of the states parties in the same manner as judgments or orders of the highest court of that state party.[216]

Evaluation

While the ITLOS has dealt expeditiously with the proceedings that have been brought before it to date, it remains strikingly underused. In the 13 years since its establishment, only 15 sets of proceedings have been initiated. Nine of these were prompt release cases, one of which was discontinued upon agreement by the parties. Four were requests for provisional measures under article 290(5) of UNCLOS, made pending the establishment of an arbitral tribunal under Annex VII to UNCLOS. Besides these, only one judgment on the merits has been issued, in the *M/V 'Saiga' (No 2) Case*, which also gave rise to a request for provisional measures under article 290(1). The SBDC remains dormant. At the end of December 2009, one case was on the Tribunal's docket concerning the maritime boundary between Bangladesh and Myanmar in the Bay of Bengal.[217]

The underuse of the ITLOS has to be seen in context—Part XV of UNCLOS has not so far been the basis for the submission of many disputes to any forum. Nonetheless, it is notable that the merits of the disputes that have arisen in relation to the interpretation and application of UNCLOS have been submitted to Annex VII arbitration, rather than to the ITLOS (or to the ICJ).[218] Of the Annex VII arbitrations, only two (both concerning maritime delimitation issues) have proceeded to an award on the merits.[219] The Annex VII arbitrations have in most, but not all, cases been administered by the International Bureau of the Permanent Court of Arbitration in The Hague.[220] The recourse to Annex VII arbitration can be largely explained by the fact that the states parties to

---

[216] ITLOS Statute, art 39.

[217] Dispute concerning the Maritime Boundary between Bangladesh and Myanmar, ITLOS/Press Release 140, 16 December 2009.

[218] With the exception of the *M/V 'Saiga' (No 2) Case* and the pending *Swordfish* proceedings, which were submitted to the ITLOS.

[219] *Guyana v Suriname* (Award of 17 September 2007); *Barbados v Trinidad and Tobago* (Award of 11 April 2006). Proceedings in the *MOX Plant* case were terminated; the arbitral tribunal in the *Southern Bluefin Tuna* case found that it did not have jurisdiction to decide the merits; the *Land Reclamation Activities in and around the Straits of Johor* case was settled following submission of the report of the group of independent experts established pursuant to the provisional measures order of the ITLOS of 8 October 2003.

[220] The *Southern Bluefin Tuna* case was administered by the International Centre for the Settlement of Investment Disputes (ICSID); the PCA has acted as registry in: the *MOX Plant* case (Ireland v UK), Order on Termination of Proceedings of 6 June 2008; *Guyana v Suriname*, *supra* note 219; *Barbados v Trinidad and Tobago*, *supra* note 219; and *Land Reclamation Activities in and around the Straits of Johor* (Malaysia v Singapore), Award on Agreed Terms of 1 September 2005.

the disputes in question have not made the same, or any, choice of procedure under article 287 of UNCLOS. Only 25 out of 159 states parties to UNCLOS have made a declaration indicating acceptance of the ITLOS. In these circumstances it is clear that most disputes subject to compulsory procedures entailing binding decisions under UNCLOS are likely to go to Annex VII arbitration unless and until more states parties make declarations under article 287.[221] The reference to the ITLOS, or to UNCLOS dispute settlement in general, in other agreements[222] has yet to give rise to any proceedings before the Tribunal. In the meantime, it remains of concern that the Tribunal has not yet been more fully utilized.[223]

The Rules of the Tribunal explicitly state that proceedings are to be conducted without unnecessary delay or expense,[224] and that time limits for completion of steps in the proceedings should be as short as the character of the case permits.[225] Where cases have been initiated before the Tribunal, the Rules do seem to have been applied in such a manner that the proceedings have taken place expeditiously. Prompt release cases have been dealt with within one calendar month from application to judgment;[226] and the provisional measures requests have also been considered and decided without undue delay. The fact that the Tribunal has been in a position to deal expeditiously with proceedings might nonetheless be expected at this stage given that the caseload of the Tribunal has been extremely light to date.

The Tribunal's provisional measures jurisdiction offers the possibility for innovative approaches, particularly as regards protection of the marine environment from serious harm. It is also noteworthy that in its provisional measures cases, the Tribunal appears to promote a dispute-management approach, most significantly in the *Malaysia-Singapore* case in which it ordered the establishment of a group of independent experts to study the land reclamation issues in question and to recommend measures to deal with any adverse effects.

---

[221] While no cases have yet been submitted to the International Court of Justice under the terms of Part XV of UNCLOS, the ICJ has nonetheless been seised of cases concerning maritime delimitation disputes since the entry into force of UNCLOS.

[222] See *supra* note 73.

[223] At the time of the Tribunal's establishment, some commentators questioned the need for, and the wisdom of, the establishment of a specialized tribunal addressing law of the sea disputes. See S Oda, 'Dispute Settlement Prospects in the Law of the Sea' (1995) 44 *International and Comparative Law Quarterly* 863.

[224] ITLOS Rules, art 49.

[225] Ibid, art 46.

[226] Indeed, as noted previously, in 2001 the Tribunal amended its rules to extend certain time limits in prompt release proceedings given the difficulties the original time limits caused for some parties.

A number of steps and initiatives have been taken to increase the potential lure of the ITLOS for litigants in disputes involving the law of the sea. In addition to the Chamber on Fisheries Matters and Chamber for the Marine Environment established by the ITLOS in 1997, in 2007 the ITLOS established a standing Chamber for Maritime Delimitation Disputes. The Tribunal, generally through its President, has also drawn attention to the possibility that exists for states parties to UNCLOS to submit disputes to a special chamber of ITLOS rather than to the full Tribunal should they prefer, and has highlighted the potential advantages for states parties of selecting such chambers over Annex VII arbitral tribunals. More recently, the Tribunal has also drawn attention to the potential utility of its advisory jurisdiction in relation to novel, or re-emerging, concerns relating to the law of the sea. In his statement to the 63rd session of the UN General Assembly in 2008, the President of the ITLOS, Judge Jesus, drew attention to this aspect of the Tribunal's advisory jurisdiction, observing that 'as the international community faces new challenges in ocean activities, such as piracy and armed robbery, advisory proceedings before the Tribunal on legal questions concerning the application and interpretation of provisions of the Convention may prove to be a useful tool to States'.[227]

The Tribunal and its members have been involved in a number of other initiatives designed to promote awareness of the Tribunal and its procedures. These include, since 2006, a number of regional workshops, to provide government experts working in the maritime field with insight into the procedures for the peaceful settlement of disputes related to the law of the sea, as enshrined in UNCLOS, with special attention given to the jurisdiction of the Tribunal and the procedure for bringing disputes before it.[228] The members of the Tribunal have also participated in other activities intended to develop capacity in relation to dispute settlement under UNCLOS, including through the International Foundation for the Law of the Sea Summer Academy. While thus far such initiatives have not given rise to any increase in recourse to the Tribunal by states parties to UNCLOS, it cannot be ruled out that they may do so in future.

---

[227] Statement by Judge José Luis Jesus, 5 December 2008, available at <http://www.itlos.org>.

[228] By 2008, such workshops had been held in Dakar, Senegal; Libreville, Gabon; Kingston, Jamaica; Singapore; and Buenos Aires, with further events planned in Bahrain, Cape Town, and Manila. Statement by Mr Rüdiger Wolfrum, President of the ITLOS, at the 62nd Session of the General Assembly, 10 December 2007, para 20, available at <http://www.itlos.org/start2_en.html>.

REFERENCE

SOURCES OF PREVIOUS CASE LAW, INCLUDING CASE REPORTS

Copies of the judgments and orders of the Tribunal can be obtained from the ITLOS website.

Reports of Judgments, Advisory Opinions and Orders are published by Martinus Nijhoff, as are *Pleadings, Minutes of Public Sittings and Documents.*

OFFICIAL PUBLICATIONS

Official publications of the Tribunal are published by Martinus Nijhoff.

Basic Texts/Textes de base: International Tribunal for the Law of the Sea, (Martinus Nijhoff, 2005).

Yearbook of the International Tribunal for the Law of the Sea, Martinus Nijhoff.

The Law of the Sea: Official Texts of the United Nations Convention on the Law of the Sea of 10 December 1982 and of the Agreement relating to the Implementation of Part XI of the United Nations Convention on the Law of the Sea of 10 December 1982 (United Nations, New York, 1997).

Report of the Preparatory Commission under Paragraph 10 of Resolution I Containing Recommendations for Submission to the Meeting of States Parties to be Convened in Accordance with Annex VI, art 4, of the Convention Regarding Practical Arrangements for the Establishment of the International Tribunal for the Law of the Sea, Volumes I to IV (United Nations, document LOS/PCN/152, 1995).

Press releases of the Tribunal, are available on the ITLOS website.

SELECT BIBLIOGRAPHY

The ITLOS Registry prepares and updates a *Select Bibliography on Settlement of Disputes Concerning the Law of the Sea*. This document is available on the ITLOS website at <http://www.itlos.org/start2_en.html>.

P C Rao and P Gautier (eds), *The Rules of the International Tribunal for the Law of the Sea: A Commentary* (2006).

N Klein, *Dispute Settlement in the UN Convention on the Law of the Sea* (2005).

S Rosenne, *Provisional Measures in International Law: The International Court of Justice and the International Tribunal for the Law of the Sea* (2005).

P C Rao and R Khan, *The International Tribunal for the Law of the Sea: Law and Practice* (2001).

G Eiriksson, *The International Tribunal for the Law of the Sea* (2000).

N-J Seeberg-Elverfeldt, *The Settlement of Disputes in Deep Seabed Mining: Access, Jurisdiction and Procedure before the Seabed Disputes Chamber of the International Tribunal for the Law of the Sea* (1998).

M Nordquist, S Rosenne, and L Sohn (eds), *United Nations Convention on the Law of the Sea 1982: A Commentary*, Vol 5 (1989).

Annual surveys of dispute settlement under the UN Convention on the Law of the Sea are published in, for example, the *International Journal of Marine and Coastal Law* and the *Italian Yearbook of International Law*.

ANNEX

List of states parties to UNCLOS

(as at 10 July 2009)

Albania, Algeria, Angola, Antigua and Barbuda, Argentina,* Armenia, Australia,* Austria,* Bahamas, Bahrain, Bangladesh, Barbados, Belarus, Belgium,* Belize, Benin, Bolivia, Bosnia and Herzegovina, Botswana, Brazil, Brunei Darussalam, Bulgaria, Burkina Faso, Cameroon, Canada,* Cape Verde,* Chile,* China, Comoros, Congo, Cook Islands, Costa Rica, Côte d'Ivoire, Croatia,* Cuba, Cyprus, Czech Republic, Democratic Republic of the Congo, Denmark, Djibouti, Dominica, Dominican Republic, Egypt, Equatorial Guinea, Estonia,* European Community, Fiji, Finland,* France, Gabon, Gambia, Georgia, Germany,* Ghana, Greece,* Grenada, Guatemala, Guinea, Guinea-Bissau, Guyana, Haiti, Honduras, Hungary,* Iceland, India, Indonesia, Iraq, Ireland, Italy,* Jamaica, Japan, Jordan, Kenya, Kiribati, Kuwait, Lao People's Democratic Republic, Latvia,* Lebanon, Lesotho, Liberia, Lithuania,* Luxembourg, Madagascar, Malaysia, Maldives, Mali, Malta, Marshall Islands, Mauritania, Mauritius, Mexico,* Micronesia (Federated States of), Moldova, Monaco, Mongolia, Montenegro, Morocco, Mozambique, Myanmar, Namibia, Nauru, Nepal, Netherlands, New Zealand, Nicaragua, Niger, Nigeria, Niue, Norway, Oman,* Pakistan, Palau, Panama, Papua New Guinea, Paraguay, Philippines, Poland, Portugal,* Qatar, Republic of Korea, Romania, Russian Federation, Saint Kitts and Nevis, Saint Lucia, Saint Vincent and the Grenadines, Samoa, São Tomé and Principe, Saudi Arabia, Senegal, Serbia, Seychelles, Sierra Leone, Singapore, Slovakia, Slovenia, Solomon Islands, Somalia, South Africa, Spain,* Sri Lanka, Sudan, Suriname, Sweden, Switzerland,* The Former Yugoslav Republic of Macedonia, Togo, Tonga, Trinidad and Tobago,* Tunisia,* Tuvalu, Uganda, Ukraine, United Arab Emirates, United Kingdom of Great Britain and Northern Ireland, United Republic of Tanzania,* Uruguay,* Vanuatu, Vietnam, Yemen, Zambia, Zimbabwe.

* Parties that have made a declaration under article 287 of UNCLOS choosing the ITLOS as a means for settlement of disputes.

3

THE DISPUTE SETTLEMENT SYSTEM OF
THE WORLD TRADE ORGANIZATION

Introduction

Name and seat of the body

3.1 The 1994 Agreement Establishing the World Trade Organization includes an Annex on dispute settlement entitled the 'Understanding on Rules and Procedures Governing the Settlement of Disputes'. The Dispute Settlement Understanding (DSU) of the World Trade Organization (WTO) is intended to resolve disputes arising between WTO members. The WTO is located in Geneva, Switzerland. The contact details are:

> World Trade Organization
> Centre William Rappard
> 154 rue de Lausanne
> CH1211 Geneva 21
> Switzerland
> Tel: 41 22 739 51 11
> Fax: 41 22 731 42 06
> Website: <http://www.wto.org/>

General description

3.2 The WTO is an international organization invested with powers and functions designed to promote and regulate international trade at the global level. It was established in 1995 as a new international organization to replace the less structured system of the General Agreement on Tariffs and Trade (hereinafter

GATT), which had provided, since 1948, a framework for several rounds of multilateral trade negotiations. By 31 July 2009, 153 states or 'separate customs territories' (including the European Communities) had become WTO members.

The dispute settlement system is a 'central element in providing security and predictability to the multilateral trading system'.[1] The system is intended to serve to preserve the rights and obligations of WTO members under the covered agreements, and to clarify the existing provisions of those agreements in accordance with customary rules of interpretation of public international law. The DSU provides that the recommendations and rulings of the DSB are not to add to or diminish the rights and obligations provided in the covered agreements.[2]

The Dispute Settlement Body is a political body comprising representatives from all members of the WTO.[3] It is charged with administering the dispute settlement process: it supervises the process of consultations between disputing members; establishes panels on request of a party to a dispute; adopts panel or Appellate Body (AB) reports and recommendations relating to the resolution of the dispute; maintains surveillance over the implementation of the recommendations; and may authorize trade sanctions in the face of non-compliance with adopted panel or Appellate Body recommendations.

In the event of a dispute between members of the WTO, one member may request the other to enter into consultations and should notify the DSB of this request.[4] If such consultations fail, the complaining party may request the DSB to establish an ad hoc panel.[5] In addition, each party may propose that other dispute settlement procedures (good offices, conciliation, or mediation) be employed between the parties, with the possible assistance of the Director-General (head of the WTO Secretariat).[6] Where more than one member requests

---

[1] Understanding on Rules and Procedures Governing the Settlement of Disputes (Annex 2 to the Agreement Establishing the World Trade Organization), 15 April 1994, art 3(2), 33 ILM 112 (1994) ('DSU').

[2] Ibid.

[3] The DSB is, in effect, the alter ego of the WTO General Council, comprising all WTO members. Agreement Establishing the World Trade Organization, 15 April 1994, art IV(3), 33 ILM 13 (1994) ('WTO Agreement').

[4] DSU, art 4.

[5] Ibid, arts 4(7), 5(4).

[6] Ibid, art 5. If such procedures are terminated, a complaining party may proceed to request the establishment of a panel, provided 60 days have passed since the date of receipt of the request for consultations. A request to establish a panel may be made sooner if the parties to the dispute jointly consider that the resort to good offices, mediation, or conciliation has failed to resolve the dispute. DSU, art 5(3). In 2002, the Philippines, Thailand, and the European Communities jointly requested mediation, having been unable to reach a mutually acceptable solution after three rounds of consultations. The Director-General of the WTO indicated that although the requesting members considered that the matter between them was not a 'dispute' within the terms of the DSU, they agreed that the Director-General, or a mediator designated by him, could be guided by procedures similar to those envisaged in art 5 of the DSU. *Request for Mediation by the Philippines, Thailand and the European Communities, Communication from the Director-General,*

the establishment of a panel relating to the same matter, a single panel may be established to examine the complaints.[7]

Panels conduct hearings on the dispute referred to them, and issue a report and recommendations on the merits of the case. The recommendations of a panel are not automatically binding upon the parties to the dispute. They become binding only after the report and recommendations have been adopted by the DSB. However, adoption is automatic; that is, a panel report is adopted unless a party to the dispute formally notifies the DSB of its decision to appeal or the DSB decides by consensus not to adopt the report.[8]

The panel report may be appealed, on legal grounds, before the Appellate Body, which may uphold, modify, or reverse the legal findings of the panel. Like panel reports, the reports of the Appellate Body have no binding effect until adopted by the DSB. Again, the reverse consensus rule applies, so that the AB's report will be adopted, unless the DSB decides otherwise by consensus. The WTO dispute settlement system has been described as 'quasi-judicial' in that independent and autonomous bodies adjudicate disputes while formally subject to the overall authority of the DSB.[9]

By the standards of most international courts and tribunals, proceedings in the WTO dispute settlement system are designed to be fast: the DSU acknowledges that prompt settlement of trade disputes is critical if the WTO is to be effective.[10] The DSU sets a timetable for the various stages in the dispute resolution process—from a request for consultations to delivery of the report of the panel and, if relevant, the report of the Appellate Body—that should result in disputes being resolved within one year, or 15 months in the event of an appeal.

The DSU also contains provisions for the surveillance of implementation of DSB recommendations and rulings. Members are to report to the DSB their intentions with regard to implementation, and further procedures exist under

---

WT/GC/66, 16 October 2002. Article 24(2) of the DSU provides that in dispute settlement cases involving a least-developed country member, where a satisfactory solution is not found in the course of consultations, the Director-General or the Chairman of the DSB shall offer their good offices, conciliation, and mediation, upon request of a least-developed country member, before a request for a panel is made.

[7] DSU, art 9(1). In such circumstances, should any of the parties to the dispute so request, the panel may issue separate reports. Ibid, art 9(2).

[8] Ibid, art 16(4). See also ibid, note 1 to art 2(4).

[9] G Marceau, 'Consultations and the Panel Process in the WTO Dispute Settlement System' in R Yerxa and B Wilson (eds), *Key Issues in WTO Dispute Settlement: The First Ten Years* (2005) 29. Palmeter and Mavroidis observe that 'although the WTO members, acting collectively as the DSB, continue to have the last word as a formal matter, in a practical sense the last legal word really now lies with the panels and the Appellate Body. Thus, while panels and the Appellate Body are not courts, increasingly they bear a striking resemblance to courts...' D Palmeter and P C Mavroidis, *Dispute Settlement in the World Trade Organization: Practice and Procedure* (2nd edn, 2004) at 85.

[10] DSU, art 3(3).

article 21.3(c) and article 21.5 of the DSU for resolution of implementation-related disputes. Further, article 22.6 of the DSU provides for arbitration in the event of a dispute as to the appropriate level of suspension of concessions in response to non-implementation of DSB recommendations and rulings.

The dispute settlement system of the WTO has been busy since the establishment of the WTO in January 1995.[11] By the end of July 2009, 397 requests for consultation had been initiated before the DSB, involving more than 300 distinct matters.[12] The US and the European Communities have been the most active litigants, both as complainants and respondents. More than 150 panel reports have been adopted, including more than 20 reports on article 21.5 requests relating to compliance. The Appellate Body has issued 97 reports, including 20 on appeals relating to panel reports under article 21.5.[13] Arbitrator's awards have been issued in more than 20 article 21.3(c) arbitrations (to determine a reasonable period of time for implementation of DSB recommendations) and in 17 article 22.6 arbitrations (on disputes concerning the appropriate level of suspension of concessions). While the caseload of the panels and the AB remains high, it is also clear that a large number of trade disputes are settled through consultations under the DSU or other means.

It should be noted that article 25 of the DSU specifically preserves the right of the parties to a dispute to agree to resolve their differences by way of arbitration within the WTO as an alternative means of dispute settlement, with DSU provisions in articles 21 and 22 applying *mutatis mutandis* to arbitration awards.[14]

The WTO dispute settlement system was to be reviewed by 1 January 1999.[15] The review process began in 1997, but has not yet led to any agreed conclusion.

---

[11] In addition to the WTO website, statistical data on WTO dispute settlement is available at <http://www.worldtradelaw.net>. See also K Leitner and S Lester, 'WTO Dispute Settlement 1995–2008: A Statistical Analysis' (2009) 12 *Journal of International Economic Law* 195.

[12] WTO, Chronological List of Disputes Cases, available at <http://www.wto.org/english/tratop_e/dispu_e/dispu_status_e.htm>.

[13] WTO, Dispute Settlement Statistics at: <http://www.wto.org/english/tratop_e/dispu_e/stats_e.htm> (updated to 11 June 2009); Dispute Settlement Body, *Annual Report (2008): Overview of the State of Play of WTO Disputes. Addendum*, WT/DSB/47/Add.1, 8 December 2008 (updated to 31 October 2008); <http://www.worldtradelaw.net>.

[14] DSU, art 25. See Award of the Arbitrators, *United States—Section 110(5) of the US Copyright Act—Recourse to Arbitration under Article 25 of the DSU*, WT/DS160/ARB25/1, 9 November 2001, 2001:II DSR 667. The EC requested consultations under DSU, art 4 in January 1999. A panel was established and issued a report in June 2000, which was adopted by the DSB in July 2000. As there was no agreement on the reasonable period for implementation of the panel recommendations, the EC requested arbitration under art 21(3)(c) of the DSU. Following the arbitrator's determination, the US and the EC informed the DSB that they had agreed to arbitration under art 25(2) DSU in order to establish the level of nullification or impairment of benefits to the EC as a result of the US measures at issue. The arbitrators' award was issued on 9 November 2001.

[15] Decision on the Application and Review of the Understanding on Rules and Procedures Governing the Settlement of Disputes, Ministerial Decision adopted by the Trade Negotiations Committee, 15 December 1993, available at <http://www.wto.org/english/tratop_e/dispu_e/dispu_e.htm#negotiations>.

Further negotiations on the DSU are taking place, in special sessions of the DSB, in light of the decisions adopted at the Ministerial Conference in Doha in 2001.[16] While numerous proposals have been put forward by members to improve or clarify the dispute settlement procedures, both at the panel and appellate stage, these have yet to lead to any formal amendments to the DSU.[17]

Institutional Aspects

Governing texts

Procedural law

3.3 The procedures of the WTO dispute settlement system are governed by the following texts:

- Articles III–IV, Agreement Establishing the World Trade Organization, 1994 (establishing the DSB and vesting it with dispute resolution powers) ('WTO Agreement');[18]
- Understanding on Rules and Procedures Governing the Settlement of Disputes (Annex 2 to the WTO Agreement) (outlining the procedure of the WTO dispute settlement system) ('DSU');
- Working Procedures (Appendix 3 to the DSU) (specifying the procedure for panel proceedings) ('Panel Working Procedures');
- Working Procedures for Appellate Review, as last amended with effect from 1 January 2005 (specifying the procedure of the Appellate Body) ('Appellate Body Working Procedures');[19]
- Rules of Conduct for the Understanding on Rules and Procedures Governing the Settlement of Disputes, adopted on 11 December 1996 (addressing the need to preserve the integrity, impartiality, and confidentiality of the various persons involved in the dispute settlement mechanism—including panel and Appellate Body members, experts and Secretariat staff) ('Rules of Conduct').[20]

---

[16] Ministerial Declaration, WT/MIN(01)/DEC/1, 20 November 2001, para 30.

[17] On the DSU review, see, for example, B Mercurio, 'Improving Dispute Settlement in the World Trade Organization: The Dispute Settlement Understanding Review—Making It Work?' (2004) 38 *Journal of World Trade* 795; G Sacerdoti, A Yanovich, and J Bohanes (eds), *The WTO at Ten: The Contribution of the Dispute Settlement System* (2005) at 193–265. Information on the status of the DSU negotiations and proposals submitted by members are available on the WTO website.

[18] WTO Agreement, art IV(3).

[19] Working Procedures for Appellate Review (as amended), WTO Doc WT/AB/WP/5, 4 January 2005 ('AB Working Procedures').

[20] Rules of Conduct for the Understanding on Rules and Procedures Governing the Settlement of Disputes, WTO Doc WT/DSB /RC /1, 11 December 1996 ('Rules of Conduct').

In addition, where WTO disputes involve questions governed by specific WTO agreements that provide for special or additional rules of procedure, these special or additional rules will prevail.[21]

Substantive law

The substantive law to be applied by the panel or Appellate Body is to be found **3.4** in the agreements listed in Appendix 1 of the DSU (the 'covered agreements'). Article 3.2 of the DSU provides that the recommendations and rulings of the DSB cannot add to or diminish the rights and obligations provided in the covered agreements.[22]

The DSU also provides that the WTO members recognize that the dispute settlement system serves to preserve the rights and obligations of members under the covered agreements and to clarify the existing provisions of those agreements in accordance with customary rules of interpretation of international law. In early cases the Appellate Body confirmed that the rules of treaty interpretation in articles 31 and 32 of the Vienna Convention on the Law of Treaties had attained the status of a rule of customary international law or general international law, and, as such, formed part of the customary rules which the AB was directed to apply by article 3.2 of the DSU.[23] The AB observed that this direction reflected a measure of recognition that trade rules were not to be read 'in clinical isolation from public international law'.[24]

While there is no formal rule of *stare decisis* in the DSU, there has been some debate as to reliance on previous AB or panel rulings in disputes (including pre-WTO, adopted GATT panel reports).[25] The AB has observed that the legal interpretations in adopted panel and AB reports become part of the WTO

---

[21] DSU, art 1(2). The list of specific or additional rules of procedure is enumerated in Appendix 2 to the DSU. Such specific or additional rules are not considered further in this Chapter. In case of a difference or conflict between the rules and procedures of the DSU and the specific rules and procedures on dispute settlement in one of the covered agreements, the Appellate Body has ruled that the latter take precedence as more suitable in a dispute concerning violation of a covered agreement provision, yet only where the difference effectively means that adherence to one rule would lead to violation of another provision. See Appellate Body Report, *Guatemala: Anti-Dumping Investigation Regarding Portland Cement from Mexico*, WT/DS60/AB/R, 25 November 1998, 1998:IX DSR 3767, paras 65–66.

[22] DSU, art 3(2); WTO Agreement, art IX.2.

[23] Appellate Body Report, *United States—Standards for Reformulated and Conventional Gasoline*, WT/DS2/AB/R, 20 May 1996, 1996:I DSR 3; Appellate Body Report, *Japan—Taxes on Alcoholic Beverages*, WT/DS8/AB/R, WT/DS10/AB/R, WT/DS11/AB/R, 1 November 1996, 1996:I DSR 97; Appellate Body Report, *United States—Countervailing Duties on Certain Corrosion-Resistant Carbon Steel Flat Products from Germany*, WT/DS213/AB/R and Corr 1, 19 December 2002, 2002:IX DSR 3779, paras 61–62.

[24] *Reformulated and Conventional Gasoline, supra* note 23.

[25] J Waincymer, *WTO Litigation: Procedural Aspects of Formal Dispute Settlement* (2002) at 510–511.

acquis[26] and create 'legitimate expectations' and hence should be taken into consideration when relevant in a particular dispute.[27] While previous findings are binding only as regards the resolution of the particular case between the parties to that dispute, nonetheless the Appellate Body has recognized that consistency of jurisprudence is relevant to enhancing the security and predictability to which the dispute settlement system should contribute. [28]

Organization

Composition, appointment, and disqualification of a panel

3.5 Panels are normally composed of three persons, although the parties to a dispute can request the enlargement of a panel so as to include five persons.[29] The Secretariat of the WTO proposes the nomination of panel members, normally on the basis of an indicative list of prospective panel members maintained by the Secretariat, which is composed of names put forward by the members and approved by the DSB.[30] The parties are expected to agree to this panel composition, unless they have compelling reasons for objecting.[31] No national of the disputing parties or third parties may serve as a panel member, unless the parties agree otherwise.[32]

If the parties cannot agree on the composition of the panel within 20 days from the date of the DSB's decision to establish a panel, any party may request the Director-General (the head of the WTO Secretariat) to appoint a panel, after consulting with the parties and with the Chairman of the DSB and of the relevant WTO Council.[33]

---

[26] *Alcoholic Beverages, supra* note 23; Appellate Body Report, *United States—Final Anti-Dumping Measures on Stainless Steel from Mexico*, WT/DS344/AB/R, 20 May 2008, paras 160–161. See also, for example, Appellate Body Report, *United States—Import Prohibition of Certain Shrimp and Shrimp Products—Recourse to Article 21.5 of the DSU by Malaysia*, WT/DS58/AB/RW, 21 November 2001, 2001:XIII DSR, 6481.

[27] *Alcoholic Beverages, supra* note 23.

[28] See eg *Stainless Steel, supra* note 26, paras 160–161. The AB observed that '[t]he Panel's failure to follow previously adopted Appellate Body reports addressing the same issues undermines the development of a coherent and predictable body of jurisprudence clarifying Members' rights and obligations under the covered agreements as contemplated under the DSU. Clarification, as envisaged in Article 3.2 of the DSU, elucidates the scope and meaning of the provisions of the covered agreements in accordance with customary rules of interpretation of public international law. While the application of a provision may be regarded as confined to the context in which it takes place, the relevance of clarification contained in adopted Appellate Body reports is not limited to the application of a particular provision in a specific case.'

[29] DSU, art 8(5). However, the request must be made within ten days from the establishment of the panel.

[30] DSU, art 8(4). DSU, art 8(1) lists, not exhaustively, the qualifications and experience of panellists, and art 8(2) states that the objective of selection is 'ensuring the independence of the members, a sufficiently diverse background and a wide spectrum of experience'. There is no requirement that panellists are lawyers, and generally they are not.

[31] Ibid, art 8(6).

[32] Ibid, art 8(3).

[33] Ibid, art 8(7).

Panellists serve in their individual capacities and not as governmental representatives or representative of any organization.[34]

Disqualification of a panel member

The Rules of Conduct set out principles for maintaining the integrity, impartiality, and confidentiality of dispute settlement proceedings. They are centred on rather detailed disclosure obligations and the avoidance of conflicts of interest. **3.6**

If a party to the dispute possesses information indicating a breach of the obligations of independence, impartiality, or confidentiality on the part of a panel member, or has knowledge of direct or indirect conflicts of interest which may impair the integrity, impartiality, or confidentiality of the dispute settlement process, it must submit this information promptly to the Chairman of the DSB.[35] The Chairman then transmits the information to the concerned panellists, and subsequently to all other parties. If the panellist does not withdraw, the Chair of the DSB may, after consulting with other WTO officials, the parties, and the concerned panellist, revoke the appointment of the panellist.[36]

Plenary/chambers

As noted above, panels comprise three (or exceptionally five) persons. The Appellate Body, on the other hand, hears cases in divisions of three of its seven members.[37] **3.7**

Appellate structure[38]

The Appellate Body provides a forum for appeals over 'issues of law covered in the panel report and legal interpretations developed by the panel'.[39] The AB is composed of seven members[40] elected by the DSB for a once-renewable four-year period.[41] In contrast to the panels, the AB is a standing body, although its members still operate on a part-time basis.[42] The members of the AB are all individuals of recognized authority, with demonstrated expertise in law and the subject matter of the covered agreements.[43] The membership of the AB should be **3.8**

---

[34] Ibid, art 8(9).

[35] Rules of Conduct, r VIII.

[36] Rules of Conduct, r VIII(6)–(8).

[37] DSU, art 17(1).

[38] See also *infra* para 3.37.

[39] DSU, art 17(6).

[40] On 31 July 2009, the members of the AB were: Lilia Bautista (Philippines), Ricardo Ramirez Hernandez (Mexico), Jennifer Hillman (US), Shotaro Oshima (Japan), Giorgio Sacerdoti (Italy), David Unterhalter (S Africa, Chairman), and Yuejiao Zhang (China).

[41] DSU, art 17(2). It is notable that this is a relatively short term of office as compared to other international courts and tribunals.

[42] The DSU requires that Appellate Body members are 'available at all times and on short notice'. DSU, art 17(3).

[43] DSU, art 17(3).

broadly representative of membership in the WTO,[44] but the AB members are unaffiliated with any government.[45] The AB is headed by a Chairman, elected by the members of the AB for a one-year term, which may be extended for a period of up to one year. In addition, each division is headed by a Presiding Member.[46] The original members of the AB took their oath of office on 3 December 1995.

The AB sits in divisions of three persons selected for each case on the basis of rotation, taking into account principles of random selection, unpredictability, and opportunity for all AB members to serve regardless of their national origin.[47] In contrast to the panels, there is no bar to a member of the AB sitting in a division hearing an appeal involving his or her state of nationality, and this has occurred in a number of cases. Although the AB hears appeals in divisions of three members, the Working Procedures for Appellate Review promote collegiality. AB members are to convene on a regular basis to discuss matters of policy, practice, and procedure, and all AB members are to receive all documents filed in any appeal. To ensure consistency and coherence in decision making, the division responsible for deciding each appeal is to exchange views with other AB members before finalizing the appellate report for circulation to WTO members.[48]

The procedure for disqualification of an AB member from a particular appeal is similar to that for panelists. However, the request should be presented to the AB itself, not to the Chair of the DSB; and the AB decides whether to accept or reject the request.[49]

Scientific and technical experts

3.9 A WTO panel may seek information and technical advice from any individual or body it deems appropriate, provided that the member state with jurisdiction over that person or body has been previously notified.[50] In addition, the panel may appoint an expert review group, composed of independent professional experts, and instruct it to prepare an advisory report.'[51] The rules governing the establishment and operation of an expert review group are set out in a separate Appendix to the DSU,[52] and in the Rules of Conduct.[53]

---

[44] In practice, there has, since 1995, always been an Appellate Body member from the United States and from the European Communities.
[45] DSU, art 17(3).
[46] AB Working Procedures, rr 5, 7.
[47] DSU, art 17.
[48] AB Working Procedures, r 4. See also ibid, r 11, paras 2 and 3.
[49] Rules of Conduct, r VIII(14)–(17); AB Working Procedures, r 10(5).
[50] DSU, art 13(1).
[51] Ibid, art 13(2).
[52] Ibid, Appendix 4.
[53] Rules of Conduct, Article II.1.

It is now consistent practice of WTO panels to request expert advice in different forms. However, they have not tended to appoint expert review groups, but rather to have recourse to individual experts.[54] The covered agreements may also contain specific rules on expert evidence. The SPS Agreement requires panels to seek expert advice in disputes 'involving scientific or technical issues',[55] and experts have been called upon in a number of cases involving the SPS Agreement.

Experts may be identified with the assistance of relevant intergovernmental organizations, and parties to the dispute have an opportunity to comment on or object to the appointment of experts. Experts are subject to the Rules of Conduct, including disclosure requirements.[56] The Appellate Body has emphasized the need for ensuring independence and impartiality of experts appointed by panels, noting that where there are justifiable doubts about an expert's independence and impartiality, a party's due process rights are not respected, and the panel may be held to have failed to make an objective assessment of facts as required under article 11 of the DSU.[57]

The panel (with the assistance of the Secretariat) submits questions to the experts, and the parties have an opportunity to comment on the questions submitted or to submit additional questions. The parties receive copies of the experts' reports and may submit written comments. A meeting between the panel and the experts together with the parties may also be held.[58]

Registry

All administrative services are provided to the panels by the WTO Secretariat.[59] **3.10**
Thus all written submissions to the panels are served through the Secretariat.[60]
In addition, the Secretariat provides panels with assistance on the legal, historical, and procedural aspects of each case. These services are normally provided by the Legal Affairs Division, but may also involve other specialized divisions. The

---

[54] See Marceau, *supra* note 9, at 38. Eg Panel Report, *European Communities—Measures Affecting the Approval and Marketing of Biotech Products*, WT/DS291/R, WT/DS292/R, WT/DS293/R, Add 1 to Add 9, and Corr 1, 21 November 2006, 2006:III DSR 847. The panel appointed six individual experts who submitted their reports on the subject under consideration, and their answers to the parties' comments. The appointment of the experts was based on a list of experts proposed by international organizations specializing in the field of agriculture and health after consultations with the parties.

[55] SPS Agreement, art 11(2).

[56] Rules of Conduct, r IV(1).

[57] Appellate Body Report, *United States—Continued Suspension of Obligations in the EC—Hormones Dispute*, WT/DS320/AB/R, 14 November, 2008, paras 415–484.

[58] See Palmeter and Mavroidis, *supra* note 9, at 121–123; see also, for example, the procedure on consultation of experts in *Biotech Products*, *supra* note 54, paras 7.20–7.30.

[59] DSU, art 27.

[60] Ibid, art 12(6). A similar rule applies in regard to submissions to the AB: AB Working Procedures, art 18.

Secretariat also caters for the logistical needs of the DSB and the Appellate Body. The Appellate Body is assisted by its own Secretariat, which provides administrative and legal support.

When involved in panel- or AB-related activities, staff of the WTO and AB Secretariats are subject to rules of conduct similar to those applicable to panel and AB members.[61]

Jurisdiction and access to the system

Jurisdiction of panels

3.11   *Ratione personae*   The compulsory jurisdiction of the WTO panel system encompasses all members of the WTO. Any state or separate custom territory possessing full autonomy in the conduct of its external commercial relations and over other matters covered by the WTO agreements can seek to join the WTO,[62] and will thereby subject itself to the compulsory jurisdiction of the dispute settlement system. Non-members (including non-member states, companies, and individuals) do not have a right to bring cases directly under the WTO dispute settlement system.

The AB has recognized that the DSU does not contain any explicit requirement that a member must have a 'legal interest' in order to request establishment of a panel, and did not accept that the need for such a legal interest was implied in the DSU.[63]

3.12   *Ratione materiae*   The subject-matter jurisdiction of the WTO dispute settlement mechanism includes all disputes between members arising under the 'covered agreements' listed in Appendix 1 to the DSU.[64]

Under the DSU, members affirm adherence to the principles of management of disputes applied under article XXII and article XXIII of GATT 1947.[65] Article XXIII of the GATT, or corresponding provisions of the other agreements, govern the substantive conditions for the initiation of dispute settlement

---

[61] Rules of Conduct, r IV(1).

[62] WTO Agreement, art XII.

[63] Appellate Body Report, *European Communities—Regime for the Importation, Sale and Distribution of Bananas*, WT/DS27/AB/R, 25 September 1997, 1997:II DSR 591, paras 132–38.

[64] DSU, Appendix 1. These are the WTO Agreement and the DSU itself, as well as multilateral agreements on trade in goods (including the GATT 1994) (Annex 1A to the WTO Agreement); the General Agreement on Trade in Services (Annex 1B); and the Agreement on Trade-Related Aspects of Intellectual Property Rights (Annex 1C). The covered agreements also include certain Plurilateral Trade Agreements (to which not all WTO members may be party), provided the parties to those agreements have adopted a decision setting out the terms of application of the DSU to the agreement in question, including any special or additional rules or procedures. See WTO, *A Handbook on the WTO Dispute Settlement System* (2004) at 10.

[65] DSU, art 3(1).

proceedings. A WTO member may present under article XXIII a claim, based on evidence that:

(1) a benefit accruing to it under a relevant agreement to which it is a party has been nullified or impaired;[66] or
(2) the attainment of the objective of that agreement is being impeded.

In either case, it must be demonstrated that the unwarranted result was caused by an act or omission on the part of the respondent member constituting one of the following:

(a) failure to meet obligations under the relevant agreement;
(b) application of a measure incompatible with the relevant agreement; or
(c) any other situation.

The jurisdiction of a panel is limited by its terms of reference, which define the claims at issue in the dispute.[67]

3.13 ***Ratione temporis*** The WTO dispute settlement mechanism only has jurisdiction over proceedings initiated at the DSB after the entry into force of the WTO Agreement (1 January 1995).[68]

Any party to a dispute may seek the establishment of a panel only after the expiration of a period of 60 days from the day it has submitted a request for consultations to the other party, if consultations fail to resolve the dispute.[69] However, the parties may agree to submit the request for a panel before the expiration of 60 days, or to extend that period in order to engage in good offices, conciliation, or mediation.[70] In urgent cases the establishment of a panel may be sought within 20 days.[71]

3.14 **Advisory jurisdiction** The panels only have contentious jurisdiction and cannot issue advisory opinions.

---

[66] DSU, art 3(3).

[67] DSU, art 7. See Appellate Body Report, *Brazil—Measures Affecting Desiccated Coconut*, WT/DS22/AB/R, 20 March 1997, 1997:I DSR 167 at 186, in which the AB also observed that the terms of reference fulfil an important due process objective, in that they give the parties and third parties sufficient information concerning the claims at issue on the dispute in order to allow them an opportunity to respond to the complainant's case; see also Appellate Body Report, *India—Patent Protection for Pharmaceutical and Agricultural Chemical Products*, WT/DS50/AB/R, 16 January 1998, 1998:I DSR 9, paras 92–93, in which the AB stated that '[t]he jurisdiction of the panel is established by that panel's terms of reference, which are governed by Article 7 of the DSU. A panel may consider only those claims that it has the authority to consider under its terms of reference. A panel cannot assume jurisdiction that it does not have...'

[68] DSU, art 3(11).

[69] Ibid, art 4(3). The parties must enter into consultations within 30 days; and consultations should be concluded within another 30 days: ibid, art 4(7).

[70] Ibid, art 5.

[71] Ibid, art 4(8). The parties must enter into consultations within ten days; and consultations should be concluded within 20 days.

Panels possess recommendatory powers: their reports are not binding until adopted by the DSB. However, as noted above, under the DSU the DSB must adopt panel reports (or Appellate Body reports, in the event of an appeal), unless it decides otherwise by consensus.[72] Such a reverse consensus will be difficult to achieve, since the agreement of both of the WTO members that are parties to the dispute in question will be needed.

It should be noted that only the WTO Ministerial Conference has the exclusive authority to render authoritative interpretations of the WTO Agreement and the multilateral trade agreements.[73]

Appellate jurisdiction

3.15 The Appellate Body may hear an appeal on points of law submitted by a party to panel proceedings. Third parties in panel proceedings, and other WTO members, may not institute appeals. However, members that were third parties in the relevant panel proceedings may participate in the appellate phase as third participants.[74]

The submission of any appeal must precede the decision of the DSB to adopt the report. Adoption of a panel report by the DSB must be effected within 60 days from the date of circulation of the panel report to the WTO members, but not before 20 days have passed.[75] If within that period no notice of appeal has been filed, the DSB will be expected to adopt the panel report.

The appeal must be limited to issues of law covered by the panel's report and legal interpretations developed by the panel.[76] Nonetheless, whether a panel has made an objective assessment of the facts before it, as required by article 11 of the DSU, is a legal question which falls within the scope of appellate review, if properly raised on appeal.[77] Nonetheless, the AB has acknowledged that in assessing the panel's appreciation of the evidence, it cannot base a finding of inconsistency under article 11 simply on the conclusion that it might have reached a different factual finding from the one reached by the panel. Rather, the AB will look to whether the panel has exceeded the bounds of its discretion, as the trier of facts, in its appreciation of the evidence. The AB has stated that it will not interfere lightly with the panel's exercise of its discretion.[78]

---

[72] Ibid, art 16(3), (4).

[73] WTO Agreement, art IX(2).

[74] DSU, art 17(4).

[75] Ibid, art 16(1), (4).

[76] Ibid, art 17(6).

[77] Appellate Body Report, *EC Measures Concerning Meat and Meat Products (Hormones)*, WT/DS26/AB/R, WT/DS48/AB/R, 13 February 1998, 1998:I DSR 135, at para 132.

[78] Appellate Body Report, *United States—Definitive Safeguard Measures on Imports of Wheat Gluten from the European Communities*, WT/DS166/AB/R, 19 January 2001, 2001:II DSR 717, at para 151.

The lack of remand authority in the appellate system has proved somewhat problematic.[79] Where a complainant claims violation of a number of provisions of WTO agreements, a panel, having found one violation, may, for reasons of judicial economy, decline to make findings in respect of the other claims. If the legal finding of the panel is reversed by the AB on appeal, however, the AB has no power to remand the case to the panel for consideration of the other claims. In such circumstances the AB has, in some cases, moved to 'complete the legal analysis' by examining the measure at issue in the light of other provisions, provided that there are sufficient factual findings in the panel report (or undisputed facts) to do so.[80]

Procedural Aspects

Languages

The official languages of the WTO are English, French, and Spanish. The parties may use any of the three languages in the proceedings.

3.16

Instituting proceedings

A request for panel establishment is to be presented before the DSB, after the expiration of 60 days from the date on which a request for consultations was presented to the other party to the dispute (20 days in urgent cases).[81] The request for establishment of a panel should contain the following information: whether consultations were held; the specific measure at issue; a brief summary of legal arguments necessary to present the problem clearly; and whether non-standard terms of reference are suggested and, if so, what terms are proposed.[82]

3.17

Unless it decides by consensus not to do so, the DSB must establish a panel at the latest at the DSB meeting following that at which the request for

---

[79] See V Hughes, 'The WTO Dispute Settlement System—from Initiating Proceedings to Ensuring Implementation: What Needs Improvement?' in *The WTO at Ten, supra* note 17, 193, at 223–227.

[80] See eg P van den Bossche, 'From Afterthought to Centrepiece: The WTO Appellate Body and its Rise to Prominence in the World Trading System' in *The WTO at Ten, supra* note 17, 289, at 317–319. The consistency of such an approach with the AB's mandate in art 17(6) of the DSU has been questioned. A number of proposals have been put forward in support of establishing a remand procedure. See eg P Sutherland (chairman) and others, 'The Future of the WTO: Assessing Institutional Challenges in the New Millennium', Report by the Consultative Body to the Director-General Supachai Panitchpakdi, December 2004, available at <http://www.wto.org/english/thewto_e/10anniv_e/future_wto_e.pdf>. See also J McCall Smith, 'WTO Dispute Settlement: The Politics of Procedure in Appellate Body Rulings' (2003) *World Trade Review* 21. On the limitation of appeals to issues of law, see T Voon and A Yanovich, 'The Facts Aside: The Limitation of WTO Appeals to Issues of Law' (2006) 40 *Journal of World Trade* 239.

[81] DSU, arts 4(7), (8), 5(4).

[82] Ibid, art 6.

establishment of the panel first appears as an item on the DSB agenda.[83] Upon the establishment of a panel, the DSB vests it with terms of reference.[84]

Panels operate in accordance with the Working Procedures in Appendix III to the DSU. In addition, a panel may establish additional working procedures to govern proceedings before it.[85]

Financial assistance

3.18 Parties to a dispute do not bear the costs of the panel or Appellate Body, which are met from the WTO budget,[86] but they must bear their own costs. In cases involving developing countries, the Secretariat will provide, upon request, technical and legal assistance to the developing country (or countries) party to the proceedings. Such assistance may include providing the services of a legal expert from the WTO technical cooperation services.[87] In addition, the Secretariat is obliged to conduct training seminars on the WTO dispute settlement system intended for experts from interested members.[88]

Provisional measures

3.19 The panel and AB do not have authority to issue provisional measures. However, when an urgent situation presents itself, the DSU provides for a shorter period of consultations (20 days instead of 60 days),[89] and for accelerated procedures.[90] The panel is instructed in urgent cases, including cases pertaining to perishable goods, to aim to complete its work within three months from the date of its constitution (instead of the six months allowed in normal cases).[91]

Preliminary proceedings/objections

3.20 The DSU does not expressly provide for a separate procedural stage for the raising of preliminary objections. However, in practice, preliminary objections are raised (for example, as to adequacy of consultations, inadequate specificity of the

---

[83] Ibid, art 6(1).

[84] Ibid, art 7.

[85] Working Procedures, r 11.

[86] DSU, arts 8(11), 17(8).

[87] Ibid, art 27(2). In addition to this possibility, in 2001 an Advisory Centre on WTO Law was established in Geneva. It should be noted that this Advisory Centre is independent of the WTO. It provides, *inter alia*, advice and assistance to developing country members of the WTO in respect of dispute settlement proceedings in accordance with the provisions of the Agreement establishing the Centre. The website of the Centre indicates that since 2001, the Centre had provided assistance directly in 28 cases, and in four cases had provided assistance through the hiring of external counsel, <http://www.acwl.ch/e/dispute/wto_e.aspx>, 31 July 2009.

[88] DSU, art 27(3).

[89] Ibid, art 4(8).

[90] Ibid, art 4(9).

[91] Ibid, art 12(8).

request for establishment of a panel, or lack of legal standing) at the beginning of the proceedings, and the panel generally decides them in its final report.[92]

The only preliminary procedure explicitly provided in the relevant WTO dispute settlement instruments is the disqualification procedure described in the Rules of Conduct. According to those Rules, information concerning a member of the panel, AB, or the Secretariat, or an expert providing information to a dispute settlement body, must be presented in confidentiality, at the earliest possible time, before the relevant body (the Chair of the DSB, Director-General of the WTO, or the AB).[93] The procedure for dealing with the allegations must be concluded within 15 working days from the date on which the said information was received.[94]

Written pleadings

Written submissions to the panel are presented in accordance with the time- **3.21** table set by the panel. As a general rule, panel proceedings should not exceed six months from the date that the composition and terms of reference of the panel have been agreed to the issuance of its report. In cases of urgency, the panel should aim to issue its report within three months. Where the panel considers that it cannot meet these time frames, it must inform the DSB in writing of the reasons for the delay and the estimated period within which it will issue its report. In no case should the panel proceedings exceed nine months.[95]

The proposed timetable for panel proceedings set out in the Working Procedures (Appendix 3 to the DSU) indicate much tighter time limits than those applicable in most other international courts and tribunals. The complaining party is expected to deposit its submission within three to six weeks after the establishment of the panel, and the respondent then has two to three weeks in which to submit its response. While, in principle, the complaining party files its submission first, the panel *may* decide, after consulting with the parties, that the initial submissions of both parties will be made simultaneously.[96] The initial submissions should include a presentation of the facts of the case and the elaboration of the relevant legal arguments.[97]

The first substantive meeting of the panel with the parties is normally held one to two weeks after the receipt of the respondent's submission. Thereafter, the parties should submit written rebuttals, within two to three weeks.[98] One

---

[92] See, for example, *Bananas, supra* note 63, at 3–15.
[93] Rules of Conduct, r VIII(1).
[94] Ibid, r VIII(4).
[95] DSU, art 20. However, it is not uncommon for panel proceedings to exceed this time frame in practice.
[96] Ibid, art 12(8)–(9).
[97] Ibid, Appendix 3, r 4.
[98] DSU, art 12(6); Panel Working Procedures, r 12(b).

to two weeks later, a second substantive panel meeting is held.[99] This meeting may result in a third written submission. In effect, the main written phase of the proceedings is generally to be completed within 14 weeks. The panel may also request the parties, at any time, to submit explanations in writing to specific questions.[100]

Each written document submitted by one of the parties to the panel shall also be made available to the other party (or parties) to the dispute. In cases involving developing country members, the panel is to ensure that the member has sufficient time to prepare its arguments, subject to the rule that proceedings are expected to be completed within a maximum period of nine months.[101]

It should be noted that, in addition to the Working Procedures in Appendix 3 of the DSU, a panel may establish additional working proceedings for specific proceedings.[102]

Oral arguments

3.22 The complaining member is invited to present its case orally at the first substantive meeting of the panel (usually within one to two weeks from the receipt of the response of the respondent), and the respondent will be invited at the same session to present its views.[103] At the next meeting (usually within one to two weeks from the receipt of rebuttals) the responding party shall first make an oral rebuttal, and the complaining party shall take the floor immediately thereafter.[104] The panel may address questions to the parties for oral explanation during any meeting. Panel questions are also often submitted in writing after or during the hearing, and parties given a short period of time in which to respond.[105]

Written transcripts of all oral arguments must be made available to the panel and the other party (or parties).

The conduct of WTO dispute settlement proceedings is confidential,[106] and the issue of increasing transparency of the proceedings has been a controversial one in discussions on the DSU review. In 2005, the panels examining complaints by the European Communities against the continued suspension of concessions by Canada and United States in the *Hormones* dispute ruled, at the common request of the parties to the disputes, that the panel proceedings would be open

---

[99] In certain cases, if new evidence is submitted at the second meeting, there may be third written submissions. Palmeter and Mavroidis, *supra* note 9, at 161.
[100] Panel Working Procedures, r 8.
[101] DSU, art 12(10).
[102] Panel Working Procedures, r 11.
[103] Ibid, r 5.
[104] Ibid, r 7.
[105] Ibid, r 8.
[106] DSU, arts 4(6), 14, 17(10).

to public observation by way of closed-circuit television broadcast.[107] In 2008, in appellate proceedings in the same dispute, the Appellate Body made a similar ruling for the first time, after requests from the parties.[108]

Third party intervention

Any member having a substantial interest in a case pending before the panel has **3.23** the right to join the proceedings as a third party, after serving a notification to that effect to the DSB.[109] The panel shall invite third parties to attend a special meeting (or meetings) dedicated to the presentation of third parties' views.[110] In addition, third parties may make written submissions to the panel (which are to be circulated among the parties to the dispute) and are entitled to receive a copy of the first submissions of the original parties to the case. In some proceedings, panels have granted enhanced rights to third parties.[111]

It should be noted that a WTO member who meets the required jurisdictional conditions may select to initiate separate proceedings pertaining to the

---

[107] WT/DS320/8, WT/DS321/8, *United States—Continued Suspension of Concessions in the EC-Hormones Dispute* and *Canada—Continued Suspension of Concessions in the EC-Hormones Dispute*, Communication from the Chairman of the Panels, 2 August 2005.

[108] Appellate Body, Procedural Ruling concerning the opening of the oral hearing to public observation in *US—Continued Suspension* and *Canada-Continued Suspension*, 10 July 2008. Appellate Body, *Annual Report for 2008*, February 2009, available at <http://www.wto.org/english/res_e/booksp_e/ab_annual_report08_e.pdf>. Certain third participants in the appeal objected to the opening of the oral hearing, invoking art 17(10) of the DSU to the effect that, 'The proceedings of the Appellate Body shall be confidential.' The Appellate Body reasoned, *inter alia*, that the conduct and organization of oral hearings falls within its authority pursuant to rule 27 of the Working Procedures for Appellate Review; it noted that the DSU did not specifically provide for an oral hearing at the appellate stage, such hearings having been instituted by the AB when it drew up its Working Procedures. The Appellate Body has subsequently allowed observation by the public of oral hearings in certain appellate proceedings in 2008 and 2009: for example, *EC—Bananas III (Article 21.5—Ecuador II)* and *EC—Bananas III (Article 21.5-US)*, Appellate Body Reports, *European Communities—Regime for the Importation, Sale and Distribution of Bananas—Second Recourse to Article 21.5 of the DSU by Ecuador*, WT/DS27/AB/RW2/ECU, 11 December 2008, and Corr 1 / *European Communities—Regime for the Importation, Sale and Distribution of Bananas—Recourse to Article 21.5 of the DSU by the United States*, WT/DS27/AB/RW/USA and Corr 1, 22 December 2008; Appellate Body Report, *US—Continued Existence and Application of Zeroing Methodology*, WT/DS350/AB/R, 11 February 2009; Appellate Body Report, *US—Laws, Regulations and Methodology for Calculating Dumping Margins ('Zeroing')—Recourse to Article 21.5 of the DSU by the European Communities*, WT/DS294/AB/RW, 11 June 2009, and Appellate Body Report, *US—Measures relating to Zeroing and Sunset Reviews—Recourse to Article 21.5 of the DSU by Japan*, WT/DS322/AB/RW, 18 August 2009.

[109] DSU, art 10(2).

[110] Panel Working Procedures, r 6.

[111] The Appellate Body has observed that '[a] panel's decision whether to grant "enhanced" participatory rights to third parties is thus a matter which falls within the discretionary authority of that panel. Such discretionary authority is, of course, not unlimited and is circumscribed, for example, by the requirements of due process'. Appellate Body Report, *United States— Anti-Dumping Act of 1916*, WT/DS136/AB/R, WT/DS162/AB/R, 26 September 2000, 2000: X DSR 4793, at para 150.

same matter that is the subject of an existing complaint by another member.[112] As noted previously, the DSB will refer this new case, if possible, to the original panel. In this event, the proceedings will be conducted so as to guarantee to the greatest extent possible that the rights that the parties would have had if separate proceedings had taken place would not be impaired. If one of the parties in the consolidated proceedings so requests, the panel shall issue separate reports.[113]

Third party participation is now extremely common in WTO proceedings. Some concerns have been raised by the fact that only members who participate in a dispute at the panel stage as third parties may participate in appellate proceedings.

Amicus curiae

3.24 There is no explicit provision in the DSU or other instruments governing the dispute settlement procedure as to the admissibility of *amicus curiae* submissions in panel or appellate proceedings. However, this is an issue which has emerged as a significant concern in practice.

In the *US-Shrimp* case, in 1998, the Appellate Body ruled that panels have the authority to accept and consider *amicus* briefs under articles 12 and 13 of the DSU.[114] In *US-Lead and Bismuth II*, the Appellate Body ruled that it has the authority to accept and consider *amicus* briefs, relying upon article 17(9) DSU.[115] In 2000, in *EC-Asbestos*, an Appellate Body division adopted an additional procedure pursuant to Rule 16 (1) Working Procedures for Appellate Review, for the purposes of *EC-Asbestos* only, regarding the procedure for requests to file *amicus* submissions.[116] While numerous applications were filed under the Additional Procedure, all were denied. Moreover, the adoption of the Additional Procedure provoked significant disquiet among numerous WTO members.

In *EC-Sardines* the Appellate Body accepted an *amicus* brief from a WTO member, Morocco, yet noted that it was not required to accept and consider

---

[112] DSU, art 10(4).

[113] Ibid, art 9.

[114] The Appellate Body stated that '[t]he thrust of Articles 12 and 13, taken together, is that the DSU accords to a panel established by the [Dispute Settlement Body], and engaged in a dispute settlement proceeding, ample and extensive authority to undertake and to control the process by which it informs itself both of the relevant facts of the dispute and of the legal norms and principles applicable to such facts'. Appellate Body Report, *United States—Import Prohibition of Certain Shrimp and Shrimp Products*, WT/DS58/AB/R, 6 November 1998, 1998:VII DSR 2755, at para 106.

[115] Appellate Body Report, *United States—Imposition of Countervailing Duties on Certain Hot-Rolled Lead and Bismuth Carbon Steel Products Originating in the United Kingdom*, WT/DS138/AB/R, 7 June 2000, 2000:V DSR 2595, at paras 36–42.

[116] Communication from the Appellate Body, *European Communities—Measures Affecting Asbestos and Asbestos-Containing Products*, WT/DS135/9, 8 November 2000.

briefs filed by members, rather that 'acceptance of any amicus curiae brief is a matter of discretion' which must be exercised on a case-by-case basis.[117]

It is not clear to what extent panels or the Appellate Body have made use of information or arguments contained in *amicus* briefs. The receipt of such briefs has frequently been noted in panel or Appellate Body reports, but no specific reference has been made to them thereafter.

Some WTO members have argued that the acceptance of *amicus curiae* briefs in dispute settlement proceedings impacts upon the rights of members. Significant objections have also been raised in the WTO regarding the additional burden upon parties that might be imposed by *amicus* briefs, as well as concerns about confidentiality of proceedings. Developing countries have raised particular concerns regarding the equal treatment of parties to dispute settlement proceedings, especially if faced with large numbers of *amicus* submissions. Debates about *amicus* participation have also been closely linked to wider debates regarding transparency in the WTO. A number of proposals were made in the course of the DSU's review to formalize the rules as regards the submission of *amicus* briefs in WTO proceedings.

Representation of the parties

The DSU does not explicitly address the issue of representation of the parties **3.25** before WTO panels and the Appellate Body.

In an early case, an objection was raised as to the presence of private counsel in panel proceedings. This issue was subsequently raised before the Appellate Body in the same case. The AB noted that it found

> nothing in the Marrakesh Agreement establishing the WTO ... the DSU or the Working Procedures, nor in customary international law or the prevailing practice of international tribunals, which prevents a WTO Member from determining the composition of its delegation in Appellate Body proceedings.[118]

The AB ruled that it is for a WTO member to decide who should represent it as members of its delegation in an oral hearing of the Appellate Body. It is now common for private counsel to represent parties in panel and Appellate Body proceedings.[119]

---

[117] Appellate Body Report, *European Communities—Trade Description of Sardines*, WT/DS231/AB/R, 23 October 2002, 2002:VIII DSR 3359, at para 167.

[118] *Bananas, supra* note 63, at paras 11 and 12.

[119] Marceau, *supra* note 9, at 42. Marceau notes that the Appellate Body's ruling on this issue in *EC-Bananas* was extended to panel proceedings in Panel Report, *Indonesia—Certain Measures affecting the Automobile Industry*, WT/DS54/R, WT/DS55/R, WT/DS59/R, WT/DS64/R and Corr 1–4, 23 July 1998, 1998:VI, DSR 2201, at para 14.1.

Decision

3.26 Before a panel report is issued, the parties receive the descriptive sections of the report for written comments (generally two to four weeks after the rebuttal session).[120] The parties are normally expected to submit their comments on this part within two weeks.[121]

In addition, the panel circulates between the parties an interim report before the conclusion of the final version. The interim report is generally issued within two to four weeks after the receipt of the parties' comments on the descriptive part of the report. Each party may submit (generally within a week from the date of receipt of the interim report) a written request for the panel to review precise aspects of the interim report and may also request a special review meeting for presentation of oral arguments.[122] The final report shall include a discussion of the arguments made at the interim review stage.[123] The interim review stage is confidential, and at least one panel has expressed disquiet when findings and conclusions from the interim report were made public.[124]

The final decision of the panel is in the form of a report comprising a descriptive part, including the facts of the case and a rather detailed account of the arguments of the parties, and the panel's finding and conclusions. Where a panel concludes that a measure taken by a member is inconsistent with a covered agreement, it shall recommend that the member concerned bring the measure into conformity with that agreement.[125] However, it is left to the member concerned to determine how to rectify the situation within a reasonable period of time.[126]

The report is to be adopted by the DSB within 20–60 days from the date it was circulated to the members of the WTO,[127] unless the DSB decides by way of consensus not to adopt the report or if an appeal is lodged to the Appellate Body.

Upon its adoption the report becomes binding on the parties. The parties are expected to comply promptly with the recommendations of the panel, and the DSB supervises the implementation of the recommendations.

---

[120] DSU, art 15(1); Panel Working Procedures, r 12(e).
[121] Panel Working Procedures, r 12(f).
[122] DSU, art 15(2).
[123] Ibid, art 15(3).
[124] *Biotech Products, supra* note 54, at paras 6.183–6.196.
[125] DSU, art 19(1).
[126] Marceau notes that the panel or AB may 'suggest' ways in which members might implement the recommendations, 'but these are just suggested ways in which a member could decide to implement'. Marceau, *supra* note 9, at 43.
[127] DSU, art 16(1), (4).

Appeals

As noted previously, appeals against legal conclusions of panel reports may be **3.27** lodged with the AB by any of the parties to the dispute (not including third parties).[128] There is no provision barring the prevailing party from appealing a panel report if it objects to certain aspects thereof.

Notice of appeal is to be submitted to the Secretariat and the appeal notified in writing to the DSB.[129] The Notice of Appeal must include the following information: the title of panel report under appeal; the name of appealing party; necessary details for future service of documents; and a brief statement of the nature of the appeal.[130] The latter should include identification of the alleged errors in law and legal interpretations in the panel report; a list of the legal provisions of the covered agreements that the panel is alleged to have erred in interpreting or applying; and an indicative list of the paragraphs of the panel report containing the alleged errors.[131]

Within 12 days of the Notice of Appeal, a party to the dispute other than the original appellant may join in the appeal, or appeal on the basis of other alleged errors in issues of law in the panel report and the panel's legal interpretations. Any such party must file a Notice of Other Appeal with the Secretariat and notify the DSB.[132]

The complete submission of the appellant is to be presented to the AB within seven days after the filing of the Notice of Appeal. The full submission should include the precise statement of grounds of appeal, the legal basis of arguments, and a description of the decision or ruling sought.[133] Other appellants' submissions are due within 15 days after the date of filing of the Notice of Appeal.[134] Any party to the dispute that wishes to respond may file a submission (to be lodged within 25 days after the filing of the Notice of Appeal). The responding submission should include a statement of the grounds for opposing the appeal (pertaining to each ground of the appeal and each allegation of legal error), the legal basis for arguments, and a description of the decision or ruling sought.[135]

---

[128] Ibid, art 17(4), (6).

[129] AB Working Procedures, r 20; DSU, art 16(4).

[130] DSU, r 20(2).

[131] The required content of the Notice of Appeal was revised in amendments to the Working Procedures for Appellate Review introduced with effect from 1 January 2005. The Appellate Body had sought to clarify the contents of the Notice of Appeal so that they provided adequate notice to an appellee of the nature of the appeal and allegations of error, so as to enable an appellee to exercise fully its rights of defence. The amended Working Procedures also make provision for the amendment of Notices of Appeal (r 23 *bis*). *Proposed Amendments to the Working Procedures for Appellate Review, Communication from the Appellate Body*, WT/AB/WP/W/8, 8 April 2004.

[132] AB Working Procedures, r 23 sets out the required content of the Notice of Other Appeal.

[133] Ibid, r 21.

[134] Ibid, r 23.

[135] Ibid, r 22.

Oral hearings will be conducted, as a rule, between 35 and 45 days after the filing of the notice of appeal.[136] As is the case for panels, the AB may request the parties at any time to submit answers to questions.[137]

As a general rule, the AB is expected to issue its report within 60 days from the date of notification of the appeal, and in any case not later than 90 days from that date.[138] There is no interim review stage for AB reports. AB reports (and the panel reports as adopted, modified, or reversed) are to be adopted by the DSB within 30 days from their circulation to the parties, unless the DSB decides by way of consensus not to adopt the report.

Costs

3.28 The costs of the WTO dispute settlement system are borne by the WTO. However, parties to a case must meet their own expenses.

Implementation of decision, recognition, and enforcement

3.29 The member concerned must inform the DSB within 30 days from the date of adoption of the report on its intentions as to implementation of the recommendations and rulings of the DSB. Where it is impracticable to comply immediately with DSB recommendations and rulings, members are afforded a reasonable period of time within which to comply. The DSU provides for an arbitration procedure[139] to determine what constitutes a reasonable period for this purpose, in the event that there is disagreement.[140] The arbitrator shall give his award within 90 days of the adoption of the report by the DSB.

In addition, where there is a disagreement over the existence or consistency with covered agreements of measures taken to comply with DSB recommendations and rulings, that dispute may be referred to the dispute settlement procedure under article 21.5 of the DSU, by way of resort to the original panel if possible. Panel reports on such disputes may also be subject to appeal. Issues relating to implementation may also be raised at meetings of the DSB.[141]

Where recommendations or rulings of the DSB are not implemented within a reasonable period of time, the DSU provides for a procedure for agreeing upon

---

[136] Ibid, r 27.

[137] Ibid, r 28(1).

[138] DSU, art 17(5).

[139] If the parties do not agree on an arbitrator within ten days after referring the matter to arbitration, the Director-General appoints the arbitrator, having consulted with the parties. DSU, art 21(3)(c), note 12. The arbitrator for this purpose may be an individual or a group. Single arbitrators have tended to be used, and members of the Appellate Body have served as arbitrators in this context.

[140] Ibid, art 21(3).

[141] Ibid, art 21(6).

satisfactory compensation or, as a 'last resort',[142] for authorization by the DSB of the temporary suspension of concessions or other obligations.[143] Where the member concerned disputes the appropriate level of suspension of concessions, the dispute may be referred to arbitration under article 22.6 of the DSU. Such arbitration is conducted by the original panel, if available, or by an arbitrator appointed by the Director-General. It is to be completed within 60 days after the date of the expiry of the reasonable period of time for compliance. The arbitrator's decision is to be accepted as final by the parties.[144] Once informed of the arbitrator's decision the DSB shall, upon request, grant authorization to suspend concessions or other obligations, where that request is consistent with the arbitrator's decision. Such a decision of the DSB is adopted by reverse consensus.

The range of procedures available in respect of implementation of recommendations and rulings of the DSB has given rise to certain problems of sequencing of proceedings in practice. Some of the more complex and intractable disputes that have been dealt with by the dispute settlement system have given rise to a series of panel, appellate, and arbitral proceedings under the DSU.

There is no provision in any of the WTO instruments as to the enforcement of panel or AB reports in municipal courts.

Evaluation

It is generally recognized that the dispute settlement system has been one of the key successes of the WTO. Although some concerns have been expressed about the possible disadvantages faced by developing country members participating in dispute settlement proceedings, the system has been invoked by both developed and developing country members of the WTO. While a number of cases have exceeded the strict time frames envisaged in the DSU, and others have given rise to a complex sequence of supplementary implementation-related proceedings under articles 21 and 22 of the DSU, on the whole disputes have been dealt with expeditiously. The institution of the reverse consensus procedure for the adoption of panel and Appellate Body reports has been a significant factor in developing the effectiveness and authoritativeness of the system. The Appellate Body has

---

[142] Ibid, art 3(7).

[143] Ibid, art 22. Art 22(3) sets out the principles and procedures to be applied by the complaining party in considering what concessions and obligations to suspend. The general principle is that the complaining party should first seek to suspend concessions or other obligations in the same sector(s) as that in which the panel or AB has found a violation or other nullification or impairment. If that party considers that it is not practicable or effective to suspend concessions in the same sector(s), it may seek to suspend concessions in other sectors under the same agreement, or under another covered agreement. If the party seeks to suspend concessions in another sector or under another covered agreement, it must state the reasons therefore in its request to the DSB.

[144] DSU, art 22(7).

played an important role in developing aspects of the dispute settlement system and in fostering coherent interpretation of the covered agreements.

As to the effectiveness of the dispute settlement procedures in securing compliance with WTO obligations, Wilson has noted that overall the compliance record has been 'quite positive' and that this positive record is reflected and confirmed by the low number of cases in which members have sought and received authorization to impose retaliatory measures.[145] Hughes has observed that the compliance record is 'extremely high' while there have been 'a few famous cases of very slow compliance or non-compliance'.[146]

A number of proposals have been made by members to improve the operation of the dispute settlement system in the context of the review of the DSU. These include, for example: a proposal that a standing panel body be established from which all panels would be composed;[147] the introduction of a remand power for the Appellate Body; and the introduction of formal rules to govern the admissibility of *amicus curiae* submissions. As yet no conclusions have been agreed on such proposals.

The issue of transparency of, and access to, the dispute settlement proceedings, particularly in cases involving issues of public interest, such as environmental, food safety, or health-related measures, has been one of the major bones of contention among WTO members, in very broad terms splitting developed and developing country members. Many developing country members have expressed concern that moves towards greater scope for participation for non-members might in some way add to the burden of WTO members in pursuing or defending cases, and might alter the balance of rights and obligations of the WTO members. The opening up of certain proceedings to public observation at the request of parties to the dispute, as occurred in the Appellate Body for the first time in 2008, is just a small step towards the levels of transparency that have come to be accepted in most other international courts and tribunals. Concerns around appropriate levels of transparency of and participation in the dispute settlement system relate more broadly to substantive concerns about the extent to which panels and the Appellate Body take into account in appropriate manner other relevant rules and principles of international law in deciding trade disputes.[148]

---

[145] B Wilson, 'Compliance by WTO Members with Adverse Dispute Settlement Rulings: The Record to Date' (2007) 10 *Journal of International Economic Law* 397 at 397–398. The review in the article examines the period from 1 January 1995 to 1 March 2007.

[146] V Hughes, 'The WTO Dispute Settlement System: From Initiating Proceedings to Ensuring Implementation. What Needs Improvement?' in *The WTO at Ten, supra* note 17, 193, at 229.

[147] For a discussion of this proposal, see eg (2003) 6 *Journal of International Economic Law* at 175–236.

[148] See eg J Pauwelyn, *Conflict of Norms in Public International Law: How WTO Law Relates to Other Rules of International Law* (2003); G Marceau, 'Conflicts of Norms and Conflicts of Jurisdiction: The Relationship between the WTO and MEAs and Other Treaties' (2001) 35 *Journal of World Trade* 1081.

REFERENCE

SOURCES OF PREVIOUS CASE LAW, INCLUDING CASE REPORTS

WTO *Dispute Settlement Reports* (WTO/Cambridge University Press, 1996–).

WTO Secretariat, *WTO Analytical Index: Guide to WTO Law and Practice* (2 vols) (2nd edn, WTO/Cambridge University Press, 2007).

WTO Secretariat, *WTO Dispute Settlement: One-Page Case Summaries (1995–2008).*

WTO Appellate Body Secretariat, *WTO Appellate Body Repertory of Reports and Awards 1995–2005* (Cambridge University Press, 2006). This publication is also available on-line on the WTO website.

Panel, Appellate Body, and arbitration reports are available on the WTO website.

SELECT BIBLIOGRAPHY

F Weiss, *Improving WTO Dispute Settlement Procedures: Issues and Lessons from the Practice of Other International Courts and Tribunals* (3rd edn, 2009).

M Matsushita, T Schoenbaum, and P C Mavroidis, *The World Trade Organization: Law, Practice and Policy* (2nd edn, 2006).

G Sacerdoti, A Yanovich, and J Bohanes (eds), *The WTO at Ten: The Contribution of the Dispute Settlement System* (2006).

Y Guohua, B Mercurio, and L Yongjie, *WTO Dispute Settlement Understanding: A Detailed Interpretation* (2005).

R Yerxa and B Wilson (eds), *Key Issues in WTO Dispute Settlement: The First Ten Years* (2005).

F Ortino and E-U Petersmann, *WTO Dispute Settlement System 1995–2003* (2004).

D Palmeter and P C Mavroidis, *Dispute Settlement in the World Trade Organization: Practice and Procedure* (2nd edn, 2004).

WTO Secretariat, Legal Affairs Division and the Appellate Body, *A Handbook on the WTO Dispute Settlement* (2004).

J Waincymer, *WTO Litigation: Procedural Aspects of Formal Dispute Settlement* (2002).

E-U Petersmann, *The GATT/WTO Dispute Settlement System: International Law, Organisations and Dispute Settlement* (1997).

Numerous journals publish articles addressing aspects of the WTO dispute settlement. A list of the principal journals can be found at <http://www.worldtradelaw.net/journals.htm>. The <http://www.worldtradelaw.net> website also contains summaries and analyses of WTO panel and AB reports and WTO arbitrations, as well as statistical data on the operation of the WTO dispute settlement system.

ANNEX

List of members of the WTO

(as at 31 July 2009)

Albania, Angola, Antigua and Barbuda, Argentina, Armenia, Australia, Austria, Bahrain, Bangladesh, Barbados, Belgium, Belize, Benin, Bolivia, Botswana, Brazil, Brunei Darussalam, Bulgaria, Burkina Faso, Burundi, Cambodia, Cameroon, Canada, Cape Verde, Central African Republic, Chad, Chile, China, Colombia, Congo, Costa Rica, Côte d'Ivoire, Croatia, Cuba, Cyprus, Czech Republic, Democratic Republic of the Congo, Denmark, Djibouti, Dominica, Dominican Republic, Ecuador, Egypt, El Salvador, Estonia, European Communities, Fiji, Finland, France, Former Yugoslav Republic of Macedonia, Gabon, Gambia, Georgia, Germany, Ghana, Greece, Grenada, Guatemala, Guinea, Guinea Bissau, Guyana, Haiti, Honduras, Hong Kong (China), Hungary, Iceland, India, Indonesia, Ireland, Israel, Italy, Jamaica, Japan, Jordan, Kenya, Korea, Kuwait, Kyrgyz Republic, Latvia, Lesotho, Liechtenstein, Lithuania, Luxembourg, Macau, Madagascar, Malawi, Malaysia, Maldives, Mali, Malta, Mauritania, Mauritius, Mexico, Moldova, Mongolia, Morocco, Mozambique, Myanmar, Namibia, Nepal, Netherlands (and the Netherlands Antilles), New Zealand, Nicaragua, Niger, Nigeria, Norway, Oman, Pakistan, Panama, Papua New Guinea, Paraguay, Peru, Philippines, Poland, Portugal, Qatar, Romania, Rwanda, Saint Kitts and Nevis, Saint Lucia, Saint Vincent and the Grenadines, Saudi Arabia, Senegal, Sierra Leone, Singapore, Slovak Republic, Slovenia, Solomon Islands, South Africa, Spain, Sri Lanka, Suriname, Swaziland, Sweden, Switzerland, Chinese Taipei, Tanzania, Thailand, Togo, Tonga, Trinidad and Tobago, Tunisia, Turkey, Uganda, Ukraine, United Arab Emirates, United Kingdom, United States, Uruguay, Venezuela, Vietnam, Zambia, Zimbabwe.

PART II

ARBITRATION INSTITUTIONS

Introduction

This Part surveys two specific institutions, established by intergovernmental agreements, which serve to administer international arbitral proceedings.

The Permanent Court of Arbitration was the first global institution for adjudication of international disputes. It was established by the 1899 Convention for the Pacific Settlement of International Disputes, subsequently revised by the 1907 Hague Convention of the same title. While the PCA was fairly widely used in the early years of its existence, it fell into disuse after the 1930s. However, since the 1990s, the PCA has been revitalized. In particular, the PCA has significantly developed its role as an institution for the support of arbitral proceedings, providing registry support and hosting oral proceedings. While there has remained relatively little use thus far of the arbitral procedures under the Hague Conventions and the PCA's own sets of Optional Rules for arbitration, the PCA had been heavily involved in the growing number of investor-state arbitrations, as well as in supporting the early arbitrations conducted pursuant to Annex VII of the UN Convention on the Law of the Sea. The PCA has also provided institutional and administrative support for a number of ad hoc arbitration proceedings, involving inter-state and other disputes.

The second institution considered is the International Centre for Settlement of Investment Disputes, established under the 1965 Convention on the Settlement of Investment Disputes between States and Nationals of Other States. ICSID provides an institutional framework for the establishment and operation of arbitral tribunals to decide disputes between host states and foreign investors arising out of an investment. It also provides a system for the recognition and enforcement of its arbitral awards—under the Convention, all contracting states, whether or not parties to the dispute, are required to recognize an award rendered pursuant to the Convention as binding and to enforce the pecuniary obligations imposed thereby, as if it were the final judgment of a court in that state.

ICSID too has seen a huge upsurge in activity since the first edition of this Manual was published in 1999. In large part, this has been caused by an increase in arbitration pursuant to bilateral investment treaties, as well as regional and sectoral investment rules incorporating provisions for recourse to arbitration. By the end of September 2009, 177 cases had been completed, including a large number of agreed settlements, six conciliation cases, and 19 Additional Facility arbitrations. A further 121 cases were pending, including seven Additional Facility proceedings. The annulment process, under article 52 of the ICSID Convention, had been invoked in relation to 37 arbitral awards, with proceedings pending in 17 cases. Many of the recently completed and ongoing proceedings have arisen out of the financial crisis in Argentina. The growth in ICSID's work has produced challenges for the system—in terms of both case management and coherence. The growing recourse to annulment proceedings has led to debates about the proper scope of post-award review in ICSID. In addition, the apparently expanding scope of investment arbitration has given rise to disquiet among some states parties to the 1965 Convention and in the last two years two parties, Bolivia and Ecuador, have denounced the Convention.

4

THE PERMANENT COURT
OF ARBITRATION

Introduction

Name and seat of the body

The Permanent Court of Arbitration (PCA) is located in the Peace Palace, The **4.1**
Hague, The Netherlands. The contact details of the International Bureau of the
PCA are as follows:

Permanent Court of Arbitration
Peace Palace
Carnegieplein 2
2517 KJ The Hague
The Netherlands
Tel: 31 70 302 4165
Fax: 31 70 302 4167
Email: bureau@pca-cpa.org
Website: <http://www.pca-cpa.org>

Although the headquarters of the PCA are located in The Hague, arbitrations
held under its auspices may take place in any other location agreed upon by
the parties. The PCA has, in recent years, concluded host country agreements
with a number of states to establish a legal framework under which future

PCA-administered proceedings can be conducted in the territory of the state concerned on an ad hoc basis.[1]

General description

4.2 The PCA, the first global institution for adjudication of international disputes, was established by the 1899 Hague Conference which adopted the Convention for the Pacific Settlement of International Disputes, subsequently revised by the 1907 Hague Convention of the same title.[2] By July 2009, 109 states had ratified one or both of the Hague Conventions.[3]

Chapter II of Part IV of the 1899 Convention established the PCA as an optional mechanism for peaceful settlement of disputes. Thus, while under no direct obligation to do so, any two states could agree to refer any dispute between them to the PCA for arbitration.

It is commonly noted that the Permanent Court of Arbitration is neither a court nor permanent. Rather, the PCA comprises a permanent secretariat (known as the International Bureau) which maintains a roster of potential arbitrators, named in advance by the states parties to the Hague Conventions. When a dispute is referred to arbitration under the auspices of the PCA, the parties to the dispute, with the assistance of the PCA International Bureau, establish an ad hoc arbitral tribunal—drawn from the PCA list of arbitrators or from persons outside this list. Thus the PCA does not itself issue awards, but awards and decisions are rendered by arbitral tribunals and other bodies established under the auspices of the PCA.[4]

The 1899 and 1907 Hague Conventions set out basic rules for the conduct of PCA arbitrations. From 1992 onwards, the PCA developed a series of sets of Optional Rules to govern various types of arbitration that might be submitted to it.[5] The Optional Rules reflect a range of disputes that might now come before PCA arbitral tribunals, notwithstanding the institution

---

[1] By July 2009, host country agreements were in place with Argentina, Costa Rica, India, Lebanon, Mauritius, Singapore, and South Africa, see <http://www.pca-cpa.org>. In May 2008, the PCA administered arbitral proceedings in Costa Rica under a host country agreement, PCA, *108th Annual Report—2008*, para 9. Hearings in PCA-administered cases have taken place all over the world, including in New York, Washington, DC, Toronto, Kuala Lumpur, Mumbai, Dar Es Salaam, Geneva, London, and Zagreb.

[2] Convention for the Pacific Settlement of International Disputes, 29 July 1899, ('1899 Hague Convention'); Convention for the Pacific Settlement of International Disputes, 18 October 1907 ('1907 Hague Convention').

[3] A list of states parties to the 1899/1907 Conventions is contained in the Annex to this Chapter.

[4] See Permanent Court of Arbitration, Press Release, *Abyei Arbitration: Final Award Rendered*, 22 July 2009, available at <http://www.pca-cpa.org>.

[5] The PCA Administrative Council adopted the first 'Rules of Arbitration and Conciliation for Settlement of International Disputes between Two Parties of Which Only One is a State' in 1962. These are superseded by the Optional Rules for this form of arbitration adopted in 1993.

was originally established with a view to the settlement of inter-state disputes. They are:

- Optional Rules for Arbitrating Disputes between Two States (1992) ('Inter-State Rules');
- Optional Rules for Arbitrating Disputes between Two Parties of which only One is a State (1993) ('State Non-State Rules');
- Optional Rules for Arbitration involving International Organizations and States (1996) (encompassing, *inter alia*, arbitration between two international organizations) ('IGO/State Rules');
- Optional Rules for Arbitration between International Organizations and Private Parties (1996) ('IGO/Private Parties Rules');
- Optional Rules for Arbitration of Disputes Relating to Natural Resources and/or the Environment (2001) ('Natural Resources Rules').

The Optional Rules are based on the UNCITRAL Arbitration Rules,[6] modified in order, *inter alia*, to reflect the public international law character of the disputes. Parties to a dispute that is submitted to PCA arbitration may select the appropriate set of Optional Rules to govern the arbitral procedure. They may also adapt the Optional Rules.[7] The adoption of the Optional Rules was designed to promote recourse to arbitration under the PCA by state and non-state actors. Optional Rules have also been adopted for conciliation[8] and fact-finding[9] procedures.

While this Chapter outlines the procedures for PCA arbitration set out in the Hague Conventions and in the various Optional Rules, it is important to note that in many instances the PCA Secretary-General and the International Bureau are involved in the administration of arbitrations that are not conducted under

---

[6] UN Commission on International Trade, 1976 UNCITRAL Arbitration Rules, General Assembly Resolution 31/98 of 15 December 1976. See D Caron, M Pellonpää, and L Caplan, *The UNCITRAL Arbitration Rules: A Commentary* (2006).

[7] Optional Rules for Arbitrating Disputes between Two States (1992), art 1(1) ('Inter-State Rules'); Optional Rules for Arbitrating Disputes between Two Parties of which only One is a State (1993), art 1(1) ('State/Non-State Rules'); Optional Rules for Arbitration involving International Organizations and States (1996), art 1(1) ('IGO/State Rules'); Optional Rules for Arbitration between International Organizations and Private Parties (1996), art 1(1) ('IGO/ Private Parties Rules'); Optional Rules for Arbitration of Disputes Relating to Natural Resources and/or the Environment (2001), art 1(1) ('Natural Resources Rules'). All Optional Rules are available at <http://www.pca-cpa.org/> (Documents and Resources/Rules of Procedure).

[8] PCA Optional Conciliation Rules (1996) ('Conciliation Rules'); PCA Optional Rules for the Conciliation of Disputes Relating to Natural Resources and/or the Environment (2001). All Optional Rules are available at <http://www.pca-cpa.org/> (Documents and Resources/Rules of Procedure).

[9] PCA Optional Rules for Fact-finding Commissions of Inquiry (1997), available at <http://www.pca-cpa.org/> (Documents and Resources/Rules of Procedure).

these procedures and Rules.[10] In practice, increasingly the principal activity of the revitalized PCA has been the provision of registry and other services to arbitrations conducted under other arbitration rules.[11] These include treaty-based arbitrations—such as those conducted under Annex VII to the UN Convention on the Law of the Sea[12] or under bilateral or regional investment treaties, as well as ad hoc arbitrations. In these circumstances, the PCA International Bureau may be charged with providing institutional and logistical support to the arbitral proceedings, acting as a channel of communication between the parties and the tribunal, and acting as registrar of the arbitration, including maintaining documents pertaining to the proceedings.

The 2008 Annual Report of the PCA notes that in 2008 the PCA acted as registry in 34 cases, including three inter-state arbitrations, 23 investor-state arbitrations, and eight arbitrations in which at least one party was a state, a state-controlled entity, or an intergovernmental organization.[13] The PCA has acted as registry in four inter-state arbitrations under Annex VII of the UN Convention on the Law of the Sea;[14] in the arbitration between the UK and Ireland relating to the OSPAR Convention, under that Convention's arbitration rules as modified by the parties;[15] and in a number of ad hoc inter-state arbitrations, subject to rules agreed in the parties' arbitration agreement.[16] For the first time in 2008, the PCA acted as registry in an intra-state dispute, between the government of Sudan and the Sudan People's Liberation Movement/Army, concerning delimitation of the Abyei Area between the north and south of Sudan. The PCA has also, for example, provided registry and administrative services in a number of investment disputes under Chapter 11 of the North American Free

---

[10] See eg T Van den Hout, 'Resolution of International Disputes: The Role of the Permanent Court of Arbitration—Reflections on the Centenary of the 1907 Convention for the Pacific Settlement of International Disputes' (2008) 21 *Leiden Journal of International Law* 643.

[11] Art 47 of the 1907 Hague Convention provides that: 'The Bureau is authorized to place its offices and staff at the disposal of the Contracting Powers for the use of any special Board of Arbitration. The jurisdiction of the Permanent Court may, within the conditions laid down in the regulation, be extended to disputes between non-Contracting Powers or between Contracting Powers and non-Contracting Powers, if the parties are agreed to recourse to this Tribunal.' Crawford notes that while in terms this provision appears to be limited to inter-state arbitration, the Bureau nonetheless agreed in 1934 to the use of the PCA facilities by a tribunal established under a contract between the Radio Corporation of America and China. J Crawford, 'The PCA and Mixed Arbitration', Remarks on the Occasion of the Celebration of the Centenary of the PCA, The Hague, 18 October 2007, at 2, available at <http://www.pca-cpa.org/upload/files/Crawford%20EN.pdf>.

[12] See Chapter 2.

[13] Permanent Court of Arbitration, *108th Annual Report—2008*, para 3.

[14] *MOX Plant case* (Ireland v UK), Order on Termination of Proceedings of 6 June 2008; *Guyana v Suriname*, Award of 17 September 2007; *Barbados v Trinidad and Tobago*, Award of 11 April 2006; and *Land Reclamation Activities in and around the Straits of Johor* (Malaysia v Singapore), Award on Agreed Terms of 1 September 2005.

[15] *Ireland v United Kingdom* ('*OSPAR' Arbitration*), Award of 2 July 2003.

[16] For example, *Belgium–Netherlands* ('*Iron Rhine Arbitration*'), Award of 24 May 2005; *Eritrea–Yemen*, Awards of 9 October 1998 and 17 December 1999.

Trade Agreement,[17] and in arbitrations under bilateral investment treaties conducted under UNCITRAL Rules.[18] The information available on these cases, and others administered by the PCA, may be limited, as the PCA only identifies parties and publishes awards and other information about proceedings where the parties have so agreed. Such information as is available is accessible on the PCA website and, to a lesser extent, in the Annual Reports.

In terms of arbitration under the PCA Optional Rules, the Inter-State Rules and the State/Non-State Rules have each been utilized in at least two proceedings, where the parties agreed to arbitration rules based on the PCA models.[19]

It may also be noted that the UNCITRAL Arbitration Rules provide for the Secretary-General of the PCA to act to designate an appointing authority for the appointment of arbitrators, in the event that no appointing authority has been agreed by the parties or if such authority refuses or fails to act.[20] This is a function that the Secretary-General has been called upon to fulfil on a number of occasions. The Secretary-General may also be requested to act as default appointing authority in certain cases.[21]

Institutional Aspects

Governing texts

Procedural law

The principal texts governing the activities of the PCA are the 1899/1907 **4.3** Hague Conventions for the Pacific Settlement of International Disputes. The

---

[17] See *infra* Ch 10.4. In September 2009, pending NAFTA Chapter 11 arbitrations administered by the PCA included: *Vito G. Gallo v Canada*; and *Chemtura Corporation v Canada*.

[18] For example, *Centerra Gold Inc and Kumtor Gold Company v Kyrgyz Republic*; *Saluka Investments BV v Czech Republic*; *Telekom Malaysia Berhad v Ghana*. Further information on these cases is available on the PCA website. The PCA also provided administrative support in *TCW Group Inc and Dominican Energy Holdings v Dominican Republic*, Consent Award of 16 July 2009 (an arbitration conducted under UNCITRAL Arbitration Rules pursuant to the Central America–Dominican Republic–United States Free Trade Agreement).

[19] The Rules of the *Eritrea-Ethiopia Boundary Commission* were based on the Inter-State Rules with modifications, and the *Eritrea-Ethiopia Claims Commission* Rules were based on the Inter-State Rules adapted to reflect the Commission's mandate and anticipated workload. The *Larsen v Hawaiian Kingdom* arbitration was conducted under the State/Non-State Rules (Award of 5 February 2001, para 2.1); and the *Abyei Arbitration* was conducted under the State/Non-State Rules with modifications agreed by the parties in the Arbitration Agreement (Arbitration Agreement between the Government of Sudan and The Sudan People's Liberation Movement/Army on Delimiting Abyei Area, 7 July 2008, art 1(1), available at <http://www.pca-cpa.org/upload/files/Abyei%20Arbitration%20Agreement.pdf>).

[20] UNCITRAL Arbitration Rules, art 6(2), art 7(2). At the time of writing, revisions to the UNCITRAL Arbitration Rules are under discussion, see <http://www.uncitral.org/uncitral/en/commission/working_groups/2Arbitration.html>.

[21] PCA, *108th Annual Report—2008*, para 60.

Conventions (of which the 1907 Convention is the more detailed) regulate the institutional structure of the PCA; the composition of the list of arbitrators; the composition of ad hoc tribunals; financial aspects of PCA operations; and the basic rules of procedure applicable to PCA good offices and mediation, inquiry, and arbitration proceedings (although the parties may choose not to apply them).[22]

In addition, different sets of Optional Rules of Procedure will be applicable upon the choice of the parties, as alternatives to the rules of procedure found in the Hague Conventions. The various Optional Rules for arbitration have been referred to in para 4.2 above.

If parties to an inter-state dispute agree to arbitrate under the auspices of the PCA, but fail to select an appropriate set of PCA Optional Rules, or an alternative set of rules (eg UNCITRAL Arbitration Rules), the proceedings will be governed by the rules of arbitration set out in the 1899/1907 Hague Conventions.[23]

The administration of the PCA is assigned to two standing bodies—the Administrative Council and the International Bureau. The Administrative Council comprises diplomatic representatives accredited to the Netherlands of the state parties to the Hague Conventions. The Council provides general guidance to the work of the PCA, supervises its administration and expenditure, and promulgates rules of procedure and other regulations.[24] The International Bureau serves as the operative secretariat of the PCA. It maintains the permanent roster of potential arbitrators; receives communications directed to the PCA (including requests for arbitration); and provides ongoing administrative services to the arbitral tribunals, including the provision of the facilities of the PCA building.[25]

The functioning of the Administrative Council and the International Bureau is governed by additional sets of rules.[26]

Substantive law

4.4 An arbitral tribunal established under the PCA system is generally expected to apply the substantive law agreed upon by the parties. In the absence of an agreement, the tribunal will apply either the applicable rules of general international

---

[22] 1899 Hague Convention, arts 20, 30; 1907 Hague Convention, arts 41, 51.
[23] 1899 Hague Convention, art 30; 1907 Hague Convention, art 51.
[24] 1899 Hague Convention, art 28; 1907 Hague Convention, art 49.
[25] 1899 Hague Convention, arts 22–23, 26; 1907 Hague Convention, arts 43, 44, 46, 47.
[26] Rules of Procedure of the Administrative Council, 19 September 1900; Rules concerning the Organization and Internal Working of the International Bureau of the Permanent Court of Arbitration, 8 December 1900. Both available at <http://www.pca-cpa.org>.

law or another body of law prescribed by choice of law rules.[27] Finally, with the agreement of the parties, the tribunal may also decide a case *ex aequo et bono*.

Organization

Composition, appointment, and disqualification

List of arbitrators Each party to the 1899 or 1907 Hague Convention is entitled **4.5** to nominate up to four persons of established competence in international law and high moral reputation, who have agreed to serve as PCA arbitrators, to a roster maintained by the International Bureau.[28] Two or more states may select the same persons to the list of arbitrators. The International Bureau transmits the list, as amended from time to time, to the states parties, and maintains a current list on its website. The selected individuals (referred to as members of the PCA) serve for a renewable six-year period. parties to an arbitration administered by the PCA are not bound to nominate arbitrators from the list of members of the PCA. However, in the *Abyei Arbitration*, the parties themselves limited the selection of the four party-appointed arbitrators to only those persons who were 'current or former members of the PCA or members of tribunals for which the PCA acted as registry'.[29]

The Natural Resources Rules provide for the establishment of a specialized list of arbitrators with expertise in the fields of natural resources and the environment, and such a list is maintained by the International Bureau.

Composition of the arbitral tribunal According to the Optional Rules, if the **4.6** parties to a dispute fail to agree on the number of arbitrators (ie sole arbitrator, three or five arbitrators), the tribunal shall be composed of three arbitrators.[30] In the case of a three-member tribunal, each party to the dispute is to appoint one arbitrator and the two appointed arbitrators are to agree upon the identity of the third arbitrator. In the absence of agreement on the third arbitrator, or upon failure on the part of one of the parties to appoint an arbitrator, the third arbitrator

---

[27] Inter-State Rules, art 33; State/Non-State Rules, art 33; IGO/State Rules, art 33; IGO/Private Parties Rules, art 33; Natural Resources Rules, art 33. The two Hague Conventions make a more ambiguous reference to settlement 'on the basis of respect for law': 1899 Hague Convention, art 15; 1907 Hague Convention, art 37. In cases involving international organizations, the tribunal is directed to take due account of the rules of the organization concerned and to the law of international organizations; and in cases involving private parties, the tribunal is directed to pay attention to the terms of the contracts or agreements in question and take into account the relevant trade usage. In cases involving natural resources and/or the environment, under the Natural Resources Rules the tribunal is also directed to apply national or international law and rules of law it determines to be appropriate.

[28] 1899 Hague Convention, art 23; 1907 Hague Convention, art 44.

[29] *Abyei Arbitration Agreement*, art 5.2, available at <http://www.pca-cpa.org/upload/files/Abyei%20Arbitration%20Agreement.pdf>.

[30] Inter-State Rules, art 5; State/Non-State Rules, art 5; IGO/State Rules, art 5; IGO/Private Parties Rules, art 5.

will be appointed by an appointing authority agreed upon by the parties. In the absence of such agreement, the appointing authority will be designated by the Secretary-General of the PCA (head of the International Bureau).[31] The Natural Resources Rules provide for the appointment of arbitrators in multi-party proceedings.[32]

If the parties agree to arbitrate their dispute before a sole arbitrator, they are free to agree on the identity of that arbitrator or, alternatively, to jointly designate an appointing authority. If no agreement is reached, the Secretary-General of the PCA shall designate an appointing authority, which shall appoint the sole arbitrator in consultation with the parties.[33]

If the parties agree on a five-member tribunal, each party shall nominate one arbitrator, and the two nominated arbitrators shall select the remaining three. If no agreement is reached, or if a party fails to appoint an arbitrator, the same procedures for completing the composition of the tribunal applicable to a three-member tribunal shall be resorted to.[34]

In contrast with the Hague Conventions, the Optional Rules specifically permit the selection of arbitrators who are not members of the PCA, that is to say, not listed on the permanent roster of arbitrators.[35]

In proceedings governed by the Hague Conventions rather than by the Optional Rules, the procedure of appointment is different. First, all appointed arbitrators must be members of the PCA. Furthermore, in the absence of agreement of the parties on the size and composition of the panel of Permanent Court of Arbitration arbitrators, the tribunal shall normally include five arbitrators. Each party should select two arbitrators (under the 1907 Convention, only one of the two selected arbitrators can be a national of the appointing state, or its designated member to the PCA list of arbitrators). The Umpire is then selected by the four appointed arbitrators or, in the alternative, by an agreed-upon third party.[36] If no agreement is reached in this manner, the Conventions provide for delegation of appointment power to two party-appointed third states. Under a

---

[31] Inter-State Rules, art 7; State/Non-State Rules, art 7; IGO/State Rules, art 7; IGO/Private Parties Rules, art 7.

[32] Natural Resources Rules, art 7(3)(4).

[33] Inter-State Rules, art 6; State/Non-State Rules, art 6; IGO/State Rules, art 6; IGO/Private Parties Rules, art 6. All of the rules provide for a consultation mechanism based upon the circulation of a list of potential arbitrators between the parties for objections, and designation of an arbitrator not objected to by any of the parties; or if no such arbitrator exists, designation of an arbitrator at the appointing authority's discretion (preferably, in cases involving states, not a national of any of the states parties to the dispute).

[34] Inter-State Rules, art 7; IGO/State Rules, art 7. The two other sets of Optional Rules do not provide in any case for a five-member arbitral tribunal.

[35] Inter-State Rules, art 8(3); State/Non-State Rules, art 8(3); IGO/State Rules, art 8(3); IGO/Private Parties Rules, art 8(3).

[36] 1899 Hague Convention, art 24; 1907 Hague Convention, art 45.

unique approach, the 1907 Convention provides, as a last resort, that the Umpire be selected by a draw by lot from a shortlist of four members of the PCA prepared by the two designated third parties (excluding citizens or nominees to the PCA of either party to the dispute).[37]

Under the 1907 Hague Convention, the parties may agree to arbitrate their dispute in an expedited summary procedure. In that case, the tribunal must normally include three arbitrators (appointed in a manner similar to the method of appointment of a five-member panel).[38]

Challenge procedures   Under the various Optional Rules, a party may insti-   **4.7** tute a challenge directed against the appointment or continued service of an arbitrator, if it becomes aware of circumstances which raise justifiable doubt as to the impartiality or independence of that arbitrator.[39] If the other party agrees to the challenge, or the arbitrator withdraws from office, a new arbitrator will be appointed (in a manner similar to that in which the retiring arbitrator was appointed).[40] Otherwise, the challenge is to be presented before the tribunal's appointing authority (which might be designated exclusively for the purpose of challenge procedures). The authority shall decide on the merits of the motion.[41]

Plenary/chambers

Arbitration tribunals established under the PCA system sit in plenary. If for   **4.8** some reason one of the arbitrators in a three- or five-member tribunal fails to participate in the proceedings, he or she will normally be replaced.[42] However, the truncated tribunal may decide to continue and hear the dispute notwithstanding the arbitrator's failure to attend its meetings.[43]

---

[37] 1907 Hague Convention, art 45. Unlike the Optional Rules, no stipulation is made in either of the Hague Conventions to resolve a situation in which one of the parties refuses to appoint its two designated arbitrators.

[38] 1907 Hague Convention, arts 86, 87. The main difference between the two procedures is that in case of disagreement among the two selected arbitrators as to the identity of the third one, the arbitrators themselves (and not the designated third parties) compose the shortlist of four arbitrators to draw from. The involvement of a third party is not sought under this procedure.

[39] Inter-State Rules, art 10; State/Non-State Rules, art 10; IGO/State Rules, art 10; IGO/Private Parties Rules, art 10; Natural Resources Rules, art 10.

[40] Inter-State Rules, art 11; State/Non-State Rules, art 11; IGO/State Rules, art 11; IGO/Private Parties Rules, art 11; Natural Resources Rules, art 11. The procedure for replacement of an arbitrator is prescribed by art 13 of each set of Rules.

[41] Inter-State Rules, art 12; State/Non-State Rules, art 12; IGO/State Rules, art 12; IGO/Private Parties Rules, art 12.

[42] 1899 Hague Convention, art 35; 1907 Hague Convention, art 59; Inter-State Rules, art 13(1), (2); State/Non-State Rules, art 13(1), (2); IGO/State Rules, art 13(1), (2); IGO/Private Parties Rules, art 13(1), (2). Under art 14 to all Optional Rules for PCA arbitration, the tribunal may decree that the hearing shall be repeated in the event of replacement of an arbitrator.

[43] Inter-State Rules, art 13(3); State/Non-State Rules, art 13(3); IGO/State Rules, art 13(3); IGO/Private Parties Rules, art 13(3).

The various PCA Optional Rules and the UNCITRAL Rules all provide for the possibility of the presiding arbitrator making decisions of procedure on his or her own in certain circumstances.[44]

Appellate structure

4.9   PCA arbitral awards are final and binding, with no right of appeal.[45]

Scientific and technical experts

4.10 Under the Optional Rules, an arbitral tribunal may appoint an expert (or several experts) and instruct them to prepare a written report on specified issues. The parties must provide the expert (or experts) with any document or goods requested; and may submit additional information they wish the expert to consider. The parties shall have the opportunity to review the expert's report and the documents he or she relied on, and comment upon them in writing to the tribunal. The parties also have the right to question the expert and introduce their own expert witnesses.[46]

A specialized panel of scientific experts has been established pursuant to the Natural Resources Rules, who may be appointed as expert witnesses under the Rules.

Registry

4.11 The PCA International Bureau, headed by the Secretary-General, provides administrative services, including registry and secretarial services, and constitutes a channel of communication between the parties and the tribunal.[47] In addition, the International Bureau files documents from all PCA cases in its archives. Under the Optional Rules, upon the written request of the parties, the International Bureau shall act as a channel of communication between the parties and the tribunal, provide secretariat services, and/or serve as registry for the arbitration.[48]

Jurisdiction and access to the PCA

Ratione personae

4.12 The original jurisdiction of the PCA under the 1899/1907 Conventions was limited to inter-state disputes.[49] Furthermore, exercise of this jurisdiction

---

[44] For example, Inter-State Rules, art 31(2); State/Non-State Rules, art 31(2).

[45] 1899 Hague Convention, art 54; 1907 Hague Convention, art 81; Inter-State Rules, art 32(2); State/Non-State Rules, art 32(2); IGO/State Rules, art 32(2); IGO/Private Parties Rules, art 32(2).

[46] Inter-State Rules, art 27; State/Non-State Rules, art 27; IGO/State Rules, art 27; IGO/Private Parties Rules, art 27.

[47] 1899 Hague Convention, art 22; 1907 Hague Convention, art 43.

[48] Inter-State Rules, art 1(2); State/Non-State Rules, art 1(4); IGO/State Rules, art 1(3); IGO/Private Parties Rules, art 1(4).

[49] 1899 Hague Convention, arts 15, 21; 1907 Hague Convention, arts 37, 42. However, see *supra* note 11, regarding the 1934 case of *Radio Corporation of America v China*.

depends upon an agreement (normally, in writing) between the parties to refer a dispute to PCA arbitration. Such agreement can be made ad hoc, or in a compromissory clause found in a valid treaty.

The various Optional Rules expanded the scope of jurisdiction of the PCA. Parties to PCA arbitrations may now include states, state entities, intergovernmental organizations, and non-state entities/private parties.

The agreement to refer a dispute to the PCA may be made by way of a separate arbitration agreement or through an arbitration clause in a contract or other legal instrument. Under the Optional Rules, an arbitration clause shall be considered independent of the other terms of the document in which it is contained, for the purposes of establishing jurisdiction. Thus invalidity of the contract, agreement, or instrument shall not *ipso facto* deprive the arbitral tribunal of jurisdiction.[50]

Finally, under the sets of Optional Rules providing for the involvement of a private party, consent to the application of the rules constitutes a waiver of sovereign immunity from jurisdiction on the part of the state or international organization concerned.[51]

Ratione materiae

The potential subject-matter jurisdiction of the PCA is unlimited.[52] However, in each case the scope of jurisdiction of the arbitral tribunal is determined subject to the wording of the applicable arbitration clause (or the *compromis*). **4.13**

Ratione temporis

The various rules of procedure do not place any temporal limits upon the referral of disputes to PCA arbitration. However, such restrictions may be indicated in the instrument concluded by the parties (ie the arbitration clause or *compromis*), which establishes jurisdiction. **4.14**

Advisory jurisdiction

PCA arbitral tribunals have only contentious jurisdiction, and arbitral awards are final and binding.[53] The PCA also renders conciliatory services, under its Rules of Conciliation and fact-finding services under the 1907 Hague Convention (see para 4.31 *infra*). **4.15**

---

[50] Inter-State Rules, art 21(2); State/Non-State Rules, art 21(2); IGO/State Rules, art 21(2); IGO/Private Parties Rules, art 21(2).

[51] State/Non-State Rules, art 1(2); IGO/Private Parties Rules, art 1(2).

[52] 1899 Hague Convention, art 21; 1907 Hague Convention, art 42.

[53] 1899 Hague Convention, art 54; 1907 Hague Convention, art 81; Inter-State Rules, art 32(2); State/Non-State Rules, art 32(2); IGO/State Rules, art 32(2); IGO/Private Parties Rules, art 32(2).

Procedural Aspects

Languages

4.16 The language (or languages) of any proceedings will be agreed upon by the parties. In the absence of such agreement it will be determined by the tribunal.[54] Under the Optional Rules, the tribunal may require that the parties translate documents submitted to the tribunal into the language (or languages) of the proceedings. In the *Abyei Arbitration*, English was the official language of the arbitration. However, the parties' arbitration agreement required the PCA to publish an Arabic translation of the award, and witness testimony was conducted in English, Dinka, and Arabic.[55] The *Eurotunnel* arbitration has two official languages, English and French. The *TCW v Dominican Republic* arbitration was conducted in Spanish and English. The PCA has arranged for interpreters of various other languages as requested by the parties in other disputes.

Instituting proceedings

4.17 Under all the Optional Rules, the party initiating arbitration (ie the claimant) is to serve the other party (ie the respondent) with a notice of arbitration.

The notice of arbitration is to contain specified information, including: reference to an arbitration clause or arbitration agreement; reference to the treaty, agreement, contract, or other legal instrument (eg constituent instrument or decision of an international organization) out of which, or in relation to which, the dispute arose; the general nature of the case and indication of the amount involved; the relief or remedy sought; and a proposal as to the number of arbitrators.[56]

Under the procedures envisaged by the Hague Conventions, no formal notice of arbitration is required. Thus the parties can move at any time to establish a tribunal and draft a *compromis*.[57] Only when the tribunal is constituted and the *compromis* agreed upon should the International Bureau be notified.[58]

---

[54] 1899 Hague Convention, art 38; 1907 Hague Convention, art 61; Inter-State Rules, art 17; State/Non-State Rules, art 17; IGO/State Rules, art 17; IGO/Private Parties Rules, art 17.

[55] *Abyei Arbitration Agreement, supra* note 19, arts 7, 9(3).

[56] Inter-State Rules, art 3; State/Non-State Rules, art 3; IGO/State Rules, art 3; IGO/Private Parties Rules, art 3; Natural Resources Rules, art 3.

[57] 1899 Hague Convention, art 24; 1907 Hague Convention, art 45.

[58] 1899 Hague Convention, art 24; 1907 Hague Convention, art 46. Under the 1899 Convention, the parties should notify the International Bureau that the tribunal has been created (even if no *compromis* has been negotiated). Under the 1907 Hague Convention, if no agreement on the contents of the *compromis* is reached, the parties may authorize the tribunal to settle a *compromis*. Furthermore, under those rules, in cases brought on the basis of a general arbitration agreement (ie an agreement which refers all future inter-state disputes or certain categories of such dispute to arbitration), or a contractual debt claim presented on behalf of a national of the claimant, the tribunal is competent to draft a *compromis* acting on a request made by one party only: 1907 Hague Convention, art 53.

Financial assistance

In 1995, the Secretary-General of the PCA established a Financial Assistance **4.18**
Fund for the Settlement of International Disputes, with the approval of the
Administrative Council. The Fund comprises voluntary financial contributions
made by states, international organizations, NGOs, and natural or legal persons. Only states (or state-controlled entities) are eligible to receive financial
support, provided that they are parties to either the 1899 or the 1907 Hague
Conventions; they have concluded an agreement to refer a dispute (or disputes)
to settlement before the PCA; and they are listed on the Development Assistance
Committee (DAC) List of Aid recipients (as prepared by the OECD).

A request for financial assistance in order to facilitate recourse to PCA arbitration, conciliation, and fact finding is to be submitted by the requesting state
to the Secretary-General. The request should include: a copy of the dispute settlement agreement (in the case of a general agreement, a brief description of the
dispute); an itemized estimate of costs for which financial assistance is sought;
and an undertaking to submit an audited statement of account on the expenditure made with the received funds.[59]

The Fund is administered by the International Bureau, with the supervision of
a Board of Trustees, which must approve every request for assistance (the Board
of Trustees is to be appointed by the Secretary-General, with the approval of the
Administrative Council). In addition, the Secretary-General periodically reports
to the Administrative Council on the activities of the Fund. The PCA 2008 Annual
Report notes that since the establishment of the Fund, contributions had been
made by nine states, and six grants of assistance have been made. Norway made a
specific contribution earmarked for expenses related to the *Abyei Arbitration*.[60]

Provisional measures

Under the Optional Rules, the tribunal may order interim measures of protec- **4.19**
tion, in the form of an interim award, at the request of a party, if such measures
are viewed by the tribunal as necessary to preserve the respective rights of the
parties or the subject matter of the dispute. These measures may include, in commercial disputes, the deposit of goods with third parties or the sale of perishable
goods. Under the Natural Resources Rules, interim measures may be taken
to prevent serious harm to the environment.[61] The tribunal is also entitled to
require from the requesting party security for the costs associated with interim
measures. It is further provided in the Optional Rules that the parties are free to

---

[59] PCA Financial Assistance Fund for Settlement of International Disputes, Terms of Reference and Guidelines, as approved by the Administrative Council on 11 December 1995, para 6.

[60] PCA, *108th Annual Report—2008*, para 32.

[61] Natural Resources Rules, art 26(1).

agree to restrict the power of the tribunal to issue interim awards; and may seek interim protection in alternative venues as well.[62]

The 1899/1907 Hague Conventions do not expressly provide for a similar authority to issue interim measures of protection.

Preliminary proceedings/objections

4.20 The various sets of Optional Rules provide for a preliminary procedure to establish the arbitral tribunal's jurisdiction. A plea alleging lack of competence of the tribunal must be raised in the written pleadings, at the statement or defence stage (or in the reply to a counter-claim). The tribunal should normally rule on the plea concerning its jurisdiction as a preliminary matter. However, it may also defer its decision to the final award, by joining jurisdictional issues to the merits.[63]

In addition, challenge proceedings against an arbitrator, made in pursuance of the Optional Rules, must be initiated within 30 days from the appointment of the challenged arbitrator, or within 30 days from the date the circumstances constituting the basis for the challenge became known to the challenging party.[64] The Hague Conventions do not provide for a preliminary procedure.

Written pleadings

4.21 After the notice of arbitration, and once the tribunal has been constituted and has directed the order of proceedings, the written stage of the proceedings (conducted in pursuance with the Optional Rules) opens with the statement of claim submitted by the claimant to the respondent, the arbitrators, and the International Bureau. The statement of claim should include, *inter alia*: a statement of facts supporting the claim; the points at issue; and the relief or remedy sought.

The claimant should attach to the statement of claim all relevant documents, including those supporting the jurisdictional basis of the PCA arbitral tribunal. In addition, the claimant may indicate further documents or evidence it intends to submit in the future.[65]

In reply, the respondent will submit to the other party and the tribunal a statement of defence, together with supporting documents, and make reference to additional documents or evidence it intends to submit.[66]

---

[62] Inter-State Rules, art 26; State/Non-State Rules, art 26; IGO/State Rules, art 26; IGO/Private Parties Rules, art 26; Natural Resources Rules, art 26.

[63] Inter-State Rules, art 21; State/Non-State Rules, art 21; IGO/State Rules, art 21; IGO/Private Parties Rules, art 21; Natural Resources Rules, art 21.

[64] Inter-State Rules, art 11(1); State/Non-State Rules, art 11(1); IGO/State Rules, art 11(1); IGO/Private Parties Rules, art 11(1).

[65] Inter-State Rules, art 18; State/Non-State Rules, art 18; IGO/State Rules, art 18; IGO/Private Parties Rules, art 18; Natural Resources Rules, art 18.

[66] Inter-State Rules, art 19(2); State/Non-State Rules, art 19(2); IGO/State Rules, art 19(2); IGO/Private Parties Rules, art 19(2); Natural Resources Rules, art 19(2).

The respondent may also include in its statement of defence (or, if the tribunal allows it, in a subsequent statement) a counter-claim arising out of the same treaty, agreement, contract, or other legal instrument, or a claim for set-off, which relies upon a claim arising from the said instrument. The counter-claim or set-off claim statement should meet the procedural requirements applicable to an ordinary statement of claim.[67]

The parties may amend or supplement their written submissions at any time, unless the tribunal considers those amendments as inappropriate given the delay in their introduction, the prejudice they cause to the other party, or any other circumstances. In no case can the claim be amended in a manner that exceeds the jurisdiction of the tribunal.[68] Finally, the tribunal is authorized to decide whether additional submissions in writing are required.[69]

The Hague Conventions provide for a less detailed procedure. However, their rules also call for submission of written pleadings in the form of communication of cases, replies, and counter-cases, with all relevant documents attached. Pleadings must be submitted to the tribunal and a certified copy made for the other party.[70]

Under the Optional Rules and the Hague Conventions, the timetable for submission of pleadings will be determined by the tribunal (except under the 1907 Hague Convention which calls upon the parties to introduce a timetable for submissions in the *compromis*).[71] However, under the Optional Rules, such periods should not normally exceed 90 days (45 days in cases involving a state and a non-state actor) for each submission.[72]

Oral arguments

The parties are entitled, under the Optional Rules, to request oral hearings and the presentation of evidence by witnesses (including expert witnesses). In the absence of such a request, the tribunal will decide whether to hold oral hearings, or conduct the proceedings solely on the basis of written submissions, documents, and other material.[73] If witnesses are to be heard, each party is to

4.22

---

[67] Inter-State Rules, art 19(3)–(4); State/Non-State Rules, art 19(3)–(4); IGO/State Rules, art 19(3)–(4); IGO/Private Parties Rules, art 19(3)–(4).

[68] Inter-State Rules, art 20; State/Non-State Rules, art 20; IGO/State Rules, art 20; IGO/Private Parties Rules, art 20.

[69] Inter-State Rules, art 22; State/Non-State Rules, art 22; IGO/State Rules, art 22; IGO/Private Parties Rules, art 22.

[70] 1899 Hague Convention, arts 39–40; 1907 Hague Convention, arts 63–64.

[71] 1899 Hague Convention, art 49; 1907 Hague Convention, art 63; Inter-State Rules, arts 18(1), 19(1), 22; State/Non-State Rules, arts 18(1), 19(1), 22; IGO/State Rules, arts 18(1), 19(1), 22; IGO/Private Parties Rules, arts 18(1), 19(1), 22.

[72] Inter-State Rules, art 23; State/Non-State Rules, art 23; IGO/State Rules, art 23; IGO/Private Parties Rules, art 23.

[73] Inter-State Rules, art 15(2); State/Non-State Rules, art 15(2); IGO/State Rules, art 15(2); IGO/Private Parties Rules, art 15(2).

communicate to the tribunal and the other party the names and addresses of the witnesses it intends to introduce, at least 30 days in advance.[74]

Under the Hague Conventions, proceedings include oral discussions. The parties are entitled to present orally to the tribunal all arguments relevant to the defence of their case; and the tribunal may put questions to them on their presentation.[75] However, if the parties choose to conduct the proceedings in summary procedure there will normally be no oral hearings.[76]

Under the Hague Conventions and the Optional Rules, oral hearings are conducted *in camera* unless the parties agree otherwise.[77] However, under the Hague Conventions, agreement of the parties is not sufficient to make the proceedings public and an additional decision of the tribunal is required.

Third party intervention

4.23   While generally third party intervention in PCA proceedings is not permissible, there is no reason why a dispute between more than two parties could not be referred to the PCA, with the agreement of all parties.[78] The various Optional Rules contain guidelines for their adaptation to multi-party proceedings.[79] Special agreement will be necessary, including on the method of appointment of arbitrators and costs. The Secretary-General of the International Bureau has expressed his willingness to render assistance to the parties to a multi-party dispute in the adaptation of the Optional Rules to the dispute.

An exception to the general rule precluding third party intervention may be found in the two Hague Conventions. In disputes involving the interpretation of treaties to which other states are parties, the parties to the dispute are to notify those other states, which will have the right to intervene in the proceedings.

---

[74] Inter-State Rules, art 25(2); State/Non-State Rules, art 25(2); IGO/State Rules, art 25(2); IGO/Private Parties Rules, art 25(2).

[75] 1899 Hague Convention, arts 45, 47; 1907 Hague Convention, arts 70, 72.

[76] 1907 Hague Convention, art 90.

[77] Inter-State Rules, art 25(4); State/Non-State Rules, art 25(4); IGO/State Rules, art 25(4); IGO/Private Parties Rules, art 25(4); Natural Resources Rules, art 25(4); 1899 Hague Convention, art 41; 1907 Hague Convention, art 66. In the *Abyei Arbitration*, for example, it was agreed that the media should be admitted to the oral hearings before the tribunal, while a portion of the hearing might be closed at the discretion of the tribunal for security reasons. *Abyei Arbitration, supra* note 19, art 8(6). The proceedings were broadcast live on the PCA website, and the video archives remain available to the public there.

[78] See eg the *Eurotunnel Arbitration*, involving two states and two private parties; *1. Centerra Gold Inc. (Canada) and 2. Kumtor Gold Company (Krygrz Republic) v The Kyrgyz Republic*, and *1. TCW Group Inc. and 2. Dominican Energy Holdings L.P. v The Dominican Republic* for examples of cases involving two claimants and one respondent. The PCA is also currently administering an inter-state dispute involving five states parties, the details of which remain confidential.

[79] *Guidelines for adapting the Permanent Court of Arbitration Rules to Disputes arising under Multilateral Agreements and Multiparty Contracts.* The Natural Resources Rules are designed to accommodate multi-party proceedings.

In this case, the award shall be considered equally binding for them.[80] The Conventions do not specify rules of procedure to regulate such intervention. However, the parties to a particular dispute may do so, either in their underlying arbitration agreement or in agreed procedural rules.[81]

Amicus curiae

There is no provision in the Hague Conventions or the Optional Rules govern-   **4.24**
ing the issue of *amicus curiae* briefs. Given the nature of PCA arbitration (involving party control over the course of the procedure), it may seem unlikely that a tribunal would accept third party *amicus curiae* briefs, unless the parties to a case so agree. Nonetheless, it is worth noting that outside the PCA context, an arbitral tribunal operating under UNCITRAL Arbitration Rules (on which the PCA Optional Rules are based) relied on article 15 of the UNCITRAL Rules when called upon to consider a request to admit an *amicus curiae* submission in an investor-state dispute under NAFTA Chapter 11. The tribunal found that the admission of *amicus* briefs could fall within its general procedural power under article 15.[82] Article 15 of the PCA Optional Rules is framed in similar terms, providing that subject to the Rules, the arbitral tribunal may conduct the arbitration in such a manner as it considers appropriate, provided that the parties are treated with equality and that at any stage of the proceedings each party is given a full opportunity of presenting its case.[83] In the PCA-administered *TCW v Dominican Republic* arbitration, the Central America-Dominican Republic–United States Free Trade Agreement provides for participation of third party states and non-parties, the procedural aspects of which were dealt with by the arbitral tribunal in their Procedural Order No 2.[84] Confidentiality of PCA proceedings may in practice prove a bar or significant obstacle to potential *amicus* participation, however.

Representation of parties

In relation to arbitration, under the 1907 Hague Convention the parties are   **4.25**
entitled to appoint special agents to attend the tribunal to act as intermediaries

---

[80] 1899 Hague Convention, art 56; 1907 Hague Convention, art 84.

[81] See eg Procedural Order No 2 in the *TCW v Dominican Republic* arbitration, dealing with third party states and intervening non-parties under art 20 of the Central America-Dominican Republic–United States Free Trade Agreement, <http://server.nijmedia.nl/pca-cpa.org/upload/files/12%20PO2.pdf>.

[82] *Methanex Corporation v United States of America,* Decision of the Tribunal on Petitions from Third Person to Participate as 'Amici Curiae', 15 January 2001, para 31.

[83] Inter-State Rules, art 15(1); State/Non-State Rules, art 15(1); IGO/State Rules, art 15(1); Natural Resources Rules, art 15(1).

[84] See *supra* note 81.

between themselves and the tribunal, and may retain counsel or advocates.[85] The Inter-State Arbitration Rules provide that parties shall appoint an agent and may also be assisted by persons of their choice.[86] A similar provision regarding representation and assistance is contained in the State/Non-State Rules, the IGO/State Rules, the IGO/Private Parties Rules, and the Natural Resources Rules.[87]

Decision

4.26   The final decision of the tribunal is in the form of a written award decided by the majority of arbitrators.[88] The award will state the reasons for the decision, unless the parties agreed that no reasons are to be provided.[89] Under the Optional Rules, the award will not be made public (unless the parties agree to publicize it) whereas under the Hague Conventions it will normally be publicized.[90] The award is final and binding upon the parties and is to be executed without delay.[91]

The Optional Rules allow parties to a dispute that reached a settlement agreement before the end of the proceedings to request the tribunal to record their agreement in the form of an arbitral award on agreed terms.[92]

Interpretation and revision of award

4.27   Under the Optional Rules, either party may approach the tribunal after the award has been issued and ask for interpretation of the award, correction of errors in computation, clerical or typographical errors, or request an additional award on claims presented during the proceedings but omitted from the award. Requests for interpretation or correction are to be presented within 60 days from the day the award was received by the parties (30 days in state/non-state cases); a request for an additional award should be presented within 60 days. The

---

[85]   1899 Hague Convention, art 37; 1907 Hague Convention, art 62.

[86]   Inter-State Rules, art 4.

[87]   State/Non-State Rules, art 4; IGO/State Rules, art 4; IGO/Private Parties Rules, art 4; Natural Resources Rules, art 4.

[88]   1899 Hague Convention, art 52; 1907 Hague Convention, art 78; Inter-State Rules, art 31; State/Non-State Rules, art 31; IGO/State Rules, art 31; IGO/Private Parties Rules, art 31; Natural Resources Rules, art 31.

[89]   1899 Hague Convention, art 52; 1907 Hague Convention, art 79; Inter-State Rules, art 32(3); State/Non-State Rules, art 32(3); IGO/State Rules, art 32(3); IGO/Private Parties Rules, art 32(3).

[90]   1899 Hague Convention, art 53; 1907 Hague Convention, art 80; Inter-State Rules, art 32(5); State/Non-State Rules, art 32(5); IGO/State Rules, art 32(5); IGO/Private Parties Rules, art 32(5).

[91]   1899 Hague Convention, art 54; 1907 Hague Convention, art 81; Inter-State Rules, art 32(2); State/Non-State Rules, art 32(2); IGO/State Rules, art 32(2); IGO/Private Parties Rules, art 32(2).

[92]   Inter-State Rules, art 34(1); State/Non-State Rules, art 34(1); IGO/State Rules, art 34(1); IGO/Private Parties Rules, art 34(1).

Rules provide that the tribunal should reply to requests for interpretation within 45 days from the receipt of the request and to requests for additional award within 60 days.[93] The tribunal is authorized to correct errors in the award, of the type mentioned above, on its own initiative—if acting within 30 days from the date of communication of the award.

Under the 1907 Hague Convention, the parties may normally submit any question related to the interpretation and the execution of the award to the original tribunal.[94] In addition, under both Hague Conventions, if the parties agree in the *compromis* to this effect, the tribunal may re-examine the award in light of the discovery of a new fact calculated to have a decisive influence on the award, which was unknown during the proceeding to the tribunal and to the party requesting revision. The period of time in which requests for revision can be made should be fixed in the *compromis*.[95]

Appeals

There is no right of appeal in respect of awards rendered by tribunals established **4.28** under the PCA rules.

Costs

The costs of PCA arbitration include the fees and expenses of the arbitrators, **4.29** which are to be determined by the tribunal, normally in consultation with the appointing authority. They will also include the costs of expert advice and other assistance provided to the tribunal; fees and expenses of the appointing authority; and the expenses of the Secretary-General and the International Bureau. Additionally, parties to the proceedings will incur their own costs in respect of legal representation and assistance.

Normally, under the Optional Rules and the Hague Conventions, each party incurs its own costs of arbitration (ie all of its legal expenses and an equal share of the other costs of arbitration).[96] However, under the Optional Rules, the tribunal may apportion the costs between the parties in any other reasonable manner warranted by the circumstances. Exceptions to this rule are found under the Optional Rules for Arbitrating Disputes between Two Parties of which only One is a State, and the Optional Rules for Arbitration between IGOs and Private Parties, which provide that the unsuccessful party should normally incur all

---

[93] Inter-State Rules, arts 35–37; State/Non-State Rules, arts 35–37; IGO/State Rules, arts 35–37; IGO/Private Parties Rules, arts 35–37; Natural Resources Rules, arts 35–37.

[94] 1907 Hague Convention, art 82.

[95] 1899 Hague Convention, art 55; 1907 Hague Convention, art 83.

[96] 1899 Hague Convention, art 57; 1907 Hague Convention, art 85; Inter-State Rules, arts 38–40; State/Non-State Rules, arts 38–40; IGO/State Rules, arts 38–40; IGO/Private Parties Rules, arts 38–40.

costs.[97] However, here again, the tribunal may decide to apportion costs in a different manner. The parties may enter into their own agreement with respect to the allocation of costs. For example, in the *Abyei Arbitration*, the parties agreed that the Presidency of the Republic of Sudan would direct for the payment of the cost of the arbitration from the Unity Fund 'regardless of the outcome of the arbitration'.[98]

Under the various Optional Rules the tribunal may request the parties to deposit funds in advance during the proceedings; and it may require additional deposits at a later stage of the proceedings.[99]

Execution of decision, recognition, and enforcement

4.30 PCA Optional Rules governing proceedings involving states and/or international organizations do not provide for any mechanism of enforcement. The Optional Rules do, however, state that the parties undertake to carry out the award without delay.[100]

In cases involving private parties that are governed by the Optional Rules on Arbitration between States and Non-States or between International Organizations and Private Parties, the tribunal is expected to file or register its award in accordance with the municipal arbitration laws of the country in which the arbitration took place. Such registration is intended to facilitate recognition and enforcement of the award in municipal courts.[101]

In cases involving private parties on the one hand, and entities that enjoy sovereign immunity on the other hand, the implied agreement to waiver of immunity which is stated in the Optional Rules for Arbitrating Disputes between Two Parties of which only One is a State and for Arbitration between International Organizations and Private Parties does not apply to the enforcement procedures, and a separate explicit waiver should be sought.[102]

Conciliation and fact finding under the PCA

4.31 In addition to arbitration, the PCA also offers conciliation services, under its Rules of Conciliation, and fact-finding services, under the 1907 Hague Convention.

The Rules of Conciliation, modelled after the UNCITRAL Conciliation Rules, are designed to apply in disputes in which at least one of the parties is

---

[97] State/Non-State Rules, art 40(1); IGO/Private Parties Rules, art 40(1).

[98] *Abyei Arbitration Agreement, supra* note 19, art 11(1).

[99] Inter-State Rules, art 41; State/Non-State Rules, art 41; IGO/State Rules, art 41; IGO/Private Parties Rules, art 41; Natural Resources Rules, art 41.

[100] Inter-State Rules, art 32(2); State/Non-State Rules, art 32(2); IGO/State Rules, art 32(2); IGO/Private Parties Rules, art 32(2).

[101] State/Non-State Rules, art 32(7); IGO/Private Parties Rules, art 32(7).

[102] State/Non-State Rules, art 1(2); IGO/Private Parties Rules, art 1(2).

a state, state entity, or enterprise or an international organization.[103] Conciliation takes place before a panel of one, two, or three conciliators selected with the agreement of the parties. In the absence of such agreement, the conciliators will be appointed in a manner similar to the appointment of arbitrators under the various Optional Rules.[104] The conciliator (or conciliators) is to attempt to reach an amicable settlement of the dispute and conducts proceedings towards this aim, in any manner he or she considers appropriate, taking into account the wishes of the parties.[105] At any stage of the proceedings, the conciliator may propose a settlement and assist the parties in drawing up an agreement.[106] The International Bureau shall render the conciliation proceedings any administrative support required by the parties or the conciliator (with consent of the parties).[107]

Under the 1907 Hague Convention, the International Bureau of the PCA may also provide administrative assistance to the work of Commissions of Inquiry.[108] Such proceedings may be initiated by any two states which are in dispute over points of fact.[109] A Commission of Inquiry is constituted in a manner similar to that of PCA arbitration tribunals.[110] The Commission is then authorized to conduct an investigation of the facts in dispute and issue a report, which the parties may adopt or reject.[111] Alternatively, parties to factual disputes (including non-parties to the Hague Conventions) may agree to apply the 1997 Optional Rules for Fact-finding Commissions of Inquiry.[112] These Rules do not merely intend to supplement the non-mandatory provisions of the 1907 Convention, but also form a self-contained procedural framework.

Evaluation

The PCA has experienced a notable revitalization in the period since the 1980s. Much of its success appears to hinge upon its ability to provide registry and administrative services to a wide range of arbitrations: potentially involving states, intergovernmental organizations, private parties, and other entities. The International Bureau has played an important role in promoting the use of the PCA in new contexts in recent years—particularly in relation to potential

---

[103] International Bureau of the Permanent Court of Arbitration, Introduction, *PCA Optional Rules of Conciliation* (1996) xi.
[104] Conciliation Rules, arts 3, 4.
[105] Ibid, art 7.
[106] Ibid, arts 7(4), 13.
[107] Ibid, art 8.
[108] 1907 Hague Convention, art 15.
[109] Ibid, art 9.
[110] Ibid, art 12.
[111] Ibid, art 35.
[112] Fact-Finding Rules, *supra* note 9.

disputes under multilateral environmental agreements as well as those under the compulsory arbitration procedures in the UN Convention on the Law of the Sea.

Where treaties provide for arbitration of disputes, the PCA now offers an efficient and experienced institutional support for the conduct of the arbitration.

Increasingly it appears that the PCA is being used to provide institutional support to investor-state arbitrations that may arise under bilateral, regional, or sectoral investment agreements and that take place outside the framework of the ICSID Convention.[113] In this sense it is competing with, and may provide a useful alternative to, ICSID's Additional Facility and other international commercial arbitration institutions. The fact that PCA-administered proceedings may be confidential, unless the parties agree otherwise, may be an attraction for certain disputants, but might be of concern to those who would wish to see a greater degree of transparency in the field of investment arbitration.[114]

The specific use of the Hague Convention procedures and PCA Optional Rules in arbitral proceedings remains relatively uncommon, but as noted in para 4.2 *supra*, there have been some significant cases which have taken place under relevant Optional Rules, with modifications agreed by the parties. The potential for speedy conduct of arbitral proceedings is demonstrated by the recent award in the *Abyei Arbitration*, handed down little over a year after the arbitration agreement was deposited with the PCA.

REFERENCE

SOURCES OF PREVIOUS CASE LAW, INCLUDING CASE REPORTS

Where parties agree to publication of the award, awards are published on the website of the PCA. Older PCA awards are being made available on-line through the Hague Justice Portal at <http://www.haguejusticeportal.net/>.

Printed copies of awards are available in *The Hague Court Reports Series* (James B Scott (ed), Oxford University Press, 1916–1932), where most early PCA awards are published, and more recent awards have been published in the *PCA Award Series* (TMC Asser Press).

PCA Annual Reports are available on the PCA website, as are the texts of the 1899 and 1907 Hague Conventions and the various sets of Optional Rules referred to in this Chapter.

---

[113] See Chapter 5.

[114] In contrast to ICSID, where a register of arbitrations is maintained and publicly available even if detailed information about the proceedings may be confidential (ICSID Administrative and Financial Regulations, art 22), the PCA does not disclose the identity of the parties to a dispute unless authorized by the parties to do so.

SELECT BIBLIOGRAPHY

N Ando, 'Permanent Court of Arbitration' in R Wolfrum (ed), *Max Planck Encyclopedia of Public International Law* (2008), available at <http://www.mpepil.com/>.

T van den Hout, 'Resolution of International Disputes: The Role of the Permanent Court of Arbitration—Reflections on the Centenary of the 1907 Convention for the Pacific Settlement of International Disputes' (2008) 21(3) *Leiden Journal of International Law* 643.

J van Haersolte-van Hof, 'The Revitalization of the Permanent Court of Arbitration' (2007) 54 *Netherlands International Law Review* 395.

S Rosenne (ed), *The Permanent Court of Arbitration: The Hague Peace Conferences of 1899 and 1907 and International Arbitration—Reports and Documents* (2001).

International Bureau of the Permanent Court of Arbitration, *International Alternative Dispute Resolution Past, Present and Future: The PCA Centennial Papers* (2000).

P Hamilton, H C Requena, L Van Scheltinga, and B Shifman, *The Permanent Court of Arbitration: International Arbitration and Dispute Resolution Summaries of Awards, Settlement Agreements and Reports* (1999).

B Shifman, 'The Revitalisation of the Permanent Court of Arbitration' (1995) 23 *International Journal of Legal Information* 284.

W E Butler, 'The Hague Permanent Court of Arbitration' in Mark W Janis (ed), *International Courts for the Twenty-First Century* (1992) 43–53.

A M Stuyt, *Survey of International Arbitrations 1794–1970* (1972).

M O Hudson, *International Tribunals: Past and Future* (1944).

M O Hudson, 'The Permanent Court of Arbitration' (1933) 27 *AJIL* 440.

J B Scott (ed), *The Reports to the Hague Conventions of 1899 and 1907* (1917) (containing the *travaux préparatoires* of the Conventions).

ANNEX

List of states parties to the 1899/1907 Conventions

(as at 31 July 2009)

Argentina,* Australia, Austria, Bahrain,† Belarus, Belgium, Belize,† Benin,† Bolivia, Brazil, Bulgaria, Burkina Faso, Cambodia, Cameroon, Canada, Chile, China, Colombia, Congo (Dem Rep of), Costa Rica,† Croatia,* Cuba, Cyprus,† Czech Republic,† Denmark, Dominican Republic, Ecuador,* Egypt,† El Salvador, Eritrea,† Estonia,† Ethiopia,* Fiji,* Finland,† France, Germany, Greece,* Guatemala, Guyana,† Haiti, Honduras, Hungary, Iceland, India,* Iran,* Iraq, Ireland,† Israel,† Italy,* Japan, Jordan,† Kenya,† Korea (Rep of),† Kuwait,† Kyrgyzstan, Lao People's Democratic Republic, Latvia,† Lebanon, Libyan Arab Jamahiriya,† Liechtenstein,† Lithuania,† Luxembourg, Macedonia (Former Yugoslav Rep of), Malaysia,† Malta,† Mauritius,* Mexico, Montenegro,* Morocco,† Netherlands, New Zealand,* Nicaragua, Nigeria,† Norway, Pakistan,* Panama, Paraguay, Peru,* Poland,† Portugal, Qatar,† Romania, Russian Federation, Saudi Arabia,† Senegal, Serbia, Singapore,† Slovak Republic,† Slovenia, South Africa,† Spain, Sri Lanka,* Sudan,† Suriname,† Swaziland,† Sweden, Switzerland, Thailand, Togo,† Turkey,* Uganda,† Ukraine, United Arab Emirates,† United Kingdom, United States of America, Uruguay,* Venezuela,* Zambia,† Zimbabwe.*

* Party only to the 1899 Hague Convention. † Party only to the 1907 Hague Convention.

5

THE INTERNATIONAL CENTRE
FOR SETTLEMENT OF
INVESTMENT DISPUTES

Introduction

Name and seat of the body

The International Centre for Settlement of Investment Disputes (ICSID or 'the **5.1**
Centre') was established on 14 October 1966 to provide facilities for the conciliation and arbitration of investment disputes between states and nationals of
other states. The seat of the Centre is at the principal office of the International
Bank for Reconstruction and Development. The contact details of ICSID are:

> ICSID
> 1818 H Street,
> NW MSN U3-301
> Washington, DC
> 20433
> USA
> Tel: (202) 458-1534
> Fax: (202) 522-2615
> Email: ICSIDsecretariat@worldbank.org
> Website: <http://icsid.worldbank.org/ICSID/>

ICSID is one of the institutions of the World Bank group. It was established by
the 1965 Convention on the Settlement of Investment Disputes between States

and Nationals of Other States (the 'ICSID Convention').[1] As of 31 July 2009, the ICSID Convention was in force for 144 states.[2]

Under article 62 of the Convention, ICSID arbitration proceedings are held at the seat of the Centre unless the parties agree otherwise. Article 63(a) of the Convention provides for the conclusion by ICSID of special arrangements with other appropriate institutions for the holding of proceedings at the seat of those institutions if the parties so agree. As of 1 May 2008, special arrangements had been made with nine other institutions.[3] Article 63(b) of the Convention provides that proceedings may be held at other places agreed by the parties, and approved by the tribunal, after consultation with the Secretary-General of ICSID.

General description

5.2 Under the Convention, ICSID provides facilities for conciliation and arbitration of investment disputes between contracting states and individuals and companies that are nationals of other contracting states.[4]

ICSID's organizational structure consists of an Administrative Council and a Secretariat. The Council is the Centre's governing body and is composed of one representative of each contracting state to the Convention.[5] The President of the World Bank serves as non-voting Chairman of the Council.[6] The Administrative Council is responsible for adopting the Centre's Administrative and Financial Regulations and its rules of procedure for conciliation and arbitration.[7] The Administrative Council has also approved the administrative arrangements

---

[1] Convention on the Settlement of Investment Disputes between States and Nationals of Other States, 18 March 1965, 575 UNTS 159 ('ICSID Convention'). For the legislative history, see *ICSID, Convention on the Settlement of Investment Disputes between States and Nationals of Other States, Analysis of Documents Concerning the Origin and the Formulation of the Convention* (1970).

[2] A list of contracting states as at 31 July 2009 appears in the Annex to this Chapter. Of the 144 contracting states as at 31 July 2009, one, Ecuador, had denounced the Convention and its denunciation was due to take effect on 7 January 2010: ICSID News Release, 9 July 2009. In accordance with art 75 of the Convention, the denunciation takes effect six months after the receipt of Ecuador's notice of denunciation. The denunciation of ICSID by Ecuador followed that by Bolivia which took effect on 3 November 2007. Bolivia's denunciation of the Convention raised the question as to the effect of the denunciation in relation to ICSID arbitral proceedings registered before that date. An updated list of ICSID contracting states is published by the Centre and available on the ICSID website. On 27 October 2009, Haiti ratified the ICSID Convention, and the Convention was due to enter into force for Haiti on 26 November 2009.

[3] The institutions with which such arrangements have been concluded are: the Permanent Court of Arbitration at The Hague; the Regional Arbitration Centres of the Asian-African Legal Consultative Committee at Cairo, at Kuala Lumpur, and at Lagos; the Australian Centre for International Commercial Arbitration at Melbourne; the Australian Commercial Disputes Centre at Sydney; the Singapore International Arbitration Centre; the Gulf Cooperation Council Commercial Arbitration Centre at Bahrain; and the German Institution of Arbitration.

[4] See ICSID Convention, art 25(1).

[5] See ibid, art 4(1).

[6] Ibid, art 5.

[7] Ibid, art 6.

concluded between the World Bank and ICSID.[8] The Council also elects the Secretary-General of ICSID.[9]

ICSID does not itself conciliate or arbitrate investment disputes. Rather, conciliation commissions and arbitral tribunals may be constituted for particular disputes in accordance with the provisions of the ICSID Convention. The Convention provides for the establishment of a Panel of Conciliators and a Panel of Arbitrators.[10] Each contracting state may designate four persons to each Panel, and the Chairman may designate ten persons to each panel.[11] Members of conciliation commissions and arbitral tribunals which are constituted in accordance with the Convention may be appointed from the Panels or from outside them.[12] The ICSID Secretariat maintains the Panels of Conciliators and Arbitrators, and provides institutional support to the initiation and conduct of conciliation and arbitration proceedings under the Convention. In essence, the ICSID Convention provides, *inter alia*, for a 'self-contained' framework for the arbitration of investment disputes, including provisions on the initiation and conduct of arbitration proceedings, the recognition and enforcement of awards, and the interpretation, revision, and annulment of awards.

Since 1978, ICSID has also had a set of Additional Facility Rules under which the ICSID Secretariat is authorized to administer certain proceedings between states and nationals of other states that fall outside the scope of the Convention. These include conciliation and arbitration proceedings for the settlement of investment disputes where one of the parties is not a contracting state to the ICSID Convention or a national of such a state. They also include conciliation and arbitration proceedings for the settlement of disputes that do not arise out of an investment, provided that the underlying transaction is not an 'ordinary commercial' one and at least one of the parties is a contracting state or a national of a contracting state. Fact-finding proceedings may also be conducted under the Additional Facility Rules.[13] The Additional Facility Rules comprise a principal set of Rules Governing the Additional Facility and three schedules on Fact-Finding, Conciliation, and Arbitration.

The Secretary-General of ICSID also in certain circumstances acts as the appointing authority of arbitrators for ad hoc arbitrations. This has mostly

---

[8] Ibid, art 6(1)(a)–(d).

[9] Ibid, art 10(1).

[10] Ibid, sec 4.

[11] Ibid, art 13.

[12] Appointments of conciliators or arbitrators by the Chairman of the ICSID Administrative Council under arts 30 and 38 of the Convention, respectively, must be made from the Panels, see arts 31 and 40.

[13] See Rules Governing the Additional Facility for the Administration of Proceedings by the Secretariat of the International Centre for Settlement of Investment Disputes, r 2 ('Additional Facility Rules'), available at <http://icsid.worldbank.org/ICSID/>.

been done in the context of agreements providing for arbitration under the 1976 Arbitration Rules of the United Nations Commission on International Trade Law.

By 30 September 2009, 177 cases had been completed within the ICSID framework,[14] including six conciliation cases and 19 Additional Facility arbitrations. A further 121 cases were pending, including seven Additional Facility proceedings. The annulment process,[15] under article 52 of the ICSID Convention, had been invoked in relation to 37 arbitral awards, with proceedings pending in 17 cases.

In recent years there has been a marked upsurge in the number of cases registered with ICSID. This can be attributed, in large part, to the growth in the number of arbitrations commenced pursuant to investor-state dispute settlement provisions in bilateral investment treaties (BITs). In light of the large number of arbitral tribunals now operating under ICSID's framework, there has been increased attention in recent years to procedural and substantive aspects of ICSID's arbitral process. On the procedural side, amendments to the Arbitration Rules have been adopted to facilitate efficient handling of proceedings, to take into account the increased complexity of some of the cases coming before ICSID tribunals, and to accommodate newer concerns such as greater provisions for transparency and participation in ICSID cases. On substance, there has been debate as to the desirability of consistency in the findings of arbitral tribunals dealing with similar legal issues, and consideration of whether there may be a need for additional post-award mechanisms to address such considerations. ICSID tribunals have also increasingly had to address their relationship with domestic dispute settlement procedures, as they grapple with alleged BIT violations that involve underlying contractual disputes.[16]

Institutional Aspects

Governing texts

Procedural law

5.3   The ICSID Convention provides the institutional and procedural framework for the settlement, through conciliation and arbitration, of investment disputes between governments and foreign investors and determines the scope of

---

[14] In numerous cases, a settlement had been agreed between the parties and proceedings discontinued by agreement; in some cases proceedings were discontinued where payment required under the ICSID Regulations were not duly made. See Administrative and Financial Regulations, r 14.

[15] See *infra* para 5.28.

[16] See generally Y Shany, *Regulating Jurisdictional Relations between National and International Court* (2007) at 63–77.

the jurisdiction of the Centre. Detailed rules of procedure for the institution and conduct of proceedings have been adopted pursuant to the Convention. These are:

(a) Rules of Procedure for the Institution of Conciliation and Arbitration Proceedings ('Institution Rules');

(b) Rules of Procedure for Arbitration Proceedings ('Arbitration Rules'); and

(c) Rules of Procedure for Conciliation Proceedings ('Conciliation Rules').[17]

The latest amendments to the ICSID Regulations and Rules adopted by the Administrative Council came into effect on 10 April 2006. Under the ICSID Convention, the parties are given latitude to decide the procedural framework for the conduct of proceedings. For example, arbitral tribunals ascertain the views of the parties on questions of procedure, and will apply agreements between the parties on procedural matters, except as otherwise provided in the Convention or the Administrative and Financial Regulations.[18] If any question of procedure arises which is not covered by the Convention, the rules of procedure for conciliation or arbitration proceedings, or any rules agreed by the parties, the tribunal shall decide the question.

Pursuant to the Rules Governing the Additional Facility, separate sets of procedural rules apply to proceedings brought under the Additional Facility.[19] The latter set of rules is generally similar to the rules of procedure governing ordinary ICSID proceedings.

The operations of the Administrative Council and the Secretariat are governed by ICSID Administrative and Financial Regulations.[20]

Substantive law

Under article 42 of the Convention, an ICSID tribunal must decide a dispute in accordance with such rules of law as may be agreed by the parties. In the absence of such agreement, the tribunal will apply the law of the contracting state party to the dispute (including its rules on the conflicts of laws) and such rules of

5.4

---

[17] Rules of Procedure for the Institution of Conciliation and Arbitration Proceedings ('Institution Rules'); Rules of Procedure for Arbitration Proceedings ('Arbitration Rules'); and Rules of Procedure for Conciliation Proceedings ('Conciliation Rules'). All Rules are available at <http://icsid.worldbank.org/ICSID/> (Rules/ICSID Convention, Regulations and Rules).

[18] Arbitration Rules, r 20.

[19] Additional Facility Rules, Sch C: Arbitration (Additional Facility) Rules ('Arbitration (Additional Facility) Rules'); Additional Facility Rules, Sch B: Conciliation (Additional Facility) Rules ('Conciliation (Additional Facility) Rules'). In arbitration conducted under the Additional Facility, the parties may agree to apply other sets of procedural rules only to the extent that they are consistent with the Additional Facility Rules: Arbitration (Additional Facility) Rules, art 29(2).

[20] ICSID Administrative and Financial Regulations, *ICSID Convention, Regulations and Rules*, Doc ICSID/15 (April 2006) ('Administrative Regulations'), also available at <http://icsid.worldbank.org/ICSID/> (Rules/ICSID Convention, Regulations and Rules).

international law as may be applicable. Similar choice of law principles also apply in arbitrations conducted under the auspices of the Additional Facility.[21] The tribunal may, if the parties so agree, decide a dispute *ex aequo et bono.*

Given the rise in cases initiated pursuant to bilateral investment treaty dispute settlement provisions, ICSID arbitral tribunals are increasingly called upon to interpret and apply the substantive provisions of such treaties.

Organization

Composition, appointment, and disqualification

5.5 **Panels of Conciliators and of Arbitrators** As noted above, ICSID maintains a Panel of Conciliators and a Panel of Arbitrators.[22] These are rosters, each consisting of up to four persons designated by each contracting state and up to ten persons designated by the Administrative Council Chairman, all for renewable six-year terms. Members of conciliation commissions and arbitral tribunals may be appointed from outside the panels, except in the case of the appointments by the Chairman of the Administrative Council.

5.6 **Composition of conciliation commissions and arbitral tribunals** The Centre is an administrative body under the auspices of which conciliation commissions and arbitral tribunals may be established and proceedings conducted.

A conciliation commission or arbitral tribunal will generally consist of one conciliator or arbitrator appointed by each of the disputing parties and a third, presiding, conciliator or arbitrator appointed by agreement of the parties. The provisions of the Convention give the parties considerable latitude, but ensure at the same time that the absence of agreement between the parties will not prevent the constitution of a conciliation commission or arbitral tribunal. If the commission or tribunal cannot be constituted within 90 days after notice of registration of the request has been dispatched by the Secretary-General, or such other period as the parties may agree, either party may require the Chairman of the Administrative Council to make the necessary appointment or appointments.[23] In practice, the Chairman performs this appointing authority function on the recommendation of the Secretary-General. In conciliation proceedings, the only requirement is that the commission has one or any uneven number of conciliators.[24] In the case of arbitration proceedings there is the further requirement that the majority of the members of the tribunal must be of a nationality other than the state which is a party to the dispute and of the state whose national is

---

[21] Arbitration (Additional Facility) Rules, art 54.
[22] ICSID Convention, art 13. The list of members of the Panels is available on the ICSID website.
[23] Ibid, art 38.
[24] Ibid, art 29(2)(b).

the other party to the dispute. The parties may, however, depart from this rule if each member of the tribunal (or the sole arbitrator) has been appointed by agreement of the parties.[25] Appointment procedures under the Additional Facility Rules are generally similar to those applicable in ordinary ICSID cases.[26]

ICSID conciliators are to clarify the issues in dispute between the parties and endeavour to bring about agreement between them on mutually acceptable terms. The conciliators may recommend terms of settlement to the parties, who must give any such recommendation their most serious consideration.[27] If the parties fail to reach an agreement, the conciliators must close the proceeding with a report noting the failure.[28]

In contrast, the ICSID Convention provides that the award of the arbitrators shall be binding on the parties.[29]

Challenge procedures   A party may propose to a tribunal the disqualification **5.7** of any of its members on account of any fact indicating a manifest lack of the qualities of integrity, competence, and independence required by the Convention for members of the Panels of Conciliators and of Arbitrators.[30] A proposal to disqualify an arbitrator must be made promptly, and in any event before the proceeding is declared closed. Unless the proposal relates to a majority of the members of the tribunal, the other members must promptly consider and vote on the proposal in the absence of the arbitrator concerned. If those members are equally divided, they will notify the Chairman of the Administrative Council of the proposal, of any explanation furnished by the arbitrator concerned, and of their failure to reach a decision. The Chairman will then endeavour to decide the matter within 30 days after he has received the proposal. While the proposal for disqualification is pending, the arbitral proceedings are suspended.[31]

Challenges to arbitrators have now been raised in a number of ICSID arbitrations, and a few decisions have been published.[32] In 2008, Ziadé noted that since

---

[25] Ibid, art 39.

[26] Arbitration (Additional Facility) Rules, arts 6–11. In contrast to ordinary ICSID proceedings, in which chairpersons for arbitration tribunals, who are selected by the Chairman of the Administrative Council, can come only from the Panel of Arbitrators (ICSID Convention, art 40), there is no such limitation in cases conducted under the Additional Facility auspices.

[27] ICSID Convention, art 34(1).

[28] Ibid, art 34(2).

[29] Ibid, art 53(1).

[30] Ibid, art 57.

[31] Arbitration Rules, r 9.

[32] For example, *SGS v Pakistan* (ICSID Case No ARB/01/13), Decision on Claimant's Proposal to Disqualify Arbitrator, 19 December 2002, (2005) 8 ICSID Rep 398; Suez, *Sociedad General de Aguas de Barcelona SA and Interagua Servicios Integrales de Agua SA v Argentine Republic* (ICSID Case No ARB/03/17), Decision on Proposal for Disqualification of a Member of the Arbitral Tribunal, 22 October 2007. There have been numerous other unpublished decisions. See C Harris, 'Arbitrator Bias in Investment and Commercial Arbitration' 5(4) *Transnational Dispute Management* (2008).

ICSID's establishment in 1966, there had been 30 proposals for disqualification, and of those 11 had been filed in 2007–2008.[33] Proposals for disqualification have rarely been successful, although on occasion arbitrators have withdrawn before a decision on a challenge was made.[34]

In *Vivendi v Argentine Republic,* an ad hoc annulment committee confirmed that the challenge procedure in article 57 of the Convention and article 9 of the Arbitration Rules was also applicable to the membership of ad hoc committees.[35] In considering the standard to be applied, the *Vivendi* Committee observed that 'the mere existence of some professional relationship with a party is not an automatic basis for disqualification of an arbitrator or committee member. All circumstances need to be considered in order to determine whether the relationship is significant enough to justify entertaining reasonable doubts as to the capacity of the arbitrator or member to render a decision freely and independently.'[36]

The Arbitration Rules contain a provision relating to disclosure by arbitrators before or at the first session of the tribunal, which was expanded by amendment in 2006. Each arbitrator must provide a statement of past and present professional business and other relationships (if any) with the parties as well as 'any other circumstance that might cause [his or her] reliability for independent judgment to be questioned by a party'.[37] Such disclosure constitutes a continuing obligation during the proceedings.

It is noteworthy that, in 2008, an ICSID tribunal issued a decision concerning the participation of counsel in ICSID proceedings where party appointed counsel and the President of the Tribunal were members of the same barristers' chambers in London.[38] In making this decision, the tribunal referred to its inherent powers to take measures to preserve the integrity of the proceedings, as well as to article 44 of the Convention, which permits a tribunal to decide any question of procedure not covered by the Convention or Arbitration Rules, or by any rules agreed by the parties.[39]

---

[33] N Ziadé, 'Recent Developments at ICSID' (2008) 25 *News from ICSID* 3 at 4, available at <http://icsid.worldbank.org/ICSID>. Ziadé observes, however, that six challenges were made against a single person who served as a tribunal member in related cases.

[34] Ibid.

[35] *Compania de Aguas Aconquija SA & Vivendi Universal v Argentine Republic* (ICSID Case No ARB/97/3), Decision on Challenge to the President of the Committee, (2002) 17 *ICSID Review—FILJ* 168.

[36] Ibid, para 28.

[37] Arbitration Rules, r 6(2).

[38] *Hvratska Elektroprivreda dd v Republic of Slovenia* (ICSID Case No ARB/05/24), Order Concerning Participation of Counsel, 6 May 2008.

[39] Art 44 provides that if any question of procedure arises which is not covered by the Convention, the Arbitration Rules or any rules agreed by the parties, the tribunal shall decide the question. The tribunal acknowledged that the fact that counsel and a member of the tribunal were members of the same chambers did not necessarily imply that one should always withdraw from ICSID arbitral proceedings. Nonetheless, it took into account the circumstances of the

Plenary/chambers

Unless the parties agree otherwise, the presence of a majority of the tribunal is **5.8** required at its sittings. In practice, parties often agree that the full tribunal shall be present at its sittings.[40] Parties also frequently agree that certain procedural issues may be decided by the presiding arbitrator alone.

Appellate structure

There is no appeal mechanism under the ICSID Convention. Arbitral awards **5.9** rendered under the ICSID Convention are to be binding on the parties and not subject to appeal or to any other remedy except those provided for in the Convention.[41] Four post-award remedies are provided in the Convention. These are rectification or supplementation, interpretation, revision, and annulment. A request for rectification or supplementation of the award will be submitted to the tribunal that rendered the award. If possible, a request for interpretation and revision of an award will also be submitted to the tribunal that rendered the award. If this is not possible, a new tribunal will be constituted.[42] An application to annul an award will be referred to a three-member ad hoc committee appointed by the Chairman of the Administrative Council. The committee members must be drawn from the Panel of Arbitrators. None of them may be a member of the tribunal that rendered the award, or have the same nationality of any such member. Nor may an ad hoc committee member have the nationality of the state party to the dispute or of the state whose national is a party to the dispute or have been designated to the Panel of Arbitrators by either of those states. An ad hoc committee member may, moreover, not have acted as a conciliator in the same dispute. The ad hoc committee has authority to annul the whole award or a part thereof.[43] There is no comparable annulment procedure under the Additional Facility Rules.

Scientific and technical experts

The tribunal may call upon the parties to produce experts, and the parties may **5.10** present oral testimony of expert witnesses before the tribunal. The tribunal may

---

case, in particular the facts that the respondent had retained the counsel in question after the tribunal had been established, that it had not informed the claimant or the tribunal of counsel's involvement until a very late stage, and that it had refused to disclose the scope of his involvement in the proceedings. In the circumstances, the tribunal considered that in order to avoid the risk of justifiable perception of partiality, had the respondent's counsel participated in the proceedings, the President of the tribunal would have had to resign. Referring to the immutability of properly constituted tribunals, under art 56(1) of the Convention the tribunal ordered that counsel should not participate.

[40] Arbitration Rules, r 14(2).
[41] See ICSID Convention, art 53(4).
[42] Ibid, arts 50, 51.
[43] Ibid, art 52.

also admit evidence given by an expert in a written deposition. In addition, the tribunal may, with the consent of both parties, arrange for the examination of an expert otherwise than before the tribunal itself. In that case the parties may participate in the examination.[44]

Registry

5.11 The role of the ICSID Secretariat is principally defined in the Administrative and Financial Regulations. These Regulations require the Secretariat to maintain case registers;[45] to serve as the channel of written communications between the parties and the arbitrators;[46] to administer the finances of the direct costs of the proceeding;[47] to make arrangements for hearings and other meetings of ICSID tribunals;[48] to provide 'other assistance' as requested;[49] and to perform depositary functions.[50] The Secretariat is headed by a Secretary-General elected by the Council for a period of six years.[51] The ICSID Secretariat also provides for the administrative needs of the Additional Facility.[52]

The existence, current status, and final disposition of the case are matters of public record in ICSID proceedings. Under the Administrative and Financial Regulations, the Secretary-General is required to maintain a register for each request for arbitration. The Secretary-General must enter into the register all significant data concerning the institution, conduct, and disposition of the case. The particular data concerning the method of constitution and membership of the arbitral tribunal must be entered, and in regard to any award, data concerning any request for any of the Convention's post-award remedies of rectification or supplementation, interpretation, revision, and annulment, and any stay of enforcement of the award. The Administrative and Financial Regulations provide that the registers shall be open for inspection by any person.[53] In addition, register entries for pending cases are published in the Annual Report of the Centre, on the ICSID website, and in the twice-yearly newsletter, *News from ICSID*.

---

[44] Arbitration Rules, r 36. See also Arbitration (Additional Facility) Rules, arts 42, 43. Under these provisions the tribunal may also appoint one or more experts to prepare a report and testify before it.
[45] Administrative Regulations, reg 23.
[46] Ibid, reg 25.
[47] Ibid, reg 14.
[48] Ibid, reg 26.
[49] Ibid, reg 25(c).
[50] Ibid, reg 28.
[51] ICSID Convention, art 10(1). The current Secretary-General is Meg Kinnear. She is the first Secretary-General to serve on a full-time basis (with effect from June 2009).
[52] Rules Governing the Additional Facility for the Administration of Proceedings by the ICSID Secretariat, 1978, Sch A: Administrative and Financial Rules (Additional Facility).
[53] Administrative Regulations, reg 23.

Jurisdiction and access

The principal provision regarding the jurisdiction of the Centre is article 25(1) of the ICSID Convention:

> The jurisdiction of the Centre extends to any legal dispute arising directly out of an investment, between a Contracting State (or any constituent sub-division or agency of a Contracting State designated to the Centre by that state) and a national of another Contracting State, which the parties to the dispute consent in writing to submit to the Centre. When the parties have given their consent, no party may withdraw its consent unilaterally.

Thus, while consent has been referred to as the 'cornerstone of the jurisdiction of the Centre',[54] the further requirements relating to the nature of the dispute and the parties thereto must also be met. The jurisdictional requirements have been addressed in many ICSID cases in which objections to a tribunal's jurisdiction have been raised.[55]

Ratione personae

Article 25(1) requires that one of the parties must be a contracting state and the **5.12** other party must be a 'national of another Contracting State'. The facilities of the Centre are therefore not available for disputes between non-state parties or for disputes between states; they are available only for disputes between non-state parties on the one hand and state parties on the other hand. The non-state party must be a 'national of another Contracting State'. This term covers both natural and juridical persons. Under article 25(2) of the Convention, a natural person is precluded from access to the Centre if the person, in addition to being a national of another contracting state, is also a national of the state party to the dispute. In contrast, a juridical person that is a national of the state party to the dispute may be a party to an ICSID proceeding if it and the state party to the dispute have agreed to treat the juridical person as a national of another contracting state because of foreign control.[56]

The Rules Governing the Additional Facility have expanded the application of ICSID's facilities so as to include parties that do not meet the jurisdictional requirements of the ICSID Convention. Under those rules, a state (or a constituent division or agency thereof) and a national of another state may agree to

---

[54] See International Bank for Reconstruction and Development. Report of the Executive Directors on the Convention on the Settlement of Investment Disputes between States and National of Other States, 18 March 1965, para 23, available at <http://icsid.worldbank.org/ICSID/> (Rules/ICSID Convention, Regulations and Rules).

[55] See generally C Schreuer, L Malintoppi, A Reinisch, and A Sinclair, *ICSID Convention: A Commentary* (2nd edn, 2009) at 71 et seq.

[56] See A Broches, 'The Convention on the Settlement of Investment Disputes between States and Nationals of Other States' in *Selected Essays by A Broches: World Bank, ICSID and Other Subjects of Public and Private International Law* (1995) 188 at 201.

utilize the Additional Facility, even if one of the relevant states (ie the state party to the dispute or the state of nationality of the private party) is not a party to the ICSID Convention.[57] However, prior to the initiation of proceedings, the agreement of the parties to accept the jurisdiction of the Additional Facility must be approved by the Secretary-General.[58]

Ratione materiae

5.13 The Convention requires that the dispute must be a 'legal dispute arising directly out of an investment'. The Convention does not define the term 'legal dispute' or 'investment'. In their 1965 Report on the ICSID Convention, the Executive Directors of the World Bank stated, in connection with the former term, 'that while conflicts of rights are within the jurisdiction of the Centre, mere conflicts of interests are not'. The Report said further that 'the dispute must concern the existence or scope of a legal right or obligation, or the nature or extent of the reparation to be made for breach of a legal obligation'. Although a number of definitions of 'investment' were considered at the time of the negotiation of the Convention, none was agreed upon 'given the essential requirement of consent by the parties'.[59]

As is the case in other forms of international arbitration, there can be no recourse to arbitration under the ICSID Convention unless the parties have agreed to this in writing. Once both parties have consented, neither may revoke its consent unilaterally. The consent may be given in regard to an existing dispute or with respect to a defined class of future disputes. The consent of the

---

[57] Additional Facility Rules, art 4(3).

[58] See Additional Facility Rules, art 4.

[59] A number of ICSID tribunals have elaborated upon the definition of 'investment' for the purposes of art 25. In *Fedax v Venezuela* (ICSID Case No ARB/96/3, Decision on Jurisdiction, 11 July 1997) and *Salini v Morocco* (ICSID Case No ARB/00/4, Decision on Jurisdiction, 23 July 2001), the tribunals referred to certain criteria implicated by the concept of investment, including a certain duration, regularity of profit and return, assumption of risk, substantial commitment, and a contribution to the economic development of the host state. This approach has been followed by a number of other tribunals. Others, however, have treated it with more caution, with the tribunal in *Biwater Gauff v Tanzania* observing that there was no basis for 'overly strict application of the five *Salini* criteria in every case. These criteria are not fixed or mandatory as a matter of law.' The tribunal observed that strict application of such criteria 'risks arbitrary exclusion of certain types of transaction from the scope of the Convention'. *Biwater Gauff v Tanzania*, Award, 24 July 2008, paras 312, 314. An ad hoc annulment committee has also been critical of this approach to the definition of 'investment' for the purposes of art 25 of the Convention, where it led a sole arbitrator to disregard the definition of investment in the bilateral investment treaty under which the arbitral proceedings had been brought, *Malaysia Historical Salvors v Malaysia* (ICSID Case No ARB/05/10), Decision on the Application for Annulment, 16 April 2009, paras 56–82. See also *Pantechniki S.A. Contractors and Engineers v Republic of Albania* (ICSID Case No ARB/07/21), Award of 30 July 2009, paras 35–49. See generally R Dolzer, 'The Notion of Investment in Recent Practice' in S Charnovitz, D Steger, and P van den Bossche (eds), *Law in the Service of Human Dignity: Essays in Honour of Florentino Feliciano* (2005) 261–275; D Krishnan, 'A Notion of ICSID Investment' in I Laird and T Weiler (eds), 1 *Investment Treaty Arbitration and International Law* (2008) 61.

parties need not be given in a single instrument. In the above-mentioned 1965 Report, the Executive Directors suggested that 'a host State might in its investment promotion legislation offer to submit disputes arising out of certain classes of investments to the jurisdiction of the Centre, and the investor might give his consent by accepting the offer in writing'.[60]

Many states have given consent to ICSID arbitration in bilateral investment treaties. Such treaties generally provide investors that qualify as a national of the other state broad guarantees against unfair and discriminatory treatment, expropriation, and currency transfer restrictions. This type of general consent to ICSID arbitration has also been included in the investment provisions of several multilateral treaties, including the North American Free Trade Agreement (NAFTA) and the Energy Charter Treaty. Where proceedings are initiated under such bilateral, regional, or sectoral investment treaties, the ICSID arbitral tribunal will have regard to the terms of the treaty in assessing whether the respondent has given valid consent to ICSID arbitration.

Upon ratification of the Convention, states may notify ICSID of the classes of investment disputes that they would or would not consider submitting to the jurisdiction of the Centre.[61] Seven states had made notifications to this effect by 31 July 2009.[62]

The parties to a dispute may refer to the Additional Facility a dispute that does not arise directly from an investment, subject to the prior approval of the Secretary-General, before initiation of proceedings. The Secretary-General shall approve an arbitration agreement only if he or she is satisfied that the underlying transaction has features which distinguish it from an ordinary commercial transaction.[63] However, if the Secretary-General believes that an arbitral tribunal might consider the dispute to be an investment dispute, he or she may require the parties to refer the case first to ordinary ICSID proceedings (provided that personal jurisdiction requirements have been met).[64]

Ratione temporis

The ICSID Convention and the Additional Facility Rules do not provide time limits for the submission of disputes to ICSID. This question is governed by **5.14**

---

[60] See Broches, *supra* note 52, at 207.

[61] ICSID Convention, art 25(4).

[62] Contracting States and Measures Taken by Them for the Purposes of the Convention, Notifications concerning Classes of Disputes Considered Suitable or Unsuitable for Submission to the Centre (art 25(4) of the Convention), ICSID 8-D, available at <http://icsid.worldbank.org/ICSID/> (Documents/Official Documents/Contracting States and Measures Taken by Them for the Purposes of the Convention).

[63] Additional Facility Rules, art 4(3). Ecuador made a notification under art 25(4) in December 2007 and subsequently denounced the Convention in July 2009.

[64] Ibid, art 4(4).

the parties' consent, which may be given in respect of an existing dispute, or in respect of a defined class of future disputes.

It may be noted that under the ICSID Convention, a contracting state may require the exhaustion of local administrative or judicial remedies as a condition for its consent to arbitration under the Convention.[65]

Further temporal restrictions may be imposed by the instrument in which consent to ICSID arbitration is given. For example, bilateral investment treaties frequently stipulate that the parties to an investor-state dispute must attempt to settle the dispute amicably, often for a period of six months, before invoking the other dispute settlement mechanisms provided in the treaty.[66]

Advisory jurisdiction

5.15   The Convention does not provide for the rendition by ICSID tribunals of advisory opinions. As noted above, cases may be brought for non-binding conciliation under the Convention or Additional Facility Rules or for fact finding under the Additional Facility Rules.

Procedural Aspects

Languages

5.16   The Centre has three official languages: English, French, and Spanish.[67] The parties to a proceeding are free to agree to the use of one or two of these languages in the proceeding.[68] The parties may agree on a language that is not an official language of the Centre, provided that the tribunal, after consultation with the Secretary-General, gives its approval. If two procedural languages are selected by the parties, any instruments may be filed in either language and either language may be used at the hearings, provided that the necessary arrangements are made for translation and interpretation.[69]

Instituting proceedings

5.17   The Convention sets forth procedures for the registration of requests for conciliation or arbitration, requiring the claimant, or both parties, to provide information concerning the issues in dispute, the identity of the parties, and their consent to the jurisdiction of the Centre.[70] Under the Convention, the

---

[65] ICSID Convention, art 26.
[66] See also, for example, NAFTA, arts 1116 and 1117, which impose express time limits on claims.
[67] Administrative Regulations, reg 34.
[68] Arbitration Rules, r 22(1).
[69] Ibid, r 22(2). See also Arbitration (Additional Facility) Rules, art 30.
[70] ICSID Convention, art 36.

Secretary-General is required to register the request, unless he finds, on the basis of the information contained in the request, that the dispute is manifestly outside the jurisdiction of the Centre.[71] The registration procedure serves the purpose of screening requests and is not a procedure to determine jurisdiction. As emphasized in the Report on the Convention of the World Bank's Executive Directors, 'registration of a request by the Secretary-General does not, of course, preclude a Commission or Tribunal from finding that the dispute is outside the jurisdiction of the Centre'.[72] Detailed provisions on the institution of proceedings are contained in the Institution Rules. Rule 2(1) of the Institution Rules, which Reed et al describe as a 'practical checklist for ensuring ICSID jurisdiction',[73] stipulates that the request shall:

(a) designate precisely each party to the dispute and state the address of each;
(b) state, if one of the parties is a constituent subdivision or agency of a contracting state, that it has been designated to the Centre by that state pursuant to Article 25(1) of the Convention;
(c) indicate the date of consent and the instruments in which it is recorded, including, if one party is a constituent subdivision or agency of a contracting state, similar data on the approval of such consent by that state unless it had notified the Centre that no such approval is required;
(d) indicate with respect to the party that is a national of a contracting state:
   (i) its nationality on the date of consent; and
   (ii) if the party is a natural person:
      (A) his nationality on the date of the request; and
      (B) that he did not have the nationality of the contracting state party to the dispute either on the date of consent or on the date of the request; or
   (iii) if the party is a juridical person which on the date of consent had the nationality of the contracting state party to the dispute, the agreement of the parties that it should be treated as a national of another contracting state for the purposes of the Convention; and
(e) contain information concerning the issues in dispute indicating that there is, between the parties, a legal dispute arising directly out of an investment.[74]

The request must be submitted in the form of a signed original, accompanied by five copies and a non-refundable lodging fee of US$25,000.[75] Where a request is registered by the Secretary-General, the parties are notified of the registration and invited to proceed to constitute a tribunal. A proceeding under the Convention is deemed to have been instituted on the date of the registration of the request.[76]

---

[71] Institution Rules, at r 6.
[72] Report of the Executive Directors of the World Bank, *supra* note 54, para 38.
[73] L Reed, J Paulsson, and N Blackaby, *Guide to ICSID Arbitration* (2004) at 27.
[74] Institution Rules, r 2.
[75] ICSID Schedule of Fees (1 January 2008), para 1.
[76] Institution Rules, r 6.

If the Secretary-General finds on the basis of the information in the request that the dispute is manifestly outside the jurisdiction of the Centre, he notifies the parties of the non-registration of the request with reasons.[77]

The Additional Facility Arbitration Rules set out the required content of a notice of arbitration to initiate proceedings under the Additional Facility.[78]

Financial assistance

5.18 ICSID does not offer any special programme of financial assistance to the parties to cases before it.

The ICSID Schedule of Fees sets out, *inter alia*, fees for lodging requests, administrative charges for use of the Centre, and fees and expenses of arbitrators, conciliators, and ad hoc committee members. Administrative charges of the Centre for particular proceedings may include, for example, out-of-pocket expenses, such as communications costs and charges for interpretation services.

Parties to ICSID proceedings can benefit from the infrastructure of the World Bank Group for the proceeding (for meeting rooms, for example).

Preliminary proceedings/objections

5.19 As early as possible after the constitution of the tribunal, the president will seek to ascertain the views of the parties with respect to questions of procedure.[79]

The Convention provides that any objection by a party to proceedings that a dispute is not within the jurisdiction of the Centre, or for other reasons is not within the competence of the tribunal, shall be considered by the tribunal. The tribunal determines whether to deal with the objection as a preliminary question or to join it to the merits.[80] Jurisdictional objections in ICSID proceedings are quite common and arbitral proceedings frequently incorporate a separate phase for dealing with jurisdictional objections. In some instances certain jurisdictional questions have been joined to the merits.[81]

Under the Arbitration Rules, a jurisdictional objection must be made as early as possible and in any event no later than the expiration of the time limit for the filing of the counter-memorial, unless the facts on which the objection are based are unknown to the party at that time.[82] Upon the filing of jurisdictional

---

[77] Ibid, r 6.

[78] Arbitration (Additional Facility) Rules, arts 3, 4.

[79] Arbitration Rules, r 20.

[80] ICSID Convention, art 41(2). See also Arbitration (Additional Facility) Rules, art 46.

[81] See eg *Tradex Hellas SA v Republic of Albania* (ICSID Case No ARB/94/2), Decision on Jurisdiction of 24 December 1996, (2002) 5 ICSID Rep 47.

[82] Arbitration Rules, r 41(1). Objections relating to ancillary claims must be made by the expiration of the time limit for filing of the rejoinder.

objections, the president of the tribunal fixes time limits within which the parties may file observations on the objections. The tribunal may decide to suspend proceedings on the merits.[83]

The tribunal decides whether or not there shall be a hearing on the objections to jurisdiction. The Arbitration Rules further provide that if the tribunal upholds jurisdiction or joins the objections to the merits, it shall fix time limits for the further procedures.[84] If the tribunal declines jurisdiction it shall render an award to that effect.[85] It should also be noted that the tribunal may at any stage of the proceeding, on its own initiative, consider whether the dispute before it is within the jurisdiction of the Centre and its own competence.[86]

The amendments to the Arbitration Rules of 2006 provide an additional basis for raising a preliminary objection: that the claim is 'manifestly without legal merit'.[87] A party has 30 days after a tribunal is constituted to submit such a preliminary objection and must 'specify as precisely as possible the basis for the objection'. The other party is given the right to respond, and the tribunal is required to rule on the objection at its first session or promptly thereafter. Parra has observed that:

> The Secretariat is powerless to prevent the initiation of proceedings that clear the jurisdictional threshold, but are frivolous as to the merits. This had been a source of recurring complaints from some respondent governments. One of the amendments to the ICSID Arbitration Rules made in 2006 was to introduce a procedure, in Rule 41, for the early dismissal by arbitral tribunals of patently unmeritorious claims.[88]

By July 2009, such objections had been raised in at least two proceedings, but in neither case was the objection upheld. The tribunal in *Trans-Global Petroleum Inc v Jordan* observed that as a basic principle of procedural fairness, an award under article 41(5) could only apply to a clear and obvious case, and that, through the use of the term 'manifestly', the standard was set high.[89]

---

[83] Ibid, r 41(3).

[84] Ibid, r 41(4).

[85] Ibid, r 41(6).

[86] Ibid, r 41(2).

[87] Ibid, r 41(5). Under the amended rule, parties may also agree to another expedited procedure for making preliminary objections.

[88] A Parra, 'The Development of the Regulations and Rules of the International Centre for Settlement of Investment Disputes' (2007) 41 *International Lawyer* 47 at 56.

[89] *Trans-Global Petroleum Inc v Hashemite Kingdom of Jordan* (ICSID Case No ARB/07/25), Decision on the Respondent's Objection under rule 41(5) of the ICSID Arbitration Rules, 12 May 2008, paras 88 and 92. See also *Brandes Investment Partners LP v Bolivarian Republic of Venezuela* (ICSID Case No ARB/08/03), Decision on the Respondent's Objection under rule 41(5) of the ICSID Arbitration Rules, 2 February 2009.

Provisional measures

5.20 At any time during a proceeding a party may request that provisional measures
for the preservation of its rights be recommended by the tribunal.[90] A request
for provisional measures must specify the right to be preserved and the circumstances that require such measures. The tribunal may also recommend provisional measures on its own initiative or recommend measures other than those
specified in a request. The tribunal may only recommend provisional measures,
or modify or revoke its recommendations, after giving each party an opportunity of presenting its observations. Parties to ICSID Convention arbitration
proceedings may only request judicial or other authorities to order provisional
measures if the agreement recording their consent to arbitration so stipulates.[91]
Amendments to the Arbitration Rules introduced in 2006 allow requests for
provisional measures to be submitted as soon as a dispute is registered with
ICSID, even before the tribunal has been constituted. In such circumstances,
the Secretary-General may fix time limits for the parties to submit observations
on the request, so that the issue may be considered by the tribunal promptly
upon its constitution.

Measures recommended by ICSID tribunals have included,[92] for example, a
stay of local arbitration,[93] a stay of a bankruptcy proceeding,[94] a recommendation that a state take whatever steps necessary to ensure that a public corporation
refrain from enforcing a final judgment against an ICSID claimant, as well as
measures for the preservation of evidence.[95] An ICSID tribunal has stressed that
any preliminary measure ordered by a tribunal must relate to the subject matter
of the case and not to separate, unrelated, or extraneous matters.[96] In terms of
the circumstances in which provisional measures may be recommended, tribunals appear to have acknowledged that such measures might be appropriate, for
example, where the need for them is urgent and necessary to preserve the status
quo or avoid the occurrence of irreparable harm or damage, or to prevent parties

---

[90] Arbitration Rules, r 39. While rule 39 of the Arbitration Rules states that parties may request that
provisional measures be 'recommended' by the tribunal, the tribunal in *Maffezini v Spain* suggested
that 'the tribunal's authority to rule on provisional measures is no less binding than that of a final award'.
Maffezini v Spain (ICSID Case No ARB/97/7), Procedural Order No 2, 28 October 1999, para 9.

[91] ICSID Convention, art 47; Arbitration Rules, r 39(6). See also Arbitration (Additional
Facility) Rules, art 47.

[92] A Antonietti, 'ICSID and Provisional Measures: An Overview' (2004) 21 *News from ICSID*
10 at 11.

[93] *SGS v Pakistan* (ICSID Case No ARB/01/13), Procedural Order No 2, 16 October 2002.

[94] *CSOB v Slovak Republic* (ICSID Case No ARB/97/4), Procedural Order No 4, 11 January
1999, Procedural Order No 5, 1 March 2000.

[95] *Biwater Gauff (Tanzania) Ltd v United Republic of Tanzania* (ICSID Case No ARB/05/22),
Procedural Order No 1, 31 March 2006.

[96] *Maffezini v Spain* (ICSID Case No ARB/97/7), Procedural Order No 2, 28 October 1999,
para 23.

from taking measures capable of having a prejudicial effect on the rendering or implementation of an eventual award, or that might aggravate or extend the dispute or render its resolution more difficult.[97]

Written pleadings

An arbitration proceeding under the ICSID Convention (or the Additional **5.21** Facility) generally consists of two distinct phases, comprising written and oral proceedings. A proceeding may have separate written and oral procedures in regard to such matters as a request for provisional measures and objections to jurisdiction, as well as in regard to the merits of the dispute.

In addition to the request for arbitration, the written procedure normally consists of a memorial by the requesting party, a counter-memorial by the other party, a reply by the requesting party, and a rejoinder by the other party.[98] The Arbitration Rules provide that a memorial shall contain a statement of the relevant facts, a statement of law, and the submissions. A counter-memorial, reply, or rejoinder shall contain an admission or denial of the facts stated in the last previous pleading; any additional facts, if necessary; observations concerning the statement of law in the last previous pleading; a statement of law in answer thereto; and the submissions. All written pleadings must be filed with the Secretary-General within time limits fixed by the tribunal.[99]

Oral arguments

The Arbitration Rules provide for the possibility of holding a pre-hearing con- **5.22** ference between the tribunal and the parties. Such hearing may be held at the request of the Secretary-General or at the discretion of the president of the tribunal to arrange for an exchange of information and the stipulation of uncontested facts in order to expedite the proceeding. A pre-hearing conference may also take place at the request of the parties to consider issues in dispute with a view to reaching an amicable settlement.[100]

The oral procedure consists of the hearing by the tribunal of parties and their representatives and of any witnesses and experts.[101] Unless either party objects, the tribunal may allow other persons to attend or observe all or part of the hearings subject to appropriate logistical arrangements. In such cases the tribunal establishes procedures for the protection of proprietary or privileged information. The possibility of wider attendance at the oral hearing unless a party objects

---

[97] See eg *Plama Consortium Limited v Bulgaria* (ICSID Case No ARB/03/24), Order of 6 September 2005, para 38.

[98] Arbitration Rules, r 29; Arbitration (Additional Facility) Rules, art 36.

[99] Arbitration Rules, r 31; Arbitration (Additional Facility) Rules, art 38.

[100] Arbitration Rules, r 21.

[101] Ibid, r 32.

was introduced in the 2006 amendments to the Arbitration Rules. Prior to the amendment to the Arbitration Rules, affirmative agreement of the parties was required in order to open the hearings to non-parties.[102]

The Additional Facility Arbitration Rules pertaining to oral hearings are generally similar to those governing ordinary ICSID proceedings.[103]

Third party intervention

5.23 Amendments to the Arbitration Rules in 2006 provide for non-party participation in ICSID proceedings in certain circumstances (see para 5.24 below).

Amicus curiae

5.24 Until 2006, the ICSID Convention and Rules, and the Additional Facility Rules, did not explicitly provide a procedure for the submission of *amicus curiae* briefs. Nonetheless, reflecting developments in other international tribunals, two ICSID tribunals in cases against the Argentine Republic had in 2005 and 2006 determined that in principle they had the power, under article 44 of the ICSID Convention, to admit *amicus curiae* submissions from suitable non-parties in appropriate cases.[104]

With effect from 10 April 2006, rule 37(2) of the Arbitration Rules provides that, having consulted both parties, the tribunal may allow a person or entity that is not a party to the dispute to file a written submission regarding a matter within the scope of the dispute. The tribunal has discretion whether to allow such a filing and shall consider, among other matters, the extent to which the non-disputing party submission would assist the tribunal in the determination of a legal or factual issue by bringing a perspective, particular knowledge, or insight that is different from the disputing parties. The tribunal will also consider the

---

[102] Ibid, r 32(2). See also Arbitration (Additional Facility) Rules, art 39(2). See Parra, *supra* note 83, at 56. In *Biwater Gauff v Tanzania*, the claimant objected to the presence at the oral hearings of a number of non-governmental organizations (which had been permitted to submit written statements—see *infra* para 5.24) and, under new rule 32(2), the tribunal noted that it therefore had no power to permit their presence or participation. *Biwater Gauff v Tanzania* (ICSID Case No ARB/05/22), Procedural Order No 5, 2 February 2007, paras 69–72.

[103] Arbitration (Additional Facility) Rules, arts 29, 39–43.

[104] *Suez Sociedad General de Aguas de Barcelona SA and Vivendi v Argentine Republic* (ICSID Case No ARB/03/19), Order in Response to a Petition for Transparency and Participation as *Amici Curiae*, 19 May 2005; *Agua Provinciales de Santa Fe SA and others v Argentine Republic* (ICSID Case No ARB/03/17), Order in Response to Petition for Participation as *Amici Curiae*, 17 March 2006. The considerations taken into account by the ICSID tribunals were similar to those considered by the NAFTA tribunal in *Methanex Corp v United States*, Decision of the Tribunal on Petitions for Third Persons to Intervene as 'Amici Curiae', 15 January 2001. Wider public interest considerations were cited as a significant factor. Both ICSID cases concerned the provision of water services. An earlier ICSID tribunal dealing with a claim relating to the provision of water services had denied an *amicus* request in a case against the Republic of Bolivia. *Aguas del Tunari SA v Republic of Bolivia* (ICSID Case No ARB/02/03).

extent to which the non-disputing party will consider a matter within the scope of the dispute and has a significant interest. The tribunal is to ensure that any non-disputing party submission does not disrupt the proceedings or unduly burden or unfairly prejudice either party, and that each party is given an opportunity to present observations on the non-disputing party submission. Under amended rule 37(2), the tribunal in *Biwater Gauff v Tanzania* allowed a petition for participation of non-disputing parties in February 2007, subject to certain procedural safeguards.[105]

Representation of the parties

Parties to ICSID Convention proceedings may appear in person or be represented by any other person of their choice.[106] Although legal representation is, therefore, not a requirement, parties to ICSID proceedings have generally retained counsel. **5.25**

Decision

The final decision of a tribunal is rendered in the form of an award. Under the Convention the arbitral tribunal shall decide questions by a majority of the votes of its members. The award shall be in writing and signed by the members of the tribunal who voted for it and shall deal with every question submitted to the tribunal, and state the reasons on which it is based.[107] **5.26**

The award must be drawn up and signed within 120 days after the closure of the proceeding. This period may be extended by the tribunal for a further 60 days if it would otherwise be unable to draw up the award.[108]

The Arbitration Rules set out the required content of the award, which includes: a statement that the tribunal was established under the Convention, and a description of the method of its constitution; a summary of the proceeding; a statement of the facts as found by the tribunal; the submissions of the parties; the decision of the tribunal on every question submitted to it, together with the reasons upon which the decision is based; and any decision of the tribunal regarding the cost of the proceeding.[109]

If parties to an arbitration proceeding agree to settle their dispute before the award is rendered, they may request the tribunal to record the settlement in the form of its award.[110]

---

[105] *Biwater Gauff, supra* note 102.

[106] Arbitration Rules, r 18.

[107] ICSID Convention, art 48.

[108] Arbitration Rules, r 46.

[109] Ibid, r 47. See also Arbitration (Additional Facility) Rules, art 53. However, the Additional Facility Rules require only that particular (i) be specified.

[110] Ibid, r 43(1). See also Arbitration (Additional Facility) Rules, art 53(4).

Once issued, the award is final and binding upon the parties.[111] The award will be published by ICSID only with the consent of the parties. However, the Arbitration Rules provide that ICSID shall promptly include in its publications excerpts of the legal reasoning of the tribunal.[112] In practice, now, most ICSID awards are published or otherwise made publicly accessible.

Rectification or supplementation, revision, and interpretation of awards

5.27 On the request of a party made within 45 days of the rendition of an award, the tribunal may, after notice to the other party, decide any question which it omitted to decide in the award.[113] The tribunal shall also rectify any clerical, arithmetical, or similar error in the award. The tribunal's decision shall become part of the award. If a dispute arises between the parties in regard to the meaning or scope of an award, either party may request an interpretation. A request for interpretation of an award will, if possible, be submitted to the same tribunal that rendered the award.[114]

Either party may also request revision of the award on the ground of discovery of some fact of such a nature as decisively to affect the award, provided that when the award was rendered that fact was unknown to the tribunal and to the requesting party. It is a further requirement that the requesting party's ignorance was not due to negligence.[115]

If it considers that the circumstances so require it, the tribunal may stay the enforcement of its award following the submission of a request for interpretation or revision. Under ICSID Additional Facility Rules only requests for an additional decision, correction of errors, and interpretation are possible; no provisions exist for a request for revision.[116]

Appeals/annulment

5.28 The ICSID arbitration procedure is governed exclusively by the ICSID Convention and neither the procedure nor the awards rendered under the Convention can be challenged in national courts of contracting states. As already noted, an ICSID arbitral award is binding on the parties; there is no appeal mechanism, and such awards can only be the subject of post-award remedies provided for in the Convention.

---

[111] ICSID Convention, art 53. See also Arbitration (Additional Facility) Rules, art 53(4).
[112] ICSID Convention, art 48(5); Arbitration Rules, r 48(4). There is no equivalent provision under the Arbitration (Additional Facility) Rules.
[113] ICSID Convention, art 49; Arbitration Rules, r 49.
[114] ICSID Convention, art 50; Arbitration Rules, r 50.
[115] ICSID Convention, art 51; Arbitration Rules, r 50.
[116] Arbitration (Additional Facility) Rules, arts 56–58.

A party may apply for the annulment of an award.[117] Under the Convention, such annulment is available on five limited grounds: that the arbitral tribunal was not properly constituted; that it manifestly exceeded its powers; that one of its members was corrupt; that there was a serious departure from a fundamental rule of procedure; or that the award failed to state the reasons on which it was based.

A request for annulment is referred to a three-member ad hoc committee appointed by the Chairman of the Administrative Council from the ICSID Panel of Arbitrators. Such a committee has the authority to annul the award in whole or in part on any of the stated grounds. Proceedings before the Committee are to be conducted in accordance with the procedures applicable in ordinary arbitration proceedings.[118]

By July 2009, more than 35 requests for annulment had been registered. This marks a significant increase since the publication of the first edition of this Manual in 1999, at which time there had been six such requests since ICSID's establishment, although of course this increase must be seen in the context of ICSID's higher caseload in this period. While the early annulment proceedings in ICSID provoked some disquiet that certain ad hoc committees may have gone beyond the limits of the mandate in article 52 in their review of awards,[119] in more recent proceedings ad hoc committees have tended to emphasize the limited nature of the grounds exhaustively set out in article 52, and have been at pains to stress that the annulment procedure does not constitute an appeal.[120]

There are a number of aspects of post-award review in ICSID, however, that appear to continue to cause some concern, including the following. First, the number of annulment requests in itself appears to risk proliferation and prolongation of proceedings, given that where awards are annulled in whole or in part, they may be resubmitted to further ICSID arbitration. Second, some ad hoc committees, while respecting in terms the restrictive mandate under article 52, have made statements that might be taken to imply some dissatisfaction with the limitations imposed by article 52.[121] Questions have been raised about the possible need for some form of appeal mechanism in ICSID, but this has not,

---

[117] ICSID Convention, art 52.

[118] Arbitration Rules, r 53.

[119] See eg the decision in *Klöckner v Cameroon* (ICSID Case No ARB/81/2), 3 May 1985, (1995) 2 ICSID Rep 95.

[120] See eg *Compania de Aguas del Aconquija SA and Vivendi Universal v Argentine Republic* (ICSID Case No ARB/97/3), Decision on Annulment, 3 July 2002, para 62. See *Azurix Corp. v Argentine Republic* (ICSID Case No ARB/01/12), Decision on the Application for Annulment, 1 September 2009, paras 39–56.

[121] *CMS Gas Transmission Company v The Argentine Republic* (ICSID Case No ARB/01/8), Decision of the Ad Hoc Committee, 25 September 2007, paras 136, 158.

at least as yet, given rise to concrete developments.[122] Third, a further question which arises out of the increase in annulment proceedings is the delay faced by a successful claimant in enforcing an award. Article 52(5) provides that an ad hoc committee may, if it considers the circumstances so require, stay enforcement of an award pending its decision. An applicant initiating annulment proceedings may request a stay of enforcement in its application, and in such circumstances enforcement is stayed provisionally until the committee rules on the request. In some cases, stays of enforcement have been conditioned upon provision of a guarantee or other security,[123] but in others no such security requirement has been imposed.[124]

The ICSID Additional Facility Rules do not allow for annulment procedures.[125]

Costs

5.29 The costs of ICSID proceedings include: the parties' expenses, including in particular counsel fees; fees and expenses of commission or tribunal members; and out-of-pocket expenses of the Centre.

Aside from counsel fees, which in most proceedings constitute the largest expenditure, the fees of the arbitrators and conciliators,[126] their travel and other expenses, as well as the Centre's out-of-pocket expenses are met from funds that the parties are requested to advance to ICSID at intervals of three to six months.

In the case of conciliation proceedings the fees and expenses of members of the commission, as well as the charges for the use of the facilities of the Centre, are borne equally by the parties. Each party bears any other expenses it incurs in

---

[122] See ICSID Secretariat Discussion Paper, *Possible Improvements of the Framework of ICSID Arbitration*, 22 October 2004, paras 20–23 and Annex. The establishment of an Appeals Facility suggested in the Discussion Paper was not taken up in the revisions to the rules that took effect in April 2006.

[123] See eg *Sempra Energy International v Argentine Republic* (ICSID Case No ARB/02/16), Decision on the Argentine Republic's Request for a Continued Stay of Enforcement of the Award, 5 March 2009. The arbitral tribunal in this case subsequently terminated the stay of enforcement on the basis of Argentina's failure to implement the required escrow arrangement. See Decision on Sempra Energy International's Request of the Termination of the Stay of Enforcement, 7 August 2009.

[124] See eg *Patrick Mitchell v Democratic Republic of the Congo* (ICSID Case No ARB/99/7), Decision on the Stay of Enforcement of the Award, 30 November 2004.

[125] Awards made under Additional Facility arbitration may, however, be subject to some form of review outside the framework of ICSID; see eg *Metalclad Corporation v United Mexican States* (ICSID Case No ARB(AF)/97/1), Award of 30 August 2000, 5 *ICSID Rep* 212 (2002), and *United Mexican States v Metalclad Corporation*, 2001 BCSC 664, available at <http://naftaclaims.com/Disputes/Mexico/Metalclad/MetalcladJudgement.pdf>.

[126] The Schedule of Fees (1 January 2008) provides that the fees of arbitrators, conciliators, and ad hoc committee members shall be US$3,000 per day of meetings or other work in connection with the proceedings, unless otherwise agreed between them and the parties.

connection with the conciliation proceeding. In contrast, in the case of arbitration proceedings, the tribunal will, unless the parties agree otherwise, assess the expenses incurred by the parties in connection with the proceeding, the fees and expenses of the tribunal members, and the expenses of the Centre, and decide how and by whom those expenditures shall be paid. The tribunal's decision on the apportionment of costs will form part of the award.[127]

Execution of decision, recognition, and enforcement

Once the parties have consented to ICSID arbitration they are bound to carry **5.30** out their undertaking and to abide by the award.

All contracting states, whether or not parties to the dispute, are required to recognize awards rendered pursuant to the Convention as binding and to enforce the pecuniary obligations imposed thereby, as if it were the final judgment of a court in that state.[128] Execution of the award is governed by the laws concerning execution of judgments in force in the state in which execution is sought.[129] The ICSID Convention provisions, however, do not affect the law in contracting states relating to immunity of that state or any foreign state from execution.[130]

The Convention's provisions on recognition and enforcement of awards do not apply to Additional Facility proceedings.

Evaluation

The volume of work handled by ICSID has increased enormously in the period since the first edition of this Manual, and the institution, and the tribunals operating under its auspices, have faced new challenges of a procedural and substantive nature. To a large degree, ICSID's workload over the past six or seven years has been dominated by the series of cases brought against the Argentine Republic in the aftermath of the financial crisis.[131] These have contributed to a growing sense that the impact of ICSID, as an institution, is much greater than the sum of its parts, ie the individual arbitral tribunals that decide specific disputes.

The basic ICSID framework established by the 1965 Convention has in many respects proved adaptable and effective in meeting the growing demand for the Centre's investment arbitration services. The self-contained nature of ICSID's

---

[127] ICSID Convention, art 61; Administrative Regulations, regs 14–16. See also Arbitration (Additional Facility) Rules, art 59; Administrative Rules (Additional Facility), arts 5–7.

[128] ICSID Convention, art 54(1).

[129] Ibid, art 54.

[130] Ibid, art 55.

[131] More than 40 proceedings have been initiated against the Argentine Republic in ICSID since 2001.

provisions on the recognition and enforcement of awards remains an attractive option for claimants. There remain some areas where further developments or revisions may be contemplated in the future.

In relation to some of the earliest ICSID cases, the proper scope of the annulment procedure proved one of the areas of greatest concern. While requests for annulment were few and far between from the mid-1980s through the 1990s, as ICSID's caseload has grown, there have now been numerous decisions on requests for annulment. The way in which the annulment procedure functions impacts significantly on perceptions of the fairness, effectiveness, and predictability of ICSID arbitration. In the light of the number and significance of annulment requests, proposals to further institutionalize or regularize the annulment process may merit further consideration. At the same time, however, notwithstanding disquiet over the legal findings reached in some ICSID tribunals, there appears to remain relatively little widespread support for the establishment of a standing appellate entity.

Demands for greater transparency of ICSID proceedings have already been answered to some degree through the amendment to the Arbitration Rules in 2006 allowing for non-disputing parties to participate, through written submissions, at the discretion of the tribunal. Demands for such participation seem likely to increase as ICSID tribunals deal with a wider range of issues touching on broad questions of economic development and public interest. Thus far, it does not seem that the introduction of new rules on such participation has led to any flight from ICSID to arbitral institutions that might be more protective of the privacy of arbitral proceedings.

Finally, the growth in ICSID arbitration has seen a corresponding increase in the number of practitioners involved in ICSID arbitration proceedings. As indicated already by the increase in the number of motions to disqualify arbitrators in recent years,[132] more attention is being paid to the identity and conduct of arbitrators and counsel, and to potential conflicts of interest and perceptions of bias. Investment arbitration is no longer, if it ever was, a wholly private dispute resolution process. The development and application of further principles and rules to govern potential conflicts of interests may be required to underpin the legitimacy of ICSID arbitration in the future.

---

[132] See *supra* para 5.7.

REFERENCE

SOURCES OF PREVIOUS CASE LAW, INCLUDING CASE REPORTS

Parties must give their consent to publication of ICSID awards prior to publication. However, ICSID will include excerpts of legal reasoning of arbitral tribunals in its publications, in accordance with Arbitration Rule 48(4). The awards are published in *ICSID Reports: Reports of Cases decided under the Convention on the Settlement of Investment Disputes between States and Nationals of other States, 1965* (1993–). Awards may also be published in the *ICSID Review—Foreign Investment Law Journal*.

ICSID awards and related documents can also be located on-line on the ICSID website (<http://www.icsid.worldbank.org/ICSID>) and in the *Oxford Reports on International Investment Claims* (Oxford University Press, 2008) at: <http://www.investmentclaims.com>.

SELECT BIBLIOGRAPHY

ICSID produces the *ICSID Bibliography* which is posted on the ICSID website (<http://www. worldbank.org/icsid>).

ICSID publishes the *ICSID Review—Foreign Investment Law Journal*.

Articles addressing aspects of ICSID proceedings are published in the *ICSID Review,* as well as *News from* ICSID, produced by the ICSID Secretariat. Relevant articles also appear in a wide range of other journals, updated references to which can be found in the *ICSID Bibliography*.

On the establishment, structure, and jurisdiction of ICSID, see further:

A Broches, 'The Convention on the Settlement of Investment Disputes between States and Nationals of Other States' (1972) 136(2) *Recueil des Cours* 331–410.

Books

B Binder, V Kriebaum, A Reinisch, and S Wittich (eds), *International Investment Law for the Twenty First Century: Essays in Honour of Christoph Schreuer* (2009).

Z Douglas, *International Law of Investment Claims* (2009).

R Happ and N Rubins, *Digest of ICSID Awards and Decisions 2003–07* (2009).

C Schreuer, L Malintoppi, A Reinisch, and A Sinclair, *ICSID Convention: A Commentary* (2nd edn, 2009).

I Laird and T Weiler (eds), *Investment Treaty Arbitration and International Law* (2 vols) (2008).

P Muchlinski, F Ortino, and C Schreuer (eds), *Handbook of International Investment Law* (2008).

R Hofmann and C Tams (eds), *The International Convention on the Settlement of Investment Disputes (ICSID): Taking Stock after 40 Years* (2007).

C McLachlan, L Shore, M Weiniger, and L Mistelis, *International Investment Arbitration: Substantive Principles* (2007).

R Doak Bishop, J Crawford, and M Reisman, *Foreign Investment Dispute: Cases, Materials and Commentary* (2005).

T Weiler, *International Investment Law and Arbitration: Leading Cases from the ICSID, NAFTA, Bilateral Investment Treaties and Customary International Law* (2005).

E Gaillard and Y Banifatemi, *Annulment of ICSID Awards* (2004).

N Horn and S Kröll, *Arbitrating Foreign Investment Disputes* (2004).

L Reed, J Paulsson, and N Blackaby, *Guide to ICSID Arbitration* (2004).

K V S K Nathan, *ICSID Convention: The Law of the International Centre for Settlement of Investment Disputes* (2000).

M Hirsch, *The Arbitration Mechanism of the International Center for Settlement of Investment Disputes* (1993).

S Toope, *Mixed International Arbitration* (1990).

ANNEX

List of contracting states and other signatories of the Convention

(as of 31 July 2009)

Afghanistan, Albania, Algeria, Argentina, Armenia, Australia, Austria, Azerbaijan, Bahamas, Bahrain, Bangladesh, Barbados, Belarus, Belgium, Benin, Bosnia and Herzegovina, Botswana, Brunei Darussalam, Bulgaria, Burkina Faso, Burundi, Cambodia, Cameroon, Central African Republic, Chad, Chile, China, Colombia, Comoros, Rep of Congo, Democratic Rep of Congo, Costa Rica, Côte d'Ivoire, Croatia, Cyprus, Czech Republic, Denmark, Ecuador,* Egypt, El Salvador, Estonia, Fiji, Finland, France, Gabon, The Gambia, Georgia, Germany, Ghana, Greece, Grenada, Guatemala, Guinea, Guyana, Honduras, Hungary, Iceland, Indonesia, Ireland, Israel, Italy, Jamaica, Japan, Jordan, Kazakhstan, Kenya, Rep of Korea, Rep of Kosovo, Kuwait, Latvia, Lebanon, Lesotho, Liberia, Lithuania, Luxembourg, former Yugoslav Rep of Macedonia, Madagascar, Malawi, Malaysia, Mali, Malta, Mauritania, Mauritius, Federated States of Micronesia, Mongolia, Morocco, Mozambique, Nepal, Netherlands, New Zealand, Nicaragua, Niger, Nigeria, Norway, Oman, Pakistan, Panama, Papua New Guinea, Paraguay, Peru, Philippines, Portugal, Romania, Rwanda, Samoa, Saudi Arabia, Senegal, Serbia, Seychelles, Sierra Leone, Singapore, Slovak Republic, Slovenia, Solomon Islands, Somalia, Spain, Sri Lanka, St Kitts and Nevis, St Lucia, St Vincent and the Grenadines, Sudan, Swaziland, Sweden, Switzerland, Syria, Tanzania, Timor-Leste, Togo, Tonga, Trinidad and Tobago, Tunisia, Turkey, Turkmenistan, Uganda, Ukraine, United Arab Emirates, United Kingdom of Great Britain and Northern Ireland, United States of America, Uruguay, Uzbekistan, Venezuela, Rep of Yemen, Zambia, Zimbabwe.

* Ecuador's denunciation of the ICSID Convention is due to take effect on 7 January 2010.

Haiti ratified the ICSID Convention on 27 October 2009, and thus the Convention was due to enter into force for Haiti on 26 November 2009.

PART III

INTERNATIONAL CRIMINAL COURTS AND TRIBUNALS

Introduction

International criminal courts and tribunals are the most recent family of international judicial bodies. Spectacular strides have been made in the past 17 years in the field of international retributive justice. The array of institutions currently existing is staggering, particularly considering how seldom war crimes and gross violations of human rights were prosecuted during the Cold War. In essence, within the larger order of international judicial bodies comprising all other courts examined in the Manual, international criminal courts and tribunals are different exactly because they are *criminal bodies*. Their mission is not to settle disputes, but rather to rule on international crimes (war crimes, crimes against humanity, crimes of genocide) through trials and, eventually, to determine criminal sanctions, like detention. In these international courts, states never appear as parties. Individuals are always the defendants, and the burden of the prosecution is shouldered by the Office of the Prosecutor, an organ of an international organization.

The international criminal courts and tribunals family can then be divided into four fundamental genera (in parenthesis the years in which they became operational and eventually terminated operations).

I) **Permanent International Criminal Courts**
   a) International Criminal Court—ICC (2004)
II) **Ad Hoc International Criminal Tribunals**
   a) International Criminal Tribunal for the former Yugoslavia—ICTY (1993)
   b) International Criminal Tribunal for Rwanda—ICTR (1995)

III) **International Military Tribunals**
    a)   International Military Tribunal at Nuremberg (1945–1946)
    b)   International Military Tribunal for the Far East (1946–1948)
IV) **Hybrid criminal tribunals (also known as 'mixed criminal tribunals' or 'internationalized criminal tribunals')**
    a)   Serious Crimes Panels in the District Court of Dili, East Timor (2000–2005)
    b)   Panels in the Courts of Kosovo (2001)
    c)   War Crimes Chamber of the Court of Bosnia-Herzegovina (2005)
    d)   Special Court for Sierra Leone (2002)
    e)   Extraordinary Chambers in the Courts of Cambodia (2006)
    f)   Special Tribunal for Lebanon (2009).

The fundamental feature of the *Permanent International Criminal Courts* genus is that jurisdiction of bodies belonging to this group (*ratione materiae, personae, loci,* and *temporis*) is not strictly limited. At the present time, the only permanent international criminal court existing is the ICC.[1] Its jurisdiction *ratione materiae* encompasses four categories of international crime (genocide, crimes against humanity, war crimes, and the crime of aggression),[2] while the jurisdiction *ratione temporis* includes crimes committed after the entry into force of the Statute on 1 July 2002. The jurisdiction *ratione personae* and *loci* include individuals accused of having committed crimes in the territory of a state party to the ICC Statute, or nationals of a state party regardless of where the act was perpetrated.[3] The ICC is a court with universal reach, as any sovereign state in the world might accept its jurisdiction, and the number of states that have done so (currently 110) has gradually expanded since the entry into force of its Statute.

At this point in history, there are two *Ad Hoc International Criminal Tribunals.* This genus is different from the Permanent International Courts genus in that these tribunals are created after large-scale international crimes have been committed and have limited jurisdiction to prosecute and try only those crimes. Their jurisdiction *ratione loci* is limited to the territory of specific states where particularly egregious crimes occurred, as is their jurisdiction *ratione temporis.* This feature is shared with the bodies of the *International Military Tribunals* genus, but not with the ICC. Ad Hoc International Criminal Tribunals have in common

---

[1] However, the creation of permanent criminal courts at a regional level at some point in the future cannot be entirely ruled out.

[2] The Court's jurisdiction over the crime of aggression is suspended, pending agreement among the contracting parties on the crime's definition.

[3] The Court can also try nationals of a non-party state either in the case that a state has accepted the Court's jurisdiction ad hoc (to date there have been two declarations in accordance with art 12(3), one of them by Côte d'Ivoire and one by the Palestinian National Authority) or pursuant to a decision of the Security Council, acting under Chapter VII of the UN Charter (Rome Statute, art 12(2).

with International Military Tribunals and the ICC an international structure (ie being composed of judges, prosecutors, and staff in general coming from several different states and applying international criminal standards). Yet, at the same time, they are different from International Military Tribunals because they are bodies of the United Nations, a universal organization representing all states, including those where crimes occurred, and not only the victorious powers. Ad Hoc International Criminal Tribunals, Permanent International Courts, and International Military Tribunals are purely international endeavours, created by the international community at large, and prosecutions and trials are held on behalf of humanity. Nationals of those countries where crimes occurred play a very limited role and appear before tribunals only as either suspects or victims. They are also all geared towards the prosecution of high-level political and military leaders.[4]

What distinguishes *Hybrid Criminal Tribunals* from the other three genera of international criminal tribunals is that they are not purely international. They combine in their structure, law, and procedure elements of both international and domestic criminal jurisdictions. They are usually composed of a mix of international and national staff (judges, prosecutors, and other personnel) and apply a compound of international and national substantive and procedural law. They are also not necessarily focused only on those most responsible at the highest levels of the political and military leadership.

These bodies are a very diverse genus amongst the family of international criminal courts, each body being the result of unique political and historical circumstances. However, should a finer classification be attempted, probably the genus could be divided into two sub-genera: national tribunals on to which an international element has been grafted ('internationalized domestic criminal tribunals') and tribunals that localize international criminal justice (that is to say, 'domesticated international criminal tribunals'). Placing bodies within sub-genera is ultimately a matter of choice of criteria, degree, and point of view. The 'Regulation 34 & 64' Panels in Kosovo, the War Crimes Chamber in Bosnia and Herzegovina, and the Serious Crimes Panels in East Timor belong to the former, while the Sierra Leone and Lebanon tribunals seem to belong to the latter group, with the Extraordinary Chambers in the Courts of Cambodia somehow being astride the two.

The rise of international criminal courts has resurrected and considerably expanded a whole corpus of international law, created a large and expanding cadre of legal professionals, and changed the way in which international organizations and states approach conflict prevention and resolution. All these

---

[4] A notable exception has been the initial 'bottom-up' strategy adopted by the first ICTY Prosecutor, Richard Goldstone, which resulted in the indictment, prosecution, and conviction of a number of low-level perpetrators.

developments are even more breathtaking if one considers the short timespan within which they took place and compares this to the usually glacial pace at which international law and its institutions develop.

The question is whether the family of international criminal courts will expand any further, or whether the ICC is ultimately going to make all other international courts obsolete or confined to marginal crises. On that issue, the jury is still out.

6

THE INTERNATIONAL
CRIMINAL COURT

Introduction

Name and seat of the Court

The International Criminal Court ('ICC' or 'the Court') is a permanent international criminal court with the jurisdiction to try individuals for the most serious international crimes. The seat is in The Hague, The Netherlands, and for the time being, it is located at:

6.1

Maanweg 174
2516 AB, The Hague
The Netherlands

Postal Address:
Post Office Box 19519
2500 CM, The Hague
The Netherlands
Tel: + 31 (0)70 515 8515
Fax: +31 (0)70 515 8555
Website: <http://www.icc-cpi.int/>

Communications and claims under article 15 of the Rome Statute may be addressed to:

Information and Evidence Unit
Office of the Prosecutor
Post Office Box 19519

2500 CM, The Hague
The Netherlands
Fax: +31 70 515 8555
Email: otp.informationdesk@icc-cpi.int

General overview

6.2 The idea of the establishment of a permanent international criminal court emerged for the first time in the aftermath of the First World War but such a tribunal was never established. In the aftermath of the Second World War, two ad hoc international military tribunals (the International Military Tribunal at Nuremberg and the International Military Tribunal for the Far East) were established to try individuals who committed war crimes, crimes against peace, and crimes against humanity. Shortly after the UN was founded, the International Law Commission received the mandate to codify the legal principles that emerged during the Nuremberg and Tokyo trials, but progress on this initiative was blocked during the Cold War years.

Towards the end of the 20th century, new impetus to the quest for a permanent international criminal jurisdiction with universal scope came from a variety of factors, including the end of the Cold War; the establishment of the ICTY and the ICTR and concerns about their ad hoc nature; and strong pressure from public opinion outraged by the continued impunity of egregious perpetrators of international crimes. These developments led to the adoption of the 1998 Rome Statute for the International Criminal Court ('Rome Statute' or 'Statute').[5] The Rome Statute entered into force on 1 July 2002.

To date, 110 states have ratified the Rome Statute.[6] The ICC is the only permanent international court having criminal jurisdiction over individuals accused of committing one or more of the crimes enumerated in the Statute (ie genocide, crimes against humanity, war crimes; jurisdiction over the crime of aggression depends on whether states parties to the Statute will be able to agree to a definition and the conditions under which the Court will exercise its jurisdiction over that crime, which, to date, has not happened).

The roots of the Rome Statute can be traced back directly to the ICTY and ICTR, along with a draft statute prepared in 1994 by the International Law Commission. However, the ICC is different from the ICTY and ICTR in several legal and structural features, some of which can be briefly addressed. First of all and most obviously, unlike the ICTY and ICTR, the ICC is a permanent judicial body, the jurisdiction of which is not limited by any time limits (with

---

[5] Rome Statute of the International Criminal Court, 17 July 1998, as amended on 30 November 1999, 8 May 2000, 17 January 2001, 16 January 2002, 2187 UNTS 90 ('Rome Statute').
[6] See *infra* Annex.

the caveat that all crimes must have been committed after the entry into force of the Statute, on 1 July 2002) and, at least potentially, has universal reach. Second, although the jurisdiction of the two ad hoc tribunals is not exclusive, but concurrent with that of national courts, both have primacy over national courts. Conversely, the judicial activity of the ICC is intended only to complement that of national courts. It exercises jurisdiction only when national courts are unwilling or unable genuinely to carry out the investigation or prosecution of a person accused of the crimes defined in the Rome Statute.[7] Third, while the ICTY and ICTR had their jurisdiction preset, the ICC Prosecutor is independent and can decide in which of the situations potentially falling under the Court's jurisdiction an investigation will be started.

Relationship with the United Nations

A fundamental difference between the ICC and the ICTY/ICTR is that while **6.3** the latter are subsidiary organs of the Security Council, and as such embedded in the United Nations, the ICC is not a UN organ. It is an independent and self-standing international judicial institution. Thus, once a case is handled by the Court, all states parties to the Statute, but not necessarily all UN members, must cooperate with the investigation and prosecution.[8]

Also, it is the Assembly of the State Parties, and not the Security Council, as in the case of the ICTY and ICTR, that supervises the work of the ICC. It reviews the administration of the Court, approves its budget, receives reports on its operation, and may decide to introduce changes in the structure and procedure of the Court (eg alteration to the number of judges or amendment of the Rules of Procedure and Evidence).[9] The Assembly also addresses instances of failure on the part of states parties to cooperate with the Court. A Bureau (comprising 20 members of the Assembly, representing the legal and geographical diversity of the states parties, elected for a period of three years) assists the Assembly in performing its functions.[10] The Assembly may create other subsidiary bodies, as necessary.[11]

Nevertheless, the Court has significant links to the UN. The precise terms that govern this relationship are set forth in the 'Negotiated Relationship Agreement between the International Criminal Court and the United Nations' (UN-ICC Agreement).[12] The Court cooperates closely with the UN in a number of areas.

---

[7] Rome Statute, arts 1, 17.

[8] Ibid, art 86.

[9] Ibid, arts 36(2), 51(2), 112 (2), (4).

[10] Ibid, art 112(3).

[11] Ibid, art 112(4). In fact, it established The Hague and New York Working Groups.

[12] Ibid, arts 2 and 115, *Negotiated Relationship Agreement between the International Criminal Court and the United Nations* (ICC-ASP/3/Res 1), 4 October 2004, <http://www.icc-cpi.int> (Legal Texts and Tools/'Relationship Agreement').

First, the Security Council may refer situations to the Court, including those that would not otherwise fall within the Court's jurisdiction (eg the situation in Darfur, over which the Court could not otherwise have jurisdiction because Sudan is not a state party).[13] Nevertheless, the Prosecutor is still free to decide whether to open an investigation on the referred situation, based on the evidence gathered and in accordance with the statutory requirements. The Council, acting under Chapter VI of the UN Charter, can also require the Court not to commence or proceed with an investigation for a period of 12 months, after the Council has requested the Court to that effect.[14] It may renew the request under the same conditions.[15] The Court is obliged to comply with the request of the Security Council. Also, the Court must keep the Security Council informed regarding such requests and referrals through the Secretary-General.[16]

The UN also participates in the funding of the Court, together with the states parties, in particular in relation to expenses incurred in cases initiated through referral by the Security Council.[17] The UN may also, on request from the Court, provide financial or fiscal advice to the Court.

Besides situations referred by the Security Council, the Court and the UN agreed, *inter alia*, to exchange information, share certain administrative responsibilities, and facilitate access to UN headquarters for representatives of all states parties to the Statute, representatives of the Court, and observers of the Assembly when a meeting of an Assembly is to be held.[18] In addition, the UN agreed to take necessary measures to allow the Court to exercise its jurisdiction, including waiving any privileges and immunities that an accused person may have in accordance with the Convention on Privileges and Immunities of the United Nations and relevant rules of international law, complying with requests for the testimony of UN officials, and cooperating with the Prosecutor, particularly with respect to investigations.[19] The Court may, *inter alia*, submit reports on its activities and propose agenda items to the UN.[20]

Administrative arrangements with the Special Court for Sierra Leone

6.4 The Court provides services, facilities, and support to the Special Court for Sierra Leone to conduct trial and related activities.[21] Former President of Liberia,

---

[13] Rome Statute, art 12.
[14] Ibid, art 16.
[15] Ibid.
[16] Relationship Agreement, art 17(1)(2).
[17] Rome Statute, art 115. However, in the case of the referral of the Darfur situation the UN did not contribute.
[18] eg Relationship Agreement, arts 5, 10, 11.
[19] eg ibid, arts 16 and 19.   [20] Ibid, arts 6 and 7.
[21] *Memorandum of Understanding regarding Administrative Arrangements between the International Criminal Court and the Special Court for Sierra Leone* (ICC-PRES/03-01-06), 13 April 2006, <http://www.icc-cpi.int> (Legal Text and Tools).

Charles Taylor, became the first to be tried at The Hague in 2007 pursuant to these arrangements.

Institutional Aspects

Governing texts

The principal text governing the establishment, structure, jurisdiction, and pro- **6.5**
cedure of the ICC is the Rome Statute.[22] The Court also follows the Rules of
Procedure and Evidence ('Rules of Proc & Evid'), adopted by the Assembly;[23]
and the Regulations of the Court (governing the routine operation of the Court),
adopted by the Court (and entered into force when the majority of states parties
did not raise an objection).[24] Other relevant legal documents are the Regulations
of the Office of the Prosecutor;[25] Regulations of the Office of the Registry;[26] the
Code of Professional Conduct for Counsel;[27] the Code of Judicial Ethics;[28] the
Staff Regulations;[29] and the Financial Regulations and Rules.[30]

Substantive law

The substantive law applied by the ICC primarily consists of the Statute and **6.6**
an additional instrument on Elements of Crimes (assisting the Court in the
interpretation of the crimes that fall under the Court's jurisdiction), adopted by
a two-thirds majority of the Assembly.[31]

Secondary sources of law applied by the Court are applicable treaties, principles, and rules of international law and of armed conflict;[32] general principles
of law accepted by municipal systems, including the state which has jurisdiction

---

[22] Rome Statute, *supra* note 15.

[23] Ibid, art 51. Rules of Procedure and Evidence (ICC-ASP/1/3 (PartII-A)), 9 September 2002, <http://www.icc-cpi.int> (Legal Texts and Tools).

[24] Ibid, art 52. Regulations of the Court (ICC-BD/01-01-04) 26 May 2004, <http://www.icc-cpi.int> (Legal Texts and Tools).

[25] Regulations of the Office of the Prosecutor (ICC-BD/05-01-09), 23 April 2009, <http://www.icc-cpi.int> (Legal Texts and Tools).

[26] Regulations of the Registry (ICC-BD/03-01-06), 25 September 2006, <http://www.icc-cpi.int> (Legal Texts and Tools).

[27] Code of Professional Conduct for Counsel (ICC-ASP/4/Res 1), 2 December 2005, <http://www.icc-cpi.int> (Legal Texts and Tools).

[28] The Code of Judicial Ethics (ICC-BD/02-01-05), 9 March 2005, <http://www.icc-cpi.int> (Legal Texts and Tools).

[29] The Staff Regulations (ICC-ASP/2/Res 2), 12 September 2003, <http://www.icc-cpi.int> (Legal Texts and Tools).

[30] The Financial Regulations and Rules (ICC-ASP/4/Res 10), 3 December 2005, <http://www.icc-cpi.int> (Legal Texts and Tools).

[31] Rome Statute, arts 9, 21(1)(a). To the extent that they raise substantive law issues, the Court will also apply the Rules of Proc & Evid.

[32] Rome Statute, art 21(1)(b).

over the crime;[33] and, to some extent, previous case law of the ICC.[34] In any event, norms applied by the ICC must be in conformity with internationally recognized human rights standards and must be of a non-discriminatory nature.[35]

Organization

Composition

6.7 The ICC is composed of the Judges, led by the President of the Court, and organized in Divisions (Chambers); the Office of the Prosecutor, led by the Prosecutor; and the Registry (Secretariat), led by the Registrar.

Judges

6.8 The ICC comprises 18 judges, nominated and elected by the states parties for a non-renewable term of nine years.[36] Judges should be persons of high moral character, impartiality, and integrity who possess the qualifications required for appointment to the highest judicial office in their own countries.[37] At least nine of the judges must have established competence and experience in criminal law, and at least five of the judges must have competence and relevant experience in international humanitarian law and human rights law.[38] The judges should be nationals of states parties, and no two judges can be nationals of the same state.[39] The composition of the entire bench should reflect equitable geographical distribution and represent the different legal systems of the world. Of the judges sitting on the ICC bench at the time of writing, six have been elected from the Western European and other Group of States (WEOG), three from the Latin American and the Caribbean Group of States (GRULAC), five from the African Group of States, two from the Eastern Europe Group, and one from the Asian Group.[40] When composing the bench, the need for adequate gender representation must also be taken into account.[41] Currently, nine are female and eight are male.[42]

The Presidency is responsible for the overall administration of the Court, with the exception of the Office of the Prosecutor, and for specific functions assigned

---

[33] Ibid, art 21(1)(c).

[34] Ibid, art 21(2).

[35] Ibid, art 21(3).

[36] Ibid, art 36(1), (6), (9). It was determined that at the first election, one-third of the judges will serve three years, another third six years, and the others nine years. Judges who served three years on their first term are eligible for re-election to a full term.

[37] Ibid, art 36(3)(a).

[38] Ibid, art 36(3)(b), (5).

[39] Ibid, art 36(4)(b), (7).

[40] That totals 17 judges. Judge Mohamed Shahabuddeen (Guyana) resigned on 16 February 2009 and at the time of writing had not yet been replaced. For the full list of judges, see <http://www.icc-cpi.int> (Structure of the Court/Chambers/The Judges).

[41] Rome Statute, art 36(8).

[42] See *supra* note 40.

to the Presidency in accordance with the Statute.[43] The Presidency is composed of three judges of the Court, elected to the Presidency by their fellow judges, for a once-renewable term of three years. The current President of the Court is Judge Sang-Hyun Song (Republic of Korea). Judge Fatoumata Dembele Diarra (Mali) is First Vice-President and Judge Hans-Peter Kaul (Germany) is Second Vice-President.

Disqualification of judges and Prosecutor   A judge may not participate in a   **6.9** case where his or her impartiality may be questioned. The Prosecutor or the accused person may request disqualification of a judge for lack of impartiality, or any other ground specified by the Rules of Procedure and Evidence.[44] The other members of the Court decide the motion after hearing the judge in question. A defendant may also raise challenges against the Prosecutor or a Deputy Prosecutor for lack of impartiality. In that event, the decision is taken by the Appeals Chamber of the Court, after hearing the officer under consideration.[45]

The Court may also determine whether the activities or additional occupations of a judge are compatible with the office he or she holds.[46] If the Court finds that a judge has committed serious misconduct or serious breach of his or her official duties, or that the judge is unable to exercise the official functions required by the Statute, it may recommend to the Assembly the removal of that judge from office.[47] Such a decision of the Court must be taken by a majority of two-thirds of the other judges.

Divisions/Chambers   The Chambers are composed of three Divisions—a   **6.10** Pre-Trial Division, a Trial Division, and an Appeals Division.[48] The Pre-Trial and Trial Division each comprise six judges or more, and the Appeals Division comprises five judges (including the President). The assignment of judges to Divisions is determined by the Court and based on the qualifications of the judges, the nature of the functions of each Division, and the need to preserve an appropriate combination of judges with expertise in criminal law and international law.[49] The Court deals with cases in Chambers. The Appeals Division constitutes a single Chamber; the Trial Division sits in three-judge Chambers; and cases brought before the Pre-Trial Division are heard by a single judge or a three-judge Chamber.[50]

---

[43] Rome Statute, art 38.

[44] Ibid, art 41(2).

[45] Ibid, art 42(7)–(8).

[46] Ibid, art 40(2)–(4).

[47] Ibid, art 46. The Assembly may also remove from office the Prosecutor, a Deputy Prosecutor (in pursuance to a recommendation by the Prosecutor), and the Registrar or Deputy Registrar of the Court (in pursuance to a recommendation by the Court).

[48] Ibid, art 34(b).

[49] Ibid, art 39(1). Judges assigned to the Appeals Division will serve there for their entire term. Other judges can change Divisions after the end of three years. Ibid, art 40(3).

[50] Ibid, art 39(2).

Appellate structure

6.11 Decisions of the Pre-Trial and the Trial Chamber may be appealed before the Appeals Chamber. The appeal may challenge either a decision of acquittal or conviction, a decision on the sentence of a convicted person, or other important interim decisions (eg admissibility of case; jurisdiction of the Court; and release or detention of a person subject to investigation or prosecution).[51] An appeal may be brought before the Appeals Chamber by the Prosecutor or the defendant and, in some cases, by others involved in the proceedings (eg a state party investigating the same case, representatives of the victims). The Appeals Chamber may affirm, amend, or reverse the original decision, order a new trial, or send the case back on remand to the Trial Chamber.[52]

Technical/scientific experts

6.12 The Statute clearly envisages the use of experts by the parties to the proceedings[53] and by the Court (eg request for an expert opinion or report).[54] Moreover, it specifically authorizes the Pre-Trial Chamber to appoint an expert (normally, upon request of the Prosecutor), in order to assist in the examination or testing of evidence in the pre-trial stage, if it is feared that the evidence might not be available at the time of the trial.[55]

The ICC has general competence to employ experts seconded by states parties, international organizations, and NGOs, in order to assist the Court or the Prosecution in its work. The terms of their employment are determined by the Assembly.[56]

Office of the Prosecutor

6.13 The Prosecutor constitutes a separate and independent organ of the Court, headed by a Prosecutor elected by the states parties.[57] The Office of the Prosecutor investigates the criminal allegations and prosecutes all cases before the Court. In addition, the Prosecutor (with the assistance of Deputy Prosecutors) is responsible for the management and administration of his or her Office. The first Prosecutor is Mr Luis Moreno-Ocampo from Argentina, who took office on 16 June 2003. The Office of the Prosecutor has three divisions: the Prosecution Division, headed by the Deputy Prosecutor for Prosecutions (currently Mrs Fatou Bensouda, from The Gambia, who was elected by the Assembly of States Parties on 8 September 2004); the Investigation Division, headed by the Head of Investigations (Mr Michel de Smedt, from Belgium, Acting Head of Investigations); and the Jurisdiction, Complementarity and Cooperation

---

[51] Ibid, arts 81–82.
[52] Ibid, art 83(1)–(3).
[53] See eg Ibid, arts 48(4), 93(1)(b), (2), (10)(b)(ii)(2).
[54] Ibid, art 100(1)(d).
[55] Ibid, art 56(2)(c).
[56] Ibid, art 44(4).
[57] Ibid, art 42.

Division, led by the Head of the Division (Ms Béatrice Le Fraper du Hellen, from France).

Secretariat

The Registry of the Court bears responsibility for the administration and pro- **6.14** vision of secretarial services to the ICC.[58] The Registry is headed by a Registrar elected by the Court for a once-renewable five-year term.[59] Currently, the Registrar is Ms Silvana Arbia, from Italy.[60] The Registrar maintains the records of the Court[61] and assumes responsibility over the work of the staff of the Registry. The employment of the staff of the Registry and the Office of the Prosecutor is regulated by Staff Regulations to be drafted by the Registrar (with agreement of the Presidency and the Prosecutor) and approved by the Assembly.[62] Recently, the position of Deputy Registrar was created.

A Victims and Witnesses Unit operates within the Registry and provides protective measures, security arrangements, counselling, and other assistance to witnesses and victims that appear before the Court.[63]

Jurisdiction

The Court exercises only criminal jurisdiction over individuals accused of hav- **6.15** ing committed the most serious international crimes.

Ratione personae and loci

The ICC has jurisdiction over individuals (older than 18 at the time of the **6.16** offence)[64] accused of having committed crimes on the territory (including vessels or aircrafts) of a state party to the Rome Statute (territory), or over nationals of a state party regardless of where the act was perpetrated (nationality).[65] The Court can also try nationals of a non-party state either in the case that the state has accepted the Court's jurisdiction ad hoc,[66] or pursuant to a decision of the Security Council, acting under Chapter VII of the UN Charter.[67]

To date, prosecutions appear to be based on a combination of both territory and nationality, since most of those indicted are nationals of a state party and

---

[58] Ibid, art 43(1).
[59] Ibid, art 43(2), (4)–(5).
[60] <http://www.icc-cpi.int> (Structure of the Court/Registry/Registrar).
[61] Rome Statute, art 64(10).
[62] Ibid, art 44(1)–(3).
[63] Ibid, art 43(6).
[64] Ibid, art 26.
[65] Ibid, art 12.
[66] To date there have been two declarations in accordance with art 12(3), one of them by Côte d'Ivoire and one by the Palestinian National Authority, <http://www.icc-cpi.int> (Structure of the Court/Registry/Declarations).
[67] Rome Statute, art 12(2).

have been accused of having committed crimes on the territory of a state party (typically, but not always, their own state of nationality). However, when it is a matter of either nationality or territory, so far it seems that, as a matter of prosecutorial strategy, nationality is a preferred ground. Indeed, the Prosecutor has examined the possibility of cases whose jurisdiction would rest solely on nationality, but decided not to act on them.[68] Also, it should be noted that the Security Council did not give the Court jurisdiction over acts of Sudanese nationals committed outside Sudan, even if they might have precipitated the conflict in Darfur.

The Rome Statute applies equally to all persons without any distinction based on official capacity, regardless of whether they are head of state, or government, member of a government or of parliament, elected representative, or government official. In no case are they exempt from criminal responsibility. On 14 July 2008, the Prosecutor applied for an arrest warrant for Omar Hassan Ahmad Al Bashir, the sitting President of Sudan, accusing him of genocide, crimes against humanity, and war crimes in Darfur.[69] The Pre-Trial Chamber I on 4 March 2009 issued the arrest warrant on counts of war crimes and crimes against humanity, but ruled that there was insufficient evidence to prosecute him for genocide.[70] Al-Bashir is the first sitting head of state ever indicted by the ICC. The warrant was delivered to the Sudanese government, which is, for the time being, and unless Bashir is removed from office, unlikely to execute it.

Ratione materiae

6.17   The Court has jurisdiction over four categories of international crime: genocide, crimes against humanity, war crimes, and the crime of aggression.[71] Genocide involves certain serious crimes committed with intent to destroy, in whole or in part, a national, ethnic, racial, or religious group;[72] crimes against humanity involve certain serious crimes knowingly committed against a civilian population, as part of a widespread or systematic attack;[73] and war crimes include

---

[68]   eg allegations of acts perpetrated by nationals of coalition forces during the invasion of Iraq in 2003. Communication Received by the Office of the Prosecutor of the ICC, 16 July 2003, p 2.

[69]   *Prosecutor v Al Bashir*, ICC-02/05-01/09, <http://www.icc-cpi.int> (Situations and Cases).

[70]   Ibid. The Prosecutor appealed the finding on genocide. At the time of writing, a decision had not yet been taken.

[71]   Rome Statute, *supra* note 5, art 5.

[72]   Ibid, art 6. The acts enumerated in the Statute are killing, causing serious harm, inflicting condition of life calculated to bring about physical destruction, preventing birth, and forcibly transferring children from one group to another.

[73]   Ibid, art 7. The acts enumerated in the Statute are murder, extermination, enslavement, deportation or forcible transfer, unlawful deprivation of liberty, torture; rape and other forms of serious sexual violence; collective persecution; enforced disappearances of persons; apartheid; and other similar inhumane acts causing great suffering or serious injury.

grave breaches of the 1949 Geneva Conventions and other serious violations of the laws of war.[74] While the Rome Conference accepted that aggression should be part of the Court's subject-matter jurisdiction, it proved impossible to agree upon either a definition of it or the appropriate mechanism for judicial determination of whether the crime occurred. The definitions of aggression and the conditions of its prosecution require a formal amendment of the Rome Statute, which, to date, has not been possible.

The Court is not supposed, nor designed, to try all perpetrators of the four 'core crimes'. It is concerned not only with the 'most serious crimes' but also 'those most responsible' such as generals, leaders, organizers, and instigators.[75] Low-level offenders are unlikely to attract the attention of the Prosecutor and are going to be left to national prosecution in deference to the principle of complementarity.

Although the original impetus behind the creation of the ICC came from states concerned with matters such as international drug trafficking and terrorism, there was ultimately no consensus in including the 'treaty crimes' (ie crimes proscribed in multilateral treaties, such as those dealing with terrorist crimes, drug crimes) within the jurisdiction of the Court. Eventually, they were excluded from the Statute.[76]

Ratione temporis

The ICC is only able to deal with crimes committed after the entry into force of the Statute (1 July 2002).[77] In this respect, it differs from all its predecessors, since prior international criminal tribunals were established primarily to deal with atrocities committed before their creation. Whether the Security Council could refer crimes that occurred before 1 July 2002 to the ICC, on the premiss that its authority under the UN Charter trumps any provisions under the Rome Statute, is unclear.[78]   **6.18**

---

[74] Ibid, art 8. The acts enumerated in the Statute are, *inter alia*, wilful killing, torture or inhuman treatment, wilfully causing great suffering or serious injury, extensive and unjustified destruction of property, compelling a prisoner of war to serve in the forces of a hostile army, wilful deprivation of the right to a fair trial from prisoners of war or other protected persons, unlawful deportation, transfer, or confinement and taking of hostages.

[75] Ibid, art 17(1)(d), says that the Court must declare a case inadmissible if it is not 'of sufficient gravity'. The Prosecutor is instructed to forgo prosecution when, 'A prosecution is not in the interests of justice, taking into account all the circumstances, including the gravity of the crime, the interests of victims and the age or infirmity of the alleged perpetrator, and his or her role in the alleged crime.' Ibid, art 53(2)(c).

[76] The exception is crimes committed against UN personnel (ibid, art 8(2)(e)(iii), (b)(vii), and (3)(iii)), which is a 'treaty crime' proscribed by the Convention on the Safety of United Nations and Associated Personnel, 9 December 1994, UN Doc A/49/49 (1994). However, since the Conference of the parties can revise the Rome Statute eight years after its entry into force (July 2010), the Rome Statute could be modified to include other 'treaty crimes'.

[77] Rome Statute, art 11(1).

[78] The Security Council resolution referring the Darfur situation referred explicitly to the 'situation in Darfur since 1 July 2002'. UN Doc S/RES/1693 (2005), para 1. It might be that the

The Court also lacks jurisdiction over crimes that took place before the entry into force of the Statute with respect to that state. However, the concerned state may declare ad hoc its acceptance of the jurisdiction of the Court over such crimes back to 1 July 2002.[79]

Complementarity

6.19 The jurisdiction of the Court is complementary to that of national courts.[80] The ICC does not have jurisdiction if a case that was brought before it is dealt with by a national legal system, and in particular:

(a) the case is being investigated or prosecuted in a national legal system;

(b) the case has been investigated in a national legal system and a decision not to prosecute has been adopted; or

(c) the case has been tried before a national court.[81]

However, the Court is able to exercise jurisdiction if no action is taken with regard to a case, or, if action has been or is being taken, if it considers that the national authorities are unwilling or unable to carry out a genuine investigation and/or prosecution. For instance, this can happen if the proceedings were or are intended to shield the accused person from criminal responsibility or were or are not independent and impartial, or if the national legal system has collapsed.[82]

Advisory jurisdiction

6.20 The ICC does not have advisory jurisdiction.

Procedural Aspects

Languages

6.21 The official languages of the ICC are the official languages of the UN: Arabic, Chinese, English, French, Russian, and Spanish. All main decisions are published in these languages.[83] The working languages of the Court are English and French. The Rules of Procedure and Evidence determine under what circumstances other official languages may be used as working languages.[84] The Court

---

Security Coucil was simply confirming that it could not refer a situation prior to that date, but perhaps it might be trying to reserve its authority to refer a situation prior to that date.

[79] Rome Statute, art 11(2). On 27 February 2004, Uganda made such a statement, accepting the exercise of the Court's jurisdiction for crimes committed following the entry into force of the Statute but prior to the entry into force of the Statute for Uganda (1 September 2002).

[80] Rome Statute, preamble, art 1.

[81] Ibid, arts 17(1)(a)–(c), 20(3).

[82] Ibid, arts 17, 20(3).

[83] Ibid, art 50(1).

[84] Ibid, art 50(2).

will allow the use of languages other than the working languages, if it finds a request to this effect to be justified.[85]

Instituting proceedings

The Prosecutor can receive referrals of situations from the states parties to the Statute,[86] or the Security Council.[87] The Prosecutor will then decide independently whether or not to open an investigation. Or, the Prosecutor may initiate investigations *proprio motu* on the basis of information received from any other source.[88] The *proprio motu* exercise of power of the Prosecutor is subject to review by the Pre-Trial Chamber.[89] The request is accompanied by supporting evidence.[90] The Prosecutor may seek additional information needed to substantiate the information in possession from any source deemed appropriate (eg states, international organizations, or NGOs).[91]

    6.22

All cases are brought by the Prosecutor before the Court at discretion. The Prosecutor may decide not to pursue a case if he or she considers that: (a) the case falls outside the jurisdiction of the Court; (b) the case is inadmissible; (c) there is no legal basis for an arrest warrant or summons to appear; or (d) prosecution would not serve the interests of justice. However, this decision may be reviewed by the Pre-Trial Chamber at the request of the entity that referred the situation to the Prosecutor (a state party or the Security Council), or by the Pre-Trial Chamber on its own motion, if the Prosecutor's decision is based on the conclusion that prosecution would not serve the interests of justice.[92]

Financial assistance

If a person that is the subject of investigation or prosecution does not have legal representation, he or she is entitled to have legal assistance assigned to him or her, where the interests of justice so require. If the person lacks sufficient means to pay for the legal assistance, the Court will fund it.[93] In addition, where standards

    6.23

---

[85] Ibid, art 50(3).

[86] To date, three states parties have referred situations on their territories to the ICC (the Democratic Republic of the Congo, Uganda, and the Central African Republic).

[87] Rome Statute, arts 13(a)–(b), 14(1). The Security Council, acting under Chapter VII of the UN Charter, has referred one situation on the territory of a non-state party (Darfur, in Sudan).

[88] Ibid, arts 13(c), 15(1). At the time of writing, the Prosecutor was analysing *proprio motu* situations as a preliminary step towards initiating a full investigation in Côte d'Ivoire, Kenya, Chad, Colombia, Afghanistan, Palestine, and Georgia.

[89] Ibid, art 15(4).

[90] Ibid, art 15(3).

[91] Ibid, art 15(2).

[92] Ibid, art 53.

[93] Ibid, arts 55(2)(c), 67(1)(d).

of fairness so demand, the accused is entitled to receive, free of charge, the assistance of an interpreter and any necessary translation services.[94]

Provisional measures

Warrants of arrest

6.24 At any time after the initiation of an investigation, the Prosecutor may seek from a Pre-Trial Chamber a warrant of arrest or a summons to appear.[95] An arrest warrant will be issued if the Pre-Trial Chamber is satisfied that there are reasonable grounds to believe that the person committed a crime falling under the jurisdiction of the ICC and that the arrest is necessary.[96]

The application for arrest must include the following information:

(a) the name of the person and other identifying information;
(b) a specific reference to the crimes which fall under the Court's jurisdiction that the person is alleged to have committed;
(c) a concise statement of facts which constitute the said crimes;
(d) a summary of evidence and other information which establish reasonable grounds to believe that the person committed the crimes attributed to him or her; and
(e) the reason why the Prosecutor believes that the arrest of the person is necessary.[97]

The warrant issued by the Court will specify the above particulars (a)–(c), to the extent that the Pre-Trial Chamber is convinced by the evidence presented by the Prosecutor (for instance, the Court may issue a warrant for only some of the crimes advanced by the Prosecutor).[98] At a later date, the prosecutor may request the Chamber to modify or add to the contents of the warrant of arrest.[99] In urgent cases, the Court may request provisional arrest of a person, for whom a warrant of arrest has been issued, until the Court files with the state concerned a formal request for arrest and surrender.[100]

---

[94] Ibid, arts 55(1)(c), 67(1)(f).
[95] Ibid, art 58.
[96] Necessity is to be determined on the basis of the need to achieve one of the following goals: (a) to ensure that person's appearance in trial; (b) to prevent that person from obstructing or endangering the investigation; or (c) to prevent that person from continuing to commit the same crime or a related crime arising out of the same circumstances (which is also within the jurisdiction of the Court). Ibid, art 58(1).
[97] Ibid, art 58(2).
[98] Ibid, art 58(3). This was the case of the arrest warrant against Sudan's President Bashir, *supra* note 69, where the Pre-Trial Chamber omitted the charge of genocide from the arrest warrant.
[99] Rome Statute, art 58(6).
[100] Ibid, art 92.

A request to arrest and surrender a person, based on the warrant of arrest, issued by the Court, is binding upon the states parties to the Rome Statute (but not all UN members), and they are obliged to take immediate measures to bring the person into custody and subsequently deliver him or her to the seat of the Court.[101]

A person subject to an arrest warrant may apply at any time for interim release pending trial. The decision of the Pre-Trial Chamber on the motion is subject to periodic review, and may also be re-examined at the request of the concerned person or the Prosecutor.[102] If the Pre-Trial Chamber determines that the person in question has been detained before trial for an unreasonable period of time, due to inexcusable delay on the part of the Prosecutor, it may order release of the person—with or without conditions.[103]

Unique investigative opportunity

The Prosecutor may request the Pre-Trial Chamber to order measures necessary to take advantage of a unique opportunity to take testimony or statement from a witness, or to examine, collect, or test evidence, which might not be available at the time of the trial.[104] The decision of the Pre-Trial Chamber is normally taken after hearing the accused person.[105] The Chamber may order any necessary action, taking into consideration the efficiency and integrity of the proceedings and the rights of the defendant. These orders may, *inter alia*, provide for a record to be made of the investigative proceedings, for representatives of the defence to attend them, or may involve the appointment of an ICC judge to supervise the questioning or gathering of evidence.[106] In appropriate cases, the Pre-Trial Chamber may order any of the above measures on its own initiative (even against the wishes of the Prosecutor who may bring an appeal against such a decision), or at the request of the accused person.[107]

6.25

A similar motion for provisional measures may be made in some cases by the Prosecutor, pending a decision on a challenge to admissibility or to jurisdiction. While normally investigation is to be suspended upon the institution of such a challenge, if presented by a state, the Prosecutor may seek authorization from the Court to continue with the investigation in exceptional cases. These are cases involving: (a) investigative measures in respect of evidence which might not be available later; (b) completion of an investigative step which has already begun (eg taking of testimony); or (c) prevention of the absconding of persons who are subject of a request submitted by the Prosecutor for an arrest warrant.[108]

---

[101] Ibid, arts 59, 89, 91.
[102] Ibid, art 60(2)–(3).
[103] Ibid, art 60(4).
[104] Ibid, art 56(1).
[105] Ibid, art 56(1)(c).
[106] Ibid, art 56(2).
[107] Ibid, arts 56(3), 57(3)(b).
[108] Ibid, art 19(8).

Preliminary motions and proceedings

6.26 A challenge to the admissibility of a case or to the jurisdiction of the Court can be made by the following persons:

(a) an accused person (or a person for whom an arrest warrent or summons to appear have been issued);

(b) a state with jurisdiction over the case that is investigating and/or prosecuting the case, or has already done so;

(c) a state from which acceptance of jurisdiction is required under article 12 of the Statute (ie not party to the Statute at the time of the crime).[109]

The Prosecutor may also seek a ruling from the Court on admissibility or jurisdiction;[110] and the Court may determine admissibility on its own motion (if involving questions of complementarity).[111]

Challenges should be raised before the commencement of the trial and only once.[112] However, in exceptional circumstances the Court may allow more than one challenge, or hear a challenge made after the beginning of the trial but only if the challenge alleges that the accused has already been tried for the same offence.[113] Challenges on behalf of states must be raised at the earliest opportunity and the Prosecutor will suspend the investigation until the Court renders its decision on such challenges.[114] Challenges made before the confirmation of charges (see *infra*) are to be brought before the Pre-Trial Chamber, while subsequent challenges will be presented to the Trial Chamber. In any event, decisions on challenges may be appealed before the Appeals Chamber.[115]

If the Prosecutor informs a state that he or she intends to investigate crimes which fall under its jurisdiction, that state may then request the Prosecutor to defer investigation because the case is being investigated or has already been investigated by that state. The request must be made within one month from receiving notice from the Prosecutor's Office.[116] If the Prosecutor believes that the requesting state is unwilling or unable to carry out the investigation, he or she may apply to the Pre-Trial Chamber for authorization of investigation despite the request for deferment.[117] The state concerned, or the Prosecutor, may appeal before the Appeals Chamber against a decision of the Pre-Trial Chamber on the application for authorization of investigation.[118]

The Prosecutor must obtain authorization before starting a *proprio motu* investigation. The Pre-Trial Chamber, acting on a request of the Prosecutor, will grant such authorization only if satisfied that the material submitted to it

---

[109] Ibid, art 19(2).
[110] Ibid, art 19(3). [111] Ibid, art 19(1). [112] Ibid, art 19(4).
[113] Ibid, art 19(4). [114] Ibid, art 19(5). [115] Ibid, art 19(6).
[116] Ibid, art 18(1)–(2). [117] Ibid, art 18(2). [118] Ibid, art 18(4).

constitutes a reasonable basis for investigation proceedings and that the case seems to fall under the jurisdiction of the Court.[119]

Furthermore, at the end of the investigation, the Prosecutor will present the charges against the accused person to the Pre-Trial Chamber for confirmation.[120] If the Pre-Trial Chamber finds, after hearing the Prosecution and the accused person, that the evidence establishes substantial grounds to believe that the person has committed the crimes charged, it will confirm the charges and enable the case to be brought before the Trial Chamber.[121] At confirmation hearings, the Prosecutor must support each charge with sufficient evidence. The accused may object to the charges, challenge the evidence, and present evidence on his or her own behalf.[122] The Chamber may confirm or decline to confirm the charges, in part or in whole, and may suggest to the Prosecutor to gather more evidence or amend the charges.[123] The Prosecutor may request the Pre-Trial Chamber, at a later date, to permit modification of the charges.[124]

Written pleadings

6.27 The charges raised by the Prosecutor are presented to the Court and to the defendant in the form of a document.[125] According to the Statute, the defence is entitled to submit to the Court a written statement in reply to the charges.[126]

Oral phase

6.28 The trial begins with the reading of the charges and a plea of guilty or not guilty by the accused person.[127] The accused must be present at trial, even those parts of it that are held in camera.[128]

If the accused person admits guilt, the Court may convict him or her after being satisfied that the person understands the charges and the implication of admission, that the admission was made voluntarily, and that it is supported by evidence.[129]

If the accused person pleads not guilty, hearings will take place under conditions of equality between the parties and each party will submit evidence relevant to the case, including its witnesses.[130] The Court can order, on its own initiative, that further evidence be produced.[131] The Statute explicitly provides that the accused will be given the opportunity to introduce witnesses on his or her behalf and to examine the witnesses against him or her.[132] Furthermore, the Prosecutor must disclose the evidence in his or her possession to the defence, as soon as practicable.[133] The accused will be able to make an unsworn oral statement in his or

---

[119] Ibid, art 15(4).
[120] Ibid, art 61.   [121] Ibid, art 61(1), (7).   [122] Ibid, art 61(5)–(6).
[123] Ibid, art 61(7).   [124] Ibid, art 61(9).   [125] Ibid, art 61(3)(a).
[126] Ibid, art 67(1)(h).   [127] Ibid, art 64(8)(a).   [128] Ibid, arts 63, 67(1)(d).
[129] Ibid, art 65.   [130] Ibid, art 69(3).   [131] Ibid, arts 64(6)(d), 69(3).
[132] Ibid, art 67(1)(e).   [133] Ibid, art 67(2).

her defence;[134] although he or she has the right to refuse to testify and remain silent without this conduct being held against the defence.[135]

The specific procedures of the trial are determined by the Trial Chamber, after consulting with the parties.[136] However, the Chamber must ensure that the trial takes place without undue delay.[137] Trials will be held in public, unless special circumstances require that some of the session will be closed to the public (in order to protect victims, witnesses, or confidential or sensitive information offered as evidence).[138]

Third party intervention/multiple proceedings

6.29   The Statute permits states and certain interested persons to intervene in certain stages of the proceedings, in connection with decisions that affect their interests. For instance, a state with jurisdiction over the crime, which is investigating and/ or prosecuting the same matter or has already done so, and any state the consent of which is required for investigation (the state in which the crime took place and the state of nationality of the suspect, if they were not parties to the Statue at the time of the crime) may challenge the admissibility of the case or the jurisdiction of the Court.[139] These states may also bring an appeal against a decision on admissibility or jurisdiction to the Appeals Chamber.[140]

Or, in the event that the Prosecutor requests from the Pre-Trial Chamber authorization to take investigative steps in the territory of a state party without its cooperation because that state is clearly unable to execute a request for cooperation, the state concerned will be heard before the Chamber. It will also be entitled to submit an appeal to the Appeals Chamber against the decision of the Pre-Trial Chamber.[141] Also, if a state believes that disclosure of certain information or documents is prejudicial to its national security interests, it may intervene in the proceedings and notify the Prosecutor or the Court of its objection to disclosure.[142] Upon failure to reach an agreement on the matter, the Court will decide whether refusal to cooperate is in accordance with the concerned state's obligations under the Statute.[143]

---

[134] Ibid, art 67(1)(h).
[135] Ibid, art 67(1)(g).
[136] Ibid, art 64(3)(a).
[137] Ibid, art 67(1)(c).
[138] Ibid, art 64(7).
[139] Ibid, art 19(2)(b)–(c).
[140] Ibid, arts 18(4), 19(6), 82(1)(a).
[141] Ibid, arts 57(3)(d), 82(2).
[142] Ibid, art 72(4)–(6).
[143] Ibid, art 72(7). If the Court finds that the state concerned violated its obligations under the Statute it may order disclosure of the information, make appropriate inference in the trial of the accused, and bring the matter to the attention of the Assembly or the Security Council.

As to multiple proceedings, the Statute envisages charges being brought in the same proceedings against multiple defendants, and the Court is authorized to join or sever charges brought against more than one accused person.[144]

Amicus curiae

There are no explicit provisions in the Statute of the ICC concerning the intro- **6.30** duction of *amicus curiae* briefs. The Statute only provides that the Court can ask for information and documents from an intergovernmental organization,[145] and arguably from other sources as well (particularly, during consideration of the issue of reparations).[146] It should also be kept in mind that investigation by the Prosecutor could be prompted by any information delivered to him or her.

The introduction of *amicus curiae* briefs and other submissions is explicitly covered in the Rules of Procedure and Evidence.[147] A Chamber may, if it considers it desirable for the proper determination of the proceedings, invite or grant leave to a state, organization, or person to submit, in writing or orally, any observation on any issue that the Chamber deems appropriate.[148] This may occur at any stage of the proceedings.[149] The Prosecutor and defence have the opportunity to respond to such observations.[150] Written observations are filed with the Registrar, who provides copies to the Prosecutor and defence. The Chamber determines what time limits apply to the filing of such observations.[151]

Representation of parties

A person to be questioned regarding a crime within the jurisdiction of the ICC **6.31** has the right to have legal assistance of his or her choosing, or if he or she does not have legal assistance, to have legal assistance assigned in any case where the

---

[144] Ibid, art 64(5).

[145] Ibid, art 87(6).

[146] Ibid, arts 69(3), 75(3).

[147] Rules of Proc & Evid, rule 103.

[148] Ibid, rule 103(1). In the case of the situation in Darfur, Sudan, a year after the referral by the Security Council, investigation was proceeding slowly, the Office of the Prosecutor alleging that investigations in Darfur could not be conducted because of the security situation. In July 2006, the Pre-Trial Chamber assigned to the Darfur situation decided to seek a second opinion (Situation in Darfur, Sudan (ICC-02/05), *Decision Inviting Observations in Application of Rule 103 of the Rules of Procedure and Evidence*, 24 July 2006). Two *amici curiae* were asked for their views: Professor Antonio Cassese, chair of the UN Commission of Inquiry whose report triggered the Darfur referral, and Louise Arbour, UN High Commissioner for Human Rights. In the *Lubanga* case, the Court denied leave to intervene to the Women's Initiatives for Gender Justice. *Lubanga* (ICC-01/04-01/06-480), *Decision on Request Pursuant to Rule 103(1) of the Statute*, 26 September 2006.

[149] Rules of Proc & Evid, rule 103(1).

[150] Ibid, rule 103(2).

[151] Ibid, rule 103(3).

interests of justice so require. If the person concerned does not have sufficient means to pay for such assistance, it shall be provided free of charge.[152]

In trials, the accused shall be entitled to conduct his or her defence in person, or through legal assistance of the accused's own choosing. Where the accused does not have legal assistance, this may be assigned by the Court where the interests of justice so require, without payment if necessary.[153]

Also, representatives of the victims and other interested persons should be heard before the Court rules on the issue of reparations to the victims.[154] The representatives of the victims, as well as bona fide owners of property adversely affected by forfeit of the convicted person's proceeds, property, or assets, may appeal an order for reparations.[155]

Decision

6.32 The decision of the Trial Chamber on the merits of the case is based on evaluation of the evidence submitted and discussed before the Court and upon assessment of the entire proceedings.[156] The decision is given in writing and read in public (in full, or in a summary version).[157] It contains findings on the evidence presented and the Chamber's conclusions.[158] If no unanimity is achieved, the decision is taken by a majority vote and the opinion of the minority judges is appended to the decision.[159]

The decision cannot exceed the facts and circumstances alleged in the charges.[160] If the accused is convicted, the Court will also consider the sentence to be imposed upon him or her. The sentence will be determined on the basis of the evidence and submissions made during trial or during a special session, convened by the Court, in which evidence and submission relevant to the sentence will be presented.[161] When deciding the sentence, the Court will consider, *inter alia*, the gravity of the crime and the individual circumstances of the convicted person (including time already served for the same crime).[162] In addition, the Court may decide, if requested or

---

[152] Rome Statute, art 55(2)(c).
[153] Ibid, art 67(1)(d).
[154] Ibid, art 75(3).
[155] Ibid, art 82(4).
[156] Ibid, art 74(2).
[157] Ibid, art 74(5).
[158] Ibid.
[159] Ibid, art 74(3), (5).
[160] Ibid, art 74(2).
[161] Ibid, art 76(1)–(2). The sentences that the Court may impose are imprisonment of up to 30 years or life imprisonment, a fine and forfeit of proceeds or property derived from the crime (without affecting the rights of third parties). If a person is found guilty for more than one crime, the Court will impose a separate penalty for each crime and a cumulative penalty which cannot exceed 30 years or life imprisonment (nor fall short of the highest separate sentence pronounced). Ibid, art 78(3).
[162] Ibid, art 78(1)–(2).

acting *proprio motu* in exceptional circumstances, to order reparations to be made to the victims of the crimes. Such a decision will be taken after hearing the convicted person, representatives of the victims, and other interested persons and states. The reparations will be collected from the convicted person or, where appropriate, from a special Trust Fund maintained by the Assembly.[163]

Revision of judgment

The convicted person, or, if dead, another person on his or her behalf, or the **6.33** Prosecutor, acting on behalf of the convicted person, may apply to the Appeals Chamber to review a final judgment if one of the following has occurred:

(a) new evidence has been discovered which (i) was not available at the time of the trial for reasons that cannot be attributed to the applying party; and (ii) is sufficiently important to have probably influenced the verdict;

(b) it has been newly discovered that decisive evidence relied upon in trial was false, forged, or falsified;

(c) one or more of the judges committed in relation to the case a serious act of misconduct or a serious breach of duty, which could justify their removal from office.[164]

If the Appeals Chamber finds merit in the application it may reconvene the original Trial Chamber, refer the case to a new Trial Chamber, or retain jurisdiction. The proceedings will then be resumed, and after hearing the parties the Court will decide whether the judgment should be revised.[165] If the Court finds that a miscarriage of justice has occurred, it may award compensation to the person who suffered punishment due to the conviction.[166]

Appeal

An appeal over a decision of the Trial Chamber on the guilt or acquittal of the **6.34** accused person can be brought by the Prosecutor or the convicted person (or the Prosecutor acting on that person's behalf). The appeal must allege one of the following flaws in the decision:

(i)   procedural error;

(ii) error of fact;

(iii) error of law; or

(iv) any other ground that affects the fairness or reliability of the proceedings or decision (this can be advanced only on behalf of the convicted person).[167]

---

163 Ibid, arts 75(1)–(3), 79.
164 Ibid, art 84(1).   165 Ibid, art 84(2).
166 Ibid, art 85(2).   167 Ibid, art 81(1).

The Prosecutor or the convicted person may also appeal against a sentence, arguing that it is disproportionate to the crime.[168] The convicted person may also appeal against an order for reparations.[169] In addition, a party to a case may appeal against the following decisions of the Pre-Trial or Trial Chamber:

(a) decision on admissibility or jurisdiction;
(b) decision granting or denying release to a person investigated or prosecuted;
(c) decision of the Pre-Trial Chamber, acting *proprio motu*, to order measures in relation to a unique investigative opportunity (only the Prosecutor can appeal on this ground);
(d) any decision that might significantly affect the fair and expeditious conduct of the proceedings or the outcome of the trial, in relation to which the Pre-Trial or Trial Chamber is of the opinion that an appeal may materially advance the proceedings.[170]

In addition, an appeal can be presented by other interested states and persons in the following cases:

(a) a state may appeal a decision to authorize investigation within its territory without its cooperation;
(b) states challenging the admissibility of the case or the jurisdiction of the Court may appeal a relevant decision of the Pre-Trial or Trial Chamber;
(c) the representatives of the victim and a bona fide owner of property adversely affected by a forfeit of the convicted person's proceeds, property, or assets may appeal an order on reparations.[171]

On appeal, the Appeals Chamber has all the powers of the Trial Chamber.[172] If it finds that the proceedings below were unfair in a way that affected the reliability of the decision or the sentence, or if it finds a factual, legal, or procedural error, which materially affected the decision or the sentence, it may order one of the following:

(a) reversal or amendment of the decision or sentence;
(b) a new trial before a different Trial Chamber.[173]

If necessary, the Appeals Chamber may permit the introduction of new evidence before it, or send the case on remand to the original Trial Chamber to determine factual issues and report back to the Appeals Chamber accordingly.[174] If during an appeal against the sentence the Court finds grounds to set aside the conviction, in part or in whole, or if during appeal against the conviction the Court finds grounds to reduce the sentence, it may invite the parties to submit their

---

[168] Ibid, art 81(2)(a).
[169] Ibid, art 82(4).   [170] Ibid, art 82(1).   [171] Ibid, arts 19(6), 82(2)(4).
[172] Ibid, art 83(1).   [173] Ibid, art 83(2).   [174] Ibid, art 83(2).

arguments on the issue, and may decide the matter.[175] However, in no case will an appeal submitted by one party only result in that party's detriment.[176]

The judgment of the Appeals Chamber states the reasons on which it is based, and is delivered in public. If no unanimity is reached between the judges, the view of the minority will be indicated and judges may append their separate or dissenting opinions on questions of law.[177]

A convicted person will normally remain in custody during the appeal, and in exceptional circumstances an acquitted person will also remain in detention.[178] The execution of other aspects of the sentence will be suspended for the duration of the appeal.[179]

Costs

Every party to criminal proceedings before the ICC bears its own expenses. As **6.35** indicated above, the accused will be provided with legal and linguistic assistance free of charge, if necessary. The costs of the activities of the Court conducted in the territory of a state, in cooperation with it, will normally be incurred by that state, except for certain expenses that will be borne by the Court.[180]

Enforcement of sentences

The Court has no prison and must rely upon states parties for the enforcement of **6.36** sentences of imprisonment.[181] Thus sentence of imprisonment will be served in the territory of a state designated by the Court, which has volunteered to accept sentenced persons.[182] Failing an offer from a state party, the host state (ie the Netherlands) is saddled with the responsibility. To date, two states, Austria[183]

---

175 Ibid, art 81(2)(b)(c).
176 Ibid, art 83(2).
177 Ibid, art 83(4).
178 Ibid, art 81(3).
179 Ibid, art 81(4).
180 Ibid, art 100(1). The measures that the Court will fund are travel and security of witnesses, experts, and persons in custody of the state concerned; translation, interpretation, and transcription; travel and subsistence of Court and Prosecution personnel; expert opinion or report requested by the Court; transport of person surrendered to the jurisdiction of the Court; and extraordinary costs. In the event that a state will request cooperation from the Court in relation to proceedings conducted under that state's laws, the Court will bear all ordinary expenses. Ibid, arts 93(10), 100(2).
181 The detention centre in Scheveningen, on the outskirts of The Hague, is used only to detain accused persons pending and during the trial.
182 Rome Statute, art 103. When designating a state the Court will take into account the principle of equitable distribution of responsibilities by states; the conformity of prison conditions to international standards; the views of the sentenced person; and his or her nationality.
183 *Agreement between the International Criminal Court and the Federal Government of Austria on the enforcement of sentences of the International Criminal Court*, 27 October 2005 (ICC-PRES/01-01-05), <http://www.icc-cpi.int> (Legal Texts and Tools/Official Journal).

and the United Kingdom,[184] have agreed to provide prison facilities for the enforcement of sentences imposed by the Court. The state in which the sentence of imprisonment is being carried out is bound by the decision of the Court and cannot modify the sentence, nor extradite the convict to a third state that wishes to prosecute or punish him or her (but with the Court's approval).[185] The Court may, however, transfer a convicted prisoner to any state other than that originally or subsequently designated (or the host state).[186]

The conditions of imprisonment must conform to the relevant international standards and will be supervised by the Court. The Court has agreed, *inter alia*, to allow the International Committee of the Red Cross (ICRC) unlimited access to detainees and all parts of the detention centre to ensure that they are treated humanely and in conformity with widely accepted international standards governing the treatment of persons deprived of liberty.[187] For the same purpose, the ICRC may also visit sentenced persons transferred to a state of enforcement in accordance with bilateral enforcement agreements concluded between the ICC and a state of enforcement.

The Court will review an imprisonment sentence after two-thirds of the sentence has been served (or 25 years in the case of life imprisonment), and at subsequent dates to be determined by the Rules of Procedure and Evidence. In reviewing the sentence, the Court will consider the level of cooperation of the convicted person with the Court and other factors indicating clear and significant change of circumstances justifying the reduction of the sentence.[188]

Fines and forfeits ordered by the Court will be recognized and enforced in the territory of the states parties in accordance to their laws, and without prejudice to the rights of bona fide third parties. The property forfeited or, where appropriate, the proceeds of its sale (or the sale of other property of the convicted person of comparable value) will be transferred to the Court.[189]

After a person is convicted or acquitted by the ICC, he or she may not be tried again for the same conduct before another court, national or international, or before the ICC itself.[190]

---

[184] *Agreement between the Government of the United Kingdom of Great Britain and Northern Ireland and the International Criminal Court on the enforcement of sentences imposed by the International Criminal Court*, 8 November 2007 (ICC-PRES/04-01-07), <http://www.icc-cpi.int> (Legal Texts and Tools/Official Journal).

[185] Rome Statute, arts 105, 108.

[186] Ibid, art 104.

[187] *Agreement between the International Criminal Court and the International Committee of the Red Cross on Visits to Persons deprived of Liberty Pursuant to the Jurisdiction of the International Criminal Court*, 29 March 2006 (ICC-PRES/02-01-06), <http://www.icc-cpi.int/menus/icc/legal texts and tools/official journal/>.

[188] Rome Statute, art 110.

[189] Ibid, art 109.

[190] Ibid, art 20(1)–(2).

Evaluation

The main challenge all new judicial bodies face is to build a reputation of impartiality and effectiveness. The International Criminal Court is still a very young institution. The Rome Statute entered into force in July 2002. The Court started operating slowly as its key positions were filled, staff was hired, and all the necessary internal procedures were adopted. The Prosecutor initiated the first investigations in 2004 and the first trials began only recently.

To date, the Rome Statute has been ratified by more than half of all states in the world (110 out of less than 200), a considerable success considering the novelty, scale, and ambition of the project. However, ratifications are mostly concentrated in Western and Central Europe, Latin America, and Africa. Looking at the map of ratifications, it is evident that the main challenge the ICC faces nowadays is to gain acceptance in the Islamic world (only Jordan, Afghanistan, and Uzbekistan have ratified), and in Central, Southern, and Eastern Asia (besides the aforementioned states, Cambodia, Mongolia, Japan, and South Korea are the only member states in this part of the world). However, more crucially, it still needs to gain support of major powers such as Russia, China, and, crucially, the United States, whose acrimonious opposition campaign during the administration of President George W Bush threatened to kill it. Although there are signals that the United States under President Barack Obama is willing to adopt a more favourable attitude towards the ICC, ratification of the Rome Statute by the United States is not to be expected any time soon. For all these reasons, and considering that Western and Central Europe and Latin American are in this age relatively stable and peaceful, the ICC is likely to concentrate its attention on Africa for the time being.

Indeed, to date, all cases currently pending before the ICC refer to situations in African countries (Uganda, Central African Republic, Democratic Republic of the Congo, and Sudan). Two more African situations, in Côte d'Ivoire and Kenya, are currently under scrutiny by the Office of the Prosecutor. The focus on Africa has been used by opponents of the ICC as evidence of its partiality and politicization. On the other hand, supporters of the Court ask where else the ICC should have started its work if not in Africa, the most troubled continent of the world, with several conflicts (international and civil) ravaging dozens of millions of lives for more than a decade. Partially to answer these challenges, recently the Office of the Prosecutor started looking at situations in Afghanistan, Colombia, and Palestine to determine whether an official investigation is warranted. Likewise, the indictment of Sudan's President Omar al-Bashir, an unprecedented event, was denounced by leaders in the Islamic world and Africa as dangerous meddling in regional affairs by former colonizing powers. At the same time, it was applauded by supporters of the ICC and the ideals it embodies as the beginning of the end of impunity for international crimes, as evidence of the impartiality of the ICC, and its capacity to withstand vigorous political pressure.

To date, the Court has issued public arrest warrants for 13 people. Of these, two have died and four are in custody, awaiting trial. Seven remain free, including al-Bashir, who openly defies the ICC with the support of the member states of the African Union who, in July 2009, agreed not to cooperate in his arrest. Of course, the al-Bashir situation is exceptional and the ICC should not be judged solely on whether it will manage to secure his arrest and surrender, but also on its capacity to deter international crimes and contribute positively to international peace and security, which is still to be proved.

When the Statute of the ICC was adopted in Rome in 1998 it was locked. Reservations were excluded and amendments were barred until eight years after its entry into force. The eight-year freeze expires in July 2010. At the time of writing, states parties to the Rome Statute are holding preliminary discussions preparing for the revision conference in Kampala, Uganda. Some states and NGOs have stated that the Review Conference should be an opportunity for stocktaking and not necessarily for amending the Statute. Although no clear agenda for the Conference exists yet, it is foreseeable that the definition of the crime of aggression and the conditions under which it may be prosecuted will constitute one of the main issues on the agenda. Other items that will likely be considered are the provision in article 124 of the Rome Statute that allows states upon ratification of the Statute not to subject their nationals to the jurisdiction of the Court for seven years with regards to war crimes and the addition of terrorism and drug crimes to the Court's jurisdiction.

REFERENCE

SOURCES OF CASE LAW,
INCLUDING CASE REPORTS

- Official Journal of the ICC: <http://www.icc-cpi.int/Menus/ICC/Legal+Texts+and+Tools/Official+Journal/>.
- Official website of the ICC: <http://www.icc-cpi.int/>.

SELECT BIBLIOGRAPHY

A Cassese (ed), *The Oxford Companion to International Criminal Justice* (2009).

J Cerone, 'U.S. Attitudes toward International Criminal Courts and Tribunals' in C Romano (ed), *The Sword and the Scales: The United States and International Courts and Tribunals* (2009) 131.

C Stahn and G Sluiter (eds), *The Emerging Practice of the International Criminal Court* (2009).

International Bar Association Human Rights Institute, *Balancing Rights: The International Criminal Court at a Procedural Crossroads. An International Bar Association Human Rights Institute Report* (2008).

B N Schiff, *Building the International Criminal Court* (2008).

O Triffterer (ed), *Commentary on the Rome Statute of the International Criminal Court* (2nd edn, 2008).

International Federation for Human Rights, *Victims' Rights before the International Criminal Court: A Guide for Victims, their Legal Representatives and NGOs* (2007).

W A Schabas, *An Introduction to the International Criminal Court* (3rd edn, 2007).

F Razesberger, *The International Criminal Court: The Principle of Complementarity* (2006).

M C Bassiouni (ed), *The Legislative History of the International Criminal Court, Transnational* (2005).

A Cassese et al (eds), *Rome Statute for an International Criminal Court: A Commentary* (2 vols, 2002).

L Sadat, *The International Criminal Court and the Transformation of International Law: Justice for the New Millennium* (2002).

M H Arsanjani, 'The Rome Statute of the International Criminal Court' (1999) 93 *Am J Int'l L* 22.

ANNEX

States parties to the Rome Statute

(as at 14 September 2009)

Afghanistan, Albania, Andorra, Antigua and Barbuda, Argentina, Australia, Austria, Barbados, Belgium, Belize, Benin, Bolivia, Bosnia and Herzegovina, Botswana, Brazil, Bulgaria, Burkina Faso, Burundi, Cambodia, Canada, Central African Republic, Chad, Chile, Colombia, Comoros, Congo, Cook Islands, Costa Rica, Croatia, Cyprus, Czech Republic, Democratic Republic of the Congo, Denmark, Djibouti, Dominica, Dominican Republic, Ecuador, Estonia, Fiji, Finland, France, Gabon, Gambia, Georgia, Germany, Ghana, Greece, Guinea, Guyana, Honduras, Hungary, Iceland, Ireland, Italy, Japan, Jordan, Kenya, Latvia, Lesotho, Liberia, Liechtenstein, Lithuania, Luxembourg, Madagascar, Malawi, Mali, Malta, Marshall Islands, Mauritius, Mexico, Mongolia, Montenegro, Namibia, Nauru, Netherlands, New Zealand, Niger, Nigeria, Norway, Panama, Paraguay, Peru, Poland, Portugal, Republic of Korea, Romania, Saint Kitts and Nevis, Saint Vincent and the Grenadines, Samoa, San Marino, Senegal, Serbia, Sierra Leone, Slovakia, Slovenia, South Africa, Spain, Suriname, Sweden, Switzerland, Tajikistan, The Former Yugoslav Republic of Macedonia, Timor-Leste, Trinidad and Tobago, Uganda, United Kingdom, United Republic of Tanzania, Uruguay, Venezuela, Zambia.

7

THE AD HOC INTERNATIONAL
CRIMINAL TRIBUNALS:
ICTY AND ICTR

Introduction

Name and seat of the body

7.1 The 'International Tribunal for the Prosecution of Persons Responsible for Serious Violations of International Humanitarian Law Committed in the Territory of the former Yugoslavia since 1991', also known as the International Criminal Tribunal for the former Yugoslavia (ICTY), is located in The Hague, The Netherlands. The address is:

> International Criminal Tribunal for the former Yugoslavia
> Churchillplein 1
> 2517 JW The Hague
> The Netherlands
> Tel: 31 70 416 5000
> Website: <http://www.icty.org/>

The 'International Criminal Tribunal for the Prosecution of Persons Responsible for Genocide and Other Serious violations of International Humanitarian Law Committed in the Territory of Rwanda and Rwandan Citizens Responsible for Genocide and Other Such Violations Committed in the Territory of Neighbouring States, between 1 January 1994 and 31 December 1994', also known as the International Criminal Tribunal for Rwanda (ICTR), is located in Arusha, Tanzania. The address is:

International Criminal Tribunal for Rwanda
Arusha International Conference Centre
PO Box 6016
Arusha, Tanzania
Tel: 1 212 963 2850, or 255-27-2505000/2565062
Fax: 1 212 963 2848, or 255-27-250-4000/4373
Website: <http://www.ictr.org>

General overview

The International Criminal Tribunal for the former Yugoslavia (ICTY) and the **7.2** International Criminal Tribunal for Rwanda (ICTR) were established respectively in 1993 and 1994 by the UN Security Council, acting under Chapter VII of the UN Charter, as an ad hoc measure to contribute to the restoration and maintenance of peace in the former Yugoslavia and in Rwanda.[1] As subsidiary organs of the UN Security Council, the ICTY's and ICTR's task is prosecution and trial of persons accused of serious violations of international humanitarian law committed in the territory of the former Yugoslavia since 1991, and in Rwanda in the course of, or in relation to, the 1994 civil war. The ICTY started operating in 1994 and the ICTR in 1995.

The ICTY/ICTR were established as temporary institutions, set up for the specific purpose of investigating crimes committed during the wars in the former Yugoslavia and Rwanda and prosecuting those responsible. This was done at a time when the domestic judicial systems in the former Yugoslavia and Rwanda were not able or willing to do so themselves.

Although the ICTY/ICTR and national courts have concurrent jurisdiction over the crimes specified in the statutes, the ICTY/ICTR have primacy over national courts: at the request of the ICTY/ICTR, national courts must defer to the tribunal.[2] However, by 2003, the tribunals were operating at full capacity while the various national judicial systems in the regions demonstrated varying degrees of intent to improve their ability to handle war crimes cases.

---

[1] The ICTY was established by SC Res 827, 25 May 1993, UN Doc S/Res/827 (1993) ('ICTY Statute'). The ICTR was established by SC Res 955, 8 November 1994, UN Doc S/Res/955 (1994) ('ICTR Statute'). The statute of each tribunal is attached to the Security Council creating each. Both Statutes have been amended, by a series of Security Council resolutions, several times. At the time of this writing, the most recent version of the ICTY Statute, as last amended on 29 September 2008 by Resolution 1837, was available at <http://www.icty.org/> (Legal Library). The most recent version of the ICTR Statute, as last amended on 13 October 2006 by Resolution 1717, was available at <http://www.ictr.org/> (Basic Legal Texts).

[2] ICTY Statute, art 9; ICTR Statute, art 8.

Consequently, a plan known as the 'completion strategy' was drafted by the tribunals, at the request of the Security Council.

The plan was endorsed by the UN Security Council in resolutions 1503 and 1534, and it consists of three phases (investigations, trials, appeals) and target dates for the completion of the tribunals' mandate.[3] In the case of the ICTY, the first deadline that was successfully met was the completion of all investigations by 31 December 2004.[4] The ICTR concluded investigations earlier than its deadline. The second was the completion of all trials by the end of 2008. At the end of 2008, the ICTY President informed the Security Council that the majority of trials would be completed during 2009 and that, due to the late arrests of accused and the sheer complexity of certain cases, a small number would continue into the first part of 2010.[5] The current ICTY goal is to complete all proceedings by 2012. The majority of appeals are on track to be concluded by the end of 2011 with a small number to spill over into 2012.[6] Conversely, the ICTR, for several reasons, including the fact that several fugitives were apprehended recently and management issues, is having greater problems meeting the goals of the 'completion strategy'. The latest report of the ICTR President to the Security Council does not contain a firm date for completion of judicial activities: 'Apart from *Karemera et al.*, trial activities in 2010 should be limited to contingency planning for possible delays of the trials scheduled for the last months of 2009, for reactions to orders from the Appeals Chambers and possible hearings for the purpose of evidence preservation. For the rest, the Trial Chambers will focus in 2010 on the judgment drafting in all remaining cases.'[7]

Institutional Aspects

Governing texts

Procedural law

7.3 The principal legal texts governing the activities of the tribunals are very similar, if not altogether identical. The main ones are the Statute[8] and the Rules

---

[3] UN Security Council Resolution 1503 (2003) and 1534 (2004).

[4] <http://www.icty.org/> (Aout the ICTY/Completion Strategy).

[5] Ibid. Security Council Resolution 1877 (2009) extended judges' term of appointment until December 2010.

[6] Ibid.

[7] Letter dated 14 May 2009 from the President of the International Criminal Tribunal for Rwanda addressed to the President of the Security Council, S/2009/247, para 74.

[8] See ICTY Statute, *supra* note 1; ICTR Statute, *supra* note 1.

of Procedure and Evidence.[9] Other texts governing proceedings and other important aspects of the work of the tribunals include the Rules governing the Detention of Persons awaiting Trial and Appeal before the Tribunal or otherwise Detained on the Authority of the Tribunal (Rules of Detention); the Regulations to Govern the Supervision of Visits to and Communications with Detainees; the Directive on the Assignment of Defence Counsel (Defence Counsel Directive); and the Code of Professional Conduct for Defence Counsel appearing before the International Tribunal.[10]

Substantive law

Unlike the case of the Statute of the International Court of Justice,[11] or the **7.4** Rome Statute of the International Criminal Court,[12] there is no distinct provision defining the sources of the 'applicable law' to be applied by the tribunals. The UN Secretary-General Report to the Security Council, which eventually became the ICTY Statute, suggested that 'the international tribunal should apply rules of international humanitarian law which are beyond any doubt part of customary law ...'.[13] The emphasis on customary law is due to the fact that the Statute, established in 1993, is retrospective in nature. Under the principle of legality, the Statute itself could not serve as a criminal code providing a basis for the applicable law for crimes committed prior to its enactment in May 1993. Therefore, only violations of international humanitarian law that unequivocally exist as crimes under customary international law at the time of their commission are prosecutable. Again, by way of contrast, the ICC Rome Statute can serve as a criminal code because the Rome Statute is prospective, providing that the temporal jurisdiction of the ICC relates to crimes committed in violation of its provisions after its entry into force on 1 July 2002. The ICTY Statute and the Secretary-General's Report point to the following international humanitarian law treaties as sources for those rules, which are considered to undoubtedly have become a part of customary international law: (1) the four Geneva Conventions

---

[9] Rules of Procedure and Evidence of the International Tribunal for the Prosecution of Persons Responsible for Serious Violations of International Humanitarian Law Committed in the Territory of the Former Yugoslavia since 1991, UN Doc IT/32/Rev 42, adopted on 29 June 1995 and amended through 24 July 2009, available at <http://www.icty.org> (Legal Library/'Rules of Procedure (ICTY)'); Rules of Procedure and Evidence, International Criminal Tribunal for Rwanda, adopted on 29 June 1995 and amended through 14 March 2008, available at <http://www.ictr.org/> (Basic Legal Texts/'Rules of Procedure (ICTR)').

[10] All these documents are available at <http://www.icty.org> (Legal Library) and <http://www.ictr.org/> (Basic Legal Texts).

[11] ICJ Statute, art 38(1).

[12] Rome Statute, art 21, which not only identifies the relevant sources of substantive law but also sets out a hierarchy.

[13] The Statute of the International Tribunal for the Former Yugoslavia was initially set out as an annex to Report of the Secretary-General pursuant to Paragraph 2 of Security Council Resolution 808 (1993), UN Doc S/25704 & Add 1 (1993), 32 ILM 1192 (1994).

of 12 August 1949; (2) the Hague Convention (IV) Respecting the Laws and Customs of War on Land and the Regulations annexed thereto of 18 October 1907; (3) the Convention on the Prevention and Punishment of the Crime of Genocide of 9 December 1948; and (4) the Charter of the International Military Tribunal of 8 August 1945.[14]

Besides these instruments, both tribunals have made resort to sundry other sources, including general principles of law, previous international practice, their own case law, and cases of other international courts and tribunals, such as the International Court of Justice or the European Court of Human Rights, but only as persuasive and compelling authorities.

Organization

Composition

7.5 The tribunals consist of the judges, divided in three Trial Chambers (divided into sections) for each tribunal, and a shared Appeals Chamber; the Office of the Prosecutor (OTP); and a Registry.[15] There is no separate police or investigative section, and the responsibility of the investigation falls on the OTP. No particular provision is made for defence counsel in the statutes. With few exceptions, they are funded by the tribunals and account for a very significant part of the budget of the institutions, although they operate largely autonomously and without much formal structure.[16]

Judges

7.6 Both tribunals comprise 16 permanent, full-time, judges.[17] Seven of the permanent judges (five of the ICTY, including the President who is member ex officio, and two of the ICTR) are members of the Appeals Chamber, which is common to both tribunals and is located in The Hague, albeit it travels to Arusha for hearings.[18] Also, the Security Council decided to establish a pool of *ad litem* judges

---

[14] See below 'Jurisdiction ratione materiae'. The Trial Chamber in *Tadić* (IT-94-1-T, Judgment, 7 May 1997) affirmed that the Statute's purpose is not to enumerate the applicable law; rather, it is to establish the ICTY's competence for the crimes enumerated in arts 2–5, which are beyond any doubt part of customary international law.

[15] ICTY Statute, art 11; ICTR Statute, art 10.

[16] It is only in 2002, in accordance with decisions taken by the Plenary of the Judges, that the ICTY established an Association of Defence Counsels of the ICTY. Tenth Annual Report of the ICTY, UN Doc A/58/297-S/2003/829, annex, para 11. The Rules of Procedure were revised to require counsel defending accused before the ICTY to belong to the Association. Rules of Procedure (ICTY), r 44(A)iii. The ICTR Rules do not contain any such provisions, but there is also an Association of Defence Counsel in Arusha, of which most counsel are members.

[17] ICTY Statute, art 12(1); ICTR Statute, art 11(1). SC Resolution 1878 (2009) authorized two ICTR judges to work on a part-time basis.

[18] Under the Rules of Procedure and Evidence, judges are required to rotate on a regular basis between the Trial Chambers and the Appeals Chamber. Rules of Procedure (ICTY and ICTR), r 27(A). This, however, has not taken place in the practice of the ICTR.

to increase capacity of the tribunals and thus expedite trials.[19] The ICTY has 12 *ad litem* judges, while the ICTR has nine.[20]

Three permanent judges and a maximum at any one time of nine *ad litem* judges serve in each Trial Chamber.[21] Each Trial Chamber to which *ad litem* judges are assigned may be divided into sections of three judges each, composed of both permanent and *ad litem* judges. For each appeal the Appeals Chamber is composed of five of its members.[22]

The permanent and *ad litem* judges must be persons of high moral character, impartiality, and integrity.[23] They must possess the qualifications required for the highest judicial offices in their respective countries.[24] The judges must have established competence in criminal law and international law, including international humanitarian law and human rights law.[25]

Both the permanent judges and the *ad litem* judges are elected for a renewable term of four years by the UN General Assembly from a list of candidates prepared by the Security Council from the nominees of the states.[26] No two permanent judges and no two *ad litem* judges may be nationals of the same state (albeit *ad litem* judges may have the same nationality as permanent judges).[27]

During any term, *ad litem* judges are appointed as needed by the Secretary-General, upon the Tribunal President's request, to serve in the Trial Chambers for one or more trials for a cumulative period of up to three years (the limit being set at three years to make them not eligible for UN pension).[28] During their appointment period, *ad litem* judges enjoy the same powers, privileges, immunities, exemptions, and facilities of a permanent judge of the Tribunal.[29] However, the *ad litem* judges are not eligible for election as, or to vote in the election of, the President of the Tribunal or the Presiding Judge of a Trial Chamber.[30] They also do not have the power to adopt procedure and evidence rules, although they must be consulted before the adoption of these rules. They do not have power to review an indictment, nor to consult with the President in assignment of judges or in relation to pardon or commutation of sentence.[31]

---

[19] In the case of the ICTY, this was done by SC Res 1329 (2000). In the case of the ICTR, SC Res 1431 (2002).

[20] ICTY Statute, art 12(1); ICTR Statute, art 11(1).

[21] ICTY Statute, art 12(2); ICTR Statute, art 11(2).

[22] ICTY Statute, art 12(3); ICTR Statute, art 11(3).

[23] ICTY Statute, art 13; ICTR Statute, art 12.

[24] Ibid.

[25] Ibid.

[26] ICTY Statute, art 13 *bis*, 13 *ter*; ICTR Statute, art 12 *bis*, 12 *ter*.

[27] ICTY Statute, art 12(1); ICTR Statute, art 11(1).

[28] ICTY Statute, art 13 *ter;* ICTR Statute, art 12 *ter.* In practice, most of the ICTR *ad litem* judges have had their mandate prolonged by decisions of the Security Council because they were engaged in multi-accused trials (still without getting entitlement to pension).

[29] ICTY Statute, art 13(1) *quater*; ICTR Statute, art 12(1) *quater.*

[30] ICTY Statute, art 13(2) *quater*; ICTR Statute, art 12(1) *quater* .

[31] Ibid.

The permanent judges of the Tribunal elect a President[32] and a Vice-President,[33] both of who may be re-elected once. The President is generally responsible for the administrative functions of the tribunal, in which capacity he or she, *inter alia*, coordinates the work of the chambers, supervises the activity of the Registry, and presides at the plenary meeting as well as in the Appeal Chamber.[34] In addition, he is responsible for the enforcement and commutation of sentences.[35]

7.7 Disqualification of judges A judge may not sit on a trial or appeal in a case in which he or she has a personal interest or where his or her impartiality can be otherwise questioned.[36] In any such circumstance, the judge must withdraw and the President will assign another judge to the case.[37] In practice, the test used by the tribunals has been the 'reasonable apprehension of bias'.[38] Judges benefit from a presumption of impartiality, which can only be rebutted on the basis of adequate and reliable evidence.[39]

Any party may apply to the Presiding Judge of a Chamber for the disqualification of a judge of that Chamber.[40] The Presiding Judge will confer with the judge in question and report to the President.[41] Following the Presiding Judge's report, if necessary the President will appoint a panel of three judges drawn from other chambers to report its decision on the merits of the application.[42] If the decision is to uphold the application, the President will assign another judge to sit in the place of the judge in question.[43]

A judge can sit on a trial for which he or she has reviewed the indictment.[44] Furthermore, such a judge will not be disqualified for sitting as a member of the Appeals Chamber to hear any appeal in that case.[45] No judge, however, may sit on any appeal in a case where that judge sat as a member of the Trial Chamber.[46]

---

[32] ICTY Statute, art 14(1); ICTR Statute, art 13(1); Rules of Procedure (ICTY and ICTR), rr 18, 20.

[33] Ibid.

[34] ICTY Statute, art 14(2); ICTR Statute, art 13(2); Rules of Procedure (ICTY and ICTR), r 19.

[35] Rules of Procedure (ICTY), rr 103, 123–125.

[36] Rules of Procedure (ICTY and ICTR), r 15(A).

[37] Ibid.

[38] *Prosecutor v Karemera*, Case ICTR-98-44-T, Decision on Motion by Nzirorera for Disqualification of Trial Judges, 17 May 2004; *Prosecutor v Furundžija*, Case IT-95-17/1-A, AC Judgment of 21 July 2000, paras 189–190.

[39] *Prosecutor v Akayesu*, Case ICTR-96-4-A, AC Judgment of 1 June 2001, para 91.

[40] Rules of Procedure (ICTY and ICTR), r 15(B). There have been several cases of applications for disqualification in the practice of the tribunals, but none succeeded. See eg *Prosecutor v Šešelj*, Case IT-03-67-PT, Decision on Motion for Disqualification, 10 June 2003; *Furundžija, supra* note 38, para 200; *Prosecutor v Delalić*, Case IT-96-21-A, AC Judgment of 20 February 2001, paras 697–699, 707.

[41] Rules of Procedure (ICTY and ICTR), r 15(B).

[42] Ibid.

[43] Ibid.

[44] Rules of Procedure (ICTY and ICTR), r 15(C).

[45] Ibid.

[46] Ibid, r 15(D).

Plenary/chambers

The judges meet in plenary to elect the President and the Vice-President; **7.8** to adopt and amend the Rules of Procedure and Evidence; to decide upon matters relating to the internal functioning of the tribunal; to adopt the Annual Report of the tribunal; and to determine or supervise the conditions of detention.[47]

The President designates for the next six months a roster of six judges. Any given month, there is one duty judge to whom indictments, warrants, and other submissions not pertaining to a case already assigned to a Chamber will be transmitted for review.[48] In addition, some of the responsibilities of the Trial Chamber can be exercised by a designated member of that Chamber, such as handling motions and conducting status conferences.[49] *Ad litem* judges are attached to the Trial Chambers and may adjudicate in pre-trial matters in cases other than those they have been assigned to try.[50]

The duty judge is in charge of reviewing indictments and dealing with all matters concerning cases not yet assigned to a Trial Chamber, or urgent applications made out of the normal Registry hours.[51] For the coordination of pre-trial proceedings, the Presiding Judge of the Trial Chamber may designate from among its members a pre-trial judge.[52] The pre-trial judge may be entrusted with some of the Trial Chamber's pre-trial functions, such as handling motions, conducting pre-trial conferences, and monitoring the disclosure procedure.[53]

The trials are dealt with by three-judge Trial Chambers and each appeal is heard and decided by five Appeals Chamber's judges.[54]

Appeals structure

While the Nuremberg and Tokyo tribunals had none, the ICTY and ICTR have **7.9** been endowed with an Appeals Chamber, shared by both tribunals, since the onset.

Technical/scientific experts

The Rules of Procedure and Evidence envisage the broad use of experts and, to **7.10** date, dozens of linguistic, forensic, historical, and other experts have testified before the tribunals. The Trial Chamber may order the medical, psychiatric, or psychological examination of the accused *proprio motu* or at the request of either

---

[47] Ibid, r 24.
[48] Ibid, r 28.
[49] Ibid, r 65 *bis*.
[50] ICTY Statute, art 13 quarter (1)(d); ICTR Statute, art 12 quarter (1)(d).
[51] Rules of Procedure (ICTY and ICTR), rr 28(A), (B), (C).
[52] Ibid, r 65 *ter* (A).
[53] Ibid, r 65 *ter* (C).
[54] ICTY Statute, art 12(2)–(3); ICTR Statute, art 11(2)–(3).

party.[55] Such examinations are conducted by one or more experts entrusted by the Registrar, selected from a list of experts maintained by the Registry.[56] The parties may also present statements of experts as evidence.[57]

The Prosecutor

7.11   The 'Prosecutor' is a distinct and independent organ of the tribunal. The functions are to investigate and prosecute.[58] The Prosecutor is appointed by the Security Council on nomination by the Secretary-General, and has to meet the same requirements of high moral character and high level of competence and experience as judges.[59] The Prosecutor serves for a four-year term and is eligible for reappointment.

The Prosecutor directs the Office of the Prosecutor (OTP). The staff of the OTP are appointed by the Secretary-General on the recommendation of the Prosecutor.[60]

When the ICTR was established, instead of being given its own prosecutor it shared that of the ICTY. A Deputy Prosecutor, based in Kigali/Arusha, ensured a continuous presence of the OTP on the ground. However, under the ICTR's Completion Strategy, on 15 September 2003 a separate Prosecutor's office was established for the ICTR.[61]

Secretariat

7.12   A Registry is responsible for the administration and servicing of each tribunal.[62] The Registry is headed by the Registrar appointed by the Secretary-General for a renewable term of four years.[63] The Registrar is assisted by a Deputy Registrar.[64] The Registrar assists the judges, the chambers, the plenary, and the Prosecutor in the performance of their functions and serves as their general channel of communication.[65] The Registrar regularly reports his or her activities to the judges meeting in plenary, and to the Prosecutor.[66]

Under rule 34 of the Rules of Procedure, an additional organ, the 'Witnesses and Victims Support Section' (as called at the ICTR) and the 'Victims and

---

[55] Rules of Procedure (ICTR and ICTY), r 74 *bis*.

[56] Ibid.

[57] For the rules governing disclosure of evidence given by experts, see ibid, r 94 *bis*.

[58] ICTY Statute, art 16.1; ICTR Statute, art 15.1.

[59] ICTY Statute, art 16.4; ICTR Statute, art 15.4.

[60] ICTY Statute, art 16.5; ICTR Statute, art 15.5.

[61] UN Security Council Res 1503 (2003). The current Prosecutor for the ICTR is Hassan Bubacar Jallow (the Gambia). The Deputy Prosecutor is Bongani Majola.

[62] ICTY Statute, art 17(1); ICTR Statute, art 16(1); Rules of Procedure (ICTY and ICTR), r 33.

[63] ICTY Statute, art 17(3); ICTR Statute, art 16(3).

[64] Rules of Procedure (ICTY and ICTR), rr 31 and 32.

[65] Ibid, rr 33, 35, 36.

[66] Ibid, r 33(C).

Witnesses Section' (as called at the ICTY), was set up under the Registrar's authority.[67] This unit recommends protective measures for victims, ensures that they receive relevant support, and develops short- and long-term plans for the protection of witnesses.[68]

The Registry is also responsible for administering and supervising the detention of prisoners for whom final judgment has not been rendered. Those are detained at a facility situated within a Dutch prison in Scheveningen, near The Hague, in the case of the ICTY, and at a similar facility in Arusha in the case of the ICTR.

Jurisdiction

Ratione personae and loci

The ICTY has jurisdiction over *individuals* of any nationality accused of serious **7.13** violations of international humanitarian law committed in the territory of the former Yugoslavia,[69] while the ICTR has jurisdiction over the same but committed in the territory of Rwanda.[70] Violations committed in states neighbouring Rwanda may also be prosecuted before the Tribunal if the perpetrator was a Rwandan citizen.[71] The tribunals have no jurisdiction over states, legal persons, and organizations.

Neither the ICTY nor the ICTR statutes contain any provisions concerning a minimum age for prosecution. Be that as it may, in practice there does not appear to have been any prosecution of individuals who were near the age of 18 at the time of the commission of the offence.[72]

Unlike the Rome Statute of the ICC, the statutes of the ICTY and ICTR do not limit prosecution to those 'bearing the greatest responsibility' or the upper echelons of the decision-making chain. The matter of the importance of the offenders is entirely left to the discretion of the Prosecutor. The first trials at the ICTY were confirmed mostly to low-level offenders, and guards at prison camps, but the focus shifted later on as the war in the former Yugoslavia ended and increasingly powerful indictees were apprehended. Moreover, as the need to bring operations of the Tribunal to an end became apparent at the beginning of the 2000s, the threshold for selecting crimes was raised. In the case of the

---

[67] Ibid, r 34.

[68] Ibid.

[69] ICTY Statute, arts 1 and 6.

[70] ICTR Statute, art 1 and 5.

[71] ICTR Statute, arts 1 and 7. This aspect of the ICTR's jurisdiction has not proved relevant in any prosecutions since all indictments concerned events in Rwanda.

[72] eg Drazen Erdemović, the youngest to appear before the ICTY, was 23 when he participated in the Srebrenica massacre. *Prosecutor v Erdemović,* Case IT-96-22-A, Sentencing Judgment of 5 March 1998, para 16.

ICTY a new standard was adopted with the Security Council Resolution 1504 of 2003, focusing not only on the objective ground of the 'seriousness' of the offences occurred, but also, expressly, on the subjective degree of responsibility of the suspected author of the alleged crimes. Security Council Resolution 1504 notably reads that the ICTY should concentrate on 'the most senior leaders suspected of being most responsible for crimes' within its jurisdiction.[73] At the ICTR, conversely, prosecutorial strategy has been from the outset focused on persons in leadership positions.[74]

Ratione materiae

7.14 The ICTY's competence is limited to the following group of crimes:[75]

(a) grave breaches of the Geneva Conventions of 12 August 1949;[76]

(b) violations of the laws or customs of war;[77]

(c) genocide;[78]

---

[73] UNSC Res 1504 (28 August 2003), preamble.

[74] See *infra* 'Evaluation' section.

[75] It must be noted that some of the crimes, for example genocide, may entail individual criminal liability as well as the responsibility of a state. As the individual criminal liability does not exclude state responsibility and vice versa, the same act of genocide could be the subject of parallel and simultaneous legal proceedings before the International Court of Justice and the tribunal. See eg *Application of the Genocide Convention on the Prevention and Punishment of the Crime of Genocide* (Bosnia and Herzegovina v Serbia and Montenegro), ICJ Judgment of 26 February 2007.

[76] ICTY Statute, art 2. The following acts against persons or property protected by the Geneva Conventions of 12 August 1949 may be prosecuted before the ICTY:

(a) wilful killing;

(b) torture or inhuman treatment, including biological experiments;

(c) wilfully causing great suffering or serious injury to body or health;

(d) extensive destruction and appropriation of property, not justified by military necessity and carried out unlawfully and wantonly;

(e) compelling a prisoner of war or a civilian to serve in the forces of a hostile power;

(f) wilfully depriving a prisoner of war or a civilian the rights of fair and regular trial;

(g) unlawful deportation or transfer or unlawful confinement of a civilian;

(h) taking civilians as hostages.

[77] ICTY Statute, art 3. Prosecutable violations include, but are not limited to:

(a) employment of poisonous weapons or other weapons calculated to cause unnecessary suffering;

(b) wanton destruction of cities, towns, or villages, or devastation not justified by military necessity;

(c) attack, or bombardment, by whatever means, of undefended towns, villages, dwellings, or buildings;

(d) seizure of, destruction, or wilful damage done to institutions dedicated to religion, charity, and education, the arts and sciences, historic monuments, and works of art and science;

(e) plunder of public or private property.

[78] ICTY Statute, art 4. Genocide, conspiracy to commit genocide; direct and public incitement to commit genocide; attempt to commit genocide and complicity in genocide, committed

(d) crimes against humanity.[79]

The ICTR's competence is limited to the prosecution of the following groups of crimes:

(a) genocide;[80]

(b) crimes against humanity;[81]

(c) violations of article 3 common to the Geneva Conventions and of Additional Protocol II.[82]

Ratione temporis

The temporal jurisdiction of the ICTY extends from 1 January 1991 onwards, **7.15** with no temporal limitation,[83] while the temporal scope of the ICTR's jurisdiction

---

with intent to destroy, in whole or in part, a national, ethnical, racial, or religious group are prosecutable. Acts constituting genocide include:
(a) killing members of the group;
(b) causing serious bodily or mental harm to members of the group;
(c) deliberately inflicting on the group conditions of life calculated to bring about its physical destruction in whole or in part;
(d) imposing measures intended to prevent births within the group;
(e) forcibly transferring children of the group to another group.

[79] ICTY Statute, art 5. The following can be prosecuted before the ICTY when committed in armed conflict against any civilian population:
(a) murder;
(b) extermination;
(c) enslavement;
(d) deportation;
(e) imprisonment;
(f) torture;
(g) rape;
(h) persecutions on political, racial, and religious grounds;
(i) other inhumane acts.

[80] ICTR Statute, art 2. For the specifics, see *supra* note 78.

[81] ICTR Statute, art 3. For the specifics, see *supra* note 79. However, note that the ICTR Statute differs from the ICTY Statute in the fact that it does not limit prosecution of crimes against humanity to those committed during armed conflict. 'The International Tribunal for Rwanda shall have the power to prosecute persons responsible for the following crimes when committed as part of a widespread or systematic attack against any civilian population on national, political, ethnic, racial or religious grounds...'

[82] ICTR Statute, art 4: '...violations shall include, but shall not be limited to:
(a) Violence to life, health and physical or mental well-being of persons, in particular murder as well as cruel treatment such as torture, mutilation or any form of corporal punishment;
(b) Collective punishments;
(c) Taking of hostages;
(d) Acts of terrorism;
(e) Outrages upon personal dignity, in particular humiliating and degrading treatment, rape, enforced prostitution and any form of indecent assault;
(f) Pillage;
(g) The passing of sentences and the carrying out of executions without previous judgement pronounced by a regularly constituted court, affording all the judicial guarantees which are recognized as indispensable by civilised peoples;
(h) Threats to commit any of the foregoing acts.'

[83] ICTY Statute, art 8.

is narrower, covering only the period between 1 January 1994 and 31 December 1994.[84]

7.16 **Relationship with national courts** The ICTY and ICTR, on the one hand, and national courts, on the other, have concurrent jurisdiction to prosecute persons for the violations of international humanitarian law falling within the tribunals' jurisdiction.[85] Such concurrence is, however, subject to the primacy of the ICTR and ICTY. At any stage of the procedure, the tribunals may request a national court to defer competence in their favour.[86] The state concerned is obliged to comply with such a request.

The concurrent jurisdictional provisions in the statutes are completed by the Rules of Procedure and Evidence, which provide that in the event of an investigation or criminal proceedings instituted in the courts of any state, the Prosecutor may propose to the Trial Chamber designated by the President that a formal request be made that such court defer to the competence of the tribunal.[87] The criteria to be considered by the Prosecutor in requesting such a deferral differ in the case of the ICTY and ICTR.

In the case of the ICTY, the Prosecutor may initiate a request for deferral if:

(a) the act in question is characterized as an ordinary crime in the national proceedings;
(b) there is a lack of impartiality and independence, or the investigations or proceedings are designed to shield the accused from international criminal liability, or the case is not diligently prosecuted; or
(c) the matter involves factual or legal questions which may have implications for proceedings before the tribunal.[88]

In the case of the ICTR, the Prosecutor is to consider the seriousness of the offence; the status of the accused at the time of the alleged offences; and the general importance of the legal questions involved in the case.

The power of the tribunals to insist upon deferral of cases pending before national courts had a certain significance in the early years of their operations,

---

[84] ICTR Statute, art 7. In November 1992, at a political rally, Leon Musegera made a speech that has been cited for its contribution to the genocidal campaign unleashed 18 months later. By 1 January 1994, he had fled the country and obtained refugee status in Canada. The Prosecutor apparently considered that the ICTR did not have temporal jurisdiction over Musugera and his speech. In June 2005, the Supreme Court of Canada described Musugera's 1992 speech as a crime against humanity: *Musugera v Canada* (MCI), 2005 SCC 40.
[85] ICTY Statute, art 9(1); ICTR Statute, art 8(1).
[86] ICTR Statute, art 8(2). ICTY Statute, art 9(2).
[87] Rules of Procedure (ICTY and ICTR), rr 9 and 10.
[88] Ibid.

since they actually used it to obtain custody of their first suspects.[89] Yet, in more recent years, the emphasis has been rather upon sending cases back to national courts, to make it possible for the ICTY and ICTR to meet the 'completion strategy' goals.

Thus, in 2003, Rule 11 *bis* was modified to allow a Chamber, after the confirmation of the indictment and either *proprio motu* or upon request of the Prosecution, to refer a case to a state (i) in whose territory the crime was committed; or (ii) in which the accused was arrested; or (iii) having jurisdiction and being willing and adequately prepared to accept such a case. To ensure consistency in the standard applied for referring cases, the ICTY has adopted the practice of appointing one 'Referral Bench', composed of three permanent judges, which deals with all referral decisions in the first instance.[90]

To date, the ICTY has referred back to the national courts of the former Yugoslavia cases concerning 13 accused, most of which are still ongoing, under the Tribunal's continuous watch. It can be roughly estimated that this has allowed the Tribunal to save about three years of work. In the case of the ICTR, two of the accused have been transferred to French courts, while to date all requests of transfer to Rwanda have been denied.

The statutes of the tribunals declare also that no person can be tried before a national court for acts in respect of which he or she has already been tried before the tribunal (*non bis in idem*).[91] A person who has been tried by a national court for acts constituting serious violations of international humanitarian law may subsequently be tried by the tribunal only if the act in question was characterized as an ordinary crime in the national proceedings; or the national court proceedings were not impartial or independent, or the proceedings were designed to shield the accused from international criminal responsibility, or was not diligently prosecuted.[92]

No cases in which suspects have been tried by the international tribunals subsequent to a national prosecution have ever presented themselves under these provisions.

Advisory jurisdiction

These tribunals do not have advisory jurisdiction.   **7.17**

---

[89] eg *Tadić* (IT-94-1-D), Decision of the Trial Chamber on the Application by the Prosecutor for a Formal request for Deferral to the Competence of the International Tribunal in the matter of Duško Tadić, 8 November 1994. In the case of the ICTR, for instance, on 11 January 1996, Trial Chamber II authorized a deferral request filed by the Prosecutor with respect to proceedings in Belgian courts against Elie Ndayambaje, Joseph Kanyabashi, and Alphonse Higaniro. First Annual Report of the ICTR, UN Doc 1/51/399-S/1996/778, annex, para 33.
[90] ICTY Rules of Procedure, r 11 *bis* (C).
[91] ICTY Statute, art 10(1); ICTR Statute, art 9(1).
[92] ICTY Statute, art 10(2); ICTR Statute, art 9(2).

Procedural Aspects

Languages

7.18   The working languages of the ICTY and ICTR are English and French,[93] while all courtroom proceedings are simultaneously interpreted into the national languages: Serbo-Croatian at the ICTY and Kinyarwandan at the ICTR. Judgments are generally issued initially in only one of the official languages (usually, but not always, English).

The accused and other persons appearing before the tribunal have a right to use their own language through the entire procedure.[94] The accused must be informed of all charges and the details of the proceedings in a language which he or she understands. The accused and other persons involved in the proceedings are entitled to the free assistance of an interpreter if they cannot understand the languages of the tribunal.[95] A copy of the judgment and of the judges' opinions must be served on the accused in a language that he or she understands if in custody.[96]

Counsel for the accused may apply to a judge or Chamber for leave to use a language other than the two working ones.[97] If permission is granted, the expenses of interpretation and translation are borne by the tribunal.[98]

Instituting proceedings

7.19   Proceedings at the ICTY and ICTR are initiated by the Prosecutor only.[99] There is no referral by states or the UN Security Council, like in the case of the ICC. Unsurprisingly, criticism of the broad discretionary powers the Prosecutor enjoys in deciding which cases are going to be prosecuted has been constant throughout the life of the ad hoc tribunals. Specifically, there have been complaints that the Prosecutors have sometimes been influenced by political considerations or pressures from the Security Council to prosecute certain groups more than others, or to avoid others altogether.[100]

---

[93] ICTY Statute, art 33; ICTR Statute, art 31; Rules of Procedure (ICTY and ICTR), r 3(A).

[94] Rules of Procedure (ICTY and ICTR) r 3(B)–(D).

[95] ICTY Statute, art 21(4)(a), (f); ICTR Statute, art 20(4)(a); Rules of Procedure (ICTY and ICTR), rr 42(A)(ii) and 43(i).

[96] ICTY Rules of Procedure, r 98 *ter* (D).

[97] Rules of Procedure (ICTY and ICTR), r 3(C).

[98] Ibid.

[99] However, the 'completion strategy' forcing an end to investigations is a significant limit to the Prosecutor's discretionary powers.

[100] By and large the Prosecutor did not account for investigative priorities at either tribunal. One notable exception is when, in 2000, the ICTY Prosecutor publicized her internal report counselling against an indictment with respect to the war crimes imputable to NATO forces during the 1999 Kosovo campaign. 'Committee established to Review the NATO bombing Campaign Against the Federal republic of Yugoslavia, Final Report of the Prosecutor', The Hague, 13 June 2000, PR/PIS/510-e.

The investigation of crimes is initiated and carried out by the Prosecutor ex officio based on information from any source.[101] The Prosecutor has broad powers of investigation, such as the power to question suspects, witnesses, and victims, and to collect evidence and conduct on-site investigations.[102] The Prosecutor may seek the assistance of the authorities of any state, as well as any relevant international body, including INTERPOL, and request such orders from a Trial Chamber or a judge as may be necessary. States are under a general obligation to cooperate for the fulfilment of the request.[103]

Upon determination that a prima-facie case exists, the Prosecutor prepares an indictment and transmits it to a judge of the Trial Chamber for confirmation.[104] The indictment must contain a concise statement of the facts and the crimes with which the accused is charged. If the judge is satisfied that a prima-facie case has been established, the judge confirms the indictment.[105] If not so satisfied, the judge may request additional material, adjourn the review to give the Prosecutor the opportunity to modify the indictment, or dismiss the indictment.[106]

The Prosecutor may amend the indictment:

(i)   at any time before its confirmation, without leave;
(ii) between its confirmation and the assignment of the case to a Trial Chamber, with leave of the judge who confirmed the indictment, or a judge assigned by the President; and
(iii) after the assignment of the case to a Trial Chamber, with the leave of the Trial Chamber hearing the case or a judge of that Chamber, after having heard the parties.[107]

The indictment may be withdrawn under similar conditions.[108]

Financial assistance

A person subject to investigation or prosecution has a right to legal assistance **7.20** without payment, provided he or she cannot pay for it, as well as to free assistance of an interpreter or other translation services, but in this case there is no choice of counsel. The Registrar assigns a lawyer (and, at the ICTY, a second

---

[101] ICTY Statute, art 18(1); ICTR Statute, art 17(1).
[102] ICTY Statute, art 18(2); ICTR Statute, art 17(2); Rules of Procedure (ICTY and ICTR), r 39.
[103] Ibid.
[104] ICTY Statute, arts 18(4) and 19(1); ICTR Statute, art 17(4) and 18(1).
[105] ICTY Statute, art 19(1); ICTR Statute, art 18(1); Rules of Procedure (ICTY and ICTR), r 39(iii), (iv).
[106] ICTY Statute, art 19(1); Rules of Procedure (ICTY and ICTR), r 47(F).
[107] Rules of Procedure (ICTY and ICTR), r 50(A).
[108] Rules of Procedure (ICTY and ICTR), r 51(A).

co-counsel in some circumstances)[109] drawing from a list of available counsels deemed eligible.[110]

Preliminary motions and proceedings

7.21 The commencement of proceedings before the tribunals is subject to confirmation of indictment by a judge. Once the indictment is confirmed, the judge may, at the request of the Prosecutor, issue such orders and warrants as may be necessary for the conduct of the trial.[111] Once the accused has been detained and transferred to the seat of the tribunal, the President assigns the case to a Trial Chamber.[112] The accused must be brought before the Trial Chamber without delay and must be formally charged at an initial appearance.[113] There is no trial *in absentia*.

At the initial appearance of the accused, subsequent to the reading of the indictment, the accused is called upon to enter a plea of guilty or not guilty on each count.[114] If the accused fails to enter a plea, or pleads not guilty, the Trial Chamber instructs the Registrar to set a date for trial.[115] If the accused pleads guilty, and the Trial Chamber is satisfied that the guilty plea was made freely; is informed; is unequivocal; and is based on sufficient facts for the crime and the accused's participation in it, the Trial Chamber may enter a finding of guilt and instruct the Registrar to set a date for the sentencing hearing.[116]

During the pre-trial phase both the Prosecutor and the defence must reciprocally disclose evidence.[117] In order to ensure an expeditious trial, the Trial Chamber holds a pre-trial conference and may hold a pre-defence conference whereby the parties clarify and finalize their trial positions.[118] For example, disputed questions of facts and law, and lists of witnesses may be filed.

The defence can file preliminary motions in writing, no later than 30 days after the Prosecutor delivers the indictment and all supporting materials to the defence.[119] Such motions may challenge jurisdiction; allege defects in the form of the indictment; seek the severance of counts joined in one indictment or seek separate trials; or raise objections based on the refusal of a request for assignment of counsel.[120]

---

[109] ICTY Directive on the Assignment of Defence Counsel, art 16(c).
[110] ICTY Statute, art 21(4)(d), (f); ICTR Statute, art 20(4)(d), (f); Rules of Procedure (ICTY and ICTR), r 42(A)(i), (ii).
[111] ICTY Statute, art 19(2); ICTR Statute, art 18(2).
[112] Rules of Procedure (ICTY and ICTR), r 62.
[113] Ibid.
[114] Ibid, r 62(A)(iii).
[115] Ibid, r 62(A)(iii), (iv) (v).
[116] Ibid, r 62(B).
[117] Ibid, rr 66, 67.
[118] Ibid, rr 73 *bis* and 73 *ter*.
[119] Ibid, r 72(A).
[120] Ibid. ICTR Rules of Procedure, rr 73 *bis*, 73 *ter*, 72(A).

The motions must be disposed of no later than 60 days after they were filed and before the commencement of the opening statements of the trial.[121] A decision on motions challenging jurisdiction can generally be appealed as a matter of right.[122] Decisions on other preliminary motions are appealable only where a leave has been granted by the Trial Chamber.[123]

Provisional measures

There are a sundry of measures the Prosecutor can take, or request a Pre-Trial **7.22** Chamber to take, during the investigation and pre-trial phase including requesting any state to arrest a suspect or an accused provisionally; to seize physical evidence; and to take all necessary measures to prevent the escape of a suspect or an accused, injury to or intimidation of a victim or a witness, or the destruction of evidence.[124] The Prosecutor can take measures of protection of victims and witnesses and transfer of detained witnesses.[125] The state concerned must comply with any such request.

Warrant of arrest

A warrant of arrest and any other orders, summons, subpoenas, warrants, and **7.23** transfer orders as may be necessary for the purposes of the investigation or for the preparation of the trial are issued by a judge or a Trial Chamber at the request of either the prosecutor or the defence, or *proprio motu*.[126] A state to which the warrant is transmitted must promptly comply therewith.[127] Once detained by the state concerned, the accused must be transferred to the seat of the tribunal.[128] The obligation of the state to transfer or surrender the accused prevails over restrictions of national extradition laws.[129] If, within a reasonable time after the warrant of arrest or transfer no action has been taken by the state concerned, the tribunal, through the President, may notify the Security Council.[130]

Once detained, an accused may not be released except upon an order of a Chamber.[131] The Trial Chamber may issue the order only after giving the host

---

[121] Rules of Procedure (ICTY and ICTR), rr 72(A), 73 *bis*, 73 *ter*.

[122] Ibid, r 72(B)(i).

[123] Ibid, r 72(B)(ii).

[124] Ibid, r 40.

[125] Ibid, rr 90, 90 *bis*. See also, rr 69, 75.

[126] Ibid, r 54. Under the Rules of Procedure (ICTY and ICTR), the Prosecutor is also empowered to 'take all necessary measures to prevent the escape of a suspect or an accused', meaning that arrest can take place at the initiative of the Prosecutor alone, without any involvement of the judges of the Tribunal. Ibid, r 40.

[127] ICTY Statute, art 29; ICTR Statute, art 28; Rules of Procedure (ICTY and ICTR), r 56.

[128] Rules of Procedure (ICTY and ICTR), rr 55(C)(i) and 57.

[129] Ibid, r 58.

[130] Ibid, r 59(B).

[131] Ibid, r 65(A).

country and the state to which the accused seeks to be released the opportunity to be heard.[132] Furthermore, the Trial Chamber must be satisfied that the accused will appear for trial and, if released, will not pose a danger to any victim, witness, or other person.[133] To that end, the Trial Chamber may impose conditions on release, including the execution of a bail bond.[134]

Any decision rendered by the Trial Chamber regarding release is subject to appeal as a right.[135] The Prosecutor may apply for a stay of a decision by the Trial Chamber to release a suspect on the basis that the Prosecutor intends to appeal the decision.[136] Where the Trial Chamber grants a stay of its decision the Prosecutor must file his or her appeal within one day from that decision.[137]

Transfer and provisional detention of suspects

7.24 During an investigation, the Prosecutor may request an order by a judge for the transfer to and provisional detention of a suspect in the tribunal's detention unit.[138] A judge may order the provisional detention and the transfer to the detention units of the tribunal if the following conditions are met:

(a) the Prosecutor has already requested a state to arrest the suspect provisionally, or the suspect is otherwise detained by a state;

(b) after hearing the Prosecutor, the judge considers that there is a reliable and consistent body of material which tends to show that the suspect may have committed a crime over which the tribunal has jurisdiction; and

(c) the judge considers provisional detention a necessary measure to prevent the escape of the suspect, injury to or intimidation of a victim or witness, the destruction of evidence, or to be otherwise necessary to the investigation.[139]

The provisional detention may not exceed 30 days, but may be renewed twice at the request of the Prosecutor after an *inter partes* hearing and the suspect assisted by counsel.[140] Thereafter, if the indictment has not been confirmed and an arrest warrant signed, the suspect is released or, if appropriate, returned to the state authorities to which the request was originally made.[141]

Upon showing that a major impediment does not allow a state to keep a suspect in custody or to prevent his escape, the Prosecutor may apply to a judge for an order to transfer the suspect to and detain him provisionally at the seat of the tribunal or another place decided by the Bureau (a body composed of the

---

132 Ibid, r 65(B).   133 Ibid.   134 Ibid, r 65(C).
135 Ibid, r 65(D).   136 Ibid, r 65(E).   137 Ibid, r 65(F).
138 Ibid, r 40 *bis* (A).   139 Ibid, r 40 *bis* (B).
140 Ibid, r 40 *bis*.   141 Ibid.

President, the Vice-President, and the Presiding Judges of the Trial Chambers).[142] Due to an urgent necessity to act, the provisional detention can be ordered by a judge without considering whether a prima-facie case may be established. Once detained, however, the suspect may immediately apply for review of the decision by a Trial Chamber.[143] The suspect must be released if the Chamber so rules, or the Prosecutor fails to prepare an indictment within 20 days of the transfer.[144]

Written phase

The charges raised by the Prosecutor must be presented to the tribunal and to the   **7.25**
accused in written form.[145] The indictment sets forth the name and particulars of the suspect, and must contain a concise statement of the facts of the case and of the crime with which the suspect is charged.[146] The defence is entitled to submit a written statement to the tribunal in reply to the indictment.

Preliminary motions must always be submitted in writing.[147]

Oral phase

As mentioned above, the reading of the charges and the plea of guilty or not   **7.26**
guilty take place during the preliminary proceedings. A trial is conducted only if the accused pleads not guilty.

At the beginning of the trial each party may make an opening statement.[148] This is followed by the presentation of evidence and the hearing of witnesses.[149] Examination-in-chief, cross-examination, and re-examination are allowed in each case.[150] A judge may, at any stage, put any questions to the witness.[151] The Trial Chamber may order either party to produce additional evidence and may summon witnesses *proprio motu*.[152]

After the presentation of all evidence both the prosecutor and the defence may present a closing argument.[153] The Prosecutor may thereafter present a rebuttal and the defence a rejoinder.[154] When both parties have completed their presentation the presiding judge closes the hearing and the Trial Chamber retires for deliberation.[155]

All proceedings before the Trial Chamber, except for the deliberations, are held in public.[156] The Trial Chamber may exclude the press and the public only for reasons of public order or morality; safety, security, or non-disclosure of the

---

[142] Ibid, r 40(B).
[143] Ibid, r 40(C).   [144] Ibid, r 40(D).   [145] Ibid, rr 47 and 53 *bis*.
[146] Ibid, r 47(C).   [147] Ibid, r 72(A).   [148] Ibid, r 84.
[149] Ibid, r 85(A).   [150] Ibid, r 85(B).   [151] Ibid.
[152] Ibid, r 98.   [153] Ibid, r 86(A).   [154] Ibid, r 86(A).
[155] Ibid, r 87(A).   [156] Ibid, r 78.

identity of a victim or witness; or protection of the interests of justice.[157] The Trial Chamber, however, must make public the reasons for a closed session.[158]

Third party intervention/multiple proceedings

7.27 The Rules of Procedure and Evidence allow only a very limited role for third parties in the proceedings.

As the tribunals have primacy over national courts, states cannot intervene for the purpose of asserting interest in prosecuting a crime concurrently tried (the Trial Chamber may, however, suspend the indictment pending the proceedings before national courts, if it considers it appropriate).[159]

A state directly affected by a Trial Chamber's interlocutory decision may seek review of that decision if the decision concerns issues of general importance relating to the tribunal's powers.[160] If the Appeals Chamber considers this request admissible it may suspend the execution of that decision.[161]

In proceedings concerning restitution of property, third parties with a lawful interest in that property must be given an opportunity to justify their claim before the Trial Chamber.[162] Claims for victim compensation, on the other hand, may only be adjudicated by competent national courts.[163] In respect of such claims victims or other persons on behalf of them have no right to be heard by the tribunal.[164] In this respect the ICTY/ICTR differ from the ICC which gives victims a role, albeit limited, during the trial.[165]

Persons accused of crimes committed in the course of the same transaction may be jointly charged and tried.[166] Two or more crimes may be joined in one indictment if the series of acts were committed in the same transaction and by the same person.[167]

Amicus curiae

7.28 The Trial and Appeals Chambers may, if it is considered desirable for the proper determination of the case, invite or grant leave to a state, organization, or person to appear before it and make submission on any issue specified by the chambers.[168] In the practice of the ad hoc tribunals, *amicus curiae* briefs have been submitted by states, international organizations, NGOs, and individual academics. For instance, at the ICTY, *amicus* briefs were submitted in the *Tadić* case by the Federal Republic of Germany (on deferral to the ICTY) and the

---

[157] Ibid, r 79.
[158] Ibid, r 79(B).
[159] Ibid, rr 11, 11 *bis* (A).
[160] Ibid, r 108 *bis* (A).
[161] Ibid, r 108 *bis* (C).
[162] Ibid, r 105(B), (C).
[163] Ibid, r 106(A), (B).
[164] Ibid, r 106(A), (B).
[165] See *supra* Chapter 6.
[166] Rules of Procedure (ICTY and ICTR), r 48.
[167] Ibid, r 49.
[168] Ibid, r 74.

United States (on legality of creation of the ICTY).[169] At the ICTR, *amicus* briefs were submitted, for example, by Belgium, arguing for an order of transfer of an accused to Belgium for trial instead of his release.[170] In several cases, leave to submit *amicus* briefs was denied.[171]

Representation of the parties

An accused has the right to be tried in his or her presence and to defend himself **7.29** or herself in person or through legal assistance of his or her choosing or to have legal assistance assigned without payment if he or she does not have sufficient means.[172] When questioned, a suspect has the right to be assisted by counsel of his or her choice or to be assigned legal assistance without payment if he or she does not have sufficient means.[173]

Decision

A majority of judges are required to reach a decision in the Trial or Appeals **7.30** Chamber.[174] The judgment must be delivered in public and be accompanied by a reasoned opinion in writing to which separate and dissenting opinions may be appended.[175]

A finding of guilt can be reached only if the majority of the judges of the Chamber is satisfied that the guilt has been proved beyond reasonable doubt.[176] The Chamber also must determine the penalty to be imposed on each count for the convicted person, if found guilty.[177] It can indicate whether such sentences will be served consecutively or concurrently.[178] It may also decide to exercise its power to impose a single sentence reflecting the totality of the criminal conduct of the accused.[179]

The ICTY/ICTR cannot sentence to death. The only available penalty affecting life and liberty is imprisonment, for a maximum term up to the convicted person's life.[180] In determining the terms of imprisonment the Trial Chamber

---

[169] *Prosecutor v Tadić*, Case IT-94-1-D, Decision of the Trial Chamber on the Application by the Prosecutor for a Formal Request for Deferral to the Competence of the International Tribunal; Second Annual Report of the ICTY, UN Doc A/51/292-S/1996/65, annex.

[170] *Prosecutor v Ntuyahaga*, Case ICTR-98-40-T, Decision on the Prosecutor's motion to Withdraw the Indictment, 18 March 1999.

[171] eg *Prosecutor v Hadžihasanović*, Case IT-01-47-PT, Decision on Joint Challenge to Jurisdiction, 12 November 2002.

[172] ICTY Statute, art 21(4)(d); ICTR Statute, art 20(4)(d).

[173] Rules of Procedure, r 42(A)(i); ICTR Rules of Procedure, r 42(A)(i).

[174] ICTY Statute, art 23(2); ICTR Statute, art 22(2).

[175] ICTY Statute, art 23(2); ICTR Statute, art 22(2).

[176] Rules of Procedure (ICTY and ICTR), r 87(A).

[177] Ibid, r 87(C).

[178] Ibid.

[179] Ibid.

[180] ICTY Statute, art 24(1); Rules of Procedure r 101(A). ICTR Statute, art 23(1); Rules of Procedure (ICTY and ICTR), r 101(A).

has taken into consideration many factors, including the gravity of the offence, the individual circumstances of the convicted person, aggravating or mitigating circumstances (including substantial cooperation with the Prosecutor), the general practices regarding prison sentences in the courts of Rwanda and the former Yugoslavia, and the extent to which any penalty imposed by any state on the convicted person for the same act has already been served.[181] In practice, the ICTY has imposed lenient sentences, as compared to what most national jurisdictions would do, but also as compared to what the ICTR did, rarely imposing life sentencing, despite the fact that many of those appearing before the tribunals were responsible for the most serious international crimes.[182]

In addition to imprisonment, the Trial Chamber may order the return to the rightful owner of any property and its proceeds acquired by criminal conduct.[183] As noted above, compensation to victims, based on the finding of guilt by the tribunal, may only be rendered by national courts.[184]

Appeal

7.31 A Trial Chamber decision on guilt or acquittal, or the terms of sentence, can be appealed before the Appeals Chamber by the convicted person or the Prosecutor on the grounds of an error on a question of law or an error of fact that caused a miscarriage of justice.[185]

Some interlocutory decisions can also be challenged, but normally appeal in these cases is subject to a leave.[186] The Trial Chamber may grant leave if the decision involves an issue that would significantly affect the fair and expeditious conduct of the proceedings or the outcome of the trial and for which an immediate resolution by the Appeals Chamber may materially advance the proceedings.[187]

On appeal, the Appeals Chamber holds a hearing, based on the record of appeal and the briefs of the appellant and the respondent.[188] The Appeals

---

[181] ICTY Statute, art 24(2); ICTR Statute, 23(2); Rules of Procedure (ICTY and ICTR), r 101(B).

[182] eg Drazen Erdemović was sentenced to five years for his active participation in summary executions, many of which were attributed to him alone, during the Srebrenica massacre of 1995. Bosnian-Serb leader Biljana Plavšić, one of the masterminds of the ethnic cleansing in Bosnia Herzegovina, was sentenced to 11 years.

[183] ICTY Statute, art 24(3); ICTR Statute, art 23(3).

[184] Rules of Procedure (ICTY and ICTR), r 106.

[185] ICTY Statute, art 25(1); ICTR Statute, art 24(1). However, the standard of appellate review has been elaborated by the jurisprudence of the tribunals, which specified, *inter alia*, that an appeal cannot be used to have a trial de novo. *Prosecutor v Kupreškić*, Case IT-95-16-A, AC Judgment of 23 October 2001, para 22.

[186] See eg Rules of Procedure (ICTY and ICTR), rr 77(J) (contempt of the tribunal), 91(I) (false testimony). See also Rules of Procedure (ICTY and ICTR), rr 72(B), 77(d), 91(J); Rules of Procedure (ICTY), r 65(D), 116 *bis* (a); Rules of Procedure (ICTR), art 117.

[187] Rules of Procedure (ICTY and ICTR), r 72(B)(ii).

[188] Ibid, rr 109 and 111–113; Rules of Procedure (ICTY), r 117; Rules of Procedure (ICTR), r 118.

Chamber authorizes such evidence only if it finds that the additional evidence was not available at trial, is relevant and credible, and could have been a decisive factor in reaching the decision at trial.[189]

The Appeals Chamber reaches its judgment by majority.[190] It may affirm, reverse, or revise the Trial Chamber's decision.[191] In appropriate circumstances the Appeals Chamber may order that the accused be retried.[192]

Revision of judgments

Where a new fact has been discovered which was not known to the moving party **7.32** at the time of the proceedings, and could not have been discovered through the exercise of due diligence, the defence, or within one year of the final judgment, the Prosecutor may apply for revision of the judgment.[193] If the Chamber finds that the new fact could have been a decisive factor in reaching the underlying decision, the reviewing Chamber pronounces a further judgment after hearing the parties.[194] The judgment on review can be appealed.[195]

Costs

The costs of the trial are borne by the tribunal. The tribunal's expenses are cov- **7.33** ered by the budget of the United Nations in accordance with article 17 of the United Nations Charter.[196]

Enforcement of sentences

Imprisonment is served in a state designated by the tribunal from a list of states **7.34** which have indicated to the Security Council their willingness to accept convicted persons.[197] The imprisonment must be in accordance with the applicable law of the state concerned, subject to the tribunal's supervision.[198] Transfer of

---

[189] Rules of Procedure (ICTY and ICTR), r 115(A). Subsequent to the conviction of the Croatian General Blaškić, the Government of Croatia made available an enormous volume of documentary material, aimed at exculpating him. The Appeals Chamber concluded that the Trial Chamber had committed reviewable error in its assessment of the facts, but acknowledged that the additional evidence admitted on appeal confirmed this. *Blaškić* (IT-95-14-A), Judgment, 24 July 2004, paras 335–348.

[190] Rules of Procedure (ICTY), r 117(b). Rules of Procedure (ICTR), r 118(B).

[191] ICTY Statute, art 25(2); ICTR Statute, art 24(2).

[192] Rules of Procedure (ICTY and ICTR), r 117(C); Rules of Procedure (ICTR), r 118(C). On 28 August 2008, the Appeals Chamber ordered the retrial of *Prosecutor v Muvunyi*, Case ICTR-2000-55-55A, para 171. The new trial started in July 2009.

[193] ICTY Statute, art 26; Rules of Procedure (ICTR), r 120(A).

[194] Rules of Procedure (ICTY and ICTR), r 120.

[195] Ibid, r 121.

[196] ICTY Statute, art 32; ICTR Statute, art 30.

[197] ICTY Statute, art 27; ICTR Statute, art 26; Rules of Procedure (ICTY and ICTR), r 103.

[198] ICTY Statute, art 27; ICTR Statute, art 26; Rules of Procedure (ICTY and ICTR), r 104.

the convicted person must take place as soon as possible after the time limit for appeal has elapsed.[199] The tribunal supervises all sentences of imprisonment.[200] A convicted person may become eligible for pardon or commutation of the sentence, to the extent that this is provided for under the applicable law of the state of imprisonment. If this happens, the state concerned is to notify the tribunal. The President, in consultation with the judges, then decides on the matter 'on the basis of the interests of justice and the general principles of law'.[201]

ICTY prisoners have been sent to serve prison terms to Norway, Germany, Austria, Denmark, Finland, France, Italy, Spain, Sweden, and the United Kingdom.[202] ICTR prisoners have been sent to Mali, Benin, and one to Italy.[203]

Restitution of property ordered by the tribunal is to be effected by competent national authorities.[204]

Evaluation

The creation of the ICTY and ICTR was unprecedented in many ways. It was the first time since the International Military Tribunals of Nuremberg and Tokyo, established after the Second World War, that individuals had been held accountable by an international court for perpetrating mass atrocities. And, this was also the first time that such a tribunal was created by the international community, and not just the victors of war. One cannot underestimate the impact of the work of these two tribunals on international law and its institutions, on the development of international criminal law, and, in general, on the way in which conflicts and their aftermath are conceptualized and approached at all levels of decision making.

For what concerns international adjudication and rule of law, the ICTY/ ICTR spurred the birth of a whole new family of international courts and tribunals. Indeed, both the success and limitations of the ICTY/ICTR gave impetus to the creation of the International Criminal Court and several hybrid criminal tribunals in various parts of the world.

The ICTY/ICTR resurrected the notion of international criminal law, long dormant during the Cold War. Being the first truly international criminal court, the ICTY played a path-breaking role in crafting international procedural law.

---

[199] Rules of Procedure (ICTY and ICTR), r 103(B).
[200] Ibid, r 104.
[201] ICTY Statute, art 28; ICTR Statute, art 27.
[202] See generally ICTY Annual Reports, available at <http://www.icty.org/> ('About ICTY'/'Reports and Publications').
[203] See generally ICTR Annual Reports, available at <http://www.ictr.org/> ('About the Tribunal'/'Annual Reports to the General Assembly').
[204] Rules of Procedure (ICTY and ICTR), r 105(F), (G).

Both the ICTY and the ICTR further refined over the years their procedures, in a learning-by-doing process that provided the foundation for subsequent generations of international criminal bodies. Also, the ICTY and ICTR, through their decisions, helped define key concepts in international humanitarian law.

For instance, the ICTY, in the *Krstić* case, clarified what constitutes a part of a group for the purposes of defining genocide.[205] In the *Čelebići* case, it declared that international criminal liability is not based only on genocide, crimes against humanity, and war crimes, but also includes *jus cogens*, or peremptory norms of international law.[206] It also held that prohibitions that have reached the level of *jus cogens*, such as torture, are also international crimes. Later, it helped identify the three elements of torture common to most definitions of torture.[207] The ICTY has also held that individuals fighting as part of an armed, non-state group bear individual responsibility for war crimes.[208] In the *Galić* case, terror was recognized as a war crime by an international tribunal for the first time.[209] The case concerned the responsibility of Stanislav Galić, Commander of the Bosnian Serb Army besieging Sarajevo from 1992 to 1994, for the campaign of shelling and sniping conducted against the civilian population of Sarajevo. This case required elaboration of the elements of the crime of 'acts or threats of violence the primary purpose of which is to spread terror among the civilian population', which had never been adjudicated by an international tribunal prior to this case. One of the important features of this case was the analysis of whether such a conduct is prohibited and criminalized under customary international law. Finally, in addition to substantiating existing international law, the Tribunal has developed legal doctrines and standards specific to international criminal tribunals. One noteworthy example includes the development of the joint criminal enterprise theory of individual criminal responsibility, particularly in the *Kvočka* judgment.[210]

In the *Akayesu* case, the ICTR was the first international tribunal to interpret the definition of genocide contained in the Convention for the Prevention and Punishment of the Crime of Genocide (1948). The guilty plea and subsequent conviction of the former Prime Minister of Rwanda, Jean Kambanda, was the first time that an accused person acknowledged guilt for the crime of genocide before an international tribunal. It was also the first time that a head of government was

[205] *Prosecutor v Krstic*, Case IT-98-33-A, AC Judgment of 19 April 2004, at paras 5–38.
[206] *Delalić, supra* note 40, 2001, para 172, fn 225.
[207] *Prosecutor v Kunarac, Kovac and Vukoc*, Case IT-96-23 & IT-96-23/I-A, AC Judgment, 12 June 2002, para 142.
[208] *Prosecutor v Dusko Tadić*, Case IT-94-1-AR-72, AC Decision on the Defence Motion for Interlocutory Appeal on Jurisdiction, 2 October 1995, at paras 95–137. See also *Prosecutor v Furundžija*, Case IT-95-17/I-T, Judgment of 10 December 1998, para 153.
[209] *Prosecutor v Galić*, Case IT-98-29-A, Judgment of 5 December 2003.
[210] *Prosecutor v Kvočka et al*, Case IT-98-30/1-T, Judgment of 2 November 2001.

convicted for the crime of genocide.[211] The ICTR also defined the crime of rape and emphasized that rape and sexual violence may constitute genocide in the same way as any other act of bodily or mental harm, as long as such acts were committed with the intent to destroy a particular group.[212] In the *Media* case, it emphasized the important guarantees of the right to freedom of expression but noted that it was 'critical to distinguish between the discussion of ethnic consciousness and the promotion of ethnic hatred'. This case resulted in the first judgment since the conviction of Julius Streicher at Nuremberg where the role of the media has been examined in the context of international criminal law.[213]

As to the impact on the ground in Yugoslavia and Rwanda (on victims, on perpetrators, on politics, and ultimately on peace and stability in the long run), the debate is still open. It will be ultimately for historians to issue a verdict. In the meantime, the list of indictees of the ICTY, totalling 161 all of which but two have been apprehended, is remarkable, including Slobodan Milošević, the Prime Minister of Yugoslavia, Milan Babić, President of the Republika Srpska Krajina; Ramush Haradinaj, former Prime Minister of Kosovo; Radovan Karadžić, former President of the Republika Srpska; Ratko Mladić, former Commander of the Bosnian Serb Army and Ante Gotovina, former General of the Croatian Army.[214] The record of the ICTR is no less impressive, including amongst the 87 indicted, the former Prime Minister, several members of the cabinet, a series of majors (bourgmestres) and other governmental and local administrators, journalists of the Radio Télévision Libre des Mille Collines (RTLM), a Rwandan radio station which played a significant role during the Rwandan Genocide, and senior officers of the Rwandan army (Forces Armées Rwandaises) and Interhamwe (a Hutu paramilitary organization).[215]

---

[211] *Prosecutor v Kambanda*, Case ICTR 97-23-S (1998).

[212] *Prosecutor v Akayesu*, Case ICTR-96-4-T (1998). The ICTY, too, rendered judgments recognizing rape and other forms of sexual violence as crimes against humanity, war crimes, underlying acts of genocide and persecutions, and enslavement as a form of torture. See, for instance, *Furundžija, supra* note 208, paras 174–186; *Prosecutor v Kunarac, Kovac and Vukoc*, Case IT-96-23, Judgment of 22 February 2001, paras 436–460.

[213] *Prosecutor v Nahimana*, ICTR-99-52-T (2003).

[214] As of 28 May 2009, the ICTY indicted 161 persons; 120 accused were tried in 86 cases, and their proceedings, at the time of this writing, were concluded, leading to 11 acquittals (in eight cases), 60 sentencings (in 48 cases), 13 referrals to national jurisdictions, while 36 (in 22 cases) had their indictments withdrawn or died during trial. In the case of ongoing proceedings at the time of writing, 12 were before the Appeals Chamber (in five cases); 21 currently at trial (seven cases); six at pre-trial stage (four cases); two still at large (two cases). <http://www.icty.org/> (Cases/Key Figures).

[215] The figures for the ICTR are 87 indictments, broken down as follows: 44 accused tried in 35 judgments; 14 accused in five cases where judgment delivery was awaited at the time of this writing; four accused in one case where trial was closed but closing arguments were yet to be heard; six ongoing trials; six accused whose trial was still to begin, and 13 fugitives. *Letter dated 14 May 2009 from the President of the International Criminal Tribunal for Rwanda addressed to the President of the Security Council* (S/2009/247).

REFERENCE

SOURCES OF CASE LAW,
INCLUDING CASE REPORTS

Reports of judgments of the ICTY can be found on the tribunals' websites.

ICTY: <http://www.icty.org> ('Cases'). *See also* ICTY, *Judicial Reports/Recueils Judiciaires* (1999–).

ICTR: <http://www.ictr.org/> ('Cases').

SELECT BIBLIOGRAPHY

International Criminal Tribunal for Yugoslavia—United Nations Interregional Crime and Justice Research Institute (UNICRI), *ICTY Manual on Developed Practices* (2009), available at <http://www.icty.org> (About ICTY/Reports and Publications/ Publications).

E Møse, 'The ICRT's Completion Strategy: Challenges and Possible Solutions' (2008) 6 (4) *J Int'l Crim Just* 667–679.

D Orentlicher, *Shrinking the Space for Denial: The Impact of the ICTY in Serbia* (2008), available at <http://www.soros.org/initiatives/osji/articles_publications/ publications/serbia_20080520>.

V Peskin, *International Justice in Rwanda and the Balkans: Virtual Trials and the Struggle for State Cooperation* (2008).

V Tochilovsky, *Jurisprudence of the International Criminal Courts and the European Court of Human Rights: Procedure and Evidence* (2008).

H Abtahi and G Boas (eds), *The Dynamics of International Criminal Justice: Essays in Honour of Sir Richard May* (2006).

K N Calvo-Goller, *The Trial Proceedings of the International Criminal Court* (2006).

Human Rights Watch, *Looking for Justice: The War Crimes Chamber in Bosnia and Herzegovina* (2006).

W Schabas, *The UN International Criminal Tribunals* (2006).

L J van den Herik, *The Contribution of the Rwanda Tribunal to the Development of International Law* (2005).

K Khan and R Dixon, *Archbold International Criminal Courts: Practice, Procedure and Evidence* (2005).

E Møse, 'Main Achievements of the ICTR' (2005) 3 (4) *J Int'l Crim Just* 920–943.

E Neuffer, *The Key to my Neighbour's House: Seeking Justice in Bosnia and Rwanda* (2003).

F Mègret, *Le Tribunal pènal international pour le Rwanda* (2002).

A Klip and G Sluiter (eds), *Annotated Leading Cases of International Criminal Tribunals* (1999–).

8

HYBRID INTERNATIONAL CRIMINAL TRIBUNALS: THE SPECIAL COURT FOR SIERRA LEONE, THE EXTRAORDINARY CHAMBERS IN THE COURTS OF CAMBODIA, AND THE SPECIAL TRIBUNAL FOR LEBANON

Introduction

Name and seat of the body

8.1 The Special Court for Sierra Leone (hereafter SCSL or Special Court) is located in Freetown, Sierra Leone. The address is:

> Jomo Kenyatta Road
> New England, Freetown, Sierra Leone
> Tel: +232 22 297000 (via Italy: +39 0831 257000)
> Fax: +232 22 297001 (via Italy: +39 0831 257001)
> General: mailto:scsl-mail@un.org
> Personnel: scsl-personnel@un.org
> Outreach and Public Affairs: scsl-pressoffice@un.org
> Website: <http://www.sc-sl.org/>

The Special Court also has offices at The Hague and New York:

> PO Box 19536
> 2500CM Den Haag
> The Netherlands

Reception: +31 70 515 9750
Fax: +31 70 322 2711

Chrysler Building
405 Lexington Ave, 5th floor, Room 5090
New York, NY 10074
Tel: +1 (212) 457-1293
Fax: +1 (212) 457-4059

The Extraordinary Chambers in the Courts of Cambodia for the Prosecution of Crimes Committed during the Period of Democratic Kampuchea (hereafter ECCC or Extraordinary Chambers) are located in Phnom Penh, Cambodia. The address is:

National Road 4
Chaom Chau Commune, Dangkao District, Phnom Penh
PO BOX 71, Phnom Penh
Cambodia
Tel: (855) 23 219814
Fax: (855) 23 219841
Website: <http://www.eccc.gov.kh>

The Special Tribunal for Lebanon (hereafter STL or Special Tribunal) is located in Leidschendam, the Netherlands. The address is:

Dokter van der Stamstraat 1
Leidschendam, 2265 BC
The Netherlands
Tel: +31 (0) 70 800 3400
Website: <http://www.stl-tsl.org/>

The address of the office in Beirut is:

Beirut Field Office
Monteverde
Lebanon

General overview

During the past decade, six hybrid criminal tribunals have been created and **8.2** have become operational. In order of establishment, they are: the Serious Crimes Panels in the District Court of Dili, East Timor (2000); the Panels in the Courts of Kosovo (2001); the Special Court for Sierra Leone (2002); the War Crimes Chamber of the Court of Bosnia-Herzegovina (2005); the Extraordinary Chambers in the Courts of Cambodia (2006); and the Special Tribunal for Lebanon (2009).

This chapter addresses only the Sierra Leonean, Cambodian, and Lebanese hybrid criminal tribunals. The Serious Crimes Panels in the District Court of Dili, East Timor, ceased to operate in 2005 and therefore has only historical interest. The hybrid Panels in the Courts of Kosovo and the War Crimes Chamber of the Court of Bosnia-Herzegovina are still operational, but they are essentially national courts of those two states.[1]

Finally, it should be noted that the procedural law of the Special Court for Sierra Leone and that of the Special Tribunal for Lebanon are, in essence, similar to that of the ICTY and ICTR,[2] which in turn are a blend of criminal procedures used in common law jurisdictions (in large part) and civil law traditions (in smaller part). The procedural law of the Extraordinary Chambers, however, is based on the template of the Cambodian criminal procedure, which in turn is closely modelled on French criminal procedure.[3] Therefore, there are significant differences between the structure and operations of the Extraordinary Chambers, on the one hand, and the Special Court and Special Tribunal, on the other hand.

---

[1] In 2008, Regulation 34 and 64 Panels in the Court of Kosovo, the hybrid criminal tribunals set up under the framework of the UN Mission on Kosovo (UNMIK) and active since 2000, were replaced by hybrid panels under the aegis of the European Union Rule of Law Mission in Kosovo (EULEX Kosovo).

[2] The Statute of the SCSL actually provides that: 'The Rules of Procedure and Evidence of the International Criminal Tribunal for Rwanda obtaining at the time of the establishment of the Special Court shall be applicable *mutatis mutandis* to the conduct of the legal proceedings before the Special Court. The judges of the Special Court as a whole may amend the Rules of Procedure and Evidence or adopt additional rules where the applicable Rules do not, or do not adequately, provide for a specific situation. In so doing, they may be guided, as appropriate, by the Criminal Procedure Act, 1965, of Sierra Leone.' Statute of the Special Court for Sierra Leone, Annex to Agreement between the United Nations and the Government of Sierra Leone on the Establishment of the Special Court for Sierra Leone, 16 January 2002, art 14, 2178 UNTS 137 ('SCSL Statute'). The Statute of the Special Tribunal for Lebanon provides that the judges will adopt the rules of procedure, and '[i]n so doing, the judges shall be guided, as appropriate, by the Lebanese Code of Criminal Procedure, as well as by other reference materials reflecting the highest standards of international criminal procedure, with a view to ensuring a fair and expeditious trial'. Statute of the Special Tribunal for Lebanon, 30 May 2007, art 28.2, UN Doc S/RES/1757 (2007) ('STL Statute'). In reality, the rules of procedure and evidence of the Special Court for Sierra Leone have provided a more significant template than the Lebanese Code of Criminal Procedure, which is a mix of criminal codes of the Ottoman Empire and colonial France.

[3] Agreement between the United Nations and the Royal Government of Cambodia concerning the Prosecution under Cambodian Law of Crimes Committed during the Period of Democratic Kampuchea, 6 June 2003, art 12.1, UN Doc A/RES/57/228 (2003) ('UN-Cambodia Agreement'): 'The procedure shall be in accordance with Cambodian law. Where Cambodian law does not deal with a particular matter, or where there is uncertainty regarding the interpretation or application of a relevant rule of Cambodian law, or where there is a question regarding the consistency of such a rule with international standards, guidance may also be sought in procedural rules established at the international level.'

Institutional Aspects

Governing texts

Procedural law

For the SCSL, the sources of procedural law are: the Agreement between the **8.3**
United Nations and the Government of Sierra Leone on the Establishment of
the Special Court for Sierra Leone, signed on 16 January 2002;[4] the Statute of the
Special Court, annexed to the Agreement;[5] the Special Court Agreement (2002)
Ratification Act, as amended on 8 November 2002;[6] the Rules of Procedure and
Evidence, as amended through 27 May 2008;[7] and various practice directions
and directives and codes of conduct.[8]

For the STL, the sources of procedural law are: Security Council Resolution
1757 to which are attached both the Agreement between the United Nations
and the Lebanese Republic pursuant to Security Council Resolution 1664 of 29
March 2006 and the Statute of the Special Tribunal for Lebanon;[9] the Rules of
Procedure and Evidence, as revised through 10 June 2009;[10] and various practice directions and directives and codes of conduct.[11]

For the ECCC, the sources of procedural law are: the Agreement between
the United Nations and the Royal Government of Cambodia concerning the
Prosecution under Cambodian Law of Crimes Committed during the Period
of Democratic Kampuchea, concluded on 6 June 2003;[12] the Law on the
Establishment of the Extraordinary Chambers, as amended through 27 October
2004;[13] and the Internal Rules (ie the Rules of Procedure and Evidence), as
amended through 6 March 2009.[14]

---

[4] 2178 UNTS 137 ('UN-Sierra Leone Agreement'). The Agreement is also available at <http://www.sc-sl.org/> (Documents).

[5] Ibid.

[6] Supplement to Sierra Leone Gazette Vol CXXXIII, No 22 (25 April 2002). The Act is also available at <http://www.sc-sl.org/> (Documents).

[7] Rules of Procedure and Evidence, 16 June 2002 (as amended through 27 May 2008) ('SCSL Rules'), available at <http://www.sc-sl.org/> (Documents).

[8] All these documents are available at <http://www.sc-sl.org/> (Documents).

[9] UN Doc S/RES/1757 (2007), 30 May 2007 ('UN-Lebanon Agreement'). The Agreement and Statute are available at <http://www.stl-tsl.org/> (Documentation).

[10] STL/BD/2009/01/Rev 1 (hereinafter 'STL Rules'), available at <http://www.stl-tsl.org/> (Documentation).

[11] All these documents are available at <http://www.stl-tsl.org/> (Documentation).

[12] The UN-Cambodia Agreement is also available at <http://www.eccc.gov.kh/> (Legal Documents/Agreements).

[13] NS/RKM/1004/006 ('Law on the Extraordinary Chambers'), available at <http://www.eccc.gov.kh/> (Legal Documents/Law on ECCC).

[14] Internal Rules, 12 June 2007 (as amended through 6 March 2009) ('ECCC Rules'), available at <http://www.eccc.gov.kh/> (Legal Documents/Internal Rules and Regulations).

Substantive law

8.4   The applicable law of the SCSL contains both substantive international criminal law and Sierra Leonean law to determine whether crimes have been committed and establish punishment. In particular, the Special Court has the power to prosecute persons who committed, or ordered the commission of, crimes against humanity,[15] serious violations of article 3 common to the Geneva Conventions of 12 August 1949 for the Protection of War Victims, and of Additional Protocol II thereto of 8 June 1977,[16] and other serious violations of international humanitarian law.[17] For what concerns substantive Sierra Leonean law, the Special Court can prosecute persons who have committed offences relating to the abuse of girls under the Prevention of Cruelty to Children Act, 1926 (Cap 31),[18] or offences relating to the wanton destruction of property under the Malicious Damage Act, 1861,[19] albeit to date charges have not been laid under these articles.

The Extraordinary Chambers apply the 1948 Convention on the Prevention and Punishment of the Crime of Genocide, for what concerns the crime of genocide; the Rome Statute of the International Criminal Court, for crimes against humanity, as modified by the Law on the Establishment of the Extraordinary Chambers in the Courts of Cambodia; the 1949 Geneva Conventions,[20] and the 1956 Cambodian Penal Code for what concerns homicide, torture, and

---

[15] SCSL Statute, art 2: '. . . the following crimes as part of a widespread or systematic attack against any civilian population: a. Murder; b. Extermination; c. Enslavement; d. Deportation; e. Imprisonment; f. Torture; g. Rape, sexual slavery, enforced prostitution, forced pregnancy and any other form of sexual violence; h. Persecution on political, racial, ethnic or religious grounds; i. Other inhumane acts'. This is *mutatis mutandis* art 3 of the Statute of the ICTR.

[16] Ibid, art 3: 'These violations shall include: a. Violence to life, health and physical or mental well-being of persons, in particular murder as well as cruel treatment such as torture, mutilation or any form of corporal punishment; b. Collective punishments; c. Taking of hostages; d. Acts of terrorism; e. Outrages upon personal dignity, in particular humiliating and degrading treatment, rape, enforced prostitution and any form of indecent assault; f. Pillage; g. The passing of sentences and the carrying out of executions without previous judgment pronounced by a regularly constituted court, affording all the judicial guarantees which are recognized as indispensable by civilized peoples; h. Threats to commit any of the foregoing acts.'

[17] Ibid, art 4. These include: 'Intentionally directing attacks against the civilian population as such or against individual civilians not taking direct part in hostilities; b. Intentionally directing attacks against personnel, installations, material, units or vehicles involved in a humanitarian assistance or peacekeeping mission in accordance with the Charter of the United Nations, as long as they are entitled to the protection given to civilians or civilian objects under the international law of armed conflict; c. Conscripting or enlisting children under the age of 15 years into armed forces or groups or using them to participate actively in hostilities.'

[18] Ibid, art 5(a): 'i. Abusing a girl under 13 years of age, contrary to section 6; ii. Abusing a girl between 13 and 14 years of age, contrary to section 7; iii. Abduction of a girl for immoral purposes, contrary to section 12'.

[19] Ibid, art 5(b): 'i. Setting fire to dwelling-houses, any person being therein, contrary to section 2; ii. Setting fire to public buildings, contrary to sections 5 and 6; iii. Setting fire to other buildings, contrary to section 6'.

[20] UN-Cambodia Agreement, art 9.

religious persecution;[21] the 1954 Hague Convention for Protection of Cultural Property in the Event of Armed Conflict, for destruction of cultural property;[22] and the Vienna Convention of 1961 on Diplomatic Relations, for crimes against internationally protected persons.[23]

Unlike the Sierra Leone and the Cambodian tribunals, the Special Tribunal for Lebanon does not apply any substantive international criminal law. It rather applies the provisions of the Lebanese Criminal Code relating to the prosecution and punishment of acts of terrorism, crimes and offences against life and personal integrity, illicit associations, and failure to report crimes and offences, including the rules regarding the material elements of a crime, criminal participation, and conspiracy; and articles 6 and 7 of the Lebanese law of 11 January 1958 entitled 'Increasing the Penalties for Sedition, Civil War and Interfaith Struggle'.[24]

Organization

Composition

It is the full participation of nationals from the affected countries that clearly **8.5** sets hybrid criminal tribunals apart from all other international criminal fora. Citizens of the former Yugoslavia or Rwanda have played minor roles in prosecutions and trials at the ICTY or the ICTR. The exact balance between the national and international staff members within a hybrid criminal tribunal varies from case to case. Usually, international judges constitute the majority of the bench, but that is not always the case. Similarly, the Prosecutor and/or the Registrar of the court are foreign while the deputy is local, but, again, there are exceptions, which can only be explained by keeping in mind the particular historical and political context in which each of these bodies was created.

Judges

Disqualification of judges In the case of all hybrid criminal tribunals, a judge **8.6** may not sit on a trial or appeal in a case in which he/she has a personal interest or where his/her impartiality can be otherwise questioned.[25] Any party may apply to the presiding judge of a chamber for the disqualification of a judge of that chamber.[26] At the SCSL, the Chamber rules on the motion to disqualify

---

[21] Ibid. Chapter II of the Law on the Extraordinary Chambers refers to the 1956 Cambodian Penal Code arts 501, 503, 504, 505, 506, 507, and 508 (Homicide), 500 (torture), and 209 and 210 (Religious persecution).
[22] Law on the Extraordinary Chambers, art 7.
[23] Ibid, art 8.
[24] STL Statute, art 2.
[25] SCSL Rules, r 15(a); STL Rules, r 25(a); ECCC Rules, r 34(1).
[26] SCSL Rules, r 15(b); STL Rules, r 25(b), (c); ECCC Rules, r 34(2)–(5).

a judge. In one incident, the President of the Special Court, Judge Geoffrey Robertson, was disqualified by the other four members of the Appeals Chamber from sitting in trials of Foday Sankoh and other members of the Revolutionary United Front because in a book he penned prior to his appointment to the Court he had described Sankoh as 'the nation's butcher' and made pejorative observations about the RUF. The motion to disqualify was submitted by the defence and was supported by the Prosecutor.[27]

At the SCSL, parties can also raise the question of overall fitness of a judge to sit as a member of the Special Court. The President may refer the matter to the Council of Judges which determines whether the allegation is of a serious nature and substantiated.[28] Should it determine so, it refers the matter to the Plenary Meeting of the judges, which in turn will refer the matter to the body that did the original appointment.[29]

At the STL, if necessary, the President appoints a judge to report to him on the merits of an application for disqualification. If the President decides to uphold the application, the President assigns another judge to sit in the place of the disqualified judge.[30]

At the ECCC, an application for disqualification of a co-investigating judge is submitted to the Pre-Trial Chamber. Motions to disqualify an adjudicating judge are submitted to the Chamber in which the judge in question is sitting.[31]

8.7 **Plenary/chambers** In the case of the Special Court for Sierra Leone, international judges always constitute the majority of judges.[32] Three judges serve in the Trial Chamber. One judge is appointed by the government of Sierra Leone, whilst two judges are appointed by the United Nations Secretary-General. Five judges serve in the Appeals Chamber. Two are appointed by the government of Sierra Leone, and the other three are appointed by the Secretary-General. The five judges of the Appeals Chamber alone elect from themselves a presiding judge, who serves as President. The practice of the SCSL trial chambers is to rotate the presiding judge each year. In the *Taylor* trial, the SCSL has a fourth judge, appointed by the United Nations, serving as an alternate judge, and it is planned to have a sixth judge as an alternate in the appeals phase.

---

[27] *Prosecutor v Sesay*, Case SCSL-04-15-AR15, Decision on Defence Motion Seeking the Disqualification of Justice Robertson from the Appeals Chamber, 13 March 2004.

[28] SCSL Rules, r 16(a).

[29] Ibid, r 16(b).

[30] STL Rules, r 25(d).

[31] ECCC Rules, r 34(5). To date, at the ECCC there has been at least one motion to disqualify a Pre-Trial Chamber judge (Judge Ney Thol). The motion was rejected. However, Judge Thol has subsequently recused himself on a number of issues, in which cases the reserve judge has sat in his place.

[32] UN-Sierra Leone Agreement, art 2; SCSL Statute, art 12.

International judges also constitute the majority at the Special Tribunal for Lebanon. The Pre-Trial Chamber is composed of one international judge only. Three judges, of whom one Lebanese and two international, shall sit in the Trial Chamber (plus there are two reserve judges, one international and one Lebanese). Five judges, of whom two Lebanese and three international, shall sit in the Appeals Chamber.[33]

The Extraordinary Chambers in the Courts of Cambodia is an exception. International judges, instead of being the majority, are the minority. Yet, to make sure the judicial process does not become hostage to Cambodian politics, a crafty mechanism has been conceived to give an equal voice to the national and international components. The Extraordinary Chambers consist of a Pre-Trial Chamber (which settles disputes between the two co-Prosecutors and decides on a range of interlocutory appeals, including jurisdictional issues), a Trial Chamber, and a Supreme Court (ie the appeals chamber).[34] The Pre-Trial Chamber is composed of five judges (three Cambodian and two international); the Trial Chambers is composed of five judges (three Cambodian and two international); and the Supreme Court is composed of seven judges (four Cambodian and three international). In all cases, the presiding judge is Cambodian. Yet, all decisions require a super-majority vote: four out of five judges at the pre-trial and trial level, and five out of seven at the Supreme Court level.[35] Separate opinions are allowed.

The requirements to serve as judges of the three tribunals are the same: high moral character, impartiality and integrity, with extensive judicial experience, and independence in the performance of their functions.[36]

The UN Secretary-General appoints the judges of the Special Tribunal for Lebanon in consultation with the Lebanese government and upon the recommendation of a selection panel, made up of two judges currently sitting on, or retired from, an international tribunal, and a representative of the Secretary-General. The Lebanese judges are appointed by the Secretary-General, from a list of 12 nominees presented by the Lebanese government upon the proposal of the Lebanese Supreme Council of the Judiciary. The international judges are appointed by the Secretary-General, from nominations received from member states or other competent persons. The judges serve for a period of three years and are eligible for reappointment.

Likewise, the UN Secretary-General appoints the international judges to the SCSL, in consultation with the Sierra Leonean government, and upon the

---

[33] STL Statute, art 8.

[34] UN-Cambodia Agreement, art 3; Law on the Extraordinary Chambers, art 9.

[35] In case of motions, the effect is that to reject the motion a super-majority is required. If no super-majority is obtained on the rejection, the moving party prevails.

[36] SCSL Statute, art 13; Law on the Extraordinary Chambers, art 10; STL Statute, art 9.

recommendation, at the invitation of the Secretary-General, by states, and in particular the member states of the Economic Community of West African States and the Commonwealth. The 'Sierra Leonean' judges, that is to say, judges nominated by the government of Sierra Leone, but who might or might not be Sierra Leonean judges, are also appointed by the Secretary-General upon recommendation by the Sierra Leonean government.[37] Judges are appointed for a three-year period and may be eligible for reappointment for a further period to be determined by the Secretary-General in consultation with the Sierra Leonean government.

For the ECCC, the Cambodian Supreme Council of the Magistracy appoints all judges, as well as designating the presiding judge of each of the Extraordinary Chambers. All judges are appointed for the duration of proceedings. In the case of the international judges, in theory the UN Secretary-General submits to the Cambodian government a list of no less than seven candidates. The Supreme Council of the Magistracy appoints five sitting judges and at least two reserve judges out of those on the list. In reality, the Secretary-General submitted only one name for each international judge position. Thus, in practice, the UN designated who would sit and who would be in reserve, and the Supreme Council of the Magistracy ratified this decision.

The Prosecutor

8.8   The Office of the Prosecutor in hybrid criminal tribunals essentially functions in the same way that the Office of the Prosecutor of ad hoc and permanent international criminal courts functions. It is a separate and independent organ of the court in charge of investigating, issuing indictments (to be confirmed by a pre-trial judge or another chamber), and pleading the case against the indictee in court.

The ECCC is an exception in this regard as it separates the task of investigating from prosecuting, entrusting the former to two co-investigating judges and the latter to two co-prosecutors.[38] In particular, the co-prosecutors collect the elements of evidence and define the crimes that are to be pursued. The case file is then passed to the co-investigating judges. The co-investigating judges are impartial. They are not a party to the case, as are the prosecutor or defence. They have a duty to collect both incriminating and exculpatory evidence. Provided there is sufficient evidence, they are responsible for sending the case to the Trial Chamber for adjudication.

At the SCSL, the Prosecutor is appointed by the Secretary-General of the United Nations after consultation with the government of Sierra Leone.[39]

---

[37] Interestingly, Sierra Leone appointed to Trial Chamber II a Samoan judge (Richard Lussick) in lieu of a Sierra Leone national.

[38] UN-Cambodia Agreement, arts 5 and 6.

[39] UN-Sierra Leone Agreement, art 3(1).

The Deputy Prosecutor is appointed by the government of Sierra Leone, in consultation with the Secretary-General of the United Nations. At the time of writing, the Prosecutor, Mr Stephen Rapp from the United States, resigned and the Deputy Prosecutor, Mr Joseph Kamara from Sierra Leone, has been appointed Acting Prosecutor.

Likewise, at the STL the Prosecutor is appointed by the Secretary-General, after consultation with the government of Lebanon and upon the recommendation of a selection panel, for a renewable three-year term.[40] The current Prosecutor is Mr Daniel A Bellemare from Canada. The Prosecutor is assisted by a Lebanese Deputy Prosecutor (currently Mrs Joyce Tabet), who is appointed by the government of the Republic of Lebanon in consultation with the Secretary-General and the Prosecutor.[41]

As was noted above, the ECCC differs from other hybrid criminal tribunals because it has both prosecutors and investigating judges, and because it has two of each: a Cambodian and an international. The national Co-Prosecutor (currently Ms Chea Leang) and Co-Investigating Judge (Mr You Bunleng) are appointed by the Supreme Council of the Magistracy, and the international Co-Prosecutor (Mr William Smith, from Australia, currently serves as the Acting International Co-Prosecutor) and Co-Investigating Judge (Mr Marcel Lemonde, from France) are appointed by the Supreme Council of the Magistracy of Cambodia out of a list of two nominees submitted by the UN Secretary-General.[42]

The co-prosecutor and co-investigating judges are supposed to be in agreement about approaches to investigation and prosecution.[43] However, should that not be the case in reality, the co-prosecutors or co-investigating judges must submit in writing the reasons for their different positions to the Director of the Office of Administration.[44] The dispute is settled by a Pre-Trial Chamber of five judges (three appointed by the Supreme Council of the Magistracy, with one as President, and two appointed by the Supreme Council of the Magistracy upon nomination by the UN Secretary-General).[45] A decision of such Pre-Trial Chamber, against which there is no appeal, requires the affirmative vote of at least four judges.[46] If there is no super-majority, the investigation or prosecution proceeds.[47]

---

[40] UN-Lebanon Agreement, art 3; STL Statute, art 11(3).

[41] UN-Lebanon Agreement, art 3(3); STL Statute, art 11(4).

[42] In reality, the Secretary-General forwarded only one name for the co-investigating judge position, that of Mr Lemonde.

[43] UN-Cambodia Agreement, arts 5(4), 6(4).

[44] Ibid, art 7.

[45] Ibid, art 7(2).

[46] Ibid, art 7(3).

[47] Ibid, art 7(4).

Secretariat

8.9 As in the case of all other international criminal tribunals, judges, defence, and prosecution are supported by the Registry, which is in charge of the non-judicial aspects of the tribunals' work. Typically, the Registry also includes various divisions in charge of court management, defence, detention, the library, translations, outreach and public affairs, security, procurement, witness and victim support, and other administrative offices.

At the STL and SCSL, the Registrar is appointed by the UN Secretary-General and is a staff member of the United Nations. The current Registrar at STL is Mr David Tolbert, from the United States. Ms Binta Mansaray, from Sierra Leone, is Acting Registrar at the SCSL. The Registrars serve for a three-year term and may be eligible for reappointment for a further period to be determined by the Secretary-General in consultation, respectively, with the Sierra Leonean and Lebanese government.[48]

At the ECCC, the registry is called the 'Office of Administration'. The Director of the Office of Administration (ie the Registrar) is appointed by the Cambodian government (currently Mr Tony Kranh, Acting Director) and is responsible for the overall management of the Office of Administration, except in matters that are subject to United Nations rules and procedures.[49] The Deputy Director of the Office of Administration (Mr Knut Rosandhaug, from Norway) is appointed by the Secretary-General and is responsible for all administration of the international components of the Extraordinary Chambers, the Pre-Trial Chamber, the co-investigating judges, the Prosecutors' Office, and the Office of Administration.[50]

Technical/scientific experts

8.10 As compared to the ICTY and ICTR, there are scant provisions on experts in the constitutive instruments of hybrid criminal tribunals. The Rules of Procedure and Evidence of the STL provide only that: 'The Trial Chamber may, *proprio motu* or at the request of a Party, order a medical, psychiatric or psychological examination of the accused. In such a case, unless the Trial Chamber otherwise orders, the Registrar shall entrust this task to one or several experts whose names appear on a list previously drawn up by the Registry and approved by the Council of Judges.'[51] The Rules of Procedure of the Special Court for Sierra Leone are no less terse, simply regulating the testimony of expert witnesses.[52]

---

[48] SCSL Statute, art 16(2); STL Statute, art 12(3).
[49] UN-Cambodia Agreement, art 8(2).
[50] Ibid, art 8(3).
[51] STL Rules, r 132.
[52] SCSL Rules, r 94 *bis*.

Conversely, the ECCC has very extensive provisions about the use of experts by the Chambers.[53]

Jurisdiction

Ratione personae and loci

The personal and territorial jurisdiction of the SCSL includes those 'who bear the greatest responsibility for serious violations of international humanitarian law and Sierra Leonean law committed in the territory of Sierra Leone' and includes also those 'who, in committing such crimes, have threatened the establishment of and implementation of the peace process in Sierra Leone' while not being in Sierra Leone, like in the case of neighbouring Liberia's President Charles Taylor.[54] Resort to child soldiers was a particularly grim feature of the Sierra Leonean conflict. Thus the Statute of the Special Court excludes from jurisdiction any person who was under the age of 15 at the time of the alleged commission of the crime.[55] **8.11**

The jurisdiction of the STL is rather narrow. It includes only 'persons responsible for the attack of 14 February 2005 resulting in the death of former Lebanese Prime Minister Rafiq Hariri and in the death or injury of other persons'.[56] However, 'if the Tribunal finds that other attacks that occurred in Lebanon...are connected in accordance with the principles of criminal justice and are of a nature and gravity similar to the attack of 14 February 2005, it shall also have jurisdiction over persons responsible for such attacks'.[57]

---

[53] ECCC Rules, r 31. See also ibid, rr 80, 80 *bis*, 84, 88, 91.

[54] SCSL Statute, art 1. Paras 2 and 3 recite: '2. Any transgressions by peacekeepers and related personnel present in Sierra Leone pursuant to the Status of Mission Agreement in force between the United Nations and the Government of Sierra Leone or agreements between Sierra Leone and other Governments or regional organizations, or, in the absence of such agreement, provided that the peacekeeping operations were undertaken with the consent of the Government of Sierra Leone, shall be within the primary jurisdiction of the sending State. 3. In the event the sending State is unwilling or unable genuinely to carry out an investigation or prosecution, the Court may, if authorized by the Security Council on the proposal of any State, exercise jurisdiction over such persons.'

[55] SCSL Statute, art 7. A special regime for those who were between 15 and 18 at the time of the commission of the crime applies. Namely 'he or she shall be treated with dignity and a sense of worth, taking into account his or her young age and the desirability of promoting his or her rehabilitation, reintegration into and assumption of a constructive role in society, and in accordance with international human rights standards, in particular the rights of the child. In the disposition of a case against a juvenile offender, the Special Court shall order any of the following: care guidance and supervision orders, community service orders, counseling, foster care, correctional, educational and vocational training programmes, approved schools and, as appropriate, any programmes of disarmament, demobilization and reintegration or programmes of child protection agencies.' SCSL Statute, art 7(1)–(2).

[56] STL Statute, art 1.

[57] Ibid: 'This connection includes but is not limited to a combination of the following elements: criminal intent (motive), the purpose behind the attacks, the nature of the victims targeted, the pattern of the attacks (modus operandi) and the perpetrators.' Ibid. See also text accompanying footnote 65; STL Rules, r 12.

The jurisdiction of the ECCC includes 'senior leaders of Democratic Kampuchea' and 'those who were most responsible for the crimes and serious violations of Cambodian laws related to crimes, international humanitarian law and custom, and international conventions recognized by Cambodia'.[58] It should be noted that the ECCC jurisdiction is not limited to the territory of Cambodia but could also extend to violations of international humanitarian law and custom that occurred in neighbouring countries (eg Laos, Thailand, or Vietnam).

Ratione materiae

8.12 See above 'Substantive law'.

Ratione temporis

8.13 The temporal jurisdiction of the ECCC includes acts committed between 17 April 1975 and 6 January 1979. That is, from when the Khmer Rouge entered Phnom Penh to when they fled from the Vietnamese army.[59]

The temporal jurisdiction of the SCSL commences on 30 November 1996 (when President Ahmad Tejan Kabbah and RUF leader Foday Sankoh signed a peace accord to end the civil war), and there is no end date.[60]

The temporal jurisdiction of the STL includes the attack of 14 February 2005, and should the Tribunal find that other attacks occurred in Lebanon between 1 October 2004 and 12 December 2005, or any later date decided by the UN and the Lebanese government, and with the consent of the Security Council, and are connected in accordance with the attack of 14 February 2005, it shall also have jurisdiction over those attacks.[61]

Relationship with national courts

8.14 The SCSL and the STL have concurrent jurisdiction with the national courts of Sierra Leone and Lebanon, respectively.[62] However, like the ICTY and ICTR, the Special Court and the Special Tribunal have primacy over the national courts of the respective states. At any stage of the procedure, they may formally request a national court to defer to their competence.[63]

Both the Statute of the Special Court and that of the Special Tribunal provide that no person shall be tried before a national court (of Sierra Leone or Lebanon) for acts for which he or she has already been tried by the Special Court or the

---

[58] Law on the Extraordinary Chambers, art 2.
[59] Ibid, art 1.
[60] SCSL Statute, art 1.
[61] STL Statute, art 1.
[62] SCSL Statute, art 8(1); STL Statute, art 4(1).
[63] SCSL Statute, art 8(2); STL Statute, art 4(1)–(3); STL Rules, rr 17, 19, 20 and 21; SCSL Rules, rr 9–11.

Special Tribunal.[64] A person who has been tried by a national court may be subsequently tried by the Special Court or Special Tribunal if the national court proceedings were not impartial or independent, were designed to shield the accused from criminal responsibility, or the case was not diligently prosecuted.[65]

According to the Agreement between the UN and the Cambodian government, the ECCC is established in the existing court structure of Cambodia.[66] The question of whether the jurisdiction of the Extraordinary Chambers is shared with other non-internationalized parts of the Cambodian judicial system is controversial. On the one hand, there has been little inclination to prosecute former Khmer Rouge leadership in the regular Cambodian courts. Indeed, that is precisely the reason for the establishment of the ECCC. The possibility of any Cambodian court wishing to step in seems to be remote. Perhaps because of this, the Agreement and the Law on the Extraordinary Chambers in the Courts of Cambodia do not contain provisions on double jeopardy. Also, it should be noted that article 25 of the Agreement provides that: 'The Royal Government of Cambodia shall comply without undue delay with any request for assistance by the Co-Investigating Judges, the Co-Prosecutors and the Extraordinary Chambers, or an order issued by any of them.'[67] To the extent the judiciary of Cambodia is understood as being part of the government of Cambodia, Cambodian courts have also an obligation of cooperation with the ECCC, which, arguably, includes deferring to the ECCC. On the other hand, in the past there have been at least two trials, *in absentia,* of Khmer Rouge leaders, Pol Pot and Ieng Sary, one of which, Ieng Sary, is currently on trial before the ECCC.

Advisory jurisdiction

These tribunals do not have advisory jurisdiction.   **8.15**

Procedural Aspects

Languages

The official and working language of the Special Court for Sierra Leone is **8.16** English.[68] However, since Krio is the lingua franca of Sierra Leone, the Statute provides that the accused or suspects shall have the right to use their own

---

[64] SCSL Statute, 9(1); STL Statute, art 5(1); SCSL Rules, r 13; STL Rules, r 23.

[65] SCSL Statute, art 9(2)(b); STL Statute, art 5(2). In addition the Statute of the SCSL provides that 'a person who has been tried by a national court . . . may be subsequently tried by the Special Court if . . . the act for which he or she was tried was characterized as an ordinary crime'. SCSL Statute, art 9(2)(a).

[66] Law on the Extraordinary Chambers, art 2.

[67] UN-Cambodia Agreement, art 25.

[68] SCSL Statute, art 24; UN-Sierra Leone Agreement, art 18; SCSL Rules, r 3(a).

language.[69] Any person appearing before, or giving evidence to, the Special Court who does not have sufficient knowledge of English may ask for permission to use his/her own language.[70] The Registrar shall make any necessary arrangements for interpretation and translation.[71]

The official languages of the Special Tribunal are Arabic, English, and French. However, in any given case, the Pre-Trial Judge or a Chamber may decide that only one or two of the official languages may be used as working languages as appropriate.[72] Decisions on any written or oral submission are rendered in English or French. Judgments, sentences, decisions on jurisdiction, and other decisions which the Pre-Trial Judge or a Chamber decides that address fundamental issues are translated into Arabic.[73] As in the case of Sierra Leone, an accused shall have the right to use his/her own language during proceedings before the Pre-Trial Judge or a Chamber.[74] Other persons appearing before the Pre-Trial Judge or a Chamber—other than those appearing as counsel—who do not have sufficient knowledge of the official languages may use their own language, subject to the authorization of the Pre-Trial Judge or a Chamber.[75]

Once again, the ECCC differs slightly from the template of the two special courts. According to the UN-Cambodia Agreement, 'the official language of the Extraordinary Chambers and the Pre-Trial Chamber is Khmer'.[76] However, the *working* languages of the Extraordinary Chambers and the Pre-Trial Chamber are Khmer, English, and French.[77]

Instituting proceedings

8.17 The Office of the Prosecutor (and, in the case of the ECCC, the co-investigating judges) is an independent organ of the tribunal. In theory, the Prosecutor has broad discretionary powers in deciding who is going to be prosecuted. In reality, prosecutors in hybrid criminal tribunals are constrained by the narrowly defined

---

[69] SCSL Rules, r 3(b).

[70] Ibid, r 3(c).

[71] Ibid, r 3(d).

[72] STL Statute, art 14; STL Rules, r 10(a).

[73] STL Rules, r 10(e).

[74] Ibid, r 10(c).

[75] Ibid, r 10(d).

[76] UN-Cambodia Agreement, art 26(1). It should be noted that the UN-Cambodia Agreement provides also that translations of public documents and interpretation at public hearings into Russian may be provided by the Royal Government of Cambodia at its discretion and expense on condition that such services do not hinder the proceedings before the Extraordinary Chambers. UN-Cambodia Agreement, art 26(3). During negotiations, the Cambodian government insisted that Russian be one of the official languages, probably because many of its judicial officials were trained in Russia and speak it, but the UN refused. Art 26(3) is the compromise they reached. However, to date, the Cambodian government has shown no inclination to make use of the possibility of providing interpretation in Russian.

[77] UN-Cambodia Agreement, art 26(2); Law on the Extraordinary Chambers, art 45.

jurisdiction, by the temporary nature of the courts in which they operate, and by strict budgetary limits.

The first phase of prosecution is the investigation. At the SCSL and STL, the Prosecutor initiates proceedings. At ECCC, action is started by the co-prosecutors, but investigation is entrusted to the co-investigating judges, albeit the rules do not specify how extensive investigation by the co-prosecutors is going to be and what is going to be left to the co-investigating judges. In all cases, even before the tribunals were created, there already existed a wealth of information available about who committed what crimes, as events took place often over several years under the eyes of the international community and the United Nations. The task of individuating who the prima-facie suspects are is, therefore, much simplified.

For sake of clarity, we will treat the SCSL and STL procedures separately from the ECCC procedure. In the case of Sierra Leone and Lebanon, the Prosecutor has broad powers to investigate, such as the power to question suspects, witnesses, and victims, and to collect evidence and conduct on-site investigations, to seek the assistance of the authorities of any state, as well as any relevant international body, including INTERPOL, and to request such orders from a Trial Chamber or a judge as may be necessary.[78]

Upon determination that a prima-facie case exists, the Prosecutor prepares an indictment and transmits it to a judge of the Trial Chamber for confirmation.[79] The indictment must contain a concise statement of the facts and the crimes with which the accused is charged. If the judge is satisfied that a prima-facie case has been established, the indictment is confirmed. A confirming judge may approve or dismiss each count contained in an indictment. If not, the judge may request additional materials, adjourn the review to give the Prosecutor the opportunity to modify the indictment, or dismiss the indictment. The Prosecutor may amend the indictment at any time before it is confirmed without leave. Once the indictment has been confirmed and before the assignment of the case to a Trial Chamber, the Prosecutor may amend the indictment with leave of the confirming judge or a judge assigned by the President if not 'improper prejudice' ensues for the accused. After the assignment of the case to a Trial Chamber, leave of the Trial Chamber hearing the case or a judge of that Chamber must be sought to amend the indictment, and leave granted only after having heard the parties.[80] The indictment may be withdrawn under similar conditions.[81]

Proceedings start differently at the ECCC. That is largely due to the fact that Cambodian criminal procedure is much more similar to French criminal

---

[78] STL Rules, r 61; SCSL Rules, r 39.
[79] STL Rules, r 68; SCSL Rules, r 47.
[80] SCSL Rules, r 50; STL Rules, r 71.
[81] SCSL Rules, r 51; STL Rules, r 72.

procedure than to the criminal procedure of international criminal courts. The investigative stage begins with a preliminary investigation by the co-prosecutors, on their own motion or at the request of one of the parties, such as defence or the 'civil parties' (ie victims), to determine whether there is evidence showing that crimes within the jurisdiction of the ECCC were committed, and to identify potential suspects and witnesses.[82] Should the co-prosecutors have reason to believe that crimes within the jurisdiction of the ECCC have been committed, they will file an 'Introductory Submission' with the co-investigating judges.[83] The Introductory Submission specifies the facts, the type of offences alleged, the applicable law, and the name of any person to be investigated if any have already been identified.[84]

Once the Introductory Submission has been filed, the co-investigating judges investigate only those facts stated in the Introductory Submission. They cannot investigate new facts, unless they have received a Supplementary Submission from the co-prosecutors.[85] The co-investigating judges have the power to charge any person against whom there is clear and consistent evidence indicating that such person may be criminally responsible for the commission of a crime referred to in the Introductory Submission or the Supplementary Submission, even when such persons were not named in the submission.[86]

The co-investigating judges investigate any incriminating or exculpatory evidence.[87] They may take any investigative action such as question suspects; interview victims and witnesses; seize physical evidence; seek expert opinions; conduct on-site investigations; issue summonses, arrest warrants, detention orders; take any appropriate measures to provide for the safety and support of potential witnesses and other sources; seek information and assistance from any sources they deem appropriate (eg states, the United Nations, intergovernmental or non-governmental organizations).[88]

During the investigation, the parties (co-prosecutors, defence, and civil parties) may also request the co-investigating judges to make such orders or undertake such investigative actions considered necessary for the conduct of the investigation.[89] Should the co-investigating judges not agree with the request, they shall issue a reasoned rejection order as soon as possible and, in any event,

---

[82] ECCC Rules, r 50.
[83] Ibid, r 53.
[84] Ibid, r 53(1).
[85] Ibid, rr 55(2), 55(3).
[86] Ibid, r 55(4).
[87] Ibid, r 55(5).
[88] Ibid.
[89] Ibid, r 55(10).

before the end of the judicial investigation. The order can be appealed before the Pre-Trial Chamber.[90]

Once the co-investigating judges consider that the investigation has been concluded, they notify all the parties (co-prosecutors, defence, and civil parties) who have 15 days to request further investigative action.[91] Again, should the co-investigating judges decide to reject such requests, they shall issue a reasoned order, which is subject to appeal before the Pre-Trial Chamber. Once this period has expired, been waived, or the appeal has been heard by the Pre-Trial Chamber, the co-investigating judges forward the case file to the co-prosecutors, who issue a written final submission requesting the co-investigating judges to either indict the charged person or dismiss the case.

The co-investigating judges issue a 'Closing Order', either issuing an indictment or dismissing the case because the acts in question do not amount to crimes within the jurisdiction of the ECCC; or because the perpetrators of the acts have not been identified; or if there is insufficient evidence against the charged person.[92] Either way, the co-investigating judges are not bound by the co-prosecutors' final submission. The indictment is subject to appeal only by the co-prosecutors, while the Dismissal Order can be appealed by the co-prosecutors and civil parties. Where no appeal is filed against a Closing Order, the co-investigating judges will forward the case to the Trial Chamber or, in case of a dismissal, to the Office of Administration for archiving.[93]

From this moment, the co-investigating judges do not play any further role in the case. However, should new evidence become available after a Dismissal Order, the investigation may be reopened by the co-investigating judges at the initiative of the co-prosecutors.[94]

Financial assistance

In the case of the three hybrid criminal tribunals, an indigent person subject to **8.18** investigation or prosecution has a right to free legal assistance.[95] The Registrar assigns and pays for the services of a lawyer, drawing from a list of available counsels deemed eligible.[96]

Preliminary motions and proceedings

The commencement of court proceedings before all international criminal **8.19** courts, including the hybrid criminal tribunals, is subject to confirmation of the

---

[90] Ibid.
[91] Ibid, r 66(1). [92] Ibid, r 67.
[93] Ibid, r 69. [94] Ibid, r 70.
[95] STL Rules, r 59(a); SCSL Rules, r 45(b)(ii); ECCC Rules, r 22(1)(b).
[96] STL Rules, r 59(b); SCSL Rules, r 45(c); ECCC Rules, r 11(2)(d).

indictment by a judge. At the ECCC the co-investigating judges confirm the indictment. At the Special Court a 'designated judge' does so, and at the Special Tribunal for Lebanon a 'Pre-Trial Judge' reviews the indictment. Once the indictment is confirmed, the judge may, at the request of the Prosecutor, issue such orders and warrants as may be necessary for the conduct of the trial.[97]

At the Special Court for Sierra Leone and the ECCC, there is no trial *in absentia*. The accused must be brought before the Trial Chamber without delay and must be formally charged at an initial appearance.[98] However, the Special Tribunal for Lebanon differs not only from the other hybrid criminal tribunals but also from all other international criminal tribunals as it allows trial in the absence of the accused (other than the refusal of the accused to attend or waiver in writing of the right to attend) if he/she has not been handed over to the Tribunal by the state authorities concerned, or if he/she has absconded or otherwise cannot be found and all reasonable steps have been taken to secure his/her appearance before the Tribunal and to inform him/her of the charges confirmed by the Pre-Trial Judge.[99] In case of conviction *in absentia*, if the accused has not designated a defence counsel of his/her choosing, he/she has the right to be retried in his/her presence before the Special Tribunal, unless he/she accepts the judgment.[100]

At the initial appearance of an accused before the Special Court and Special Tribunal, charges are read and the accused is instructed to enter a plea to the charges.[101] This is typical in common law criminal procedure. However, at the ECCC, which, again, is based on civil law criminal procedure, there exists no guilty plea. Rule 89 of the Rules of Procedure and Evidence at the ECCC provides that: 'The President shall declare the substantive hearing open. The President shall order the Greffiers to read the counts against the Accused...Before any Accused is called for questioning, the Co-Prosecutors may make a brief opening statement of the charges against the Accused. The Accused or his/her lawyers may respond briefly.'

At the SCSL and STL, the Prosecutor must disclose evidence during the pre-trial phase.[102] At the SCSL, defence disclosure of its evidence to the Prosecutor before the defence case is discretionary, and at the STL it appears to be mandatory.[103] In order to ensure an expeditious trial, the Trial Chamber holds a

---

[97] SCSL Rules, r 54; STL Rules, r 77.

[98] SCSL Statute, art 17(4)(d); SCSL Rules, rr 60, 61; ECCC Rules, r 81(1). There are exceptions, of course, for instance when the accused refuses to attend proceedings or cannot for medical reasons.

[99] STL Statute, art 22(1). See also STL Rules, rr 206–209.

[100] STL Statute, art 22.3.

[101] Ibid, art 20(1); STL Rules, rr 98–100; SCSL Rules, rr 61 and ff.

[102] STL Rules, rr 110–114; SCSL Rules, rr 66–70.

[103] See SCSL Rule 73 *bis* (which reads a Chamber 'may' order); STL Rule, r 112(a) (which reads the Defence 'shall' provide).

pre-trial conference and may hold a pre-defence conference whereby the parties clarify and finalize their trial positions.[104]

After the Prosecutor delivers the indictment and all supporting materials to the defence, the defence can file preliminary motions in writing.[105] Such motions may challenge jurisdiction; allege defects in the form of the indictment; seek the severance of counts joined in one indictment or seek separate trials; or raise objections based on the refusal of a request for assignment of counsel.

The motions are disposed before the commencement of the opening statements of the trial. A decision on motions challenging jurisdiction can generally be appealed as a matter of right.[106] Other decisions on preliminary motions, which are not on jurisdiction, but rather on form of the indictment, severance, and similar issues, can be appealed when they involve an issue that would significantly affect the fair and expeditious conduct of the proceedings or the outcome of the trial.[107]

Provisional measures

As in the case of all international criminal bodies, there are several measures the Prosecutor (or the co-investigating judge) can take, or request a Pre-Trial Chamber or a designated judge to take, during the investigation and pre-trial phase. For instance, the Prosecutor (and/or co-investigating judge at the ECCC) may request that a state arrest a suspect or an accused and place him in custody in accordance with the laws of that state; or to seize physical evidence; or to take all appropriate measures to prevent the escape of a suspect or an accused, injury to or intimidation of a victim or witness, or the destruction of evidence.[108]   **8.20**

Written phase

There are several steps that can only be taken in writing. For instance, the indictment ('Closing Order' at the ECCC) is always in writing.[109] Motions are generally in writing albeit some can be done orally.[110] At the SCSL and STL, the Prosecutor and defence are required to file pre-trial and pre-appeal briefs.[111] The   **8.21**

---

[104] STL Rules, rr 127–129; SCSL Rules, rr 73 *bis* and *ter.*

[105] STL Rules, r 90(a); SCSL Rules, r 72(a). No later than 30 days in the case of Lebanon, and 21 days in the case of Sierra Leone. Ibid.

[106] STL Rules, r 90(b)(i); SCSL Rules, r 72(e).

[107] STL Rules, r 90(b)(ii); SCSL Rules, r 72(F).

[108] See, for instance, STL Rules, rr 62, 64, 77–85; SCSL Rules, rr 40, 41, 54–59; ECCC Rules, rr 29 42, 43, 44, 61, 63, 64.

[109] SCSL Rules, r 47; STL Rules, r 68; ECCC Rules, r 67.

[110] See eg STL Rules, r 126(b).

[111] For the pre-trial brief see SCSL Rules, rr 73 *bis* and *ter* (the Trial Chamber has discretion to ('may') order the defence, and has done so in practice. STL Rules, r 91. For the pre-appeal briefs see STL Rules, rr 181–183; SCSL Rules, rr 111–113.

Prosecutor should detail a summary of the evidence that the Prosecutor intends to bring regarding the commission of the alleged crime and the form of responsibility incurred by the accused for each count. The brief shall include any admissions by the parties, as well as a statement of matters that are not in dispute; the list of witnesses the Prosecutor intends to call; and the list of exhibits the Prosecutor intends to offer stating, where possible, whether the defence has any objection as to authenticity. The pre-trial brief of the defence must address factual and legal issues including, in general terms, the nature of the accused's defence, and the matters which the accused disputes in the Prosecutor's pre-trial brief and the reasons why. At the close of evidence, the parties file a final trial brief.[112]

Oral phase

8.22 At the beginning of the trial each party may make an opening statement.[113] After that, witnesses and evidence is introduced by each party. Testimony is always given orally and in court, but written testimony can be admitted in some cases.[114] After the presentation of all evidence both the Prosecutor and the defence may present a closing argument.[115]

All proceedings before the Trial Chamber, except for the deliberations, are held in public.[116] The Trial Chamber may exclude the press and the public only for reasons of public order or morality; safety; security or non-disclosure of the identity of a victim or witness; or protection of the interests of justice.[117]

The judgment is delivered orally in public, and is followed by a reasoned opinion in writing to which separate and dissenting opinions may be appended.[118]

Third party intervention/multiple proceedings

8.23 The Rules of Procedure and Evidence of hybrid criminal tribunals allow only a very limited role for third parties in the proceedings. The role of *amicus curiae* is addressed below. The main exception is the role played by victims.

At the SCSL (as well as at the ICTY and ICTR), victims appear only as witnesses. They have no standing and their legal representatives play no role in proceedings. In the case of the STL and ECCC (as well as the ICC), victims are to play a substantial role. A victim is defined as a person 'who has suffered physical, material, or mental harm as a direct result of an attack within the

---

[112] See SCSL Rules, r 86(b); STL Rules, r 147(b).

[113] STL Rules, r 143; SCSL Rules, r 84; ECCC Rules, r 89(2) *bis*.

[114] STL Rules, rr 149(f), 155, 158; SCSL Rules, rr 71, 85(d). See also ECCC Rules, rr 91 and 25–26.

[115] SCSL Rules, r 86; ECCC Rules, r 94; STL Rules, r 147. At the STL, the Prosecutor may thereafter present a rebuttal and the defence a rejoinder. Ibid.

[116] SCSL Rules, r 78; STL Rules, r 136; ECCC Rules, r 79(6).

[117] SCSL Rules, r 79; STL Rules, r 137; ECCC Rules, r 79(6)(b).

[118] STL Statute, art 23; SCSL Statute, art 18; ECCC Rules, rr 101(2), 102.

Tribunal's jurisdiction'.[119] Persons claiming to be victims of a crime within the tribunal's jurisdiction may request the Pre-Trial Judge, in the case of STL, or the co-investigating judge or Trial Chamber, in the case of the ECCC, to be granted the status of victims participating in the proceedings.[120] At the ECCC, victims who have been given such status are called 'Civil Parties' (from French 'Partie Civile').[121] After hearing the Prosecutor and the defence, the judge to whom the request was made rules on the matter, taking into consideration several factors.[122] The Pre-Trial Judge may limit the number of victims entitled to express their views and concerns in proceedings and may appoint one or more common legal representatives for multiple victims (or representatives for indigent victims).[123] Victims may appeal the decision of the Pre-Trial Judge.[124]

Victims participating in proceedings are entitled, for instance, to receive documents filed by the parties; request the Chamber (Trial or Appeal) to call witnesses or to tender other evidence; cross-examine witnesses and file motions and briefs; and file written submissions at the sentencing stage relating to the impact of crimes on the victims.[125] Both the STL and ECCC are equipped with a unit to assist the participation of victims and their legal representatives.[126]

At the STL and SCSL, persons accused of crimes committed in the course of the same transaction may be jointly charged and tried.[127] At the SCSL, there have been three main 'joint trials': against the leaders of the Armed Forces Revolutionary Council (*Prosecutor v Brima, Kamara and Kanu*), those of the Civil Defence Forces (*Prosecutor v Fofana and Kondewa*), and those of the Revolutionary United Front (*Prosecutor v Sesay, Kallon and Gbao*).[128] Also, two or more crimes may be joined in one indictment if the series of acts were committed in the same transaction and by the same person.[129]

---

[119] STL Rules, r 2. The STL limits the definition of victims to natural persons, while the ECCC enlarges it to 'legal entities'. ECCC Rules, Glossary, 'Victim'.

[120] STL Rules, r 86(a); STL Statute, art 17; ECCC Rules, r 23.

[121] ECCC Rules, Glossary, 'Civil Party'.

[122] STL Rules, r 86(b). See also ECCC Rules, r 23(2).

[123] STL Rules, rr 87(c),(e); ECCC Rules, r 23(8). At the ECC, victims may also choose to organize their Civil Party action by becoming members of a Victims' Association. ECCC Rules, r 23(9).

[124] STL Rules, r 86 (d); ECCC Rules, r 23(4).

[125] STL Rules, r 87. See eg ECCC Rules, rr 23(6), 31(20), 56(10), 59, 74(4), 80, 83, 113.

[126] At the STL, the relevant unit is called the 'Victim Participation Unit'. STL Rules, r 51. At the ECCC, it is called the 'Victims Unit'. ECCC Rules, r 12.

[127] STL Statute, art 11(1); SCSL Rules, r 48; STL Rules, r 70(a). At the time of writing, at the ECCC the prosecution is planning a joint trial of at least four suspects. Whether the other organs of the ECCC will agree to this move remains to be seen.

[128] See <http://www.sc-sl.org/> (Cases).

[129] SCSL Rules, r 49; STL Rules, r 70(b).

Amicus curiae

8.24 In the case of these hybrid criminal tribunals, a Chamber (or in the case of the ECCC, a co-investigating judge) may, if considered desirable for the proper determination of the case, invite or grant leave to any state, organization, or person to make submissions as *amicus curiae* on any issue specified.[130] The SCSL Rule on *amicus curiae* relies on these same general terms. The rules on *amicus curiae* of the Special Tribunal for Lebanon and the ECCC are more specific, adding that *amicus curiae* submissions must be in writing; that the Court can allow *amici* (states, organization, or persons) to appear before it; and that the parties shall have the opportunity to respond to any submissions made by *amicus curiae* or third parties.[131]

This is the classical role played by *amici curiae*: to provide information the judges believe desirable for the proper determination of the case. However, the Rules of Procedure of the STL and those of the ECCC also add other unorthodox roles for the *amicus*. For instance, in the case of the STL, the Prosecutor may file a motion for a ruling by the Pre-Trial Judge that an attack that occurred in Lebanon between 1 October 2004 and 12 December 2005 is 'connected' to the Hariri attack, the focus of the subject-matter jurisdiction of the Tribunal ('Connected Case Submission'). The Prosecutor may appeal the ruling by the Pre-Trial Judge, in which case the Appeals Chamber may request the Head of the Defence Office to nominate an independent counsel as *amicus curiae* to act in opposition to the Prosecutor's appeal.[132] The need for an appointment of an *amicus curiae* for the defence on a connected case decision can be explained by the fact that, at that point in time in the case, there is still no accused who can oppose the Prosecution's appeal.

Another example from the STL is when the Pre-Trial Judge or a Chamber has reason to believe that a person may be in contempt of the Tribunal and the Prosecutor indicates a preference not to investigate the matter or submit an indictment, or in the view of the Pre-Trial Judge or the Chamber the Prosecutor has a conflict of interest with respect to the relevant conduct, the Registrar may be directed to appoint an *amicus curiae* to investigate the matter and report back to the Pre-Trial Judge or the Chamber as to whether there are sufficient grounds for contempt proceedings.[133]

In the case of the ECCC, in the Closing Order, the co-investigating judges make any necessary decisions concerning sealed items and, for this purpose, may

---

[130] SCSL Rules, r 74; STL Rules, r 131; ECCC Rules, r 33.

[131] STL Rules, r 131; ECCC Rules, r 33. *Amici* can appear before the tribunal only in the case of Lebanon.

[132] STL Rules, r 11(d).

[133] STL Rules, r 134(c)(ii). See also ibid, r 152(b)(ii), (c)(ii); SCSL Rules, r 77(c)(iii) on contempt allows for the appointment of 'experienced independent counsel' for purposes of investigating allegations of contempt.

grant leave or invite the submission of *amicus curiae* briefs.[134] Or, when the judgment is pronounced, the Chamber makes any necessary decisions concerning sealed items and, for this purpose, it may grant leave or invite the submission of *amicus curiae* briefs.[135]

Representation of the parties

An accused has the right to defend himself/herself in person or to be assisted by **8.25** counsel of his/her choice or to be assigned legal assistance without payment if he/she does not have sufficient means.[136] The ECCC does not have specific rules regulating self-representation. The STL limits the right to self-defence by giving the Pre-Trial Judge, the Trial Chamber, or the Appeal Chamber the power to impose counsel, to represent or otherwise assist the accused, whenever the judges find that this is necessary in the interests of justice and to ensure a fair and expeditious trial.[137]

Hybrid tribunals are equipped with autonomous units within the Registry to ensure the rights of the suspects and indictees. At the STL and SCSL these units are called 'Defence Office', while at the ECCC the name is 'Defence Support Section'. These units provide, *inter alia*, legal advice and assistance during the arrest and preliminary detention phases and before the suspect has exercised the right to choose a counsel; legal assistance to indigent suspects and indictees; lists of qualified criminal defence counsels from which suspects and indictees can select their own; and assistance to counsels, where appropriate.[138] Counsels are accorded immunities necessary to carry out their functions freely and independently.[139]

Conduct of counsels before hybrid criminal tribunals is regulated by special codes of professional conduct.[140] When counsels engage in conduct that is offensive, abusive, frivolous, obstructs the proceedings, and otherwise fails to meet

---

[134] ECCC Rules, r 67(6).

[135] Ibid, r 99.

[136] UN-Cambodia Agreement, art 13(1); Law on the Extraordinary Chambers, art 35 new (d); ECCC Rules, r 22; SCSL Statute, art 17(4)(d); STL Statute, arts 15(c), 16.4(d).

[137] STL Rules, r 59(f).

[138] SCSL Rules, r 45; STL Statute, art 13, STL Rules, rr 57–59; ECCC Rules, rr 11, 22.

[139] In particular, the counsel shall be accorded: (a) immunity from personal arrest or detention and from seizure of personal baggage; (b) inviolability of all documents relating to the exercise of his or her functions as a counsel of a suspect or accused; (c) immunity from criminal or civil jurisdiction in respect of words spoken or written and acts performed in his or her capacity as counsel. Such immunity shall continue to be accorded after termination of his or her functions as a counsel of a suspect or accused'. UN-Sierra Leone Agreement, art 14(2); UN-Lebanon Agreement, art 13(2); Law on the Extraordinary Chambers, art new 42(3). The SCSL and STL add also 'Immunity from any immigration restrictions during his or her stay as well as during his or her journey to the Court and back.' UN-Sierra Leone agreement, art 14(2)(d); UN-Lebanon Agreement, art 13(2)(d).

[140] See *supra* notes 8 and 11.

acceptable standards of professional competence and/or ethics, the judge or Chamber may, after giving the counsel in question a warning, impose sanctions, such as fines and/or non-payment of fees, and/or refuse audience.[141] The judge or Chamber may also communicate any misconduct to the professional body regulating the conduct of the counsel in the counsel's national jurisdiction.[142]

Decision

8.26 When the parties have completed their presentation of the case, the Presiding Judge declares the hearing closed, and the Trial Chamber deliberates in private.[143] A majority (at the ECCC a super-majority) of judges is required to reach a decision in the Trial or Appeals Chamber.[144] The judgment is delivered in public and is accompanied by a reasoned opinion in writing to which separate and dissenting opinions may be appended.[145] A finding of guilt can be reached only if the majority (again, at the ECCC a super-majority) of the judges finds that guilt has been proved beyond reasonable doubt.[146]

Should the indictee be found guilty, or, in the case of the SCSL and STL, but not in the case of the ECCC, should the indictee enter a guilty plea, the Chamber also must determine the penalty or sentence to be imposed for each count upon which the accused has been convicted. In case of multiple sentences, it can indicate whether such sentences will be served consecutively or concurrently.[147]

Like all international criminal tribunals, hybrid criminal tribunals cannot impose the death penalty. In the case of the STL and ECCC, imprisonment is for a maximum term up to the convicted person's life.[148] In the case of the SCSL, the Rules of the Court require that any sentence of imprisonment be a specific number of years.[149] Thus no 'life' sentence exists at the SCSL as such, albeit an indictee might be sentenced to a term that far exceeds normal life spans. The Prosecutor and the defence can submit to the Trial Chamber any relevant

---

[141] STL Rules, r 60(a); SCSL Rules, rr 46(a–c); ECCC Rules, r 38.

[142] STL Rules, r 60(b); SCSL Rules, r 46(d); ECCC Rules, r 38(2). There have already been at least two instances at the ECCC of cases of misconduct communicated to the professional body regulating the conduct of the counsel in the counsel's national jurisdiction, one to the Paris Bar and one to the Alaska Bar.

[143] SCSL Rules, r 87(a); STL Rules, r 148(a); ECCC Rules, r 96.

[144] STL Statute, art 23; SCSL Statute, art 18; UN-Cambodia Agreement, art 4; Law on the Extraordinary Chambers, art 14.

[145] STL Statute, art 23; SCSL Statute, art 18; ECCC Rules, rr 101(2), 102.

[146] SCSL Rules, r 87(a); STL Rules, r 148(a); ECCC Rules, r 87(1).

[147] SCSL Rules, r 101(c); STL Rules, r 171(d). At the STL, the Chamber can 'exercise its power to impose a single sentence reflecting the totality of the criminal conduct of the accused'. Ibid.

[148] STL Statute, art 24; SCSL Statute, art 19; UN-Cambodia Agreement, art 10; Law on the Extraordinary Chambers, art 38. At the ECCC, the minimum penalty is five years. Ibid, art 39. Juvenile offenders cannot be sentenced to imprisonment at the SCSL. SCSL Rules, r 101(a).

[149] SCSL Rule, r 101.

information that may assist the judges in determining the appropriate sentence.[150] Factors taken into consideration are the gravity of the offence;[151] the individual circumstances of the convicted person;[152] the aggravating and mitigating circumstances, including cooperation with the Prosecutor;[153] and the extent to which any penalty imposed by any court of any state has already been served.[154] Credit shall be given for any period which the convicted person was detained in custody pending transfer to the court, and during trial or appeal before transfer.[155] Also, practice regarding prison sentences in Sierra Leone and at the ICTR will be taken into account at the SCSL. Similarly, such practices in Lebanon will be taken into account at the STL.[156] To date, of the three hybrid criminal tribunals, only the SCSL has sentenced its convicts. Compared to the ICTY and also the ICTR, there have been several lengthy sentences handed down.[157]

In addition to imprisonment, the Trial Chamber of the three hybrid criminal tribunals may order property forfeiture, including the proceeds thereof, and confiscation of any asset acquired unlawfully or by criminal conduct.[158] In the case of the Lebanon and Sierra Leone courts, compensation and restitution to victims, based on the finding of guilt by the tribunal, may only be rendered by national courts.[159] In the case of the ECCC, the Chamber itself shall make any decisions on any Civil Party claims.[160]

Appeal

An Appeals Chamber (at the ECCC, this is called 'the Extraordinary Chamber **8.27** of the Supreme Court') hears appeals from persons convicted by a trial chamber or from the Prosecutor. At the ECCC, the Civil Party or the co-prosecutors can also appeal.[161] The grounds for appeal include an: 'error on a question of law' or

---

[150] STL Rules, r 171(a); SCSL Rules, r 100 (a).
[151] SCSL Statute, art 19(2); STL Statute, art 24(2).
[152] Ibid.
[153] SCSL Rules, r 101(b)(i–ii); STL Rules, r 172(b)(i–ii).
[154] SCSL Rules, r 101(b)(iii); STL Rules, r 172(b)(iv).
[155] SCSL Rules, r 101(d); STL Rules, r 172(c); ECCC Rules, r 99.1.
[156] SCSL Statute, art 19(1); STL Statute, art 24(2); STL Rules, r 172(a)(iii). Since the ECCC is part of the courts of Cambodia, arguably it will also follow general Cambodian practices in determining sentencing.
[157] Sesay was sentenced to 52 years; Alex Tamba Brima and Santigie Borbor Kanu to 50; Brima Kamara to 45; Kallon to 40; Gbao to 25; Kondewa to 20; Fofana to 15.
[158] SCSL Statute, art 19(3); SCSL Rules, r 104; Law on the Extraordinary Chambers, art 39. The absence of provisions about forfeiture of property in the STL is explained by the nature of the crimes prosecuted by that Tribunal.
[159] SCSL Rules, r 105; STL Statute, art 25.
[160] ECCC Rules, r 100.
[161] STL Statute, art 26; Law on the Extraordinary Chambers, art 36 new; SCSL Statute, art 20.

an 'error of fact'.[162] The Statute of the SCSL also adds a procedural error, albeit procedural errors are arguably also errors on a question of law.[163]

Time limits for filing appeals at the STL and ECCC are generally 30 days from the date on which the judgment, sentence, or decision was pronounced.[164] At the SCSL, the time limit is 14 days, with some exceptions.[165]

The Appeals Chamber holds appeal hearings and issues decisions based on the record of appeal and the briefs of the parties.[166] A party may apply by motion to present additional evidence that was not available at trial.[167] The Appeals Chamber can authorize the admission of such evidence if it finds that consideration of additional evidence is in the interest of justice.[168]

The Appeals Chamber reaches its judgment by majority (or, at the ECCC, super-majority). A reasoned opinion in writing is required, to which separate or dissenting opinions may be appended.[169] The Appeals Chamber may affirm, reverse, or revise the decisions taken by the Trial Chamber.[170] The Special Court and the Special Tribunal may also order a retrial.[171]

Revision of judgments

8.28 Where a party discovers a new fact which was not known at the time of the proceedings before the Trial Chamber or Appeals Chamber and which could

---

[162] STL Statute, art 26(1)(a) and (b); Law on the Extraordinary Chambers, art 36 new; SCSL Statute, art 20(1)(a) and (b). The SCSL Statute adds: 'The judges of the Appeals Chamber of the Special Court shall be guided by the decisions of the Appeals Chamber of the International Tribunals for the former Yugoslavia and for Rwanda. In the interpretation and application of the laws of Sierra Leone, they shall be guided by the decisions of the Supreme Court of Sierra Leone.' SCSL Statute, art 20(3).

[163] SCSL Statute, art 20(1)(c).

[164] STL Rules, r 177. Rule 178 specifies that: 'A State directly affected by an interlocutory decision of the Pre-Trial Judge or of the Trial Chamber may, within fifteen days from the date of the decision, file a request for review of the decision by the Appeals Chamber if that decision concerns issues of general importance relating to the powers of the Tribunal.' See also ECCC Rules, r 107(1). In the case of a decision relating to detention, bail, or protective measures, the time limit is 15 days. ECCC Rules, r 107(2). In the case of a decision ordering release from provisional detention, it is 24 hours. ECCC Rules, r 107(3).

[165] SCSL Rules, r 108. The exceptions are appeals decisions on contempt of the court (r 77); false testimony (r 91); misconduct of counsel (r 46); bail (r 65); decisions on motions (r 73(B)). In these cases, the time limit is seven days.

[166] STL Rules, rr 179, 181–185; SCSL Rules, rr 109–114; ECCC Rules, rr 106, 108, 109.

[167] SCSL Rules, r 115(a); STL Rules, r 186(a).

[168] SCSL Rules, r 115(b). The STL Rules list as criteria for admissibility of additional evidence: was not available at trial; could not have been discovered with the application of due diligence; is relevant and credible; could be a decisive factor in reaching the decision.

[169] STL Statute, art 23; SCSL Statute, art 18; STL Rules, r 188(b); SCSL Rules, r 118(b). At the ECCC Supreme Court Chamber, a ruling on appeal requires a majority of five judges. ECCC Rules, r 111(6). See also ibid, rr 111(1), 101(2).

[170] STL Statute, art 26(2); Law on the Extraordinary Chambers, art 36 new; SCSL Statute, art 20.2.

[171] STL Rules, r 188(c); SCSL Rules, r 188(c). The constitutive instrument of the ECCC provides that the Supreme Court Chamber 'shall not return the case to the Extraordinary Chamber of the trial court', thus seemingly ruling out retrials. Law on the Extraordinary Chambers, art 36 new.

have been a decisive factor in reaching the decision, the convicted person or the Prosecutor may submit an application for a review of the judgment.[172]

At the Special Court for Sierra Leone and the Special Tribunal for Lebanon, the Appeals Chamber rules upon an application for review. At the ECCC, it is the original Chamber that decided the case that rules on such applications for review.[173] If the Chamber in question agrees that the new material evidence, if proved, could have been a decisive factor in reaching a decision, in the case of the SCSL and STL it may reconvene the Trial Chamber or retain jurisdiction over the matter,[174] while in the case of Cambodia it can only retain jurisdiction and cannot reconvene a trial chamber.[175] In all cases, the judgment on review may be appealed.[176]

Costs

The costs of prosecution, trial, and detention are borne by the hybrid crim- **8.29** inal tribunals. The majority, and in some cases the totality, of the expenses of the hybrid criminal tribunals are covered by voluntary contributions from UN member states and international organizations. In this regard, hybrid criminal tribunals differ from the ICTY, the ICTR, and the ICC, whose expenses are paid by all UN member states or all states parties to the Rome Statute, through regular, general assessments.

The Special Court for Sierra Leone is funded entirely from voluntary contributions in cash and in kind.[177] To date, more than 40 states, representing all geographic areas of the world, have contributed. The United States, the United Kingdom, the Netherlands, and Canada have contributed each more than US$10 million, and Germany, Ireland, the European Commission, Sweden, Norway, France, Denmark, and Finland have contributed each between US$1 million and US$10 million.[178]

---

[172] SCSL Rules, r 120. The Rules of Procedure of the Special Tribunal for Lebanon add that the material new evidence which has been discovered must not have been known to the moving party at the time of the proceedings and could not have been discovered through the exercise of due diligence. STL Rules, r 190(A). The Rules of the ECCC add also that ground for revision is if that decisive evidence, taken into account at trial and upon which the conviction depends, was false, forged, or falsified; or one or more of the judges who participated in a judicial investigation or a conviction committed, in that case, an act of serious misconduct or serious breach of duty of sufficient gravity to justify the removal of that judge or those judges. ECCC Rules, r 112. Also in Lebanon, the Prosecutor's right to request a revision lapses one year after the final judgment has been pronounced, while that of the defence does not lapse. STL Rules, r 190(a).
[173] ECCC Rules, r 112(2); STL Statute, art 27(2); SCSL Statute 21(2).
[174] SCSL Statute, art 21(2); STL Statute, art 27(2).
[175] STL Rules, r 191; ECCC Rules, r 112(3). At the ECCC, a revision decision shall require the affirmative vote of at least five judges. Ibid.
[176] SCSL Rules, r 122; STL Rules, r 192.
[177] UN-Sierra Leone Agreement, arts 6, 7.
[178] <http://www.sc-sl.org/>; The Special Court for Sierra Leone at a Glance (2009) at 6.

Fifty-one per cent of the costs of the Special Tribunal for Lebanon are borne by voluntary contributions from states, while the government of the Lebanese Republic finances 49 per cent of the costs.[179] The STL began functioning on 1 March 2009. At the time of writing, contributions were in hand to finance the Tribunal for only the first 12 months of its operations, until March 2010.[180]

In the case of the ECCC, expenses are shared between the government of Cambodia, on the one hand, and, on the other, the United Nations and donor states.[181] To date, about 88 per cent of the expenses have been covered by states (Japan, India, Thailand, the Netherlands, New Zealand, Switzerland, Australia, France) and international organizations (UN and European Commission), while the remaining 12 per cent have been covered by the government of Cambodia.[182]

Enforcement of sentences

8.30 In the case of the Special Tribunal for Lebanon, any imprisonment is to be served in a state designated by the Tribunal from a list of states that have indicated their willingness to accept convicted persons.[183] Transfer of the convicted person must take place as soon as possible after the time limit for appeal has elapsed.[184] The STL, or a body designated by it, supervises all sentences of imprisonment.[185] The STL has not yet concluded any enforcement agreements.

In the case of Sierra Leone, imprisonment is to be served in principle in that country.[186] However, should circumstances preclude the enforcement of sentences in Sierra Leone itself, the place of imprisonment for each convicted person shall be designated by the President of the Special Court, after confirmation from each requested state that entered into an agreement with the Court of the willingness and ability to receive a designated convicted person for the full

---

[179] <http://www.stl-tsl.org/> (About the STL).

[180] Ibid.

[181] Law on the Extraordinary Chambers, art 44 new: 'The expenses and salaries of the Extraordinary Chambers shall be as follows: 1. The expenses and salaries of the Cambodian administrative officials and staff, the Cambodian judges and reserve judges, investigating judges and reserve investigating judges, and prosecutors and reserve prosecutors shall be borne by the Cambodian national budget; 2. The expenses of the foreign administrative officials and staff, the foreign judges, Co-investigating judge and Co-prosecutor sent by the Secretary-General of the United Nations shall be borne by the United Nations; 3. The defence counsel may receive fees for mounting the defence; 4. The Extraordinary Chambers may receive additional assistance for their expenses from other voluntary funds contributed by foreign governments, international institutions, non-governmental organizations, and other persons wishing to assist the proceedings.' For the details of UN contributions, see UN-Cambodia Agreement, art 17.

[182] <http://www.eccc.gov.kh/> (Finances).

[183] STL Rules, r 174(a).

[184] STL Rules, r 174(b); SCSL Rules, r 103(c).

[185] STL Rules, r 175.

[186] SCSL Rules, r 103(a).

length or a portion of his/her sentence.[187] To date, the SCSL has signed sentence enforcement agreements with Finland, Rwanda, Sweden, and the UK.[188]

In the case of the ECCC, imprisonment is to be served in Cambodia only, as there is no provision for serving a sentence in any other state. Nothing, however, prevents the government of Cambodia from entering into such agreements in the future.

At the SCSL and STL, a convicted person may become eligible for pardon or commutation of the sentence, to the extent that this is provided for under the applicable law of the state of imprisonment. If this happens, the state concerned is to notify the tribunal in question (or its likely residual mechanism if after the closure of the tribunal in question). The President, in consultation with the judges, then decides on the matter 'on the basis of the interests of justice and the general principles of law'.[189] In the case of the ECCC, the government of Cambodia is barred from requesting any amnesty or pardon for any person convicted for crimes under the jurisdiction of the Extraordinary Chambers.[190]

Evaluation

As much as in the case of the ICC, the evaluation of hybrid criminal courts treated in this Chapter ought to take into account their novelty. The Special Court for Sierra Leone started operating in 2002, the Extraordinary Chambers in 2006, and the Special Tribunal for Lebanon in 2009.

In 2003, the Prosecutor of the Special Court for Sierra Leone issued 13 indictments, and no new indictments are expected before it concludes operations at the end of March 2011. Of the accused, two died before they could be tried.[191] Of the remaining 11 accused, five have been tried, and their appeals

---

[187] SCSL Rules, r 103(A).
[188] <http://www.sc-sl.org/> (Documents 'Sentence enforcement agreements').
[189] SCSL Rules, rr 123–124; STL Rules, rr 194–196.
[190] UN-Cambodia Agreement, art 11(1); Law on the Extraordinary Chambers, art 40 new.
[191] Foday Saybana Sankoh, the leader of the Revolutionary United Front, was indicted on 7 March 2003 on 17 counts of crimes against humanity, violations of art 3 common to the Geneva Conventions and of Additional Protocol II, and other serious violations of international humanitarian law. Sankoh died in custody of natural causes on 29 July 2003. On 8 December 2003, the Prosecutor formally withdrew the indictment. Sam Bockarie, former Battlefield Commander of the Revolutionary United Front, was indicted on 7 March 2003 on 17 counts of crimes against humanity, violations of art 3 common to the Geneva Conventions and of Additional Protocol II, and other serious violations of international humanitarian law. Bockarie was killed in Liberia in May 2003. On 8 December 2003, the Prosecutor formally withdrew the indictment.

concluded.[192] Three are currently in the appeals phase.[193] Another accused, the former Liberian President Charles Taylor is, at the time of writing, being tried away from the seat of the Special Court, in The Hague.[194] One indictee remains a fugitive.[195]

To date, the co-investigating judges of the Extraordinary Chambers have charged five persons: Kaing Guek Eav Duch (S-21 Director); Nuon Chea (Deputy Secretary of the Communist Party of Kampuchea); Ieng Sary (Minister of Foreign Affairs of Democratic Kampuchea); Ieng Thirith (Minister of Social Affairs of Democratic Kampuchea); Khieu Samphan (President of Democratic Kampuchea). At the time of writing, only one trial (Duch) was in progress.

---

[192] The trials of three former leaders of the Armed Forces Revolutionary Council (*Prosecutor v Brima, Kamara and Kanu*) and of two members of the Civil Defence Forces (*Prosecutor v Fofana and Kondewa*) have been completed, including appeals. On 20 June 2007, Brima, Kanu, and Kamara were each convicted of 11 counts. These were acts of terrorism; collective punishments; extermination; murder; rape; outrages upon personal dignity; physical violence; conscripting or enlisting children under the age of 15 years into armed forces or groups, or using them to participate actively in hostilities; enslavement; and pillage. This was the first time ever that an international court ruled on charges related to child soldiers, and the first time an international court delivered a guilty verdict for the military conscription of children. On 19 July 2007, Alex Tamba Brima and Santigie Borbor Kanu were sentenced to 50 years in jail, while Brima Kamara was sentenced to 45 years. On 22 February 2008, the Appeals Chamber denied their appeal and reaffirmed the verdicts. *Prosecutor v Alex Tambar Brima, Brima Bazzy Kamara, Santigie Borbor Kanu*, Case SCSL-2004-16, available at <http://www.sc-sl.org/> (Cases).
On 2 August 2007, Kondewa and Fofana were convicted of murder, cruel treatment, pillage, and collective punishments. Kondewa was further found guilty of use of child soldiers. On 9 October 2007, the Court decided on the punishment. Kondewa was sentenced to eight years' imprisonment. Fofana received six years. The Prosecutor had asked for 30 years' imprisonment for both. The Court imposed a lesser sentence because it recognized some mitigating factors, including the Civil Defence Forces'—to which Kondewa and Fofana belonged—efforts to restore Sierra Leone's democratically elected government. On 28 May 2008, the Appeals Chamber overturned convictions of both defendants on the collective punishments charge as well as Kondewa's conviction for the use of child soldiers. However, the Appeals Chamber also entered new convictions against both for murder and inhumane acts as crimes against humanity. The Appeals Chamber also enhanced the sentences against the two, with the result that Fofana will serve 15 years and Kondewa will serve 20 years. *Prosecutor v Fofana and Kondewa*, Case SCSL-2004-14, available at <http://www.sc-sl.org/> (Cases).
[193] On 25 February 2009, Issa Sesay, Augustine Gbao, and Morris Kallon, three former leaders of the Revolutionary United Front (RUF), were found guilty of murder, enlistment of child soldiers, amputation, sexual slavery, and forced marriage. The three were all convicted on charges of forced marriage, the first such convictions ever handed down by an international criminal court. Sentences were handed down on 8 April 2009. Sesay was sentenced to 52 years, Kallon to 40, and Gbao to 25. The trial is currently in the appeal phase. *Prosecutor v Sesay, Kallon and Gbao*, Case SCSL-2004-15, available at <http://www.sc-sl.org/> (Cases).
[194] *Prosecutor v Taylor*, Case SCSL-03-01.
[195] Johnny Paul Koroma, the former leader of the Armed Forces Revolutionary Council, was indicted on 7 March 2003 on 17 counts of war crimes and crimes against humanity. Koroma fled Freetown in January 2003. His fate and whereabouts are unknown. There are rumours that he might be deceased. In May 2008, the Plenary of Judges amended the Rules of Procedure and Evidence to allow a case, where a person had been indicted by the Special Court, to be referred for trial to another state jurisdiction should Koroma be apprehended after the Special Court ceases operations. See SCSL Rules, r 11 *bis*.

Whether more suspects should be investigated and indictments issued is a major point of contention between the national and international components of the ECCC. In September 2009, the Office of the Co-Investigating Judges received three further introductory submissions from the Office of the Co-Prosecutor to open investigations on five new suspects (who, according to Court rules, cannot thus far be named). The submissions were sent following a Pre-Trial Chamber ruling which resolved the ongoing prosecutorial disagreement on the question of additional investigations.[196] Be that as it may, more than 30 years have passed since the Khmer Rouge rule in Cambodia and most of those responsible have already passed away anyway, including the Khmer Rouge leader Pol Pot and Ta Mok, also known as 'Brother Number Five' or 'The Butcher'.[197]

Finally, the Special Tribunal for Lebanon started operating in March 2009 and, to date, has not issued any indictments. While it is not possible to predict how many individuals in the end will be indicted, the relatively narrow subject-matter jurisdiction of the Special Tribunal and the political ramifications of the situation will likely result in numbers of indictees comparable to those prosecuted by the Special Court and the Extraordinary Chambers.[198] Considering several of those likely to be indicted are not in Lebanon, it remains to be seen how many will eventually be surrendered to the Special Tribunal to serve any sentencing.

---

[196] Chea Leang, the National Prosecutor, had objected to the request of the former International Co-Prosecutor Robert Petit to forward new submissions to the Office of the Co-Investigating Judges. The dispute was submitted to the Pre-Trial Chamber in December 2008, but the Pre-Trial Chamber was unable to make a binding decision with the required super-majority of four out of five judges. However, r 71(4)(c) of the ECCC Rules of Procedure provides that the action proposed by the International Co-Prosecutor shall be executed in case the Pre-Trial Chamber cannot reach a super-majority decision. The public redacted version of the 'Considerations of the Pre-Trial Chamber Regarding the Disagreement Between the Co-Prosecutors Pursuant to Internal Rule 71' is available at <http://www.eccc.gov.kh/> (Legal Documents/Court Documents/Pre-Trial Chamber).

[197] Case 001/18-07-2007/ECCC-TC.

[198] In 2005, the United Nations Security Council adopted Resolution 1595 to send an investigative team to look into Hariri's assassination. This team was headed by German judge Detlev Mehlis and presented its initial report to the Security Council on 20 October 2005. The Mehlis Report implicated a network of Syrian and Lebanese officials, with special focus on Syria's military intelligence chief Assef Shawkat and Syrian President Bashar al-Assad's brother-in-law. The Security Council extended the mandate for the investigation, which was to end in December 2008, until 28 February 2009. The Eleventh Report was issued on 10 December 2008 and is available at <http://www.stl-tsl.org/> (Registry/Documentation/Background documents/UN Fact-Finding mission).

On 29 April 2009, the Special Tribunal ordered the immediate and unconditional release of the only four suspects arrested during the investigation, for complete absence of reliable proof against them. These were General Jamil Mohammad Amin el-Sayyed (head of General Security), General Ali Salah el-Dine el-Hajj (chief of internal security forces, the Lebanese police force), Brigadier-General Raymond Fouad Azar (head of Army Intelligence), and Brigadier-General Mostafa Fehmi Hamdane (head of the presidential guard). Considered as Syria's main rule-enforcing agents at the time, they have spent nearly three years and eight months in detention after Lebanese authorities arrested them on 1 September 2005, and during that period no charges were ever pressed against them.

The number of indicted individuals and trials is not the only way to evaluate the record of hybrid criminal courts nor necessarily the most insightful. It is also necessary to hold them against the expectations that the international community had when they were created. The hybrid criminal courts genus grew largely as a reaction to the perceived failure of the ad hoc criminal tribunals (ICTY-ICTR), which had been accused of being slow, inefficient, bottomless pits into which hundreds of millions of dollars were thrown every year, and removed from the victims and the places where crimes had been committed.

The promise of hybrid international tribunals was to deliver justice exactly tailored to the needs of the situation: close to the victims and incorporating locals in the court's structure and with budgets and management tightly controlled. Again, while hybrid courts are probably still too new to justify any firm conclusion, it is already evident that they might fall well short of the stated goals and probably suggest that the criticism levelled against the ad hoc tribunals was based on unrealistic expectations.

To begin with, there is little evidence that hybrid courts are significantly less expensive or more rapid that ad hoc criminal courts. Over about 15 years of operation, the ICTY and ICTR have respectively indicted 161 and 87 individuals, many of which ranked highly within the political and military cadres of Yugoslavia and Rwanda. Only two indictees of the ICTY and 13 of the ICTR remain at large. To this, one must add the fundamental contribution that both tribunals made to the strengthening and expansion of international criminal law. The price has been about US$2.8 billion over 15 years, or about US$11.2 million per indictee.

In comparison the Special Court for Sierra Leone, which originally was created to operate for only three years with an US$80 million budget, has now entered its eighth year of operations with a total cost of well above US$150 million to pay for just 13 indictments and 11 trials. The cost per indictee of the Special Court for Sierra Leone is remarkably very similar, if not higher, to that of the ICTY-ICTR. Moreover, the fact that hybrid tribunals are funded on the basis of voluntary contributions, as contrasted to assessed contributions, as in the case of the ICTY-ICTR or ICC, makes them harder to manage and creates an incentive for free-riding and race to the bottom between donors. Besides, savings at hybrid courts are done at the expense of those who can hardly protest: the defendants. The conclusion is that there is no such thing as inexpensive and fast criminal justice, neither internationally nor, arguably, nationally.

Second, the idea that hybrid courts will bring justice close to the victims has gradually given way to pragmatic considerations. The trial of former President of Liberia Charles Taylor was moved to The Hague, to the ICC premises, for reasons of security. Placing the Special Tribunal for Lebanon in Lebanon itself was never an option. At most, nearby Cyprus or Italy were considered, but eventually it was decided that the best location was again in a suburb of The Hague.

Third, the participation of the governments of the states where crimes occurred in the creation and administration of hybrid criminal courts has proved to be at best a mixed blessing. The long and troubled history of the creation of the Special Tribunal for Lebanon and the Extraordinary Chambers show that the UN can quickly become a hostage of local politics and used to settle national political vendettas. The often very narrow jurisdiction of hybrid courts can smack of blindsided and personalized justice, giving rise to toxic accusations of partiality.

Therefore, one might wonder whether hybrid criminal tribunals will pass down to history as a temporary patch to avoid impunity for certain particularly heinous crimes while the ICC gradually expands its jurisdiction and gains momentum, or whether they are here to stay. The answer is not straightforward.

First, one should consider that because of their polymorphous nature there is virtually no situation in which a kind of hybrid tribunal could not be imagined. Flexibility and customizability are probably the greatest assets of hybrid criminal tribunals. They can be made to fit any country or suspect. For instance, hybrid criminal tribunals have been proposed for the Rwanda-like situation in Burundi in the 1990s, for the terrorist bombings in Iraq since the US-led invasion, and for Sudan, as an alternative to prosecution by the ICC. They can be created ad hoc to prosecute crimes against internationally protected persons, or other international crimes created by treaties, and even in fields other than international criminal law (such as terrorist and drug crimes). This consideration alone should warrant against dismissing hybrid criminal tribunals as a historical anomaly.

Second, it should be considered that the jurisdiction of the ICC will never be complete. Even in an unrealistic scenario where all states of the world have accepted its jurisdiction, it will never cover crimes committed before the entry into force of the Rome Statute, and since international crimes have no statute of limitations, at least for this very reason, hybrid criminal tribunals will not be totally crowded out by the ICC for a long time. There are also potential points of overlap, if one considers that the jurisdiction of the Special Court for Sierra Leone or the Special Tribunal for Lebanon have no temporal limitations forward.

Still, when considering the outlook for hybrid criminal tribunals, one should probably distinguish between the two basic genera: the 'domesticated international courts' and the 'internationalized domestic courts'. The aim of 'internationalized domestic courts', like those in Kosovo, East Timor, and Bosnia-Herzegovina, which have not been treated in this Chapter, is not solely to prosecute international crimes, but also to buttress the national judiciary and the rule of law in the affected country. Overall, as long as the United Nations, or regional organizations, will take over ad interim the exercise of sovereign powers in territories, and as long as they are given broad mandates, as contrasted to mere peacekeeping functions, it is likely that hybrid courts will not remain isolated experiments in international criminal justice.[199]

However, the future of 'domesticated international courts', like those treated in this Chapter, is much more uncertain. Their failure might lead to the reconsideration of the ICTY-ICTR model, or to the ultimate acceptance of the ICC as a necessity.

REFERENCE

SOURCES OF CASE LAW, INCLUDING CASE REPORTS

Legal instruments of the hybrid criminal tribunals can be found on their respective websites.

SCSL: <http://www.sc-sl.org/>.

ECCC: <http://www.eccc.gov.kh>.

STL: <http://www.stl-tsl.org/>.

Reports of judgments of the SCSL and ECCC can be found on those websites, too. The SCSL is currently the only one with a sizeable case law of the three hybrid tribunals considered in this section. For a digest of its jurisprudence, see C Laucci, *Digest of Jurisprudence of the Special Court for Sierra Leone: 2003–2005* (2007).

SELECT BIBLIOGRAPHY

E Cimiotta, *I Tribunali Penali Misti* (2009).

J Ciorciari and A Heindel (eds), *On Trial: The Khmer Rouge Accountability Process* (2009).

P Kermani Mendez, 'The New Wave of Hybrid Tribunals: A Sophisticated Approach to Enforcing International Humanitarian Law or an Idealistic Solution with Empty Promises?' (2009) 20 *Criminal Law Forum* 1, 53–96.

M Mugraby, 'The Syndrome of One-time Exceptions and the Drive to Establish the Proposed Hariri Court' in S Haugbolle and A Hastrup (eds), *The Politics of Violence, Truth and Reconciliation in the Arab Middle East* (2009).

F Mégret, 'A Special Tribunal for Lebanon: The UN Security Council and the Emancipation of International Criminal Justice' (2008) 21 (2) *Leiden J Int'l L* 485–512.

Office of the United Nations High Commissioner for Human Rights, *Rule-of-Law Tools for Post-conflict States: Maximizing the Legacy of Hybrid Courts* (2008).

C Tofan, *The Establishment of the Hariri Tribunal* (2008).

---

[199] Still, it should be noted that since the 2000s the UN has shied away from such comprehensive operations, preferring missions with a lighter footprint, as in the case of Afghanistan. See generally C Trenkov-Wermuth, *United Nations Justice: Legal and Judicial Reform in Governance Operations* (2010).

D Cohen, "Hybrid" Justice in East Timor, Sierra Leone, and Cambodia: "Lessons Learned" and Prospects For the Future' (2007) 43 *Stan J Int'l L* 11–38.

A Lelarge, 'Le Tribunal spécial pour le Liban' (2007) 53 *Annuaire français de droit international* 397–428.

S Linton, 'Putting Cambodia's Extraordinary Chambers into Context' (2007) 11 *Sing YB Int'l L* 195–259.

A-C Martineau, *Les Juridictions pénales internationalisées: un nouveau modèle de justice hybride* (2007).

'Symposium: The Special Tribunal for Lebanon' (2007) 5 *J Int'l Crim Just* 5.

H Ascensio, *Les Juridictions pénales internationalisées: Cambodge, Kosovo, Sierra Leone, Timor Leste* (2006).

W Schabas, *The UN International Criminal Tribunals: The Former Yugoslavia, Rwanda and Sierra Leone* (2006).

'Symposium: International Criminal Tribunals in the 21st Century' (2006) 21 *Am U Int'l L Rev* 4.

'Symposium: Cambodian Extraordinary Chambers. Justice at Long Last?' (2006) 4 (2) *J Int'l Crim Just*.

T Fawthrop and H Jarvis, *Getting away with Genocide? Elusive Justice and the Khmer Rouge Tribunal* (2005).

C Romano, A Nollkaemper, and J Kleffner (eds), *Internationalized Criminal Courts and Tribunals: Sierra Leone, East Timor, Kosovo, and Cambodia* (2004).

K Ambos and M Othman (eds), *New Approaches in International Criminal Justice: Kosovo, East Timor, Sierra Leone and Cambodia* (2003).

L Dickinson, 'The Promise of Hybrid Courts' (2003) 97 *Am J Int'l L* at 295.

PART IV

REGIONAL ECONOMIC INTEGRATION BODIES/FREE TRADE AGREEMENTS

Introduction

The adjudicative bodies addressed in this Part reflect the growing trend towards regional arrangements for economic cooperation and integration and the consequential need for dedicated dispute settlement arrangements. The jurisdiction of the regional courts and tribunals in this Part generally includes:

- complaints against member states of the relevant community for non-compliance with its rules, which may generally be brought by community institutions or by other member states;
- complaints against the institutions of the community themselves, which may generally be brought by member states or other institutions established within the community;
- preliminary references by domestic courts of the member states for the interpretation of specific aspects of the law of the relevant community.

Numerically, the family of judicial bodies and dispute settlement systems of regional economic communities is the largest. One can count at least two dozen such bodies. However, most of these never actually started functioning, or, after timid beginnings, were abandoned and have not been used for years, or are active but only minimally. These include, to name a few, the Court of Justice of the Common Market for Eastern and Southern Africa;[1] the Court of Justice of the African Union;[2] the Court of Justice of the Economic Community

---

[1] <http://about.comesa.int/> (Institutions/COMESA Court of Justice).
[2] <http://www.africa-union.org/> (Organs/The African Court of Justice).

of West African States;[3] the Court of Justice of the West African Economic and Monetary Union;[4] the East African Court of Justice;[5] the Judicial Board of the Organization of Arab Petroleum Exporting Countries;[6] the Court of Justice of the Economic Community of Central African States;[7] the Court of Justice of the Arab Maghreb Union;[8] the Court of Justice of the African Economic Community; the Southern Africa Development Community Tribunal;[9] and the Central American Court of Justice (Corte Centroamericana de Justicia).[10]

This Part contains a large section on judicial bodies and dispute settlement systems of regional economic communities. All those addressed in this section are active.[11] The Part is divided into two sub-chapter. The first comprises courts of the European Economic Area, namely the European Court of Justice (renamed, after the entry into force of the Treaty of Lisbon, Court of Justice of the European Union) and the European Free Trade Association Court. The second sub-chapter comprises five courts and dispute settlement systems of other regional economic communities and agreements: the Caribbean Court of Justice; the Andean Tribunal of Justice; the Economic Court of the Commonwealth of Independent States; the North American Free Trade Agreement; and the Mercosur dispute settlement system.

In a way, the European Court of Justice (ECJ) is the mother of all judicial bodies of regional economic communities. Not only is it the longest standing and in many ways most successful of all, entrenching and, at times, driving the European process of integration, but it has also provided the template, acknowledged or unacknowledged, of many other courts of regional economic integration agreements. Thus significantly more space is devoted to it in this Part than to the other courts.

The principal function of the ECJ is to ensure the uniform interpretation and application of European Community/European Union law by member states and institutions. The ECJ consists of three courts: the Court of Justice properly called, the Court of First Instance (CFI), and the European Civil Service Tribunal. The ECJ is among the busiest institutions considered in this Manual: since its establishment its three components have decided a combined total of

---

[3] <http://www.ecowas.int/>.

[4] <http://www.uemoa.int/>.

[5] <http://www.eac.int/> (Organs of the Community/The East African Court of Justice).

[6] <http://www.oapecorg.org/> (About us/OAPEC Structure).

[7] <http://www.ceeac-eccas.org/>.

[8] <http://www.maghrebarabe.org/>.

[9] <http://www.sadc.int/>.

[10] <http://www.sica.int/> (Órganos e Instituciones/La Corte Centroamericana de Justicia). It should not be confused with the Corte de Justicia Centroamericana, which existed between 1908 and 1918.

[11] Two active courts not covered in this edition of the Manual are the Common Court of Justice and Arbitration of the Organization for the Harmonization of Business Law in Africa (OHADA) (see <http://www.ohada.org/>) and the Benelux Court of Justice (see <http://www.courbeneluxhof.be/>).

about 15,000 cases, about 1,000 in 2008 alone.[12] The potential subject matter of disputes brought to the ECJ is vast in scope, and includes institutional issues such as the legal basis of community legislation and the proper exercise of powers by community institutions.

The European Free Trade Association (EFTA) is a sub-regional trade bloc, created in 1960 as an alternative for European states who are either unable or unwilling to join the EC/EU. Over time, most EFTA states joined the EC/EU. Nowadays, EFTA members are Iceland, Liechtenstein, Norway, and Switzerland. The EFTA has its own court (EFTA Court).

The European Economic Area (EEA) was established in 1994, between EFTA member states and EC/EU member states, to allow EFTA states to participate in the European single market without joining the EC/EU.[13] Thus the EEA is a two-pillar structure: the EC/EU and the EFTA. Because the EEA Agreement extended most of the European Community single market to the participating EFTA states, EEA law is largely identical to EC law. The EFTA Court's jurisprudence is de facto based on the case law of the Court of Justice of the European Communities (ECJ). Hence, the two separate courts are treated within the same sub-chapter.

The five courts and dispute settlement systems discussed in the sub-chapter 'Courts of Justice of Other Economic Communities' are a mixed group. They include courts whose structure and jurisdiction resembles that of the ECJ (eg the Andean Tribunal of Justice and, to a certain extent, the Economic Court of the Commonwealth of Independent States); hybrid courts that combine ECJ-like functions to that of national highest court of appeal (eg the Caribbean Court of Justice); dispute settlement systems that do not rely on permanent courts but rather on a series of ad hoc arbitral panels (eg NAFTA dispute settlement procedures); and systems that added a permanent court structure, somewhat similar to that of traditional regional economic agreements, to the NAFTA ad hoc arbitration model (eg the Mercosur dispute settlement system with the Ad Hoc Arbitral Tribunals and the Permanent Tribunal of Review).

Overall, the bodies reviewed in this Part are notable for the sophisticated mechanisms they provide for the settlement of disputes in a specialized area of regional law, as well as for the mechanisms most of them provide, by way of preliminary references and opinions, for the uniform interpretation and application of regional economic law in the domestic legal systems of member states. While, in contrast to the WTO, a number of the courts reviewed here provide some direct recourse to dispute settlement procedures for natural and legal persons directly affected by the law in question, access is by no means unlimited.

---

[12] ECJ, *Annual Report* (2008) 100–101; CFI, *Annual Report* (2008) 190; CST, *Annual Report* (2008) 215. Available at <http://curia.europa.eu/> (Court of Justice, Court of First Instance, Civil Service Tribunal/Statistics of Judicial Activity).

[13] Switzerland opted out of the EEA and is not subject to the EFTA Court jurisdiction.

9

COURTS OF THE EUROPEAN ECONOMIC AREA

1. THE EUROPEAN COURT OF JUSTICE/ COURT OF JUSTICE OF THE EUROPEAN UNION

Introduction

Name and seat of the body

The European Court of Justice is based in Luxembourg at the following address: **9.1.1**

Boulevard Konrad Adenauer
L-2925 Luxembourg
Tel: (352) 43 03-1
Fax: (352) 43 03-2600
Email: info@curia.europa.eu
Website: <http://www.curia.europa.eu>

The European Court of Justice (hereafter referred to as the ECJ or the Court of Justice) is also known as the Court of Justice of the European Communities. After the entry into force of the Treaty of Lisbon, in December 2009, it has been officially renamed 'Court of Justice of the European Union'.

General overview

The ECJ is the principal judicial organ of the European Union (EU), notably **9.1.2** its component part the European Community (EC). It was established by the

European Coal and Steel Community Treaty in 1951, and started operating in 1952.[14] Article 220 of the EC Treaty provides that the ECJ 'shall ensure that in the interpretation and application of this Treaty the law is observed'. In essence, within its jurisdiction, the ECJ reviews the legality of the acts of the institutions of the European Union; ensures that member states comply with their obligations under EU law; and ensures uniform interpretation and implementation of EU law by ruling on requests of interpretation of EU law submitted by national courts.

The ECJ consists of three courts: the Court of Justice properly called, the Court of First Instance (CFI), and the European Civil Service Tribunal. The Court of First Instance was created in 1988 (operative since 1989).[15] Its function is to act as first level of jurisdiction over direct actions brought by natural or legal persons and also to adjudicate cases that fall under its original jurisdiction (mostly trademark and competition cases). The Civil Service Tribunal was created in 2004 (operative since 2005) to adjudicate in disputes between the European Union and its employees.[16] This section addresses only the Court of Justice and the Court of First Instance.

Since their establishment, approximately 15,000 judgments have been delivered by the three courts, making the judicial system of the EU/EC the one with the largest case law of all international courts.

Institutional Aspects

Governing texts

9.1.3   The organization and operation of the Court of Justice are essentially governed by the Treaty Establishing the European Community (hereinafter EC Treaty)[17] and by the Treaty on European Union (hereinafter EU Treaty),[18] as amended by

---

[14] Treaty Establishing the European Coal and Steel Community, 18 April 1951, 261 UNTS 140.

[15] Council Decision 88/591, Establishing a Court of First Instance of the European Communities, 24 October 1998, 1988 OJ (C 187).

[16] Treaty of Nice, art 225a, 26 February 2001, 2001 OJ (C 80), provides for the creation of 'judicial panels' in certain specific areas to lessen the load of the Court of Justice and the Court of First Instance. The European Civil Service Tribunal was established by Council Decision 2004/752, 2004 OJ (L 333) 7. An appeal against a ruling of the Civil Service Tribunal lies with the CFI, but only on a point of law, and, in exceptional cases, the Court of Justice.

[17] Treaty Establishing the European Community, 7 February 1992 (as amended through 26 February 2001), 2006 OJ (C 321) 37 ('EC Treaty').

[18] Treaty on European Union, 7 February 1992 (as amended through 26 February 2001), 2006 OJ (C 321) 5 ('EU Treaty'). The EU Treaty (also known as the Maastricht Treaty) was signed after final negotiations between the members of the European Economic Community and established the European Union. A separate protocol of the treaty led to the creation of the Euro and the Three Pillars of the European Union. The European Community ('Economic' was removed from its name) became incorporated into the European Union as one of the 'pillars' and encompassed the economic, social, and environmental policies. The other two 'pillars' are Common Foreign and Security Policy, and Police and Judicial Cooperation in Criminal Matters. European Navigator, <http://www.ena.lu/> (last visited 27 September 2009).

the Treaty of Amsterdam.[19] The EU Treaty sets the limits of the jurisdiction of the ECJ concerning Police and Judicial Cooperation in Criminal Matters.[20] The ECJ Treaty describes the structure of the Court and the Court's jurisdiction in matters relating to the EC Treaty.[21]

The current version of the Statute (1 March 2008), covering both the Court of Justice and the CFI, is the one contained in the Protocol on the Statute of the Court of Justice adopted in Nice on 26 February 2001.[22] All the provisions of the EC Treaty that refer to the Court of Justice also apply to the Court of First Instance, unless provided differently by the Statute of the Court of Justice.[23]

Under article 223 of the EC Treaty, the Court of Justice establishes its Rules of Procedure.[24] The Rules must be approved by the European Council, acting by a qualified majority.[25] The current version of the Rules of Procedure of the Court of Justice is the one amended on 13 January 2009,[26] and completed by the Supplementary Rules.[27] The current version of the CFI Rules of Procedure is the one amended on 7 July 2009.[28]

Other relevant legal texts, which are all available on the ECJ's or the CFI's homepage, that should be mentioned are the Instructions to the Registrar of the Court of Justice (3 October 1986);[29] Practice Directions relating to direct actions and appeals;[30] Information Note on References from National Courts

---

[19] Treaty of Amsterdam amending the Treaty on European Union, the Treaties Establishing the European Communities and Certain related Acts, 2 October 1997, 1997 OJ (C 340) 1.

[20] EU Treaty, art 35.

[21] Ibid, arts 220–245.

[22] Protocol on the Statute of the Court of Justice annexed to the Treaty on European Union, to the Treaty Establishing the European Community and to the Treaty Establishing the European Atomic Energy Community, in accordance with art 7 of the Treaty of Nice, amending the Treaty on European Union, the Treaties establishing the European Communities and certain related acts, 26 February 2001, 2001 OJ (C 80) 1, as amended by Council Decision 2003/624 of 15 July 2003, 2003 OJ (L 188) 1, by art 13(2) of the Act concerning the conditions of accession of 16 April 2003, 2003 OJ (L 236) 37, Council Decisions of 19 and 26 April 2004, 2004 OJ (L 132) 1, 5, and 2004 OJ (L 194) 3 (corrigendum), Council Decision 2004/752 of 2 November 2004, Establishing the European Union Civil Service Tribunal, OJ (L 333) 7 and 2004 OJ (L 103) 54, by Council Decision 2005/694 of 3 October 2005, 2005 OJ (L 266) 60, by art 11 of the Act concerning the conditions of accession of 25 April 2005, 2005 OJ (L 157) 203, and by Council Decision of 20 December 2007, 2007 OJ (L 24) 42). Available at <http://curia.europa.eu/> (Court of Justice/Procedure).

[23] EC Treaty, art 224.

[24] Ibid, art 223.

[25] Ibid.

[26] The Rules of Procedure of the Court of Justice of the European Communities of 19 June 1991, 1991 OJ (L 176) 7 and 1992 OJ (L 383) 117 (corrigenda) ('ECJ ROP').

[27] Done at Luxembourg on 4 December 1974, 1974 OJ (L 350) 29, with amendments through 21 February 2006 [2006 OJ (L 72) 1].

[28] 1991 OJ (L 136); corrigendum published in 1991 OJ (L 317) 34.

[29] Available at <http://curia.europa.eu/jcms/jcms/Jo2_7031/> (Court of Justice/Procedure).

[30] Ibid.

for a Preliminary Ruling;[31] Notes for the guidance of Counsel;[32] Advice to counsel appearing before the Court;[33] Court of First Instance Practice Directions to parties, of 17 July 2009; and Advice to counsel appearing before the Court.[34]

Organization

9.1.4 Under article 221 of the EC Treaty, the Court of Justice must consist of one judge per member state (currently 27 judges).[35] The judges are appointed by the governments of the member states for a six-year renewable term. They are chosen from among lawyers who possess the qualifications required for appointment to the highest judicial offices in their home countries, or who are of recognized competence. Their independence and impartiality must also be beyond doubt.[36]

The judges of the Court elect one of themselves as President of the Court for a renewable term of three years.[37] The President designates the judges to act as rapporteurs in the various cases, presides at hearings and deliberations of the full Court or the Grand Chamber, and directs the work of the Court and its staff. Vassilios Skouris (Greece) was elected President of the Court of Justice in 2003.

Eight Advocates-General assist the Court.[38] It is the role of the Advocates-General to propose to the Court, in complete independence, a legal solution to the cases for which they are responsible. They do not take part in the Court's deliberations. The Advocate-General's opinion, although often in fact followed, is not binding on the Court. The Advocates-General are full members of the Court but they are not judges. The qualifications they are required to possess are equal to those required to become a judge of the Court.[39]

The Court of Justice appoints the Registrar, whose responsibility is to manage the departments of the Court under the authority of the President.[40]

The Court may sit as a full court, in a Grand Chamber of 13 judges or in Chambers of three or five judges.[41] The Court sits as a full court in the particular cases prescribed by the Statute of the Court (proceedings to dismiss the European Ombudsman or a Member of the European Commission who has failed to fulfil

---

[31] 2005 OJ (C 143) 1.
[32] Available at <http://curia.europa.eu/> (Court of Justice/Procedure).
[33] Ibid.
[34] Available at <http://curia.europa.eu/> (Court of First Instance/Procedure)
[35] EC Treaty, art 221.
[36] Ibid, art 223.
[37] Ibid.
[38] Ibid, art 222. The Council, acting unanimously, may increase the number of Advocates-General, should the Court so request.
[39] Ibid, art 223.
[40] Ibid.
[41] ECJ ROP, art 11.

his or her obligations, etc) and where the Court considers a case of exceptional importance.[42] It sits in a Grand Chamber when a member state or an institution which is a party to the proceedings so requests, and in particularly complex or important cases.[43] Other cases are heard by Chambers of three or five judges.[44]

The Court of First Instance consists of at least one judge per member state (currently 27).[45] The Statute of the Court of Justice determines the number of judges and provides that the members of the Court of First Instance may be called upon to perform the task of an Advocate-General[46] Other aspects of the composition of the Court of First Instance, such as the method for appointment of judges, election of President, and duration of tenure, are the same as for the Court of Justice.[47] Currently, Marc Jaeger (Luxembourg) holds the Presidency of the Court of First Instance.

Jurisdiction

The Treaty of Maastricht, which established the European Union, divided EU policies into three main areas called 'pillars'. Judicial supervision of legal acts of the European Union by the ECJ is essentially limited to the so-called 'Community' pillar, the one inherited from the EC, and which concerns economic, social, and environmental policies. The ECJ has no jurisdiction over acts under the second pillar, Common Foreign and Security Policy,[48] while it has very limited jurisdiction for what concerns the third pillar: Police and Judicial Cooperation in Criminal Matters.[49]

9.1.5

For what concerns the division of competences between the ECJ and the CFI, the ECJ has reserved jurisdiction for actions under articles 230 (actions for annulment) and 232 (actions for failure to fulfil obligations) of the EC Treaty

---

[42] ECJ Statute, art 16.

[43] Ibid.

[44] Ibid.

[45] EC Treaty, art 224; ECJ Statute, art 48.

[46] ECJ Statute, arts 48–49. For instance, D A O Edward in *Automec Srl v Commission*, Case T-24/90, 1992 ECR II-2223 and in *Asia Motor France v Commission*, Case T-28/90, 1992 ECR II-2285.

[47] EC Treaty, art 224.

[48] EU Treaty, art 46 does not provide the Court with any jurisdiction under this pillar.

[49] This pillar was originally named 'Justice and Home Affairs'. EU Treaty, art 46(b) states that the Court of Justice has jurisdiction on acts taken under the third pillar but only if jurisdiction has been accepted ad hoc by member states. Moreover, under EU Treaty, art 35(3), member states have a choice as to whether to limit the possibility of making a reference to the national court of last instance only or to allow any national court to make a reference. For current information as to which member states have accepted the Court's jurisdiction over acts under the third pillar and which option they selected, see <http://curia.europa.eu/> (Court of Justice/Procedure/Jurisdiction of the Court of Justice to give preliminary rulings on police and judicial cooperation in criminal matters). Direct actions against 'third pillar' acts can be brought under EU Treaty, art 35(6) by a member state or the Commission against a framework decision or decision. Moreover, EU Treaty, art 35(1) provides for an indirect way of challenging third pillar acts by providing the Court jurisdiction to give preliminary rulings *inter alia* on the validity of framework decisions or decisions.

that are brought by a member state against the European Parliament and/or against the Council (with the exception of those that are heard by the CFI) or by one Community institution against the other.[50] Conversely, the CFI has jurisdiction to hear direct actions brought by member states against the Commission; action brought by member states against the Council in the field of state aid and anti-dumping as well as against implementing acts; actions for damages; actions based on contracts which give the CFI jurisdiction; and actions relating to Community trade marks.[51]

The ECJ has multiple heads of jurisdiction, making a precise but succinct summary difficult. In short, cases can be brought before the ECJ either as 'direct actions' (for 'annulment', 'failure to act', and 'failure to fulfil obligations') or indirectly, as in the case of referrals for preliminary rulings from national courts, or appeals of judgments decided by the CFI.

Direct actions

9.1.6 Actions for failure to fulfil obligations When member states fail to fulfil an obligation under the EC Treaty, another member state (rarely in practice)[52] or the Commission (typically) may bring a case before the ECJ.[53] Natural or legal persons cannot bring actions for failure to fulfil obligations.

Before a case is brought, the Commission, or the member state through the Commission, must give the member state in question the opportunity to reply to the reasoned opinion on the matter given by the Commission. If the state in question does not comply with the opinion within the period laid down by the Commission, the Commission may bring the matter before the Court.[54]

If the Court finds that an obligation has not been fulfilled, the member state concerned must terminate the breach without delay. If, after new proceedings are initiated by the Commission, the Court of Justice finds that the member state concerned has not complied with its judgment, it may, upon the request of the Commission, impose on the member state a fixed or a recurring financial penalty.[55] Actions for failure to fulfil obligations constitute the vast majority of direct actions cases decided by the Court.

Under the EU Treaty, the Court of Justice has also jurisdiction to rule on any dispute between member states regarding the interpretation or the application of acts adopted by the Council whenever the dispute cannot be settled by

---

[50] Council Decision 2004/407, 2004 OJ (L 132) 5 (amending art 51 of the Court's Statute).

[51] EC Treaty, art 225(3), inserted by the Nice Treaty, also provides for the CFI to hear preliminary rulings. However, the necessary amendment of the Statute for this purpose has not yet been made at the time of writing.

[52] Ibid, art 227.

[53] Ibid, art 226.

[54] Ibid, arts 226–227.

[55] Ibid, art 228.

the Council within six months of it being referred to the Council by one of its members.[56]

Actions for annulment   By an action for annulment, the applicant seeks   **9.1.7**
the annulment of a measure (regulation, directive, or decision) adopted by a
Community institution.[57] The grounds are lack of competence, infringement of
an essential procedural requirement, infringement of the EC Treaty or of any rule
relating to its application, or misuse of powers.[58] The Court of Justice has exclusive jurisdiction over actions brought by a member state against the European
Parliament and/or against the Council,[59] or brought by one Community institution against another (eg Commission v Council).[60] Moreover, the Court has
jurisdiction to review measures adopted by the Board of Governors or the Board
of Directors of the European Investment Bank.[61] Member states, the Council,
the Commission, and the Parliament are privileged applicants as they do not
have to show any particular interest in the matter of the case to have standing.

---

[56] EU Treaty, art 35(7); ECJ ROP, art 109b.

[57] EC Treaty, art 230. With the entry into force of the Lisbon Treaty, annulment actions will
be governed by art 263 of the Treaty on the Functioning of the European Union (TFEU), which
will replace EC Treaty, art 230. Under the new provision the jurisdiction of the Court to review
Union acts would be extended. 'The Court of Justice of the European Union shall review the
legality of legislative acts, of acts of the Council, of the Commission and of the European Central
Bank, other than recommendations and opinions, and of acts of the European Parliament and of
the European Council intended to produce legal effects *vis-à-vis* third parties. It shall also review
the legality of acts of bodies, offices or agencies of the Union intended to produce legal effects *vis-
à-vis* third parties. It shall for this purpose have jurisdiction in actions brought by a Member State,
the European Parliament, the Council or the Commission on grounds of lack of competence,
infringement of an essential procedural requirement, infringement of the Treaties or of any rule
of law relating to their application, or misuse of powers.

The Court shall have jurisdiction under the same conditions in actions brought by the Court
of Auditors, by the European Central Bank and by the Committee of the Regions for the purpose
of protecting their prerogatives.

Any natural or legal person may, under the conditions laid down in the first and second paragraphs, institute proceedings against an act addressed to that person or which is of direct and
individual concern to them, and against a regulatory act which is of direct concern to them and
does not entail implementing measures.

Acts setting up bodies, offices and agencies of the Union may lay down specific conditions and
arrangements concerning actions brought by natural or legal persons against acts of these bodies,
offices or agencies intended to produce legal effects in relation to them.

The proceedings provided for in this Article shall be instituted within two months of the publication of the measure, or of its notification to the plaintiff, or, in the absence thereof, of the day
on which it came to the knowledge of the latter, as the case may be.'

[58] EC Treaty, art 230(2).

[59] ECJ Statute, art 51(a) (apart from Council measures in respect of state aid, dumping, and
implementing powers).

[60] Actions for annulment are also possible against framework decisions and decisions taken
under the third pillar. EC Treaty, art 35(6). Such action, however, can only be brought by a member state or the Commission, and within two months of the publication of the measure.

[61] EC Treaty, art 237(b), (c).

The Court of First Instance has jurisdiction, at first instance, in all other actions of this type, and particularly in actions brought by individuals. Actions brought by individuals face a strict standing requirement: the individual must prove to have been directly and individually harmed by Community legislation.[62] Also, for an action for annulment by a private party to be admissible an interest in seeing the contested measure annulled must be proved.[63] Such interest must be 'vested and present...and is evaluated as at the date on which the action is brought', and should be retained until the end of the proceedings.[64] Annulment proceedings must be instituted within two months of the publication of the measure, or of its notification to the plaintiff, or, in the absence thereof, of the day on which the plaintiff came to knowledge of the latter.[65]

If the Court rules in favour of the plaintiff, the act is declared void.[66] The Court can also grant partial annulment, but only if the annulled part can be severed from the rest of the act.[67] Also, the Court can limit the effects of voiding the act by stating which effects of the act in question which it has declared void shall be

---

[62] EC Treaty, art 230(4) provides that natural and legal persons can challenge decisions, unless they are addressed to them specifically, only if they are of direct and individual concern to them. See *Plaumann v Commission*, Case 25/62, 1963 ECR 95. More recently, see *Unión de Pequeños Agricultores v Council*, Case C-50/00P, 2002 ECR I-1125; *Jégo Quéré v Commission*, Case T-177/01, 2002 ECR II-2365.

[63] See *Antillean Rice Mills and Others v Commission*, Joined Cases T-480/93 and T-483/93, 1995 ECR II-2305, at para 59; *Pergan v Commission*, Case T-474/04, 2007 ECR II-4225, at paras 39–42.

[64] *Sniace v Commission*, Case T-141/03, 2005 ECR II-1197, at para 25; *Gordon v Commission*, Case T-175/04, Judgment of 22 December 2008, at para 27.

[65] EC Treaty, art 230(5).

[66] Ibid, art 231(1).

[67] With the entry into force of the Lisbon Treaty, annulment actions will be governed by art 263 of the Treaty on the Functioning of the European Union (TFEU), which will replace EC Treaty, art 230. Under the new provisions, the jurisdiction of the Court to review Union acts would be extended. 'The Court of Justice of the European Union shall review the legality of legislative acts, of acts of the Council, of the Commission and of the European Central Bank, other than recommendations and opinions, and of acts of the European Parliament and of the European Council intended to produce legal effects *vis-à-vis* third parties. It shall also review the legality of acts of bodies, offices or agencies of the Union intended to produce legal effects *vis-à-vis* third parties.

It shall for this purpose have jurisdiction in actions brought by a Member State, the European Parliament, the Council or the Commission on grounds of lack of competence, infringement of an essential procedural requirement, infringement of the Treaties or of any rule of law relating to their application, or misuse of powers.

The Court shall have jurisdiction under the same conditions in actions brought by the Court of Auditors, by the European Central Bank and by the Committee of the Regions for the purpose of protecting their prerogatives.

Any natural or legal person may, under the conditions laid down in the first and second paragraphs, institute proceedings against an act addressed to that person or which is of direct and individual concern to them, and against a regulatory act which is of direct concern to them and does not entail implementing measures.

Acts setting up bodies, offices and agencies of the Union may lay down specific conditions and arrangements concerning actions brought by natural or legal persons against acts of these bodies, offices or agencies intended to produce legal effects in relation to them.

considered as definitive nonetheless.[68] The institution whose act has been declared void is required to take all necessary measures to comply with the judgment.[69]

Actions for failure to act Procedurally, actions for failure to act are essen- **9.1.8** tially similar to actions for annulment.[70] Should the European Parliament, the Council, or the Commission, in infringement of the EC Treaty, fail to act, any member state or any other institution of the community may bring an action before the ECJ to have the infringement established.[71] However, such an action may be brought only after the institution concerned has been called on to act. Where the failure to act is held to be unlawful, it is for the institution concerned to take appropriate measures.[72] Also, any natural or legal person may complain to the ECJ that an institution of the Community has failed to address to that person any act other than a recommendation or an opinion.[73]

Jurisdiction to hear actions for failure to act is shared between the Court of Justice and the Court of First Instance according to the same criteria as for actions for annulment.

Non-direct actions

References for preliminary rulings To ensure uniform application of **9.1.9** Community legislation and to prevent conflicting interpretations, national courts may—and, if it is a court of last instance, must—refer the matter to the Court of Justice 'for a preliminary ruling', asking the Court to clarify a point concerning the interpretation of Community law.[74]

The Court of Justice has jurisdiction to give preliminary rulings under three different treaty provisions. The most important jurisdiction is to be found in article 234 of the EC Treaty under which the Court can at the request of any national court or tribunal give preliminary rulings on:

1. The interpretation of the EC Treaty;[75]
2. The validity and interpretation of acts of the institutions of the Community and of the European Central Bank;

The proceedings provided for in this Article shall be instituted within two months of the pub-lication of the measure, or of its notification to the plaintiff, or, in the absence thereof, of the day on which it came to the knowledge of the latter, as the case may be.'

[68] EC Treaty, art 231(2).
[69] Ibid, art 233.
[70] *Chevalley v Commission*, Case 15/70, 1970 ECR 975, at para 6.
[71] EC Treaty, art 232.
[72] Ibid, art 233.
[73] Ibid, art 232.
[74] Ibid, art 234.
[75] The Court's jurisdiction is, in principle, confined to considering provisions of Community law. See, in particular, *Ministero dell'Economia e delle Finanze v Cassa di Risparmio di Firenze SpA*, Case C-222/04, 2006 ECR I-289, at para 63.

3. The interpretation of the statutes of bodies established by an act of the Council, where those statutes so provide.

Moreover, the Court can, subject to the conditions laid down in article 35 of the EU Treaty, render preliminary rulings on the validity and interpretation of certain types of Union law.[76] Finally, article 68 of the EC Treaty sets out when the Court has jurisdiction to deal with requests for preliminary rulings on visas, asylum, immigration, and other policies related to free movement of persons (EC Treaty, Title IV). It is, in this regard, a condition that the questions on Title IV matters are raised in a case before a requesting national court against whose decisions there is no judicial remedy under national law.[77]

The name is somewhat of a misnomer in that preliminary rulings are in fact the final determination of the law in question. The Court of Justice's reply takes the form of a judgment or reasoned order. The national court to which it is addressed is bound by the interpretation given as well as all courts deciding the same case in different instances (eg if the case is appealed).[78]

Any 'court or tribunal of Member State' can request a preliminary ruling at any stage of the proceedings.[79] The matter of what constitutes a 'court or tribunal' is a matter of Union law and it is not to be determined by reference to national law.[80] In determining whether or not a body is a 'court or tribunal of Member State', the Court takes a number of issues into account, namely whether:[81]

1. it is established by law,
2. it is permanent,
3. its jurisdiction is permanent,
4. it has an adversarial procedure,
5. it applies rules of law, and
6. it is independent.

However, it should be noted that these criteria are not absolute. In *Broekmeulen v Huisarts Registratie Commissie* the ECJ ruled that a body established under the auspices of the Royal Medical Society for the Promotion of Medicine was

---

[76] See *Pupino*, Case C-105/03, 2005 ECR I-5285, at paras 19 and 28; *Santesteban Goicoechea*, Case C-296/08 PPU, 2008 ECR I-6307, at para 36; *Katz v Sós*, Case C-404/07, Judgment of 9 October 2008, at para 29.

[77] See *Roda Golf & Beach Club SL*, C-14/08, Judgment of 25 June 2009, at paras 25–29.

[78] See eg *Fratelli Pardini SpA v Ministero del Commercio con l'Estero and Banca Toscana (Lucca branch)*, Case 338/85, Opinion of Advocate General Darmon, 1988 ECR 2041, at para 11.

[79] EC Treaty art 234.

[80] *Corbiau v Administration des Contributions*, Case C-24/92, 1993 ECR I-1277, at para 15.

[81] *Dorsch Consult Ingenieurgesellschaft v Bundesbaugesellschaft Berlin*, Case C-54/96, 1997 ECR I-04961 at 23.

a 'court or tribunal' within the meaning of the Treaty, even though it was a private association.[82]

Conditions of admissibility are that the national court must have real and substantial doubts as to the interpretation of Community law and the question referred must be of relevance for the decision of the main proceedings.

As to the form which referrals for preliminary rulings must follow, any form allowed by the national procedural law is acceptable.[83] Referrals should exclusively deal with the relevant point of interpretation or validity and contain a statement of the facts which are essential to a full understanding of the legal significance of the main proceedings; an exposition of the national law which may be applicable; a statement of the reasons prompting the national court to refer the question or questions to the ECJ; and, where appropriate, a summary of the arguments of the parties.

It is through referral jurisdiction European citizens can challenge Community rules which affect them indirectly, or not specifically. Although the reference can be made only by a national court, all the parties to the proceedings before the national court, the member states, and the European institutions may take part in the proceedings before the Court of Justice.

Many important principles of Community law have been established by preliminary rulings, sometimes in reply to questions referred by national courts of first instance.[84] In recent years, preliminary rulings have become the largest part of the docket of the Court of Justice.

Procedural Aspects

Languages

All 23 languages of the EU are working languages at the ECJ. In all direct **9.1.10** actions, the language used in the application will be the 'language of the case', that is the language in which the proceedings will be conducted. With references for preliminary rulings, the language of the case is that of the national court which made the reference to the Court of Justice. Oral proceedings at hearings are interpreted simultaneously, as required, into the various official languages of

---

[82] *C Broekmeulen v Huisarts Registratie Commissie*, Case 346/80, 1981 ECR 2311.

[83] For the details, see Information Note on References from National Courts for a Preliminary Ruling, *supra* note 31.

[84] eg *Rewe-Zentral AG v Bundesmonopolverwaltung fur Branntwein*, Case 120/78, 1979 ECR 649 (better known as '*Cassis de Dijon* case'). The lowest common denominator approach forced the European countries to work towards harmonization of trade by creating community standards.

the European Union. The judges deliberate, without interpreters, in a common language which, traditionally, is French.

Commencement of proceedings and the written procedure

9.1.11   Whatever the type of case, there is always a written stage and usually an oral stage, which takes place in open court. However, a distinction must be drawn between references for preliminary rulings and direct actions.

   In both types of action, a judge-rapporteur, appointed by the President, is responsible for monitoring the progress of the case.[85]

In references for preliminary rulings

9.1.12   Referrals for preliminary rulings by the ECJ from national courts generally are in the form of a judicial decision in accordance with national procedural rules. When that request has been translated into all the Community languages by the Court's translation service, the Registry notifies it to the parties to the national proceedings, and also to all the member states and the institutions. A notice is published in the Official Journal of the European Union stating, *inter alia*, the names of the parties to the proceedings and the content of the questions. The parties, the member states, and the institutions of the European Union have two months within which to submit written observations to the Court of Justice. [86]

In direct actions

9.1.13   Direct actions before the Court are brought by application addressed to the Registry. The Registrar publishes a notice of the action in the Official Journal, setting out the applicant's claims and main arguments. At the same time, the application is served on the responding party, which has one month within which to file a statement in defence. The applicant may lodge a reply, and the defendant a rejoinder, the time allowed being one month in each case. The time limits for lodging these documents must be complied with unless an extension is granted by the President.

Hearings

Preparatory inquiries and the report for the hearing

9.1.14   In all proceedings, once the written procedure is closed, the parties are asked to state, within one month, whether and why they wish a hearing to be held. After reading the preliminary report of the judge-rapporteur and hearing the views of the Advocate-General, the Court decides during a weekly administrative meeting whether any preparatory inquiries are needed, what type of division

---

[85]   ECJ ROP, art 9.
[86]   ECJ Statute, art 23.

or chamber the case should be assigned to, whether a hearing should be held, for which the President will fix the date, and whether an Advocate-General will present an opinion. The judge-rapporteur summarizes in a report for the hearing the facts alleged and the arguments of the parties and of any interveners. The report is made public at the hearing in the language of the case.[87]

Public hearing and the Advocate-General's opinion

9.1.15

The case is argued at a public hearing, before the bench and the Advocate-General, if the Advocate-General responsible for the case has been requested to deliver an opinion. The judges and the Advocate-General may ask the parties any questions they consider appropriate. Some weeks later, the Advocate-General delivers his opinion before the Court of Justice, again in open court. This marks the end of the oral procedure.[88] Again, not every case necessarily involves the participation of the Advocate-General. The Court might decide that no opinion is necessary.[89] Nor does the Court necessarily follow the Advocate-General's opinion.[90]

Judgments

9.1.16

The judges deliberate on the basis of a draft judgment drawn up by the judge-rapporteur.[91] Each judge of the division or chamber concerned may propose changes. Decisions of the Court of Justice are taken by majority and no record is made public of any dissenting opinions.[92] Judgments are signed by all the judges who took part in the deliberation and their dispositive part is read in a public hearing.[93]

Special forms of procedure

Reasoned orders

Where a question referred for a preliminary ruling is identical to a question   **9.1.17**
on which the Court has previously decided, or where the answer to the question admits no reasonable doubt, or may be deduced from existing case law, the Court of Justice may give its decision by way of a reasoned order, citing in particular a previous judgment relating to that question or the relevant case law.[94]

---

[87] The ECJ Statute (art 20) still provides that the report will be read at the hearing. The practice has long been discontinued.
[88] ECJ Statute, art 20.
[89] Ibid (this arrangement was introduced in 2003).
[90] See *supra* para 9.1.4.
[91] ECJ Statute, art 20.
[92] ECJ ROP, art 27.
[93] Ibid, art 64.
[94] Ibid, art 104(3).

The expedited procedure

9.1.18　The expedited procedure enables the Court to give its rulings quickly in very urgent cases by reducing the time limits and omitting certain steps in the procedure. On application by one of the parties, the President of the Court may decide, after hearing the other parties, whether the particular urgency of the case requires the use of the expedited procedure. Such a procedure can also be used for references for preliminary rulings. In that case, the application is made by the national court seeking the preliminary ruling. [95]

Application for interim measures

9.1.19　In cases other than referrals for preliminary rulings, the Court of Justice may prescribe any necessary interim measures.[96] Actions brought before the Court do not have suspensory effects per se. However, should the Court of Justice consider that circumstances so require, it may order that application of the contested act be suspended.[97]

　　Application to suspend the operation of any measure adopted by an institution and any other interim measures are admissible only if made by a party to a case before the Court and the request relates to that case.[98] The application shall state the subject matter of the proceedings, the circumstances giving rise to urgency, and the pleas of fact and law establishing a prima-facie case for the interim measures applied for.[99]

　　The President of the Court has considerable powers when it comes to interim measures. The application is served on the opposite party, and the President prescribes a short period within which that party may submit written or oral observations.[100] The President may grant the application even before the observations of the opposite party have been submitted.[101] This decision may be varied or cancelled even without any application being made by any party.[102] Also, the President may order a preparatory inquiry.[103] Finally, the President can either decide on the application himself or refer it to the Court.[104]

　　The decision on the application shall take the form of a reasoned order, from which no appeal shall lie.[105] As in the case of provisional measures in most international courts, unless the order fixes the date on which the interim measure is to lapse, the measure shall lapse when final judgment is delivered.[106] Also, the order shall have only an interim effect, and shall be without prejudice to the decision of the Court on the substance of the case.[107]

---

[95]　Ibid, art 62a.　　[96]　EC Treaty, art 243.　　[97]　Ibid, art 242.
[98]　ECJ ROP, art 83.　　[99]　Ibid, 83(2).　　[100]　Ibid, 84(1).
[101]　Ibid, 84(2).　　[102]　Ibid, 84(2).　　[103]　Ibid, 84(2).
[104]　Ibid, 85.　　[105]　Ibid, 86(1).　　[106]　Ibid, 86(3).
[107]　Ibid, 86(4).

Appeal

Appeals may be brought before the Court of Justice against judgments and orders of the Court of First Instance. Appeals are limited to points of law only. If the appeal is admissible and well founded, the Court of Justice sets aside the judgment of the Court of First Instance. Where the state of the proceedings so permits, the Court may itself decide the case. Otherwise, the Court must refer the case back to the Court of First Instance, which is bound by the decision given on the appeal.[108]

9.1.20

In exceptional circumstances, decisions of the Court of First Instance on appeals from the European Union Civil Service Tribunal may be reviewed by the Court of Justice.

Costs

There are no fees for proceedings before the Court of Justice.[109] The Court does not cover the fees and expenses of the lawyers representing the parties. However, a party who is wholly or in part unable to meet the costs of the proceedings may at any time apply for legal aid.[110] The application must be accompanied by all necessary evidence establishing the need.[111]

9.1.21

A decision as to costs shall be given in the final judgment or in the order which closes the proceedings.[112] The unsuccessful party shall be ordered to pay the costs if they have been applied for in the successful party's pleadings.[113] The Court may order a party, even if successful, to pay costs which the Court considers that party to have unreasonably or vexatiously caused the opposite party to incur.[114]

Enforcement of judgments

In the EC/EU, Community law is implemented and enforced primarily at the national level. Through its case law, the Court of Justice has established the principle of direct effect of Community law. National governments and their administrations and courts are obliged to apply Community law in full within

9.1.22

---

[108] ECJ Statute, art 61.
[109] 'Proceedings before the Court shall be free of charge, except that:
    (a) where a party has caused the Court to incur avoidable costs the Court may, after hearing the Advocate General, order that party to refund them;
    (b) where copying or translation work is carried out at the request of a party, the cost shall, in so far as the Registrar considers it excessive, be paid for by that party on the scale of charges referred to in Article 16(5) of these Rules.' ECJ ROP, art 72.
[110] Ibid, art 76(1).
[111] Ibid.
[112] Ibid, art 69(1).
[113] Ibid, art 69(2).
[114] Ibid, art 69(3).

their sphere of competence and to protect the rights conferred on citizens by that law,[115] and not to apply any conflicting national provision, whether prior or subsequent to the Community provision.[116]

The Court of Justice works in conjunction with the national courts, which are the ordinary courts applying Community law. Any national court or tribunal which is called upon to decide a dispute involving Community law may, and sometimes must, submit questions to the Court of Justice for a preliminary ruling.

The Court has also established the principle of the liability of member states for breach of Community law. Any breach of Community law by a member state may be brought before the Court. If the Court rules against the states, and the Commission considers that the member state concerned has not taken the measures required by the judgment, after having given that state the opportunity to submit its observations, the Commission issues a reasoned opinion. If non-compliance still persists, then the Commission can bring the matter before the Court, seeking an order mandating the state to pay a periodic penalty and/or a fixed sum.[117]

REFERENCE

SOURCES OF CASE LAW, INCLUDING CASE REPORTS

Each case is allocated a case number on the day it is referred to the Court. Cases before the Court of Justice have the prefix C; those before the Court of First Instance have the prefix T.

Judgments and the opinions of the Advocates-General are available on the ECJ's website on the day they are pronounced or delivered.[118] They are, in most cases, subsequently

---

[115] See *NV Algemene Transporten Expeditie Onderneming van Gend & Loos v Netherlands Inland Revenue Administration*, Case 26/62, 1963 ECR 1 (establishing that provisions of the EC treaties are capable of creating legal rights which could be enforced by both natural and legal persons before the courts of the Community's member states).

[116] See *Flaminio Costa v ENEL*, Case 6/64, 1964 ECR 585 (establishing the principle of supremacy of Community law over national law).

[117] EC Treaty, art 228. Since 2006, it has been the practice of the Commission to request both lump sum payments and periodic penalties. *Commission v French Republic*, Case C-304/02, 2005 ECR I-6263. See also Communication by the Commission on Financial Penalties for Member States who Fail to Comply with Judgments of the European Court of Justice, SEC (2005) 1658 (13 December 2005).

[118] <http://curia.europa.eu/>.

published in print in the European Court Reports.[119] All relevant legal texts regulating law and procedure of the ECJ can be found on the ECJ's website.

SELECT BIBLIOGRAPHY

K Alter, *The European Court's Political Power: Selected Essays* (2009).

A Türk, *Judicial Review in EU Law* (2009).

P Craig and G de Búrca, *EU law: Text, Cases, and Materials* (4th edn, 2008).

A Arnull, *The European Union and its Court of Justice* (2nd edn, 2006).

K P E Lasok et al, *Judicial Control in the EU: Procedures and Principles* (2004).

K Alter, *Establishing the Supremacy of European Law: The Making of an International Rule of Law in Europe* (2001).

K P E Lasok, *The European Court of Justice: Practice and Procedure* (2nd edn, 1994).

---

[119] Before the creation of the Court of First Instance, all case law was published in a single volume of the European Court Reports. The Court Reports now consist of three volumes: the judgments and opinions of the Court of Justice, together with the opinions of the Advocates-General, are published in Volume I; the judgments of the Court of First Instance are published in Volume II; and there is a separate publication for the case law in staff cases. EUR-Lex—Simple Search, <http://eur-lex.europa.eu/>.

2. THE EUROPEAN FREE TRADE
ASSOCIATION COURT

Introduction

Name and seat of the body

9.2.1 The European Free Trade Association Court, also known as the EFTA Court, is based in Luxembourg at the following address:

> 1, rue du Fort Thüngen
> L-1499 Luxembourg
> Tel: (+352) 42 10 81
> Fax: (+352) 43 43 89
> Email: eftacourt@eftacourt.lu
> Website: <http://www.eftacourt.lu>

General overview

9.2.2 The European Economic Area (EEA) was established on 1 January 1994 between member states of the European Free Trade Association (EFTA), the European Community (EC), and all member states of the European Union (EU). It allows EFTA countries to participate in the European single market without joining the EU. The European Free Trade Association Court (hereinafter EFTA Court) is a supranational court covering the three European Free Trade Association (EFTA) members who are also members of the European Economic Area (EEA). At present, they are Iceland, Liechtenstein, and Norway. Switzerland is an EFTA member but not a member of the EEA.

The citizens and economic operators of the three states have access to the internal market of the European Union under the EEA Agreement. The EEA legal order is, however, separated from the EC legal order. Enforcement of EEA law could have been carried out by the European Court of Justice (ECJ). However, as there were significant legal difficulties in giving Union institutions powers over non-members, the EFTA Court was set up to perform a role which is similar to that of the ECJ.

Institutional Aspects

Governing texts

The governing texts of the EFTA court are the EEA Agreement,[120] the Agreement **9.2.3** between the EFTA States on the Establishment of a Surveillance Authority and Court of Justice (ESA/Court Agreement),[121] and in particular Protocol 5 (Court's Statute), and the Rules of Procedure (the current version is that of 1 January 2008).[122] Other relevant documents are the Instructions to the Registrar and Guidance for Counsel.[123] The EFTA Court's Statute and its Rules of Procedure are modelled on those of the Court of Justice of the European Communities.

As indicated, the EEA has a two-pillar structure: the European Community (EC) constituting one pillar and the three participating EFTA states the other. In substance, the EEA Agreement has extended most of the EC single market to the participating EFTA states. EEA law is therefore largely identical to EC law. In order to secure a level playing field for individuals and economic operators in both pillars, special homogeneity provisions have been laid down in the EEA Agreement and in the Surveillance and Court Agreement. Under these rules, the EFTA Court shall follow the relevant case law of the ECJ on provisions of Community law that are identical in substance to provisions of EEA law rendered prior to the date of signature of the EEA Agreement (2 May 1992) and shall pay due account to the principles laid down by the Court of Justice of the European Communities' relevant case law rendered after that date. The EFTA Court's jurisprudence is in fact based on the case law of the Court of Justice of the European Communities (ECJ). The ECJ, CFI, and EFTA Court have not only emphasized the need for a uniform interpretation of EC and EEA law, but have also actively seen to it that homogeneity be preserved.[124]

---

[120] Agreement on the European Economic Area, 2 May 1992, 1994 OJ (L 1) 3 ('EEA Agreement').

[121] Agreement on the Establishment of a Surveillance Authority and Court of Justice, 2 May 1992, 1994 OJ (L 344) 3 ('ESA/Court Agreement').

[122] Adopted by the EFTA Court on 4 January and 1 February 1994 ('EFTA Court ROP'). The Rules were subsequently amended by decisions of the EFTA Court of 22 August 1996 and 20 September 2007, available at <http://www.eftacourt.int/> (The Court/Procedure).

[123] Available at <http://www.eftacourt.int/> (The Court/Procedure).

[124] See eg *Erla María Sveinbjörnsdóttir v The Government of Iceland*, Case E-9/97, 1998 (C 84) 5, a reference for advisory opinion, where the Court stated that '[r]eference is essentially made to the case law of the ECJ establishing the principle of liability under Community law, the similarities between the EEA Agreement and the EC Treaty, the homogeneity objective of the EEA Agreement, the recognition of the important role that individuals will play through the exercise

Organization

9.2.4 The EFTA Court has been essentially modelled after the ECJ, the main difference being that there are no Advocates-General. The Court consists of three judges (one per member state) and six ad hoc judges (two per member state). The judges are nominated by the member states and appointed by their governments collectively through common accord for six years. The judges elect their President for a term of three years.[125]

> Currently, the judges are:
> Carl Baudenbacher (Liechtenstein)—President
> Thorgeir Örlygsson (Iceland)
> Henrik Bull (Norway)

The ad hoc judges are:

> Ingibjörg Benediktsdóttir (Iceland)
> Nicole Kaiser (Liechtenstein)
> Ola Mestad (Norway)
> Martin Ospelt (Liechtenstein)
> Benedikt Bogason (Iceland)
> Bjørg Ven (Norway)

The Registrar, responsible for the administration of the Court and for certain procedural and other issues, is Skúli Magnússon, from Iceland.

Jurisdiction

9.2.5 The EFTA Court has jurisdiction over the following:

1. Actions for failure to fulfil obligations. These are brought by the EFTA Surveillance Authority (the counterpart of the Commission in the EC/EU) against a member state for infringement of the EEA Agreement or the Surveillance and Court Agreement. As in the case of the EC/EU, proceedings before the Court are preceded by a procedure conducted by the EFTA Surveillance Authority, which gives the member state the opportunity to reply to the complaints against it. If the exchange does not settle the matter, the EFTA Surveillance Authority may bring an action before the EFTA

---

of their rights in judicial proceedings and the stated intention of ensuring equal treatment of individuals and economic operators'. See also *Opel Austria GmbH v Council of the European Union*, Case T-115/94, 1997 ECR II-39ff, at paras 107 and 108; and *Bellio F.lli Srl v Prefettura di Treviso*, Case C-286/02, 2004 ECR, I-3465, at para 34: '[b]oth the Court and the EFTA Court have recognised the need to ensure that the rules of the EEA Agreement which are identical in substance to those of the Treaty are interpreted uniformly'.

[125] EFTA Court ROP, arts 2–9.

Court. If the Court finds that an obligation has not been fulfilled, the EFTA state concerned must terminate the breach without delay.

2. Disputes between two or more EFTA states regarding the interpretation or application of the EEA Agreement or the Agreement on a Standing Committee of the EFTA states.

3. Actions for annulment brought by an EFTA state or an individual or legal person against a decision of the EFTA Surveillance Authority.

4. Actions for failure to act brought by an EFTA state or a natural or legal person against the EFTA Surveillance Authority.

5. Similarly to ECJ preliminary rulings, the EFTA Court has jurisdiction to give advisory opinions on the interpretation of the EEA Agreement upon a request of a national court of an EEA/EFTA state. The referring national court will then decide the case before it based on the EFTA Court's answer.

Procedural Aspects

Languages

Proceedings before the Court are always in English, except in cases where an **9.2.6** advisory opinion is sought by a national court of an EFTA state party to the EEA. In the latter case, the opinion of the Court will be in English and in the national language of the requesting court. Written proceedings consist of the communication to the parties of applications, statements of case, defences and observations, and replies, if any, as well as all papers and documents in support or of certified copies of them. Communications are made by the Registrar in the order and within the time laid down in the Rules of Procedure of the Court.

The oral proceedings consist of the hearing by the Court of agents, advisers, and lawyers, as well as the hearing, if any, of witnesses and experts.[126] The oral hearing is almost always held in English.

Instituting proceedings

A case is brought before the Court by a written application addressed to the **9.2.7** Registrar. The application includes, among other things, the subject matter of the dispute, the form of order sought, and a brief statement of the pleas in law on which the application is based.

The application must be accompanied, where appropriate, by the measure the annulment of which is sought or by any other relevant documents. If the documents are not submitted with the application, the Registrar shall ask the party concerned to produce them within a reasonable period, but in that event

---

[126] Protocol 5 to the ESA/Court Agreement on the Statute of the EFTA Court, art 18.

the rights of the party shall not lapse even if such documents are produced after the time limit for bringing proceedings.[127]

Hearing

9.2.8 The hearing in court is public, unless the Court, of its own motion or on application by the parties, decides otherwise for serious reasons.[128] The deliberations of the Court are confidential and no separate or dissenting opinion may be published.

Third party intervention

9.2.9 Any EFTA state, the EFTA Surveillance Authority, the European Community, and the European Community Commission may intervene in cases before the Court. The same right to intervene is also open to any person establishing an interest in the result of any case submitted to the Court, except in cases between EFTA states or between EFTA states and the EFTA Surveillance Authority. An application to intervene is limited to supporting the form of order sought by one of the parties.[129]

Judgment

9.2.10 The Court decides by majority vote. Judgments must state the reasons on which they are based and contain the names of the judges who took part in the deliberation.[130]

Unlike preliminary rulings by the ECJ, advisory opinions of the EFTA Court are not legally binding on the requesting national courts. However, in practice, they are being followed.

An application for revision of a judgment may be made to the Court on discovery of a fact which is of such nature as to be a decisive factor, and which, when the judgment was given, was unknown to the Court and to the party claiming the revision. No application for revision may be made after the lapse of ten years from the date of the judgment.[131]

REFERENCE

SOURCES OF CASE LAW, INCLUDING CASE REPORTS

Judgments of the Court are published in the EFTA Court Reports. They are also available online at <http://www.eftacourt.int> (Cases).

---

[127] Ibid, art 19.   [128] Ibid, art 27.   [129] Ibid, art 36.
[130] Ibid, art 32.   [131] Ibid, art 40.

SELECT BIBLIOGRAPHY

C Baudenbacher, 'The EFTA Court, the ECJ, and the Latter's Advocates General: A Tale of Judicial Dialogue' in A Arnull, P Eeckhout, and T Tridimas (eds), *Continuity and Change in EU Law: Essays in Honour of Sir Francis Jacobs* (2008) 90–122.

EFTA Court, *EFTA Court Texts: Relating to the Organization, Jurisdiction and Procedure of the Court* (2008).

EFTA Court, *The EFTA Court: Legal Framework, Case Law, and Composition, EFTA Court* (3rd edn, 2008) (available at <http://www.eftacourt.int/> (The Court/ Publications)).

C Baudenbacher et al (eds), *The EFTA Court: Ten Years On* (2005).

T Ingadottir, 'The EEA Agreement and Homogeneous Jurisprudence: The Two Pillar Role Given to the EFTA Court and the Court of Justice of the European Communities' (2002) 2 *The Global Community: Yearbook of International Law and Jurisprudence* 193–202.

Evaluation

The European legal system has some unique attributes that make it distinct from all other genera of international courts and that largely explain its reach and success. Access is far wider than most international adjudicative bodies, with states, the European Commission, and private litigants empowered to use the system to challenge directly or indirectly, via national courts and preliminary rulings, European and national policies. Wide access, in turn, gives the ECJ and EFTA Court more opportunities to influence national policies and to develop European law incrementally, a strategy key in building support for jurisprudence and enhancing the overall effectiveness of the European legal system.

But it has not always been like that. Since its early and modest beginnings with the establishment of the European Coal and Steel Community Treaty in 1951, the European legal and institutional landscape has constantly evolved, expanding both territorially, from six states to nowadays 27, and in scope. The European Court of Justice has evolved with the system. Indeed, it has been said that 'the transformation of the European legal system has turned the European Court of Justice into probably the most influential international legal body in existence'.[132] At times, arguably, it has driven this evolution by gradually expanding jurisdiction. Its structure has changed over time as the number and complexity of cases swelled, by first giving rise to a two-level system of jurisdiction, with the creation of the Court of First Instance in 1998, and then the Civil Service Tribunal in 1989. The EFTA Court has changed, too, but in a different way as the EFTA gradually lost members to first the

---

[132] K Alter, *Establishing the Supremacy of European Law: The Making of an International Rule of Law in Europe* (2001) 229.

European Community and nowadays the European Union. At the time of writing, Iceland was considering starting accession negotiations with the EU. If successful, that might leave the EFTA Court jurisdiction over only Norway (which, in its history, declined twice to join the EC and is unlikely to do so any time soon) and Liechtenstein.

The latest milestone in the ever-changing European legal framework is the Treaty of Lisbon (also known as the Reform Treaty), which amended both the EC Treaty and the EU Treaty.[133] The Treaty of Lisbon changed the EC/EU institutions and their functions in several major respects, including more qualified majority voting in the EU Council; increased involvement of the European Parliament in the legislative process; elimination of the pillars system; and creation of a President of the European Council and a High Representative for Foreign Affairs to present a united position on EU policies.

Of course, the Treaty of Lisbon affects the European Court of Justice, too, both on the surface and on core aspects. The name will change from 'Court of Justice of the European Communities' to 'Court of Justice of the European Union'. The new Court will include the 'Court of Justice', the 'General Court' (essentially the Court of First Instance renamed), and any other specialized courts, besides the already existing Civil Service Tribunal (now called the European Union Civil Service Tribunal) that might be created in due time with the agreement of the European Parliament, for instance in patent law.[134]

Besides structural reforms, the Treaty of Lisbon improves access to justice before the European courts for one important category of cases. Currently, individuals can challenge the legality of certain EU acts directly before the Court of First Instance, if it can be shown that the act is of 'direct and individual concern' to the plaintiff.[135] The Treaty of Lisbon removes the requirement of 'individual concern' when a person or business challenges 'a regulatory act which does not entail implementing measures'.[136] This covers certain regulations that previously were almost impossible to challenge.

Yet, the most radical changes are in the dramatic expansion of the jurisdiction of the Court of Justice of the European Union, bringing it one step closer to becoming a true superior court of a federal union of states, like the US Supreme Court. Under the new system, the Courts' jurisdiction will include all the activi-

---

[133] Treaty of Lisbon Amending the Treaty on European Union and the Treaty Establishing the European Community, 13 December 2007, art 48(7) 2007 OJ (C 306) 1 ('Treaty of Lisbon') adopted on 13 December 2007, entered into force on 1 December 2009. The consolidated version of the Treaty of Lisbon, together with the amended version of the EU Treaty and the EC Treaty (renamed Treaty on the Functioning of the European Union—TFEU) can be found at <http://register.consilium.europa.eu/> (Treaty of Lisbon).

[134] Treaty of Lisbon, art 17; TFEU, arts 257 and 262.

[135] See *supra* note 62.

[136] TFEU, art 263.

ties of the Union, including justice and home affairs and judicial and police cooperation, with the sole exception of common foreign and security policy.[137]

It might extend to human rights, too. Indeed, the Treaty of Lisbon amends article 6 of the Treaty on European Union to provide for recognition of the Charter of Fundamental Rights.[138] While the text of the Charter has not been incorporated into the Treaty directly, article 6 provides that: 'The Union recognizes the rights, freedoms and principles set out in the Charter of Fundamental Rights of the European Union... which shall have the same legal value as the Treaties.'[139] The Charter covers a whole raft of traditional human rights, drawn from those set out in the European Convention on Human Rights (ECHR). It also covers social and economic rights and principles and contains modern rights, such as the right of access to information in relation to the EU institutions and the protection of personal data. These rights are not new to the EU legal system, and the Treaty does not change the legal effect or enforceability of those rights. The Charter does not create new general rights under national law and only applies when national governments are implementing EU law. However, the fact that they will have the same legal value as the EU treaties is significant as, over time, they might lead the Court of Justice to develop human rights jurisprudence parallel to that of the European Court of Human Rights. In fact, the amended EU Treaty provides that: 'Fundamental rights, as guaranteed by the European Convention for the Protection of Human Rights and Fundamental Freedoms and as they result from the constitutional traditions common to the Member States, shall constitute general principles of the Union's law.'[140] It remains to be seen where the process of convergence of the two principal European international courts will lead to and whether the reformed Court of Justice of the European Union will be able to function as effectively as it did when it had far less member states and a considerably narrower subject-matter jurisdiction.

---

[137] Treaty of Lisbon, art 24. The exceptions include the Court's jurisdiction to monitor compliance with art 40 of the Treaty of Lisbon and to review the legality of certain decisions as provided for by art 275.2 of the Treaty on the Functioning of the European Union. Ibid.

[138] Charter of Fundamental Rights of the European Union, art 1, 2000 OJ (C 364) 1, 10, available at <http://www.europarl.europa.eu/> (Charter). It was originally proclaimed by EU institutions at the Nice Inter-Governmental Conference in December 2000, revised on 12 December 2007.

[139] EU Treaty, art 6.

[140] EU Treaty, art 6(3). Protocol 30, art 1.1, provides that: 'The Charter does not extend the ability of the Court of Justice of the European Union, or any court or tribunal of Poland or of the United Kingdom, to find that the laws, regulations or administrative provisions, practices or action of Poland or of the United Kingdom are inconsistent with the fundamental rights, freedoms and principles that it reaffirms.'

10

COURTS OF JUSTICE OF OTHER ECONOMIC COMMUNITIES

1. THE CARIBBEAN COURT OF JUSTICE

Introduction

Name and seat of the body

10.1.1 The Caribbean Court of Justice (CCJ) is a hybrid judicial body acting as both an international court of a regional economic integration agreement (ie the Caribbean Community—CARICOM) and a national court of last instance shared by several Caribbean states. The Court is located in the Republic of Trinidad and Tobago at:[1]

> 134 Henry Street
> PO Box 1768
> Port of Spain
> Republic of Trinidad and Tobago
> Tel: 1-868-623-2CCJ(2225)

---

[1] Agreement Establishing the Seat of the Caribbean Court of Justice and the Offices of the Regional Judicial and Legal Services Commission between the Government of Trinidad & Tobago and the Caribbean Community, 30 April 1999, available at <http://www.caribbeancourtofjustice.org/> (Court Instruments). Yet, 'as circumstances warrant, the Court may sit in the territory of any other Contracting Party'. Agreement Establishing the Caribbean Court of Justice, 14 February 2001, art III.3 ('CCJ Agreement'), available at <http://www.caribbeancourtofjustice.org/> (Court Instruments).

Email: info@caribbeancourtofjustice.org
Website: <http://www.caribbeancourtofjustice.org>

General overview

The CCJ was established on 14 February 2001 by the Agreement Establishing **10.1.2**
the Caribbean Court of Justice ('CCJ Agreement').[2] To date, the CCJ Agreement
has been ratified by 12 members of the Caribbean Community (hereinafter
Contracting Parties), including: Antigua and Barbuda; Barbados; Belize;
Dominica; Grenada; Guyana; Jamaica; St Kitts and Nevis; St Lucia; St Vincent
and the Grenadines; Suriname; and Trinidad and Tobago.[3]

The CCJ is a hybrid judicial body, combining elements of both domestic and
international courts. Like the European Court of Justice, it is an international
judicial body because it settles disputes between Contracting Parties and community institutions over the interpretation and application of the 2001 Revised
Treaty of Chaguaramas of the Caribbean Community ('Revised Treaty') establishing the Caribbean Single Market and Economy.[4] At the same time, it is a
national court of appeal, acting as last instance of jurisdiction for Caribbean
states that have accepted its jurisdiction. As of August 2009, only two states,
Guyana and Barbados, had accepted the CCJ's appellate jurisdiction. The CCJ
replaces the Judicial Committee of the Privy Council, sitting in the United
Kingdom, which used to be the Caribbean's highest appellate court. Since its
inauguration on 16 April 2005, the Court has received 51 cases: 48 as appellate court and three under its original jurisdiction (resulting in six judgments,
including decisions of preliminary matters).[5]

Institutional Aspects

Governing texts

The two principal texts governing the Caribbean Court of Justice are the CCJ **10.1.3**
Agreement[6] and the Revised Treaty of Chaguaramas.[7] The Revised Treaty
establishes the original jurisdiction of the Court and determines its composition

---

[2] CCJ Agreement, *supra* note 1.
[3] <http://www.caribbeancourtofjustice.org/> (About).
[4] Revised Treaty of Chaguaramas Establishing the Caribbean Community including the
CARICOM Single Market and Economy, 5 July 2001 ('Revised Treaty of Chaguaramas'), available at <http://www.caribbeancourtofjustice.org>.
[5] <http://www.caribbeancourtofjustice.org> (Judgments).
[6] CCJ Agreement, *supra* note 1.
[7] Revised Treaty of Chaguaramas, *supra* note 4.

and its relationship to the CARICOM. The appellate jurisdiction of the Court is governed exclusively by Part III of the CCJ Agreement.[8]

The rules regulating the Court's procedure are outlined in the Caribbean Court of Justice (Original Jurisdiction) Rules, as last amended on 14 July 2006;[9] and the Caribbean Court of Justice (Appellate Jurisdiction) Rules, as last amended on 1 April 2008.[10]

Other relevant documents are the Practice Directions; the Protocol relating to the Tenure of Judges; the Protocol on the Privileges and Immunities of the Caribbean Court of Justice and the Regional Judicial and Legal Services Commission; the Protocol to the Agreement Establishing the Caribbean Court of Justice relating to Security of Tenure of Members of the Regional Judicial and Legal Services Commission; and the Revised Agreement Establishing the Caribbean Court of Justice Trust Fund Agreement Establishing the Caribbean Court of Justice.[11]

Organization

Composition

10.1.4 Under the CCJ Agreement, the Court is composed of the President and no more than nine judges.[12]

The Court may sit in such number of divisions as may be directed by the President.[13] In the case of the exercise of both of its jurisdictions, the Court is considered duly constituted provided that it consists of no less than three judges and represents an uneven number of judges.[14] This notwithstanding, in the exercise of its original jurisdiction, a sole judge appointed by the Chairman (ie the most senior of the judges appointed by the President) is sufficient, although this judge's decisions may be reviewed by a panel of no more than five judges.[15]

10.1.5 **Eligibility** The Agreement also outlines eligibility requirements for the office of judge. Besides the customary requirements of high moral character and

---

[8] The Revised Treaty does not provide for the Court's appellate jurisdiction because it is not a requirement for operation of the Caribbean Common Market.

[9] Caribbean Court of Justice (Original Jurisdiction) Rules ('Original Jurisdiction Rules'), available at <http://www.caribbeancourtofjustice.org> (Rules).

[10] Caribbean Court of Justice (Appellate Jurisdiction) Rules ('Appellate Jurisdiction Rules'), available at <http://www.caribbeancourtofjustice.org> (Rules).

[11] Available at <http://www.caribbeancourtofjustice.org> (Court instruments).

[12] CCJ Agreement, art IV.1. As of August 2009, the Court is composed of seven judges: President: Michael de la Bastide (Trinidad and Tobago), Rolston Nelson (Trinidad and Tobago), Duke Pollard (Guyana), Adrian Saunders (St Vincent and the Grenadines), Desiree Bernard (Guyana), David Hayton (UK), and Jacob Wit (Netherland Antilles).

[13] Ibid, art IV.3.

[14] Ibid, art XI.1; Appellate Jurisdiction Rules, r 2.2.

[15] Ibid, art XI.4–5.

integrity, the Agreement adds 'intellectual and analytical ability' and 'understanding of people and society'.[16] The pool of candidates from which judges can be drafted is wider than in the case of any international court. Indeed, any judge of a court of unlimited jurisdiction in civil and criminal matters in the territory of a Contracting Party or in some part of the Commonwealth, or in a state exercising civil law jurisprudence common to Contracting Parties, or a court having jurisdiction in appeals from any such court, is eligible for appointment.[17] Besides this large group, under the Agreement individuals engaged in the practice or teaching of law for 15 years within one of the member CARICOM states *or* in some part of the Commonwealth *or* in a state exercising civil law jurisprudence common to the Contracting Parties are eligible.[18] At least three of the judges other than the President must possess expertise in international law, including international trade law.[19]

Appointment and removal   A feature setting the CCJ apart from most other   **10.1.6**
international courts is how judges are selected and appointed. With the exception of the President of the Court, who is appointed by the qualified majority vote of three-quarters of the Contracting Parties,[20] CCJ judges are appointed by a majority vote of an institution called the Regional Judicial and Legal Services Commission (RJLSC).

The RJLSC is established by article V of the Agreement and assumes primary responsibility for overseeing the Court. The RJLSC's specific responsibilities include: (1) making appointments to the office of judge of the Court; (2) making appointments of officials and employees for the CCJ; (3) determining the terms and conditions of service of officials and employees; and (4) terminating appointments in accordance with the provisions of the Agreement.[21] The Commission comprises: the President of the Court (Chairman of the Commission); two persons jointly nominated by the Organization of the Commonwealth Caribbean Bar Association and the Organization of Eastern Caribbean States (OECS) Bar Association; one chairman of Judicial Services Commission of a Contracting Party; the Chairman of a Public Service Commission of a Contracting Party; two persons from civil society nominated jointly by the Secretary-General of the Community and the Director-General of the OECS; two distinguished jurists nominated jointly by the Dean of the Faculty of Law of the University of the West Indies, the Deans of the Faculties of Law of any of the Contracting Parties and the Chairman of the Council of Legal Education; and two persons nominated jointly by the Bar or Law Associations of the Contracting Parties.[22]

---

[16] Ibid, art IV.11.
[17] Ibid, art IV.10.   [18] Ibid.   [19] Ibid, art IV.1.
[20] Ibid, art IV.6.   [21] Ibid, art V.3.   [22] Ibid, art V.1.

Judges hold office indefinitely, but only until the age of 75.[23] The President of the Court is appointed by a qualified majority vote of three-quarters of the Contracting Parties on the recommendation of the Commission.[24] The President serves for a period of seven years (non-renewable).[25]

Judges may be removed from office only for inability to perform the functions of their office, whether arising from illness or any other cause or for misbehaviour.[26] A judge other than the President shall be removed from office by the Commission if the question of the removal of the judge has been referred by the Commission to a tribunal; and the tribunal has advised the Commission that the judge ought to be removed from office for inability or misbehaviour.[27] The President shall be removed from office by the Heads of Government on the recommendation of the Commission.[28]

If at least three Heads of Government in the case of the President jointly represent to the other Heads of Government, or if the Commission decides in the case of any other judge, that the question of removing the President or the judge from office ought to be investigated, then the Heads of Government or the Commission appoint a tribunal which consists of a chairman and not less than two other members, selected by the Heads of Government or the Commission from among persons who hold or have held office as a judge of a court of unlimited jurisdiction in civil and criminal matters in some part of the Commonwealth, or in a state exercising civil law jurisprudence common to Contracting Parties, or a court having jurisdiction in appeals from any such court.[29] The tribunal advises the Heads of Government or the Commission, as the case may be, whether the President or the judge ought to be removed from office.[30]

Jurisdiction

Original jurisdiction

10.1.7 The original jurisdiction of the CCJ is very similar to that of other regional economic integration agreement courts, and in particular the ECJ. The Revised Treaty of Chaguaramas assigns the CCJ a central role in the Caribbean Single Market and Economy. Much like the ECJ, the Court fulfils its role in two ways. First, it settles disputes between Contracting Parties; or between Contracting

---

[23] The Agreement originally provided for the age limit of 72. Ibid, art IX.2. However, this limit was extended by the Protocol Relating to the Tenure of Judges, 26 May 2007, available at <http://www.caribbeancourtofjustice.org/> (Court Instruments).

[24] CCJ Agreement, art IV.6.

[25] Ibid, art IX.1.

[26] Ibid, art IX.4.

[27] Ibid, art IX.5.2

[28] Ibid, art IX.5.1.

[29] Ibid, art IX.6.a.

[30] Ibid, art IX.6.b.

Parties and the Community; and/or between individuals and Contracting Parties or Community institutions on the implementation of CSME law and regulations.[31] Standing of natural and legal persons is limited. It is granted only with special leave of the Court provided that the Court determines that the Treaty intended a right to be conferred for the benefit of the person directly; that the person has suffered a prejudice in respect to enjoyment of the benefit; that the Contracting Party entitled to espouse the claim of the person in question has either omitted or declined to do so, or expressly agreed that the person may bring the claim before the Court; and, finally, that the Court finds that the interest of justice so requires.[32]

The substantive law to be applied in the exercise of the Court's original jurisdiction is the applicable rules of international law.[33] However, the Court may also employ other principles of law or equity where necessary.[34] Judgments of the Court are legally binding precedent for parties in proceedings before the Court unless judgments have been subject to revision.[35]

Second, the CCJ considers referrals for preliminary rulings from national courts (including the Eastern Caribbean Supreme Court). Whenever a national court of a Contracting Party is seized of an issue 'whose resolution involves a question concerning the interpretation or application of the Treaty', and if the national court in question determines that resolution of the issue is necessary to deliver a judgment, it must refer the question to the Court for determination before delivering its own judgment.[36]

Advisory jurisdiction

10.1.8 The Court has exclusive jurisdiction to deliver advisory opinions concerning the interpretation and application of the Treaty establishing the CARICOM and its revisions. Request for advisory opinions can be made only by the Contracting Parties or the Community.[37]

Appellate jurisdiction

10.1.9 Besides sharing the traits common to most courts of regional economic integration agreements, the CCJ is also a national court. As of August 2009, only two Contracting Parties—Guyana and Barbados—have accepted the CCJ's

---

[31] Art 211 of the Revised Treaty grants the CCJ *compulsory* and *exclusive* jurisdiction to hear and determine disputes concerning the interpretation and application of the Treaty. Revised Treaty of Chaguaramas, art 211.

[32] CCJ Agreement, art XXIV.

[33] Ibid, art XVII.

[34] Revised Treaty of Chaguaramas, art 217.

[35] CCJ Agreement, art XXII.

[36] Revised Treaty of Chaguaramas, art 214; CCJ Agreement, art XVI.

[37] CCJ Agreement, art XIII.

appellate jurisdiction. Others might follow. Haiti and Suriname might be less likely to do so, at least for the time being, as they have distinct legal systems based on civil law tradition.[38]

The CCJ can hear appeals against decisions of the courts of appeals of states that have accepted this kind of jurisdiction only in the following cases: (1) final decisions in civil proceedings in excess of 25,000 Eastern Caribbean currency; (2) final decisions in proceedings for dissolution or nullity of marriage; (3) final decisions in civil proceedings which involve the interpretation of the Constitution of the Contracting Party; (4) issues arising under the Constitution of a Contracting Party for protection of fundamental rights; (5) final decisions relating to the determination of any question for which a right of access to the superior court of a Contracting Party is expressly provided by its Constitution; and (6) such other cases as may be prescribed by any law of a Contracting Party.[39] In addition, appeals may be granted by leave from the court of appeal of a Contracting Party if: (1) the question on appeal involves an issue of great general or public importance; or (2) the law of the Contracting Party prescribes a right to seek the leave of the Court.[40]

The Court's appellate jurisdiction is not retroactive and does not apply to national court decisions deemed at the time of the Agreement's entry into force to be final.[41] The substantive law to be applied in the Court's exercise of appellate jurisdiction is the municipal law of the referring court, which is in essence British common law.

Appellate structure

10.1.10   There are no appeals against decisions of the CCJ, or various levels of jurisdiction within the CCJ. All decisions of the Court are final and binding.

Procedural Aspects

Languages

10.1.11   The official language of the Court is English, which is used in written and oral proceedings in records, judgments, and advisory opinions of the Court.[42] In the case of Contracting Parties in which the first language is not English, that party

---

[38]   Haiti has a French-based legal system and Suriname has a Dutch-based legal system while all other Contracting Parties have British-based legal systems. The CCJ has been largely modelled on the British common law model, therefore making difficult the integration of states whose legal system is based on the civil law legal tradition.

[39]   CCJ Agreement, art XXV.2.

[40]   Ibid, art XXV.3.

[41]   Ibid, art XXV.5.

[42]   Original Jurisdiction Rules, r 7.1.

shall be entitled to conduct its case in its first language and the Court Registrar shall provide for an interpreter.[43]

Instituting proceedings

Original jurisdiction

For proceedings initiated by a Contracting Party of a Member of the Community, **10.1.12** the originating application shall:

1. identify the parties to the dispute;
2. give an address for service of process;
3. establish the grounds for the Court's jurisdiction;
4. state the precise nature of the claim, a full statement of the facts, and the contentions on which the claim is based;
5. specify the remedy sought;
6. list and annex all documents supporting the claimant's claim; and
7. be dated and signed by the party's attorney-at-law or agent.[44]

If proceedings are started by a private person, the applicant must file an application for special leave, annexed to a copy of the originating application. The application for special leave shall outline the reasons why the applicant feels the requirement for *locus standi* of private entities are met (discussed above).[45]

In case of referrals to the CCJ for a preliminary ruling, the national court sends the request to the Registrar of the Court.[46] The referral must:

1. state the question the Court is asked to consider;
2. explain how the referred question is relevant to the issues in the proceedings before the national court;
3. identify the parties to the proceedings and give an address for service; and
4. give an account for the legal and factual background necessary for full understanding of parts (1) and (2).[47]

Requests for advisory opinions must be submitted in writing. The request must include:

1. a clear and succinct statement of the point upon which the opinion is sought;
2. a statement of the facts germane to the issue raised; and
3. the respective legal submissions on the issues raised.[48]

---

[43] Ibid, at rule 7.3.
[44] Ibid, rule 10.2.
[45] Ibid, rule 10.4.
[46] Ibid, rule 11.1.
[47] Ibid, rule 11.2.
[48] Ibid, rule 11.3.

Appellate jurisdiction

10.1.13   Under the Court's appellate jurisdiction, proceedings commence with the filing of a notice of appeal. For a notice of appeal to be filed, the party must have
first been granted a leave to appeal by the lower national court.[49] An application
for leave to appeal must be submitted to the lower court no later than 30 days
from the date of the judgment, must state the facts necessary to satisfy that the
applicant has a right of appeal, and must be signed by the applicant and his/her
attorney-at-law.[50]

An applicant may also apply for special leave to appeal directly to the CCJ.
An application for special leave must be made within 42 days of the date of judgment from which special leave is sought or within 21 days of a judgment refusing
a leave to appeal by the lower court.[51] The application to the CCJ for special leave
must include: (1) facts necessary to enable the Court to determine whether special leave ought to be granted; (2) the grounds of appeal which it is proposed to
argue; and (3) a signature by the applicant and his/her attorney-at-law.[52]

Financial assistance

10.1.14   In the exercise of the Court's appellate jurisdiction, applicants may apply for
financial assistance. To do so, the applicant must file, together with the application for special leave, an affidavit stating that the applicant's maximum net
worth is, in the case of a Barbados national, $10,000 Barbados dollars and, in the
case of a Guyanese national, $250,000 Guyanese dollars.[53] The applicant must
also show that he has an arguable ground of appeal.[54]

Interim measures

10.1.15   When the Court is exercising its original jurisdiction, an application for interim
measures may be filed by either party at the time of the originating application or at any time thereafter. The application should: (1) establish the right in
support of which the measures are sought; (2) explain why interim measures
are needed and the possible consequences if not prescribed; and (3) specify the
terms of the order sought. As soon as practicable, the Registrar of the Court shall
serve the opposing party with the application and grant a short period for the
party to make written submissions. Unless the application for interim measures
is uncontested, the Court will order a hearing. However, in exceptional cases,
the Court may also prescribe interim measures before receiving written or oral

---

[49] Appellate Jurisdiction Rules, rr 10.1, 10.2.
[50] Ibid, r 10.3.
[51] Ibid, r 10.4.
[52] Ibid, r 10.5.
[53] Ibid, r 10.6.
[54] Caribbean Court of Justice (Appellate Jurisdiction) (Amendment) Rules 2008, r 10.17.

submissions from the opposing party. The order granting interim measures shall include a date upon which the measures are to lapse.[55]

Preliminary objections/proceedings

In the exercise of its original jurisdiction, at any time, the Court may dismiss a **10.1.16** case where it is clear that it lacks jurisdiction or where the action is manifestly inadmissible, without taking further steps in the proceedings. A defendant may also apply to the Court for decision on a preliminary objection based on a procedural matter. The defendant's application must state the facts and law relied on for the objection. The Court will then specify a time period within which the opposite party must file written submissions, after which the Court will set a date for a hearing on the preliminary objection. Except in limited cases, no further preliminary objections can be made after the parties are notified by the Registrar of the date for the hearing.[56]

Decision

Decisions are taken by majority of the judges of the Court or division hearing the **10.1.17** case.[57] A distinctive feature of the original jurisdiction of the CCJ is the prohibition of *non liquet*. Article XVII of the Agreement bars the Court from refusing to determine a matter on the grounds of 'silence or obscurity of the law'. Also, the CCJ constitutive instrument is distinctive insofar as it creates a sort of *stare decisis* rule whereby judgments of the Court are legally binding precedents for parties, not only those in the given case but any party in any proceedings before the Court.[58]

Intervention by third parties

In the exercise of the Court's original jurisdiction, whenever the construction of **10.1.18** a convention to which member states and persons other than those concerned in the case are parties is in question, the Registrar notifies all such states and persons forthwith.[59] If a Contracting Party, the Community, or private person then considers that it has a substantial interest of a legal nature which may be affected by a decision of the Court, it may apply to intervene.[60] An application for leave to intervene must be filed within six weeks of the applicant having been notified of the originating application.[61] The Court's decision on the application would

---

[55] Original Jurisdiction Rules, r 12.2.
[56] Ibid, r 22.2.
[57] CCJ Agreement, art IV.4.
[58] Ibid, art XXII.
[59] Ibid, art XVIII.2.
[60] Ibid, art XVIII.1.
[61] Original Jurisdiction Rules, r 14.2.

appear to be non-reviewable.[62] Furthermore, if a party successfully intervenes in Court proceedings, the Court's judgment is equally binding on the intervening party.[63]

Revision of decision

10.1.19 The Agreement provides for revision of judgments made under the Court's original jurisdiction but only when some decisive fact unknown to the Court at the time the judgment was given is discovered,[64] and in any event only within six months of the discovery of the new fact,[65] and no later than five years from the date of the judgment.[66] Besides, ignorance of the fact should not be due to negligence on the part of the applicant.[67]

Costs

10.1.20 Like most international courts, there are no fees, other than filing fees, for proceedings before the CCJ. However, the CCJ is unlike any other international court in the way its operational expenses are covered. A Trust Fund, administered by an independent Board of Trustees, has been established and capitalized in the sum of US$100 million, so as to enable the recurrent expenditure of the Court to be financed by income from the fund.[68]

The parties bear their own litigation costs. However, the Court may order the unsuccessful party to pay the successful party's pleadings and may also elect to have any party pay the opposing party's costs where the Court determines that the party has unreasonably caused the opposing party to incur them.[69]

Enforcement of judgments

10.1.21 Member states, Organs, Bodies of the Community, or persons to whom a judgment of the Court applies shall comply with the judgments.[70] A Contracting Party to the Agreement commits to take all necessary steps, including enactment of legislation, to ensure enforcement of a judgment, decree, order, or sentence of the Court as if it were a judgment of a superior court of that Contracting Party.[71]

---

[62] On the face of it, art XX of the CCJ Agreement seems to apply only to final judgments.
[63] CCJ Agreement, art XVII.
[64] Ibid, art XX.1.
[65] Ibid, art XX.4.
[66] Ibid, art XX.5.
[67] Ibid, art XX.
[68] <http://www.caribbeancourtofjustice.org> (About).
[69] Original Jurisdiction Rules, r 30.1.
[70] CCJ Agreement, art XV.
[71] Ibid, art XXVI.

REFERENCE

SOURCES OF CASE LAW, INCLUDING CASE REPORTS

Decisions and relevant legal instruments of the CCJ can be found on the Court's website: <http://www.caribbeancourtofjustice.org/about.htm>.

SELECT BIBLIOGRAPHY

D M Aaron, 'Reconsidering Dualism: The Caribbean Court of Justice and the Growing Influence of Unincorporated Treaties in Domestic Law' (2007) 6 *The Law and Practice of International Courts and Tribunals* 233–268.

A Saunders, 'The Caribbean Court of Justice and the Legal Profession: Promoting a Caribbean Jurisprudence' (2007) 33 *Commonwealth Law Bulletin* 681–689.

D O'Brien, 'The Caribbean Court of Justice and its Appellate Jurisdiction: A Difficult Birth' (2006) *Public Law* 344–363.

D Bascombe, 'The Introduction of the Caribbean Court of Justice and the Likely Impact on Human Rights Standards in the Caribbean Commonwealth' (2005) 31 *Commonwealth Law Bulletin* 117–125.

D O'Brien, 'The Caribbean Court of Justice and Reading Down the Independent Constitutions of the Commonwealth Caribbean: The Empire Strikes Back' (2005) 10 *European Human Rights L Rev* 607–627.

Honorable Sir D Simmons, 'The Caribbean Court of Justice: A Unique Institution of Caribbean Creativity' (2005) 29 *Nova L Rev* 171.

R A Abdullah Khan, 'The Caribbean Court of Justice and Referrals from National Courts: Unavoidable Supremacy?' (2004) 5 *Griffin's View on International and Comparative Law* 26–38.

S A McDonald, 'The Caribbean Court of Justice: Enhancing the Law of International Organizations' (2004) 27 *Fordham Int'l L J* 930.

R P Hamilton, 'A Guide to Researching the Caribbean Court of Justice' (2002) 27 *Brook J Int'l L* 531.

2. THE ANDEAN COMMUNITY TRIBUNAL OF JUSTICE

Introduction

Name and seat of the body

10.2.1 The Andean Community Tribunal of Justice (Tribunal de Justicia de la Comunidad Andina) is located in Quito, Ecuador,[72] at:

> Calle Augusto Egas No 33-65 y Bosmediano
> Sector Bella-Vista
> Quito, Ecuador
> Tel: (593) 2446448
> Fax: (593) 2922462
> PO Box: 17079054
> Email: tjca@tribunalandino.org.ec
> Website: <http://www.tribunalandino.org.ec>

General overview

10.2.2 The Andean Community Tribunal of Justice (ATJ) is the judicial body of the Andean Community. It was established in 1979 and became operative in 1984.

The Andean Community (previously known as the Andean Pact) is a subregional economic and social integration arrangement created in 1969 by the Cartagena Agreement.[73] Presently, the Andean Community is composed of four member states—Bolivia, Colombia, Ecuador, and Peru—and five associate members—Chile, and the four Mercosur member states, Argentina, Brazil,

---

[72] Treaty Establishing the Andean Tribunal of Justice, 22 May 1979, as amended by the Protocol of Cochabamba, 28 May 1996, art 5, ('ATJ Treaty'), available at <http://www.comunidadandina.org> (Treaties); Statute of the Andean Community Tribunal of Justice, 22 June 2001, art 6 ('ATJ Statute'), available at <http://www.tribunalandino.org.ec/> (Normativa del Tribunal).

[73] Andean Subregional Integration Agreement, 26 May 1969, 8 ILM 910 ('Cartagena Agreement').

Paraguay, and Uruguay. Chile withdrew in 1976, and Venezuela acceded in 1973 and then withdrew in 2006.

Since 1969, the Andean Community has experienced numerous changes. In 1993, the members of the Andean Pact formed a free trade area. Trade in services, particularly transportation, was also liberalized. In 1996, the member states decided to reform the Cartagena Agreement. The Protocol of Trujillo introduced several changes.[74] The Andean Community was created and replaced the Andean Pact. A new institutional framework, the Andean Integration System (AIS), was created.[75] The main bodies of the AIS currently include: the Andean Council of Presidents; Andean Council of Foreign Affairs Ministers; Andean Community Commission; Andean Community Secretariat-General; Andean Parliament; Andean Development Corporation; Latin American Reserve Fund; and the Andean Community Tribunal of Justice.[76]

The Andean Tribunal's structure and competences are largely modelled on those of the European Court of Justice. The Tribunal is the principal judicial organ of the Andean Community.[77] Its duties include ensuring the legality of Community provisions, compliance with Community laws by member states and Community institutions, and interpreting Andean Community laws to ensure that they are applied uniformly in the territories of the member states. After the European Court of Justice and the European Court of Human Rights, the Andean Tribunal of Justice is the international judicial body with the largest number of total cases decided (1,569, up to 2007).[78] Ninety per cent of these relate to intellectual property rights.[79]

Institutional Aspects

Governing texts

The organization and operation of the Andean Tribunal of Justice are essentially governed by the 1969 Cartagena Agreement (Acuerdo de Integración

10.2.3

---

[74] Modifying Protocol of the Andean Subregional Integration Agreement (Cartagena Agreement), 10 March 1996, 273 Official Gazette of the Cartagena Agreement (1997) ('Protocol of Trujillo').

[75] The AIS is designed to allow for effective coordination among its component bodies and institutions in order to maximize sub-regional Andean integration, promote its external projection, and strengthen the actions related to the integration process. Cartagena Agreement, Ch II, art 7.

[76] Ibid, Ch II, art 6. Almost all of the Andean bodies and institutions were created during the first ten years of the integration process (in the 1970s), except for the Andean Council of Presidents, which was set up in 1990. <http://www.comunidadandina.org/ingles/quienes/brief.htm>.

[77] ATJ Statute, art 4.

[78] <http://www.tribunalandino.org.ec/> (Estadisticas/Notas informativas).

[79] L Helfer, K Alter, and F Guerzovich, 'Islands of Effective International Adjudication: Constructing an Intellectual Property Rule of Law in the Andean Community' (2009) 109 *American Journal of International Law* 1, 2.

subregional Andino),[80] as modified by subsequent protocols, and in particular the Protocol of Trujillo,[81] which expanded the Tribunal's jurisdiction to labour disputes, arbitration, and actions for failure to act; the 1979 Treaty Creating the Tribunal of Justice (Tratado de Creación del Tribunal de Justicia de la Comunidad Andina),[82] as modified by the 1996 Protocol of Cochabamba (hereinafter ATJ Treaty);[83] the Tribunal's Statute (Estatuto del Tribunal de Justicia de la Comunidad Andina), as approved on 22 June 2001, by the Andean Council of Foreign Ministers (Decision 500);[84] and the Tribunal's Rules of Procedure (Reglamento Interno del Tribunal de Justicia de la Comunidad Andina).[85] Other relevant documents include the 'Guide for the submission of requests for preliminary rulings by national courts'.[86]

The legal system of the Cartagena Agreement consists of:

(a) the Cartagena Agreement, its Protocols, and additional instruments;
(b) the Treaty Creating the Andean Tribunal and its Amending Protocols;
(c) the Decisions of the Andean Council of Foreign Ministers and of the Commission of the Andean Community;
(d) the Resolutions of the Secretariat-General of the Andean Community; and
(e) the Industrial Complementarity Agreements and any such other agreements as the member states may adopt among themselves within the context of the Andean sub-regional integration process.[87]

Organization

Composition

10.2.4 The Tribunal comprises four judges, one for each member state of the Andean Community.[88] Each member state presents a list containing three candidates.

---

[80] Cartagena Agreement, *supra* note 73.

[81] Protocol of Trujillo, *supra* note 74.

[82] Treaty Establishing the Andean Tribunal of Justice, 22 May 1979, 18 ILM 1203 (1979).

[83] *Supra* note 72.

[84] ATJ Statute, *supra* note 72.

[85] Statute and Rules are available at <http://www.tribunalandino.org.ec/> (Normativa del tribunal). The Rules are drafted and adopted by the Court. ATJ Treaty, art 15.

[86] (Nota Informativa sobre el Planteamiento de la Solicitud de Interpretación Prejudicial por los órganos judiciales nacionales), Gaceta Oficial del Acuerdo de Cartagena, No 694, 3 August 2001, p 4, available at <http://www.tribunalandino.org.ec/> (Notas Informativas).

[87] ATJ Treaty, art 1.

[88] According to art 7 of the Cartagena Agreement, the Court of Justice is composed of five judges. However, in the light of the withdrawal of Venezuela from the Andean Community, the Andean Council of Foreign Ministers by Decision 633 (adopted on 12 June 2006) modified the Treaty by providing that the number of judges is equal to the number of member states of the Community, which is, at present time, four. <http://www.comunidadandina.org> (Normativa).

The judges are appointed by unanimous decision of the member states.[89] As in the case of all international courts, candidates must possess a good moral reputation and fulfil the necessary conditions for exercising the highest judicial functions in their respective countries or be highly competent jurists.[90]

Judges are appointed for a six-year term and may be re-elected only once.[91] They carry out the function of President by rotation.[92]

The judges appoint the Registrar (Secretario) for a once-renewable three-year term.[93] Currently, the Registrar is Isabel Palacios Leguizamón (Colombia). All member states rotate to have one of their citizens as Registrar.[94]

It should be noted that the Andean Council of Foreign Ministers, in consultation with the Tribunal, has the power to create the position of Advocate-General, to such number and with such powers as may be established for that purpose in the Tribunal's Statute.[95]

Judges may be removed from office at the request of the government of a member country, via the government of Ecuador,[96] only if, in the exercise of their duties, they commit a serious violation listed in the Tribunal's Statute. These are: manifest misconduct; any action incompatible with the position; repeated failure to fulfil duties inherent in the function; carrying out professional activities other than teaching or academic duties; breach of the oath.[97]

Jurisdiction

The jurisdiction of the Andean Tribunal is largely similar to that of other courts **10.2.5** of regional economic integration agreements, with some significant exceptions. Jurisdiction is also exclusive. According to article 42 of the Treaty Creating the Tribunal, member states 'shall not submit any dispute that may arise from the application of provisions comprising the legal system of the Andean Community to any court, arbitration system or proceeding whatsoever except for those stipulated in this Treaty'. However, member states or bodies and institutions of the Andean Integration System may submit to the stipulations of the Treaty Creating the Tribunal to judicial bodies other than the Andean Tribunal in the case of disputes with third countries.[98]

---

[89] ATJ Treaty, art 7.
[90] Ibid, art 6. Currently the judges are: President: Carlos Jaime Villarroel Ferrer (Bolivia); Oswaldo Salgado Espinoza (Ecuador), Ricardo Vigil Toledo (Peru), and Leonor Perdomo Perdomo (Colombia).
[91] Ibid, art 8.
[92] ATJ Statute, art 14.
[93] ATJ Treaty, arts 14–15.
[94] ATJ Statute, art 17.
[95] ATJ Treaty, art 8; ATJ Statute, art 142.
[96] ATJ Statute, art 12.
[97] ATJ Treaty, art 10; ATJ Statute, art 11.
[98] ATJ Treaty, art 42.

Actions for annulment (acciones de nulidad)

10.2.6   The ATJ has the authority to void decisions of the Andean Council of Foreign Ministers, the Commission of the Andean Community, and Resolutions of the Secretariat-General, or agreements concluded between member states within the framework of the Community when inconsistent with the Andean Community legal system, or *ultra vires*.[99] Actions for annulment can be brought by member states, the Council of Foreign Ministers, the Commission of the Andean Community, the Secretariat-General, or private parties.[100]

Member states can bring actions for annulment only if they have not voted in favour of the adoption of the challenged decision or agreement.[101] Private parties, be they individuals or legal entities, can bring actions for annulment only if the decision or agreement at issue affects their subjective rights or legitimate interests.[102]

Actions for annulment must be brought before the Tribunal within two years from the date the decision or agreement becomes effective.[103] After two years, acts and other decisions of the Community can still be challenged, but only via a national court. The national court then requests a preliminary ruling from the Tribunal of Justice of the Andean Community regarding the legality of the given act. The case is suspended until the Andean Tribunal has issued its decision, which the national judge must adopt.[104]

Up to the end of 2007, the ATJ had considered 46 actions for annulment.[105]

Actions for failure to fulfil obligations (acciones de incumplimiento)

10.2.7   Actions for failure to fulfil obligations can be brought by the Andean Secretariat-General against any member state, by any member state against another member state, and by natural and legal persons against member states. Member states' actions that can be challenged include the adoption of national laws inconsistent with the Andean legal system, lack of implementation of norms of the Andean legal system, or any other acts or omissions that hinder or block the implementation of the Andean legal system.[106]

If the Secretariat-General believes that a member state has committed any of the above, it informs the state in writing. The state has 60 days to respond to the allegations.[107] After receiving the state's reply, the Secretariat-General issues

---

[99] ATJ Treaty, art 17; ATJ Statute, arts 101–106.
[100] ATJ Treaty, art 17.
[101] Ibid, art 18.
[102] Ibid, art 19.
[103] Ibid, art 20.
[104] Ibid.
[105] <http://www.tribunalandino.org.ec/> (Estadisticas/Acciones de Nullidad).
[106] ATJ Statute, art 107.
[107] ATJ Treaty, art 23; ATJ Statute, arts 107–120.

a decision on whether it deems the state in violation of its legal obligations.[108] If the Secretariat-General decides that this is the case, it requests a decision on the matter from the ATJ.[109] Any member state affected by the failure to fulfil obligations of another state can join the Secretariat-General in the action.[110]

If a member state considers that another member state has failed to comply with its obligations under the legal system of the Andean Community, it may file a claim with the Secretariat-General.[111] As is the case when the Secretariat-General acts *proprio motu*, the state is then given an opportunity to reply. If that does not resolve the matter, the Secretariat-General refers the matter to the Tribunal or, if the Secretariat-General fails to do so, the member state that initiated the action may bring the matter directly to the Tribunal.[112]

Natural or legal persons may raise the issue of failure to fulfil obligations by a member state, but only when they are affected directly, at any time before national courts,[113] or to the Tribunal via the Secretariat-General according to the procedure described above.[114]

Until the end of 2007, the ATJ had considered 105 actions for failure to fulfil obligations.[115]

Actions for failure to act (recursos por omisión)

The Council of Foreign Affairs Ministers, the Andean Community Commission or the Secretariat-General, member states, and natural or legal persons whose subjective rights and legitimate interests are affected may request the ATJ to issue a ruling ordering the Council of Foreign Affairs, the Andean Community Commission, or the Secretariat-General to fulfil an obligation expressly mandated under any of the instruments of the Andean Community legal system.[116] The Tribunal must issue a ruling on the matter within 30 days.[117] The ruling must be published in the Official Gazette of the Cartagena Agreement and state the form, way, and period in which the body in question shall fulfil its obligations.[118] Up to the end of 2007, the ATJ had considered six actions for failure to act.[119]

10.2.8

---

[108] Ibid.
[109] Ibid.
[110] Ibid.
[111] ATJ Treaty, art 24.
[112] Ibid.
[113] Ibid, art 31.
[114] Ibid, art 25.
[115] <http://www.tribunalandino.org.ec/> (Estadisticas/Acciones de Incumplimento).
[116] ATJ Treaty, art 37; ATJ Statute, arts 129–134.
[117] ATJ Treaty, art 37.
[118] Ibid.
[119] <http://www.tribunalandino.org.ec/> (Estadisticas/Acciones de Incumplimento).

Preliminary rulings (interpretaciones prejudiciales)

10.2.9   In order to ensure the uniform application of provisions comprising the legal system of the Andean Community, it is the responsibility of the Tribunal to make preliminary rulings on such provisions when requested by national judges.[120] The Tribunal's ruling is limited to specifying the contents and scope of provisions on the basis of relevant facts in the case pending before the national court.[121] However, the Tribunal may not interpret the contents and scope of national law, nor judge the facts in dispute.[122]

National courts may request preliminary rulings by the Andean Tribunal if they are not the last instance of jurisdiction.[123] If the Tribunal does not render the preliminary ruling before the national court's decision is due, the national court may rule without waiting for the Andean Tribunal to issue the ruling.[124] However, if the national court is a court of last instance, then the national court must suspend proceedings and request a preliminary ruling from the Tribunal.[125] Arguably, the failure of a national court that is a court of last instance to request a preliminary ruling from the Tribunal might be considered a violation of due process, which could render null and void the judgment of the national court. At the international level, that would amount to a failure of the state concerned to fulfil its obligations under the Andean Community agreements.

Preliminary rulings by the Andean Tribunal are binding and must be adopted by the requesting national court.[126] The Andean Community member states ensure that national judges observe the Andean Tribunal's preliminary rulings.[127]

Preliminary rulings are, by far, the largest part of the Andean Tribunal's docket. Until the end of 2007, the ATJ had considered 1,407 requests for a preliminary ruling.[128]

Arbitration

10.2.10   The Andean Tribunal may arbitrate disputes arising from the application or interpretation of contracts or agreements concluded between institutions of the Andean Integration System or between these and third parties, or between private parties.[129] This jurisdiction is voluntary. Parties need to agree to arbitration.[130]

---

[120] ATJ Treaty, art 32; ATJ Statute, art 121.
[121] ATJ Treaty, art 34.
[122] Ibid.
[123] ATJ Treaty, art 33; ATJ Statute, art 122.
[124] ATJ Treaty, art 33; ATJ Statute, art 123.
[125] Ibid.
[126] ATJ Treaty, art 35; ATJ Statute, art 127.
[127] ATJ Treaty, art 36; ATJ Statute, art 128.
[128] <http://www.tribunalandino.org.ec/> (Interpretaciones Prejudiciales).
[129] ATJ Treaty, art 38.
[130] Ibid.

It should also be noted that private parties may request the Secretariat-General to arbitrate disputes arising from private contracts governed by the legal system of the Andean Community.[131] Arbitral awards of the ATJ and the Secretariat-General are binding, final, and given full legal effect under the domestic laws of the member states.[132] However, to date the Andean Tribunal has not yet exercised this kind of jurisdiction.

Administrative jurisdiction

Finally, the Andean Tribunal has jurisdiction to hear disputes between the Institutions of the Andean Community and its employees.[133] **10.2.11**

Appellate structure

There are no appeals against decisions of the Andean Tribunal, or various levels of jurisdiction within the Andean Tribunal. All decisions of the Tribunal are final and binding, once published in the Official Gazette. **10.2.12**

Procedural Aspects

Languages

The official language of the Andean Tribunal is Spanish.[134] Languages and dialects of indigenous groups can be used in acts before the Tribunal, as long as they are translated into Spanish; a notarized translation being necessary only when requested by a party or by the Tribunal itself.[135] **10.2.13**

Instituting proceedings

All cases must be filed in writing, addressed to the President of the Tribunal through the Registrar, and in three copies.[136] Cases can be filed by email or fax, but the applicant must still send the original within three days by mail.[137] Applications must be signed and the signature notarized.[138] The information that should be included in the application varies according to what kind of jurisdiction the Tribunal is requested to exercise. Once a case has been filed with the Tribunal, it is assigned by the President to a judge rapporteur (*juez sustanciador*).[139] **10.2.14**

---

[131] Ibid.
[132] ATJ Treaty, art 39.
[133] ATJ Treaty, art 40; ATJ Statute arts 135–139.
[134] ATJ Statute, art 34.
[135] Ibid.
[136] Ibid, art 45.
[137] Ibid.
[138] Ibid.
[139] Ibid, art 37.

Financial assistance

10.2.15   There is no provision for financial assistance.

Interim measures

10.2.16   The filing of an action for annulment per se does not affect the legal validity of the contested act.[140] However, the Tribunal, at the request of the applicant, can order temporary suspension of the contested act or any other interim measure deemed necessary.[141] The Tribunal can request the applicant to post a bond to ensure that, should the Tribunal not find the contested measure illegal, those who might have suffered damages caused by the suspension of the measure are compensated.[142]

Preliminary objections/proceedings

10.2.17   Preliminary objections must be included in the reply to the filing by the applicant, which is due within 40 days.[143] The applicant has ten days to reply to the preliminary objections, after which the Tribunal will rule.[144]

   The Tribunal may, either *proprio motu* or at the request of either party, merge two or more cases when it deems it useful to issue a single judgment.[145] Merger can be done up to the moment when the parties file their final submissions, before the Tribunal begins deliberations.[146]

Intervention by third parties/*amicus curiae*

10.2.18   Anyone who has a substantive legal interest in the case or might be affected negatively by the outcome of the case can intervene in proceedings.[147] However, intervention in the TJA is more like that of an *amicus curiae* rather than that of a full-intervener. Indeed, the intervener is not bound by the decision of the Tribunal.[148]

Public hearing

10.2.19   All hearings are public unless the Tribunal, *proprio motu* or at the request of either party, decides to hold closed-door hearings.[149]

---

[140]   Ibid, art 105.
[141]   Ibid.
[142]   Ibid.
[143]   Ibid, art 61. See also ibid, arts 56–57.
[144]   Ibid, art 61.
[145]   Ibid, art 63.
[146]   Ibid.
[147]   Ibid, art 72.
[148]   Ibid.
[149]   Ibid, art 82.

Decision

Decisions are taken by a majority of three judges out of four.[150] No separate or dissenting opinions are allowed.[151] In case of decisions declaring void acts of the Community institutions, the Tribunal will specify the time frame within which the given Community institution must act to ensure implementation of the Tribunal's decision.[152]

10.2.20

Revision

Only decisions on actions for failure to fulfil obligations are subject to revision.[153] Requests for revision are admissible only when filed by a party to the case, refer to issues that would have decisively influenced the decision, and where unknown to the requesting party at the time the case was decided.[154] Requests for revision must be filed within 90 days of the date on which the requesting party became aware of the decision and in no case after one year of the decision. Requests for revision do not interrupt the enforcement of the original decision.[155]

10.2.21

Costs

The expenses of the Tribunal are paid by the Andean Community member states, as assessed by the Commission upon preparation of the Community's budget.[156] There are no fees for proceedings before the Tribunal.[157] The parties can be charged for costs the Tribunal might incur for photocopying, visits, or expert opinions, according to tariffs established by the Tribunal.[158] The parties bear their respective litigation costs. However, the Tribunal may decide otherwise, if so requested by one of the parties.[159] Moreover, it may allocate costs caused by the production and evaluation of evidence differently.[160]

10.2.22

Enforcement of judgments

Once decisions of the Tribunal have been published in the Official Gazette, they are final and binding and have direct effect in the territory of member states

10.2.23

---

[150] Ibid, art 32. There is no provision as to what would happen in the case of a 2-2 split vote.
[151] Ibid, art 90.
[152] Ibid, art 106.
[153] Ibid, art 95.
[154] Ibid.
[155] Ibid.
[156] Ibid, art 26.
[157] Ibid, art 38.
[158] Ibid.
[159] Ibid, art 90.
[160] Ibid, art 81.

without need of further incorporation or exequatur.[161] Judgments on actions for failure to fulfil obligations brought by legal or natural persons can be brought before a national judge with a request for damages.[162]

Were the Tribunal to decide that the member state has not complied with its obligations, the state has 90 days to take the necessary steps to give effect to the judgment.[163] Should a member state fail to give full effect to the Tribunal's judgment, the Tribunal has the power to summarily decide what benefits accruing from the Cartagena Agreement the other member states can suspend, in whole or in part.[164] However, should the restriction or suspension of the benefits of the Cartagena Agreement worsen the situation to be resolved or fail to be effective, the Tribunal is free to order the adoption of other measures.[165] A verdict of non-compliance issued by the Tribunal constitutes ground for the claimant to present a request before a national judge for compensation for any damages or loss that may be due.[166]

REFERENCE

SOURCES OF CASE LAW, INCLUDING CASE REPORTS

All cases decided by the ATJ, as well as the basic legal texts governing its structure and functioning, are published in the Official Journal of the Andean Community (Gaceta Oficial del Acuerdo de Cartagena). They are also available on the Tribunal's website: <http://www.tribunalandino.org.ec>.

SELECT BIBLIOGRAPHY

L Helfer, K Alter, and F Guerzovich, 'Islands of Effective International Adjudication: Constructing an Intellectual Property Rule of Law in the Andean Community' (2009) 103 *Am J Int'l L* 1–46.

R Yong and A Camilio, 'Enhancing Legal Certainty in Colombia: The Role of the Andean Community' (2008–2009) 17 (2) *J Int'l L and Practice* 377–400.

M Benlolo-Carabot, N Susani, A-L Vaurs-Chaumette, and P Daillier, 'La Jurisprudence des tribunaux des organisations d'intégration latino-américaines' (2007) 53 *Annuaire français de droit international* 718–777.

---

[161] ATJ Treaty, art 41; ATJ Statute, art 91. The same applies to arbitration awards and the arbitration awards of the General Secretariat.

[162] ATJ Statute, art 110.

[163] ATJ Treaty, art 27; ATJ Statute, art 111.

[164] ATJ Treaty, art 27; ATJ Statute, art 119.

[165] Ibid.

[166] ATJ Treaty, art 30.

R J Garrón Bozo, 'El control de constitucionalidad y el control de comunitariedad de las normas de derecho comunitario derivado andino' (2007) 13 *Anuario de derecho constitucional latinoamericano* 761–771.

R Vigil Toledo, 'La compentencia arbitral del Tribunal de Justicia y de la Secretaría General de la Comunidad Andina' (2007) 13 *Anuario de derecho constitucional latinoamericano* 773–783.

J A Quindimil López, *Instituciones y derecho del la Comunidad Andina* (2006).

R A Suárez Arcila, 'Dispute Settlement within the Andean Community' (2005) 6 *Griffin's View on International and Comparative Law* 49–57.

M Baquero-Herrera, 'The Andean Community: Finding Her Feet within Changing and Challenging Multidimensional Conditions' (2004) 10 *L & Bus Rev Am* 577.

R Vigil Toledo, 'La consulta prejudicial en el Tribunal de Justicia de la Comunidad Andina' (2004) 10 *Anuario de Derecho Constitucional Latinoamericano* 939.

R Vigil Toledo, 'La Solución de Controversias en el Derecho Comunitario Andino', in Julio Lacarte and Jaime Granados (eds), *Settlement of Inter-governmental Trade Disputes: Multilateral and Regional Approaches* (2004) 159–171.

M Tangarife Torres, *Derecho de la Integración en la Comunidad Andina* (2002).

3. THE MERCOSUR DISPUTE SETTLEMENT SYSTEM

Introduction

Name and seat of the body

10.3.1 The seat of the Permanent Tribunal of Review (in Spanish 'Tribunal Permanente de Revisión') is the city of Asunción, Paraguay. Conversely, Ad Hoc Arbitral Tribunals (in Spanish 'Tribunal Ad Hoc del Mercosur')[167] and Groups of Experts to settle disputes between private parties and Mercosur states may meet in any city within Mercosur states.[168] Contact details for the Mercosur Secretariat are as follows:

> Dr Luis Piera 1992
> Piso 1
> Edificio MERCOSUR
> CP 11.200
> Montevideo, Uruguay
> Tel & Fax: (+ 598 2) 410.09.58/418.05.57
> Website: <http://www.mercosur.int/>

Contact details for the Tribunal Permanente de Revisión (Permanent Tribunal of Review—PTR) are:

> Mcal. López y Gral. Santos
> Edificio 'Villa Rosalba'
> Asunción, Paraguay

---

[167] While the literal translation from Spanish is 'Mercosur Ad Hoc Tribunal', we prefer translating to 'Ad Hoc Arbitral Tribunals' as the use of the singular might wrongly suggest that there exists a permanent Ad Hoc Arbitral Tribunal. In reality, the Mercosur Secretariat facilitates the creation of ad hoc arbitral panels to settle disputes.

[168] Protocol of Olivos, 18 February 2002, art 38, 42 ILM 4 (2003) ('PO'); Rules of Procedure of the Protocol of Olivos, art 52, 15 December 2003, CMC/DEC Nº37/03 ('PO RoP').

Tel & Fax: (595 21) 221.411/221.417/221.435/221.448
Email: secretaria@ PTRmercosur.org
Website: <http:// PTRmercosur.org>

General description

The Mercosur (short for Mercado Común del Sur) is a regional economic inte- **10.3.2**
gration organization comprising Argentina, Brazil, Paraguay, and Uruguay. It
was created in 1991 by the Treaty of Asunción,[169] later amended by the 1994
Protocol of Ouro Preto.[170] Like all regional economic integration agreements,
the aim of Mercosur is the creation of a common market to promote free trade
and integration of the economies of the member states. Mercosur is the world's
third largest regional trading bloc, after the European Community and NAFTA,
and it might further expand (Venezuela signed a membership agreement on 17
June 2006).[171] In 2003, Mercosur members signed a cooperation agreement
with the Andean Community, declaring their intention to move towards integration of the two common markets, and eventually all of South America.[172]
Currently, Bolivia, Chile, Colombia, Ecuador, and Peru have associate member
status in Mercosur.

The 1991 Treaty of Asunción contained a rudimentary dispute settlement
system, simply providing for negotiations and then mediation by the Common
Market Group, the executive body of Mercosur coordinated by the Ministries
of Foreign Affairs of the member states.[173] The Treaty of Asunción also provided
that Mercosur states shall adopt a permanent dispute settlement system for the
common market before 31 December 1994.[174] The Protocol of Brasilia of 17
December 1991 created an interim dispute settlement system.[175] It provided for
direct negotiations between the parties to a dispute and, if negotiations fail, it
empowered the Common Market Group to suggest a solution by consulting a
panel of experts to obtain technical advice or to resort to an arbitral tribunal.

---

[169] Treaty of Asunción Establishing a Common Market, 26 March 1991, 30 ILM 1041 (1991)
('Treaty of Asunción').

[170] Protocol of Ouro Preto on the Institutional Structure of Mercosur, 17 December 1994, 34
ILM 1244 (1994) ('OP Protocol').

[171] The accession agreement can be found at <http://www.mercosur.int/> (Protocolo de
Adhesión de la República Bolivariana de Venezuela al MERCOSUR). Before entering into force,
the accession agreement needs to be ratified by the Brazilian and Paraguayan parliaments which,
to date, has yet been done.

[172] Agreement on Economic Complementarity (Acuerdo de Complementación Económica)
No 56 between the Andean Community and MERCOSUR, 16 October 2003, available at
<http://www.sice.oas.org/>.

[173] Treaty of Asunción, Annex III.

[174] Ibid, para 3.

[175] Protocol of Brasilia for the Settlement of Disputes, 17 December 1991, 36 ILM 691
(1997).

Between 1997 and 2005, ten arbitrations were held within the framework of the Protocol of Brasilia.[176]

The 1994 Protocol of Ouro Preto modified the institutional structure of Mercosur and, concerning dispute settlement, it entrusted the task of settling disputes arising out of non-compliance by member states with Mercosur agreements with a newly established Mercosur Trade Commission.[177] The Mercosur Trade Commission settled a number of disputes, mostly brought by private parties against Mercosur member states, but remained an untoward procedure.

The 2002 Protocol of Olivos, which entered into force on 1 January 2004, created a new system that took elements introduced by the Brasilia and Ouro Preto Protocols and expanded them by creating the Permanent Tribunal of Review.[178] This is the current dispute settlement system available in Mercosur.[179] It is essentially a three-tier system. First, the parties try to settle disputes by direct negotiations.[180] If, after 15 days and unless the parties agree otherwise, the dispute is not settled or settled only partially, arbitral proceedings can be initiated by any party to the dispute.[181] Alternatively, the parties then may agree to refer the dispute to the Common Market Group for consideration.[182] The Common Market Group gives the parties to the dispute an opportunity to present their respective positions and may request, when considered necessary, the advice of experts.[183] Within 30 days, the Group makes recommendations that, whenever possible, are specific and detailed with a view towards solving the dispute.[184] Other Mercosur states not involved in the dispute may also request the intervention of the Common Market Group.[185] The second tier of the dispute settlement procedure is made of Ad Hoc Arbitral Tribunals (AHAT), and their awards can eventually be appealed to a standing judicial body, the Permanent Tribunal of Review (the third tier of the system).

In general, the Mercosur dispute settlement system resembles that of the WTO. However, there are also major differences. First, should the states parties to a dispute so agree, the dispute can be directly submitted for final adjudication

---

[176] Awards can be found at <http://www.mercosur.int/> (Solución de Controversias/Laudos de Tribunals ad hoc conforme al Protocolo de Brasilia).

[177] OP Protocol, *supra* note 170.

[178] PO, *supra* note 168.

[179] Ibid, art 55. Art 53 of the Protocol of Olivos provides that: 'Before the end of the common external tariff convergence process, the State Parties shall review the current dispute settlement system, in order to adopt the Permanent Dispute Settlement System for the Common Market referred to in Annex III of the Treaty of Asunción.'

[180] Ibid, art 4.

[181] Ibid, art 6.

[182] Ibid.

[183] Ibid, art 6.2.i.

[184] Ibid, arts 7.1, 8.

[185] Ibid, arts 6.3, 7.2.

to the PTR, without having to go first through an ad hoc arbitral panel.[186] Second, the dispute settlement procedure is open not only to Mercosur states but also to private parties. Natural or legal persons can file claims with the National Chapter of the Common Market Group of the state where they have their usual residence or place of business. Claims can be filed about the adoption or application, by any Mercosur state, of legal or administrative measures having a restrictive, discriminatory, or unfair competition effect in violation of Mercosur law.[187] The National Chapter of the Common Market Group that receives the complaint engages in consultations with the National Chapter of the Common Market Group of the state charged with the violation.[188] If the dispute is not settled within 15 days, the National Chapter of the Common Market Group forwards the claim directly to the Common Market Group.[189] The Common Market Group calls upon a Group of Experts to issue an opinion within 30 days.[190] The Group of Experts gives the claimant and the state in question the opportunity to be heard and to submit their arguments at a hearing.[191] The Group of Experts submits its opinion to the Common Market Group.[192] If the Group of Experts is unanimous in finding a violation, any other state party may request the adoption of corrective measures. If this request is not complied with within 15 days, the claiming state party may resort directly to the arbitration procedure.[193] If no unanimity is reached, the complaint is dismissed.[194] However, that does not bar subsequent arbitral proceedings initiated by Mercosur states.[195]

It should be noted that Mercosur states also can refer disputes falling within the scope of application of the Protocol of Olivos to the dispute settlement system of the World Trade Organization or other preferential trade systems that the Mercosur states parties may have entered into, provided that the parties to the dispute agree on that forum.[196]

Institutional Aspects

Governing texts

The legal documents regulating the Mercosur dispute settlement procedure **10.3.3** are the Protocol of Olivos[197] and a series of decisions of the Common Market Council, in particular the Rules of the Protocol of Olivos[198] and other rules

---

[186] Ibid, art 23.
[187] Ibid, arts 39, 40.   [188] Ibid, art 41.   [189] Ibid, art 41.2.
[190] Ibid, art 42.2.   [191] Ibid, art 42.3.   [192] Ibid, art 44.1.
[193] Ibid, art 44.1.i   [194] Ibid, art 44.1.iii.   [195] Ibid, art 44.2.
[196] Ibid, art 1.2.   [197] *Supra* note 168.   [198] PO RoP, *supra* note 168.

governing particular aspects of the Mercosur dispute settlement procedure.[199] The internal administration of the PTR is regulated by a series of decisions of the Common Market Group and the Common Market Council.[200]

The applicable law includes the Treaty of Asunción,[201] the Protocol of Ouro Preto,[202] other relevant protocols and agreements concluded within the framework of the Treaty of Asunción,[203] the Decisions of the Common Market Council,[204] the Resolutions of the Common Market Group and the Instructions of the Mercosur Trade Committee,[205] as well as the applicable principles and provisions of International Law.[206] Ad Hoc Arbitral Tribunals, or the PTR when acting as a direct single instance, can decide the dispute *ex aequo et bono*, if the parties so agree.[207]

Organization

Composition

10.3.4 **Arbitrators and members of the PTR**   Ad Hoc Arbitral Tribunals are composed of three arbitrators.[208] Each state party to the dispute appoints one from a list.[209] Each Mercosur state nominates 12 arbitrators to be included in the list, which is managed by the Administrative Secretariat of the Mercosur.[210] The third arbitrator, who is also the Presiding Arbitrator, is chosen by agreement between the parties[211] from a separate list. Each Mercosur state designates four arbitrators of this list.[212] Should the parties not be able to agree on the third arbitrator, the Administrative Secretariat of the Mercosur shall draw from the list, excluding nationals of the states involved in the dispute.[213]

---

[199] See eg CMC/DEC 30/05 (Rules of procedure of the PTR); CMC/DEC 30/04 (Rules of procedure of ad hoc arbitral tribunals); CMC/DEC 23/04 (Procedure for exceptionally urgent cases); CMC/DEC 02/07 (Rules regulating request by national supreme courts of advisory opinions of the PTR). All these documents are available at <http://www.mercosur.int> (Normativa/Decisiones).

[200] Available at <http://www.mercosur.int/> (Normativa/Resoluciones).

[201] Treaty of Asunción, *supra* note 169.

[202] OP Protocol, *supra* note 170.

[203] Available at <http://www.mercosur.int/> (Tratados, Protocolos y Acuerdos).

[204] Available at <http://www.mercosur.int/> (Normativa/ Decisiones).

[205] Available at <http://www.mercosur.int/> (Normativa/Resoluciones).

[206] PO, art 34.1.

[207] Ibid, art 34.2.

[208] Ibid, art 10.

[209] Ibid, art 10.2.

[210] Ibid, art 11.

[211] Ibid, art 10.3.

[212] Ibid, art 11.2. It should be noted that at least one of the arbitrators designated by each state party for inclusion in the list shall not be a national of any of the states parties of the Mercosur. Ibid.

[213] Ibid, art 10.3.ii.

The PTR is composed of five members. Each of the four Mercosur states appoints one for a twice-renewable two-year term.[214] The fifth member is chosen unanimously by Mercosur states from a list that includes eight members, each of the Mercosur states having nominated two.[215] The fifth member is appointed for a three-year non-renewable term.[216] If the Mercosur states cannot agree on the choice of the fifth member, the Administrative Secretariat of the Mercosur draws from the same list.[217]

The PTR operates in chambers of three members. Two of them are nationals of each of the states participating in the dispute and the third one, the Presiding Member, is chosen by the Director of the Administrative Secretariat of Mercosur by draw from the remaining PTR members that are not nationals of the states involved in the dispute.[218] Where the dispute involves more than two Mercosur states, or when the PTR hears cases directly and not as the court of appeal, five members sit in the case.[219]

The members of the PTR are permanently available to act whenever they are called upon to do so.[220] The arbitrators of the Ad Hoc Arbitral Tribunals and of the PTR are lawyers serving impartially and independently. They have recognized expertise in the fields that may be the subject matter of disputes, and are familiar with the body of Mercosur regulations.[221]

Criteria for disqualification of arbitrators or members of the PTR include having represented any of the states parties to a dispute in previous steps of the dispute settlement or procedure; or having a direct interest in the dispute and its outcome; or having represented anyone during the preceding three years who have a direct interest in the dispute and its outcome; or not being sufficiently independent from the authorities of the states parties to the dispute.[222]

The Group of Experts hears claims brought by natural or legal persons and is composed of three members selected from a list of 24 experts.[223] Each Mercosur state appoints six persons having recognized expertise in issues that may be the subject matter of the claim.[224]

---

[214] Ibid, art 18.
[215] Ibid, art 18.3.
[216] Ibid.
[217] Ibid. Currently, the members of the PTR are Carlos María Correa (Argentina), João Grandino Rodas (Brazil), Roberto Ruiz Díaz Labrano (Paraguay), and Roberto Puceiro Ripoll (Uruguay). The fifth member for the period 15 December 2008 to 15 December 2011 is Jorge Luiz Fontoura Nogueira (Brazil).
[218] Ibid, art 20.
[219] Ibid, art 20.2; PO RoP, art 39.2.
[220] PO, art 19.
[221] Ibid, art 35.
[222] PO RoP, art 19.1.
[223] PO, art 43.
[224] Ibid.

10.3.5 Registry Registrar services for Ad Hoc Arbitral Tribunals are provided for by the Administrative Secretariat of Mercosur. The PTR's Registry (Secretaría del Tribunal) is headed by the Registrar (Secretario), currently Mr Santiago Deluca from Argentina.[225]

Jurisdiction

10.3.6 The subject-matter jurisdiction of the Arbitral Tribunals, the PTR, and the Group of Experts includes adjudicating disputes arising out of the interpretation, application, or breach of the Treaty of Asunción, the Protocol of Ouro Preto, the protocols and agreements executed within the framework of the Treaty of Asunción, the Decisions of the Common Market Council, the Resolutions of the Common Market Group, and the Instructions of the Mercosur Trade Commission.[226] To date, the Ad Hoc Arbitral Tribunals have rendered awards in two disputes.[227] The PTR has yet to decide a dispute brought to it directly.

Advisory jurisdiction

10.3.7 The PTR has advisory jurisdiction as well.[228] To date, the PTR has given three advisory opinions.[229] Requests for advisory opinions can concern the Treaty of Asunción, Protocol of Ouro Preto, and any other protocols or agreements concluded within the framework of the Treaty of Asunción, decisions of the Common Market Council, resolutions of the Common Market Group, and Directives of the Mercosur Trade Commission. They cannot concern matters being addressed by the dispute settlement procedure.[230]

Advisory opinions can be requested by the Common Market Council, the Common Market Group, or the Mercosur Trade Commission.[231] The PTR cannot consider requests for advisory opinions from single Mercosur states. Only all Mercosur states, acting jointly, can do so.[232] High national courts can request

---

[225] PO RoP, art 35.

[226] PO, art 1.

[227] Award in the case between Uruguay and Argentina over *Transit over the Bridges Gral, San Martín y Gral, and Artigas*; Award in the case between Uruguay and Argentina over the *Import Ban of Remodeled Tires*. Both awards are available at <http://tprmercosur.org/> (Solución de Controversias/ Laudos). In both cases, the awards were appealed before the PTR (see *infra* note 237).

[228] PO, art 3; PO RoP, arts 2–13.

[229] Advisory Opinion (Opinión Consultiva) No 01/2007, *Norte S.A. Imp. Exp. c/Laboratorios Northia Sociedad Anónima, Comercial, Industrial, Financiera, Inmobiliaria y Agropecuaria s/Indemnización de Daños y Perjuicios y Lucro Cesante* (requested by the Supreme Court of Paraguay); Opinión Consultiva No 01/2008, *Sucesión Carlos Schnek y otros c/Ministerio de Economía y Finanzas y otros.* (requested by the Supreme Court of Uruguay); Opinión Consultiva No 01/2009, *Frigorífico Centenario S.A. c/Ministerio de Economía y Finanzas y otros* (requested by the Supreme Court of Uruguay). All opinions are available at <http://www.mercosur.int/> (Solución de Controversias/Opiniones Consultivas).

[230] PO RoP, art 12.

[231] Ibid, art 3.1.

[232] Ibid, arts 3.1, 3.2.

advisory opinions, too, but the scope of their requests is limited to legal interpretation of Mercosur treaties and acts only.[233] The PTR has 45 days to render
the opinion.[234] Advisory opinions do not have binding force for the requesting
state or Mercosur organ.[235]

Appellate structure

Any of the parties to a dispute may file a motion for appeal with the PTR against
the award of an Ad Hoc Arbitral Tribunal within 15 days of the notification
of the award.[236] To date, the PTR has decided two appeals.[237] Only points of
law can be raised during the appeal.[238] Decisions *aequo et bono* of the Ad Hoc
Arbitral Tribunal cannot be appealed.[239] There is no appeal against decisions of
the PTR when the dispute has been brought before it directly.[240] The other party
has 15 days to reply to the motion.[241] The PTR decides within 30 days of the
receipt of the reply.[242] It may confirm, modify, or revoke the award of the Ad Hoc
Arbitration Tribunal; its decision is final and binding.[243]

10.3.8

Procedural Aspects

Languages

Spanish and Portuguese are the official and working languages in all Mercosur
dispute settlement proceedings.[244]

10.3.9

Instituting proceedings

All cases must be filed in writing to the Administrative Secretariat of Mercosur.[245] Requests for advisory opinions are submitted in writing to the Registry

10.3.10

---

[233] Ibid, art 4.
[234] Ibid, art 7.
[235] Ibid, art 11.
[236] PO, art 17.
[237] Award 02/2006, *Impedimentos a la Libre Circulación derivado de los Cortes en Territorio
Argentino de Vías de Acceso a los Puentes Internacionales Gral. San Martín y Gral. Artigas* (Appeal
of Argentina against the Award of 21 June 2006); Award 01/2005, *Prohibición de Importación
de Neumáticos Remoldeados Procedentes del Uruguay* (Appeal of Uruguay against the Award of
25 October 2005). Both appeals are available at <http://www.mercosur.int/> (Solución de
Controversias/Opiniones Consultivas).
[238] PO, art 17.2.
[239] See *supra* note 207.
[240] PO, art 23.2.
[241] Ibid, art 21.
[242] Ibid, art 21.2.
[243] Ibid, art 22.
[244] Ibid, art 56.
[245] PO RoP, art 18.

of the PTR.[246] Motions for appeal against arbitral awards must be presented simultaneously to the Administrative Secretariat of Mercosur and the Registry of the PTR.[247] Natural or legal persons file claims in writing with the National Chapter of the Common Market Group of the state party where they have their usual residence or place of business.[248]

Financial assistance

10.3.11 There is no provision for financial assistance.

Interim measures

10.3.12 Whenever well-grounded suppositions exist that the continuation of a given situation may cause severe and irreparable damage to one of the parties to the dispute, at the request of the interested party the Ad Hoc Arbitral Tribunals may order provisional measures be taken.[249] In exceptional cases, involving goods that are perishable or that would otherwise lose their value within a short time, requests for provisional measures are heard by the PTR with all its five members sitting.[250] Interim measures can be discontinued at any time by the Ad Hoc Arbitral Tribunal.[251] In case of motions for appeal against arbitral awards, provisional measures that have not been discontinued prior to the award remain in force until the PTR decides to lift them.[252]

Intervention by third parties/*amicus curiae*

10.3.13 If two or more of the states parties hold the same position in a dispute, they may appear jointly before the Ad Hoc Arbitral Tribunal and appoint an arbitrator jointly.[253]

Decision

10.3.14 The Ad Hoc Arbitral Tribunal, or the PTR, if seized directly, decides the case within 60 days.[254] The term may be extended by decision of the Ad Hoc Arbitral Tribunal by a maximum of 30 additional days.[255] The PTR has 30 days to

---

[246] Ibid, arts 3.2, 3.3.
[247] Ibid, art 36.1.
[248] Ibid, art 46.
[249] PO, art 15.1.
[250] Ibid, arts 2, 24. Urgent proceedings are regulated by CMC/Dec 23/04.
[251] PO, art 15.2.
[252] Ibid, art 15.3
[253] Ibid, art 13.
[254] Ibid, arts 16, 23.1.
[255] Ibid.

decide on appeals and, likewise, it has the power to extend the term by up to 15 days.[256]

The awards of the Ad Hoc Arbitral Tribunal and of the PTR are adopted by a majority vote. The arbitrators are not allowed to specify the grounds for their dissenting votes. All deliberations are also confidential and remain so at all times.[257]

Revision

Any of the states parties involved in the dispute may request a clarification of the decision, or the way in which the decision is supposed to be enforced, of the Ad Hoc Arbitral Tribunal or the PTR.[258] The Ad Hoc Arbitral Tribunal or the PTR decide on the request within 15 days.[259] To date, the PTR has issued one clarification of a judgment it rendered in an appeal case.[260]   **10.3.15**

Costs

Any expenses and fees incurred in connection with the activity of the arbitrators are borne by the state appointing them. The expenses of the presiding arbitrator are borne equally by the states parties involved in the dispute, unless the Court decides otherwise.[261] Likewise, any expenses and fees incurred in connection with the activity of the PTR are borne equally by the states involved in the dispute, unless the Court decides otherwise.[262]   **10.3.16**

Any expenses arising from the involvement of the Group of Experts, including experts' honoraries, translation, and other costs, are borne as determined by the Common Market Group or, if no agreement is reached, are borne equally by the parties directly involved in the claim.[263]

Enforcement of judgments

The states parties to the Treaty of Asunción and the Protocol of Olivos[264] recognize as binding, *ipso facto* and with no need for a special agreement, the   **10.3.17**

---

[256] Ibid, art 21.2.
[257] Ibid, art 25.
[258] Ibid, art 28.
[259] Ibid.
[260] Award 01/2006, *Prohibición de Importación de Neumáticos Remoldeados procedentes de Uruguay* (request of clarification presented by Argentina of the award of the TRP of 20 December 2005), available at <http://www.mercosur.int/> (Solución de Controversias/Laudos).
[261] PO, art 36.1.
[262] Ibid, art 36.2.
[263] Ibid, art 43.3; PO RoP, art 53.
[264] PO, art 54: 'Adhesion to the Treaty of Asunción shall ipso jure constitute adhesion to this Protocol. Denunciation of this Protocol shall ipso jure constitute denunciation of the Treaty of Asunción.'

jurisdiction of the Ad Hoc Arbitral Tribunals formed in each case, as well as the jurisdiction of the PTR.[265]

All decisions of the Ad Hoc Arbitral Tribunals and the PTR are binding on the states involved in the dispute as from the time of their notification.[266] The decisions are enforced in the way and with the scope and term determined therein.[267]

Should one party or parties not take the measures requested in the decision, or take measures different from those indicated in the decision, the other party or parties can refer the matter to the Ad Hoc Arbitral Tribunal in question, or the PTR.[268] To date, the PTR has issued a judgment on such an issue.[269] Moreover, the prevailing party may start applying temporary countermeasures (up to one year) with the aim of inducing compliance with the award, such as the interruption of concessions or other similar obligations owed to the other party.[270] The countermeasure should target obligations in the same sector or sectors affected by non-compliance with the decision. Should the state consider that impracticable or ineffective, it may interrupt concessions or obligations in another sector, but in that case the decision must be motivated.[271]

Should the party against which countermeasures have been taken consider them disproportional, or should it feel that countermeasures in a different sector are not warranted, it can challenge them before the Ad Hoc Arbitral Tribunal, or to the PTR, depending on which body rendered the decision in question.[272] To date, the PTR has issued a judgment on such a matter.[273] In analysing proportionality, the Ad Hoc Arbitral Tribunal or the PTR take into account, among other things, the volume and/or value of trade in the sector concerned, as well as any other damage or factor that may have had an influence on the determination of the level or amount of compensatory measures.[274] Countermeasures must be adjusted according to the eventual decision of the relevant body within ten days, unless provided otherwise.[275]

---

[265] Ibid, art 33.

[266] Ibid, art 26.

[267] Ibid, arts 27, 29.

[268] Ibid, art 30.

[269] Award 01/2008, *Divergencia sobre el cumplimiento del Laudo No 1/05 (Art 30 Protocolo de Olivos)* (Uruguay v Argentina), available at <http://www.mercosur.int/> (Solución de Controversias/Laudos).

[270] PO, art 31.

[271] Ibid, art 31.2.

[272] Ibid, art 32.

[273] Award 01/2007, *Prohibición de importación de neumáticos Remoldeados procedentes del Uruguay* (Uruguay v Argentina) (Request for a decision on the disporportionality of counter-measures). Available at <http://www.mercosur.int/> (Solución de Controversias/Laudos).

[274] PO, art 32.2.ii.

[275] Ibid, art 32.3.

REFERENCE

SOURCES OF CASE LAW, INCLUDING CASE REPORTS

All cases decided by the Ad Hoc Arbitral Tribunals or the PTR are available on <http://PTRmercosur.org/> (Solución de Controversias). They are also published in the Official Bulletin of the Mercosur (Boletín Oficial del Mercosur), available at <http://www.mercosur.int/> (Boletín Oficial).

SELECT BIBLIOGRAPHY

N Lavranos and N Vielliard, 'Competing Jurisdictions between MERCOSUR and WTO' (2008) 7 (2) *The Law and Practice of International Courts and Tribunals* 205–234.

A Pastori Fillol, 'Comentarios al primer laudo del Tribunal Permanente de Revisión del Mercosur sobre la aplicación en exceso de medidas compensatorias' in Waldemar Hummer (ed), *Mercosur y Unión Europea* (2008).

N Susani, *Le Règlement des différends dans le Mercosur: un système de droit international pour une organisation d'intégration* (2008).

B Olmos Giupponi, 'El sistema de solución de controversias de Mercosur: análisis de la situación actual y propuestas para el future' in Carlos R Fernández Liesa (ed), *Tribunales internacionales y espacio iberoamericano* (2007).

R E Vinuesa, 'The MERCOSUR Settlement of Disputes System' (2006) 5 (1) *The Law and Practice of International Courts and Tribunals* 77–87.

R E Vinuesa, 'Enforcement of Mercosur Arbitration Awards within the Domestic Legal Orders of Member States' (2005) 40 (3) *Tex Int'l L J* 425–442.

4. THE NORTH AMERICAN FREE TRADE AGREEMENT DISPUTE SETTLEMENT SYSTEM

Name and seat of the body

10.4.1 Contact details for the NAFTA Secretariat, which comprises Canadian, Mexican, and US sections, are as follows:

NAFTA Secretariat Canadian Section
Royal Bank Centre
90 Sparks Street
Suite 705
Ottawa, Ontario
K1P5B4
Tel: 1 613 992 9388
Fax: 1 613 992 9392

Secretariado del TLCAN Sección Mexicana
Blvd Adolfo Lopez Mateos 3025, 2° Piso
Col Heroes de Padierna
CP10700, Mexico DF
Tel: 525 629 9630
Fax: 525 629 9637

NAFTA Secretariat
US Section
Room 2061
14th Street and Constitution Avenue, NW
Washington, DC 20230
Tel: 1 202 482 5438
Fax: 1 202 482 0148
Website: <http://www.nafta-sec-alena.org>

General description

10.4.2 In 1992 Canada, the USA, and Mexico concluded the North American Free Trade Agreement (NAFTA),[276] establishing the North American Free Trade Area. The Agreement removes trade barriers and promotes economic cooperation between the three participating states. Supervision over the implementation of NAFTA is

---

[276] North American Free Trade Agreement, 17 December 1992, 32 ILM 289 and 605 (1993) ('NAFTA').

under the primary responsibility of a Free Trade Commission (comprising ministerial representatives of the parties) assisted by a permanent Secretariat.[277] Most disputes arising under NAFTA are to be assigned by the Free Trade Commission to ad hoc dispute settlement panels, roughly similar to the GATT/WTO dispute settlement panels. Disputes concerning antidumping and countervailing duties are to be dealt with by different machinery involving bi-national panels.

The general dispute settlement procedure (Chapter 20 of the NAFTA Agreement)

The dispute settlement provisions of NAFTA apply to any dispute between the states parties concerning: (1) the interpretation or application of NAFTA; or (2) allegations that the application of an actual or proposed measure taken by a party is inconsistent with its NAFTA obligations, or would cause impairment or nullification of certain benefits that the complaining party expects to attain under NAFTA.[278] Once a dispute has arisen, the parties must first enter into consultations.[279] If no solution is found within a fixed period of time, the complaining party may request the convening of the Free Trade Commission (comprising the Trade Ministers of the parties), which will put its good offices at the disposal of the parties in order to facilitate a settlement.[280] If the parties fail to reach agreement within a fixed period of time, any party can request the Commission to establish an ad hoc arbitration panel.[281]

10.4.3

A panel comprises five independent experts. Each party is to select two persons, who are citizens of the other party to the dispute, and the chairperson is selected by agreement of the parties.[282] According to NAFTA, to facilitate the selection process, the parties should maintain a permanent roster of potential arbitrators (comprising up to 30 qualified persons) appointed with the consent of all states parties.[283] However, in practice a formal roster has never been established, resulting in ad hoc appointment processes subject to considerable delays. The appointment of an arbitrator who is not on the roster may be challenged by the other party.[284]

The procedure taken by the panels follows closely that of GATT/WTO panels (see Chapter 3). After hearings conducted in pursuance of the Commission's

---

[277] NAFTA, arts 2001, 2002.

[278] Ibid, art 2004.

[279] Ibid, art 2006.

[280] Ibid, art 2007.

[281] Ibid, art 2008. The normal period before establishment of a panel is 30 days from the date the Commission was first convened to discuss the dispute.

[282] Ibid, art 2011. If no agreement is reached, one of the parties, designated by lot, will appoint the chair. However, the appointing party cannot select a person of its own nationality.

[283] Ibid, art 2009.

[284] Ibid, art 2011.3.

Model Rules of Procedure[285] (from which the parties may agree to deviate), an initial report is published. The parties may submit their comments on the report and, subsequently, the panel issues a final report containing factual and legal findings.[286]

The reports are binding upon the parties. They are to be executed, preferably through non-implementation or removal of the unlawful measure, but alternatively through compensation. In case of failure to comply with the report, the complaining party may exercise trade sanctions against the recalcitrant party.[287] To date, three reports have been published under the general dispute settlement procedure outlined in Chapter 20 of the NAFTA Agreement.[288]

Antidumping and countervailing duties bi-national panels (Chapter 19 of the NAFTA Agreement)

10.4.4 Chapter 19 of NAFTA introduces a separate dispute settlement mechanism for review of final administrative decisions by national authorities of the three member states related to the imposition of antidumping and countervailing duties. The central feature of this mechanism is the establishment of ad hoc bi-national panels to review domestic administrative determinations relating to antidumping and countervailing duties. A special section of the Secretariat of the Free Trade Commission facilitates the operation of the bi-national panel system.[289]

A state party to NAFTA may request the establishment of a bi-national panel in two situations:

(1) if another party has adopted a statutory amendment which is inconsistent with the GATT (or certain specified side agreements) or the object and purpose of NAFTA,[290] or has the function and effect of overturning a bi-national panel decision (and is also inconsistent with the GATT and/or NAFTA);[291]

(2) if a determination of a competent domestic authority on antidumping or countervailing duties is incompatible with the domestic law of the importing state, as would have been applied by a domestic court of review.[292]

---

[285] Model Rules of Procedure for Chapter Twenty of the North American Free Trade Agreement and Supplementary Procedures Pursuant to Rule 35 on the Availability of Information, 13 July 1995, available on the NAFTA Secretariat's website: <http://www.nafta-sec-alena.org>.

[286] NAFTA, arts 2016, 2017.

[287] Ibid, arts 2018, 2019. The proportionality of trade sanctions may be the subject of separate panel proceedings.

[288] <http://www.nafta-sec-alena.org/> (Dispute Settlement/Decisions and Reports).

[289] NAFTA, art 1908.

[290] Ibid, arts 1902.2(d), 1903.1(a). Subsection 2(d)(ii) defines the purpose and object of the NAFTA Agreement as: 'to establish fair and predictable conditions for the progressive liberalization of trade among the Parties to this Agreement, while maintaining effective and fair disciplines on unfair trade practices'.

[291] Ibid, art 1903.1(b).

[292] Ibid, art 1904.2.

Such panels can also be established in relation to a dispute on antidumping or countervailing duties upon the request of the importing state, acting on its own initiative, or acting on the request of a person that would have had legal standing before equivalent domestic challenge procedures.[293]

Bi-national panels comprise five independent and qualified experts, who are normally to be selected from a roster of at least 75 persons.[294] Each party is to select two panel members and the fifth is to be agreed upon or, failing agreement, nominated by a party chosen by lot.[295]

The procedure of bi-national panels requested to examine statutory amendments is governed by Annex 1903.2 to the NAFTA Agreement, which entails procedures similar to those of the general panel machinery (the panels, or the parties, acting jointly, are to decide on supplementary rules of procedure).[296] In the event of failure to comply with decisions of a bi-national panel on statutory amendments, the complaining state is free to adopt comparable legislation or equivalent executive action to the violating amendments, or even to terminate its participation in NAFTA.[297]

Bi-national panels established to review administrative determinations are to apply the same standards of review that a domestic court would have applied.[298] They conduct their business in accordance with fixed rules of appellate procedure that have been agreed upon by the states parties.[299] A private litigant is to have the same procedural rights before a bi-national panel as he or she would have had before a comparable domestic review tribunal.[300] The supervision of the mechanism of bi-national panels reviewing administrative determinations is assigned to two ad hoc bodies: the Extraordinary Challenge Committee (composed of three members, selected by the parties from a roster of 15 senior judges or former judges), which may be requested to review the integrity of the mechanism;[301] and a Special Committee (composed in a similar manner to the Extraordinary Challenge Committee), which oversees state compliance in relation to the operation of the mechanism. To date, three cases have been decided under the Extraordinary Challenge Committee procedure.[302] A Special Committee is to

---

[293] Ibid, art 1904.5.

[294] Ibid, Annex 1901.2. The parties may also select non-roster panel members; however, in this case, the other party has a right to disqualify up to four non-roster candidates.

[295] Ibid, Annex 1901.2, art 3.

[296] Ibid, Annex 1903.2, art 1.

[297] Ibid, art 1903.3(b).

[298] Ibid, art 1904.3.

[299] Ibid, art 1904 Panel Rules.

[300] Ibid, arts 1904.5, 1904.7.

[301] Ibid, art 1940.13. Grounds for extraordinary challenge (ECC) are: (1) gross misconduct, conflict of interest, or other violation of rules of conduct by a panel member; (2) serious departure on the part of the panel from a fundamental rule of procedure; (3) if a panel manifestly exceeded its powers, authority, or jurisdiction. Only states may initiate ECC proceedings.

[302] <http://www.nafta-sec-alena.org/> (Dispute Settlement/Decisions and Reports).

be established if one party alleges that the other party impeded the work of the bi-national panel or failed to comply with the panel's decision.[303] The Special Committee may approve sanctions against the non-complying party.

To date, 120 cases have been referred to bi-national panels.[304]

Investment disputes (Chapter 11 of the NAFTA Agreement)

10.4.5   Chapter 11 of NAFTA sets out the applicable rules relating to investment. Within its framework it is also possible for an investor of a member state to institute arbitral proceedings for resolution of disputes which may arise with the host state. It is, however, first necessary to have attempted to settle the claim through consultation or negotiation,[305] and to have waited until at least six months have elapsed after the events giving rise to a claim.[306] Pursuant to the provisions of this section, an investor may submit the claim to arbitration under the Additional Facility Rules of ICSID.[307] It is also possible to submit the dispute to arbitration under the UNCITRAL rules.[308]

Alternatively, the investor may choose the remedies available in the host country's domestic courts. An important feature of the Chapter 11 arbitral provisions is the enforceability in domestic courts of final awards by arbitration tribunals.

To date, 16 Chapter 11 arbitration proceedings have been instituted against the US, 12 against Canada, and 12 against Mexico.[309]

Dispute settlement under the NAFTA side agreements on Environment and Labor

10.4.6   In 1993 Canada, Mexico, and the United States concluded two side agreements to the NAFTA: the North American Agreement on Environmental Cooperation (NAAEC)[310] and the North American Agreement on Labor Cooperation (NAALC).[311] In the case of both agreements, there are substantially two dispute

---

[303] NAFTA, art 1905. Grounds for a motion to establish a Special Committee are if a party has: (1) prevented the establishment of a panel; (2) prevented the panel from rendering its decision; (3) prevented the implementation of a panel decision; or (4) failed to provide an opportunity for panel or judicial review.

[304] <http://www.nafta-sec-alena.org/> (Dispute Settlement/Decisions and Reports).

[305] NAFTA, art 1118.

[306] Ibid, art 1120.

[307] Neither Mexico nor Canada is party to the ICSID convention, therefore the fall-back option is reliance on the Additional Facility Rules of ICSID which cover disputes with states that are not party to ICSID.

[308] Ibid, art 1120(1). For ICSID arbitration see *supra* para 2.5.

[309] <http://www.state.gov/> (Bureaus-Offices Reporting Directly to the Secretary/Office of the Legal Adviser/International Claims and Investment Disputes (L/CID)/NAFTA Investor-State Arbitrations).

[310] North American Agreement on Environmental Cooperation, 8–14 September 1993, 32 ILM 1480 ('NAAEC').

[311] North American Agreement on Labor Cooperation, US-Can-Mex, 8–14 September 1993, 32 ILM 1499 ('NAALC').

settlement procedures. One handles complaints by any of the three states parties that another party has violated obligations under either side agreement, which are handled first by conciliation carried out by a Council made of cabinet-level state representatives, and eventually by Arbitral panels.[312] The other addresses complaints by private parties alleging that a state party is failing to enforce effectively its environmental or labour laws.[313] Complaints are filed with a tri-national Secretariat in the case of the environmental side agreement, or with the National Administrative Offices (NAOs) created by each government within their own labour ministry to implement the labour side agreement. Both procedures result in an investigation of the matter by the body to which the complaint was referred, an attempt to find a mutually satisfactory outcome, and the preparation of a report that might be made publicly available.[314]

The Secretariat of the Commission for Environmental Cooperation, which receives complaints under the NAAEC, is located at:

393 rue St-Jacques Ouest, bureau 200
Montreal, Quebec
H2Y 1N9 Canada
Tel: 1 514 350-4300
Fax: 1 514 350-4314
Email: msilva@ccemtl.org
Website: <http://www.cec.org/>

Complaints under the labour side agreement need to be filed with the respective National Administrative Offices:

Inter-American Labour Cooperation
Labour Branch
Human Resources and Social Development Canada
165 Hotel de Ville
Place du Portage, Phase II
Hull, Quebec K1A 0J2, Canada
Tel: (819) 953-8860
Fax: (819) 953-8494
Website: <http://www.hrsdc.gc.ca/>

Under-Coordinator for Hemispheric Labor Policy
Secretariat of Labor and Social Welfare
Periférico Sur 4271, Edificio A, Planta Baja
Col. Fuentes del Pedregal. Del. Tlalpan

---

[312] NAALC, arts 27–41; NAAEC, arts 22–36.

[313] NAALC, arts 21–26; NAAEC, arts 14–15.

[314] For the procedures under each agreement see, in the case of the NAAEC, <http://www.cec. org/> (Citizens Submissions on Enforcement Matters) and, in the case of the NAALC, <http:// new.naalc.org/> (The NAALC/Rules of Procedure).

14149 México, DF, México
Tel: (5255) 5645-22-18
Fax: (5255) 5645-42-18
Email: oanmex@stps.gob.mx

US Department of Labor
200 Constitution Ave NW, Room S-5303
Washington, DC 20210, USA
Tel: (202) 693-4887
Fax: (202) 693-4851
Email: otla@dol.gov
Website: <http://www.dol.gov/ilab/programs/nao/main.htm>

As of March 2004, 28 public communications about complaints by private parties over alleged violations of the labour side agreement had been released.[315] As of August 2009, a total of 69 submissions had been submitted by private parties alleging violations of the environmental side agreements.[316]

REFERENCE

SOURCES OF CASE LAW, INCLUDING CASE REPORTS

All cases decided under the various NAFTA dispute settlement procedures can be found at <http://www.nafta-sec-alena.org> (Dispute Settlement/Decisions and Reports).

SELECT BIBLIOGRAPHY

D A Gantz, *Regional Trade Agreements: Law, Policy and Practice* (2009).
J Graubart, *Legalizing Transnational Activism: The Struggle to Gain Social Change from NAFTA's Citizen Petitions* (2008).
B Appleton, *NAFTA: Text and Selected Documents* (2007).
C Leathley, *International Dispute Resolution in Latin America: An Institutional Overview* (2007).
C H Brower II et al (eds), *NAFTA Chapter Eleven Reports* (2006).
R G Finbow, *The Limits of Regionalism: NAFTA's Labour Accord* (2006).
M N Kinnear, *Investment Disputes under NAFTA: An Annotated Guide to NAFTA Chapter 11* (2006).
G C Hufbauer, *NAFTA Revisited: Achievements and Challenges* (2005).
R Folsom, *Accord de libre échange nord-américain* (2004).
T Weiler, *NAFTA Investment Law and Arbitration: Past Issues, Current Practice, Future Prospects* (2004).

---

[315] <http://www.naalc.org/> (Public Communications/Table).
[316] <http://www.cec.org/> (Citizens Submissions on Enforcement Matters/Status).

5. THE ECONOMIC COURT OF THE COMMONWEALTH OF INDEPENDENT STATES

Introduction

Name and seat of the body

The Economic Court of the Commonwealth of Independent States **10.5.1**
(Ekonomicheskij Sud Sodruzhestva Nezavisimih Gosudarstv, hereinafter
'ECCIS' or Economic Court) is located at the following address:

17 Kirov Street
Minsk, Belarus, 2200550
Tel: +375-17-206-61-08
Fax: +375-17-206-62-07
Website: <http://www.sudsng.org>

General description

The Economic Court of the Commonwealth of Independent States was cre- **10.5.2**
ated on 6 July 1992, by the Agreement on the Status of the Economic Court
(hereafter ECCIS Agreement).[317] It began functioning in 1994. The Court is
an organ of the Commonwealth of Independent States (CIS), a regional organization coordinating actions between members in the field of trade, finance,
lawmaking, and security, and grouping together nine former republics of the
Soviet Union.[318] Eight of these (Armenia, Belarus, Kazakhstan, Kyrgyzstan,

---

[317] Agreement on the Status of Economic Court of CIS, 6 July 1992, <http://www.sudsng.org/
documents/> (in Russian).

[318] The CIS is an organizational framework providing for political and economic relations
between former USSR republics. It was created in 1991 (see Agreement on the Establishment of
the Commonwealth of Independent States, 21 December 1991, <http://www.therussiansite.org/
legal/laws/CISagreement.html> (unofficial English translation)). The organization's structures
were consolidated in 1993 with the conclusion of the CIS Charter. Charter of the Commonwealth

Moldova, Russia, Tajikistan, and Uzbekistan, but not Azerbaijan) have ratified the ECCIS Agreement and the appended 'Court Regulation', as the Court's Statute is called.[319] Following the establishment of the Eurasian Economic Community ('EurAsEC') in 2004,[320] which aims to create a fully fledged common market, the Economic Court of the Commonwealth of Independent States was also given jurisdiction over disputes involving the five CIS member states which now comprise the EurAsEC (Belarus, Kazakhstan, Kyrgyzstan, Russia, and Tajikistan).[321]

Institutional Aspects

Governing texts

10.5.3 The work of the Court is governance by the 1992 Agreement on the Status of the Economic Court and the appended ECCIS Statute (or Regulation).[322] In addition, in 1997 the Court adopted its Rules of Procedure.[323]

Organization

Composition

10.5.4 Under the ECCIS Agreement, the Court is to be composed of judges selected by the different member states in accordance with their individual national judicial nomination procedures for positions in the highest commercial and arbitration courts. In practice, not all of the member states have exercised the right to nominate a judge, and the Court is currently manned by five judges only (all holding the nationality of EurAsEC member states). Judges are elected for a ten-year term.[324]

---

of Independent States, 22 January 1993, <http://www.sudsng.org/> (Documents) (in Russian). For more information on the CIS, see <http://www.cis.minsk.by/main.aspx?uid=74>.

[319] ECCIS Statute/Regulation ('ECCIS Statute'), appended to Agreement on the Status of Economic Court of CIS, 6 July 1992, <http://www.sudsng.org/> (Documents)(in Russian).

[320] Agreement between the Commonwealth of Independent States and Eurasian Economic Community about assuming by the Economic Court of the Commonwealth of Independent States the Functions of the Court of the Eurasian Economic Community, 3 March 2004, <http://www.sudsng.org/> (Documents) (in Russian).

[321] Uzbekistan's membership in EurAsEC was suspended in 2008.

[322] See *supra* notes 317, 319.

[323] Rules of Procedure of the Economic Court of the CIS, art 28, 12 Vestnik Vysshego Arbitrazhnogo Suda Rossiiskoi Federatsii [Bulletin of the Supreme Arbitration Court of the Russian Federation] 64 (1994), as revised in 1997 ('ECCIS Rules of Procedure').

[324] The current composition of the Court is: President: F Abdulloev (Tajikistan); Judges: S Z Zholdybaev (Kazakhstan), T N Molchanova (Russia), A S Kerimbayeva (Kyrgyzstan), and L E Kamenkova (Belarus).

The Court can sit in Chambers, Full Court, and Plenum (being a joint body comprising all ECCIS judges and the Chief Justices of the highest commercial courts, courts of arbitration, and other highest government bodies of the member states, designated to settle economic disputes). It was originally planned that the Chambers would handle the inter-state cases brought before the Court, whilst the Full Court would hear requests for interpretation. However, given the limited number of judges currently sitting on the Court all hearings are now conducted before the Full Court. The Plenum was designed to serve primarily as an appellate body hearing appeals from ECCIS judgments in contentious cases.[325] To date, however, no appeals have been made. Therefore, annual meetings of the Plenum are dedicated to discussions on the operation of the Court, and the review of reform proposals.

Jurisdiction

Contentious jurisdiction

Article 3 of the ECCIS Statute grants the Court jurisdiction over disputes **10.5.5** arising out of:

1. implementation of 'economic obligations'[326] provided by treaties and acts of the Council of Heads of State, Council of Heads of Governments, and other Commonwealth institutions;
2. a conflict between legal acts taken by member states in the economic sphere, and agreements and acts of the Commonwealth;
3. other disputes arising out of agreements between member states and acts of the CIS institutions if the agreement or act has an arbitration clause specifying the Economic Court as a method for dispute resolution.

Although the ECCIS constitutive instruments are silent on the point, arguably CIS states party to the ECCIS Agreement, or EurAsEC states, refer any other kind of dispute to the Court by way of a special agreement.

Article 4 of the ECCIS Statute provides that judgments of the Economic Court must be based on 'the provisions of agreements and other acts of the Commonwealth of Independent States, as well as on other applicable normative

---

[325] ECCIS Statute, para 10.

[326] The term 'economic obligations' has been broadly construed by the Court as obligations concerning tangible benefits that have monetary value, such as transfers of goods, monetary resources, and services. Such obligations can be assumed by the CIS states not only in the sphere of trade, production, finance, or transport, but also in relation to their cooperation in humanitarian, ecological, cultural, and other spheres. Case C-1/1-97, Vestnik Vysshego Arbitrazhnogo Suda RF (Vestn. VAS) [The Highest Arbitration Court of the RF Reporter] 1997, No 2, p 99.

acts'. The 1997 Rules of Procedure further describe the legal basis for the Court's decisions by providing the list of governing texts:

(1) international treaties in force between the disputing states;
(2) CIS acts;
(3) rules contained in the legislative acts of the former USSR which are mutually applied by the contesting states;
(4) national legislation of the contesting states;
(5) international conventions, whether general or particular, establishing rules expressly recognized by the disputing states;
(6) generally recognized principles of international law and international custom, as evidence of a general practice accepted as law;
(7) general principles of law recognized in member states of the Commonwealth;
(8) rulings of the Plenum of the Economic Court, and other decisions of the Economic Court that have precedential value.

Until June 2009, the Court had heard only ten contentious cases. Of these, four were found inadmissible and one was discontinued.

Advisory jurisdiction

10.5.6 The Court also has advisory jurisdiction over interpretation of agreements, and other acts of the Commonwealth and its institutions (including non-economic CIS instruments), and can issue opinions at the request of: the highest legislative and executive organs of member states; their highest economic and commercial courts; or CIS institutions.[327] Advisory opinions are issued by the Full Court, but are not binding in nature.

Advisory opinions are the bulk of the Court's docket: 83 out of a total of 93 cases considered since it started operating in 1994.

---

[327] ECCIS Statute, art 5. In practice, the Court has shown considerable flexibility in the types of entities it allowed to request advisory opinions. For instance, Opinion No 07/95, *Interpretation of the CIS Agreement on the International Legal Guarantees for the Activities of the Inter-State Television Company MIR*, was requested by MIR, a multinational, corporation controlled by a government. Opinion No 07/95, Vestnik Vysshego Arbitrazhnogo Suda RF [Vestn VAS] [The Highest Arbitration Court of the RF Reporter] 1995; in Opinion No 09/95/C-1/2-96, the General Confederation of Trade Unions, a non-governmental organization, requested an interpretation of the CIS Agreement on Mutual Recognition of Rights and Compensation to Injured Workers. The Court recognized the applicant as a CIS institution. Opinion No 09/95/C-1/2-96, Vestnik Vysshego Arbitrazhnogo Suda RF [Vestn VAS] [The Highest Arbitration Court of the RF Reporter] 1996.

Procedural Aspects

Languages

10.5.7 Proceedings before the Court are conducted in Russian,[328] and are subject to strict time limits (which in practice are often not followed).[329] They are normally open to the public, and the judgments are usually published in full (although the Court may decide to publish parts thereof only).

Instituting proceedings

10.5.8 Proceedings before the Economic Court against any CIS member state may be initiated by another CIS member state,[330] or a CIS institution.[331] The states parties to the ECCIS Agreement are deemed to have *ipso facto* accepted the Court's jurisdiction; nevertheless, other CIS member states may also agree to adjudicate before the Court. Third parties may intervene in the proceedings in order to protect their legal interests.[332]

Decision

10.5.9 Individual opinions in contentious cases are not allowed.[333] In the case of advisory opinions, they are allowed and may be appended to the conclusions of the majority. In practice, however, judgments are normally issued as the joint opinion of the bench, without any dissents.

---

[328] ECCIS Rules of Procedure, art 28.

[329] Ibid, art 58.

[330] ECCIS Statute, art 3. Formally, the Court has jurisdiction only over disputes between CIS member states. In practice, however, there have been cases where disputes referred to the Court were not purely intergovernmental in nature. For instance, in Case No C-1/15-96 a dispute between Russia and Kazakhstan was triggered by provincial governments and private parties entering into private contracts on the basis of the Russian-Kazakhstan 1992 Agreement on Principles of Trade and Economic Cooperation. The Court held that it had jurisdiction to decide the case because the obligations assumed by commercial entities and subsequently approved by the governments must be treated as obligations assumed by the governments. Case C-1/15-9624, Vestnik Vysshego Arbitrazhnogo Suda RF [Vestn VAS] [The Highest Arbitration Court of the RF Reporter] 1996.

[331] ECCIS Statute, art 3. The main CIS institutions are: Council of the Heads of State, Council of the Heads of Government, Inter-Parliamentary Assembly, Council of Foreign Ministers, Council of Defence Ministers, Economic Council and the Economic Court. For the full list of CIS institutions, see <http://www.cis.minsk.by>.

[332] A F Douhan et al, 'Ekonomicheskij Sud Sodruzhestva Nezavisimih Gosudarstv 15 Let' (2008), <http://sudsng.org> (in Russian).

[333] ECCIS Rules of Procedure, art 86.

In three out of five contentious cases decided by the Court (all against Kazakhstan), the judgment has not yet been complied with.

REFERENCE

SOURCES OF CASE LAW, INCLUDING CASE REPORTS

All judgments and opinions of the Court are published in Russian, in *Sodruzhestvo Informatsionnii Vestnik* (Commonwealth Information Bulletin), the official CIS publication. They are also published in *Vestnik Vysshego Arbitrazhnogo Suda Rossijskoj Federacii* (Information Bulletin of the Highest Arbitration Court of the Russian Federation).

The official website of the Court includes all the decisions of the Court, general information, and news: <http://www.sudsng.org>.

In 2008, the ECCIS published a report on its first 15 years of activity, entitled 'Economic Court of the Commonwealth of Independent States: 15 Years'. The report includes all judgments, advisory opinions, and rulings and biographies of the present judges. It is currently available only in Russian.

SELECT BIBLIOGRAPHY

A F Douhan et al, 'Ekonomicheskij Sud Sodruzhestva Nezavisimih Gosudarstv: 15 Let' (2008), <http://sudsng.org/download_files/publication/pub15year/kniga_itog1.pdf> (in Russian).
G M Danilenko, *The Economic Court of the Commonwealth of Independent States* (1999) 31 *NYU J Int'l L & Pol* 893.

Evaluation

The European Court of Justice is a model, but also an exception, within the large and heterogeneous family of judicial bodies and dispute settlement systems of regional economic communities. While many regional courts share jurisdictional and procedural traits with the ECJ and have been created explicitly or implicitly with that template in mind, most of them have failed to replicate the success of their European peer. Indeed, those considered in this sub-chapter are only relatively successful.

They are success stories if compared to the more than a dozen regional economic courts that have been established but never actually started functioning, those that, after timid beginnings, were abandoned and have not been used for years, or those that are active at barely detectable levels.[334] But when compared to the ECJ, which has managed to establish itself as a central focus, if not the

---

[334] See *supra* Introduction to Part IV.

driving force, of the economic and political integration of Europe, it is evident that they are struggling to various degrees and for various reasons and are still far from entrenched.

Of course, it is difficult to generalize. Each judicial body or dispute settlement mechanism is a unique case. It is also unclear to what extent the underachievement of these adjudicative bodies and dispute settlement systems is the cause or effect of problems affecting the regional organization within which they operate. Be that as it may, problems of underutilization and lukewarm acceptance of rulings notwithstanding, regional economic courts often show remarkable degrees of effectiveness, even though only on certain selected topics or in certain aspects of their oft diversified jurisdiction.[335]

For instance, the overwhelming majority (more than 90 per cent) of decisions of the Andean Tribunal of Justice are preliminary rulings on cases referred by national courts. Of those, about 90 per cent concern intellectual property issues. The Andean Tribunal of Justice has helped to establish intellectual property as a 'rule of law island' in the Andean Community where national judges, administrative officials, and private parties actively participate in regional litigation and conform their behaviour to Andean rules.[336] However, in the vast seas surrounding this island, by contrast, Andean rules remain riddled with exceptions, underenforced, and often circumvented by domestic actors. Out of 1,569 decisions until 2007, only 52 were from cases brought against the Community (46 actions for annulment and six for failure to act) and only 105 against Andean member states for failure to fulfil obligations.

The same 'islands of effectiveness' phenomenon also can be found in other regional courts considered in this Chapter. For instance, the Caribbean Court of Justice is both an international court and a national court. It is an international court ECJ-like when it acts under its original jurisdiction deciding matters of Caribbean Community law. It is a national court of last instance when it hears appeals against decisions of national supreme courts, as the Judicial Committee of the Privy Council, sitting in the United Kingdom, used to do. To date, more than 90 per cent of the caseload of the Caribbean Court of Justice are appeals and, for that matter, against rulings of only two Caribbean states (Guyana and Barbados). So far, the CCJ has considered only three cases under its original ECJ-like jurisdiction.

---

[335] Granted, the ECJ too considers more cases under some heads of jurisdiction than under others. However, imbalances are not as marked as in the case of other regional economic integration agreements courts. For instance, in 2008, the ECJ rendered 288 preliminary rulings, but also decided 207 actions for failure to fulfil obligations. ECJ Annual Report, 2008, pp 79–107, available at <http://curia.europa.eu/> (Court of Justice/Statistics of Judicial Activity).

[336] See generally Helfer, Alter and Guerzovich, *supra* note 79 at section 10.2.3.

Likewise, while the Economic Court of the Commonwealth of Independent States has both contentious and advisory jurisdiction, to date it has issued 83 advisory opinions and considered only ten contentious cases, of which only five progressed to the merits stage. Moreover, if one considers that advisory opinions of the ECCIS are not binding and that in the five contentious cases it ruled, in three the ruling was not complied with, it is clear that the ECCIS is having troubles being fully embraced and accepted by CIS member states.

The imbalance is also evident in the case of NAFTA. The dispute settlement procedure between the states parties (Chapter 20) is rarely used. The overwhelming majority of cases decided under NAFTA dispute settlement procedures are antidumping and countervailing duties considered by bi-national panels (120) and investment disputes brought by private investors against the host state (40). The complaints procedure under the North American Agreement on Environmental Cooperation has been used more than twice as much as the one under the North American Agreement on Labor Cooperation (69 to 28).

Finally, the Mercosur dispute settlement procedure remains largely underutilized with a very modest record of two arbitral awards and two appeals, three advisory opinions, and two other decisions (clarification of a ruling and proportionality of countermeasures) over five years of operation. The fact that the Mercosur dispute settlement system is not to the exclusion of other dispute settlement procedures, in particular those of the WTO, might explain the modest mark.

So far most, if not all, scholarly literature about judicial bodies and dispute settlement mechanisms of regional economic organizations other than the ECJ has been merely descriptive. It is difficult to find articulate assessments of the factors determining their success or failure. Legal scholars and political scientists have preferred focusing on the ECJ success story. However, the pathology of regional economic courts can be as illuminating as success stories to determine what are the factors under which international courts thrive and can be effective.

PART V

HUMAN RIGHTS BODIES

Introduction

This Part of the Manual addresses courts and quasi-judicial bodies established in order to monitor the compliance of states with different human rights treaties. Five of the surveyed courts and commissions operate at the regional level under the auspices of regional political organization. (In addition, the annexes to the chapters on the European Court of Human Rights and African Human Rights Courts and Commission briefly introduce two other regional committees of lesser prominence.) Four other surveyed bodies operate under UN auspices at the global level; one further set of global complaint procedures operates under the auspices of the International Labour Organization. All 12 bodies discussed below were established after the conclusion of the Second World War, and illustrate the growth in concern for human rights at the international and regional level during this period.

The regional mechanisms reviewed in this Part generally comprise commissions and courts entrusted with receiving, investigating, and/or adjudicating complaints. The first to be established was the European Court of Human Rights ('ECtHR'), which is entrusted with monitoring the compliance of member states of the Council of Europe with their obligations under the 1950 European Convention on Human Rights, and the Protocols thereto. Under the original text of the Convention, a two-tier enforcement mechanism was established, consisting of two organs—(1) the European Commission on Human Rights ('Commission') and (2) the European Court of Human Rights. Under this system, petitions from individuals, NGOs, or states alleging violations of the Convention had to be brought, initially, before the Commission. Following the entry into force of the 11th Protocol to the Convention in 1998, the Commission was abolished, and most of its functions transferred to the Court. As a result, claimants (namely states and individuals) may now submit applications directly to the Court.

The ECtHR deals with complaints by states and individuals concerning the protection of human rights by the 47 states parties to the European Convention. Upon receipt of an application, the Court determines its admissibility and, if admissible, attempts to secure a friendly settlement of the dispute on the basis of respect for the human rights set out in the Convention and Protocols thereto. If no settlement is reached, a Chamber of the Court will hear the case and issue a binding judgment, which in exceptional cases may be referred for second review before an enlarged chamber (the Grand Chamber). Since its establishment, the Court has received more than 200,000 petitions.

An Annex to the Chapter on the ECtHR provides some basic information on another Council of Europe human rights mechanism—the collective complaints procedure under the 1995 Protocol to the European Social Charter, which authorizes the European Committee on Social Rights to receive complaints from human rights and labour organizations alleging the violation of social rights by states that have ratified the 1961 European Social Charter and the 1995 Protocol (almost 60 complaint proceedings have been initiated before the Committee to date).

The Inter-American human rights system discussed in Chapter 12 incorporates a two-tiered system similar to that originally utilized under the European Convention. Thus the Inter-American Commission on Human Rights and the Inter-American Court of Human Rights are entrusted with monitoring and adjudicating the human rights practices of the 24 states parties to the 1969 American Convention of Human Rights (concluded under the auspices of the Organization of American States). All complaints are first brought to the Commission, which examines the admissibility of the complaint, investigates the allegations against the state party concerned, makes recommendations to states parties, and, if appropriate, prepares a report on the case. The Commission may decide to pursue the complaint by bringing a claim against a state party (which has accepted such jurisdiction) before the Court. Twenty-one states have issued the required declarations of acceptance. Since 1979 the Court has received more than 200 cases, while the Commission has dealt with more than 20,000 complaints since its establishment.

The African Commission on Human Rights described in Chapter 13 is an expert body intended to ensure compliance with the 1981 African Charter on Human and People's Rights, which now functions under the institutional framework of the African Union (the successor of the Organization of African Unity). It disseminates information on human rights in Africa, and receives periodic reports from the states parties to the African Charter. The Commission is also authorized to receive communications from state and non-state actors alleging violation of the human rights guaranteed by the African Charter. The procedure for handling communications involves investigation of the factual claims of the parties by the Commission, and the issuance of recommendations on the merits in the form of observations or a report. Since its establishment, the African Commission has received some 400 communications from individuals and NGOs. In contrast, the inter-state communication procedure before the Commission has hardly ever been used.

In June 1998, the member states of the OAU adopted a Protocol on the establishment of a Court of Human and People's Rights, thereby offering the possibility of complementing the Commission's work with judicial remedies. The Protocol entered into force in 2004, and judges were elected for the Court in 2006. The Court has not yet issued any decision (a first case was brought before the Court only in 2008). What's more, the African Union decided in 2004 to merge the new human rights court with the African Court of Justice (an economic integration court). A Protocol to that effect was adopted in 2008, but has not yet entered into effect. The new Court of Justice and Human Rights is expected to begin operation in the coming years.

An Annex to Chapter 13 briefly addresses another African Union mechanism for protecting human rights—the complaints procedure under the 1990 African Charter for the Rights and Welfare of the Child, which establishes a Committee of Experts, and authorizes it to receive complaints alleging violations of the 1990 Charter. This complaints mechanism has hardly ever been invoked, and its effectiveness is still unclear.

The next body reviewed in this Part (in Chapter 14) is the UN Human Rights Committee (HRC), established under the 1966 International Covenant on Civil and Political Rights. The Covenant entered into force in 1976 and has now been ratified by 164 states. The Committee receives and studies periodic reports from states parties as to their implementation of the standards set out in the Covenant, and may issue general comments on the provisions of the Covenant. Where a state party has accepted its competence to do so, the Committee may also receive communications from states and/or individuals alleging violations of human rights by that state party. So far 113 states have accepted the competence of the Committee (under the Optional Protocol) to receive communications from individuals, and 48 states have authorized it to receive inter-state communications. The Committee has received almost 2,000 individual complaints and has issued views on almost 700 cases. No inter-state communication, however, has even been lodged with the HRC.

The three other UN committees more briefly reviewed in this Part, in various subsections of Chapter 15, have been established to monitor compliance with particular human rights treaties: (1) The 1966 International Convention on the Elimination of All Forms of Racial Discrimination (CERD Committee); (2) the 1984 Convention Against Torture and other Cruel, Inhuman or Degrading Treatment or Punishment (CAT Committee); and (3) the 1979 Convention on the Elimination of All Forms of Discrimination against Women (CEDAW Committee). The CERD Committee examines periodic reports of the 173 states parties to the CERD Convention. It may also address complaints presented against states parties either by other states, or by individuals or groups of individuals. Inter-state complaints are permitted under the Convention itself, while the submission of complaints by individuals or groups requires prior acceptance by the state concerned of the competence of the CERD Committee to receive such complaints. To date, the CERD Committee has received 43 individual complaints, but no inter-state communications.

The CAT Committee may hear inter-state or individual complaints provided the states parties concerned have accepted the jurisdiction of the CAT Committee to receive such complaints. So far the Committee has received almost 400 communications and has published its views on the merits of more than 150 of them. In addition, the CAT Committee considers periodic reports by the states parties on measures taken to implement the Convention, and may also investigate countries suspected of engaging in a systematic practice of torture (where relevant information has been received from reliable sources) without any formal complaint being made. A 2002 Protocol to the CAT creates a new sub-committee for the purpose of conducting on-site visits of detention facilities.

The last UN Committee surveyed in this Part is the CEDAW Committee, whose powers to review individual communications and conduct investigations of systematic violations of CEDAW have been enumerated in a 1999 Optional Protocol (which entered into force in 2000). Ninety-eight CEDAW member states have ratified the Optional Protocol and 20 communications have already been registered with the Committee.

It should be noted that a new complaint mechanism has more recently been created under another UN human rights treaty—the 2006 Convention on the Rights of Persons with Disabilities (whose Additional Protocol entered into force in 2008)—and that two other complaints mechanisms, under the 1990 Convention on the Protection of the Rights of All Migrant Workers and Members of Their Families (MWC) and the 1966 International Covenant on Economic, Social and Cultural Rights (ICESCR), are in the process of being created. As none of these three new mechanisms is yet active, they have not been covered in this edition of the Manual.

The last global mechanism reviewed here is the representation and complaints procedure of the International Labour Organization (ILO). ILO member states report periodically on measures taken to implement the various ILO

Conventions to which they are party and these are reviewed by a Committee of Independent Experts. In addition, representations or complaints may be made to the ILO alleging failure of member states to comply with relevant ILO Conventions, or freedom of association standards. These complaints, which may be made by states, delegates to the ILO General Conference, and domestic and international employers' or workers' associations are dealt with by the ILO Governing Body, or subsidiary bodies established by it. One of these subsidiary bodies (the Committee on Freedom of Association) has received to date almost 3,000 complaints.

11

THE EUROPEAN COURT
OF HUMAN RIGHTS

Introduction

Name and seat of the Court

11.1 The European Court of Human Rights ('ECtHR' or 'the Court') is a permanent court entrusted with monitoring the compliance of member states of the Council of Europe with their obligations under the European Convention on Human Rights. The Registry of the Court operates within the organizational framework of the Council of Europe and is located at the following address:

> European Court of Human Rights
> Conseil de l'Europe
> F-67075 Strasbourg CEDEX
> France
> Tel: 33 3 88 41 20 18
> Fax: 33 3 88 41 27 30
> Website: <http://www.dhcour.coe.fr>

General description

11.2 The European Convention of Human Rights ('the ECHR' or 'the Convention') was adopted within the framework of the Council of Europe in 1950,[1] an

---

[1] Convention for the Protection of Human Rights and Fundamental Freedoms, 4 November 1950, ETS 5 (1950), as amended by Protocol No 11, 11 May 1994, ETS 155 (1994) ('ECHR').

organization designed to bring European states into closer association.[2] The institutional link between the Council of Europe, based in Strasbourg (France), and the ECHR remains to this day. The Council's Committee of Ministers is responsible for monitoring the implementation of judgments of the Court. States interested in joining the Council of Europe must undertake a political commitment to ratify the Convention.[3]

The Convention and the Protocols thereto which have been adopted subsequently enumerate fundamental rights and freedoms which the contracting parties undertake to respect and secure. The original text of the Convention introduced a two-tier enforcement mechanism, intended to ensure compliance with its prescribed human rights standards. This mechanism consisted of two organs, the European Commission of Human Rights ('Commission') and the Court.

Under the original system, petitions from individuals, NGOs, or states alleging violations of the Convention were initially to be brought before the Commission. The Commission examined the admissibility of the petition and attempted to find a friendly settlement. Under certain conditions the Commission and the complaining states could refer the case to the Court on behalf of the complainant.

Following the entry into force of the 11th Protocol to the Convention on 1 November 1998, the Commission was abolished and most of its functions transferred to the Court. As a result of this Protocol, individual applicants can now submit cases directly to the Court.[4]

The Court deals with complaints by states and individuals concerning the protection of human rights by the 47 states parties to the Convention. Upon receipt of an application, the Court determines its admissibility and, if admissible, attempts to secure a friendly settlement of the dispute on the basis of respect for the human rights set out in the Convention and Protocols thereto.[5] If no settlement is reached, a Chamber of the Court hears the case and issues a binding judgment, which in exceptional cases may be referred for additional review before an enlarged 'Grand Chamber'.

Between the start of the Court's operation in 1959 and the entry into force of the 11th Protocol in 1998, the ECtHR dealt with over 1,000 petitions, nearly all of which were initiated by private parties. About two-thirds of these cases were adjudicated on their merits, and in almost 500 instances a violation of the Convention was found.

---

[2] Statute of the Council of Europe, 5 May 1949, preamble, ETS 1.
[3] See eg F Benoît-Rohmer and H Klebes, *Council of Europe Law: Towards a Pan-European Legal Area* (2005) 31.
[4] ECHR, arts 33, 34.
[5] Ibid, arts 38, 39.

With the introduction in 1998 of the system permitting direct access of individuals to the Court, the number of applications has sharply increased, crossing the 200,000 mark in 2007. The vast majority of these applications were either declared inadmissible or are still pending (116,800 cases were pending in November 2009); still, the Court has rendered some 10,000 judgments during the last decade.[6]

Upon the entry of force of the 14th Protocol (which was concluded in 2004),[7] some important procedural innovations will take place—including changes in the terms of judicial service, composition of benches, grounds for dismissal of cases, and the participation of the EU in the Convention. Given Russia's current refusal to ratify the Protocol, however, the 14th Protocol's future appears to be uncertain (considering that protocols must be ratified by all member states). In order to break the deadlock, the Committee of Ministers adopted in 2009 Protocol 14 *bis*—an instrument designed to introduce on an interim basis some of the reforms provided for in the 14th Protocol (relating to bench composition and powers of admissibility committee) for those member states interested, pending the entry into force of the latter.[8] Protocol 14 *bis* entered into force on 1 October 2009.

Institutional Aspects

Governing texts

Procedural law

11.3 The principal text governing the operation of the ECtHR is the ECHR, as amended by the 11th Protocol.[9] The Convention establishes the Court and determines its composition, jurisdiction, and the general contours of its procedure. More specific rules of procedure are enumerated in the Rules of Court, adopted in November 1998 (and amended since, on a number of occasions),[10] though the Court may derogate from these rules where appropriate after consultation with the

---

[6] For statistical reports on the judicial activities of the Court, see <http://www.echr.coe.int/ECHR/EN/Header/Reports+and+Statistics/Statistics/Statistical+information+by+year>.

[7] Protocol No 14 to the Convention for the Protection of Human Rights and Fundamental Freedoms, amending the Control System of the Convention, 13 May 2004, ETS 194 (2004).

[8] Protocol No 14 *bis* to the Convention for the Protection of Human Rights and Fundamental Freedoms, 27 May 2009, ETS 204 (2009).

[9] The operation of the Court would be subject to additional important modifications after the entry into force of the 14th Protocol (some changes have already been introduced with respect of proceedings involving member states that ratified Protocol 14 *bis*).

[10] Rules of Court, 4 November 1998 ('Rules of Court'), available at <http://www.echr.coe.int> (Basic Texts).

parties.[11] In addition, the President of the Court may issue Practice Directions, pursuant to Rule 32 of the Rules of Court, which primarily relate to document submissions and hearings. (Four Practice Directions have been issued to date.)[12]

One may also mention the Agreement on Treatment to be accorded by States to Persons participating in proceedings before the Court, an agreement to which 35 member states have acceded.[13] This agreement is designed to guarantee certain immunities to the relevant persons, and to facilitate their access to the Court.

Substantive law

The substantive law to be applied by the ECtHR consists of the rights and freedoms listed in Section I of the ECHR, and Protocols 1,[14] 4,[15] 6,[16] 7,[17] 12,[18] and 13.[19]   **11.4**

Organization

Composition and judges

The Court is composed of judges, equal in number to the number of states parties to the Convention.[20] At present there are 47 judges.[21] Judges must be persons of high moral character who possess qualifications required for appointment to a high judicial domestic office, or are considered to be juris-consults of recognized competence.[22] Each state party is entitled to nominate three candidates for service on the Court (who may or may not be its nationals), and the Parliamentary Assembly of the Council of Europe further elects one judge in respect of a given   **11.5**

---

[11] Ibid, r 31.

[12] The existing Practice Directions are available at <http://www.echr.coe.int> (Basic Texts).

[13] European Agreement relating to Persons Participating in Proceedings of the European Court of Human Rights, 5 March 1996, ETS 161 (1996).

[14] Protocol to the Convention for the Protection of Human Rights and Fundamental Freedoms, 20 March 1952, ETS 9 (1952).

[15] Protocol No 4 to the Convention for the Protection of Human Rights and Fundamental Freedoms, 16 September 1963, ETS 46 (1963).

[16] Protocol No 6 to the Convention for the Protection of Human Rights and Fundamental Freedoms, 28 April 1983, ETS 114 (1983).

[17] Protocol No 7 to the Convention for the Protection of Human Rights and Fundamental Freedoms, 22 November 1984, ETS 155 (1984).

[18] Protocol No 12 to the Convention for the Protection of Human Rights and Fundamental Freedoms, 4 November 2000, ETS 177 (2000).

[19] Protocol No 13 to the Convention for the Protection of Human Rights and Fundamental Freedoms, 3 May 2002, ETS 187 (2002).

[20] ECHR, art 20.

[21] For the full current composition of the Court, see <http://www.echr.coe.int> (The Court/ Judges of the Court).

[22] ECHR, art 21(1).

country.[23] Despite their nomination by states (normally their state of national-ity) the judges serve on the bench in an individual capacity.[24]

The term of office is a renewable six-year period and retirement age is 70.[25] Protocol 14 would change this state of affairs and enable judges to serve a single nine-year term only.[26] This reform in the term of service would arguably strengthen the judicial independence of serving judges.[27]

The Court is headed by a President and two Vice-Presidents elected for three-year terms.[28] The quorum for plenary sessions of the Court is two-thirds of the judges.[29]

11.6   Disqualification of judges   Judges may not participate in cases in which they have a personal interest, in which they were previously involved as representa-tives of one of the parties or other interested persons (or as member of a dispute settlement or investigation body), with regards to which they have expressed prejudicial opinions, or where there exists other reasons to doubt their inde-pendence or impartiality.[30] A judge who becomes aware of a reason that war-rants his or her withdrawal from the case should notify the President of the relevant Chamber accordingly. In the event of doubt as to the propriety of the judge's participation in the proceedings, the matter will be decided by the rele-vant Chamber (or Committee).[31]

Judges must refrain from engaging in any activity which is incompatible with their independence, impartiality, or the demands of their office. Judges are to report to the President any additional activities in which they engage, and the latter may request the judge concerned to forgo that activity, or to bring the mat-ter to the attention of the plenary Court.[32] Any judge may bring to the plenary

---

[23] Ibid, art 22(1). In order to improve the gender balance on the Court, the Parliamentary Assembly decided in 2005 not to consider single-sex lists of candidates (unless the sex in ques-tion is under-represented on the Court). Parliamentary Assembly, Resolution 1426 (2005) on Candidates for the European Court of Human Rights. However, the Court opined that the Resolution violates the rights of the states parties under the Convention. *Advisory Opinion on Certain Legal Questions concerning the Lists of Candidates submitted with a view to the Election of Judges to the European Court of Human Rights*, delivered by the ECtHR on 12 February 2008.
[24] ECHR, art 21(2).
[25] Ibid, art 23(1), (6). Retired judges will continue to deal with cases on which they sat prior to their retirement. Ibid, art 23(7).
[26] Protocol 14, art 2 (amending ECHR, art 23).
[27] Council of Europe, Protocol No 14 to the Convention for the Protection of Human Rights and Fundamental Freedoms, amending the Control System of the Convention: Explanatory Report, at para 50, <http://conventions.coe.int/Treaty/EN/Reports/Html/194.htm>.
[28] ECHR, art 26(a); Rules of Court, r 8. The current President of the Court is Jean-Paul Costa (France).
[29] Rules of Court, r 20(2).
[30] Ibid, r 28(2).
[31] Ibid, r 28(4).
[32] ECHR, art 21(3); Rules of Court, r 4. This rule applies, *mutatis mutandis*, with regard to ad hoc judges or retired judges that continue to sit on some cases. Rules of Court, r 28(2)(c).

Court a motion against another judge who has allegedly ceased to fulfil the conditions for service on the bench. A majority of two-thirds is required to dismiss a judge under these circumstances.[33]

In 2008, the Court adopted a new Resolution on Judicial Ethics, which codifies and develops existing standards of judicial independence and impartiality, addressing *inter alia* issues such as maintenance of the secrecy of deliberations, judicial freedom of expression, and honours and decorations.[34]

Plenary/chambers   The Court hears cases in committees of three judges **11.7** (reviewing the admissibility of applications), in chambers composed of seven judges and two substitute judges (the nine judges form a 'Section'), or in the Grand Chamber which comprises 17 judges and three substitute judges.[35] The plenary Court determines the composition of the Grand Chamber, the four or more Sections from which the seven-judge chambers are formed for each case (with the other judges of the Section sitting as substitutes), and the Presidency of these Sections (referred to in the ECHR as Chamber Presidents).[36] The Sections are composed with due regard to the need for geographical and gender balance, and should be representative of the different legal systems of the states parties.[37] All chambers will include the judges elected by the state party involved in the case.[38] If no such judge is available, the state concerned may appoint an ad hoc judge meeting the qualifications for appointment to the Court to sit in the specific case.[39] The various Sections establish Committees from within their members for one-year terms to review the admissibility of applications.[40]

The Grand Chamber is to include ex officio the President and Vice-Presidents of the Court and the Presidents of the different Sections. When the Grand Chamber is dealing with a case on referral, after it was already reviewed by a Chamber (see para 11.8 below), judges who sat on the first-in-time Chamber

---

[33] ECHR, art 24; Rules of Court, r 7.

[34] European Court of Human Rights, Resolution on Judicial Ethics, 23 June 2008, <http://www.echr.coe.int/NR/rdonlyres/1F0376F2-01FE-4971-9C54-EBC7D0DD2B77/0/Resolution_on_Judicial_Ethics.pdf>.

[35] ECHR, art 27(1); Rules of Court, r 24(1).

[36] ECHR, art 26(b),(c); Rules of Court, rr 8, 24–26. The Rules provide that Vice-Presidents of Sections are also to be elected and will replace the Presidents of the Sections if they cannot preside over a case (eg in a case involving the President's state of nationality or the state that nominated him or her to the Court) or prevented from sitting on the Grand Chamber: Rules of Court, rr 12–13, 24(5)(a). When appointing Presidents and Vice-Presidents, the Court will strive to reach balanced representation of the two sexes. Ibid, r 14.

[37] Rules of Court, r 25(2).

[38] ECHR, art 27(2); Rules of Court, rr 24(2)(b), 26(1)(a).

[39] ECHR, art 27(2); Rules of Court, r 29. If several states parties involved in the case have a common interest, the President of the Court will invite them to appoint an ad hoc judge in common. Rules of Court, r 30.

[40] ECHR art 27(1); Rules of Court, r 27.

are not eligible to sit on the Grand Chamber (with the exception of Section presidents and judges elected in respect of the states concerned).[41]

Cases will normally be heard before a seven-judge Chamber. However, when a case raises a serious question affecting the interpretation of the Convention or Protocols, or a question which might result in a judgment which is inconsistent with previous judgments of the Court, the Chamber may relinquish its jurisdiction in favour of the Grand Chamber. This is possible only if none of the parties to the case submits a reasoned objection within one month of being notified of the intent to relinquish jurisdiction.[42]

Following the entry into force of Protocol 14 (and for the states that ratified Protocol 14 *bis*, following the entry into force for them of that Protocol), admissibility decisions could be issued by single judges (who may not be a judge elected with regard to the respondent state). The Committee of Ministers may reduce, after the entry into force of Protocol 14, the number of judges in chambers from seven to five, for a fixed period of time.[43]

Judgment review

11.8   The Grand Chamber can hear cases on referral at the request of any party to a case decided by a seven-judge Chamber. A request for referral to the Grand Chamber of a case already decided by a Chamber will, however, be granted only in exceptional cases, such as where a panel of five Grand Chamber judges accepted that the case raises a serious question affecting the interpretation of the Convention or Protocols, or a serious issue of general importance.[44] In *K and T v Finland,* the Court held that reference of cases to the Grand Chamber leads to the setting aside of the original Chamber judgment and its replacement by the new Grand Chamber judgment. Hence, it is impossible to refer mere parts of a case which has already been decided to the Grand Chamber,[45] and following referral, the Grand Chamber retains all of the powers possessed by the Chamber which originally reviewed the case.[46]

Scientific and technical experts

11.9   The parties to a case before the Court may ask to introduce the testimony of expert witnesses. The ECtHR may also summon experts on its own initiative,

---

[41] ECHR, art 27(3).

[42] Ibid, art 30; Rules of Court, r 72.

[43] Protocol 14, art 6.

[44] ECHR, art 43; Rules of Court, r 73. The decision of the panel is final and binding on the Grand Chamber. *Pisano v Italy,* Judgment of 24 February 2002 at para 26.

[45] *K and T v Finland,* 2001-VII ECHR at paras 140–141. See also *Göç v Turkey,* 2002-V ECHR at paras 35–37; *Perna v Italy,* 2003-V ECHR, at paras 23–24; *Azinas v Cyprus,* 2004-III ECHR at para 32; *Cumpănă v Romania,* Judgment of 17 December 2004, at para 66; *Sisojeva v Latvia,* Judgment of 15 January 2007, at para 61.

[46] *Pisano, supra* note 44, at para 28.

or following a request by a third party.[47] In addition, the Court may approach any person or institution and request it to provide to the Court information, an opinion, or a report on a specific issue.[48]

The Court can decide to pass on its powers of pre-trial inquiry to a delegation of judges. In this event, the Chamber hearing the case will set up a delegation comprising one or more of its judges to conduct investigations related to the case at hand; the Chamber may also appoint experts to assist the delegation.[49]

During the presentation of any expert testimony the judges participating in the hearing may question the experts (the parties may also do so subject to the control of the President of the Chamber, or the head of the delegation).[50] In the event that a party objects to the invitation of a specific expert witness to appear before the Court, the matter will be decided by the President of the Chamber, or the head of the delegation.[51]

Registry

The administration of the Court is facilitated by its Registry, which is headed **11.10** by the Registrar.[52] The Registrar is elected by the plenary Court for a renewable five-year term,[53] and is assisted by two Deputy Registrars,[54] as well as Section Registrars and Deputy Registrars appointed for each Section of the Court.[55] The Registrar is responsible for the work of the Registry and for the Court's archives, communications with the Court, and dissemination of information concerning the Court.[56] The staff of the Registry is to be designated by the Secretary-General of the Council of Europe with the agreement of the Court's President or Registrar.[57]

Jurisdiction of and access to the Court

Ratione personae

Any state party to the Convention may bring to the Court a case against any other **11.11** state party, which is alleged to have breached the provisions of the Convention

---

[47] As of 2003, matters relating to expert testimony and reports are regulated by an Annex to the Rules Concerning Investigations. Rule A1 of the Annex governs the powers of the Chamber to summon experts or to authorize a delegation of judges to exercise such powers on its behalf.
[48] Annex Concerning Investigations, r A1(2).
[49] Ibid, r A1(3).
[50] Ibid, r A7(1)–(2).
[51] Ibid, r A7(5).
[52] ECHR, art 25. The current Registrar is Erik Fribergh (Sweden).
[53] Ibid, art 26(e); Rules of Court, r 15(1), (2).
[54] Rules of Court, r 16.
[55] Ibid, r 18.
[56] Ibid, r 17.
[57] Ibid, r 18(3).

or the Protocols.[58] Individuals, NGOs, and groups of individuals who claim to have been victims of a human rights violation[59] may also bring a case against the state party which has committed the alleged violation.[60]

Ratione materiae

11.12 In both inter-state cases and individual applications, the Court may only address complaints alleging a breach of the provisions of the Convention and Protocols by a state party.[61]

Ratione temporis

11.13 A case must be presented to the ECtHR within six months from the date on which domestic remedies were exhausted (the 'exhaustion' rule), and the final decision of the competent domestic authorities rendered (the 'six months' rule').[62] The 'exhaustion' rule is designed 'to afford the Contracting States the opportunity of preventing or putting right the violations alleged against them before those allegations are submitted to the Court',[63] and is premised on the assumption that there

---

[58] ECHR, art 33.

[59] The ECtHR and Commission have construed the term 'victim' narrowly as implying the person directly affected by the challenged act or omission. Hence, the Court has held that an individual cannot bring an *actio popularis* against a law *in abstracto*: *Klass v Germany* (1978) 2 EHRR 214. In addition, the Commission has declined on several occasions to regard organizations bringing complaints on behalf of their members, specific persons, or the general public, as victims under the Convention: eg *Church of X v UK* (1969) App No 3798/68, 12 Yearbook of the European Convention on Human Rights 306. At the same time, the Court held that victimhood can be established even if no prejudice was caused by the violation (although lack of prejudice would impact the remedies issued)—unless the state acknowledged the violation and redressed it. *Aydin v Turkey*, 2000-III ECHR; *Amur v France*, 1996-III ECHR 846 at para 36; *Lüdi v Switzerland* (1992) Eur Ct H R (Ser A) No 238, at para 34; *Brumărescu v Romania*, 1999-VII ECHR at para 50; *Siliadin v France*, Judgment of 27 July 2005, at para 62.

[60] ECHR, art 34. Under the old system, which existed until 1998, complaints presented to the Commission by individuals could be brought to the Court by the Commission, or an interested state party. Only individuals from states parties to Protocol 9 could forward the complaint to the Court after it had been dealt with by the Commission: Convention for the Protection of Human Rights and Fundamental Freedoms, 4 November 1950, art 48, ETS 5 (1950); ECHR, Protocol No 9 to the European Convention for the Protection of Human Rights and Fundamental Freedoms, 6 November 1990, ETS 140 (1994).

According to art 34, the states parties undertake 'not to hinder in any way the effective exercise' of the right of individual complaint. In its case law, the Court construed this as requiring states to allow individual applicants to communicate freely with the Court without being subjected to any form of pressure to withdraw or modify their complaint. *Akdivar v Turkey*, 1996-IV EHRR 1192, para 105; *Aksoy v Turkey*, 1996-VI EHRR 2260, at para 105; *Ilaşcu v Moldova*, Judgment of 8 July 2004, at para 480. See also *infra* para 11.18.

[61] ECHR, arts 33–34.

[62] Only violations committed by a state after the entry into force of the ECHR may be alleged with respect to it. *Blečic v Croatia*, Judgment of 8 March 2006.

[63] *Scordino v Italy (no 1)*, Judgment of 29 March 2006, para 141; *Selmouni v France*, 1999-V Eur Ct HR 149, at para 74.

are effective local remedies.[64] Still, the rule appertains to ordinary remedies and does not include a requirement to apply for exceptional remedies such as motion for retrial, or supervisory-review.[65] Remedies need to be exhausted only if they relate to the alleged breach and are, in the context of the case, available, accessible, sufficiently certain in theory and practice, offer reasonable prospects of success, and whose invocation can be reasonably expected from the applicant.[66] The burden of proving the existence of unexhausted local remedies lies with the respondent government;[67] if this burden is met, the applicant is required to demonstrate that the remedies were exhausted, that they were inadequate or ineffective, or that exceptional circumstances warrant dispensing with the requirement.[68]

The 'six months' rule is designed to promote values of legal finality and certainty, and to facilitate the establishment of the facts of the case.[69] The six-month period is calculated from the date on which a final local decision was issued,[70] or in the event of a lack of local remedies, from the date of the act or measure complained against.[71] In the event of a continuing violation, the period starts at the date of cessation of the violation.[72]

In all events, the Court held that the 'six months' and 'exhaustion' rules should be applied in a manner that is mindful of the facts of the specific case, is not excessively formalistic, and does not hinder an effective exercise of the right

---

[64] *Kudła v Poland*, 2000-XI Eur Ct HR 197, para 152; *Selmouni, supra* note 63, at para 74.

[65] *Berdzenishvili v Russia*, Decision of 29 January 2004.

[66] See eg *Kozacioğlu v Turkey*, Judgment of 19 February 2009, paras 39–40; *Borzhonov v Russia,* Judgment of 22 January 2009, para 33; *Nikolaishvili v Georgia*, Judgment of 13 January 2008, para 108; *Scordino, supra* note 63, at paras 141–142; *İlhan v Turkey*, 2000-VII Eur Ct HR 267, para 59. *Dalia v France*, 1998-I Eur Ct HR 76, para 38; *Aksoy, supra* note 60, at para 52; *Akdivar, supra* note 60, at para 68; *Vernillo v France*, 1991 Eur Ct HR (ser A), No 198, para 27. Hence, for example, there is no need to pursue remedies that are essentially the same as remedies that have been unsuccessfully sought. *Kozacioğlu, supra*, at paras 40, 43. *Riad v Belgium*, Judgment of 24 January 2008, para 84. In the same vein, there is no need to pursue civil remedies in deprivation of the right to life cases. See eg *Shakhgiriyeva v Russia*, Judgment of 8 January 2008, para 128.

[67] *Kozacioğlu, supra* note 66, at para 39; *V v UK*, 1999-IX Eur Ct HR 111, para 57; *Akdivar, supra* note 60, at para 68.

[68] *Akdivar, supra* note 60, at para 68. The example cited in the *Akdivar* case for such exceptional circumstances was total passivity of state authorities in the face of serious allegations. This appears to refer, however, to the effectiveness of the remedy in question.

[69] *Varnava v Turkey*, Judgment of 18 September 2009, para 156; *Koval v Ukraine*, Decision of 30 March 2004; *Kirk v UK*, Decision of 15 May 1996 (EHR Commission).

[70] The Commission has clarified that the six-month period is to be calculated from the time of service of the written final judgment to the applicant and not from the date of its oral reading. *Worm v Austria*, 83 D&R 17 (1995).

[71] *Koval, supra* note 69.

[72] Ibid. Still in *Varnava*, the Court distinguished between ongoing violations that arise out of one specific act (such as in the case of disappearances) and ongoing violations arising out of repetitive measures (such as in the case of constant intrusion of privacy by legislation). In the first category of cases, the Court will need to ensure that no long periods of delay should be tolerated without good reason. *Varnava, supra* note 69, at paras 157–159.

to apply to the Court.[73] Still, there are limits to this flexibility, and the applicant is expected to comply with domestic laws and procedures relating to the remedies sought.[74]

Advisory jurisdiction

11.14 The Court may render an advisory opinion on the interpretation of the Convention and Protocols, at the request of the Committee of Ministers.[75] Opinions can only deal with procedural questions and may not deal with matters concerning the scope of the substantive rights and freedoms enumerated in the Convention and Protocols, or any other matter which may be raised in ordinary proceedings before the Court.[76] Indeed, in 2004, the Court refused to grant an advisory opinion on the question of whether member states in the Convention could join other regional human rights mechanisms offering less robust human rights protections, citing concerns that the same question may be raised in the admissibility stage of the Court's ordinary proceedings.[77]

A request for an advisory opinion is to be filed with the Registry and should contain *inter alia* the question on which the opinion of the Court is sought; and all relevant documents.[78] The states parties are then invited, within time limits fixed by the President, to submit their comments on the matter to the Court.[79] The Registry communicates all submissions to the Committee of Ministers and to the states parties.[80] The President may invite the parties who have submitted written comments to present oral arguments before the Grand Chamber, which will render the opinion.[81] Opinions must be reasoned and can include, where relevant, separate or dissenting opinions.[82]

---

[73] *Nikolaishvili, supra* note 66, at para 109; *Aksoy, supra* note 60, at para 53. *Cardot v France*, 1991 Eur Ct HR (ser A), No 200, para 34. For example, the applicant cannot be expected to file two successive applications to the Court, if domestic appeal is available for one of his heads of claims but unavailable for the other. In such a case, the second head of claim is admissible notwithstanding the passage of more than six months from the date of the final decision. *Fernandez-Molina v Spain*, Decision of 8 October 2002 (extracts).

[74] *Cardot, supra* note 73, at para 34.

[75] ECHR, art 47(1). The power to issue advisory opinions was granted to the Court in Protocol No 2 to the Convention for the Protection of Human Rights and Fundamental Freedoms, 6 May 1963, ETS 44 (1963).

[76] ECHR, art 47(2).

[77] Decision on the Competence of the Court to Give an Advisory Opinion, 2 June 2004 (ECtHR). The case revolved around the compatibility of the participation of Russia and other former Soviet Union republics in both the ECHR and the Convention on Human Rights and Fundamental Freedoms of the Commonwealth of Independent States.

[78] Rules of Court, r 83.

[79] Ibid, rr 84, 85(1).

[80] Ibid, r 85(2).

[81] Ibid, r 86.

[82] ECHR, art 49; Rules of Court, r 88.

So far, the Court has been requested to issue advisory opinions only twice. It accepted one request and rejected the other.

Procedural Aspects

Languages

The official languages of the Court are English and French.[83] However, the ini- **11.15** tial correspondence of applicants to the Court may be undertaken in any of the official languages of the states parties.[84] In addition, the President of the Chamber may authorize the parties to use one of official languages of the states parties other than English or French. Responsibility for interpretation or translation of the pleadings of private applicants then normally rests on the Registry; and responsibility for the cost of interpreting or translating the pleadings of the state party rest with that party.[85] Witnesses, experts, and other persons appearing before the Court may use their own language if they do not possess sufficient knowledge of the official languages. In that event, the Registrar will arrange for interpretation or translation.[86]

Instituting proceedings

All cases before the Court are initiated by way of a written application.[87] In inter- **11.16** state cases, the application must include the following details: name of state party against which the application is made; statement of facts; statement of the alleged violations of the Convention and relevant arguments; statement on compliance with admissibility requirements (exhaustion of domestic remedies and the six months rule); object of the application and indication of any claims for just satisfaction to the injured party; name and address of applicant's agent; and copies of relevant documents (in particular, decisions relating to the object of the application).[88]

An application filed by a natural or legal person should contain the following information: name, date of birth, nationality, sex, occupation, and address of applicant; name, occupation, and address of the representative; name of state party against which the application is made; succinct statement of facts; succinct statement of the alleged violations of the Convention and relevant arguments;

---

[83] Rules of Court, r 34(1).
[84] Ibid, r 34(2).
[85] Ibid, r 34(3), (4). In exceptional cases, the President may require the private party to assume the interpretation and translation costs.
[86] Ibid, r 34(6).
[87] Ibid, r 45(1).
[88] Ibid, r 46.

succinct statement of compliance with conditions of admissibility (including information on whether other international investigations or settlement procedures have been previously invoked); object of the application and indication of claims for just satisfaction to the applicant; and copies of relevant documents (in particular, decisions relating to the object of the application).[89]

Financial assistance

11.17 The President of the Chamber may grant free legal aid to an applicant pursuant to a request by the applicant, or on the President's own motion.[90] The President must be satisfied, however, that the proper conduct of a case before the Court justifies legal aid and that the applicant has insufficient means to meet the costs entailed by the proceedings.[91] The latter determination will be based on a financial statement on the means available to the applicant to be submitted by him or her, and upon which the respondent state may be invited to comment.[92]

Once a decision to grant legal aid has been adopted, the Registrar will fix a rate of legal fees in accordance with a pre-existing legal aid scale, and determine the level of other expenses to be paid.[93] The grant will also cover, where necessary, representation before the Grand Chamber.[94] The President may revoke or modify a grant of legal aid in the event of a change in the circumstances underlying the previous decision.[95]

Interim measures

11.18 The Chamber, or its President, may indicate interim measures to be adopted by the parties. It may do so at the request of a party, any other concerned person, or acting *proprio motu*.[96] The adoption of interim measures must be justified by the existence of 'an imminent risk of irreparable damage'[97] and the consequent need to ensure effective exercise of the right of individual application to the Court, as well as the effective examination of the application by the latter.[98]

---

[89] Ibid, r 47. Application forms are available on the Court's website at <http://www.echr.coe.int/ECHR/EN/Header/Applicants/Apply+to+the+Court/Application+pack>.

[90] Rules of Court, r 91.

[91] Ibid, r 92.

[92] Ibid, r 93.

[93] Ibid, rr 94, 95.

[94] Ibid, r 91(2).

[95] Ibid, r 96.

[96] Ibid, r 39(1).

[97] *Mamatkulov v Turkey*, 2005-I Eur Ct HR 293, para 104. Interim measures have been mostly issued in extradition and deportation cases involving allegations of violations of the right to life and the prohibition against torture.

[98] Ibid, at para 128. Still, the fact that the Court was able to effectively review the application does not necessarily mean that the obligation to comply with interim measures was met. *Shamayev v Georgia*, 2005-III Eur Ct HR 153, para 478; *Olaechea Cahuas v Spain*, Judgment of 10 August 2006, para 81; *Shtukaturov v Russia*, Judgment of 27 March 2008, para 147.

In the past, the Court has construed the indication of interim measures by the Commission as lacking formally binding power.[99] However, in *Mamatkulov* (2003) the Court embraced a more robust approach in relation to Court-issued interim measures, and held that parties 'must comply with such measures and refrain from any act or omission that will undermine the authority and effectiveness of the final judgment'.[100] Furthermore, it was held in a subsequent case that the obligation to comply with interim measures should be treated as a matter of urgency.[101]

The Chamber will notify the Committee of Ministers of the interim measures it has indicated and may request information from the parties on their implementation.[102] In all urgent cases, the Registrar, acting with authorization of the President, will inform the state party concerned as soon as possible that an application which aims to secure an object requiring urgent protection has been filed.[103]

Proceedings

Initial examination by a judge rapporteur

Before reviewing the merits of an application, the Court must ascertain the **11.19** admissibility of the case. The initial examination of the application is undertaken by a judge rapporteur, appointed by the President of the Section to which the case was assigned (in individual applications) or by the Chamber (in inter-state cases).[104] In cases brought before the Grand Chamber, the judge rapporteur is to be appointed by its President.[105]

If the judge rapporteur considers the individual application to be inadmissible, he or she may decide (subject to the directions of the President of the Section) not to refer the case to a Chamber, but rather to a three-judge Committee.[106] In inter-state cases, the judge rapporteur receives the written observations of the parties to the case and then submits a report to the relevant Chamber on the admissibility of the case.[107] In cases submitted by individuals, the judge rapporteur may request the parties to offer additional information or evidence within fixed time limits before submitting the report on admissibility.

---

[99] *Cruz Varas v Sweden* (1991) 14 EHRR 1.
[100] *Mamatkulov v Turkey*, Judgment of 6 February 2003, para 110. The decision was reaffirmed by the Grand Chamber in 2005.
[101] *Paladi v Moldova*, Judgment of 10 March 2009, para 98.
[102] Rules of Court, r 39(2)–(3).
[103] Ibid, r 40.
[104] Ibid, rr 48(1), 49(2). Where the application appears on its face to be inadmissible, the Registry may forward it directly to a Committee of judges (see *infra* para 11.20).
[105] Ibid, r 50. In inter-state cases the President of the Grand Chamber may appoint more than one judge rapporteur.
[106] Ibid, r 49(3)(b).
[107] Ibid, rr 48, 49(3).

Proceedings on admissibility

11.20 In inter-state cases the decision on admissibility is to be taken by the Chamber designated by the President of the Section to which the case was assigned.[108] The President of the Section will also invite the respondent party to submit to the Registrar written observations on the question of admissibility, which are to be communicated to the applicant for a reply in writing.[109] The Chamber may request additional written observations from the parties within time limits fixed by the President of the Chamber after consulting with the parties.[110] The Chamber will hold oral hearings if one or more of the parties so request, or on its own motion.[111]

In individual applications referred to a Committee, the latter may declare the application inadmissible only by a unanimous vote, and only after considering the judge rapporteur's report.[112] If the Committee is not unanimous that the case should be dismissed, it will refer the case to a Chamber to decide the question of admissibility.[113] The Chamber may strike the case out of the list of cases at once, or decide to give notice to the respondent state. In this event, it may invite the parties to submit written observations within time limits fixed by the President of the Chamber.[114] Where appropriate, the Chamber may invite the parties, at the parties request or on its own motion, to participate in oral hearings.[115]

A Chamber decision on admissibility must provide reasons and indicate the majority by which it was rendered.[116] Still, even in cases where a finding of admissibility has been reached, the Court may adopt a finding of inadmissibility at any subsequent stage of the proceedings.[117] Moreover, in exceptional cases, the Court may decide to join the decision on admissibility to the merits stage.[118]

The grounds for inadmissibility of an application to the Court (from any source) are the following:

(a) failure to exhaust domestic remedies in accordance with the rules of international law;[119]

---

[108] ECHR, art 29(2); Rules of Court, r 51(1).
[109] Rules of Court, r 51(3).
[110] Ibid, r 51(4), (6).
[111] Ibid, r 51(5).
[112] ECHR, art 28; Rules of Court, r 53(2).
[113] ECHR, art 29(1); Rules of Court, r 53(3).
[114] Rules of Court, r 54(1), (2).
[115] Ibid, r 54(3).
[116] Ibid, r 56(1).
[117] ECHR, art 35(4).
[118] Ibid, art 29(3); Rules of Court, r 54A(1).
[119] ECHR, art 35(1). See *supra* para 11.13.

(b) failure to submit the case within six months from the date on which the final decision of the competent domestic authorities was adopted (the 'six months' rule).[120]

In individual applications, the Court will also refuse to entertain cases for the following reasons:

(c) the application is anonymous;[121]
(d) the application is substantially the same as one which has already been examined by the Court, or submitted to another international investigation or settlement procedure, and contains no new relevant information;[122]
(e) the application is incompatible with the provisions of the Convention or Protocols, manifestly ill-founded, or an abuse of the right to make an application.[123]

In addition, the Court may, at any time, strike out an application if it reaches the conclusion that the applicant is no longer interested in pursuing the matter, the case has been resolved, or the Court is no longer justified to review the application provided that the requirement to respect human rights does not require a continuation of the review process.[124]

Upon the entry into force of Protocol 14 a number of changes relating to admissibility procedures will be effected. First, single judges will be authorized

---

[120] ECHR, art 35(1). See *supra* para 11.13.

[121] ECHR, art 35(2)(a) However, the Court has admitted at least on one occasion an anonymous complaint, which included verifiable facts which enabled the respondent parties to identify the individuals in question (without learning their true names). *Shamayev v Georgia and Russia*, Decision of 16 September 2003.

[122] ECHR, art 35(2)(b). Claims raising identical issues but brought by different applicants before more than one international forum would not be barred by this article. *Folgerø v Norway*, Decision of 14 February 2006.

[123] ECHR, art 35(3). Claims raising allegations not covered by the substantive or jurisdictional provisions of the Convention may be deemed 'incompatible with the provisions of the Convention'. See eg *Matveyev v Russia*, Decision of 14 December 2004; *X v Germany*, 23 D&R (1967) 51 (EHR Commission). General and unsubstantiated allegations would normally be deemed as manifestly ill-founded (see eg *Cazacu v Moldova*, Judgment of 23 October 2007, para 26), as are applications based on weak evidence or untenable legal propositions (see eg *Basnet v UK*, Judgment of 24 June 2008, paras 69–70; *Stici v Moldova*, Judgment of 23 October 2007, para 34; *Gliha v Slovenia*, Judgment of 6 September 2007, at para 1; *Makuc v Slovenia*, Judgment of 31 May 2007, paras 177–179; *Osoian v Moldova*, Judgment of 28 February 2006; *Çetinkaya v Turkey*, Judgment of 5 January 2006, para 2). Abuse of the right to application has been found in those very few cases where the application was knowingly based on untrue facts. See eg *Akdivar, supra* note 60, at paras 53–54; *Varbanov v Bulgaria*, 2000-X Eur Ct HR 225, para 36. In the same vein, the persistent use of insulting or provocative language may also be viewed as abuse of the right of application. *Chernitsyn v Russia*, Judgment of 6 April 2006, para 25; *Duringer v France*, 2003-II Eur Ct HR 341.

[124] ECHR, art 37(1). For example, in *Association SOS Attentats* it was held that a legal settlement between Libya and terror victims renders it unjustified to continue proceedings against the French government for granting Libya legal immunity for claims over the terror acts covered by the settlement. *Association SOS Attentats v France*, Decision of 4 October 2006.

to declare the inadmissibility of complaints (this procedure is already employed with regard to cases involving states parties to Protocol 14 *bis*).[125] Second, committees of three judges will be authorized, when acting unanimously, to dispose of the merits of admissible applications so long as the question at hand has already been 'the subject of well-established case-law' (this change too is already available in cases involving state parties to Protocol 14 *bis*).[126] This introduces within the context of the admissibility stage a summary adjudication procedure for repetitive cases. Third, a new inadmissibility ground has been added. Where the applicant 'has not suffered a significant disadvantage', the Court may dismiss the application unless such dismissal would be inconsistent with the need to secure respect for human rights or the case 'has not been duly considered by a domestic tribunal'.[127]

Written pleadings

11.21   After a case has been declared admissible, the President of the Chamber will fix time limits and the order for the filing of written pleadings on the merits and additional evidence (in inter-state cases, after consulting with the parties).[128] In inter-state applications the President may, with the agreement of the parties, order that written pleadings will be dispensed with.[129] Unless the President of the Chamber decides otherwise, claims for just satisfaction for injury are to be specifically set out in the written observations on the merits.[130] Such claims must enumerate the particulars of the damage, costs, and expenses, and include supporting documents.[131]

Oral pleadings

11.22   A hearing will take place if the Chamber decides it is necessary, or if one of the parties to the case so requests. In cases initiated by individual application, however, the Chamber may decide not to conduct hearings if the merits of the case have been addressed at hearings held at the admissibility stage, or in cases where the Chamber considers hearings to be unnecessary for examination of the

---

[125] Protocol 14, art 7; Protocol 14 *bis*, arts 2–3, 3.

[126] Protocol 14, art 8; Protocol 14 *bis*, art 4. If needed, the Committee members may invite the judge elected in respect of the respondent state to sit on the Committee instead of one of the Committee members. Such a need may arise if the discussion of the merits of the application could benefit from the presence of a judge familiar with the law and practice of the respondent state. Explanatory Report to Protocol 14, *supra* note 27, at para 71, <http://conventions.coe.int/Treaty/EN/Reports/Html/194.htm>.

[127] Protocol 14, art 12.

[128] Rules of Court, rr 58(1), 59.

[129] Ibid, r 58(1).

[130] Ibid, r 60.

[131] Ibid, r 60(2).

matter.[132] Once it is decided that oral hearings will be held, the President of the Chamber is to fix the relevant procedure.[133]

Oral hearings before the Court will be public unless, in exceptional circumstances, the Court decides otherwise.[134] The Court may decide to hold hearings in camera following a reasoned request of a party, any other concerned person, or on its own motion.[135] The circumstances which the ECtHR may consider when deciding to hold proceedings in camera must relate to the moral interest, public order, or national security in a democratic society, the interests of juveniles, the protection of private lives, or other interests of justice.[136]

Third party intervention

Upon notice to the respondent state that a case has been found admissible, the **11.23** Registrar will also notify accordingly the state of nationality of the applicant (if different from the respondent state).[137] The latter is entitled to intervene in the case, submit written comments, and participate in the oral proceedings.[138] Unless it has been decreed otherwise by the President of the Chamber, the state in question should exercise its right of intervention within 12 weeks from the date on which it was notified of the application (or, in Grand Chamber cases, from the date of notification of the referral of the case to the Grand Chamber).[139]

In addition, the President of the ECtHR or the Chamber may invite, in the interest of the proper administration of justice, states parties other than the applicant's state of nationality or any person concerned with the outcome of the case who is not the applicant to submit written comments to the Court and, in exceptional cases, to participate in the hearings.[140] NGOs and other interested natural or legal persons may utilize this procedure to submit information to the Court as *amicus curiae*, even before the application has been declared admissible.[141]

A third party seeking permission to intervene may submit to the Court a reasoned request indicating the nature of its interest in the case within 12 weeks from the date on which the respondent state was notified of the application (or, in exceptional cases, another period of time designated by the President of the

---

[132] Ibid, rr 58(2), 59(3).
[133] Ibid, rr 58(2), 59(4).
[134] ECHR, art 40(1); Rules of Court, r 63(1).
[135] Rules of Court, r 63(1), (3).
[136] Ibid, r 63(2).
[137] Ibid, r 44(1)(a).
[138] ECHR, art 36(1).
[139] Rules of Court, r 44(1)(b), 3(a).
[140] ECHR, art 36(2); Rules of Court, r 44(2)(a).
[141] See eg *Malone v UK* (1984) 7 EHRR 14. A summary of all significant cases submitted to the Court is published on the Court's website upon notice to the relevant governments.

Chamber).[142] In Grand Chamber cases, the 12-week period starts after notification of the decision to refer the case to the Grand Chamber.[143]

Permission to intervene may be granted subject to conditions and time limits set by the President of the Chamber.[144] As is the case with intervention by the applicant's state of nationality, the original parties to the case are entitled to respond to any comments submitted by the third party intervener.[145]

Multiple proceedings

11.24   The Rules of Court permit the submission of applications by more than one applicant party, or against more than one respondent party.[146] Furthermore, the Court may order either at the request of the parties, or on its own motion, to join the consideration of two or more applications, or to join hearings related to these applications.[147]

Amicus curiae

11.25   As indicated above (para 11.23), the Court may permit any person concerned with the outcome of the case (including NGOs) to intervene as *amicus curiae* and submit written comments to the Court.[148]

Representation of parties

11.26   States parties are to be represented by agents, who may have the assistance of advocates or counsel.[149] Under article 34 of the ECHR, persons, non-governmental organizations, or groups of individuals may initially present applications either by themselves or through a representative. Such a representative for an applicant shall be an advocate authorized to practise in any of the states parties to the ECHR, and resident in the territory of any of them, or any other person approved by the President of the Chamber.[150] Unless the President of the Chamber decides otherwise, an applicant must be represented at any hearing decided on by the Chamber, or for the purpose of proceedings following a decision to notify the

---

[142] Rules of Court, r 44(2)(b).
[143] Ibid, r 44(3)(a).
[144] Ibid, r 44(4).
[145] Ibid, r 44(5).
[146] See eg ibid, r 30(1) (appointment of common ad hoc judge to more than one applicant or respondent state party). See also ibid, rr 46, 47(l)(c).
[147] Ibid, r 42.
[148] ECHR, art 36(2); Rules of Court, r 44(2). See also M Frigessi di Rattalma, 'NGOs before the European Court of Human Rights: Beyond *Amicus Curiae* Participation' in T Treves et al (eds), *Civil Society, International Courts and Compliance Bodies* (2005) 57; N Vajic, 'Some Concluding Remarks on NGOs and the ECHR', ibid at 97–102.
[149] Rules of Court, r 35.
[150] Ibid, r 36 (1), (4)(a).

respondent state of the application.[151] The President of the Chamber may, however, give leave for the applicant to present his or her own case.[152] In exceptional instances, where the President considers that the circumstances or the conduct of the advocate or other representative so warrants, the President of the Chamber may direct that a representative of an applicant be replaced.[153] Such a direction might be made at any stage during the proceedings.

Decision

The decisions of the ECtHR are issued in the form of legally binding judgments **11.27** or decisions.[154] Final judgments are to contain, *inter alia*, an account of the procedure; the facts of the case; a summary of the parties' submissions; reasons for the judgment in point of law; operative provisions; and a decision on costs (if one has been adopted).[155] If necessary, the judgment will include a statement as to which text is authentic.[156] The judgment may be read at a public hearing. In all events, it is notified in writing to the parties and made available to the general public on-line.[157] Any judge on the bench may append his or her separate, concurring, or dissenting opinion to the judgment.[158]

Where just satisfaction is properly requested and raised in the proceedings, the Court may include in the judgment a ruling on that matter.[159] Alternatively, the Court may reserve its decision on remedies and order that further proceedings be conducted, preferably before the same Chamber.[160] The Court may also encourage the parties to the judgment to negotiate a settlement on the issue of just satisfaction and the equitability of such settlement will be reviewed by the Court.[161]

Just satisfaction will only be awarded where the domestic law of the state party fails to afford full satisfaction for the injury suffered. It may encompass both pecuniary and non-pecuniary damages. With regard to pecuniary harm, the applicant must show a clear causal connection between the violation of rights and the harm.[162] Still, the Court may make detractions from the sums due to

---

[151] Ibid, r 36(2).
[152] Ibid, r 36(3).
[153] Ibid, r 36(4)(b).
[154] ECHR, art 45(1).
[155] Rules of Court, r 74(1).
[156] Ibid, r 74(1)(l).
[157] ECHR, art 44(3); Rules of Court, rr 76(2), 77(2), (3), 78.
[158] ECHR, art 45(2); Rules of Court, r 74(2).
[159] ECHR, art 41.
[160] Rules of Court, r 75(1), (2).
[161] Ibid, r 75(3), (4). According to ECHR, art 37 (1) *in fine,* the ECtHR must ensure that any settlement is consistent with respect for human rights.
[162] *Z v UK,* 2001-V 2001-V Eur Ct HR 1, para 119; *Çakıcı v Turkey,* 1999-IV Eur Ct HR 583, para 127; *Barberà v Spain,* Eur Ct HR (Ser A), No 285-C (1994), para 16. See also Practice Direction on Just Satisfaction Claims, issued on 28 March 2007, para 7.

the applicant in certain cases (such as where the applicant contributed to the unlawful situation by his or her own fault, or where the general public interest would be harmed).[163] Where a precise calculation of damages is impossible, the Court will exercise its discretion in awarding equitable levels of satisfaction.[164] Non-pecuniary harm, designed to compensate for non-material harm (such as pain and suffering) is also assessed on an equitable basis in light of the standards developed by existing case law.[165] In any event, the Court may consider the level of damages awarded in national Courts, but is not bound by such levels.[166]

Interpretation and revision of judgment

11.28 A party to a case decided by the ECtHR may request interpretation of the judgment within one year of its delivery.[167] The request must state the exact points in the operative provisions of the judgment which require interpretation. It is to be filed with the Registrar and presented before the original Chamber (or, if impossible, before the available judges of that Chamber with other judges selected by the President of the Court by a draw of lots).[168] The Chamber may reject the motion on the grounds that there is no reason warranting its consideration, or it may invite the other parties to the case to submit written comments within fixed time limits.[169] If necessary, the Chamber may hold oral hearings. The decision on interpretation will be rendered in the form of a new judgment.[170]

If a clerical error, error in calculation, or another obvious mistake has been found in the judgment, the Court on its own motion, or at the request of a party, may rectify the error. Such a request must be submitted within one month from the delivery of judgment.[171]

If a fact which might have had a decisive influence on the outcome of the case is discovered after the judgment has been rendered, any party may request the Court to revise the judgment.[172] The request must be made within six

---

[163] Practice Direction, *supra* note 162, at para 2.

[164] *Smith and Grady v UK* (Just Satisfaction), 2000-IX Eur Ct HR 193, paras 18–19; *The Sunday Times v UK (no 1)* (Article 50), Eur Ct HR (Ser A), No 38 (1980), para 15.

[165] Practice Direction, *supra* note 162, at paras 14–15.

[166] *Z v UK*, *supra* note 162, at para 120. Practice Direction, *supra* note 162, at para 3.

[167] Rules of Court, r 79(1). The Court has held that the authority to interpret judgment is inherent. *Ringheisen v Austria*, Eur Ct HR (Ser A), No 13 (1973), para 13.

[168] Rules of Court, r 79(2), (3).

[169] For example, the Court will decline a request for interpretation of a legal term already interpreted by the Court in previous cases (eg *Giacomon v Italy*, Decision of 6 October 1998), a request which seeks to interpret a clear point (eg *Allenet de Ribemont v France*, 1996-III Eur Ct HR 903, para 23), or that seeks in effect to modify the judgment (eg *Hentrich v France*, 1997-IV Eur Ct HR 1285, para 16).

[170] Rules of Court, r 79(4).

[171] Ibid, r 81.

[172] The new evidence must be, however, of sufficient weight to support the applicant's version of events. *Pardo v France*, 1997-III Eur Ct HR 735, para 15. It should also be relevant to the decisive reasons that supported the Court's judgment. *Gustafsson v Sweden*, 1998-V Eur Ct HR 2084, para 29.

months from discovery of the new fact, and will be reviewed only if that fact was unknown to the Court and the requesting party at the time when the judgment was delivered, and could not have reasonably been discovered then.[173] The request for revision is to be filed with the Registrar and will be referred to the original Chamber if possible.[174] The Chamber may reject the request at once, or invite comments from the other parties and hold hearings where necessary. The final decision on the motion is to be issued in the form of a new judgment.[175] In practice, however, the Court has subjected requests for revision to strict scrutiny, and expressed great reluctance to reopen final judgments.[176]

Request for a rehearing

A party to a case that has been decided by a seven-judge Chamber may request, **11.29** in exceptional circumstances, that the case be referred to the Grand Chamber. The request must demonstrate that the judgment raises a serious question affecting the interpretation of the Convention or Protocols, or a serious issue of general importance which merits consideration by the Grand Chamber.[177]

The request must be made in writing and filed with the Registry within three months from the date of delivery of the judgment. It is then to be referred to a panel of five Grand Chamber judges that will decide the application on the basis of the existing case file.[178] Reasons need not be given for refusal of such requests, and the Grand Chamber has no authority to review the panel's decision.[179] If the panel accepts the request, the Grand Chamber will hear the case in accordance with the ordinary procedure of the Court, and will render a new judgment that fully replaces the Chamber judgment.[180]

Costs

The operational costs of the Court are covered by the Council of Europe.[181] **11.30** Each party to a case is responsible for costs associated with the summoning of

---

[173] Rules of Court, r 80(1). Applicants who were manifestly on notice during the proceedings of the existence of certain facts cannot rely upon them in subsequent revision proceedings. *McGinley v UK*, 2000-I Eur Ct HR 321, para 36.

[174] Rules of Court, r 80(2), (3). Here, too, the President will select by lot judges to complete the composition of the original Chamber, if necessary. Note that rule 102 provides for a special transitional procedure to govern request for revision pertaining to judgments issued before the entry into force of Protocol 11. In such cases, a new Chamber will be formed by the President of the Section so authorized by the President of the Court.

[175] Ibid, r 80(4).

[176] See eg *McGinley, supra* note 173, at para 30.

[177] ECHR, art 43(1); Rules of Court, r 73(1).

[178] ECHR, art 43(2); Rules of Court, r 73(2).

[179] *Pisano, supra* note 44, paras 26–27.

[180] ECHR arts 43(3), 44(1); Rules of Court, rr 71, 73(3). For more details, see *supra* para 11.8.

[181] ECHR, art 50.

witnesses and experts on his or her behalf, and with other measures for taking evidence adopted by the Court at his or her request. Nonetheless, the Court may decide to otherwise allocate these costs (ie to order the other party, a third party, or the Council of Europe to bear them).[182] With regard to legal costs and other expenses, the Court may award them to the applicant if a request for their reimbursement is included within the claim for just satisfaction.[183]

Enforcement of judgments

11.31   Final judgments of the Court are binding upon the states parties.[184] All judgments of the Grand Chamber are final. Judgments of ordinary Chambers are final if: the parties waive the right to request referral to the Grand Chamber; a Grand Chamber panel has rejected the request for reference; or no request for reference to the Grand Chamber was filed within three months from the date of delivery of the judgment.

The states parties must execute the judgment subject to supervision by the Committee of Ministers of the Council of Europe.[185] According to statistics published by the Council of Europe in reference to 2007, deadlines for just satisfaction payments were not met in only 7 per cent of cases; still, in more than 60 instances, payments were delayed for more than five years.[186] (The respective figures for 2008 are 5 per cent and 79.)[187] The level of state compliance with general measures required by the Court, however (legislative changes for example), appears to be lower and slower.[188]

Evaluation

The European Court of Human Rights is in many ways a success story: it has been able to generate a large number of important decisions which have dramatically advanced the protection of human rights in Europe,[189] to attract good levels of compliance,[190] and to contribute thereby to European political

---

[182]   Rules of Court, r A5(6).

[183]   Practice Direction, *supra* note 162 , paras 16–21.

[184]   ECHR, art 46(1).

[185]   Ibid, art 46(2).

[186]   Council of Europe—Committee of Ministers, *Supervision of the Execution of Judgments of the European Court of Human Rights: 1st Annual Report—2007* (2008) 219, 233.

[187]   Council of Europe—Committee of Ministers, *Supervision of the Execution of Judgments of the European Court of Human Rights: 2nd Annual Report—2008* (2009) 52, 65.

[188]   See eg MW Janis et al, *European Human Rights Law: Texts and Materials* (3rd edn, 2008) 105–106.

[189]   See eg ibid at 114.

[190]   Council of Europe—Committee of Ministers, *Supervision of the Execution of Judgments of the European Court of Human Rights: 1st Annual Report—2007* (2008) 10; L R Helfer and A M Slaughter, 'Toward a Theory of Effective Supranational Jurisprudence' (1997) 107 *Yale LJ* 273, 296.

integration.[191] As indications of its success, one may note the sharp increase in the number of states subject to the Court's jurisdiction over the last 50 years, the move from optional to compulsory jurisdiction (consolidated in 1998 with the entry into force of Protocol 11), attempts by other regional organizations to emulate the ECtHR's structure, and the inclination of international and domestic courts to rely heavily on its jurisprudence.[192]

Moreover, the Court is responsible for groundbreaking developments relating to the status of individual applicants, which have had significant impact on other international courts and tribunals. The ECtHR serves as a model of a supra-national court, which allows natural and legal persons a broad right of access. Since individuals often serve effectively as 'private attorney-generals',[193] the level and quality of law application and law enforcement through the Court is unprecedented in its scope.

Still, the Court increasingly finds itself a victim of its own success. The sharp rise in the number of applications referred to the Court (in 1997—the last full year in which the old pre-Protocol 11 system operated—less than 5,000 cases were submitted to the Commission; in 2008 some 50,000 cases were submitted to the Court) has extended the Court's resources beyond their maximum capacity. As a result, the backlog of cases has already crossed the 100,000 mark, and this situation continues to deteriorate. Even if Protocol 14—the comprehensive reform Protocol that reduces the number of judges per case, expedites the disposition of repetitive claims, and introduces new grounds for inadmissibility— enters into force any time soon,[194] it is questionable whether it in itself offers sufficient solutions for the Court's capacity problems. Moreover, the removal of violations entailing insignificant disadvantages from the Court's docket (provided that local courts had reviewed the application in question) may transform the nature of the Court into a kind of constitutional court, thus limiting its substantive reach and comprehensive accessibility.[195]

Finally, it should be noted that with the eastwards expansion of the Council of Europe and with it the Court's jurisdiction, the profile of typical cases has changed from cases involving cutting-edge social problems (such as treatment

---

[191] See eg G Nolte, 'European and US Constitutionalism: Comparing Essential Elements' in G Nolte (ed), *European and US Constitutionalism* (2005) 3, 5.

[192] See eg J G Merrills, *The Development of International Law by the European Court for Human Rights* (2nd edn, 1993) 20.

[193] See eg E A Young, 'Institutional Settlement in a Globalizing Judicial System' (2005) 54 *Duke LJ* 1143, 1153.

[194] Protocol 14. Russia is the only contracting state that has not yet ratified the Protocol. Its entry into force requires ratification by all contracting states.

[195] S Greer, *The European Convention on Human Rights: Achievements, Problems and Prospects* (2007) 165–167.

of homosexuals and transgenders,[196] abortion issues,[197] proselytizing,[198] and immigrants' rights[199]) to cases revealing violation of the most basic human rights (involving torture,[200] disappearances,[201] lack of due process,[202] etc). Such changes present a significant challenge to the Court. It remains to be seen whether the Court's record of effectiveness and accumulated legitimacy can be maintained in these new political circumstances.[203]

REFERENCE

SOURCES OF CASE LAW

The judgments of the ECtHR are published by the Court's Registry in *Publications of the European Court of Human Rights, Judgments and Decisions.*

Decisions of the former Commission were reported in a series titled *Decisions and Reports of the European Commission on Human Rights.* Recent decisions of the Court can be found on the Court's website.

Judgments of the Court can also be found in *European Human Rights Reports* (EHRR) (European Law Centre Ltd, 1979–) and the *Yearbook of the European Convention on Human Rights*/European Commission and European Court of Human Rights (Martinus Nijhoff, 1960–) (selected decisions only).

All judgments and decisions are also available on-line at <http://www.echr.coe.int/ECHR/EN/Header/Case-Law/HUDOC/HUDOC+database/>.

SELECT BIBLIOGRAPHY

D J Harris, M O'Boyle, and C Warbrick, *Law of the European Convention on Human Rights* (2nd edn, 2009).
E L Abdelgawad, *The Execution of Judgments of the European Court of Human Rights* (2nd edn, 2008).
M W Janis et al, *European Human Rights Law: Texts and Materials* (3rd edn, 2008).
S Greer, *The European Convention on Human Rights: Achievements, Problems and Prospects* (2007).
F G Jacobs and Robin C A White, *The European Convention on Human Rights* (4th edn, 2006).

---

[196] See eg *Norris v Ireland*, Eur Ct HR (Ser A), No 142 (1988); *Rees v UK*, Eur Ct HR (Ser A), No 106 (1986).

[197] See eg *Open Door v Ireland*, Eur Ct HR (Ser A), No 246-A (1992).

[198] See eg *Kokkinakis v Greece*, Eur Ct HR (Ser A), No 260-A (1993).

[199] See eg *Ahmut v Netherlands*, 1996-VI Eur Ct HR 2017; *Abdulaziz v UK*, Eur Ct HR (Ser A), No 94 (1985).

[200] See eg *Aydin, supra* 59; *Jabari v Turkey*, 2000-VIII Eur Ct HR149 (2000).

[201] See eg *Osmanoglu v Turkey*, Judgment of 24 January 2008; *Bazorkina v Russia*, Judgment of 27 July 2006.

[202] See eg *Shanelnik v Ukraine*, Judgment of 19 February 2009.

[203] See M W Janis, 'Russia and the "Legality" of Strasbourg Law' (1997) 8 *EJIL* 3.

A H Robertson and J G Merrills, *Human Rights in Europe: A Study of the European Convention on Human Rights* (4th edn, 2001).

P van Dijk and G H J van Hoof, *Theory and Practice of the European Convention on Human Rights* (3rd edn, 1998).

L Clements, *European Human Rights: Taking a Case under the Convention* (1996).

T Zwart, *The Admissibility of Human Rights Petitions: The Case Law of the European Commission of Human Rights and the Human Rights Committee* (1994).

R Beddard, *Human Rights and Europe* (3rd edn, 1993).

J E S Fawcett, *The Application of the European Convention on Human Rights* (2nd edn, 1987).

ANNEX I

List of states parties to the ECHR

(as of August 2009) [47 in total]

Albania, Andorra, Armenia, Austria, Azerbaijan, Belgium, Bosnia and Herzegovina, Bulgaria, Croatia, Cyprus, Czech Republic, Denmark, Estonia, Finland, France, Georgia, Germany, Greece, Hungary, Iceland, Ireland, Italy, Latvia, Liechtenstein, Lithuania, Luxembourg, the former Yugoslav Republic of Macedonia, Malta, Moldova, Monaco, Montenegro, Netherlands, Norway, Poland, Portugal, Romania, Russia, San Marino, Serbia, Slovak Republic, Slovenia, Spain, Sweden, Switzerland, Turkey, Ukraine, United Kingdom.

ANNEX II

The Collective Complaint System under the European Social Charter

General information

Name and seat of the body

The European Committee on Social Rights is an independent expert body established to monitor compliance with the 1961 European Social Charter and its subsequent revisions.[204] It can be contacted at:

Secretariat of the European Social Charter
Council of Europe
Directorate General of Human Rights and Legal Affairs
Directorate of Monitoring
F-67075 Strasbourg CEDEX France

---

[204] European Social Charter, 18 October 1961, 529 UNTS 89, ETS 35 ('Social Charter'). A revised version of the Social Charter and amending Protocols entered into force on 1 July 1999: European Social Charter (Revised), 3 May 1996, ETS 163 ('Revised Social Charter').

Tel: +33 (0) 38841-3258
Fax: +33 (0) 38841-3700
Email: Social.Charter@coe.int
Website: <http://www.coe.int/t/dghl/monitoring/socialcharter/default_en.asp>

Description

The European Social Charter was concluded in 1961 within the framework of the Council of Europe, and entered into force on 26 February 1965.[205] Under the Charter and its 1988 Additional Protocol, states parties undertake to direct their policy towards the attainment of conditions in which a detailed list of economic and social human rights (enumerated in Part I of the Charter), may be effectively realized. States parties must additionally consider some of these rights as legally binding upon them.[206] At present, there are 40 states parties to the Social Charter and the Revised Social Charter (13 of which are also parties to the 1988 Additional Protocol).

The Social Charter is supervised mainly through a system of regular state reporting. The examination of reports is carried out by the Committee of Independent Experts, which in November 1998 renamed itself the European Committee of Social Rights ('ECSR' or 'the Committee'). The Committee comprises 15 experts of the highest integrity and with recognized competence in international social questions. They are elected by the Council of Europe's Committee of Ministers from a list of nominees put forward by the states parties to the Charter.[207] Experts serve on the Committee for a renewable term of six years.[208] The Committee receives administrative services from a section of the Secretariat of the Council of Europe (the Directorate of Human Rights).

The states parties submit periodic reports on the implementation of the Social Charter to the ECSR, and the Committee communicates its conclusions on the degree of state compliance to the political organs of the Council of Europe (namely the Governmental Committee and the Committee of Ministers).[209] In 1995, a Protocol was concluded ('Collective Complaints Protocol'), granting the ECSR quasi-judicial responsibilities. The Complaints

---

[205] Ibid.

[206] Part I of the Social Charter lists broad rights and principles which need to be pursued as a matter of policy. Part II enumerates rights with greater detail, and the parties undertake to accept ten articles (or 45 numbered paragraphs) as binding upon them (including at least five basic rights): Social Charter, art 20(1). In addition, parties to the Additional Protocol to the Social Charter undertake to implement at least one more right: Additional Protocol to the European Social Charter, 5 May 1988, ETS 128. Under the Revised Social Charter, each state party is bound by six or more basic rights and a total of at least 16 articles (or 63 numbered paragraphs).

[207] Social Charter, art 25(1). The original number of experts on the Committee was seven. It was subsequently agreed to increase that number to nine: Protocol amending the European Social Charter, 10 October 1991, art 3, ETS 142. In 2001, the number was raised again by the Committee of Ministers to 15. COE Doc CM/Del/Dec(2001) 751 (2001) at 17. The current membership of the Committee of Experts is: President: Ms Polonca Končar (Slovakia); Vice-Presidents: Mr Andrzej Swiatkowski (Poland) and Mr Colm O'Cinneide (Ireland); General Rapporteur: Mr Jean-Michel Belorgey (France); Members: Ms Csilla Kollonay Lehoczky (Hungary), Mr Lauri Leppik (Estonia), Ms Monika Schlachter (Germany), Ms Birgitta Nyström (Sweden), Ms Lyudmila Harutyunyan (Armenia), Mr A Rüçhan Isik (Turkey), Mr Petros Stangos (Greece), Mr Alexandru Athanasiu (Romania), Mr Luis Jimena Quesada (Spain), and Ms Jarna Petman (Finland).

[208] Social Charter, art 25(2).

[209] Ibid, arts 21, 22, 27 (Revised Social Charter, art C).

Protocol provides for a system of collective complaints by certain domestic and international NGOs to the ECSR.[210] The Protocol entered into force on 1 July 1998 and 14 states are now bound by it.

Under the Collective Complaints Protocol the ECSR may receive complaints alleging unsatisfactory application of the Charter on the part of states parties to the Protocol.[211] The procedure is governed by the 1998 Protocol and by the Rules adopted by the Committee.[212] Complaints are to be made using one of the official languages of the Council of Europe (or in the case of domestic NGO complainants, any other language).[213] The Committee will receive written pleadings from the complainant, the state complained against, and third parties (for example, other states parties to the Collective Complaints Protocol, and international organizations of employers or trade unions with observer status before the Governmental Sub-Committee).[214] The ECSR may hold oral hearings on the case, either at its own initiative or at the request of one of the parties.[215]

At the end of the proceedings, the Committee is to prepare a report on the compliance of the state complained against with the applicable Charter (or Protocol) obligations.[216] The report is then communicated to the Committee of Ministers and the Parliamentary Assembly of the Council of Europe, and will be published within four months from its conclusion.[217] If the Committee finds that the Charter has not been applied in a satisfactory manner, the Committee of Ministers shall adopt a recommendation by a majority of two-thirds of those voting.[218] In that event, the state concerned is expected to inform the ECSR in its next periodic report on the measures it has taken to give effect to the recommendations of the Committee of Ministers.[219]

To date, 58 complaints have been submitted to the ECSR. As at the end of 2008, the ECSR has published 50 admissibility decisions, and 38 decisions on the merits of complaints submitted to it.

JURISDICTION

The ECSR may receive complaints alleging unsatisfactory application of the Social Charter or the 1988 Protocol, filed against states parties to these instruments and the Collective Complaints Protocol, by any of the following organizations: (i) international organizations of employers and trade unions;[220] (ii) international NGOs which have consultative status with the Council of Europe if included on a list drawn up by the Governmental Committee, and then only in respect of matters in which they have 'particular competence' (inclusion on

---

[210] Additional Protocol to the European Social Charter providing for a System of Collective Complaints, 9 November 1995, ETS 158 ('Complaints Protocol').

[211] Complaints Protocol, arts 1, 11.

[212] Rules of the European Committee of Social Rights (adopted on 24 March 2004), <http://www.coe.int/t/dghl/monitoring/socialcharter/ESCRrules/Rules_en.pdf> ('ECSR Rules').

[213] ECSR Rules, r 24.

[214] Complaints Protocol, arts 6, 7.

[215] Ibid, art 7(4); ECSR Rules, r 33.

[216] Complaints Protocol, art 8(1); ECSR Rules, r 35. According to the Rules, publication on the Council of Europe website shall be tantamount to transmittal to the Parliamentary Assembly.

[217] Complaint Protocol, art 8(2).

[218] Ibid, art 9(1).

[219] Ibid, art 10; ECSR Rules, r 36.

[220] Complaints Protocol, art 1(a).

the list is valid for four years, but can be renewed upon application);[221] (iii) 'representative' national organizations of employers and trade unions[222] (whether they are 'representative' or not is to be decided in the admissibility proceedings); and (iv) other types of 'representative' national NGOs only after a special optional declaration by the respective respondent government allowing such complaints, and again only in respect of matters in which those NGOs have 'particular competence'.[223]

Reference

Sources of jurisprudence

The conclusions of the ECSR are published on the Committee's website. The website also includes a Digest of the Case Law of the Committee (<http://www.coe.int/t/dghl/monitoring/socialcharter/Digest/DigestSept2008_en.pdf>).

Books

D Harris and J Darcy, *The European Social Charter* (2nd edn, 2003).
D Gomien, D Harris, and L Zwaak, *Law and Practice of the European Convention on Human Rights and the European Social Charter* (1996).

Articles

H Cullen, 'The Collective Complaints System of the European Social Charter: Interpretative Methods of the European Committee of Social Rights' (2009) 9 *Human Rights Law Review* 61.

A Nolan, 'Addressing Economic and Social Rights Violations by Non-state Actors through the Role of the State: A Comparison of Regional Approaches to the "Obligation to Protect"' (2009) 9 *Human Rights Law Review* 225.

D Marcus, 'The Normative Development of Socio-Economic Rights through Supranational Adjudication' (2006) 42 *Stanford Journal of International Law* 53.

R R Churchill and U Khaliq, 'The Collective Complaints System of the European Social Charter: An Effective Mechanism for Ensuring Compliance with Economic and Social Rights?' (2004) 15 *European Journal of International Law* 417.

C Mac Amhlaigh and M Nedelka, 'Forty Years of the European Social Charter: Celebration or Commiseration?' (2001) 1 *University College of Dublin Law Review* 67.

Y Shany, 'Stuck in a Moment in Time: The International Justiciability of Economic, Social and Cultural Rights' in D Barak-Erez and A Gross (eds), *Exploring Social Rights: Between Theory and Practice* (2007) 77.

---

[221] Ibid, art 1(b).
[222] Ibid, art 2(c).
[223] Ibid, art 2(1).

ANNEX III

States parties to the Social Charter 1961 and to the Revised Social Charter

(as of August 2009)

Albania, Andorra, Armenia, Austria,* Azerbaijan, Belgium, Bosnia and Herzegovina, Bulgaria, Croatia,* Cyprus, Czech Republic,* Denmark,* Estonia, Finland, France, FYROM,* Georgia, Germany,* Greece,* Hungary, Iceland,* Ireland, Italy, Latvia,* Lithuania, Luxembourg,* Malta, Moldova, Netherlands, Norway, Poland,* Portugal, Romania, Slovakia, Slovenia, Spain,* Sweden,* Turkey, Ukraine, United Kingdom.*

* States parties only to the 1961 Charter.

ANNEX IV

States parties to the Collective Complaint Protocol

(as of August 2009)

Azerbaijan, Bulgaria, Croatia, Cyprus, Finland,* France, Greece, Ireland, Italy, Netherlands, Norway, Portugal, Slovenia, Sweden.

* States that have accepted the competence of the ECSR to receive complaints from representative national NGOs other than employers and trade union organizations.

12

THE INTER-AMERICAN COURT OF HUMAN RIGHTS AND THE INTER-AMERICAN COMMISSION ON HUMAN RIGHTS

Introduction

Name and seat of the Court and Commission

12.1 The Inter-American Court of Human Rights ('IAHR Court' or 'the Court') is a judicial body which has been entrusted with both contentious and advisory jurisdiction. It possesses contentious jurisdiction over certain Organization of American States ('OAS') member states that have joined the 1969 American Convention on Human Rights ('American Convention' or 'IAHR Convention') and accepted the power of the Court to monitor their compliance with the IAHR Convention. Under its advisory jurisdiction, the Court may interpret those human rights treaties to which OAS member states are parties.

The Court is located in San José, Costa Rica, at the following address:

Inter-American Court of Human Rights
Apdo 6906-1000
San José
Costa Rica
Tel: (506) 234-0581 or 225-3333
Fax: (506) 234-0584
Email: corteidh@sol.racsa.co.cr
Website: <http://corteidh-oea.nu.or.cr/ci/>

The Court's work is supported by the Inter-American Commission on Human Rights ('IAHR Commission')—an OAS organ entrusted with the mandate to promote and protect the fundamental rights of persons under the jurisdiction of OAS member states. Amongst other functions it prepares and publishes reports on the situation of human rights in particular member states; special thematic reports; and reports on individual cases that it may decide to refer to the IAHR Court for adjudication. The Commission is located in Washington, DC, at:

CIDH-OEA
1889 F St, NW
Washington, DC 20006
USA
Tel: (202) 458-6002
Fax: (202) 458-3992
Website: <http://www.oas.org/>

General description

The IAHR Court is the principal judicial body entrusted with monitoring and **12.2** adjudicating the human rights practices of states parties to the 1969 American Convention,[1] which was concluded under the organizational framework of the OAS. The Convention entered into force in 1978 and the Court was officially inaugurated in 1979.

The Inter-American Commission on Human Rights operates alongside the Court. The Commission pre-dates the Court and has been active since 1959.

Once the Commission decides to open a case regarding an alleged violation of the 1948 American Declaration of the Rights and Duties of Man (adopted by all OAS members),[2] or the 1969 Convention, it determines whether it satisfies the admissibility requirements. If it does, it places itself at the disposal of the parties for the purpose of attempting to reach a friendly settlement. If no friendly solution is reached it issues a report on the merits, including its conclusions as to whether the Declaration and/or the Convention have been violated, and issues a number of recommendations, which it sends to the state in question. The state has three months to comply with the recommendations, during which either the Commission or the state may choose to refer the case to the Court. Such a referral may be made where the case involves an alleged violation

---

[1] American Convention on Human Rights, 22 November 1969, OASTS 36; OAS Off Rec OEA/Ser L/V/II 23, Doc 21, Rev 6 (1979); reprinted in 9 ILM 673 (1970) ('American HR Convention').

[2] American Declaration of the Rights and Duties of Man, OAS Res XXX, adopted by the Ninth International Conference of American states (1948), reprinted in Basic Documents Pertaining to Human Rights in the Inter-American System, OEA/Ser L.V/II.82 Doc 6 Rev 1 (1992) at 17 ('American HR Declaration').

of the Convention by a state party which has either permanently accepted the jurisdiction of the Court, or is willing to accept it ad hoc for the purpose of resolving the particular case.

As noted above, the Court has contentious and advisory jurisdiction. The Court possesses contentious jurisdiction over the 21 states parties to the American Convention that have declared their acceptance *ipso facto* of its compulsory jurisdiction, and over other states parties that may accept its jurisdiction for specific cases on an ad hoc basis.[3] In addition, any member state and the Commission can request the Court for an advisory opinion on any matter relating to human rights in the Americas.[4]

In contentious cases, the Court (which is not bound to accept the facts as found by the Commission) investigates and determines whether or not the defendant state has violated the human rights of the victim or victims. If the Court finds a violation, it may decide to award reparations. To date, the Court has issued 196 judgments and some 15 additional cases are currently pending. The Commission has opened more than 20,000 cases since 1965.

Institutional Aspects

Governing texts

Procedural law

12.3 The principal text governing the structure, role, and powers of the IAHR Court is Chapter VIII of the American Convention. The Convention establishes the Court, determines its composition and jurisdiction, and outlines its procedure. Other more specific rules regulating the operation of the Court can be found in the following instruments:

- Statute of the Inter-American Court on Human Rights ('the Statute');[5]
- Rules of Procedure of the Inter-American Court on Human Rights ('Rules of Procedure').[6]

The IAHR Commission has its own Statute and Rules of Procedure.[7]

---

[3] American HR Convention, art 62.

[4] Ibid, art 64.

[5] Statute of the Inter-American Court on Human Rights, OAS Res 448 (DC-O/79), OAS Official Records OEA/Ser P/IX.0.2/80, Vol 1, at 98 ('IAHR Court Statute').

[6] Rules of Procedure of the Inter-American Court on Human Rights, 2000 (as amended in 2009) ('IAHR Court Rules of Procedure'), available at <http://www.corteidh.or.cr/regal_ing.pdf>.

[7] Statute of the Inter-American Commission on Human Rights, OAS Res 447 (IX), OAS Official Records OEA/Ser P/IX.0.2/80, Vol 1 ('IAHR Commission Statute'), available at <http://www.cidh.org/Basicos/English/Basic17.Statute%20of%20the%20Commission.htm>; Rules of

Substantive law

The substantive law to be applied by the IAHR Court, when exercising its con- **12.4**
tentious jurisdiction, is to be found in Part I of the American Convention on
Human Rights, the San Salvador Protocol,[8] the Protocol to Abolish the Death
Penalty,[9] the Inter-American Convention to Prevent and Punish Torture,[10]
the Inter-American Convention on Forced Disappearance of Persons,[11] the
Inter-American Convention on the Prevention, Punishment and Eradication
of Violence Against Women,[12] and the Inter-American Convention on
the Elimination of All Forms of Discrimination Against Persons with
Disabilities.[13] When exercising its advisory competence, the Court may interpret any other human rights treaties that OAS member states are party to.[14]

The IAHR Commission may also review complaints involving the human
rights practices of OAS member states that are not parties to the American
Convention on Human Rights.[15] In cases brought against such states, the
Commission applies the American Declaration of the Rights and Duties of
Man, which is considered to be part of the definition of human rights included
in the OAS Charter and therefore binding on member states.[16]

Procedure of the Inter-American Commission on Human Rights ('IAHR Commission Rules
of Procedure'), available at <http://www.cidh.org/Basicos/English/Basic18.Rules%20of%20
Procedure%20of%20the%20Commission.htm>.

[8] Additional Protocol to the American Convention on Human Rights in the area of
Economic, Social and Cultural Rights, 7 November 1988, art 8(a), arts 13, 19(6), OAS Official
Records OAS/Ser L V/II 92, Doc 31 Rev 3 ('ESCR Protocol'). The Court has held that when
interpreting the American Convention it will emphasize the objective meaning of the text
and its individual-protecting objective. *Restrictions to the Death Penalty (Arts. 4(2) and 4(4)
American Convention on Human Rights)*, Advisory Opinion of 8 September 1983, I/A CHR
(Series A), No 3 at para 50; *The Effect of Reservations on the Entry into Force of the American
Convention on Human Rights (Arts. 74 and 75)*, Advisory Opinion of 24 September 1982, I/A
CHR (Series A), No 2 at para 29.
[9] Protocol to the American Convention on Human Rights to Abolish the Death Penalty, 8
June 1990, OAS TS No 73 (1990) ('Death Penalty Protocol').
[10] Inter-American Convention to Prevent and Punish Torture, 9 December 1985, OAS TS No
67 ('IA Torture Convention').
[11] Inter-American Convention on Forced Disappearance of Persons, 9 June 1994, 33 ILM
1529 (1994) ('IA Disappearances Convention').
[12] Inter-American Convention on the Prevention, Punishment and Eradication of
Violence Against Women, 9 June 1994, 33 ILM 1534 (1994) ('IA Violence against Women
Convention').
[13] Inter-American Convention on the Elimination of All Forms of Discrimination
Against Persons with Disabilities, 7 June 1999, OAS Doc AG/RES 1608 ('IA Disabilities
Convention').
[14] American HR Convention, art 64(1).
[15] IAHR Commission Statute, art 20.
[16] The Commission must give particular attention to arts 1–4, 18, 25, 26 of the American HR
Declaration: IAHR Commission Statute, art 20(a).

Organization

Composition

12.5 **IAHR Court** The IAHR Court comprises seven judges who are nationals of different OAS states (not necessarily states which are parties to the Convention).[17] They are elected by the states parties to the American Convention on Human Rights for a renewable six-year term.[18] Judges should be jurists of the highest moral authority, of recognized competence in the area of human rights, and must have the required qualifications for service in the highest judicial office of their state of nationality (or in the state that proposed them as candidates). In the event that a state party to a case does not have a judge of its nationality on the bench, it may appoint an ad hoc judge.[19]

The Court elects a President and Vice-President for a renewable two-year term.[20]

12.6 **IAHR Commission** The Commission comprises seven members of high moral character and recognized competence in the field of human rights.[21] They are elected by the member states of the OAS for a term of four years, which is renewable once.[22] No two commissioners can be of the same nationality.[23] The Commission elects a Chairman and two Vice-Chairmen for one-year terms (renewable once every four-year period).[24]

12.7 **Disqualification of judges** Judges cannot sit in a case pending before the Court if they (or their family members) have a direct interest in it, or if they had

---

[17] American HR Convention, art 52; IAHR Court Statute, art 4. The current composition of the Court is: President: Cecilia Medina Quiroga (Chile); Vice-President: Diego García Sayán (Peru); Judges: Sergio Garcia Ramirez (Mexico), Manuel E Ventura Robles (Costa Rica), Leonardo A Franco (Argentina), Margarette May Macaulay (Jamaica), and Rhadys Abreu Blondet (Dominican Republic).

[18] American HR Convention, arts 53, 54; IAHR Court Statute, arts 5(1), 7.

[19] American HR Convention, art 55; IAHR Court Statute, art 10; IAHR Court Rules of Procedure, art 19. Ad hoc judges have been appointed in numerous cases. In one case, the Court refused to allow a state to appoint an ad hoc judge because the appointment was made after the expiration of the period of time required in the Rules of Procedure. *Sawhoyamaxa Indigenous Community v Paraguay*, Judgment of 29 March 2006, I/A CHR (Series C) No 146, para 15. Judges ad hoc do not always share the nationality of the appointing state. See eg *Trujillo-Oroza v Bolivia*, Judgment of 26 January 2000, I/A CHR (Series C) No 64.

[20] IAHR Commission Statute, art 14; IAHR Commission Rules of Procedure, arts 6, 8.

[21] American HR Convention, art 34; IAHR Commission Statute, art 2. The current membership of the Commission is: Chair: Luz Patricia Mejía Guerrero (Venezuela); Vice-Chairs: Víctor E. Abramovich (Argentina) and Felipe González (Chile); Members: Paolo G Carozza (US), Sir Clare Kamau Roberts (Antigua and Barbuda), Paulo Sérgio Pinheiro (Brazil), and Florentín Meléndez (El Salvador).

[22] American HR Convention, arts 36, 37; IAHR Commission Statute, arts 3, 6.

[23] American HR Convention, art 37(2); IAHR Commission Statute, art 7.

[24] IAHR Commission Statute, art 14; IAHR Commission Rules of Procedure, arts 6, 8.

previously taken part in it whether as lawyers, members of a dispute settlement body, or in any other capacity.[25]

If the judge in question refuses to withdraw from the case after being advised to do so by the President, the Court may decide to disqualify him or her.[26] In the event that a judge has become unfit to serve (ie if he or she takes certain positions in a domestic executive branch or in an international organization, or is in a situation that might prevent him or her from discharging a judge's official functions, or that might affect his or her independence or impartiality or the dignity or prestige of the office), the Court can decide to remove the judge from a specific case, and may recommend to the General Assembly of the OAS to remove that judge from office.[27]

Similarly, members of the Commission who fail to fulfil the duties of their office or engage in functions which are incompatible with their service in the Commission may be removed from office by the General Assembly of the OAS, acting upon the recommendation of five other Commission members.[28]

Plenary/chambers   The IAHR Court sits in plenary (the quorum for delib-   **12.8**
eration consists of five judges).[29] All the judgments, advisory opinions, and 'the interlocutory decisions that put an end to a case or proceedings' should be adopted by the plenary Court.[30]

The Commission also adopts decisions in a plenary (quorum of four members), although it may conduct some preparatory parts of its work in working groups of not more than three members.[31]

Appellate structure

The inter-American human rights system does not have an appellate structure   **12.9**
and decisions of the Court are final and binding.[32] However, a case dealt with by the Commission may be brought to the Court for additional review by an unsatisfied state party.

Technical/scientific experts

The Court may hear, on its own motion, any evidence it considers helpful. This   **12.10**
includes obtaining the opinion of an expert witness either at the request of the

---

[25] IAHR Court Statute, art 19(1). Judges have recused themselves on a number of past occasions. See eg *Las Palmeras v Colombia*, Judgment of 4 February 2000, I/A CHR (Series C) No 67 at para 18.
[26] IAHR Court Statute, art 19(2), (3).
[27] American HR Convention, art 73; IAHR Court Statute, art 18.
[28] American HR Convention, art 73; IAHR Commission Statute, arts 8, 10; IAHR Commission Rules of Procedure, art 4.
[29] IAHR Court Statute, art 21(1); IAHR Court Rules of Procedure, art 14.
[30] *Restrictions to the Death Penalty, supra* note 8, at para 17.
[31] IAHR Commission Statute, art 17; IAHR Commission Rules of Procedure, arts 16, 18.
[32] American HR Convention, art 67.

parties or on the Court's own initative.[33] A party who believes that the expert appointed by the Court (or his or her family member) has a direct interest in the outcome of the case, or was previously involved in the dispute in any capacity, may ask for the expert to be disqualified within ten days from his or her appointment.[34] The Court will rule on the challenge.

Secretariat

12.11 The administrative needs of the Court are served by the Secretariat of the Court headed by a Secretary.[35] The Court elects the Secretary for a renewable five-year term,[36] and the rest of the staff of the Secretariat is appointed by the Secretary-General of the OAS, in consultation with the Secretary of the Court. The Secretary is responsible, *inter alia*, for: communicating the decisions of the Court; taking minutes at its meetings; dealing with the correspondence of the Court; directing the administration of the Court (in pursuance of the instructions of the President); preparing draft rules, programmes, and budget; and supervising the work of the Court staff.[37]

The IAHR Commission receives secretarial services from a special unit in the General Secretariat of OAS, headed by an Executive Secretary.[38] The Secretariat of the Commission is responsible, *inter alia* for: preparing draft reports and resolutions; distributing documents among the members of the Commission; receiving petitions; requesting information from governments; and assisting the Commission in the performance of its functions.[39]

Jurisdiction and admissibility

Ratione personae

12.12 **IAHR Commission** Any person, group of persons, or NGO (recognized under the laws of at least one member state of the OAS) may submit a petition

---

[33] IAHR Court Rules of Procedure, art 50. The Court has made extensive use of expert evidence in a number of cases. See eg *Saramaka People v Suriname*, Judgment of 28 November 2007, I/A CHR (Series C) No 172 (Court relied in its decision on seven expert opinions presented to it by the Commission, the alleged victims, and the state); *Neira Alegra v Peru*, Judgment of 19 September 1996, I/A CHR (Series C) No 29 at para 34; *El Amparo v Venezuela*, Judgment of 14 September 1996, I/A CHR (Series C) No 28 at paras 12, 28 (in both cases, the Court appointed actuarial experts to facilitate the calculation of reparations due to the victims); *Gangaram Panday v Suriname*, Judgment of 21 January 1994, I/A CHR (Series C), No 16 at paras 30, 55 (Court requested and received expert reports from the national forensic evidence institutions of Costa Rica and Venezuela); *Fairén-Garbi and Solís-Corrales v Honduras*, Judgment of 15 March 1989, I/A CHR (Series C) No 6 at paras 38, 156 (Court appointed a handwriting expert and relied on his report in its decision).
[34] American HR Convention, art 53.
[35] Ibid, art 59; IAHR Court Statute, art 14.
[36] IAHR Court Rules of Procedure, art 7.
[37] Ibid, art 10.
[38] American HR Convention, art 40; IAHR Commission Statute, art 21.
[39] IAHR Commission Rules of Procedure, arts 12, 13.

to the Commission alleging a violation of the American Convention by a state party.[40] Any state party may accept, by way of a declaration, the competence of the Commission to receive claims against it from another member state.[41] Such declarations (submitted under article 45(1) of the Convention) may be unrestricted in time, or for a limited period of time, or for one specific case. In any event, only states that have also made declarations under article 45(1) may bring communications to the Commission.[42] Persons, groups of persons, and NGOs may also present to the Commission communications against OAS member states not parties to the Convention, alleging violation of fundamental human rights.[43] Only complaints brought against states parties to the Convention can be subsequently forwarded to the Court.

IAHR Court   The IAHR Court has jurisdiction over claims against states   **12.13**
that have accepted its jurisdiction. Consent to the jurisdiction of the Court can be expressed through a general declaration of *ipso facto* acceptance of jurisdiction pursuant to article 62(1) of the Convention, through ad hoc declarations, or through a special agreement.[44] As mentioned above, 21 states parties to the Convention have made general declarations accepting the Court's jurisdiction.

Only states parties and the Commission may bring a case before the Court.[45] Where declarations of acceptance of jurisdiction under article 62(1) require reciprocity, only states that have also made a declaration under the same article may present an inter-state claim against the respondent state.

Petitioners and/or representatives of the victims participate alongside the Commission in the proceedings before the Court. In particular, they are allowed to submit briefs and present oral arguments on the merits.[46]

Ratione materiae

Both the IAHR Court and Commission are competent to address all ques-   **12.14**
tions concerning the alleged violation or the interpretation and application of the human rights enumerated in the American Convention, in addition to some relevant provisions found in the San Salvador Protocol, the Protocol to

---

[40] American HR Convention, art 44.
[41] Ibid, art 45.
[42] Ibid, art 45(2).
[43] IAHR Commission Statute, art 20.
[44] American HR Convention, art 62. Once compulsory jurisdiction is accepted it cannot be withdrawn (the state can release itself from the Court's jurisdiction only by denouncing the American Convention in its entirety). *Constitutional Court v Peru*, Judgment of 24 September 1999. I/A CHR (Series C) No 55 at paras 38–40; *Ivcher-Bronstein v Peru*, Judgment of 24 September 1999, I/A CHR (Series C) No 54 at para 50. Still declarations of acceptance can be limited by conditions pertaining to reciprocity, period of validity, and specific cases. American HR Convention, art 62(2).
[45] American HR Convention, art 61.
[46] IAHR Court Rules of Procedure, art 24.

Abolish the Death Penalty, the Inter-American Convention to Prevent and Punish Torture, the Inter-American Convention on Forced Disappearance of Persons, the Inter-American Convention on the Prevention, Punishment and Eradication of Violence Against Women, and the Inter-American Convention on the Elimination of All Forms of Discrimination Against Persons with Disabilities.[47] With regard to OAS member states who are not parties to the American Convention, the IAHR Commission may review the observation of fundamental human rights standards under general international law, with particular reference to the American Declaration of the Rights and Duties of Man.[48]

Admissibility[49]

12.15 **IAHR Commission** The Commission may admit cases under the Convention only if the following conditions are met:[50]

(a) the individual whose rights have been violated must have exhausted the remedies existing under the domestic laws of the state concerned, in accordance with international law (except in cases where the defendant state failed to observe due process in its domestic procedures; prevented the exhaustion of remedies; or if there has been unwarranted delay in providing a final judgment under domestic procedures);

(b) the petition must have been lodged within six months from the date on which the individual whose rights were violated was notified of the final judgment in his or her case;

(c) the petition or inter-state communication must not be pending before another international dispute settlement procedure;

(d) the alleged violation must be attributable or imputable to the state complained against.

---

[47] American HR Convention, arts 44, 45(1), 62(3); ESCR Protocol, art 19(6); Death Penalty Protocol, *supra* note 9; IA Torture Convention, *supra* note 10; IA Disappearances Convention, *supra* note 11; IA Violence against Women Convention, *supra* note 12 (article 12 of the Convention explicitly authorizes the IAHR Commission to investigate complaints of violation); IA Disabilities Convention, *supra* note 13.

[48] IAHR Commission Statute, art 20. See eg *Victims of the Tugboat '13 de Marzo' v Cuba*, Case 11.436, Inter-Am CHR 45, OEA/Ser L/V/II, Doc 95, Rev 7 (1996) (finding that Cuba violated arts 1, 8, 18 of the American Declaration). For a discussion of the authoritative status of the Declaration, see *Interpretation of the American Declaration of the Rights and Duties of Man within the Framework of Article 64 of the American Convention on Human Rights*, Advisory Opinion of 14 July 1989, I/A CHR (Series A) No 10 at paras 41–43.

[49] See also *infra* para 12.24.

[50] American HR Convention, art 46. It is also necessary that the alleged violation took place at a time when the Convention (or relevant Protocol) was in force with respect to the state concerned.

IAHR Court   The IAHR Court can receive cases relating to states that have   **12.16**
accepted its jurisdiction only after proceedings at the Commission have failed to
yield an appropriate result.[51]

Advisory jurisdiction

The IAHR Court may render non-binding advisory opinions at the request of   **12.17**
any OAS member state or authorized OAS organ, acting within the scope of its
competence.[52] The subject matter of such an opinion can encompass the interpretation of the American Convention and other human rights treaties applicable in the territory of the member states to the OAS.[53] The request for an
advisory opinion may be denied by the Court because *inter alia* 'the issues raised
deal mainly with international obligations assumed by a non-American State
or with the structure or operation of international organs or bodies outside the
inter-American system; or because granting the request might have the effect
of altering or weakening the system established by the Convention in a manner
detrimental to the individual human being'.[54]

The request for an advisory opinion should specify with precision the question on which the opinion of the Court is sought, in addition to the considerations giving rise to the request.[55] Requests submitted by OAS organs other than
the Commission must also specify the relationship between the question and
their sphere of competence. If the request pertains to a treaty other than the
American Convention, the request should also include the name of the treaty
and a list of parties thereto.[56] Where the compatibility of domestic legislation
with the Convention is at issue, the request should refer to the provisions of the
law to which the advisory opinion should relate, and a copy of the legislation
must be attached to the request.[57]

Upon initiation of advisory proceedings, the Secretary will send copies of
the request to all OAS member states, the Commission, the Secretary-General

---

[51] American HR Convention, art 61(2). See eg *Viviana Gallardo* et al, Decision of 13 November
1981, I/A CHR Ser A No G 10181 (involving rejection by the Court of an attempt by a state
accused of a human rights violation to bring a case on its own initiative directly to the Court).

[52] American HR Convention, art 64. The Court has stated that the goal of the advisory process is
'to assist the American States in fulfilling their international human rights obligations and to assist
the different organs of the inter-American system to carry out the functions assigned to them in this
field'. *'Other Treaties' subject to the advisory jurisdiction of the Court (Art. 64 American Convention on
Human Rights)*, Advisory Opinion of 24 September 1982, I/A CHR (Ser A) No 1 at para 25.

[53] The advisory jurisdiction of the Court also encompasses bilateral and multilateral treaties, treaties which are not primarily human rights instruments, and treaties whose membership
includes non-OAS parties. *'Other Treaties', supra* note 52, at para 52.

[54] Ibid, at para 52.

[55] IAHR Court Rules of Procedure, art 64.

[56] Ibid, art 65.

[57] Ibid, art 66. See eg *Proposed Amendments of the Naturalization Provisions of the Constitution
of Costa Rica*, Advisory Opinion of 19 January 1984, I/A CHR (Ser A) No 4.

of the OAS, and all relevant OAS organs. The President will fix time limits for the submission of written observations,[58] and the Court will decide whether to hold oral proceedings on the request. The advisory opinion will be delivered in a manner similar to the delivery of judgment.[59] Dissenting or separate opinions may be published in addition to the opinion of the majority.[60]

To date, 19 advisory opinions have been rendered by the Court.

Procedural Aspects

Languages

12.18   The official languages of the Court, Commission, and the OAS are Spanish, English, French, and Portuguese.[61] The Court and Commission may select any of the official languages to be its working language (or languages).[62] The usual working languages of the Court are English and Spanish. The Court may however replace the working language for any specific case with the language of one of the parties to the case (provided that it is also an official language). In cases where a person appearing before the Court is not fluent in the working language, the Court can authorize him or her to use another language and it will arrange for a translator and interpreter.[63]

Instituting proceedings

IAHR Commission

12.19   Petitions to the Commission are to be made in writing and are to include *inter alia*: an account of the act or situation which is denounced (specifying place and date of the alleged violation and, if possible, name of victims and any officials that might have appraised the act or situation); information on whether domestic remedies have been exhausted or if it has been impossible to exhaust them; and information on whether the complaint has been submitted to other international settlement proceedings.[64]

The Secretariat or the Commission may ask the petitioner to complete any information omitted from its petition.[65] If the Commission finds the petition prima-facie admissible it will require the government concerned to

---

[58] IAHR Court Rules of Procedure, art 67.
[59] Ibid, art 68.
[60] Ibid, art 69(3).
[61] IAHR Court Rules of Procedure, art 21(1); IAHR Commission Rules of Procedure, art 22(1).
[62] IAHR Court Rules of Procedure, art 21(2); IAHR Commission Rules of Procedure, art 22(1). The Court's decision is to be reviewed each year and the Commission's every two years.
[63] IAHR Court Rules of Procedure, art 21(4).
[64] IAHR Commission Rules of Procedure, art 28.
[65] Ibid, arts 26, 29.

provide information on the case within two months (which may be extended by the Commission by not more than one more month).[66] In urgent cases, the Commission will ask the government concerned to provide it with information in the promptest manner.[67]

IAHR Court

A case is brought before the IAHR Court by a written application prepared in all **12.20** of the working languages.[68] The application will contain *inter alia*: a statement of the facts; supporting evidence; particulars of witnesses and expert witnesses; and legal arguments.[69] Applications presented by the Commission shall also include a copy of the Commission's report.

After a preliminary review of the application, the President may instruct the applicant to correct any deficiencies within 20 days.[70] The Secretary will forward a notice of the application to the judges of the Court, the respondent state, the Commission (if it is not the applicant), and the alleged victim.[71] The victim or his or her representative will then have two months to submit a brief to the Court containing pleadings, motions, and evidence. The fact that an application has been filed will also be communicated to the states parties to the Convention and the Secretary-General of the OAS.[72] The respondent state will have two months from the date on which it was presented with the victim's brief (approximately four months from the date of the submission of the original application) in order to reply to the application and the brief.[73]

Financial assistance

There is no programme of financial assistance under the framework of the **12.21** American human rights system.

Precautionary and provisional measures

IAHR Commission

In urgent cases, when irreparable harm to persons is likely, the Commission **12.22** may request the concerned government to take provisional precautionary

---

[66] Ibid, art 30(2), (3).
[67] Ibid, art 30(4).
[68] IAHR Court Rules of Procedure, art 33. In the event that a party submits the application in only one of the working languages, it must provide translated copies in the other official languages within 30 days from the date of filing of the original application.
[69] Ibid, art 34.
[70] Ibid, art 35.
[71] Ibid, arts 36, 37.
[72] Ibid, art 36(3).
[73] Ibid, art 39.

measures.[74] The decision to request such measures is to be taken by the Commission as a whole or, when it is not in session, by the Chair (and in his or her absence, by one of the Vice-Chairs) after consulting with the other members of the Commission. The Commission has expressed the view that OAS member states are required to comply with the precautionary measures it prescribes.[75]

IAHR Court

12.23 The Court is authorized to order provisional measures in cases of extreme gravity and urgency, if such measures are necessary to avoid irreparable harm to persons.[76] The fact that the Commission has already issued precautionary measures in relation to the same issue creates a presumption in favour of the necessity for issuing provisional measures.[77]

The Court may order measures at the request of a party, at the request of the Commission (in matters not yet submitted to the Court), at the request of the alleged victim, or acting on its own initiative.[78] When considering the application for provisional measures, the Court may solicit expert opinions, reports, or other relevant data.[79]

The request for provisional measures is to be submitted by any means of communication to any judge or to the Secretariat, and transmitted to the President. The latter (after consulting with some or all of the judges) can call upon the government concerned to adopt the necessary temporary measures for ensuring the effectiveness of any order that the Court may issue at a later date pursuant to the request for provisional measures.[80]

In all events, provisional measure orders are legally binding.[81] States are to report to the Court on their compliance with such orders, and the Commission and the order's 'beneficiaries' may submit their observations to the Court on the

[74] IAHR Commission Rules of Procedure, art 25. See eg *Maya Indigenous Communities of the Toledo District v Belize*, IAHR Commission Report No 40/04 (2004), 13 IHRR 553 (2006) at para 8; *Dann v US*, IAHR Commission Report No 75/02 (2002); 10 IHRR 1143 (2003) paras 14–25 (describing a failure by the US to comply with prescribed precautionary measures).
[75] See eg *Detainees in Guantanamo Bay, Cuba*, Letter by the President of the IAHR Commission of 13 March 2002, available at <http://www1.umn.edu/humanrts/cases/guantanamo-2003.html>; *Garza v US*, IAHR Commission Report No 52/01 (2001) at para 117, available at <http://www.cidh.org/annualrep/2000eng/chapteriii/merits/USA12.243a.htm>.
[76] American HR Convention, art 63(2); IAHR Court Rules of Procedure, art 26(1). According to the Court's case law, provisional measures will be issued in exceptional circumstances only. See eg *Chunima v Guatemala*, Order of 1 August 1991, para 6(b), available at <http://www.corteidh.or.cr/docs/medidas/chunima_se_03_ing.pdf>.
[77] See *Digna Ochoa and Plácido et al v Mexico*, Order of 17 November 1999 at para 6, available at <http://www.corteidh.or.cr/docs/medidas/dignaochoa_se_01_ing.pdf>.
[78] American HR Convention, art 63(2); IAHR Court Rules of Procedure, art 26(1), (2), (3).
[79] IAHR Court Rules of Procedure, art 26(5), (8).
[80] Ibid, art 26(4), (6). See eg *Chunima v Guatemala*, Order of the President of 15 July 1991, available at <http://www.corteidh.or.cr/docs/medidas/chumina_se_01_ing.pdf>.
[81] See *Constitutional Court (Peru)*, Provisional Measures, Order of 14 August 2000, at para 14, available at <http://www.corteidh.or.cr/docs/medidas/tribunal_se_02_ing.pdf>.

states' reports.[82] Instances of non-compliance and any appropriate recommendations are reported by the Court to the General Assembly of the OAS.[83]

Provisional measure orders can be extended over time and/or amended to cover more subjects of protection, or to remove protection from subjects who no longer face a serious and urgent risk.[84]

Preliminary proceedings

IAHR Commission

Before reviewing the merits of a petition or inter-state communication, the Commission must first consider the admissibility of the complaint. The following questions are considered: **12.24**

(a) whether domestic remedies have been exhausted and, if not, whether there are grounds to exempt the petitioner from this requirement;[85]
(b) whether the deadline for presentation of a petition (six months after the conclusion of domestic proceedings) has elapsed;[86]
(c) whether the petition is also pending before another international settlement procedure to which the state complained against is subject, or constitutes a duplication of a petition pending or settled in the past by the Commission or another international organization;[87] and
(d) whether there are other grounds for inadmissibility.[88]

The Commission will normally issue and publish a preliminary decision on admissibility. In special cases it may issue a single report including findings on both admissibility and merits.[89]

IAHR Court

A party to the case may file a preliminary objection to the admissibility of the case or to the jurisdiction of the Court, and submit it with their answer to the application.[90] **12.25**

---

[82] IAHR Court Rules of Procedure, art 26(7).

[83] Ibid, art 26(10).

[84] See eg the many orders issued over 13 years in the *Colotenango. Colotenango (Guatemala)*, Order of 12 July 2007, available at <http://www.corteidh.or.cr/docs/medidas/colotenango_se_13_%20ing.pdf>; *Plan de Sánchez Massacre in favour of Members of the Community Studies and Psychosocial Action (ECAP) Team (Guatemala)*, Order of 26 November 2007, para 7, available at <http://www.corteidh.or.cr/docs/medidas/plandesanchez_se_06_%20ing.pdf>.

[85] IAHR Commission Rules of Procedure, art 31.

[86] Ibid, art 32. Where no prompt and effective domestic remedies are available, the Commission will verify whether the petition has been filed within reasonable time under the circumstances of the case.

[87] IAHR Commission Rules of Procedure, art 33.

[88] Ibid, art 34(b), (c). Other grounds for inadmissibility include: lack of factual basis which alleges a human rights violation, the complaint being manifestly groundless or out of order, and inadmissibility by reason of supervening evidence.

[89] IAHR Commission Rules of Procedure, art 37.

[90] IAHR Court Rules of Procedure, art 38(1).

The objection should include facts, legal arguments, and supporting evidence *inter alia*.[91] The other party may present a brief response to any objections to the Court's jurisdiction within 30 days.[92] The filing of preliminary objections does not suspend proceedings on the merits.[93] The Court may convene a hearing on the objections and decide upon them. It may also decide, for the sake of judicial economy, to join its decision on preliminary objections to the decision on the merits.[94]

As indicated above, a party to a case may request the disqualification of a judge. Such a request must be filed with the Court before the first hearing of the case, or at the first possible opportunity, if a relevant disqualifying factor becomes subsequently known.[95]

Written phase

IAHR Commission

12.26 After finding the petition admissible (or after adopting a decision to defer admissibility to the merits stage), the Commission will invite the petitioner to submit in writing, within two months, his or her additional observations on the merits of the case. The government complained against will be subsequently invited to respond and to submit within two further months its written observations.[96] Submission periods may be extended in appropriate cases by the Executive Secretariat by an additional month.[97]

IAHR Court

12.27 Within two months from receiving the application, the respondent must provide an answer, in writing, to the application.[98] The answer must address the same issues as the application and should be prepared in a similar format. At any time before the opening of the oral proceedings, the parties may request the President of the Court to allow them to present additional written pleadings. The President may permit such pleadings and fix time limits for their presentation.[99]

Oral arguments

IAHR Commission

12.28 The Commission may decide to conduct oral hearings on its own initiative or at the request of an interested party submitted at least 50 days before the beginning

---

[91] Ibid, art 38(2).
[92] Ibid, art 38(4).
[93] Ibid, art 38(3).
[94] Ibid, art 38(5), (6).
[95] Ibid, art 20.
[96] IAHR Commission Rules of Procedure, art 38(1).
[97] Ibid, art 38(2).
[98] IAHR Court Rules of Procedure, art 39.
[99] Ibid, art 40.

of the relevant session of the Commission.[100] At the hearing, the parties may present new documents, expert opinions, and evidence. The Commission may also decide to receive oral testimonies of witnesses or experts (whether at the request of the party or acting on its own initiative).[101] The hearings should be conducted in accordance with the 'equality of arms' principle[102] and be public in nature (unless exceptional circumstances prevail).[103]

IAHR Court

The President of the IAHR Court will call oral hearings if necessary, and pre-   **12.29**
scribe the order of the presentations.[104] The judges may question all persons appearing before the Court. In addition, the representatives of the parties, the Commission, and the alleged victim may question any person that the Court decides to hear, including the alleged victims, witnesses, or experts.[105] Such questioning is, however, subject to the control of the President of the Court (although the Court can overrule him or her on some issues). The hearings of the Court are public, unless the Court decides otherwise due to exceptional circumstances.[106]

In its case law, the Court has emphasized that the state complained against cannot rely on the failure of the complainant to present evidence that cannot be obtained without the state's cooperation.[107]

Third party intervention/multiple proceedings

Traditionally, procedures before the IAHR Court or Commission did not offer   **12.30**
the possibility of third party intervention. One may note, however, that the Commission is instructed to appear as a representative of the 'public interest' in all cases.[108] Moreover, a recent amendment to the Court's Rules of Procedure

---

[100] IAHR Commission Rules of Procedure, arts 38(5), 59, 62(1). The decision to convoke a hearing will be made by the President of the Commission at the proposal of the General Secretary.

[101] IAHR Commission Rules of Procedure, art 63(1).

[102] Ibid, art 64(2), (4), (5).

[103] Ibid, art 66.

[104] IAHR Court Rules of Procedure, arts 42, 43.

[105] Ibid, art 44.

[106] IAHR Court Statute, art 24(1). For example, in *Velásquez-Rodríguez* the Court heard in a closed session the testimony of members of the Honduran military. *Velásquez-Rodríguez v Honduras*, Judgment of 29 July 1988, I/A CHR (Series C) No 4 at para 33.

[107] See eg *Gangaram-Panday, supra* note 33, at para 49; *Godínez Cruz v Honduras*, 20 Judgment of January 1989, I/A CHR (Series C) No 5 at para 141; *Velásquez-Rodríguez, supra* note 106, at para 135.

[108] IACHR Court Statute, art 28; IAHR Court Rules of Procedure, art 34(3). See also *Viviana Gallardo, supra* note 51, explanation of vote by Judge Piza Escalante, at para 4 (the IAHR Commission has 'a sui generis role, purely procedural, as an auxiliary of the judiciary, like that of a "Ministerio Público" of the inter-American system for the protection of human rights').

allows victims to intervene in the proceedings and submit pleadings, motions, and evidence throughout the process.[109]

As regards multiple proceedings, there is no bar against bringing a complaint on behalf of more than one person and/or state to the Commission or to the Court (provided that jurisdictional conditions have been met). Furthermore, the Commission may combine and process in a single set of proceedings any petitions dealing with the same facts and persons,[110] and the Court may order the joinder of interrelated cases.[111]

Amicus curiae

12.31 The Court's Rules of Procedure now provide for the submission of *amicus* briefs by persons unrelated to the case who wish to present to the Court information relating to the relevant facts or legal considerations.[112] *Amicus curiae* briefs must be submitted before the passage of 15 days from the day of the public hearing of the case or, if no hearing takes place, before the passage of 15 days from the date on which the parties' final written submissions were requested. The parties will receive copies of the *amicus* briefs.

Representation of parties

12.32 States parties who come before the Court are to be represented by an agent, who may be assisted by any persons of his choice.[113] The Commission shall be represented by the delegates it has designated.[114] Victims may participate in the proceedings either in person or through their duly accredited representatives. In the event of a multiplicity of victims, they should agree on a single intervener to act on their behalf (if they do not reach agreement, the Court will decide on the matter for them).[115]

Decision

IAHR Commission

12.33 The Commission issues a report on the merits including its conclusions of fact and law, and determination on whether the Declaration, the Convention, or

---

[109] IAHR Court Rules of Procedure, art 24. In cases where there are multiple victims, a single intervener will be appointed to represent their interests. At least one of the judges has referred to the victim's representatives as the 'true complainant' in the case. *El Amparo, supra* note 33, dissenting opinion of Judge Cançado Trindade, at note 10.

[110] IAHR Commission Rules of Procedure, art 29(d).

[111] IAHR Court Rules of Procedure, art 29.

[112] Ibid, arts 2,(3), 41. In practice, the Court has long admitted *amicus curiae* briefs. See eg *Compulsory Membership in an Association Prescribed by Law for the Practice of Journalism*, Advisory Opinion of 13 November 1985, I/A CHR (Ser A) No 5.

[113] IAHR Court Rules of Procedure, art 22.

[114] Ibid, art 23.

[115] Ibid, art 24.

another instrument has been violated.[116] In cases involving a finding of violation, the Commission will first issue a preliminary confidential report with recommendations which the violating state should comply with, in addition to a designated time frame for compliance. Only after that period of time expires may the Commission adopt the report and publish it.[117] The Commission may follow up on any of the recommendations specified in its reports.[118]

In the case of states parties to the Convention, the decision on the merits—known as an 'Article 50 Report'—is transmitted to the state, which then has three months to implement the recommendations contained therein, and to inform the Commission thereof. In the case of states parties that have accepted or are willing to accept the jurisdiction of the Court ad hoc, the Commission may—during this period—refer the case for adjudication (after consulting with the petitioners).[119] If the case has not been referred to the Court, the Commission publishes a final decision—known as an 'Article 51 Report'—in its Annual Report to the General Assembly of the OAS.[120]

The Court has declared that states parties to the American Convention have an obligation to make every effort to apply the recommendations of a protection organ such as the Commission.[121]

IAHR Court

Unlike the Commission, the Court issues its final decisions in the form of judgments. The judgment will include *inter alia*: a description of the procedural history of the case, factual and legal findings, and a decision, if any, on costs.[122] The judgment is decided by a majority of the judges.[123] Judges may append dissenting or separate opinions to the judgment.[124] If a violation of the Convention was found, the Court will order the respondent state to take measures so that the injured party may be ensured the enjoyment of the rights or freedoms which were violated.[125] In appropriate cases, where the judgment did not address the question of reparations, the Court will set time limits and the format for proceedings aimed at securing a separate judgment on the question of reparations to

12.34

---

[116] American HR Convention, art 50(1); IAHR Commission Rules of Procedure, art 43.
[117] IAHR Commission Rules of Procedure, art 43(2).
[118] Ibid, art 46.
[119] Ibid, art 43(3).
[120] American HR Convention, art 51.
[121] *Loayza Tamayo v Peru*, Judgment of 17 September 1997, I/A CHR (Series C) No 33 at para 80. This decision reversed earlier decisions which did not recognize a legal obligation to implement Commission reports. See eg *Caballero Delgado and Santana v Columbia*, Judgment of 8 December 1995, I/A CHR (Series C) No 22 at para 67.
[122] IAHR Court Rules of Procedure, art 59(1).
[123] IAHR Court Statute, art 23(2).
[124] IAHR Court Rules of Procedure, art 59(2).
[125] American HR Convention, art 63(1).

the injured party.[126] If the parties have reached an agreement on reparations, the Court is to verify the fairness of the agreement.[127] If not, then a hearing on reparations and costs takes place, leading to a separate judgment on the matter.[128]

Interpretation and revision of judgments

12.35 In the event of disagreement over the meaning or scope of the judgment, any party to a case may request the Court to interpret it.[129] The request must be filed with the Secretariat within 90 days from the date of notification of the judgment and must state with precision the issues which require interpretation.[130] The Secretary will transmit the request to both the states parties to the case and the Commission, and will invite them to submit written comments within a time limit fixed by the President of the Court.[131] The Court (preferably of the same composition as that which rendered the original judgment)[132] will determine which procedure to follow with regard to the request, and will deliver interpretation of the request in the form of a judgment.[133]

The Convention and other relevant instruments do not address the possibility of a revision of the judgment. Still, in one case, the Court opined that review of final judgments would be possible in exceptional circumstances, where it is shown that important facts on which the judgment relied were false, or that the judgment has been procured by improper means.[134]

Appeal

12.36 There is no appeal from judgments of the IAHR Court. The judgments are final and binding.[135]

Costs

12.37 Proceedings before the Court and Commission are free of charge for the parties. Traditionally, the parties have assumed their own expenses, including the

---

[126] IAHR Court Rules of Procedure, art 60(1).

[127] Ibid, art 60(2).

[128] See generally V M Rodriguez Rescia, 'Reparations in the Inter-American System for the Protection of Human Rights', 5 *ILSA J Int'l & Comp L* (1999) 583, 590–591.

[129] American HR Convention, art 67. See *Velásquez-Rodríguez v Honduras*, Judgment of 17 August 1990, I/A CHR (Series C) No 9 at para 26 ('The interpretation of a judgment involves not only precisely defining the text of the operative parts of the judgment, but also specifying its scope, meaning and purpose based on the considerations of the judgment').

[130] American HR Convention art 67; IAHR Court Rules of Procedure, art 62(1).

[131] IAHR Court Rules of Procedure, art 62(2).

[132] Ibid, art 62(3). See also *Velásquez-Rodríguez, supra* note 129, at para 12.

[133] IAHR Court Rules of Procedure, art 62(5).

[134] *Genie-Lacayo v Nicaragua*, Order of 13 September 1997, I/A CHR (Series C) No 45 at para 12.

[135] American HR Convention, art 67.

cost of producing any evidence they request.[136] Still, the Court is authorized to award costs for the purpose of covering expenses incurred by the claimants and/ or victims before domestic courts and inter-American human rights organs.[137] Indeed, the Court has held that where violation of the Convention has been found, the victim should be compensated for all necessary and reasonable costs associated with invoking the IAHR machinery.[138] More recently, the Court has also awarded victims with costs for expenditures associated with the exhaustion of local remedies.[139]

Enforcement of judgments

States parties participating in a case before the IAHR Court must comply with its judgment.[140] In the event that the Court awards damages against a state party, this part of the judgment may be enforced against the state concerned by the same domestic procedures governing the execution of judgments against the state.[141]   **12.38**

Evaluation

Although modelled after the organs constituting the European human rights mechanism, the record of achievement of the IAHR Court and Commission is less impressive than that of their European counterparts. The number of cases brought before the Court is far smaller than the number of cases brought before the European Court, and the impact and prestige of the IAHR machinery falls short of that of the ECHR. The reasons for these differences are quite obvious. First, and foremost, the political climate in which the inter-American system has operated for a good part of its existence has been extremely difficult, confronting dictatorships, a culture of impunity, and a series of economic crises. Moreover, two of the region's 'heavy weights' and potential leaders in the field of human rights (namely, the US and Canada) have not, to this very day, joined the Convention. As a result, the ability of the Court and the Commission to push for the reforms required for better protection of human rights in its member states has, at times, been very limited.

---

[136]   IAHR Court Rules of Procedure, arts 48, 50(2).
[137]   Ibid, arts 56(2), 59(1)(h).
[138]   *Garrido and Baigorria v Argentina*, Judgment of 27 August 1998, I/A CHR (Ser C) No 39 at paras 79–80.
[139]   See *Saramaka People, supra* note 33, at para 204; *Miguel Castro-Castro Prison v Peru*, Judgment of 25 November 2006, I/A CHR (Series C) No 160 at para 455.
[140]   American HR Convention, art 68(1).
[141]   Ibid, art 68(2).

Second, the jurisdictional structure of the IAHR system has not kept up with developments in Europe. Although recent amendments to the IAHR Court have strengthened the procedural status of victims in judicial proceedings, the lack of direct access to the Court by individual complainants,[142] and the cumbersome two-level process involving the Commission and Court, limits the effectiveness of the system. This is so notwithstanding some of the system's exceptional features which have no parallel in Europe (such as a broad right of standing for individuals before the Commission,[143] a broad authority for the Court to issue advisory opinions,[144] and jurisdiction of the Commission over states not parties to the Convention).

Still, a number of positive signs of progress can be noted. The democratization of Latin America in recent decades and the increasing willingness of the Commission to refer cases to the Court have improved the system's performance. Recent procedural reforms designed to improve access to the Court by victims and *amicus curiae*, and to shorten the length of the proceedings, may translate into more transparent, accessible, and effective process. Indeed, the steadily increasing flow of cases to the Commission and the even more pronounced flow to the Court are indicative of the increased success of the IAHR Court and Commission in consolidating their authority and credibility across large cross-sections of the region's states and inhabitants.

In all events, the extremely important normative contribution of the IAHR system to the development of international human rights on both a regional and a global level should be acknowledged. Some of the Commission's reports on indigenous peoples' rights and human rights in times of conflict have made exceptional contributions to the international human rights movement.[145] In the same vein, the IAHR Court has established groundbreaking jurisprudence on legal issues such as the positive obligations of states to protect human rights, the invalidity of amnesties for perpetrators of international crimes, and fair trial guarantees.[146]

---

[142] The limitation on access by individuals to the Court has been referred to by one of the judges as a 'repugnant matter'. *Viviana Gallardo, supra* note 51, explanation of vote by Judge Piza Escalante, at para 8. See also A A Cançado Trindade, 'The Consolidation of the Procedural Capacity of Individuals in the Evolution of the International Protection of Human Rights: Present State and Perspectives at the Turn of the Century' (1998) 30 *Colum Human Rights L Rev* 1, 27.

[143] See eg *Castillo-Petruzzi et al v Peru*, Judgment of 4 September 1998, I/A CHR (Series C) No 41, concurring opinion of Judge Cançado Trindade, at paras 24–28; Cançado Trindade, *supra* note 142.

[144] *Other Treaties, supra* note 52, at para 14 ('Article 64 of the Convention confers on this Court an advisory jurisdiction that is more extensive than that enjoyed by any international tribunal in existence today').

[145] See eg 'Report on the Situation of Human Rights of a Sector of the Nicaraguan Population of Miskito Origin', OAS/Ser L/V/II.62. Doc 10 Rev 3 and Doc 26, Washington, DC, 1984; *Abella v Argentina*, Case No 11.137, Report No 5/97, Annual Report of the IAHR Commission 1997.

[146] See eg *Velásquez-Rodríguez, supra* note 106; *The Right to Information on Consular Assistance: In the Framework of the Guarantees of the Due Process of Law*, Advisory Opinion OC-16/99 of 1 October 1999, I/A CHR (Series A) No 16; *Barrios Altos v Peru*, Judgment of 14 March 2001, I/A CHR (Series C) No 75.

REFERENCE

CASE REPORTS

Judgments of the IAHR Court are published in a series titled *Inter-American Court of Human Rights Reports* and are available on the internet.

Reports of the Commission can be found on the Commission's website and, in addition, in two commercial publications: the *Inter-American Yearbook on Human Rights* (Martinus Nihoff) and Buergenthal and Norris's *Human Rights: The Inter-American System.*

SELECT BIBLIOGRAPHY

Books

J M Pasqualucci and T Buergenthal, *The Practice and Procedure of the Inter-American Court of Human Rights* (2003).

S Davidson, *The Inter-American Human Rights System* (1997).

D J Harris and S Livingstone (eds), *The Inter-American System of Human Rights* (1998).

Association of the Bar of the City of New York, *The Inter-American Commission on Human Rights: A Promise Unfulfilled*—A report by the Committee on International Human Rights (1993).

T Buergenthal, *Protecting Human Rights in the Americas: Selected Problems* (3rd edn, 1990).

Articles

J L Cavallaro and S E Brewer, 'Reevaluating Regional Human Rights Litigation in the Twenty-First Century: The Case of the Inter-American Court' (2008) 102 *Am J Int'l L* 768.

C Grossman, 'The Inter-American System of Human Rights: Challenges for the Future' (2008) 83 *Ind LJ* 1267.

M H Tan, 'Upholding Human Rights in the Hemisphere: Casting down Impunity through the Inter-American Court of Human Rights' (2008) 43 *Tex Int'l LJ* 243.

T Buergenthal, 'New Upload: Remembering the Early Years of the Inter-American Court of Human Rights' (2005) 37 *NYU J Int'l L & Pol* 259.

C M Cerna, 'The Inter-American System for the Protection of Human Rights' (2001) 95 *ASIL Proc* 75.

V M Rodriguez Rescia, 'Reparations in the Inter-American System for the Protection of Human Rights' (1999) 5 *ILSA J Int'l & Comp L* 583.

D J Padilla, 'The Inter-American Commission on Human Rights of the Organisation of American States: A Case Study' (1993) 9 *American U J Int'l Law and Pol'y* 95.

C Medina, 'The Inter-American Commission on Human Rights and the Inter-American Court of Human Rights: Reflections on a Joint Venture' (1990) 12 *Human Rts Q* 439.

C Grossman, 'Proposals to Strengthen the Inter-American System of Human Rights' (1989) 32 *German Year Book of International Law* 264.

D Shelton, 'Improving Human Rights Protections: Recommendations for Enhancing the Effectiveness of the Inter-American Commission and Inter-American Court of Human Rights' (1988) 3 *American U J Int'l Law and Pol'y* 323.

M D Vargas, 'Individual Access to the Inter-American Court of Human Rights' (1984) 16 *NYU J Int'l L & Pol* 601.

T Buergenthal, 'The Inter-American Court of Human Rights' (1982) 76 *Am J Int'l L* 231.

R E Norris, 'Bringing Human Rights Petitions before the Inter-American Commission' (1980) 20 *Santa Clara L Rev* 733.

ANNEX

List of states parties to the American Convention on Human Rights

(as of September 2009)

Argentina;* Barbados; Bolivia;* Brazil;* Chile;* Colombia;* Costa Rica;* Dominica; Dominican Republic;* Ecuador;* El Salvador;* Grenada; Guatemala;* Haiti*; Honduras;* Jamaica*; Mexico;* Nicaragua;* Panama;* Paraguay;* Peru*; Suriname;* Uruguay;* Venezuela.*

Trinidad and Tobago has withdrawn from the American Convention, effective 26 May 1999.

* States that recognize the competence of the IAHR Court.

OAS MEMBER STATES NOT PARTIES TO THE AMERICAN CONVENTION ON HUMAN RIGHTS

Antigua and Barbuda, Bahamas, Belize, Canada, Cuba, Guyana, Saint Lucia, Saint Vincent and the Grenadines, St Kitts and Nevis, Trinidad and Tobago, United States of America.

13

THE AFRICAN COMMISSION AND COURT ON HUMAN AND PEOPLES' RIGHTS

Introduction

Name and seat of the body

The African Commission on Human and Peoples' Rights ('African HR **13.1** Commission' or 'Commission') is an expert body intended to ensure compliance with the African Charter on Human and Peoples' Rights ('African Charter').[1] The headquarters of the Commission are at the following address:

> African Commission on Human and Peoples' Rights
> 31 Bijilo Annex Layout
> Kombo North District, Western Region
> PO Box 673
> Banjul
> The Gambia
> Tel: 220 4410 505 – 6
> Fax: 220 4410504
> Email: achpr@achpr.org
> Website: <http://www.achpr.org/>

Sessions of the Commission are alternated between Banjul, The Gambia, and other venues offered by different states parties to the Charter.

---

[1] African Charter on Human and Peoples' Rights, 27 June 1981, OAU Doc CAB/LEG/67/3 Rev 5, 21 ILM 58 (1982) ('African HR Charter').

The African Court on Human and Peoples' Rights ('African HR Court' or 'Court') was established in 1998[2] as a judicial body authorized to adjudicate complaints brought against those member states of the African Charter which have accepted the jurisdiction of the Court.

The Court is temporarily situated at the following address:

The African Court on Human and Peoples' Rights
TANAPA Phase II
Dodoma Road
PO Box 6274
Arusha
United Republic of Tanzania
Tel: 255-272-050134/138
Fax: 255-272-050112
Email: registry@african-court.org
Website: <http://www.african-court.org>

After the entry into force of a 2008 Protocol on the merger of the African HR Court and the African Court of Justice,[3] human rights cases will be addressed by the human rights section of the new African Court of Justice and Human Rights. The new Court is expected to sit in the same place in which the African HR Court is currently seated.[4]

General description

13.2 The African Commission was established under article 30 of the 1981 African Charter and began its operation in November 1987. It has certain supervisory powers over all 53 states parties to the African Charter. Until 2000, the Commission functioned under the institutional framework of the Organization of African Unity (OAU). With the establishment of the African Union (AU) in 2000, it has assumed the powers and responsibility of the OAU vis-à-vis the Commission (and references in the Charter and the other constitutive instruments to the OAU should now be read as references to the AU).

The Commission's task is to promote and ensure respect for human rights in Africa. It disseminates information on human rights in Africa (by sponsoring research and conferences among other means)[5] and receives periodic reports

---

[2] Protocol to the African Charter on the Establishment of the African Court on Human and Peoples' Rights, 9 June 1998, OAU Doc OAU/LEG/AFCHPR/PROT (III) ('Court Protocol').

[3] Protocol on the Statute of the African Court of Justice and Human Rights, 1 July 2008, ('ACJHR Protocol'), available at <http://www.africa-union.org> (Documents/Treaties, Conventions and Protocols).

[4] S Sceats, 'Africa's New Human Rights Court: Whistling in the Wind?' Chatham House International Law Briefing Paper 09/01, available at <http://www.chathamhouse.org.uk/files/13587_bp0309sceats.pdf>, at 11.

[5] African HR Charter, art 45(1)(a).

from the states parties to the African Charter on measures taken to give effect to the human rights obligations prescribed therein.[6] Furthermore, the Commission is authorized to receive communications from both state and non-state actors alleging violation of the rights enumerated in the African Charter.[7] The procedure for handling communications involves investigation by the Commission of the factual claims of the parties and the issuance of recommendations on the merits, published in the form of a report.[8] Where a communication lodged by a person or entity other than a state party alleges the existence of serious, massive, and repeated violations of human and peoples' rights or an emergency situation, an in-depth study involving proactive investigation by the Commission may be undertaken with the approval of the Assembly of Heads of State and Government of the OAU (Assembly).[9] Reports of the Commission are not formally binding upon states parties; however, the Commission has taken the position that its decisions should be viewed as authoritative interpretations of the African Charter.[10]

Since its establishment, the Commission has received about 400 communications from individuals and NGOs. At the same time, the inter-state communication procedure before the Commission, and the in-depth study procedure, has hardly been used.[11]

In June 1998, the member states of the OAU adopted a Protocol on the establishment of a Court of Human and Peoples' Rights ('Protocol on the Court').[12] The Protocol entered into force in 2004 and the first judges were elected in 2006. The African Union decided in 2004, however, to merge the African HR Court with the not-yet-functioning African Court of Justice (a Court that the AU Constitutive Instrument designated as the judicial organ of the AU),[13] thereby creating a new African Court of Justice and Human Rights ('ACJHR' or 'the

---

[6] Ibid, art 62.

[7] Ibid, arts 47, 55.

[8] Ibid, arts 52, 58. The Commission has, on a few occasions, mediated an amicable settlement of the complaint, although its constitutive instruments do not address this possibility in cases initiated by non-state actors. See F Viljoen, 'Communications under the African Charter: Procedure and Admissibility' in M Evans and R Murray (eds), *The African Charter on Human and Peoples' Rights: The System in Practice 1986-2006* (2nd edn, 2008) at 76, 80–85.

[9] African HR Charter, art 58(1), (2), (3).

[10] R Murray, *The African Commission on Human and Peoples' Rights and International Law* (2000) at 54–55.

[11] Viljoen, *supra* note 8, at 76. The only inter-state communication ever published by the Commission is *DRC v Burundi, Rwanda and Uganda*, Comm No 227/99, AHPR Commission 20th Activity Report (2006), Annex IV, at 111. In-depth studies were requested by the Commission on a number of occasions, but were never approved by the Assembly. Viljoen, *supra* note 8, at 79.

[12] See *supra* note 2.

[13] Constitutive Act of the African Union, 11 July 2000, art 18 ('AU Constitutive Act'), available at <http://www.africa-union.org> (Documents/Treaties, Conventions and Protocols). The Protocol establishing the Court of Justice was concluded on 11 July 2003, and is also available at <http://www.africa-union.org> (Documents/Treaties, Conventions and Protocols).

new Court'). An instrument to that effect was adopted in 2008 but has not entered into force as yet.[14]

In late 2009, the African HR Court issued judgment in the first case presented before it (dismissing the case for lack of jurisdiction).

Institutional Aspects

Governing texts

Procedural law

13.3   The principal text governing the composition, mandate, and procedure of the African Commission is Part II of the African Charter. Other provisions regulating the work of the Commission are to be found in the Rules of Procedure of the Commission.[15] The operation of the African HR Court is governed by the Protocol on the Court and Interim Rules of Court, adopted in 2008.[16] With the entry into force of the Statute of the newly merged ACJHR, the Statute and Rules of Procedure promulgated thereunder shall govern the work of the new Court.[17]

Substantive law

13.4   When handling communications, the Commission reviews the compliance of member states with the provisions of the African Charter. In construing the Charter, the Commission is instructed to draw inspiration from other sources of international human rights law including, *inter alia*, the Charters of the UN and the OAU (subsequently replaced by the AU Constitutive Act), the Universal Declaration of Human Rights, and also African, UN, and other instruments on human rights to which African states are parties (or, alternatively, members of UN-specialized agencies that adopted such instruments).[18] The Commission is also to take into consideration other international conventions setting out norms recognized by AU member states, African practices (which conform to international human rights standards), customs generally accepted as law, general

---

[14]   See *supra* note 3. The instruments establishing the African Court of Justice and the African HR Court have entered into force separately.

[15]   Rules of Procedure of the African Commission on Human and Peoples' Rights, 6 October 1995, available at <http://www1.umn.edu/humanrts/africa/rules.htm> ('Commission Rules'). The Commission is currently preparing a revised version of the Rules that would be harmonized with the Rules of Procedure of the new ACJHR.

[16]   Interim Rules of Court, 20 June 2008 ('Interim Rules'), available at <http://www.african-court.org> (Basic Documents).

[17]   Statute of the African Court of Justice and Human Rights, Annex to CJHR Protocol, art 27 ('ACJHR Statute').

[18]   African HR Charter, art 60.

principles of law recognized by African states, as well as legal precedents and doctrine.[19]

Under the 1998 Protocol, the Court is to apply the Charter and any relevant human rights instruments adopted by the states concerned.[20] The parallel provision introduced in the relevant part of the ACJHR Statute refers explicitly to the Charter, as well as to the 'the Charter on the Rights and Welfare of the Child, the Protocol to the African Charter on Human and Peoples' Rights on the Rights of Women in Africa, or any other legal instrument relating to human rights, ratified by the States Parties concerned'.[21]

Organization

Composition

The Commission comprises 11 persons, all of whom are nationals of different **13.5** states parties to the African Charter.[22] The members of the Commission are nominated by the states parties (each party may nominate two candidates—at least one of them must be a national of the nominating state) and elected by the AU Assembly for a renewable period of six years.[23] Members of the Commission must be persons of the highest reputation, and be known for their high morality, integrity, impartiality, and competence in the field of human and peoples' rights. It is preferable that Commission members be equipped with legal experience also.[24] The members sit on the Commission in their personal capacity.[25] A Chairman and a Vice-Chairman are elected from within the Commission's ranks. Those elected serve in office for a renewable two-year period.[26] In the past, questions have been raised concerning the independence and objectivity of some Commissioners, who served on the Commission while holding concurrently senior positions in their states' executive branch.[27]

---

[19] Ibid, art 61. See eg *Centre for Free Speech v Nigeria*, Comm No 206/97, AHPR Commission 14th Activity Report (2000–2001), Annex V, at 81, 84 (finding a violation of the Charter and the UN Basic Principles on the Independence of the Judiciary).

[20] Court Protocol, art 7.

[21] ACJHR Statute, art 28(c).

[22] African HR Charter, arts 31(1), 32, 34. The present composition of the Commission is: Chair: Ms Reine Alapini-Gansou (Benin); Members: Mr Musa Ngary Bitaye (Gambia); Ms Catherine Dupe Atoki (Nigeria); Mr Mohammed Fayek (Egypt); Ms Zainabo Sylvie Kayitesi (Rwanda); Mr Mohamed Khalfallah (Tunisia); Ms Soyata Maiga (Mali); Mr Mumba Malia (Zambia); Ms Faith Pansy Tlakula (South Africa); and Mr Yeung Kam John Yeung Sik Yuen (Mauritiania). One spot on the Commission is vacant and needs to be filled.

[23] African HR Charter, arts 33, 34, 36; Commission Rules, r 11.

[24] African HR Charter, art 31(1).

[25] Ibid, art 31(2); Commission Rules, r 11(2).

[26] African HR Charter, art 42(1); Commission Rules, r 17.

[27] G Baricako, 'The African Charter and African Commission on Human and Peoples' Rights' in M Evans and R Murray (eds), *The African Charter on Human and Peoples' Rights: The System in Practice 1986–2006* (2nd edn, 2008) at 1, 9.

The Court comprises 11 judges, all of whom are nationals of different AU states.[28] Judges should be jurists of high moral character with recognized practical, judicial, or academic ability in the field of human and peoples' rights. They are elected by the Assembly upon nominations made by the states parties to the Protocol on the Court (each state may propose three candidates, at least two of whom must be its nationals).[29] In selecting judges the Assembly must ensure that the bench as a whole is representative of the main different regions and legal traditions in Africa,[30] and that adequate gender representation is achieved.[31] The judges serve a six-year term (renewable once) and elect a President and Vice-President for a two-year period (also renewable once).[32]

The new ACJHR will comprise 16 judges of different nationalities. Eight of them will serve in the new Court's Human Rights Section and the rest will serve in the General Affairs Section.[33] The full Court will elect a President and Vice-President (each of whom must serve in a different Section of the Court), who will preside, *inter alia*, over sessions in their respective Sections.[34] Judges in the new Court will also be elected for a six-year term (renewable once) and shall serve on a part-time basis.[35] The President and Vice-President shall be elected for a three-year period (also renewable once) and shall serve during that time on a full-time basis.[36]

13.6   **Disqualification of members**   A Commission member must not participate in the consideration of a communication in which he or she has a personal interest or has participated in any previous capacity in the adoption of a decision relating to the same case.[37] In such circumstances, the member concerned should voluntarily withdraw or be removed from the case by a decision of the Commission.[38] If a member of the Commission has ceased to carry out his or her official functions, the other members may decide unanimously to remove that member from office. In this case, the Chairman will notify this decision to the AU Chairperson, who will then declare the seat vacant.[39]

---

[28]   Court Protocol, art 11. The current composition of the Court is: President: Mr Jean Mutsinzi (Rwanda); Vice-President: Ms Sophia A B Akuffo (Ghana); Members: Mr Modibo Tounty Guindo (Mali); Mr Hamdi Faraj Fanoush (Libya); Mr El Hadji Guisse (Senegal); Ms Kellelo Justina Masafo-Guni (Lesotho); Mr Bernard Ngoepe (South Africa); Mr Gerard Niyungeko (Burundi); Dr Fatsah Ouguergouz (Algeria); and Joseph Nyamihana Mulenga (Uganda). Mr Githu Muigai (Kenya) resigned from the Court in July 2009 and needs to be replaced.

[29]   Court Protocol, arts 12, 14.

[30]   Ibid, art 14(2).

[31]   Ibid, arts 12(2), 14(3).

[32]   Ibid, arts 15, 21.

[33]   ACJHR Statute, arts 3, 16.

[34]   Ibid, art 22.

[35]   Ibid, art 8.

[36]   Ibid, arts 22(1), 8(4).

[37]   Commission Rules, r 109(1).

[38]   Ibid, rr 109(2), 110.

[39]   Ibid, r 14(1).

Under the 1998 Protocol, a judge may not participate in a case in which his or her state of nationality is involved. (Note that this rule stands in contradistinction to rules found in the constitutive instruments of the ECtHR and IAHR Court, which encourage the participation of judges in cases involving their state of nationality).[40] Additionally, a judge may not sit in a case in which he or she was involved as a party representative, a member of another dispute settlement body, or in any other capacity.[41] The Court may decide unanimously (with the exception of the judge concerned) to suspend or remove a judge from office if his or her other activities interfere with the judge's independence or impartiality, or are incompatible with the requirements of the office.[42] The Assembly may, however, overrule such a decision.[43]

Comparable provisions govern the independence and impartiality of judges under the new ACJHR Statute.[44] Furthermore, the new Statute explicitly enshrines judicial independence by providing that 'the Court and its Judges shall not be subject to the direction or control of any person or body'.[45]

Plenary/chambers   The Commission conducts most of its business in plenary (with the quorum being seven members);[46] however, it may also create subsidiary bodies (such as committees, sub-commissions, and working groups), to whom it may delegate some of its functions.[47] In reviewing communications, the Commission may establish working groups of three members each to make recommendations to the plenary session of the Commission on the admissibility of communications, or on the contents of the Commission's observations and reports.[48]

13.7

The African HR Court also sits in plenary (with seven judges constituting the necessary quorum).[49] The new ACJHR will, however, normally sit in Sections of eight judges.[50] A Section may nevertheless decide to refer a case to the full Court.[51] Moreover, Sections will be authorized to create chambers, and to conduct some of their judicial business through them, in accordance with the future Rules of Procedure.[52]

---

[40] Court Protocol, art 22.
[41] Ibid, art 17(2).
[42] Ibid, arts 18, 19(1).
[43] Ibid, art 19(2).
[44] ACJHR Statute, arts 13, 14.
[45] Ibid, art 12(3).
[46] African HR Charter, art 42(3); Commission Rules, r 43.
[47] Commission Rules, rr 28, 29.
[48] Ibid, rr 115, 120(1), (3).
[49] Court Protocol, art 23.
[50] ACJHR Statute, art 16.
[51] Ibid, art 18.
[52] Ibid, art 19.

Appellate structure

13.8   Under the 1998 Protocol, the Court is authorized to hear cases which have already been reviewed by the Commission.[53] The future relationship between the Commission and the new ACJHR will be sorted out in the Rules of Procedure which are currently being prepared by both institutions. The new Court's Statute merely provides that the relationship will be one of 'complementarity' both vis-à-vis the Commission and the African Committee of Experts on the Rights and Welfare of the Child[54] (a committee monitoring compliance with the African Charter on the Rights and Welfare of the Child).[55]

Technical/scientific experts

13.9   There is no explicit provision under the various instruments governing the work of the Commission which addresses participation of experts in communication proceedings, although the Charter authorizes the Commission to invite any person 'capable of enlightening it' to present before it.[56] In practice, expert opinions have been admitted in a few cases.[57]

According to the 1998 Protocol, parties to African HR Court proceedings can introduce expert opinions as part of the evidence they submit to the Court.[58] By contrast, the 2008 ACJHR Statute omits all reference to expert opinions or testimony. One may assume that the matter will be regulated in the future Rules of Procedure.

Secretariat

13.10   The administrative needs of the Commission are fulfilled by the Chairperson of the AU (previously, the Secretary-General of the Organization of African Unity), who provides the Commission with the necessary staff, means, and services.[59]

---

[53] Court Protocol, art 5; Interim Rules, r 29. Although the Protocol and the Rules are less than clear on the actual nature of the 'complementary relations' between the African HR Court and the Commission, it appears to be based on the modality of relations that existed between the ECtHR and the European Commission until 1998 (and still exists in the relations between the I/A Court and Commission). See Viljoen, *supra* note 8, at 131. Interestingly, the Court may also refer inadmissible cases back to the Commission. Court Protocol, art 6(3).

[54] ACJHR Statute, art 27(2).

[55] African Charter on the Rights and Welfare of the Child, 11 July 1990, OAU Doc CAB/LEG/24.9/49 (1990) ('Charter on Rights of the Child'). The Committee of Experts is authorized to receive communications relating to any matter covered by the Charter. Ibid, art 44. See more on the Committee of Experts in Annex V of this Chapter.

[56] African HR Charter, art 46.

[57] See eg *Rencontre Africaine pour la Défense de Droit de l'Homme v Zambia*, Comm No 71/92, AHPR Commission 10th Activity Report (1996–1997), Annex X, at 61; *Interights v Botswana*, Comm No 240/2001 (2004), AHPR Commission 17th Activity Report (2003–04), Annex VII, at 95.

[58] See Court Protocol, art 26(2).

[59] African HR Charter, art 41; Commission Rules, r 22(3). For a critical discussion of the Secretariat's performance, see Baricako, *supra* note 27, at 12–16; F Adolu 'A View from the Inside: The Role of the Secretariat', ibid at 316–343.

The head of the Secretariat of the Commission is the Secretary, appointed by the AU Chairperson, in consultation with the Chair of the Commission. *Inter alia*, the Secretary assists members of the Commission in the exercise of their functions; serves as a channel of communication to and from the Commission; is the custodian of the archives of the Commission; keeps a record of all communications; notifies the members of the Commission on issues submitted to him or her; and makes arrangements (under instructions from the AU Commission Chairperson) for the meetings of the Commission.[60] In practice, the Secretariat has been chronically underfunded and understaffed by the OAU and AU and has had to solicit funding from non-African sources.

The African HR Court has its own registry and staff, headed by a Registrar.[61] In the same vein, the new ACJHR will also have its own registry.[62]

Jurisdiction

Ratione personae

African Commission   The Commission may receive communications against **13.11** states parties to the African Charter, which are submitted by: (1) another state party[63] or (2) any other source.[64] In the latter case, the Commission may consider the communication only if the majority of its members decides to do so.[65]

African Court   The African HR Court has jurisdiction over cases brought by **13.12** the following claimants:

(1) the Commission;
(2) the state party that lodged a complaint to the Commission;
(3) the state party against which the complaint has been lodged;
(4) the state party whose citizen is a victim of human rights violations; and
(5) any African intergovernmental organization.[66]

Although the Protocol does not explicitly require that a claim be brought only against an African Charter member state which is also a party to the Protocol,

---

[60] Commission Rules, rr 22(4), 23, 27.
[61] Court Protocol, art 24.
[62] ACJHR Statute, art 22(4).
[63] African HR Charter, arts 47, 49.
[64] Ibid, art 55. African and NGOs may thus present communications to the Commission and have done so on many occasions. See eg *Malawi African Association v Mauritania*, Comm No 54/91 (2000), AHPR Commission 13th Activity Report (1999–2000), Annex V, at 138; *Amnesty International v Zambia*, Comm No 212/98, ACPHR 12th Activity Report (1998–1999), Annex V, at 76. Private individuals, other than the immediate victim of the violation, may also seize the Commission. Viljoen, *supra* note 8, at 103–104.
[65] African HR Charter, art 55(2).
[66] Court Protocol, art 5(1).

such an interpretation is sensible, since only such states will be bound by judgments of the Court.[67]

The Court will also be authorized to receive cases brought directly to it (arguably, without first seizing the Commission) by individuals or NGOs with observer status before the Commission (a more stringent *jus standi* standard than that applied in the Commission proceedings, which are open to all NGOs), if the state against which the complaint has been made submitted a declaration under article 34(6) of the Protocol, recognizing the competence of the Court to receive such claims.[68] So far, however, only two states have submitted such declarations.[69]

The new ACJHR will enjoy, by and large, similar jurisdictional powers over human rights issues to that of the African HR Court: cases against member states may be brought by other member states (who have ratified the Statute), by the Commission, or by other accredited African IGOs or AU organs.[70] In addition, the Statute also authorizes the Committee of Experts on the Rights and Welfare of the Child and African national human rights institutions to bring claims before it.[71] Nevertheless, the Statute retains the restrictive rule which limits the right of individuals and NGOs to bring cases directly to the Court to those instances in which a declaration of consent has been given by the state complained against.[72]

Ratione materiae

13.13 **African Commission**   The jurisdiction of the Commission encompasses all cases where a state party or other competent applicant has good reasons to believe that another state party has violated the provisions of the Charter.[73] Following the adoption of the Protocol to the African Charter on the Rights of Women in Africa,[74] the Commission was invested with temporary jurisdiction (pending the establishment of the Court) to monitor the implementation of this instrument too. Arguably, such powers include the review of communications against

---

[67] Ibid, art 30.
[68] Ibid, arts 5(3), 34(6).
[69] Sceats, *supra* note 10, at 10.
[70] ACJHR Statute, arts 29, 30.
[71] Ibid, art 30(c), (e).
[72] Ibid, art 30(f); ACJHR Protocol, art 8.
[73] African HR Charter, arts 47, 49, 55–56. The Charter is not clear on the subject matter of complaints submitted by persons or bodies other than states parties. Nonetheless, in practice, these communications address human rights violations under the Charter. In *Jawara* the Commission held that individual complaints need not raise serious or massive violations of the Charter and that sporadic violations may also be raised. *Jawara v Gambia*, Comm No 147/95, ACHPR 13th Activity Report (1999–2000), Annex V, at 96, 102.
[74] Protocol to the African Charter on Human and Peoples' Rights on the Rights of Women in Africa, 13 September 2000, adopted by the 2nd Ordinary Session of the Assembly of the African Union, AU Doc CAB/LEG/66.6 (2000).

member states that ratified the Protocol.[75] Furthermore, such powers of review should probably continue to reside with the Commission in regard of member states that have not accepted the Court's jurisdiction to accept individual petitions.

Communications may sometimes lead to an in-depth study of a human rights situation in a particular African country (as opposed to the ordinary review procedure resulting in the Commission's observations). In such cases, the communication must indicate, either on its own or together with other communications, the existence of a series of serious or massive violations of human rights, or a state of emergency. The Commission should then refer the case to the Assembly, to obtain its authorization to conduct an in-depth study.[76] In actual practice, after a number of failed attempts to obtain the Assembly's consent for an in-depth situation study, the Commission stopped utilizing this procedure.[77]

African Court   Under the Protocol, the Court's jurisdiction extends to all   **13.14** cases and disputes concerning the interpretation and application of the African Charter, the Protocol on the Court, or any human rights instrument ratified by the states concerned.[78] The ACJHR Statute similarly governs 'the interpretation and the application of the African Charter, the Charter on the Rights and Welfare of the Child, the Protocol to the African Charter on Human and Peoples' Rights on the Rights of Women in Africa, or any other legal instrument relating to human rights, ratified by the States Parties concerned'.[79] Such a broad basis of jurisdictions has already raised concerns about jurisdiction conflicts between the new African courts and other international human rights complaint procedures.[80]

Ratione temporis

African Commission   In cases involving communications from 'other   **13.15** sources'—ie presented by non-state actors—the complaint must be lodged only after the exhaustion of domestic remedies (unless the domestic procedures are unduly prolonged).[81] Moreover, the communication should be submitted within a reasonable time from the date on which local remedies were exhausted.[82]

---

[75] Viljoen, *supra* note 8, at 96.
[76] African HR Charter, art 58.
[77] Viljoen, *supra* note 8, at 79.
[78] Court Protocol, art 3(1).
[79] ACJHR Statute, art 28(c).
[80] See eg C Heyns, 'The African Regional Human Rights System: In need of reform?' (2001) *African Human Rights Law Journal* 155, 167.
[81] African HR Charter, art 56(5).
[82] Ibid, art 56(6).

The Commission may deal, as a rule, with an inter-state communication only after the complaining state has addressed a written communication to the other state concerned, thereby drawing its attention to the possible violation.[83] The Commission can be seized only after the expiration of three months from the date on which the original communication was received by the state complained against, and only if the matter has not been settled.[84] In exceptional cases of patent violations, however, the state complainant may refer the case to the Commission immediately.[85] Inter-state communications should also meet the requirements of the exhaustion of local remedies rule.[86]

All communications must cover events that took place after the entry into force of the relevant human rights instrument for the state complained against.[87]

13.16 **African Court**   In principle, the same temporal requirements of admissibility applicable to Commission proceedings also apply to the African HR Court.[88] This includes exhaustion of domestic remedies and probably also an obligation to file a claim within a reasonable time after exhausting domestic remedies. The precise division of labour between the ACJHR and the Commission will be addressed in the Rules of Procedure of the Court. Given the complementarity between the Court and the Commission it might be expected that a case will be brought before the Court only after it has been dealt with by the Commission, although the current text of the Court's Statute does not require this.[89] Cases currently pending before the Commission appear to be outside the scope of the ACJHR's temporal jurisdiction which is arguably prospective in nature (unless such cases reveal ongoing human rights violations); by contrast, the 2008 Protocol regulates the transfer of cases from the African HR Court to the new ACJHR.[90]

Advisory jurisdiction

13.17   The Commission is authorized to interpret the provisions of the African Charter at the request of a state party, an AU institution, or an African organization

---

[83] Ibid, art 47.

[84] Ibid, art 48.

[85] Ibid, art 49.

[86] Ibid, art 50.

[87] See eg *Pagnoulle v Cameroon*, Comm No 39/90, AHPR Commission 10th Activity Report (1996–1997), Annex X, at 52, 54 ('the Commission cannot pronounce on the equity of court proceedings that took place before the African Charter entered into force in Cameroon'). Still, the Commission held in the same case that it may exercise jurisdiction over continuing violations— including ones originating in pre-ratification events.

[88] Court Protocol, art 6(2). See also Viljoen, *supra* note 8, at 131 (Court should not rigidly apply the admissibility requirements).

[89] I Kane and A C Motala, 'The Creation of a New African Court of Justice and Human Rights' in M Evans and R Murray (eds), *The African Charter on Human and Peoples' Rights: The System in Practice 1986–2006* (2nd edn, 2008) at 406, 430–431.

[90] ACJHR Protocol, art 5.

recognized by the AU.[91] The Rules of Procedure do not specify a procedure for consideration of interpretation requests and the procedure seems to be defunct.[92]

The African HR Court has the power to render advisory opinions at the request of AU member states or organs or any African organization recognized by the AU,[93] provided that the same matter is not being dealt with by the Commission. Such an opinion is to be reasoned and every judge may produce his or her dissenting opinion.[94]

The new ACJHR will also have broad substantive advisory powers covering 'any legal question'.[95] Only AU organs are authorized to request advisory opinions from the new Court; still, states and IGOs that are entitled to participate in contentious proceedings may also participate in pending advisory proceedings.[96]

Procedural Aspects

Languages

13.18 The working languages of the Commission are Arabic, English, French, and Portuguese.[97] All working languages may be used before the Commission and translated into all other working languages. A person who addresses the Commission in a language which is not a working language must arrange for translation into one of the working languages.[98]

Whilst the 1998 Court Protocol is silent on the matter, the new ACJHR's official and working languages will be the same as those of the AU.[99]

Instituting proceedings

13.19 A case is initiated before the Commission by way of a written communication. Communications submitted by non-state parties ('other sources') should contain *inter alia*: the personal details of the author; the Charter provisions that

---

[91] African HR Charter, art 45(3).

[92] In practice, the Commission has adopted, on its own initiative, several resolutions aimed to elucidate unclear provisions of the Charter without, however, suggesting that this was an exercise of its advisory jurisdiction under the Charter.

[93] Court Protocol, art 4. Viljoen takes the position that the term 'African organizations' also encompasses African NGOs. Viljoen, *supra* note 8, at 130.

[94] Court Protocol, art 4.

[95] ACJHR Statute, art 53.

[96] Ibid, art 54.

[97] Commission Rules, r 34.

[98] Ibid, r 35.

[99] AU Constitutive Act, art 25 (specifying that Arabic, English, French, Portuguese, and 'African languages' will be the Union's working languages 'if possible').

were allegedly violated; the underlying facts; and information on exhaustion of local remedies and any parallel international proceedings.[100] If the applicability of the African Charter to the communication is in doubt, the Commission, through its Secretary, may request clarification and/or additional information from the author within fixed time limits.[101]

Inter-state communications must also contain a detailed and comprehensive statement on (a) the actions denounced and (b) provisions of the Charter allegedly violated.[102] Moreover, as noted above, the inter-state communication must normally be made first to the state party complained against, with a copy to the Chairs of the AU and the Commission.[103] After a period of three months in which no settlement has been reached (except in cases of a clear violation), the complaining state must send a notification of its intent to submit the dispute to the Commission. The notification is to be sent to the two Chairs and a copy must be sent to the other state involved.[104] It should include *inter alia* information on the correspondence between the two states, and information regarding the exhaustion of domestic remedies, as well as any parallel international proceedings.[105]

Financial assistance

13.20 Financial assistance is not available for participants in proceedings before the Commission. Under the Protocol on the Court, however, the Court will provide free legal representation to a party to a case before it, where the interests of justice so require.[106] A similar provision exists under the new ACJHR Statute.[107]

Provisional measures

13.21 During proceedings involving individual communications, the Commission may indicate its views on whether interim measures are needed to avoid irreparable damage to the alleged victim.[108] The Commission (or the Chairperson when the Commission is not at session) may also indicate other desirable interim measures necessary to protect the interests of the parties or the proper conduct of the proceedings.[109] Provisional (or interim) measures are not formally binding upon the parties; nevertheless, in the *Saro-Wiwa* case, the Commission held that

---

[100] Commission Rules, r 104(1).
[101] Ibid, r 104.
[102] Ibid, r 88(2).
[103] Ibid, r 88(1).
[104] African HR Charter, art 48; Commission Rules, r 92.
[105] Commission Rules, r 93(2).
[106] Court Protocol, art 10(2).
[107] ACJHR Statute, art 52(2).
[108] Commission Rules, r 111(1).
[109] Ibid, r 111(2), (3).

failure to comply with provisional measures entails a violation of the African Charter.[110]

The Protocol establishing the Court allows it to adopt provisional measures in cases of extreme gravity and urgency, if such measures are needed to avoid irreparable harm to persons.[111] A similar provision also exists under the new ACJHR Statute.[112]

Preliminary proceedings

Before reviewing the merits of a communication, the Commission must make a decision on the question of admissibility.[113] In practice, however, the Commission first acknowledges the fact that it was seized by communications before discussing their admissibility.[114] **13.22**

In the case of a communication presented by a non-state actor, the Commission must verify the following requirements for the admissibility of the communication:[115]

(a) it indicates the name of the authors (even if they wish the Commission to protect their anonymity);
(b) it is compatible with the AU Constitutive Instrument or with the African Charter on Human and Peoples' Rights;[116]
(c) it is not written in disparaging or insulting language directed at the state concerned (or its institutions) or the AU;[117]
(d) it is not based exclusively on mass media reports;
(e) local remedies have been exhausted (unless the application of such remedies is clearly unduly prolonged);[118]

---

[110] *International PEN v Nigeria,* Comm No 137/94, AHPR Commission 12th Activity Report (1998–1999), Annex V, at 62, 72–73.

[111] Court Protocol art 27(2).

[112] ACJHR Statute, art 35.

[113] African HR Charter, arts 50, 56; Commission Rules, r 118.

[114] Commission Rules, rr 93, 102. For criticism, see Viljoen, *supra* note 8, at 77–78 (opining that the 'seizing' procedure is meaningless yet leads to an unnecessary delay of six months in the consideration of all communications).

[115] African HR Charter, art 56; Commission Rules, r 116.

[116] According to Viljoen, the two compatibility requirements (with the Charter and Constitutive Instrument) should be understood as cumulative, not alternative, in nature. Viljoen, *supra* note 8, at 95.

[117] For criticism of the 'no disparaging language' admissibility requirement, see C A Odinkalu, 'The Individual Complaints Procedure of the African Commission on Human and Peoples' Rights: A Preliminary Assessment' (1998) 8 *Transnational Law and Contemporary Problems* 359, 382.

[118] Viljoen opines that the victim, not the communication author (if other than the victim), should be expected to exhaust local remedies. Viljoen, *supra* note 8, at 112. He also notes that the exhaustion requirement can be waived with regard to complaints alleging serious or massive violations. Ibid at 119–120.

(f) it is submitted within a reasonable time after the exhaustion of local remedies, or after the Commission became seized of the matter; and

(g) it does not deal with matters already settled by the states involved in accordance with the Charter of the UN, the AU Constitutive Instrument, or the African Charter on Human and Peoples' Rights.[119]

The Commission may be assisted in its consideration of the admissibility of the complaint by working groups composed of three members of the Commission (or less). Working groups may recommend to the plenary Commission whether or not to admit the communication.[120] The Commission (or working group) may request additional written information or observations on admissibility from the state concerned or the author of the communication within fixed time limits.[121] In any event, the Commission cannot declare a communication admissible unless the state party has received an opportunity to submit its observations on the question of admissibility (within not more than three months from receiving the communication).[122]

In cases brought by states, the Committee must also be satisfied that a number of conditions have been met, such as: that the preliminary stage of direct communications between the two states (in accordance with article 47 of the Charter) has been exhausted; that the three months' time limit from the date of the original communication has expired; and that domestic remedies have been exhausted, in accordance with international law principles.[123]

The African HR Court has been instructed to rule on the admissibility of cases before 'taking into account the provisions of article 56' (ie the article governing the admissibility of non-state communications to the Commission) and after consulting with the Commission where necessary.[124] It has been suggested in the literature that this formulation affords the Court discretion on the matter of admissibility.[125] The new ACJHR Statute does not address the issue of admissibility, thus leaving the matter for its future Rules of Procedure.

---

[119] In practice, the Commission tended to construe this limit broadly and to dismiss or suspend review of communications simultaneously pending before other dispute settlement procedures (but not yet settled by them). See eg *Interights v Eritrea,* Comm No 233/99, ACHPR 16th Activity Report (2002–2003) at 76.

[120] Commission Rules, r 115. The Commission started utilizing working groups in 1999.

[121] Ibid, r 117(1). The Commission normally allocates three months for the submission of additional information and two months for follow-up requests. Viljoen, *supra* note 8, at 90.

[122] Commission Rules, r 117(2), (4).

[123] African HR Charter, arts 47, 48; Commission Rules, r 97. For a discussion, see Viljoen, *supra* note 8, at 134–137.

[124] Court Protocol, art 6.

[125] See eg Viljoen, *supra* note 8, at 131.

Written phase

Communications from non-state actors

In the event that the Commission decides that the communication is admissible, **13.23** the state complained against will be given three months to submit in writing its explanation or statement clarifying the issue under consideration, and also indicating, if possible, remedial measures it intends to apply.[126] The explanation and the statement will then be made available to the author of the communication, who will be entitled to submit, within fixed time limits, a written response including additional information and observations.[127]

Inter-state communications

Upon receipt of the original communication (before the seizing of the **13.24** Commission), the state complained against must present a written reply to the complaining state within three months.[128] The reply must include *inter alia* written explanations, declarations, or statements relating to the issues raised; possible indications and measures that are to be taken to end the situation denounced; and an indication of appellate procedures in use, or still available.[129]

After the Commission has been seized of the communication, both parties are entitled to submit written observations, according to a procedure to be determined by the Commission.[130] In addition, the Commission may request the parties to provide further information or observations in writing, within fixed time limits.[131]

The Interim Rules governing proceedings before the African HR Court require the filing of applications and evidence in writing.[132] The Interim Rules also authorize the Court to request the parties to file additional documents and written explanations.[133] The 2008 ACJHR Statute is silent on the conduct of written proceedings and seems to delegate the matter to the new Court's future Rules of Procedure.

Oral phase

The parties to a case brought by a state may present their oral submissions **13.25** before the Commission.[134] The Commission may also, and on its own initiative,

---

[126] Commission Rules, r 119(2).
[127] Ibid, r 119(3).
[128] African HR Charter, art 47; Commission Rules, r 90(1).
[129] African HR Charter, art 47; Commission Rules, r 90(2).
[130] African HR Charter, art 51(2); Commission Rules, r 100(1).
[131] African HR Charter, art 51(1); Commission Rules, r 99.
[132] Interim Rules, r 34. See also Court Protocol, art 26.
[133] Interim Rules, r 41.
[134] African HR Charter, art 51(2); Commission Rules, r 100(1).

request the parties (through the Secretary) to appear before it and provide information or comments.[135] Such presentation is to be made within fixed time limits and according to a procedure determined by the Commission.[136] The Commission has additionally developed a practice of affording oral hearings in cases initiated by communications received from other sources. Prior to the session in which it proposes to take the oral hearing, the Commission issues hearing notices to the parties notifying them of the venue and time for the hearing.

The consideration of communications by the Commission is conducted in private sessions, which are not open to the public.[137] In contrast, the African HR Court and the ACJHR will normally sit in public.[138] The 1998 Protocol and the Interim Rules explicitly provide for submission of oral evidence to the Court, whereas the ACJHR Statute is silent on the matter.[139]

Third party intervention/multiple proceedings

13.26 The various instruments regulating the work of the Commission do not specifically provide for, or exclude, third party intervention. (The Commission has yet to receive or consider any such request or application.) Furthermore, under the African Charter there is no impediment against two or more parties filing a communication together against a state party. In cases brought by persons or entities other than states parties, the Commission may decide to consider two or more communications jointly, if it deems this to be useful.[140]

Under the Protocol on the Court, any state party with an interest in a case can make a request to join the proceedings.[141] In the same vein, the ACJHR Statute provides for a right to intervene for member states and Union organs who may be affected by the decision in the case.[142] The Court may also invite member states, AU organs, or any other person to participate in the written or oral proceedings if such participation will be 'in the interest of the effective administration of justice'.[143]

Amicus curiae

13.27 In investigating a communication the Commission may receive information from the AU Commission Chairperson or from any person capable of enlightening it.[144]

---

[135] African HR Charter, art 51(1); Commission Rules, r 99.
[136] Commission Rules, r 100(3).
[137] Ibid, rr 96(1), 106.
[138] Court Protocol, art 10(1); ACJHR Statute, art 39.
[139] Court Protocol, art 26(2); Interim Rules, rr 45–47.
[140] Commission Rules, r 114(2).
[141] Court Protocol, art 5(2).
[142] ACJHR Statute, art 49(1). Any interpretative decision by the Court will be equally binding on the parties and the intervening party. Ibid, art 49(2).
[143] Ibid, art 49(3).
[144] African HR Charter, art 46.

A similar power can be found with regard to admitting information from interested states and specialized institutions of the AU.[145]

Although the involvement of *amicus curiae* is not explicitly regulated in the constitutive instruments of the African HR Court and the ACJHR, the latter Court's broad powers of intervention could serve to facilitate the participation of some *amicus curiae* in proceedings before it.[146]

Representation of parties

States parties to the Charter have the right to be represented during the consideration of a relevant issue by the Commission, and to submit observations orally and in writing.[147] The Commission also authorizes authors of other communications to be represented if they so choose.

13.28

Under the African HR Court Protocol, any party to a case shall be entitled to be represented by a legal representative of that party's choice. Free legal representation may be provided where the interests of justice so require.[148] Similar provisions can be found in the ACJHR Statute.[149]

Decision

In cases brought by non-state applicants, the Commission will normally prepare observations, made on the basis of the information submitted to it by the parties.[150] Such observations take the form of a judicial decision, and contain a description of the facts, procedures, party arguments, and legal findings. The Commission now often specifies what remedies would be appropriate to rectify a violation of the Charter.[151]

13.29

As noted above, in cases where the Commission believes that the communication, alone or together with other communications, reveals a series of serious or massive human rights violations or a case of emergency, it may notify the Assembly accordingly.[152] The Assembly may then request the Commission to conduct an in-depth study of the situation. The factual findings of such a study, as well as the recommendations of the Commission, will be prepared in the form of a report.[153] In practice, the in-depth reporting procedure has never been followed through.

---

[145] Commission Rules, rr 71, 73.

[146] ACJHR Statute, art 49(3); Interim Rules, r 46(1).

[147] Rules of Procedure, art 100.

[148] Court Protocol, art 10(2).

[149] ACJHR Statute, arts 36, 52(2).

[150] Commission Rules, r 120(2).

[151] See eg *Institute of Human Rights and Development in Africa v Angola*, Comm No 292/2004, AHPR Commission 23rd–24th Activity Report (2006–2008), Annex II, at 86, 106–107; *The Social and Economic Rights Action Center v Nigeria*, Comm No 155/96, AHPR Commission 15th Activity Report (2001–2002), Annex V, at 31, 43–44.

[152] African HR Charter, art 58.

[153] Ibid, art 58(2); Commission Rules, r 120(3).

In cases brought by states, if no amicable settlement has been reached the Commission will prepare a report within 12 months from the date on which it was seized.[154] The report will include the decisions and conclusions of the Commission on the merits of the case.[155]

Decisions of the Commission are not binding. Moreover, under the Charter, reports of the Commission should remain confidential until the Assembly decides to publish them.[156] However, the Commission may, through the Secretary, issue press releases on its activities, which include, *inter alia*, information on the decisions of the Commission on communications presented before it.[157] In practice, the Commission's Activity Reports made to the AU Assembly of Heads of State and Government that include the text of the Commission's decisions on the communications brought before it are now routinely published.

The African HR Court is expected to present its decisions within 90 days from the end of deliberations. The decision will be prepared in the form of a reasoned judgment, which will then be publicized.[158] Any judge may deliver his or her separate or dissenting opinion with the judgment.[159] Similar provisions exist under the ACJHR Statute.[160]

Interpretation and revision of judgments

13.30 There are no explicit provisions under the instruments governing the work of the Commission that allow for interpretation or revision of observations or reports adopted by the Commission. An exception is found with regard to decisions on admissibility of complaints, which the Commission may reconsider at a later date, if requested to do so.[161]

Under the 1998 Protocol on the Court, parties to a case may request interpretation of a judgment, or its revision, in the light of new evidence.[162] Similar provisions can be found in the ACJHR Statute.[163]

Appeal

13.31 There are currently no avenues of appeal from decisions of the Commission. This is bound to change with the operationalization of the African HR Court and/or the ACJHR. Still, the exact relationship between the two courts and

---

[154] African HR Charter, art 52; Commission Rules, r 101(1).
[155] Commission Rules, r 101(3).
[156] African HR Charter, art 59(2); Commission Rules, r 108.
[157] Commission Rules, r 96.
[158] Court Protocol, art 28(1), (5)–(6).
[159] Ibid, art 28(7).
[160] ACJHR Statute, arts 43, 44.
[161] Rules of Procedure, r 118(2).
[162] Court Protocol, art 28(3), (4).
[163] ACJHR Statute, arts 47, 48.

the Commission, including the specific extent to which the courts will exercise appellate jurisdiction over the decisions of the Commission, is yet to be determined.[164]

Costs

Proceedings before the Commission are free of charge, but the parties must bear their own expenses. A similar rule has been incorporated into the ACJHR Statute.[165]   **13.32**

Enforcement of decisions

Decisions of the African Commission are not binding and thus are not subject to enforcement procedures. In contrast, judgments of the African HR Court and the new ACJHR will be binding upon the parties and states will have to comply with judgments within time periods fixed by the Court. Moreover, states parties to the Protocol on the Court and the ACJHR Statute will be obliged to guarantee the execution of the Court's judgments.[166] The latter instrument also confers enforcement powers on the AU Assembly of Heads of State and Government.[167]   **13.33**

Evaluation

The African machinery for human rights protection is weaker than its European and even inter-American counterparts. This is so despite the fact that the scope of personal and subject-matter jurisdiction of the African human rights system is broader than any other regional human rights institution—it covers 53 countries, is available to complainants other than the actual victims of human rights violations, and encompasses a broad range of human rights (including economic and social rights and instruments other than the African Charter). The relative weakness of the African Commission (currently the only regularly functioning part of the African human rights machinery) can be attributed to a number of structural problems, such as the limited budget of the Commission, the short duration of Commission sessions, the inadequate facilities from which it works, understaffing of its Secretariat, the limited publicity afforded to the Commission's work (although there has been considerable improvement in this regard in recent years), and the political controls over the work of the Commission which AU organs may exercise, pursuant to the African HR Charter.[168] More fundamentally,

---

[164] Court Protocol, art 8; ACJHR Statute, art 27(2).

[165] ACJHR Statute, art 52(1).

[166] Court Protocol, art 30; ACJHR Statute, art 46(2), (3).

[167] ACJHR Statute, art 46(4).

[168] This was compounded in the early years of the Commission by the appointment of several serving members of the national executive as Commissioners. Baricako, *supra* note 27, at 9.

however, it appears that the limited success of the African HR Commission is closely tied to broader problems surrounding the processes of democratization, good governance, and economic development in the African continent. Without real enforcement powers, the Commission has to rely on its informal ability to prod and persuade African governments to adopt better practices; and its ability to do so is heavily dependent on the goodwill and capabilities of the relevant states—both often lacking in practice. The type of violations brought before the Commission—including state sanctioned violence, ethnic and gender discrimination, and political repression[169]—further complicate the challenges presented before the Commission. So, while the Commission's record has certainly improved over the years (notably, its work has become more efficient, well organized and publicized, and some of its jurisprudence is certainly impressive),[170] it has not transformed itself into a powerful legal and political actor on the African or global scene, on a par with other regional human rights institutions.

Although the move by the AU to stronger institutions—most notably, the creation of the African HR Court and the future ACJHR—should be seen as a move in the right direction, it is probably too soon to assess its actual implications for the protection of human rights in Africa. The subsuming of the African HR Court within the ACJHR before the first Court had a chance to adjudicate cases (and before the economic efficiency arguments underlying the merger of the African Court of Justice and the African HR Court had been put to actual test) does not seem to bode well for the project of establishing a strong African human rights court.[171] In addition, the unclear relationship between the Court and Commission suggests that the Court is still very much a 'half-baked' idea. Finally, the limits placed on the Court's ability to hear cases brought by individuals and NGOs put in question the actual commitment of the drafter to creating a robust court that could hold African governments accountable for their human rights records.

REFERENCE

CASE REPORTS

The observations of the Commission are published in the *Review of the African Commission on Human & Peoples' Rights* (seven volumes to date) and in the Annual Activity Reports (1987–).

---

[169] See eg *Institute of Human Rights and Development in Africa v Angola*, Comm No 292/2004, AHPR Commission 23rd–24th Activity Report (2006–2008), Annex II, at 86; *PEN v Nigeria*, *supra* note 110, at 62.

[170] See eg *Social and Economic Rights Center v Nigeria*, *supra* note 151, at 31; *Amnesty International v Zambia*, Comm No 212/98, ACPHR 12th Activity Report (1998–1999), Annex V, at 76.

[171] For a critical description of the chain of events which led to the merger of the two courts, see Kane and Motala, *supra* note 89, at 408–417.

SELECT BIBLIOGRAPHY

Books

M Evans and R Murray (eds), *The African Charter on Human and Peoples' Rights: The System in Practice 1986–2006* (2nd edn, 2008).

F Viljoen, *International Human Rights Law in Africa* (2007).

F Ouguergouz, *The African Charter on Human and Peoples Rights: A Comprehensive Agenda for Human Dignity and Sustainable Democracy in Africa* (2003).

U Oji Umozurike, *The African Charter on Human and Peoples' Rights* (1997).

E A Ankumah, *The African Commission on Human and Peoples' Rights* (1996).

J Matringe, *Tradition et modernité dans la Charte Africaine des Droits de l'Homme et des Peuples: étude du contenu normatif de la Charte et de son apport a la théorie du droit international des droits de l'homme* (1996).

E Yemet Valere, *La Charte Africaine des Droits de l'Homme et des Peuples: étude comparative* (1996).

F Ouguergouz, *La Charte Africaine des Droits de l'Homme et des Peuples: une approche juridique des droits de l'homme entre tradition et modernité* (1993).

N S Rembe, *The System of Protection of Human Rights under the African Charter on Human and Peoples' Rights: Problems and Prospects* (1991).

Articles

S T Ebobrah, 'The Admissibility of a Case before the African Court on Human and People's Rights: Who Should do What' (2009) 3 *Malawi Law Journal* 87.

U O Umozurike, 'The African Charter on Human and People Rights: Suggestions for More Effectiveness' (2007) 13 *Annual Survey of International and Comparative Law* 179.

F Viljoen and L Louw, 'State Compliance with the Recommendations of the African Commission on Human and Peoples' Rights, 1994–2004' (2007) 101 *American Journal of International Law* 1.

M Killander, 'Confidentiality versus Publicity: Interpreting Article 59 of the African Charter on Human and People's Rights' (2006) 6 *African Human Rights Law Journal* 572.

B T Nyanduga, 'Focus: Twenty Years after the Entry into Force of the African Charter on Human and People's Rights: Conference Paper' (2006) 6 *African Human Rights Law Journal* 255.

G Mukundi Wachira and A Ayinla, 'Twenty Years of Elusive Enforcement of the Recommendations of the African Commission on Human and People's Rights: A Possible Remedy' (2006) 6 *African Human Rights Law Journal* 465.

M Peschardt Pedersen, 'Standing and the African Commission on Human and Peoples' Rights' (2006) 6 *African Human Rights Law Journal* 407.

A P Van der Mei, 'The Advisory Jurisdiction of the African Court on Human and Peoples' Rights' (2005) 5 *African Human Rights Law Journal* 27.

F Ouguergouz, 'The Establishment of an African Court of Human and Peoples' Rights: A Judicial Premiere for the African Union' (2005) *African Yearbook of International Law* 79.

F Viljoen, 'A Human Rights Court for Africa, and Africans' (2004) 30 *Brooklyn J of Intl L* 30.

C Heyns, 'The African Regional Human Rights System: In Need of Reform?' (2001) 1 *African Human Rights Law Journal* 155.

N J Udombana, 'Towards the African Court on Human and Peoples' Rights: Better Late than Never' (2000) 3 *Yale Human Rights Development LJ* 45.

M Mutua, 'The African Human Rights Court: A Two-Legged Stool?' (1999) 21 *HRQ* 342.

H Boufrik, 'La Cour Africaine des Droits de l'Homme et des Peuples: un organe judiciaire au service des droits de l'homme et des peuples en Afrique' (1998) 10(1) *Revue africaine de droit international et comparé*.

G J Naldi and K Magliveras, 'Reinforcing the African System of Human Rights: The Protocol on the Establishment of a Regional Court of Human and Peoples' Rights' (1998) 16 *Netherlands Human Rights Quarterly* 431–456.

M Mubiala, 'La Cour Africaine des Droits de l'Homme et des Peuples: mimétisme institutionnel ou avancée judiciaire?' (1998) *Revue générale de droit international public* 765.

C A Odinkalu and C Christensen, 'The African Commission on Human and Peoples' Rights: The Development of its Non-State Communication Procedures' (1998) 20 *Human Rights Quarterly* 235.

A E Anthony, 'Beyond the Paper Tiger: The Challenge of a Human Rights Court in Africa' (1997) 32 *Texas International Law Journal* 511.

I A Badawi El-Sheikh, 'The African Commission on Human and Peoples' Rights: A Call for Justice' in K Koufa (ed), *International Justice*, XXVI Thesaurus Acroasium (1997).

R Murray, 'Decisions by the African Commission on Individual Communications under the African Charter on Human and Peoples' Rights' (1997) 46 *ICLQ* 412.

P Amoah, 'The African Charter on Human and Peoples' Rights: An Effective Weapon for Human Rights?' (1992) 4 *African Journal of International & Comparative Law* 226.

K El Madmad, 'Les Droits des femmes dans la Charte Africaine des Droits de l'Homme et des Peuples' (1993) *Afrique* 2000.

O Okere, 'The Protection of Human Rights in Africa and the African Charter on Human and People's Rights: Comparative Analysis with the European and American Systems' (1984) 6 *Human Rights Quarterly* 141.

ANNEX I

List of 53 states parties to the African Charter on Human and Peoples' Rights

(as of September 2009)

Algeria; Angola; Benin; Botswana; Burkina Faso; Burundi; Cameroon; Cape Verde; Central African Republic; Chad; Comoros; Congo; Côte d'Ivoire; Democratic Republic of Congo; Djibouti; Egypt; Equatorial Guinea; Eritrea; Ethiopia; Gabon; The Gambia; Ghana; Guinea; Guinea-Bissau; Kenya; Lesotho; Liberia; Libya; Madagascar; Malawi; Mali; Mauritania; Mauritius; Mozambique; Namibia; Niger; Nigeria; Rwanda; São Tomé and Principe; Senegal; Seychelles; Sierra Leone; Somalia; South Africa; Sudan; Swaziland; Tanzania; Togo; Tunisia; Uganda; Western Sahara (Sahrawi Arab Democratic Republic); Zambia; Zimbabwe.

ANNEX II

List of 25 states parties to the 1998 Protocol establishing the African HR Court

(as of September 2009)

Algeria, Burkina Faso,* Burundi, Comoros, Côte d'Ivoire, Gabon, Gambia, Ghana, Kenya, Lesotho, Libya, Malawi,* Mali, Mauritania, Mauritius, Mozambique, Niger, Nigeria, Rwanda, Senegal, South Africa, Tanzania, Togo, Tunisia, Uganda.

*States that have recognized the competence of the Court to admit petitions from individuals and NGOs.

ANNEX III

States that have ratified the 2003 African Court of Justice Protocol

(as of September 2009)

Algeria, Comoros, Egypt, Gabon, Gambia, Lesotho, Libya, Mali, Mauritius, Mozambique, Niger, Rwanda, South Africa, Sudan, Tanzania, Tunisia.

ANNEX IV

States that have ratified the 2008 ACJHR Protocol

(as of September 2009)*

Libya, Mali.

* The Protocol will enter into force upon the submission of 15 ratifications.

ANNEX V

The African Committee of Experts on the Rights and Welfare of the Child

INTRODUCTION

Name and seat of the body

The African Committee of Experts on the Rights and Welfare of the Child ('the Committee of Experts' or 'the Committee') is an expert body entrusted with monitoring compliance with the 1990 African Charter on the Rights and Welfare of the Child.[172] The Committee's Secretariat is located at:

Department of Social Affairs
Commission of the African Union
African Union Headquarters
PO Box 3243
Roosevelt Street (Old Airport Area)
W21K19 Addis Ababa
Ethiopia
Tel: (251) 11 551 35 22 (Direct)
Fax: + (251) 11 553 57 16
Email: dsocial@africa-union.org

Committee sessions generally take place at the AU headquarters in Addis Ababa, although the Committee may, and in fact has, convened in other locations.

General information

The Committee comprises 11 experts nominated by the states parties to the 1990 Charter and elected by the AU Assembly of Heads of State and Government.[173] The Committee has general awareness-raising and standard-setting mandates;[174] but it is also authorized to review periodic reports submitted by states parties.[175]

In addition, the Committee may receive communications from: 'any person, group or non-governmental organization recognized by the Organization of African Unity, by a Member State, or the United Nations', in relation to the 1990 Charter.[176] This complaint procedure is governed by the Committee's Rules of Procedure,[177] which refer in turn to more specific Guidelines.[178] According to the Guidelines, communications to the Committee would be deemed admissible only if submitted by a victim or on his or her behalf (though the victim's consent can sometimes be presumed).[179] Other conditions of admissibility generally mirror those controlling the submission of communications to the African Commission, such as: compatibility with the 1990 Charter and the AU Constitutive Act; alleged facts not based merely on media reports; absence of parallel international proceedings; exhaustion of local remedies; no excessive delay in submission; and use of inoffensive language.[180]

---

[172] Charter on Rights of the Child, *supra* note 55.

[173] Ibid, arts 33, 34. The current membership of the Committee is: Chair: Ms Seynabou Ndiaye Diakhate (Senegal); Vice-Chair: Ms Marie Chantal Koffi Appoh (Côte d'Ivoire); Members: Ms Boipelo Lucia Seitlhamo (Botswana); Ms Martha Koome (Kenya); Mrs Mamosebi T Pholo (Lesotho); Mr Moussa Sissoko (Mali); Mrs Dawlat Ibrahim Hassan (Egypt); Mr Cyprien Adébayo (Benin); Mrs Agnès Kabore (Burkina Faso); Mrs Andrianirainy Rasamoely (Madagascar); and Mrs Maryam Uwais (Nigeria).

[174] Charter on Rights of the Child, art 42.

[175] Ibid, art 43.

[176] Ibid, art 44.

[177] Rules of Procedure of the Committee of Experts on the Rights and Welfare of the Child, AU Doc Cmttee/ACRWC/II.Rev 2 (2003).

[178] Guidelines for the Consideration of Communications Provided for in Article 44 of the African Charter on the Rights and Welfare of the Child, AU Doc ACERWC/8/4 (2006).

[179] Ibid, Ch 2, art 1(I).

[180] Ibid, Ch 2, art 1(III).

Interestingly, the Committee may (in exceptional cases) address communications against AU member states not parties to the 1990 Charter, on the basis of other relevant human rights instruments.[181] The Guidelines authorize the Committee to delegate parts of the work relating to the review of communications (including follow-up) to a working group and/or a rapporteur.[182] Review procedures are generally confidential.[183] According to the Guidelines, the Committee may also issue provisional measures to prevent harm to potential or actual child victims.[184] Finally, the Guidelines encourage the participation of the children (those concerned by the communication) in the process.[185] So far, the Committee has been presented with very few communications, and has not issued decisions in relation to any of them.[186]

The 1990 Charter also provides for a process of investigation into country situations,[187] and the Committee has also issued Guidelines for conducting such investigations, which provide for on-site missions.[188] This procedure has not been used to date.

List of 45 States Parties to the African Charter on the Rights and Welfare of the Child (as of September 2009)

Algeria; Angola; Benin; Botswana; Burkina Faso; Burundi; Cameroon; Cape Verde; Chad; Comoros; Congo; Côte d'Ivoire; Egypt;* Equatorial Guinea; Eritrea; Ethiopia, Gabon; The Gambia; Ghana; Guinea; Guinea-Bissau; Kenya; Lesotho; Liberia; Libya; Madagascar; Malawi; Mali; Mauritania; Mauritius; Mozambique; Namibia; Niger; Nigeria; Rwanda; Senegal; Seychelles; Sierra Leone; South Africa; Sudan; Tanzania; Togo; Uganda; Zambia; Zimbabwe.

* States who have excluded through reservation the power of the Committee to review communications lodged against them (see <http://www.crin.org/RM/acrwc.asp>)

Select bibliography

Books

J Sloth-Nielsen, *Children's Rights in Africa* (2008).

Articles

J Sloth-Nielsen and B D Mezmur, 'Win Some, Lose Some: The 10th Ordinary Session of the African Committee of Experts on the Rights and Welfare of the Child' (2008) 8 (1) *African Human Rights Law Journal* 207.

---

[181] Ibid, Ch 2, art 1(II).
[182] Ibid, Ch 2, art 2(II), Ch 3, art 4.
[183] Ibid, Ch 3, art 3(I).
[184] Ibid, Ch 2, art 2(IV).
[185] Ibid, Ch 3, art 3.
[186] M Affa'a Mindzie, 'Regional Protection of Child Rights in Africa' (2007) *Pambazuka News*, Issue No 328, <http://pambazuka.org/en/category/comment/44416>.
[187] Charter on Rights of the Child, art 45.
[188] Guidelines for the Conduct of Investigation Provided for in Article 55 of the African Charter on the Rights and Welfare of the Child, AU Doc ACERWC/8/5 (2006) (a French Version is available at <http://www.africa-union.org/child/Autres%20documents/Directives%20 Enquetes%20-%20Final%20-%20French.pdf>).

B D Mezmur, 'The African Committee of Experts on the Rights and Welfare of the Child: An Update' (2006) 6 *African Human Rights Law Journal* 549.

A Lloyd, 'How to Guarantee Credence: Recommendations and Proposals for the African Committee of Experts on the Rights and Welfare of the Child' (2004) 12 *The International Journal of Children's Rights* 21–40.

C F J Doebbler, 'A Complex Ambiguity: The Relationship between the African Commission on Human and Peoples Rights and other African Union Initiatives Affecting Respect for Human Rights' (2003) 13 *Transnational Law and Contemporary Problems* 7.

A Lloyd, 'Evolution of the African Charter on the Rights and Welfare of the Child and the African Committee of Experts: Raising the Gauntlet' (2002) 10 *The International Journal of Children's Rights* 179.

14

THE HUMAN RIGHTS COMMITTEE

Introduction

Name and seat of the body

The Human Rights Committee (HRC or 'the Committee') is an independent expert **14.1**
body established to monitor compliance with the International Covenant on Civil
and Political Rights (ICCPR).[1] It is located in the UN headquarters in Geneva:

Human Rights Committee
Office of the High Commissioner for Human Rights
Palais des Nations, United Nations
8–14 Avenue de la Paix
1211 Geneva 10
Switzerland
Tel: (41) 22 917 9000
Fax: (41) 22 917 9022
Website: <http://www.unhchr.ch>

General description

The HRC was established under the 1966 ICCPR, which entered into force in **14.2**
1976. It is an independent expert body, entrusted with powers of supervision
over the implementation of the ICCPR, which has been ratified by 164 states.

---

[1] International Covenant on Civil and Political Rights, 16 December 1966, art 28, UN GA
Res 2200 A (XXI), GAOR, 21st Session, Supp No 16 (A/6316) 52, reprinted in UN Doc A/
CONF 32/4 ('ICCPR').

The HRC reports to the General Assembly of the UN (through the Economic and Social Council), conducts its sessions in UN facilities, is financed by the UN budget, and receives all administrative services from the UN Office of the High Commissioner for Human Rights.

The Committee serves three main functions. It receives periodic reports from the states parties to the ICCPR on their compliance with the human rights standards set out in the Covenant and issues observations therein. It also issues 'general comments' on the provisions of the Covenant.[2] In addition, the HRC may receive communications from individuals and/or states alleging violations of human rights by states parties to the ICCPR that have accepted the competence of the HRC to review such petitions.[3] So far 113 states have accepted the jurisdiction of the HRC to receive individual communications and 48 states have authorized the HRC to receive inter-state complaints. The procedure for dealing with communications is essentially quasi-judicial (in inter-state cases, the HRC may also provide its good offices in an attempt to find an amicable solution or facilitate conciliation). The HRC admits evidence, receives submissions, and makes its views available to the parties. These views are not binding upon the states parties.

To date the HRC has received 1,871 individual complaints. It has considered communications on their merits and issued its views on some 667 cases, finding a breach of the ICCPR in 531 cases (80 per cent of the time). The rest of the communications have been found inadmissible, were discontinued, or are still pending before the HRC. By contrast, no inter-state communication has ever been lodged with the HRC.

Institutional Aspects

Governing texts

Procedural law

14.3   The principal texts governing the structure, responsibilities, and competence of the HRC are the ICCPR and the Optional Protocol. The Optional Protocol authorizes the HRC to address individual communications and outlines the procedure for handling such complaints. As indicated above, the Optional Protocol has been adopted by 113 of the states parties to the ICCPR. Other rules governing the work of the HRC are to be found in the HRC Rules of Procedure.[4]

---

[2] ICCPR, art 40.

[3] Ibid, art 40; Optional Protocol to the International Covenant on Civil and Political Rights, UN GA Res 2200 A (XXI), GAOR, 21st Session, Supp No 16 (A/6316) 59 ('Optional Protocol').

[4] Rules of Procedure of the Human Rights Committee, UN Doc CCPR/C/3/Rev 8, 22 September 2005 ('Rules of Procedure').

Substantive law

The substantive law to be applied by the HRC comprises the human rights provisions found in Parts I–III of the ICCPR. Additionally, for the 71 states parties that have adopted the Second Optional Protocol on Abolishing the Death Penalty, the provisions of that Protocol will also be applicable.[5] **14.4**

Organization

Composition

The HRC comprises 18 independent experts, who are nationals of different states parties to the ICCPR.[6] The members of the Committee are nominated and elected by the states parties (each party may nominate two of its nationals) for a renewable period of four years.[7] They should be persons of high moral character having recognized competence in the area of human rights.[8] The composition of the entire Committee should reflect equitable geographical distribution and represent the variety of forms of civilization and legal systems;[9] it is also desirable that some members will have a legal background.[10] **14.5**

The Committee elects from within its members a Bureau consisting of a Chairman, three Vice-Chairmen, and a Rapporteur.[11] (The officers serve a renewable two-year term.)[12] The Committee meets three times a year in either Geneva or New York for three-week sessions.

Disqualification of Committee members HRC members are expected not to participate in a case involving an individual communication if he or she has a personal interest or previous involvement in the case in any capacity.[13] In this event, the member is to withdraw voluntarily or be removed from sitting on that case, by a decision of the Committee.[14] **14.6**

---

[5] Second Optional Protocol to the International Covenant on Civil and Political Rights, Aiming at the Abolition of the Death Penalty, 15 December 1989, GA Res 128 (44), UN Doc A/RES/44/128.

[6] ICCPR, arts 28, 31(1). The current membership of the HRC is Mr Abdelfattah Amor (Tunisia); Mr Mohammed Ayat (Morocco); Mr Lazhari Bouzid (Algeria); Mr Prafullachandra Natwarlal Bhagwati (India); Ms Christine Chanet (France); Mr Ahmad Amin Fathalla (Egypt); Mr Yuji Iwasawa (Japan); Ms Helen Keller (Switzerland); Mr Rajsoomer Lallah (Mauritius); Mr Zonke Zanele Majodina (South Africa); Ms Iulia Antoanella Motoc (Romania); Mr Michael O'Flaherty (Ireland); Mr Jose Luis Perez Sanchez-Cerro (Peru); Mr Rafael Rivas Posada (Columbia); Sir Nigel Rodley (UK); Mr Fabián Omar Salvioli (Argentina); Mr Krister Thelin (Sweden); Ms Ruth Wedgwood (US).

[7] ICCPR, arts 29, 30(4), 32(1).

[8] Ibid, art 28(2).

[9] Ibid, art 31(2).

[10] Ibid, art 28(2).

[11] Rules of Procedure, r 17.

[12] ICCPR, art 39(1); Rules of Procedure, r 18.

[13] Rules of Procedure, r 90(1).

[14] Ibid, rr 90(2), 91.

If a member of the Committee has ceased to carry his or her official functions as a member of the Committee, the other members may decide unanimously to remove him or her from office. In this case, the Chairman will notify the Secretary-General of the UN accordingly, and the latter will declare the seat vacant.[15]

14.7 **Plenary/chambers** The HRC sits in plenary (a quorum of 12 members is required).[16] Nonetheless, the Committee may establish subsidiary bodies and delegate parts of its functions to such bodies.[17] For instance, the admissibility of individual communications to the HRC may be determined by a working group of five members (if the members of the working group decide so unanimously).[18]

Appellate structure

14.8 The ICCPR does not have an appellate structure and there is no avenue for recourse against recommendations of the HRC. Still, decisions on admissibility may be revisited at the request of the concerned state party.[19]

Technical/scientific experts

14.9 There is no explicit provision under the various instruments governing the work of the HRC that permits involvement by experts (other than the Committee members) in the proceedings.

Secretariat

14.10 Responsibility for administration of the HRC lies with the Secretary-General of the UN.[20] The Secretary-General provides the Committee with the staff and facilities that comprise the HRC's secretariat. Since 1997, overall responsibility for the administration of the HRC (and the other treaty bodies) has been assigned by the UN General Assembly to the Office of the High Commissioner for Human Rights.

The secretariat, *inter alia*, arranges for the meetings of the HRC;[21] receives communications to the Committee and registers them;[22] circulates documents between the members of the HRC;[23] requests additional information from the complainant (if necessary);[24] and informs the concerned parties of various procedural decisions taken by the Committee.[25]

---

[15] ICCPR, art 33(1); Rules of Procedure, r 13(1).
[16] ICCPR, art 39(2)(a); Rules of Procedure, r 37.
[17] Rules of Procedure, r 62.
[18] Ibid, rr 93(2), 95.
[19] Ibid, r 99(4).
[20] ICCPR, art 36; Rules of Procedure, r 23.
[21] Rules of Procedure, r 25.
[22] Ibid, r 75.
[23] Ibid, rr 76, 84–85.
[24] Ibid, r 86.
[25] Ibid, rr 81(2), 99(1).

Jurisdiction

Ratione personae

The HRC may receive communications relating to states parties that have **14.11**
accepted the jurisdiction of the Committee. Under the ICCPR and Optional
Protocol, a separate declaration is required for each of the two heads of jurisdiction of the HRC—ie those involving individual and inter-state communications.
The HRC may receive individual communications directed against states that
have accepted the Optional Protocol.[26] In addition, a declaration made by a state
party under article 41 of the ICCPR (recognizing the inter-state competence of
the Committee) enables the HRC to receive communications against that state,
if presented by another state which has also made an article 41 declaration.[27]

Individual communications may be brought only by individuals who are
subject to the jurisdiction of the state complained against and who claim to be
victims of a human rights violation under the Covenant.[28]

Ratione materiae

Communications to the HRC can address any violation of the rights enumerated **14.12**
in the ICCPR (in the case of individual communication)[29] or any failure to fulfil
the obligations of the ICCPR (in the case of an inter-state communication).[30]

A complaint against a state that has adopted the Second Optional Protocol
may also allege breach of a relevant provision thereunder (unless, upon ratification, the ratifying state has restricted the application of the communication
mechanism in cases involving the Second Optional Protocol).[31]

Ratione temporis

The HRC may only consider alleged violations of human rights that have **14.13**
occurred after the date of entry into force of the Covenant and the First Optional
Protocol for the state complained against (unless the alleged violation is one
which, despite occurring before this date, continues to have effects).[32]

---

[26] Optional Protocol, art 1.
[27] ICCPR, art 41(1).
[28] Ibid, arts 1, 2. See *Diergaardt v Namibia,* Comm No 760/1997, UN Doc CCPR/C/69/
D/760/1997 (2000) at para 10.3 ('there is no objection to a group of individuals, who claim to be
commonly affected, to submit a communication about alleged breaches of these rights'). See also
*A Group of Associations for the Defence of the Rights of Disabled and Handicapped Persons in Italy v
Italy*, Comm No 163/1984, GAOR, 39th Session, Supp No 40, at 198.
[29] Optional Protocol, art 1. But see *Lubicon Lake Band v Canada*, Comm No 167/1984, UN
Doc Supp No 40 (A/45/40) at 1 (1990) (individuals cannot submit claims alleging violations of
the right to self-determination provided for in article 1 of the ICCPR).
[30] ICCPR, art 41(1).
[31] Second Optional Protocol, arts 4, 5. No state has entered a reservation to that effect.
[32] See eg *Yurich v Chile*, Comm No 1078/2002, UN Doc CCPR/C/85/D/1078/2002 (2005).

The HRC can deal with any communication only after all available domestic remedies have been exhausted (unless such remedies are unreasonably prolonged).[33] The other temporal conditions governing the admissibility of complaints depend on whether the communication was lodged by an individual or a state. Where individual communications are involved, no limitation period is provided; however where inter-state communications are involved, a state may present a communication against another state only after the expiration of six months from the date of notifying the state complained against (in writing) that it has failed, in the opinion of the complainant, to give effect to a provision of the Covenant.[34]

Other international claims

14.14 An individual communication may be presented only if the same matter is not simultaneously pending before any another international procedure of investigation.[35] Several states have entered reservations extending the scope of the aforementioned *lis alibi pendens* reservation so as to also encompass communications raising a matter already addressed in proceedings that were concluded before other international procedures of investigation.[36]

Advisory jurisdiction

14.15 Generally speaking the HRC does not have an advisory jurisdiction. The Committee has, however, issued 33 'general comments' on the Covenant, which serve as important interpretative pronouncements on the meaning and scope of the provisions of the Covenant.[37]

Procedural Aspects

Languages

14.16 The official languages of the HRC are Arabic, Chinese, English, French, Russian, and Spanish (ie the official languages of the UN).[38] All official languages, except

---

[33] ICCPR, art 41(l)(c); Optional Protocol, arts 2, 5(2)(b).

[34] ICCPR, art 41(l)(a),(b).

[35] Optional Protocol, art 5(2)(a). This excludes procedures reviewing the general human rights situation in a particular country. The term 'same matter' has been construed by the Committee with some flexibility. See eg *Pallach v Spain,* Comm No 1074/2002, UN Doc CCPR/C/80/D/1074/2002 (2004) at para 6.2; *Glaziou v France,* Comm No 452/1991, UN Doc CCPR/C/51/D/452/1991 (1994) at para 7.2.

[36] See reservations by Croatia, Denmark, France, Germany, Iceland, Ireland, Italy, Luxembourg, Malta, Moldova, Norway, Poland, Romania, Russia, Slovenia, Spain, Sri Lanka, Sweden, Turkey, and Uganda.

[37] The general comments of the HRC are available at <http://www2.ohchr.org/english/bodies/hrc/comments.htm>.

[38] Rules of Procedure, r 28.

Chinese, are also the working languages of the Committee (but in actual practice only English, French, and Spanish are used). Discussions in the HRC are translated into all working languages. A person who addresses the Committee in a non-official language must arrange for translation into one of the working languages.[39]

Instituting proceedings

A case is brought before the HRC by way of a written communication. **14.17** Communications submitted by individuals under the Optional Protocol should include, *inter alia*, information on the author of the communication; the factual and legal basis of the claim; and information on compliance with admissibility requirements.[40] If the communication is lacking in details or is unclear, the Secretary-General of the UN may request additional information or clarifications from the author within a designated time frame.[41]

An inter-state communication alleging failure to comply with the Covenant should also include information on admissibility, including details on prior steps taken to ensure settlement of the dispute.[42]

Financial assistance

Financial assistance is not available for participants in HRC proceedings. **14.18**

Interim measures

In cases involving individual communications, the HRC may, at any time **14.19** during the proceedings, inform the state party concerned of the view of the Committee on whether interim measures are desirable in order to prevent irreparable damage to the alleged victim.[43] Although such recommendation is not formally binding upon the state party concerned, the HRC has held that state parties are required to adopt *appropriate measures* to give effect to the Views of the Committee, including on the 'desirability of interim measures of protection',[44] and are subject to an implicit obligation to refrain from taking 'any action that

---

[39] Ibid, rr 29, 30.
[40] Optional Protocol, art 5(2)(a); Rules of Procedure, r 86(1).
[41] Rules of Procedure, rr 84(2), 86(1), (2).
[42] Ibid, r 74.
[43] Ibid, r 92. Interim measures can be recommended even before a decision on admissibility has been taken. Furthermore, a member of the HRC that serves as Special Rapporteur on New Communications and Interim Measures may request the state party to refrain from adopting harmful measures before the Committee had the chance to review the request for interim measures. According to the jurisprudence of the Committee, the irreparable nature of the harm in question should be determined on a case-by-case basis. *Stewart v Canada,* Comm No 538/1993, UN Doc CCPR/C/58/D/538/1993 (1996) at para 7.7.
[44] *Bradshow v Barbados*, Comm No 489/1992, UN Doc CCPR/C/51/D/489/1992 (1994) at para 5.3. See also *Roberts v Barbados,* Comm No 504/1992 , UN Doc CCPR/C/51/D/504/1992 (1994) at para 6.3.

would prevent or frustrate the Committee in its consideration and examination of the communication'.[45] Furthermore, it held that the lawfulness of risk-creating measures that run contrary to interim measures issued by the Committee will be 'scrutinized in the strictest light'.[46] The upshot of this appears to be that failure to comply with interim measures is deemed by the HRC to constitute a violation of both the Covenant and the Optional Protocol.[47]

Preliminary proceedings

14.20 The Committee is to decide as soon as possible on the admissibility of the complaint.[48] In the case of individual communications, the question of admissibility is handled by the full Committee or by a working group of five or more members. The working group may unanimously declare a communication admissible or inadmissible. In the event of the latter occurrence, however, the declaration has to be confirmed by the Committee.[49] The Committee may also designate members as Special Rapporteurs on New Communications and Interim Measures to prepare the consideration of communications by the Committee.[50] The full Committee or working groups must confirm that:

(a) the communication is not anonymous and emanates from an individual (or individuals) who was subject at the relevant times to the jurisdiction of a state party to the Optional Protocol;

(b) the individual in question has sufficiently substantiated that he or she has been a victim of a violation by that state party of a human right prescribed by the Covenant—in cases where the alleged victim is unable to submit the communication himself or herself, the communication may be submitted on his or her behalf;

(c) the communication does not constitute an abuse of the right of submission;

(d) the communication is not incompatible with the provisions of the ICCPR;

---

[45] *Shukurova v Tajikistan*, Comm No 1044/2002, UN Doc CCPR/C/86/D/1044/2002 (2006) at para 6.1. See also *Weiss v Austria*, Comm No 1086/2002, UN Doc CCPR/C/77/D/1086/2002 (2002) at para 7.2. But see *Schedko v Belarus*, Comm No 886/1999, UN Doc CCPR/C/77/D/886/1999 (1999) at para 8.1 (execution of a complainant was not a violation per se of the Optional Protocol).

[46] *Ahani v Canada*, Comm No 1051/2002, UN Doc CCPR/C/80/D/1051/2002 (2004) at para 8.1.

[47] See *Piandiong v Philippines*, Comm No 869/1999, UN Doc CCPR/C/70/D/869/1999 (2000) at paras 5.1–5.2.

[48] ICCPR, art 41 (l)(c); Optional Protocol, art 5(2).

[49] Rules of Procedure, rr 93, 95(1).

[50] Ibid, r 95(3).

(e) the same matter is not the subject of another pending international procedure of investigation or settlement;

(f) the individual has exhausted all available domestic remedies, or the application of these remedies is unreasonably prolonged.[51]

Normally, the state party complained against will be requested to submit written explanations and statements addressing issues relating to both the admissibility and the merits of the communication, but in exceptional cases the Committee, the working group, or the special rapporteur can decide to request a written reply on admissibility only.[52] The state party that receives a request for a written reply (on admissibility or admissibility and merits) may apply in writing, within two months, for the communication to be rejected as inadmissible, setting out the grounds of inadmissibility. The Committee, the working group, or the special rapporteur may decide, because of the special circumstances of the case, to extend the time for the submission of the reply until the Committee has ruled on the question of admissibility.[53] In all events, if the Committee decides that a communication is inadmissible under the Protocol it shall communicate its decision through the Secretary-General to the author of the communication and the state party concerned, as soon as possible.[54]

In inter-state cases, the Committee must make the following determinations:

(a) that both involved states made appropriate declarations under article 41 of the ICCPR;

(b) that a six-month time limit from the date of the initial communication has expired; and

(c) that domestic remedies have been exhausted, as required by international law, or that their application is unreasonably prolonged.[55]

Written phase

Individual communications

After the communication has been received, the state complained against **14.21** will be given six months to submit written explanations or statements to the Committee.[56] The Committee, working group, or special rapporteur may request the state party or author of the communication to submit additional

---

[51] Optional Protocol, art 5(2), Rules of Procedure, r 96.
[52] Rules of Procedure, r 97(2).
[53] Ibid, r 97(3).
[54] Ibid, r 98(1).
[55] ICCPR, art 41(l)(c); Rules of Procedure, r 74. That latter rule also requires the states concerned to report on 'any other procedure of international investigation or settlement resorted to by the States parties concerned'. It is not clear whether this purports to introduce a new ground of inadmissibility in inter-state cases that is not mentioned in the Covenant.
[56] Rules of Procedure, r 97(2).

written information or observations relevant to the admissibility or merits of the communication within specified time limits.[57] Each party may also be given an opportunity to comment on submissions made by the other party (within separately fixed time limits).[58]

Inter-state communications

14.22 States which are parties to a dispute before the HRC may present written submissions on their behalf when the communication involving them is being considered.[59] The Committee will determine the procedure for making these submissions, after consulting with the parties.[60] Furthermore, during its handling of the communication, the Committee may request the involved states to supply it with additional relevant information, including written observations on their behalf.[61] Such requests will be made through the Secretary-General and will indicate a time limit for the submission of the information.

Oral phase

14.23 The parties to an inter-state case before the HRC are entitled to make oral representations before the Committee.[62] The Committee will determine the procedure for making such submissions, after having consulted with the parties.[63] The HRC may also request the introduction of additional oral information or observations by the parties, within fixed time limits.[64]

There are no provisions for oral proceedings under the Optional Protocol or the Rules of Procedure governing the consideration of individual communications. Meetings of the HRC in which communications are considered are not public.[65]

Third party intervention/multiple proceedings

14.24 The various instruments governing the work of the HRC do not provide for third party intervention. As to multiple proceedings, the Optional Protocol does not preclude the submission of communications by more than one person adversely affected by violation of human rights.[66] Furthermore, the Committee may consider two or more communications jointly, if it deems this to be appropriate.[67]

---

57 Ibid, r 97(4).
58 Ibid, r 91(6).
59 ICCPR, art 41(l)(g); Rules of Procedure, r 81(1).
60 Rules of Procedure, r 81(3).
61 ICCPR, art 41(1)(f); Rules of Procedure, r 80.
62 ICCPR, art 41(1)(g); Rules of Procedure, r 81(1).
63 Rules of Procedure, r 81(3).
64 Ibid, r 80.
65 ICCPR, art 41(1)(d); Optional Protocol, art 5(3); Rules of Procedure, rr 88, 102.
66 Optional Protocol, art 1.
67 Rules of Procedure, r 94(2).

Amicus curiae

There is no explicit provision in any of the relevant instruments permitting the **14.25** submission of *amicus curiae* briefs to the HRC. So far the Committee has not admitted submissions of this kind.

Representation of parties

The communication should be submitted personally by the individual claiming **14.26** to be a victim, or by that individual's representative. Additionally, a communication may be submitted on behalf of an alleged victim when it appears that the individual in question is unable to submit the communication personally.[68]

Decision

In relation to cases brought by individual complainants, the Committee will receive **14.27** information from the parties on both admissibility and merits and, after considering the communication in the light of all written information, it formulates its Views on the matter.[69] Normally, such Views include the details of the complaint; the submissions of the parties; any interim decisions taken by the Committee; the facts as proven before the Committee; conclusions as to whether any provisions of the ICCPR were violated; the legal reasoning; and, in some cases, an operative part indicating the actions necessary to restore compliance with the ICCPR. The Views of the Committee are not formally binding; still, the Committee has repeatedly conveyed to states the expectation that they take appropriate measures to give legal effect to its Views since they reflect the Committee's interpretation of the Covenant.[70]

In inter-state cases, the HRC must prepare a report within 12 months of the date in which the communication has been brought before it.[71] If a friendly settlement has been reached between the states parties involved in the proceedings, the report should briefly describe the facts of the case and the solution reached. If no solution was agreed upon, the report will state the facts of the case and will have attached to it the written and oral submissions of the parties. With the agreement of the parties, the HRC may appoint a Conciliation Committee to continue to deal with the dispute.[72]

The decisions of the HRC are taken by a majority of the members participating in the consideration of the communication[73] (although the HRC usually operates by way of consensus). Members of the HRC may append to the Views

---

[68] Ibid, r 96(b).
[69] Optional Protocol, art 5(4); Rules of Procedure, r 100(1).
[70] *Bradshow, supra* note 44, at para 5.3; *Roberts, supra* note 44, at para. 6.3.
[71] ICCPR, art 41(l)(h); Rules of Procedure, r 82(1).
[72] ICCPR, art 42; Rules of Procedure, r 83.
[73] ICCPR, art 39(2)(b); Rules of Procedure, r 51 (including note to rule 51).

of the Committee their individual opinions.[74] The Views of the Committee are communicated to the individual and to the state party concerned.[75]

Interpretation and revision of decisions

14.28   The relevant instruments regulating the work of the HRC do not permit requests for interpretation or revision of the Views of the Committee. Still, a communication declared inadmissible by the HRC may be resubmitted to the Committee if the reasons for inadmissibility are no longer applicable.[76] In the same vein, a finding of admissibility may be revisited on the basis of new information produced by the relevant state.[77]

Appeal

14.29   There is no avenue of appeal with respect to decisions of the HRC.

Costs

14.30   Proceedings before the HRC are free of charge. However, the parties must bear their own expenses.

Enforcement of decisions

14.31   The decisions of the Committee are not binding upon the parties, and as a result cannot be enforced without their consent. However, the HRC designates a Special Rapporteur for Follow-Up on Views to monitor the measures adopted by the relevant states parties to give effect to the Committee's Views.[78] The special rapporteur may make such contacts and take action as appropriate for the due performance of the follow-up mandate, and is to make such recommendations for further action by the Committee as may be necessary.

Evaluation

The HRC is the only active human rights complaints body with broad subject-matter jurisdiction and potentially universal reach: the ICCPR contains a catalogue of human rights, comparable in its scope to the list of rights protected under the European, Inter-American, and African human rights instruments. Furthermore, its membership includes states from across all regions of the world

---

[74] Rules of Procedure, r 100.
[75] Ibid, r 100(4).
[76] Rules of Procedure, r 98(2).
[77] Ibid, r 98(2).
[78] Ibid, r 101(1).

and has been steadily increasing over the years (113 states are now subject to its individual complaints jurisdiction—more than double the number subject to the jurisdiction of any regional court). Given these wide-ranging powers of jurisdiction and in view of the impressive stature of numerous Committee members (some of the world's most prominent international jurists and human rights experts have been members of the Committee at times), one would have expected the Committee to emerge as a central human rights complaints body. Still, the Committee has not, until now, been able to establish itself as a focal point for human rights adjudication on a par with the European Court of Human Rights. This relative failure is no doubt attributed in part to the non-binding nature of the Committee's Views, which rendered the Committee a merely quasi-judicial body (as opposed to a 'real court'). It may also relate to the optional nature of the jurisdiction of the Committee under the Optional Protocol, which limits the reach of the Committee in relation to many human rights violating states.

More serious constraints to the effectiveness of the Committee, however, can arguably be found not in the formal jurisdictional powers possessed by it, but rather in the procedures it has actually embraced: the transparency-deficit in the complaint process—in particular, the conduct of complaint-related business in closed sessions and the absence of oral proceedings—has reduced public awareness of the work of the Committee and has restricted its 'public shaming' effect. Moreover, the limited time resources allocated for dispensing with the Committee's business (nine weeks per year for review of individual complaints and state periodic reports and the drafting of general comments) constitute a serious practical hurdle that undercuts the Committee's potential impact. Hence, greater resource allocation to the Committee which would enable its continuous work, combined with a reform of the Rules of Procedure, could significantly improve the stature of the Committee.

Notwithstanding the aforementioned limitations, one can point to the increasing body of complaints referred to the Committee as an indication of the growing acknowledgement of its work and of increased confidence in its usefulness. The introduction of robust follow-up procedures seems to have contributed also to improvements in the level of compliance with the Committee's Views. Moreover, the jurisprudence of the Committee offers a source of rich and often innovative analysis of human rights issues, and is a key component in the human rights movement. In particular, one may note in this regard those decisions of the Committee which advanced an understanding of the extra-territorial scope of human rights obligations,[79] limited the possibility of applying the death penalty,[80] protected

---

[79] See eg *Burgos v Uruguay*, Comm No 52/1979, UN Doc CCPR/C/OP/1 at 88 (1984).

[80] See eg *Judge v Canada*, Comm No 829/1998, UN Doc CCPR/C/78/D/829/1998 (2003); *Ng v Canada*, Comm No 469/1991, UN Doc CCPR/C/49/D/469/1991 (1994); *Pratt v Jamaica*, Comm No 210/1986 and 225/1987, UN Doc Supp No 40 (A/44/40) at 222 (1989).

group rights and interests,[81] and promoted equality for disempowered groups in society, such as women and gays.[82]

REFERENCE

CASE REPORTS

The views of the Committee on the merits and admissibility of communications are normally made public.[83] They are published in the annual report of the HRC to the General Assembly of the UN (UN Doc Supp 40). The decisions can be found in *Selected Decisions under the Optional Protocol* (UN, 1985–) and in *Official Records of the Human Rights Committee* (UN, 1993–). Many decisions can be found on the University of Minnesota Human Rights Library website <http://wwrw.umn.edu/humanrts/undocs/undocs.htm> and in the *Oxford Reports on International Law*: <http://www.oxfordlawreports.com>.

SELECT BIBLIOGRAPHY

Books

Yearbook of the Human Rights Committee (UN, 1986–).

H J Steiner, P Alston, and R Goodman, *International Human Rights in Context: Law, Politics, Morals* (3rd edn, 2007).

R Burchill, S Davidson, and A Conte, *Defining Civil and Political Rights: The Jurisprudence of the United Nations Human Rights Committee* (2004).

S Joseph, Jenny Schultz, and Melissa Castan, *The International Covenant on Civil and Political Rights: Cases, Materials, and Commentaries* (2nd edn, 2004).

W Vandenhole, *The Procedures before the UN Human Rights Treaty Bodies: Divergence or Convergence?* (2004).

A F Bayefsky, *How to Complain to the UN Human Rights Treaty System* (2003).

M O'Flaherty, *Human Rights and the United Nations: Practice before the Treaty Bodies* (1996).

M Nowak, *A Commentary on the UN Covenant on Civil and Political Rights* (1993).

D McGoldrick, *The Human Rights Committee* (1991).

P R Gandhi, *The Human Rights Committee and the Right of Individual Communication: Law and Practice* (1988).

M J Bossuyt, *Guide to the 'Travaux Preparatories' of the International Covenant on Civil and Political Rights* (1987).

Articles

R C Blitt, 'Who Will Watch the Watchdogs? Human Rights Nongovernmental Organizations and the Case for Regulation' (2005) 10 *Buff Hum Rts L Rev* 261.

---

[81] See eg *Faurisson v France*, Comm No 550/1993, UN Doc CCPR/C/58/D/550/1993(1996); *Lubicon Lake Band, supra* note 29.

[82] See eg *Toonen v Australia*, Comm No 488/1992, UN Doc CCPR/C/50/D/488/1992 (1994); *Aumeeruddy-Cziffra v Mauritius*, Comm No 35/1978, GAOR 36th Sess, Supp No 40 (A/36/40), annex XIII (1981). But see *Joslin v New Zealand*, Comm No 902/1999, UN Doc A/57/40 at 214 (2002).

[83] Rules of Procedure, r 102.

H J Steiner, 'Individual Claims in a World of Massive Violations: What Role for the Human Rights Committee?' in P Alston and K Crawford (eds), *The Future of UN Human Rights Treaty Monitoring* (2000) 15.

S Davidson, 'The Procedure and Practice of the Human Rights Committee under the First Optional Protocol on Civil and Political Rights' (1991) 4 *Canterbury Law Review* 337.

A De Zayas, J T Moller, and T Opsahl, 'Application of the International Covenant on Civil and Political Rights under the Optional Protocol by the Human Rights Committee' (1989) 26 *Comparative Judicial Review* 3.

P R Gandhi, 'The Human Rights Committee and the Right of Individual Petition' (1986) 57 *British Yearbook of International Law* 173.

D Shelton, 'Individual Complaint Machinery under the United Nations 1503 Procedure and the Optional Protocol to the International Covenant on Civil and Political Rights' in H Hannum (ed), *Guide to International Human Rights Practices* (1984).

P S Brar, 'The Practice and Procedures of the Human Rights Committee under the Optional Protocol of the International Covenant on Civil and Political Rights' (1983) 26 *Indian Journal of International Law* 506.

K Das, 'United Nations Institutions and Procedures Founded on Conventions on Human Rights and Fundamental Freedoms' in K Vasak and P Alston (eds), *The International Dimension of Human Rights* (1982).

A H Robertson, 'The Implementation System: International Measures' in Louis Henkin (ed), *The International Bill of Rights: The Covenant on Civil and Political Rights* (1981).

ANNEX

List of 165 states parties to the ICCPR

(as of September 2009)

Afghanistan, Albania, Algeria, Andorra, Angola, Argentina, Armenia, Australia, Austria, Azerbaijan, Bahamas, Bahrain, Bangladesh, Barbados, Belarus, Belgium, Belize, Benin, Bolivia, Bosnia and Herzegovina, Botswana, Brazil, Bulgaria, Burkina Faso, Burundi, Cambodia, Cameroon, Canada, Cape Verde, Central African Republic, Chad, Chile, Colombia, Congo, Costa Rica, Côte d'Ivoire, Croatia, Cyprus, Czech Republic, Democratic Republic of the Congo, Denmark, Djibouti, Dominica, Dominican Republic, Ecuador, Egypt, El Salvador, Equatorial Guinea, Eritrea, Estonia, Ethiopia, Finland, France, Gabon, Gambia, Georgia, Germany, Ghana, Greece, Grenada, Guatemala, Guinea, Guyana, Haiti, Honduras, Hungary, Iceland, India, Indonesia, Iran, Iraq, Ireland, Israel, Italy, Jamaica, Japan, Jordan, Kazakhstan, Kenya, Democratic People's Republic of Korea, Kuwait, the Kyrgyz Republic, Laos, Latvia, Lebanon, Lesotho, Liberia, Libya, Liechtenstein, Lithuania, Luxembourg, the former Yugoslav Republic of Macedonia, Madagascar, Malawi, Maldives, Mali, Malta, Mauritania, Mauritius, Mexico, Monaco, Mongolia, Montenegro, Morocco, Mozambique, Namibia, Nepal, Netherlands, New Zealand, Nicaragua, Niger, Nigeria, Norway, Panama, Papua New Guinea, Paraguay, Peru, Philippines, Poland, Portugal, Republic of Korea, Republic of Moldova, Romania, Russian Federation, Rwanda, Saint Vincent and the Grenadines, Samoa, San Marino, Senegal, Serbia, Seychelles, Sierra Leone,

Slovakia, Slovenia, Somalia, South Africa, Spain, Sri Lanka, Sudan, Suriname, Swaziland, Sweden, Switzerland, Syria, Tajikistan, Thailand, Timor-Leste, Togo, Trinidad and Tobago, Tunisia, Turkey, Turkmenistan, Uganda, Ukraine, United Kingdom, United Republic of Tanzania, United States, Uruguay, Uzbekistan, Vanuatu, Venezuela, Vietnam, Yemen, Zambia, and Zimbabwe.

ANNEX II

List of 113 states parties to the Optional Protocol

(as of September 2009)

Albania, Algeria, Andorra, Angola, Argentina, Armenia, Australia, Austria, Azerbaijan, Barbados, Belarus, Belgium, Benin, Bolivia, Bosnia and Herzegovina, Brazil, Bulgaria, Burkina Faso, Cameroon, Canada, Cape Verde, Central African Republic, Chad, Chile, Colombia, Congo, Costa Rica, Côte d'Ivoire, Croatia, Cyprus, Czech Republic, Democratic Republic of the Congo, Denmark, Djibouti, Dominican Republic, Ecuador, El Salvador, Equatorial Guinea, Estonia, Finland, France, Gambia, Georgia, Germany, Ghana, Greece, Guatemala, Guinea, Guyana, Honduras, Hungary, Iceland, Ireland, Italy, Kazakhstan, the Kyrgyz Republic, Latvia, Lesotho, Libya, Liechtenstein, Lithuania, Luxembourg, the former Yugoslav Republic of Macedonia, Madagascar, Malawi, Maldives, Mali, Malta, Mauritius, Mexico, Moldova, Mongolia, Montenegro, Namibia, Nepal, Netherlands, New Zealand, Nicaragua, Niger, Norway, Panama, Paraguay, Peru, Philippines, Poland, Portugal, Republic of Korea, Romania, Russian Federation, Saint Vincent and the Grenadines, San Marino, Senegal, Serbia, Seychelles, Sierra Leone, Slovakia, Slovenia, Somalia, South Africa, Spain, Sri Lanka, Suriname, Sweden, Tajikistan, Togo, Turkey, Turkmenistan, Uganda, Ukraine, Uruguay, Uzbekistan, Venezuela, and Zambia.

Note: Jamaica withdrew from the Optional Protocol in 1997.

ANNEX III

List of 48 states that made ICCPR, article 41 declarations accepting the competence of the HRC to receive inter-state complaints

(as of September 2009)

Algeria, Argentina, Australia, Austria, Belarus, Belgium, Bosnia and Herzegovina, Bulgaria, Canada, Chile, Congo, Croatia, Czech Republic, Denmark, Ecuador, Finland, Gambia, Germany, Ghana, Guyana, Hungary, Iceland, Ireland, Italy, Republic of Korea, Liechtenstein, Luxembourg, Malta, Netherlands, New Zealand, Norway, Peru, Philippines, Poland, Russian Federation, Senegal, Slovakia, Slovenia, South Africa, Spain, Sri Lanka, Sweden, Switzerland, Tunisia, Ukraine, United Kingdom, United States, and Zimbabwe.

15

OTHER UN TREATY BODIES

1. THE COMMITTEE ON THE ELIMINATION OF RACIAL DISCRIMINATION

Introduction

Name and seat of the body

The Committee on the Elimination of Racial Discrimination ('CERD **15.1.1**
Committee' or 'the Committee') is an independent expert body established to
monitor compliance with the 1965 International Convention on the Elimination
of All Forms of Racial Discrimination ('CERD').[1] It is located at the following
address:

> Committee on the Elimination of Racial Discrimination
> Centre for Human Rights
> Palais des Nations, United Nations
> 8–14 Avenue de la Paix
> 1211 Geneva 10
> Switzerland
> Tel: (41) 22 917 9000
> Fax: (41) 22 917 9022
> Website: <http://www.unhchr.ch>

---

[1] International Convention for Elimination of All Forms of Racial Discrimination, 21
December 1965, UN GA Res 2106A (XX), GAOR, 12th Session, Supp No 14 (A/6014) 47, UN
Doc A/CONF 32/4 ('CERD').

General description

15.1.2 The CERD Committee began its operation in 1969, following the entry into force of CERD. States parties to the Convention agree to undertake appropriate measures to eliminate racial discrimination and promote understanding between different races. The CERD Committee is entrusted with monitoring compliance of the 173 states parties with the provisions of CERD.

The Committee comprises 18 independent experts elected by states parties for four-year terms.[2] It examines periodic reports of states parties describing their implementation of CERD and submits general suggestions and recommendations to the General Assembly of the UN.[3] In addition, the Committee may address complaints presented against states parties to CERD by other states, and in some cases may consider complaints lodged by individuals or groups of individuals.[4] The complaints procedures involve quasi-judicial investigation of allegations of non-compliance with the Convention, which results in the preparation of a report by the CERD Committee containing non-binding recommendations. The work of the CERD Committee is governed by Part II of CERD, and by the Rules of Procedure adopted by the Committee.[5] According to the Rules, complaint proceedings are generally closed to the public.[6] The official languages of the CERD Committee are Chinese, English, French, Russian, and Spanish (all but Chinese are also working languages).[7] The administrative needs of the Committee are provided by the Secretary-General of the UN (through the Office of the High Commissioner for Human Rights);[8] the UN also provides its premises for the sessions of the Committee.[9]

Individual Communications

15.1.3 Since 1982 the CERD Committee has been authorized to receive communications from individuals and groups of individuals who claim to be victims of a

---

[2] CERD, art 8. The current membership is Mr Jens Hartig Danielsen (Denmark), Mr Mahmoud Abdoul-Nasr (Egypt), Mr Noureddine Amir (Algeria), Mr Alexai S Avtonomov (Russia), Mr José Francisco Cali Tzay (Guatemala), Ms Fatimata-Binta Victoria Dah (Burkina-Faso), Mr Ion Diaconu (Romania), Mr Kokou Mawuena Ika Kana (Togo), Mr Régis de Gouttes (France), Mr Huang Yong'an (China), Mr Anwar Kemal (Pakistan), Mr Dilip Lahiri (India), Mr José Augusto Lindgren Alves (Brazil), Mr Pastor Elias Murillo Martinez (Colombia), Mr Chris Maina Peter (Yanzania), Mr Pierre-Richard Prosper (US), Mr Linos-Alexander Siciliano (Greece), and Mr Patrick Thornberry (UK).

[3] CERD, art 9.

[4] Ibid, arts 11, 14.

[5] Rules of Procedure, as revised on 1 January 1989, UN Doc CERD/C/35/Rev 3 ('CERD Rules').

[6] Ibid, r 88.

[7] Ibid, r 26.

[8] CERD, art 10(3); CERD Rules, rr 21, 23.

[9] CERD, art 10(4); CERD Rules, r 5.

violation of CERD by a state party, to which jurisdiction they are subject.[10] Complaints can only be filed, however, against states that have accepted the competence of the Committee to receive individual communications by way of a declaration deposited with the UN Secretary-General. To date, 53 states have made such a declaration.

Any state party which makes a declaration accepting the competence of the Committee to hear individual complaints may establish or indicate a national body competent to receive communications alleging violations of CERD after all other domestic remedies have been exhausted. Where such national bodies exist, the complainant may only bring the case before the CERD Committee if the designated national body has failed to resolve the matter.[11] The complainant should bring the case before the CERD Committee within six months from the exhaustion of domestic remedies or, where a body has been designated to hear such complaints, six months from the failure of that body to resolve the matter.

The Committee must first ascertain the admissibility of the communication, the conditions for which are:[12] (i) it is not anonymous; (ii) it emanates from individuals subject to the jurisdiction of a state party that has made a declaration under article 14 (accepting the competence of the Committee to receive such communications); (iii) the individual complainant claims to be a victim of a violation of CERD (but in exceptional cases the communication can be submitted on behalf of such a victim); (iv) the communication is compatible with the provisions of CERD; (v) it is not an abuse of right; (vi) the individual has exhausted all domestic remedies (including the national review body), except when their application is unreasonably prolonged; and (vii) the communication was submitted within six months of the exhaustion of domestic remedies (except in the event of exceptional circumstances).

The Committee may request additional information, clarifications, and observations related to the question of admissibility from the parties.[13] If it finds the communication to be admissible, it will give the state party an opportunity to submit, within three months, its written observations and statements on the matter (including information on possible remedies); the individual will then be given the opportunity to respond to the state's contentions.[14] If deemed necessary, the Committee may invite the petitioner and the state concerned to appear before the Committee and provide additional information or answers to

---

[10] CERD, art 14(1). The Committee became competent to review individual communications immediately after ten states declared their acceptance of this power of the Committee. Ibid, art 14(9).

[11] Ibid, art 14(2), (5).

[12] Ibid, art 14(2), (5), (6)(a), (7)(a); CERD Rules, r 91.

[13] CERD Rules, r 92. A communication cannot be declared admissible unless the state complained against was given an opportunity to comment upon it.

[14] CERD, art 14(6); CERD Rules, r 94(1), (2), (4).

questions.[15] The Committee will then formulate its opinion on the case, taking into consideration all relevant information presented to it. The opinion will contain the suggestions and recommendations of the Committee, and the state party will be invited to inform the Committee, at a later date, on whether it has taken measures to implement the Committee's views.[16] A summary of the submissions of the parties and the opinion of the Committee is published in the Committee's annual report to the General Assembly and in press communiqués.[17]

To date the Committee has received 45 individual communications (almost half of them against a single country—Denmark). Of these 45 complaints, 17 were declared inadmissible, and four active complaints are still pending. The Committee found violations of CERD in ten out of the 29 cases on which it issued a report on the merits.

Inter-State Communications

15.1.4   Any state party to CERD may bring a complaint against any other state party, which has allegedly failed to give effect to the provisions of the Convention (without need for an additional manifestation of consent by the respondent state).[18] The communication is then to be transmitted to the state complained against, and the latter must provide written explanations or statements to the CERD Committee within three months from receiving the complaint.[19] In the event that the states concerned have been unable to settle the dispute between them within six months from the date on which the state complained against received the communication, either state may refer the matter again to the Committee.[20]

The Committee will address the matter only if available domestic remedies have been exhausted, or their application is unreasonably prolonged.[21] It may request further information from the states concerned[22] and it must invite them to participate in the sessions in which the communication is being considered.[23] After verifying the admissibility of the communication, the Committee is to refer

---

[15]   CERD Rules, r 94(5).

[16]   CERD, art 14(7)(b); CERD Rules, r 95.

[17]   CERD, art 14(8); CERD Rules, rr 96, 97. Selected opinions are published on the CERD Committee's website.

[18]   CERD, art 11(1).

[19]   Ibid; CERD Rules, r 69. The Rules suggest that the Committee may decide not to transfer the communication for comments in an appropriate case (eg when the complaint is patently ill-founded).

[20]   CERD, art 11(2).

[21]   Ibid, art 11(3).

[22]   Ibid, art 11(4); CERD Rules, r 70.

[23]   CERD, art 11(5); CERD Rules, r 71.

the case to a five-member ad hoc conciliation commission (comprising nationals of states parties other than the parties to the dispute; they may or may not be members of the Committee). The composition of the commission is to be agreed upon by the states parties concerned or, in the absence of such agreement, determined by the CERD Committee (which in this case elects five of its members to serve on the commission).[24] The commission will attempt to secure a friendly settlement of the dispute and, in the event of failure to reach a solution, it will send to the Committee a report containing its factual and legal findings.[25] The Committee will then forward the report to the parties, and they must declare to the Committee within three months whether they intend to comply with the recommendations of the commission.[26] After the expiry of three months, the Chairman of the Committee will circulate the commission's report and the declarations of the states parties concerned to all states parties to CERD.[27] Ongoing inter-state disputes may then be referred to the ICJ for judicial settlement.[28] So far there have been no inter-state cases under this procedure.

REFERENCE

SOURCES OF CASE LAW, INCLUDING CASE REPORTS

Relevant materials can be found on the Committee website, on the University of Minnesota Human Rights Library website, and on the Netherlands Institute for Human Rights Documentation website.

SELECT BIBLIOGRAPHY

Books

W Vandenhole, *The Procedures before the UN Human Rights Treaty Bodies: Divergence or Convergence?* (2004).

S Pritchard and N Sharp, *Petitioning the CERD Committee: Individual Complaints under the Racial Discrimination Convention* (1998).

M Banton, *International Action against Racial Discrimination* (1996).

UN Centre for Human Rights, *The Committee on the Elimination of Racial Discrimination* (1991).

N Lerner, *The UN Convention on the Elimination of All Forms of Racial Discrimination* (1980).

---

[24] CERD, art 12(1), (2); CERD Rules, rr 72–74.
[25] CERD, arts 12(l)(a), 13(1).
[26] Ibid, art 13(2); CERD Rules, r 78(1), (2).
[27] CERD, art 13(3); CERD Rules, r 78(3).
[28] CERD, art 22.

Articles

P Thronberry, 'Confronting Racial Discrimination: A CERD Perspective' *Human Rights Law Review* (2005) 5 *Hum Rts L Rev* 239.

W Felice, 'The UN Committee on the Elimination of all Forms of Racial Discrimination: Race and Economic and Social Human Rights' (2002) 24 *Human Rights Quarterly* 205–236.

S Pritchard, 'Breaking the National Sound Barrier: Communicating with the CERD and CAT Committees' (1999) *Australian Journal of Human Rights* 23.

ANNEX

List of 173 states parties to CERD

(as of September 2009)

Afghanistan, Albania, Algeria,* Andorra,* Antigua and Barbuda, Argentina,* Armenia, Australia,* Austria,* Azerbaijan,* Bahamas, Bahrain, Bangladesh, Barbados, Belarus, Belgium,* Belize, Benin, Bhutan, Bolivia,* Bosnia and Herzegovina, Botswana, Brazil,* Bulgaria,* Burkina Faso, Burundi, Cambodia, Cameroon, Canada, Cape Verde, Central African Republic, Chad, Chile,* China, Colombia, Comoros, Congo, Costa Rica,* Côte d'Ivoire, Croatia, Cuba, Cyprus,* Czech Republic,* Democratic Republic of the Congo, Denmark,* Dominican Republic, Ecuador,* Egypt, El Salvador, Equatorial Guinea, Eritrea, Estonia, Ethiopia, Fiji, Finland,* France,* FYROM,* Gabon, Gambia, Georgia,* Germany,* Ghana, Greece, Guatemala, Guinea, Guyana, Haiti, Holy See, Honduras, Hungary,* Iceland,* India, Indonesia, Iran, Iraq, Ireland,* Israel, Italy,* Jamaica, Japan, Jordan, Kazakhstan*, Kenya, Korea,* Kuwait, Kyrgyzstan, Laos, Latvia, Lebanon, Lesotho, Liberia, Libya, Liechtenstein,* Lithuania, Luxembourg,* Madagascar, Malawi, Maldives, Mali, Malta,* Mauritania, Mauritius, Mexico,* Moldova, Monaco,* Mongolia, Montenegro,* Morocco,* Mozambique, Namibia, Nepal, Netherlands,* New Zealand, Nicaragua, Niger, Nigeria, Norway,* Oman, Pakistan, Panama, Papua New Guinea, Paraguay, Peru,* Philippines, Poland,* Portugal,* Qatar, Romania,* Russia,* Rwanda, Saint Kitts and Nevis, Saint Lucia, Saint Vincent and the Grenadines, San Marino,* Saudi Arabia, Senegal,* Serbia,* Seychelles, Sierra Leone, Slovakia,* Slovenia,* Solomon Islands, Somalia, South Africa,* Spain,* Sri Lanka, Sudan, Suriname, Swaziland, Sweden,* Switzerland,* Syria, Tajikistan, Tanzania, Timor-Leste, Togo, Tonga, Trinidad and Tobago, Tunisia, Turkey, Turkmenistan, Uganda, Ukraine,* United Arab Emirates, United Kingdom, United States of America, Uruguay,* Uzbekistan, Venezuela,* Vietnam, Yemen, Zambia, Zimbabwe.

* States that have recognized the competence of the CERD Committee to receive individual communications.

2. THE COMMITTEE AGAINST TORTURE

Introduction

Name and seat of the body

The UN Committee against Torture ('CAT Committee' or 'the Committee') **15.2.1** is authorized to monitor compliance with the UN Convention against Torture and other Cruel, Inhuman or Degrading Treatment or Punishment ('CAT'), to receive applications from complainants in respect of violations of the Convention and to conduct ex officio inquiries into the practice of torture. The CAT Committee is located at:

Committee against Torture
Centre for Human Rights
Palais des Nations, United Nations
8–14 Avenue de la Paix
1211 Geneva 10
Switzerland
Tel: (41) 22 917 9000
Fax: (41) 22 917 9022
Website: <http://www.unhchr.ch>

General description

CAT was concluded in 1984 and entered into force in 1987.[29] To date, 146 states **15.2.2** have ratified or acceded to the Convention (see Annex I). Under CAT, states

---

[29] Convention against Torture and other Cruel, Inhuman or Degrading Treatment or Punishment, 10 December 1984, CA Res 39/46, 39 UN GAOR Supp (No 51), UN Doc A/39/51, at 197 (1984), 23 ILM 1027 (1984).

have undertaken to take all measures to prevent torture in their territory and/or involving any person subject to their jurisdiction. The Convention provides for the establishment of the CAT Committee in order to monitor the compliance of the states parties with their obligations under CAT.[30]

The Committee comprises ten independent experts elected by the states parties to CAT for renewable four-year terms.[31] In electing experts, factors for consideration include geographical distribution and the usefulness of some members of the Committee having legal experience, as well as of their being serving members of the Human Rights Committee.[32] No more than one representative from any given state party may be included as a member of the Committee.

The Committee considers periodic reports submitted by the states parties on the measures taken by them to implement the Convention and may issue general comments thereon.[33] The Committee can also receive communications from individuals or from the states parties alleging non-compliance with CAT by a state party which has accepted the jurisdiction of the CAT Committee to investigate such complaints.[34] In addition, where it has received information from reliable sources indicating that torture may be systematically practised, the Committee may investigate the situation.[35] A 2002 Optional Protocol also establishes a Sub-Committee for regular monitoring of detention places that operates alongside the Committee.[36]

All investigatory procedures involve the exercise of quasi-judicial powers by the Committee and the formulation of its findings in the form of a non-binding report.

The procedure applied by the CAT Committee is governed by Part II of CAT and by the Rules of Procedure adopted by the Committee (recently amended in 2002). The Secretary-General of the UN provides the CAT Committee with secretarial services (through the Office of the High Commissioner for Human Rights) and the sessions of the Committee are held in UN facilities.[37] The official and working languages of the Committee are English, French, Russian, and

---

[30] Ibid, art 17.

[31] Ibid, art 17(1), (5). The current membership is Ms Essadia Belmir (Morocco), Ms Felice Gaer (US), Mr Luis Gallegos Chiriboga (Ecuador), Mr Abdoulaye Gaye (Senegal), Mr Claudio Grossman (Chile), Ms Myran Y Kleopas (Cyprus), Mr Alexander Kovalev (Russia), Mr Fernando Marino Menendez (Spain), Ms Nora Sveaass (Norway), and Mr Xuexian Wang (China).

[32] CAT, art 17(1), (2).

[33] Ibid, art 19. Although the Committee has no explicit power to issue general comments or recommendations addressed to all states parties, it has issued until now two general comments.

[34] Ibid, arts 21, 22.

[35] Ibid, art 20.

[36] Optional Protocol to the Convention against Torture and other Cruel, Inhuman or Degrading Treatment or Punishment, 18 December 2002, GA Res A/RES/57/199 (2002), 42 ILM (2003) 26.

[37] CAT, arts 18(3), 23; UN Doc CAT/C/3/Rev 4 as revised on 9 August 2002 ('CAT Rules'), rr 4, 21, 23.

Spanish.[38] The meetings of the CAT Committee in which communications or information on systematic practice of torture are considered are normally closed to the public.[39] The Committee generally holds two working sessions in Geneva every year, usually in April/May and November.[40]

Individual Communications (Article 22 Procedure)

The CAT Committee may receive communications from individuals subject to **15.2.3** the jurisdiction of a state party that has declared its acceptance of the competence of the Committee to receive individual complaints.[41] To date, 64 states have recognized the competence of the CAT Committee in this context (see Annex III).

A communication must be submitted to the Committee by or on behalf of any person who claims to be a victim of a violation of the CAT by the state complained against.[42] This includes a relative or designated representative of the victim or any other person when it appears that the alleged victim is unable to submit the communication and the author of the communication justifies his or her acting on the victim's behalf.[43]

The Committee must first determine whether the communication is admissible.[44] This entails verification that the complainant has exhausted domestic remedies (unless the exhaustion process is unreasonably prolonged or likely to be ineffective).[45] It will also require confirmation that another international dispute settlement procedure has not been invoked in relation to the same case. This appears not to refer to the non-conventional mechanisms of the UN, such as the special rapporteurs.[46] The Committee will not accept anonymous communications (although it may accept a request by the author of the communication to have his or her name withheld if so required by the circumstances).[47] The alleged

---

[38] CAT Rules, r 26.

[39] CAT, arts 20(5), 21(l)(d), 22(6); CAT Rules, rr 89, 101.

[40] CAT Rules, rr 2, 4.

[41] CAT, art 22(1).

[42] Ibid.

[43] CAT Rules, r 107(a).

[44] CAT, art 22(5); CAT Rules, r 107.

[45] If a communication is found inadmissible, it may be resubmitted later when the grounds for inadmissibility no longer apply. CAT Rules, r 110(2).

[46] See eg *Mutombo v Switzerland*, Comm No 13/1993, UN Doc A/49/44 at 45 (1994) (Committee acknowledging the work of UN Special Rapporteurs on the general situation in Congo, but conducting an independent assessment of the risk faced by the applicant).

[47] CAT, art 22(2); CAT Rules, r 98(2)(b). The other requirements of admissibility are that: the communication emanates from a person subject to the jurisdiction of a state that had recognized the competence of the Committee to receive individual communications; it is not an abuse of right; and it is not incompatible with the provisions of CAT. Ibid, r 107.

violation must have occurred after the date when article 22 of CAT came into force for the state concerned.

The Committee may then allocate the case to a member of the Committee who will serve as a rapporteur, seeking further information and referring the case to the state party concerned. If necessary, either the rapporteur or the Committee may request the state party to adopt interim measures to protect the interests of the alleged victim.[48] The Committee may require from the individual and state concerned additional information, clarifications, and observations on the issue of admissibility.[49]

The state concerned is normally expected to submit its observations and state-ments on the merits of the communication within six months from the date it was notified of its submission.[50] The author of the communication will then be given the opportunity to respond to the state's submissions. The Committee may invite the individual and state concerned to appear before it to provide clarifi-cations or answer questions.[51] It can also address matters which it considers of relevance, notwithstanding the fact that no submissions as to such matters have been made by the parties. The Committee may also refer to information sup-plied to it by UN bodies or specialized agencies which may assist in the disposal of the case, and may also consider information provided by NGOs.[52]

After receiving the submissions of the parties, the Committee formulates its decision on the matter. Although the Committee's practice is to do so by con-sensus, members may append summaries of their individual views to those of the Committee.[53] The decision will be forwarded to the parties to the dispute, and the Committee may subsequently invite the state concerned to report on whether it has implemented the decision (although it is not formally binding).[54] Summaries of the submissions of the parties and the views of the Committee are published in its annual report to the states parties to CAT and to the General Assembly.[55]

So far the CAT Committee has dealt with 391 individual communications (more than half of them submitted against one of three countries—Canada, Sweden, and Switzerland). In 158 of these cases, the Committee submitted its

---

[48] CAT Rules, rr 108, 110(3). Although not formally binding, the Committee has held that states are expected to cooperate in good faith with the CAT communications procedure, includ-ing with interim measures requested. *TPS v Canada*, Comm No 99/1997, UN Doc CAT/C/24/ D/99/1997 (2000) at para 15.6.

[49] CAT Rules, r 109(5).

[50] CAT, art 22(3); CAT Rules, r 109.

[51] CAT Rules, r 111(4).

[52] Ibid, r 62.

[53] CAT, art 22(7); CAT Rules, r 113.

[54] CAT, art 22(7); CAT Rules, r 112(5). A member of the Committee may serve as rapporteur for follow-up procedures and recommend to the Committee follow-up measures. Ibid, r 114.

[55] CAT, art 24; CAT Rules, r 115. Selected views are published on the CAT Committee's website and at <http://www.umn.edu/homanrts/catdecisions.html/>.

Views on the merits (finding a violation only on 48 occasions); 148 cases were found inadmissible or discontinued; and 85 cases are still pending.

Inter-State Communications (Article 21 Procedure)

A state party to CAT may present to the Committee a communication against **15.2.4** another state party if both states have accepted, by way of declaration, the jurisdiction of the CAT Committee to receive inter-state complaints.[56] To date, 60 states have accepted the jurisdiction of the Committee in this context (see Annex II). The communication must allege that the respondent state has failed to fulfil its obligations under CAT. The complaining state must initially forward the complaint to the state complained against, and the latter is to respond in writing within three months. If no friendly settlement is reached within six months from the date on which the initial communication was received by the respondent state, either state may refer the matter to the CAT Committee.[57] The Committee must verify the admissibility of the complaint before considering the merits of the case. In this regard, the Committee will especially consider whether the complainant has exhausted all domestic remedies (unless the exhaustion process is unreasonably prolonged or likely to be ineffective).[58]

The CAT Committee will offer its good offices to the parties, with a view to facilitating amicable settlement based on respect for the obligations under CAT, and may establish an ad hoc conciliation commission for this purpose.[59] The parties are entitled to make oral and/or written submissions before the Committee, which may request from the parties additional information or observations, orally or in writing.[60] Within 12 months from the date on which the dispute was referred to the CAT Committee, the Committee will publish a report; where no settlement was reached this will contain a brief statement of facts, the written submissions, and a summary of the oral submissions of the parties.[61] Where settlement is reached, the report is limited to a brief statement of the facts and the solution reached. The report will then be communicated to the states parties concerned. Unsettled inter-state disputes may eventually be submitted to arbitration, or to the ICJ.[62]

No inter-state cases have been considered before the CAT Committee so far.

---

[56] CAT, art 21(1).

[57] Ibid, art 21(l)(a), (b).

[58] Ibid, art 21(l)(c); CAT Rules, r 91.

[59] CAT, art 21(1)(e); CAT Rules, r 92.

[60] CAT, art 21(l)(f), (g); CAT Rules, rr 93, 94.

[61] CAT, art 21(l)(h); CAT Rules, r 95. If a solution was found, the report will indicate its terms.

[62] CAT, art 30.

Investigation of Systematic Practice of Torture
(Article 20 Procedure)

15.2.5 The CAT Committee may also investigate allegations of the systematic practice of torture in the territory of any state party without being prompted by a formal complaint. If reliable information on the existence of such a situation is brought to the attention of the Committee by any source, it may initiate examination of the matter and invite the state concerned to submit its observations within a limited period.[63] The exhaustion of domestic remedies is not required before such allegations may be submitted to the Committee.[64] The Committee may obtain additional information from a variety of sources (eg intergovernmental organizations, NGOs, and individuals).[65] Where necessary, the Committee may authorize one or more of its members to conduct a confidential inquiry.[66]

In conducting the inquiry, the Committee shall seek the cooperation of the state party concerned.[67] The inquiry may include, with the consent of the state concerned, a visit to the territory of the state concerned and hearings of witnesses and other individuals.[68] The Committee may request the concerned government to ensure that there is no interference with such proceedings and no intimidation of any witnesses.[69] The findings of the inquiry are then presented to the Committee, which subsequently examines and then transmits them along with its own comments and suggestions, where appropriate, to the state concerned. In addition, the Committee may invite the state party to suggest any action which it might take.[70] A summary account of the investigatory proceedings may be published in the annual report of the Committee to the General Assembly.[71] Proceedings remain confidential until this stage.[72] Upon signature, ratification, or accession to CAT, a state may declare that it does not recognize the competence of the CAT Committee under article 20.[73] To date, 12 states parties maintain such declarations (see Annex I); article 20 investigations have been made public on 12 occasions.[74]

---

[63] Ibid, art 20(1); CAT Rules, r 76.
[64] See A Byrnes, 'The Committee against Torture' in P Alston (ed), *The United Nations and Human Rights* (1992) 530–533.
[65] CAT Rules, rr 76(4), 77.
[66] CAT, art 20(2); CAT Rules, r 78.
[67] CAT, art 20(3).
[68] Ibid; CAT Rules, rr 80, 81.
[69] CAT Rules, r 81(2).
[70] CAT, art 20(4); CAT Rules, r 83.
[71] CAT, art 20(5); CAT Rules, r 84. The Committee must consult with the state concerned before deciding to publish the summary account.
[72] CAT, art 20(5).
[73] Ibid, art 28.
[74] So far, article 20 procedures have been conducted with relation to Colombia, Egypt, Guatemala, Mexico, Nepal, Peru, Serbia, Sri Lanka, Togo, Turkey, Uzbekistan, and Brazil.

REFERENCE

SOURCES OF CASE LAW, INCLUDING CASE REPORTS

Relevant materials can be found on the CAT website, on the University of Minnesota Human Rights Library website, and on the Netherlands Institute for Human Rights Documentation website.

SELECT BIBLIOGRAPHY

Books

W Vandenhole, *The Procedures before the UN Human Rights Treaty Bodies: Divergence or Convergence?* (2004).
C Ingelse, *The UN Committee against Torture: An Assessment* (2001).
A Boulesbaa, *The UN Convention against Torture and Prospects for Enforcement* (1999).
UN Centre for Human Rights, *The Committee against Torture* (1992).

Articles

T Kelly, 'The UN Committee against Torture: Human Rights Monitoring and the Legal Recognition of Cruelty' (2009) 31 *Human Rights Quarterly* 777.
J Herrmann, 'Implementing the Prohibition of Torture on Three Levels: The United Nations, the Council of Europe, and Germany' (2008) 31 *Hastings Int'l & Comp L Rev* 437.
S Pritchard, 'Breaking the National Sound Barrier: Communicating with the CERD and CAT Committees' (1999) *Australian Journal of Human Rights* 23.
A Dormenval, 'UN Committee against Torture: Practice and Perspectives' (1996) 8 *Netherlands Quarterly of Human Rights* 26.
A Byrnes, 'The Committee against Torture' in P Alston (ed), *The United Nations and Human Rights* (1992) 509.

ANNEX I

List of 146 states parties to CAT

(as of September 2009)

Afghanistan,* Albania, Algeria, Andorra, Antigua and Barbuda, Argentina, Armenia, Australia, Austria, Azerbaijan, Bahrain, Bangladesh, Belarus,* Belgium, Belize, Benin, Bolivia, Bosnia and Herzegovina, Botswana, Brazil, Bulgaria,* Burkina Faso, Burundi, Cambodia, Cameroon, Canada, Cape Verde, Chad, Chile, China,* Colombia, Congo, Costa Rica, Côte d'Ivoire, Croatia, Cuba, Cyprus, Czech Republic, Democratic Republic of the Congo, Denmark, Djibouti, Ecuador, Egypt, El Salvador, Equatorial Guinea,* Estonia, Ethiopia, Finland, France, FYROM, Gabon, Georgia, Germany, Ghana, Greece, Guatemala,

Guinea, Guyana, Holy See, Honduras, Hungary, Iceland, Indonesia, Ireland, Israel,* Italy, Japan, Jordan, Kazakhstan, Kenya, Korea, Kuwait,* Kyrgyzstan, Latvia, Lebanon, Lesotho, Liberia, Libya, Liechtenstein, Lithuania, Luxembourg, Madagascar, Malawi, Maldives, Mali, Malta, Mauritania,* Mauritius, Mexico, Moldova, Monaco, Mongolia, Montenegro, Morocco,* Mozambique, Namibia, Nepal, Netherlands, New Zealand, Nicaragua, Niger, Nigeria, Norway, Panama, Paraguay, Peru, Philippines, Poland,* Portugal, Qatar, Romania, Russia, Rwanda, Saint Vincent and the Grenadines, San Marino, Saudi Arabia,* Senegal, Serbia, Seychelles, Sierra Leone, Slovakia, Slovenia, Somalia, South Africa, Spain, Sri Lanka, Swaziland, Sweden, Switzerland, Syria,* Tajikistan, Thailand, Timor-Leste, Togo, Tunisia, Turkey, Turkmenistan, Uganda, Ukraine, United Kingdom, United States of America, Uruguay, Uzbekistan, Venezuela, Yemen, Zambia.

* States that have excluded the competence of the CAT Committee to investigate systematic practice of torture under Article 20 of CAT.

ANNEX II

List of states parties to CAT that recognize the competence of the Committee to receive inter-state communications

(as of September 2009)

Algeria, Andorra, Argentina, Australia, Austria, Belgium, Bolivia, Bulgaria, Cameroon, Canada, Chile, Costa Rica, Croatia, Cyprus, Czech Republic, Denmark, Ecuador, Finland, France, Georgia, Germany, Ghana, Greece, Hungary, Iceland, Ireland, Italy, Japan, Kazakhstan, Korea, Liechtenstein, Luxembourg, Malta, Monaco, Montenegro, Netherlands, New Zealand, Norway, Paraguay, Peru, Poland, Portugal, Russia, Senegal, Serbia, Slovakia, Slovenia, South Africa, Spain, Sweden, Switzerland, Togo, Tunisia, Turkey, Uganda, Ukraine, United Kingdom, United States of America, Uruguay, Venezuela.

ANNEX III

List of states parties to CAT that recognize the competence of the Committee to receive individual communications

(as of September 2009)

Algeria, Andorra, Argentina, Australia, Austria, Azerbaijan, Belgium, Bolivia, Bosnia and Herzegovina, Brazil, Bulgaria, Burundi, Cameroon, Canada, Chile, Costa Rica, Croatia, Cyprus, Czech Republic, Denmark, Ecuador, Finland, France, Georgia, Germany, Ghana, Greece, Guatemala, Hungary, Iceland, Ireland, Italy, Kazakhstan, Korea, Liechtenstein, Luxembourg, Malta, Mexico, Monaco, Montenegro, Morocco, Netherlands, New Zealand, Norway, Paraguay, Peru, Poland, Portugal, Russia, Senegal, Serbia, Seychelles, Slovakia, Slovenia, South Africa, Spain, Sweden, Switzerland, Togo, Tunisia, Turkey, Ukraine, Uruguay, Venezuela.

3. THE COMMITTEE ON THE ELIMINATION
OF DISCRIMINATION AGAINST WOMEN

Introduction

Name and seat of the body

The UN Committee on the Elimination of Discrimination against Women   **15.3.1**
('CEDAW Committee' or 'the Committee') is authorized to monitor compliance
with the UN Convention on the Elimination of All Forms of Discrimination
against Women ('CEDAW'), to receive applications from complainants in
respect of violations of the Convention, and to conduct ex officio inquiries into
grave or discriminatory practices. The CEDAW Committee is located at:

> Committee on the Elimination of Discrimination against Women
> Centre for Human Rights
> Palais des Nations, United Nations
> 8–14 Avenue de la Paix
> 1211 Geneva 10
> Switzerland
> Tel: (41) 22 917 9000
> Fax: (41) 22 917 9022
> Website: <http://www.unhchr.ch>

General description

CEDAW was concluded in 1979 and entered into force in 1981.[75] To date, 186   **15.3.2**
states have ratified or acceded to the Convention. Under CEDAW, states undertake to adopt policies designed to eliminate discrimination against women. The
Convention provides for the establishment of the CEDAW Committee in order

---

[75] Convention on the Elimination of All Forms of Discrimination against Women, 18
December 1979, GA Res 34/180, 34 UN GAOR Supp (No 46) at 193, UN Doc A/34/46
(1979).

to monitor the compliance of the states parties with their obligations under CEDAW.[76]

The Committee comprises 23 independent experts elected by the states parties to CAT for renewable four-year terms.[77] In electing experts, factors for consideration include equitable geographical distribution and representation of different forms of civilization and the principal legal systems. The Committee may not feature more than one representative from any given country.[78]

The Committee considers periodic reports submitted by states parties describing the measures taken by them to implement the Convention and may issue general comments thereon.[79] Under the 1999 Optional Protocol to CEDAW, the Committee has also been authorized to receive communications from individuals alleging violation of CEDAW by a state party which has adopted the Optional Protocol.[80] The Committee may also investigate situations involving states parties to the Optional Protocol, where information received from reliable sources suggests that systematic violations of CEDAW have taken place.[81]

All investigation procedures involve the exercise of quasi-judicial powers by the Committee and the formulation of its findings in the form of a non-binding report.

The procedure applied by the CEDAW Committee is governed by Part V of CEDAW and the Rules of Procedure adopted by the Committee. The Secretary-General of the UN provides the CEDAW Committee with secretarial services (through the Office of the High Commissioner for Human Rights) and the sessions of the Committee are held in UN facilities.[82] The official and working languages of the Committee are Arabic, Chinese, English, French, Russian, and Spanish.[83] The meetings of the CEDAW Committee in which

---

[76] Ibid, art 17.

[77] Ibid, art 17(1), (5). The current membership is Ms Nicole Ameline (France), Ms Ferdous Ara Begum (Bangladesh), Ms Magalys Arocha Dominguez (Cuba), Ms Violet Tsisiga Awori (Kenya), Ms Barbara Evelyn Bailey (Jamaica), Ms Meriem Belmihoub-Zerdani (Algeria), Mr Niklas Bruun (Finland), Ms Saisuree Chutikul (Thailand), Ms Dorcas Coker-Appiah (Ghana), Mr Cornelis Flinterman (Netherlands), Ms Naela Mohamed Gabr (Egypt), Ms Ruth Halperin-Kaddari (Israel), Ms Yoko Hayashi (Japan), Ms Indira Jaising (India), Ms Soledad Murillo de la Vega (Spain), Ms Violeta Neubauer (Slovenia), Ms Pramila Patten (Mauritius), Ms Silvia Pimentel (Brazil), Ms Victoria Popescu (Romania), Ms Zohra Rasekh (Afghanistan), Ms Dubravka Šimonović (Croatia), and Ms Zou Xiaoqiao (China).

[78] CAT, art 17(1), (2).

[79] Ibid, arts 18, 21.

[80] Optional Protocol to the Convention on the Elimination of All Forms of Discrimination against Women, 6 October 1999, art 2, GA Res 54/4, annex, 54 UN GAOR Supp (No 49) at 5, UN Doc A/54/49 (Vol I) (2000)('Optional Protocol').

[81] Ibid, art 8.

[82] CEDAW, arts 17(9), 20(2); Rules of Procedure of the Committee on the Elimination of Discrimination against Women, UN Doc A/56/38 (Supp)(2003), as amended by UN Doc A/62/38 (2007) ('CEDAW Rules'), rr 5, 21.

[83] CEDAW Rules, r 24.

communications or information on systematic discriminatory practices are considered are normally closed to the public and confidential in nature.[84] The Committee generally holds two to three working sessions per year but may also meet for additional special sessions where warranted.[85]

Individual Communications

The CEDAW Committee may receive communications from individuals sub- **15.3.3** ject to the jurisdiction of a state party that has joined the Optional Protocol providing for the competence of the Committee to receive individual complaints.[86] To date, 98 states have ratified the Optional Protocol (see Annex).

A communication must be submitted to the Committee by or on behalf of any person who claims to be a victim of a violation of CEDAW by the state complained against. This includes a designated representative of the victim or other persons acting on behalf of the alleged victim with her consent (unless the author of the communication can justify acting on the victim's behalf without her consent).[87]

The Committee (or a working group appointed by the Committee) will first determine whether the communication is admissible.[88] This entails verification that the complainant has exhausted domestic remedies (unless their application is unreasonably prolonged or likely to be ineffective). It will also require confirmation that: previous Committee proceedings or other international dispute settlement procedures have not been invoked in relation to the same case; the communication is not incompatible with the provisions of CEDAW; it is not ill-founded, insufficiently substantiated, or an abuse of right; and the relevant facts did not occur prior to the entry into force of the Optional Protocol for the state in question.[89] The Committee will not accept anonymous communications.[90] The Committee may then allocate the case to either a working group of the Committee or a rapporteur, who may seek further information from the author of the communication or state party concerned.[91] If necessary, the Committee,

---

[84] Optional Protocol, arts 7(2), 8(5); CEDAW Rules, rr 74, 81.

[85] CEDAW Rules, r 3.

[86] Optional Protocol, art 1.

[87] Ibid, art 2; CEDAW Rules, r 68.

[88] Optional Protocol, art 4; CEDAW Rules, r 72(4). The authority of working groups to decide (unanimously) on the admissibility of a communication is provided for in CEDAW Rules, r 64(2).

[89] Optional Protocol, art 4(2). If a communication is found inadmissible, it may be resubmitted later when the grounds for inadmissibility no longer apply. CEDAW Rules, r 70(2).

[90] Optional Protocol, art 3; CEDAW Rules, r 56(3)(c). The identity of the author of the communication will be disclosed to the relevant state party only if the author consents to it. Optional Protocol, art 6(1); CEDAW Rules, r 58(5).

[91] CEDAW Rule, r 68(9).

the working group, or the rapporteur may request the state party to adopt interim measures in order to avoid irreparable harm to the alleged victim.[92] The working group may also make recommendations to the Committee on the merits of the communication.[93]

The state concerned is normally expected to submit its observations and statements on the merits of the communication within six months from the date it was notified of the communication's submission. The author of the communication and the relevant state may then be given the opportunity to submit additional explanations or statements.[94] It may also address matters which it considers of relevance, notwithstanding the fact that no submissions as to such matters have been made by the parties. It may refer to information supplied to it by UN bodies, or any other body which may assist in the disposal of the case.[95]

After receiving the submissions of the parties, the Committee formulates its Views on the matter. Members of the Committee may append summaries of their individual views to that of the Committee.[96] The decision will be forwarded to the parties to the dispute and the Committee may subsequently invite the state concerned to report on whether it has implemented the Committee's recommendations (although the recommendations are not formally binding).[97] Summaries of the submissions of the parties and the Views of the Committee are published in its annual report to the states parties to CEDAW and to the General Assembly.[98]

So far the CEDAW Committee has dealt with 20 individual communications. In seven cases it adopted Views on the merits (finding a violation on most occasions); nine cases were found inadmissible or discontinued; and four are still pending.

Investigation of Systematic Violations of CEDAW

15.3.4 The CEDAW Committee may also investigate allegations of systematic violations of CEDAW by a state party that adopted the Optional Protocol and did not submit a declaration excluding this power of the Committee.[99] The investigation will commence only if reliable information on the existence of such a

---

92 Optional Protocol, art 5(1); CEDAW Rules, r 63.
93 CEDAW Rules r 72(3).
94 Ibid, r 69(8).
95 Ibid, r 72(2).
96 Optional Protocol, art 7(3); CEDAW Rules, r 72(6).
97 Optional Protocol, art 7(4), (5); CEDAW Rules, r 73. Members of the Committee may serve as rapporteurs for follow-up procedures or serve as a working group for follow-up procedures and recommend to the Committee follow-up measures designed to ascertain that the state concerned gives effect to the Views of the Committee.
98 Optional Protocol, art 12; CEDAW Rules, r 74(10).
99 Optional Protocol, arts 8, 9; CEDAW Rules, r 76.

situation is brought to the attention of the Committee through the Secretary-General, who is to maintain a permanent register of such information.[100] The Committee should then invite the state concerned to submit its observations within a limited period of time.[101] The Committee may obtain additional information from a variety of other sources (eg intergovernmental organizations, NGOs, and individuals).[102] Where necessary, the Committee may authorize one or more of its members to conduct a confidential inquiry.[103]

In conducting the inquiry, the Committee shall seek the cooperation of the state party concerned.[104] The inquiry may include (with the concerned state's consent), a visit to the territory of the state concerned and hearings of witnesses and other individuals.[105] The Committee may request the concerned government to ensure that there is no interference with such proceedings and no intimidation of any witnesses.[106]

The findings of the inquiry will be presented to the Committee, which will examine these and then transmit them along with its own comments and recommendations to the state concerned.[107] The state concerned is expected to submit its observations on the outcome of the Committee's inquiry; and the Committee may solicit from the state additional information on follow-up measures it may have adopted in response to the inquiry.[108] A summary account of the investigation proceedings may be published in the annual report of the Committee to the General Assembly.[109] Proceedings remain confidential until this stage.

To date, no inquiries have been made public although a careful reading of the annual reports suggests that the Committee has engaged in relevant, confidential, investigation activity in some years.

REFERENCE

SOURCES OF CASE LAW, INCLUDING CASE REPORTS

Relevant materials can be found on the CEDAW website, on the University of Minnesota Human Rights Library website, and on the Netherlands Institute for Human Rights Documentation website.

---

[100] CEAW Rules, rr 77–78.
[101] Optional Protocol, art 8(1); CEDAW Rules, r 83(1).
[102] Optional Protocol, art 8(2); CEDAW Rules, r 83(3).
[103] CEDAW Rules, r 84.
[104] Optional Protocol, art 8(5); CEDAW Rules, r 85.
[105] Optional Protocol, art 8(2); CEDAW Rules, rr 86, 87.
[106] CEDAW Rules, rr 87(4), 91.
[107] Optional Protocol, art 8(3); CEDAW Rules, r 89.
[108] Optional Protocol, art 9; CEDAW Rules, r 90.
[109] Optional Protocol, art 12; CEDAW Rules, r 80. The Committee may consult with the relevant state with respect to the contents of the summary.

SELECT BIBLIOGRAPHY

Books

W Vandenhole, *The Procedures before the UN Human Rights Treaty Bodies: Divergence or Convergence?* (2004).

Articles

A Byrnes and E Bath, 'Violence against Women, the Obligation of Due Diligence and the Optional Protocol to the Convention on the Elimination of all Forms of Discrimination against Women: Recent Developments' (2008) 8 *Human Rights Law Review* 517.

A Danka, 'In the Name of Reproductive Rights: Litigating before the UN Committee on the Elimination of Discrimination against Women' (2006) 4 *Roma Rights Quarterly* 31.

H Jones and K Wachala, 'Watching over the Rights of Women' (2005) 5 *Social Policy and Society* 127.

F Gomez Isa, 'The Optional Protocol for the Convention on the Elimination of All Forms of Discrimination against Women: Strengthening the Protection Mechanisms of Women's Human Rights' (2003) 20 *Ariz J Int'l & Comp L* 291.

K Tang and J T Cheung, 'Realizing Women's Human Rights in Asia: The UN Women's Convention and the Optional Protocol' (2003) 9 *Asian Journal of Women's Studies* 9–37.

K Ritz, 'Soft Enforcement: Inadequacies of Optional Protocol as a Remedy for the Convention on the Elimination of All Forms of Discrimination against Women' (2001–2002) 25 *Suffolk Transnat'l L Rev* 191.

A F Bayefsky, 'The CEDAW Convention: Its Contribution Today' (2000) 94 *Am Soc'y Int'l L Proc* 197.

H Gilchrist, 'The Optional Protocol to the Women's Convention: An Argument for Ratification' (2000) 39 *Colum J Transnat'l L* 763.

E Herzer, 'CEDAW: After Years of Controversy, UN Adopts Compromised Individual Complaints Procedure for Women' (1999–2000) 85 *Women Law J* 23.

A Byrnes and J Connors, 'Enforcing the Human Rights of Women: A Complaints Procedure for the Women's Convention?' (1995) 21 *Brook J Int'l L* 679.

E Evatt, 'The Right to Individual Petition: Assessing its Operation before the Human Rights Committee and its Future Application to the Women's Convention on Discrimination' (1995) 89 *Am Soc'y Int'l L Proc* 227.

ANNEX

List of 98 states parties to CEDAW Optional Protocol

(as of September 2009)

Albania, Andorra, Angola, Antigua and Barbuda, Argentina, Armenia, Australia, Austria, Azerbaijan, Bangladesh,* Belarus, Belgium, Belize,* Bolivia, Bosnia and Herzegovina, Botswana, Brazil, Bulgaria, Burkina Faso, Cameroon, Canada, Colombia,* Cook Islands, Costa Rica, Croatia, Cyprus, Czech Republic, Denmark, Dominican Republic,

Ecuador, Finland, France, FYROM, Gabon, Georgia, Germany, Greece, Guatemala, Hungary, Iceland, Ireland, Italy, Kazakhstan, Korea, Kyrgyzstan, Latvia, Lesotho, Libya, Liechtenstein, Lithuania, Luxembourg, Maldives, Mali, Mauritius, Mexico, Moldova, Mongolia, Montenegro, Mozambique, Namibia, Nepal, Netherlands, New Zealand, Niger, Nigeria, Norway, Panama, Paraguay, Peru, Philippines, Poland, Portugal, Romania, Russia, Rwanda, Saint Kitts and Nevis, San Marino, Senegal, Serbia, Slovakia, Slovenia, Solomon Islands, South Africa, Spain, Sri Lanka, Sweden, Switzerland, Tanzania, Thailand, Timor-Leste, Tunisia, Turkey, Turkmenistan, Ukraine, United Kingdom, Uruguay, Vanuatu, Venezuela.

* States that have excluded the competence of the CEDAW Committee to investigate systematic practice of torture under Article 8 of the Optional Protocol.

Evaluation

The three individual complaint mechanisms surveyed in this Chapter represent a quasi-judicial procedure for addressing alleged human rights violations. Like the HRC Optional Protocol process discussed in Chapter 14, the proceedings employed by the three Committees have some obvious judicial features: the process is complainant-initiated; it includes the exchange of party submissions; and the process concludes with the publication of reasoned factual and legal findings by a neutral third party. Yet, these procedures are not fully equivalent to Court procedures. Most significantly, the decisions of the Committees are not formally binding. What's more, the conditions under which the processes take place are different from those characterizing the operation of courts: Committee members are not always lawyers; most proceedings do not include an oral phase; and the restricted session time of the Committees (a period of time in which they are also expected to fulfil a host of other compliance-inducing tasks, including the review of periodic reports and the issuance of general comments/recommendations) limits the Committees' ability to engage in in-depth fact-finding process and legal analysis. The optional nature of the process is also out of step with the increased tendency to invest international courts with compulsory jurisdiction. It is therefore not surprising that the individual complaints mechanism of the UN human rights Committees have not attracted considerable attention nor garnered significant influence—the HRC representing an exception in this regard, *inter alia* by reason of the breadth of its mandate and the quality of its membership. In fact, the jurisdictional overlap between the specific mechanisms under the three UN treaties and other, more prominent and effective mechanisms operating at the regional level or the HRC does not bode well for the Committees' future prospects.

Notwithstanding the limits of the complaint mechanism process, it still remains a useful tool for the UN human rights Committees (alongside other processes described above such as the investigation of situations of systemic violation). Most importantly, it enables the Committees to use the study of specific communications as illustrations of general human rights situations or problems afflicting the member states. The review of communications and its follow-up thus provides the Committees with another strategic avenue for prodding member states towards greater compliance with their treaty obligations. The fact that an increasing number of human rights treaties now include such a mechanism, and that a growing number of states accede thereto, suggests that treaty makers and state officials consider such procedures as relatively useful for improving compliance, and yet, sufficiently harmless so as not to seriously jeopardize their states' political interests and reputations.

While the individual complaints mechanism is useful, though not extremely successful, the inter-state complaints procedures discussed in this Chapter have fallen into complete desuetude. It is interesting to note in this respect that even the CERD inter-state procedure, which does not require consent of the respondent party for its initiation, has never been utilized. The political reluctance of states to complain against one another and the increasing availability of less politically costly compliance mechanisms (such as individual complaints) appear to constitute the main reason for the demise of the inter-state process.

16

REPRESENTATION AND COMPLAINT PROCEDURES OF THE INTERNATIONAL LABOUR ORGANIZATION

Introduction

Name and seat of the body

The International Labour Organization (ILO) is an intergovernmental organ- **16.1**
ization dedicated to the global promotion of labour standards. Among its activities, the ILO offers a number of complaint procedures designed to monitor member states' compliance with their ILO obligations. The ILO, and its secretariat—the International Labour Office—are located at:

International Labour Office
Department of Labour Standards
4, route de Morillons
CH-1211 Geneva 22
Switzerland
Tel: (41) 22 799 61 11
Fax: (41) 22 798 86 85
Email: ilo@ilo.org
Website: <http://www.ilo.org/>

General description

The International Labour Organization ('ILO') was established in 1919 **16.2**
in order to promote standards, at the international level, of domestic working

conditions and social justice with a view to thereby contributing to world peace.[1] The Organization has 183 state members. It comprises three principal organs:

(1) a General Conference of representatives of the member states (with each national delegation including two government representatives, an employers' representative, and a workers' representative);

(2) a Governing Body (comprising 28 governmental representatives, 14 employers' representatives, and 14 workers' representatives); and

(3) the International Labour Office, which is the Organization's secretariat.

The central function of the ILO is the adoption of international labour standards by way of Conventions (open to ratification by the member states) and non-binding instruments (recommendations, resolutions, declarations). In order to ensure compliance of member states with ILO standards, the ILO employs several supervisory procedures. Each state periodically reports to the ILO on the measures undertaken to give effect to the ILO Conventions it has ratified, and the reports are then subsequently reviewed by a special Committee of Independent Experts appointed by the Governing Body.[2] States, delegates to the General Conference, and domestic and international employers' and workers' associations may additionally communicate complaints or representations to the ILO alleging failure of a member state to comply with applicable ILO Conventions, or required freedom of association standards. Such communications are dealt with by the Governing Body itself, or by subsidiary bodies established by it.[3]

Representation Procedure

16.3 In accordance with Article 24 of the ILO Constitution, any employers' or workers' industrial association (such as labour unions) may submit a written representation to the International Labour Office alleging that a member state has failed to secure, in any respect, the effective observance of an ILO Convention to which the member state is party.[4] The Office will forward the representation

---

[1] Constitution of the International Labour Organization, 9 October 1946, Preamble, 15 UNTS 40 ('ILO Constitution').

[2] Ibid, art 22.

[3] See generally ILO, *Handbook of Procedures Relating to International Labour Conventions and Recommendations* (2006) at 48–53.

[4] ILO Constitution, art 24. The representation must indicate that the author is an industrial association; explicitly refer to art 24 of the Constitution; refer to the Convention to which the relevant ILO member state is party; and provide details on the alleged non-compliance. Governing Body, Standing Orders concerning the procedure for the examination of representations under Articles 24 and 25 of the Constitution of the International Labour Organization, arts 1, 2, ILO Doc GB.291/9(Rev) (2004), Appendix I ('Standing Orders'). For more information on the discretion of the Governing Body to recognize an industrial association as such, see Governing Body, Introductory Note to Standing Orders concerning the procedure for the examination

to the Governing Body.[5] If the Officers of the Governing Body (namely, the Chairman and the two Vice-Chairmen) find the representation admissible, the Governing Body will set up a subsidiary tripartite committee, composed of non-involved members of the Governing Body, to examine the matter. The Governing Body may also refer the case, where appropriate, to the Committee on Freedom of Association. The tripartite committee may invite the concerned association and government to provide it with information and statements.[6] After examining the representation, the tripartite committee will deliver a report to the Governing Body containing the committee's conclusions and recommendations.[7] The reports of the tripartite committee are usually published. The Governing Body will consider the report (in the presence of the government concerned, if not represented in the Governing Body), and will decide whether to adopt any decisions on the basis of the committee's recommendations. The Governing Body may also decide to publish the representation and the government's response thereto.[8]

The number of complaints submitted each year to the Governing Body pursuant to representation procedure has been relatively small. The Governing Body's 2007–2008 Annual Report, for example, takes note of two new representations referred to tripartite committees, and adopts the report of a tripartite committee in a third case.[9]

Complaint Procedure

Article 26 of the Constitution of the ILO authorizes a state party to bring a complaint against another member state that has allegedly failed to secure the effective observance of any ILO Convention, to which both the complaining state and the state complained against are parties.[10] The complaint is to be filed with the International Labour Office, which will refer the case to the Governing Body. The complaint procedure may also be initiated by a delegate of the Conference to the Governing Body, or by the latter body acting on its own motion.[11]

16.4

---

of representations under Articles 24 and 25 of the Constitution of the International Labour Organization, ibid, Appendix II, at paras 9–10.

  [5] ILO Constitution, art 24.
  [6] Standing Orders, arts 4, 5. The government has a right to be heard in an oral session, while the appearance of representatives of the association before the committee is at the latter's discretion.
  [7] Ibid, art 6.
  [8] ILO Constitution, art 25; Standing Orders, art 8.
  [9] ILO Governing Body, Annual Report 2007–2008, ILO Doc LC97-PR1-2008-05-0190-1-En.doc/v2 (2008) at 9–10.
  [10] ILO Constitution, art 26(1).
  [11] Ibid, art 26(4).

The Governing Body will normally establish a Commission of Inquiry to investigate the complaint. At its discretion, however, it may decide to give the government complained against an opportunity to reply to the allegations before appointing the Commission of Inquiry, and the Governing Body may further decline to appoint a Commission if the response of the said government is considered satisfactory.[12] The respondent government is entitled to participate in the meetings of the Governing Body in which the complaint is being considered.[13]

Commissions of Inquiry are composed of three independent experts.[14] There are no standing orders governing the procedure of the Commissions and each Commission determines its own procedures (subject only to the ILO Constitution and general guidance from the Governing Body). In practice, the proceedings are of a quasi-judicial nature involving the gathering of evidence, presentation of written and/or oral arguments, and, on occasion, on-site visits. On-site visits require the consent of the relevant states, but in practice this tends to be granted. The Commission of Inquiry then prepares a report containing factual findings and recommendations, and submits the report to the Governing Body.[15] Reports are published by the International Labour Office.[16]

After the report is concluded, the states involved in the proceedings will inform the International Labour Office within three months of receiving the report whether they intend to comply with it (or if not, whether they will agree to refer the case to the International Court of Justice).[17] The Governing Body may recommend to the Parties' General Conference to take appropriate implementation measures against a state party which fails to implement a report (or a judgment of the ICJ on the same matter).[18] The Governing Body may also (upon the request of the defaulting government) appoint another Commission of Inquiry in order to verify compliance with the report (or the ICJ judgment).[19] So far this inquiry process has led to the publication of 12 reports.[20]

---

[12] Ibid, art 26(2), (3).

[13] Ibid, art 26(5).

[14] Although there is no formal requirement as to the composition of the Commission of Inquiry, it has been the unchanged practice of the Governing Body to appoint three persons thereto.

[15] ILO Constitution, art 28.

[16] Ibid, art 29(1).

[17] Ibid, art 29(2).

[18] Ibid, art 33.

[19] Ibid, art 34.

[20] The Commission of Inquiry reports are available on the website: <http://www.ilo.org/ilolex/english/INQUIRY.htm>.

Complaints on Infringement of
Freedom of Association

In 1951, the Governing Body established a mechanism to supervise the imple-   **16.5**
mentation of labour standards relating to freedom of association. An employers' or workers' organization, or a government, may bring a complaint against
any ILO member state alleging an infringement of freedom of association by
that state (even if it is not a party to one of the ILO Conventions on freedom of
association).[21] An employers' or workers' association must meet one of the following conditions:[22]

(1) it is a directly interested domestic organization;
(2) it is an international organization with consultative status with the ILO; or
(3) it is an international organization to which a domestic organization directly
     affected is affiliated.

The communication is to be made in writing to the International Labour Office,
which may request additional information.[23]

The International Labour Office will communicate the complaint and the
reply of the concerned government to a permanent subsidiary committee of
the Governing Body—the Committee on Freedom of Association (CFA). The
Committee comprises nine members of the Governing Body (and an independent chair).[24] It is authorized to investigate complaints (including the conduct of
oral hearings and on-site visits, if necessary)[25] and to submit its recommendations to the Governing Body. The Governing Body may then approve the recommendations of the Committee. The reports of the Committee are published, and
the Committee may take follow-up action where needed (for example, such as
when the member state is not subject to a relevant ILO Convention that introduces periodic reporting duties).[26] In its work, the Committee gives priority to
cases involving human life or personal freedom, those affecting the trade union
movement as a whole, or those involving states of emergency.[27] The Freedom of

---

[21] Function of the ILO and mandate of the Committee on Freedom of Association, para 2,
ILO Committee on Freedom of Association, *Digest of Decisions and Principles of the Freedom of
Association Committee of the Governing Body of the ILO* (5th edn, 2006) 7.

[22] Ibid, Annex I: Special Procedures for the Examination in the International Labour
Organization of Complaints alleging Violations of Freedom of Association.

[23] CFA Procedures, para 44.

[24] Ibid, para 7; ILO, Handbook of Procedures Relating to International Labour Conventions
and Recommendations (2006) at 50–52.

[25] CFA Procedures, paras 67–69.

[26] Ibid, paras 70–74.

[27] Ibid, para 54.

Association Committee meets three times every year, and deals with over 30 cases at each meeting. To date it has examined almost 3,000 complaints.

In appropriate cases (and acting upon the recommendation of the Committee on Freedom of Association), the Governing Body may refer specific complaints for further investigation by a permanent, nine-member, independent Fact-Finding and Conciliation Commission. The Fact-Finding Commission normally works in panels of three members.[28] The procedure of the latter body is generally similar to that of the Commission of Inquiry (but there is no right of appeal to the ICJ), and its reports are also published. If the government complained against is not a party to any ILO freedom of association Convention, however, its consent to the process is required. So far the Fact-finding and Conciliation Committee has handled less than ten cases.

Evaluation

The ILO procedures briefly discussed in this Chapter present an impressive procedural diversity and a long pedigree. Still, the procedures have been utilized until now quite sparingly—only a handful of cases have been presented via the representation procedure, the complaint procedure, and the fact-finding process. What's more, their contribution to improvements in the labour practices of ILO member states appears to have been, with some notable exceptions,[29] rather minor. This may be another indication of the limits of inter-statal dispute settlement mechanisms in advancing human rights norms (notwithstanding the tripartite composition of the ILO). The limited effectiveness of the complaint procedures is also perhaps reflective of the modest time and resource constraints allocated thereto by the ILO.[30]

The Freedom of Association Committee complaint mechanism represents an important exception to the aforementioned trend. The CFA's liberal rules of personal jurisdiction, which permit the submission of complaints by a wide variety of national and international labour organizations and NGOs, have facilitated its transformation into one of the busiest human rights mechanisms existing at the global level. This 'island of jurisdiction'[31] has been widely

---

[28] Digest of Decisions, *supra* note 2, at 2.

[29] See a discussion of the ILO compliance measures against Myanmar in L R Helfer, 'Understanding Change in International Organizations: Globalization and Innovation in the ILO' (2006) 59 *Vand L Rev* 649 at 711–713.

[30] See eg S Cooney, 'Testing Times for the ILO: Institutional Reform for the New International Political Economy' (1999) 20 *Comp Lab L & Pol'y J* 365 at 375.

[31] L Helfer, K Alter, and F Guerzovich, 'Islands of Effective International Adjudication: Constructing an Intellectual Property Rule of Law in the Andean Community' (2009) 109 *American Journal of International Law* 1.

perceived as a force for the advancement of the cause of freedom of association around the world.[32]

REFERENCE

SOURCES OF CASE LAW, INCLUDING CASE REPORTS

Relevant materials can be found on the ILO website.

R Gopalakrishnan, 'Working Paper No 1: Freedom of Association and Collective Bargaining in Export Processing Zones: The Role of the ILO Supervisory Mechanisms' (2007) (International Labour Office: Geneva).

SELECT BIBLIOGRAPHY

Books

V Y Ghebali, *The ILO: A Case Study on the Evolution of UN Specialised Agencies* (1989).
E A Landy, *The Effectiveness of International Supervision* (1966).

Articles

E de Wet, 'Governance through Promotion and Persuasion: The 1998 ILO Declaration on Fundamental Principles and Rights at Work' (2008) 9 *German Law Journal* 1429.

L R Helfer, 'Monitoring Compliance with Unratified Treaties: The ILO Experience' (2008) 71 *Law and Contemporary Problems* 193.

A Wisskirchen, 'The Standard Setting and Monitoring Activity of the ILO: Legal Questions and Practical Experience' (2005) 144 *International Labour Review* 253.

L Milnichuk, 'The Circle of Labour: The NAALC, ILO, FTAA and Labour Dispute Resolution Mechanisms' (2003–2004) 1 *International Law Review* 235.

N Valticos, 'Les Conventions de l'Organisation Internationale du Travail a la croisée des anniversaires' (1996) 100 *Revue générale de droit international public* 5.

N Valticos, 'Once more about the ILO System of Supervision: In what Respect is it still a Model?' in N Blokker and S Muller (eds), *Towards More Effective Supervision by International Organisations* (1994).

L Sweptson, 'The Future of ILO Standards' (1994) 117 *Monthly Labour Review* 16.

N Valticos, 'Les Commissions d'enquête de l'Organisation Internationale du Travail' (1987) *Revue générale de droit international public*.

E A Landy, 'The implementation procedures of the ILO' (1980) 20 *Santa Clara Law Review* 633.

---

[32] See L R Helfer, 'Monitoring Compliance with Unratified Treaties: The ILO Experience' (2008) 71 *Law & Contemp Prob* 193 at 202; S Charnovitz, 'The ILO Convention on Freedom of Association and its Future in the United States' (2008) 102 *Am J Int'l L* 90 at 92. For a less generous evaluation of the record of the CFA, see J C Knapp, 'The Boundaries of the ILO: A Labor Rights Argument for Institutional Cooperation' (2003) 29 *Brooklyn J Int'l L* 369 at 380.

ANNEX

List of ILO member states

(as of September 2009)

Afghanistan, Albania, Algeria, Angola, Antigua and Barbuda, Argentina, Armenia, Australia, Austria, Azerbaijan, Bahamas, Bahrain, Bangladesh, Barbados, Belarus, Belgium, Belize, Benin, Bolivia, Bosnia and Herzegovina, Botswana, Brazil, Brunei Darussalam, Bulgaria, Burkina Faso, Burundi, Cambodia, Cameroon, Canada, Cape Verde, Central African Republic, Chad, Chile, China, Colombia, Comoros, Congo, Costa Rica, Côte d'Ivoire, Croatia, Cuba, Cyprus, Czech Republic, Democratic Republic of the Congo, Denmark, Djibouti, Dominica, Dominican Republic, Ecuador, Egypt, El Salvador, Equatorial Guinea, Eritrea, Estonia, Ethiopia, Fiji, Finland, the former Yugoslav Republic of Macedonia, France, Gabon, Gambia, Georgia, Germany, Ghana, Greece, Grenada, Guatemala, Guinea, Guinea-Bissau, Guyana, Haiti, Honduras, Hungary, Iceland, India, Indonesia, Iran, Iraq, Ireland, Israel, Italy, Jamaica, Japan, Jordan, Kazakhstan, Kenya, Kiribati, Korea, Kuwait, Kyrgyzstan, Laos, Latvia, Lebanon, Lesotho, Liberia, Libya, Lithuania, Luxembourg, Madagascar, Malawi, Malaysia, Maldives, Mali, Malta, Marshall Islands, Mauritania, Mauritius, Mexico, Moldova, Mongolia, Montenegro, Morocco, Mozambique, Myanmar, Namibia, Nepal, Netherlands, New Zealand, Nicaragua, Niger, Nigeria, Norway, Oman, Pakistan, Panama, Papua New Guinea, Paraguay, Peru, Philippines, Poland, Portugal, Qatar, Romania, Russian Federation, Rwanda, Saint Kitts and Nevis, Saint Lucia, Saint Vincent and the Grenadines, Samoa, San Marino, São Tomé and Principe, Saudi Arabia, Senegal, Serbia, Seychelles, Sierra Leone, Singapore, Slovakia, Slovenia, Solomon Islands, Somalia, South Africa, Spain, Sri Lanka, Sudan, Suriname, Swaziland, Sweden, Switzerland, Syria, Tajikistan, Tanzania, Thailand, Timor-Leste, Togo, Trinidad and Tobago, Tunisia, Turkey, Turkmenistan, Tuvalu, Uganda, Ukraine, United Arab Emirates, United Kingdom, United States, Uruguay, Uzbekistan, Vanuatu, Venezuela, Vietnam, Yemen, Zambia, Zimbabwe.

Part VI

INSPECTION, REVIEW, AND COMPLIANCE MECHANISMS IN INTERNATIONAL FINANCIAL INSTITUTIONS

Introduction

The mechanisms reviewed in this Part do not fall strictly into the categorization of 'international courts and tribunals'. They comprise a variety of mechanisms, involving a variety of fact-finding, forms of mediation and other procedures, established within international and regional development banks to provide a forum to which affected parties may bring concerns or complaints alleging that the bank in question is not complying with its own policies and procedures in respect of a specific project. These policies and procedures may relate to a range of issues, including, for example, environmental impact assessment, involuntary resettlement, protection of cultural resources, and indigenous peoples. While established within the bank itself, the mechanisms are intended to function in a manner that is independent of the bank in question.

For the purposes of this Manual, the principal interest in these types of mechanism lies in the fact that they offer an opportunity for communities or persons adversely affected by projects financed by development banks to hold those institutions to account. The mechanisms surveyed in this Part vary in nature, but have some common features. The principal limitation inherent in them is that the review that they provide normally extends only to considering the bank's compliance with its own policies and procedures in the design, appraisal, and implementation of projects. They are not generally designed to consider the adequacy of the policies and procedures themselves.

The first such mechanism, addressed in Chapter 17, is the World Bank Inspection Panel, established in 1993. The Panel may receive complaints alleging non-compliance by the Bank's Management with the Bank's own operational policies and procedures. The Panel may receive requests for review from groups of people who claim to be adversely affected by such non-compliance. If the circumstances warrant a full investigation, this is conducted by the Panel in accordance with the Panel's mandate and operating procedures. The findings and recommendations of the Panel are presented in the form of a report to the President of the Bank and the Executive Directors. It is the Board of Directors that may decide what action to take, if any, to implement the report.

Chapter 18 briefly surveys inspection, review, and compliance mechanisms established in other international and regional financial institutions. Several of these institutions have established mechanisms similar to the World Bank Inspection Panel. In addition, as experience has been gained, and new mechanisms developed, there has been a shift towards supplementary 'problem-solving' and consultation-based approaches alongside the original inspection or compliance review functions. Five such mechanisms are outlined in Chapter 18.

The Inter-American Development Bank (IDB) Independent Investigation Mechanism was established in 1994. The Mechanism is modelled on the World Bank's Inspection Panel. However, instead of a standing Inspection Panel, the IDB Mechanism establishes a roster of 15 investigators of not less than ten different nationalities from Bank member countries, from which panels may be drawn. The Bank receives requests for investigation presented to it by an affected party in the territory of a borrower/recipient. Where an investigation is conducted, it is undertaken by three members from the roster, who present their findings to the Bank's Executive Directors. The Directors make the final determination whether or not the Bank's policies have been followed, and may instruct Management to take preventive or corrective action where required. A review of the Mechanism was underway in 2009 with a view to establishing a Consultation and Investigation Mechanism.

The Asian Development Bank (ADB) established an Accountability Mechanism in 2003 to replace the Inspection Function reviewed in the first edition of this Manual. The new Mechanism comprises a consultation phase and a compliance review phase. The consultation phase of the Accountability Mechanism consists of a special project facilitator seeking to respond to specific problems and concerns of locally affected people through a range of informal and flexible methods. The compliance review phase comprises an independent three-member compliance review panel to investigate alleged violations of ADB's operational policies and procedures that have resulted in direct, adverse, and material impacts on project-affected people and to make recommendations for ensuring future compliance and reducing adverse impacts.

The International Finance Corporation (IFC) and Multilateral Investment Guarantee Agency (MIGA), part of the World Bank Group, are not subject to the procedures of the Inspection Panel outlined in Chapter 17. However, in 1999, an Office of the Compliance Advisor/Ombudsman (CAO) was established for IFC and MIGA. The Office of the CAO of the IFC and MIGA has three roles: first, responding to complaints by persons who are affected by projects and attempting to resolve the issues raised using a flexible, problem-solving approach (the Ombudsman role); second, providing a source of independent advice to the President and management of IFC and MIGA in relation to particular projects and broader environmental and social policies (the Advisory role); and third, overseeing audits of IFC's and MIGA's social and environmental performance both overall and in relation to sensitive projects, to ensure compliance with policies, guidelines, procedures, and systems (the Compliance role).

The African Development Bank (AfDB) approved the establishment of an Independent Review Mechanism in 2004, and operating rules and procedures were approved in 2006. The Mechanism comprises a Compliance Review and Mediation Unit and a roster of experts. The roster comprises three external experts, two of whom will be selected to participate in compliance review panels where such a review is authorized. The Director of the Compliance Review and Mediation Unit also participates in such panels. In addition to compliance review, the Mechanism also provides for mediation or problem-solving processes.

Finally, in 2003, the Board of Directors of the European Bank for Reconstruction and Development (EBRD) approved an Independent Recourse Mechanism (IRM), the rules of procedure for which were approved in 2004. Again, the Mechanism provides for both compliance reviews (in respect of the Bank's policies and procedures) and problem-solving initiatives. In May 2009, the Board of Directors of the EBRD approved the adoption of Rules of Procedure for a new Project Complaint Mechanism (PCM).

17

THE INSPECTION PANEL OF
THE WORLD BANK

Introduction

Contact information

17.1 The Inspection Panel of the World Bank is an independent administrative body authorized to investigate certain complaints concerning projects financed by the Bank. Its contact details are:

Executive Secretary
The Inspection Panel
1818 H Street, NW
Washington, DC 20433
USA
or
PO Box 27566
Washington, DC 20038
Tel: 1 202 458 5200
Fax: 1 202 522 0916
Email: ipanel@worldbank.org
Website: <http://www.worldbank.org/inspectionpanel>

General description

17.2 The Inspection Panel of the World Bank is a permanent body created in 1993 to review projects financed by the Bank, which are the subject of complaints alleging non-compliance by the Bank's Management with the Bank's own operational policies and procedures with respect to project design, appraisal, and/or implementation.[1] The Panel may receive requests for review from groups of people who claim to be adversely affected by such non-compliance.

Although the Panel is independent in its operation, it is assisted in its work by the administrative facilities of the World Bank, and is located at the Bank's headquarters. Furthermore, Panel recommendations to investigate complaints are subject to the formal approval of the Bank's Executive Directors.[2] The findings and recommendations of the Panel are presented in the form of a report to the President of the Bank and the Executive Directors. The Board of Directors may decide what action to take, if any, to implement the report. The Panel has no formal role in monitoring implementation of its recommendations.

When the Panel receives a request for inspection, it registers the request unless it is clearly outside the mandate of the Panel. The Bank's Management is given an opportunity to respond on how it is complying, or intends to comply, with the policies and procedures that are the subject of the complaint. The next phase is an eligibility review, in which the Panel assesses whether a full investigation is warranted, on the basis of the eligibility criteria set out in the Inspection Panel's governing instruments. If the Panel decides that an investigation is required, it makes a recommendation to this effect to the Bank's Executive Directors. The Executive Directors should approve the Panel's recommendation subject only to consideration of the eligibility criteria. One or more panelists are then charged with conducting the investigation, which generally includes site visits, expert advice, and consultations with the requester, the borrowing state, and other interested parties. The Panel submits a report to the Executive Directors, including its findings as to whether there has been non-compliance with Bank policies and procedures. The Executive Directors decide, once Management has had an opportunity to respond, what further action should be taken.

The establishment of the Inspection Panel was hailed as a significant step in providing for accountability of an international institution to groups of persons and communities affected by its activities. The Panel process has been subject to close scrutiny and some criticisms, particularly in the early stages of its operation. There have been some clarifications and adjustments to the Panel procedure over time. As of 31 July 2009, the Panel had registered 52 requests for inspection, of the 58 requests submitted; 27 investigations had been recommended, and 24 conducted.[3]

---

[1] Resolution No IBRD 93–10, Resolution No IDA 93–6, *The World Bank Inspection Panel*, 34 ILM 520 (1995) ('Panel Resolution'). Available at <http://www.worldbank.org/inspectionpanel>.

[2] There are 24 Executive Directors of the World Bank. Five are appointed by the members with the largest number of shares (currently US, Japan, Germany, France, and the UK), and the remainder are elected by the other members of the World Bank.

[3] International Bank for Reconstruction and Development, *Accountability at the World Bank: The Inspection Panel at 15 Years* (2009) at 200.

Institutional Aspects

Governing texts

Procedure

17.3 The principal text governing the operations of the Inspection Panel is the Resolution establishing the World Bank Inspection Panel, adopted on 22 September 1993 ('Panel Resolution').[4] The Resolution provides guidance on the selection of Panel members and powers of the Panel and provides general outlines of the Panel's rules of procedure. Clarifications on the meaning of the text of the Panel Resolution were made by the Executive Directors in a review of the experience of the inspection procedure completed in 1996,[5] and again in 1999.[6]

The detailed rules of procedure regulating the operation of the Panel are to be found in the Operating Procedures adopted by the Panel in 1994.[7]

Substantive law

17.4 The applicable standards to be applied by the Inspection Panel are the World Bank's operational policies and procedures. These include instructions adopted by the Management of the Bank such as 'Operational Policies', 'Bank Procedures', 'Operational Directives', which are, generally speaking, binding upon Bank employees.[8] The Panel cannot rely upon non-binding policy statements such as 'Guidelines' and 'Best Practices'.[9] In addition, as already noted, the Panel may not examine the adequacy of the policies and procedures themselves.

Organization

Composition

17.5 The Inspection Panel is composed of three members of different nationalities from countries which are members of the Bank. They are appointed by the Bank's Board of Directors, acting upon the recommendation of the President of

---

[4] Panel Resolution, *supra* note 1.

[5] Review of the Resolution establishing the Inspection Panel: Clarification of certain aspects of the Resolution, 17 October 1996, Annual Report of the Inspection Panel 29 (1 August 1996–31 July 1997) ('1996 Clarification').

[6] 1999 *Clarification of the Board's Second Review of the Inspection Panel*, available at <http://www.worldbank.org/inspectionpanel> ('1999 Clarification').

[7] Operating Procedures, Inspection Panel for the International Bank for Reconstruction and Development and the International Development Association, 19 August 1994, 34 ILM 510 (1995) ('Operating Procedures').

[8] These include the following instruments: Bank's Operational Policies; Bank Procedures and Operational Directives, and similar documents. They include Operational Policies on, for example, Environmental Assessment, Indigenous Peoples, Cultural Property, and Involuntary Resettlement. The World Bank's Operational Manual can be accessed via the Inspection Panel website.

[9] Panel Resolution, para 12.

the World Bank for a non-renewable five-year term.[10] The members of the Panel elect a Chairperson for a renewable one-year term.

Panel members are selected on the basis of the following characteristics: ability to deal with cases thoroughly and fairly; independence from Bank Management; exposure to developmental issues and living conditions in developing states; and, preferably, knowledge and experience of the operations of the World Bank.[11] Former officers of the Bank and other members of staff can be selected to serve on the Panel only after two years have elapsed since the end of their service in the World Bank Group,[12] and panellists may not be employed by the World Bank group after the end of their service on the Panel.[13]

Ineligibility of Panel members   Panel members may not participate in the hearing and investigation of any request related to a matter in which they have a personal interest, or have had significant involvement in any capacity.[14]   **17.6**

Panel members may only be removed from office by a decision of the Executive Directors, for cause.[15]

Plenary/chambers

All members of the Inspection Panel participate in the review of a request for inspection.   **17.7**

Appellate structure

There are no appeals over the recommendations of the Inspection Panel.   **17.8**

Technical/scientific experts

During the conduct of its investigation the Panel may hire independent consultants to research specific issues related to the case.[16] This commonly occurs. The Panel may also receive written or oral submissions from any independent expert (other than one hired by the Panel).[17]   **17.9**

Under the Panel Resolution, the Panel will also consult, as needed, with officers of the Bank with particular knowledge on the method of execution of the Bank's projects (Director-General, Operations Evaluation Department, and the Internal Auditor).[18] Similarly, the advice of the Legal Department of the World Bank will be sought by the Panel.[19]

---

[10] Ibid, para 2. As of 31 July 2009, the members were: Werner Kiene (Austria) (Chairperson); Roberto Lenton (Argentina); and Alf Morten Jerve (Norway). Eimi Watanabe (Japan) was to replace Werner Kiene when his term of office ended on 31 October 2009. Roberto Lenton was to be the Chairperson with effect from 1 November 2009.
[11] Panel Resolution, para 4.   [12] Ibid, para 5.   [13] Ibid, para 10.
[14] Ibid, para 6.   [15] Ibid, para 8.   [16] Operating Procedures, para 45(e).
[17] Ibid, paras 45(d), 50.   [18] Panel Resolution, para 21.
[19] Ibid, para 15; Operating Procedures, para 62.

Secretariat

17.10 The Inspection Panel is assisted in the conduct of its investigation by a small secretariat, headed by an Executive Secretary.[20] The secretariat is functionally independent of the World Bank Management and is responsible only to the Inspection Panel. The secretariat is responsible for maintaining the Panel's register and for providing administrative support to Panel operations, handling communications with requesters and potential requesters, and disseminating information regarding Panel activities and Panel reports.

Jurisdiction and access

Ratione personae

17.11 The Panel may receive requests for inspection presented to it by an affected party from the territory of the borrowing state that can demonstrate that its rights and interests have been or are likely to be directly affected by an act or omission of the Bank as a result of failure of the Bank to follow its operational policies and procedures in relation to a Bank-financed project.[21]

A request cannot be made by a single individual (or on his or her behalf), but rather must be made by a community of persons, such as an organization, association, society, or other grouping of individuals.[22] The Executive Director's 1996 Clarification explained that the term 'community of persons' implies any two or more persons who share some common interests or concerns.

The request is to be presented by the affected party, or by its local representative. In exceptional cases, where the requesting party alleges that no appropriate local representative is available, it may proceed with a foreign representative, subject to approval by the Executive Directors at the time they consider the request for inspection.[23]

A request for investigation may be made by any Executive Director in special cases of serious alleged violations of policies and procedures, and, at any time, by the Executive Directors acting as a body.[24]

Ratione materiae

17.12 The scope of the Panel's jurisdiction covers requests relating to acts or omissions of the Bank resulting from a failure on the part of the Bank to follow operational policies and procedures pertaining to the design, appraisal,

---

[20] Panel Resolution, para 11.

[21] Panel Resolution, para 12.

[22] Ibid, para 12.

[23] Ibid. See eg *Inspection Panel Investigation Report. The Qinghai Project, A Component of the China: Western Poverty Reduction Project*, 28 April 2000, available at <http://siteresources. worldbank.org/EXTINSPECTIONPANEL/Resources/CHINA-InvestigationReport.pdf>. The request for inspection was made by the International Campaign for Tibet, a US-based NGO.

[24] Panel Resolution, para 12.

and/or implementation of a project (including failure to require the borrower state to comply with its loan-related obligations with respect to such policies and procedures).[25] Such failure must have had or must threaten to have a material adverse effect.[26]

A request for an investigation made to the Panel by an Executive Director must demonstrate that a serious violation of the Bank's policies and procedures has taken place.[27]

The Panel is not authorized to deal with: complaints with respect to actions that are the responsibility of parties other than the Bank (such as the borrower); complaints against procurement decisions; requests submitted after the loan has been closed or more than 95 per cent disbursed; and requests on issues on which the Panel has previously made a recommendation, unless justified by new evidence or circumstances not known at the time of the prior request.[28]

As noted above, the Panel is not charged with reviewing the appropriateness of the policies or procedures of the Bank, but merely with ensuring that the Bank observes them. The competence of the Panel extends only to acts and omissions of the two organizations which adopted the Panel Resolution—the International Bank for Reconstruction and Development (IBRD) and the International Development Association (IDA); it does not extend to other institutions of the World Bank Group such as the International Finance Corporation (IFC) or the Multilateral Investment Guarantee Agency (MIGA).[29] However, it extends to any project or programme financed in whole or part by the IBRD or IDA.[30]

The co-financing of projects by various international and regional financial institutions raises the possibility that complaints or requests may be lodged in the inspection or related mechanisms of more than one bank in respect of the same project.[31]

Ratione temporis

The request must meet two temporal requirements: it may not be presented   **17.13** before the requesting party has taken measures to bring the issue to the attention of the Bank's Management, and the Management's response has proved to have been unsatisfactory (exhaustion of remedies);[32] and the request must not

---

[25] Panel Resolution, paras 12, 13.
[26] Panel Resolution, para 12.
[27] Ibid, para 12.
[28] Operating Procedures, para 2.
[29] On IFC and MIGA, see Chapter 18.
[30] This would include, for example, projects funded through trust funds administered by the Bank, such as the Global Environment Facility, *The Inspection Panel at 15, supra* note 3, at 28.
[31] Ibid, at 62–63. Such a situation arose in relation to the Bujagali Falls hydroelectric project in Uganda, where submissions were made to the Inspection Panel and the African Development Bank's Compliance Review and Mediation Unit, and arrangements for cooperation in review of the requests were put in place. IPN Request RQ07/1. On the African Development Bank mechanism, see Chapter 18.
[32] Panel Resolution, paras 13, 16.

be presented after the loan has been fully or substantially disbursed (at least 95 per cent of the loan sum).[33]

Advisory jurisdiction

17.14 The Inspection Panel does not have jurisdiction beyond review of requests for inspection.

Procedural Aspects

Languages

17.15 The working language of the Inspection Panel is English, but requests may be submitted in a local language where they are submitted directly by affected people and the latter are unable to obtain a translation. The Operating Procedures note that, where the request is not submitted in English, the time needed to ensure an accurate and agreed translation may delay acceptance of the request and consideration by the Panel.[34]

Instituting proceedings

17.16 Panel proceedings are initiated by a submission of a request for investigation. The request must be made in writing and submitted together with two additional copies.[35] It should include the name of the requesting party, its contact address, its signature, the date of the request, and proof of authorization to represent, in the case of requests submitted by a representative.[36] In requests brought by non-local representatives, there must also be clear evidence that no appropriate local representation is available.[37] The Panel procedures make provision for the details of the requesters to remain confidential in certain circumstances, in order to protect them from retaliatory measures.[38]

The request should also describe: the underlying facts (including the harm suffered or expected to be suffered); the steps already taken to deal with the problem; the nature of alleged acts or omissions of the Bank; the actions taken to bring the matter to the attention of Management; and Management's response to such actions.[39] No specific form is required and the request may be made by way of a letter.[40] Parties are, however, encouraged to make use of the model request form

---

[33] Ibid, para 14(c).
[34] Operating Procedures, para 8.
[35] Ibid, para 59.
[36] Ibid, paras 9, 10, 11.
[37] Ibid, para 11.
[38] *The Inspection Panel at 15, supra* note 3, at 23, 49–51.
[39] Panel Resolution, para 16.
[40] Operating Procedures, para 7.

appended to the Operating Procedures, and available on the Inspection Panel website. While the model form asks the requester to specify how it is alleged that the Bank has violated its policies and procedures, it is not essential for the requester to identify in the request the specific policies and procedures at issue. In practice, the requester may not be familiar with the specific policies of the Bank that may be relevant. The 1999 Clarification indicates merely that, as one of the eligibility criteria, the request must assert 'in substance' a serious violation.[41]

The request should be accompanied by supporting documents including: all correspondence with the World Bank staff; notes of meetings with Bank staff; a map or diagram indicating the location of the area affected by the project; and any other evidence in support of the complaint.[42] The request must be delivered by registered, certified, or hand delivered mail to the Inspection Panel or the resident representative of the Bank in the country in which the project is being executed.[43]

When the Panel receives a request, the Chairperson, on the basis of the information in the request, either registers it, asks for additional information, or finds that the request is outside the Panel's mandate. Registration of the request may be refused unless all necessary information and documentation is filed.[44] The Chairperson will also notify the requesters if it is found that the request is without doubt manifestly outside the Panel's mandate.[45]

Financial assistance

The office of the Inspection Panel offers advice on how to prepare and submit a request for inspection, and provides other necessary information required for participation in Panel proceedings.[46] The Bank does not provide additional technical assistance or funding to potential requesters.[47]

17.17

Provisional measures

The Inspection Panel is not authorized to render provisional measures.

17.18

Preliminary proceedings

As noted above, if the request is clearly outside the Panel's mandate, or if it is frivolous, it will not be registered. Otherwise the request is registered and a copy of the request is sent to the Bank's Management, which must send a response within 21 days with evidence that it has complied or intends to comply with

17.19

---

[41] 1999 Clarification, para 9(b); *The Inspection Panel at 15, supra* note 3, at 27.
[42] Operating Procedures, para 12.
[43] Ibid, para 14.
[44] Ibid, para 21.
[45] Ibid, para 22.
[46] Ibid, para 15.
[47] See 1996 Clarification.

the relevant policies and procedures.[48] The Panel evaluates the Management's response and the eligibility of the request. [49]

If the Panel is not satisfied on the basis of the response that Management is in compliance (or intends to bring itself into compliance) with Bank policies and procedures,[50] it must decide whether to recommend inspection. As part of this process, the Chairperson may appoint a member of the Panel to conduct a preliminary study of the request (including possibly an on-site inspection).[51] At this stage, the Panel does not investigate in depth the Management's actions, rather the focus of the eligibility phase is on determining whether the request qualifies for a full investigation.[52] In order to recommend an investigation, the Panel must determine that the six eligibility criteria are met. These are the criteria set out in paragraphs 12–14 of the 1993 Resolution and in paragraph 9 of the 1999 Clarification. They are as follows:

(a) the affected party consists of any two or more persons with common interests or concerns who are in the borrower's territory;
(b) the request asserts in substance that a serious violation by the Bank of its operational policies and procedures has or is likely to have a material adverse effect on the requester;
(c) the request asserts that its subject matter has been brought to Management's attention and that, in the requester's view, Management has failed to respond adequately demonstrating that it has followed or is taking steps to follow the Bank's policies and procedures;
(d) the matter is not related to procurement;
(e) the related loan has not been closed or substantially disbursed;
(f) the Panel has not previously made a recommendation on the subject matter or, if it has, the request does assert that there is new evidence or circumstances not known at the time of the prior request.

On the basis of its review of the request and the position of Management, the Panel will confirm if the eligibility criteria have been met and submit its recommendation to the Board of Executive Directors as to whether an inspection should be conducted. The recommendation should normally be submitted within 21 days from the date on which the Panel received Management's initial response.[53]

---

48 Operating Procedures, para 27.   49 Ibid, para 34.   50 Ibid.
51 Ibid, paras 24, 36. The 1999 Clarification notes that borrowers' consent for field visits for the purposes of the inspection procedure is assumed. 1999 Clarification, para 19.
52 *The Inspection Panel at 15, supra* note 3, at 27.
53 Panel Resolution, para 19; Operating Procedures, paras 29(a), 30. The 1999 Clarification stated that the original time limit, set forth in the Resolution for both Management's response to the request and the Panel's recommendation, will be strictly observed except for reasons of force majeure, ie reasons that are clearly beyond Management's or the Panel's control respectively, as may be approved by the Board on a no objection basis.

If the Panel recommends an inspection, the Board will authorize it without discussion except with respect to the specified eligibility criteria.[54]

In certain circumstances, the Panel may propose to defer its decision as to whether to recommend an investigation in order to allow time for the Bank's Management and the requesters to discuss the issues of concern and seek to achieve a resolution.[55] Without formal amendment of the Inspection Panel mechanism, this approach reflects the more 'problem-solving' approach built in to some of the newer review and inspection procedures in other development banks and, in the World Bank Group, in IFC and MIGA.[56]

Written submissions

After a decision to initiate an investigation has been taken, the Panel may request **17.20** written submissions on specific issues from the requesting party, Bank staff, and a variety of other persons and entities (other affected people, experts, government or project officials, or NGOs).[57] In addition, the requesting party and the Bank may present to the Panel or the Inspector (ie the Panel member responsible for the inspection) any supplementary information or evidence considered to be relevant to the request.[58]

Oral submissions

After a decision to initiate proceedings has been taken, the Panel may arrange **17.21** to meet or to receive oral submissions from the requester, Bank staff, and other interested persons and entities).[59] In addition, the Panel can decide to conduct public hearings in the project area,[60] or conduct visits to project sites.[61] In practice, such site visits are routine.

The Panel may also discuss its preliminary findings of fact with the requester (though not necessarily through oral submissions).[62]

Third party intervention

There is no provision for formal third party intervention in the investigation (but **17.22** see *infra* para 17.23).

---

[54] 1999 Clarification, para 9. D Bradlow, 'Private Complainants and International Organizations: A Comparative Study of the Independent Inspection Mechanisms in International Financial Institutions' (2005) 36 *Georgetown Journal of International Law*, 403, at 416 and 419.

[55] *The Inspection Panel at 15, supra* note 3, 52–55.

[56] See Chapter 18.

[57] Operating Procedures, para 45(d).

[58] Ibid, preamble, para 47.

[59] Ibid, para 45(a), (d). The additional persons and entities specified in the Operating Procedures are other affected people, government and project officials of the borrowing state, and NGO representatives.

[60] Ibid, para 45(b).   [61] Ibid, para 45 (c).   [62] Ibid, para 49.

Amicus curiae

17.23 The Panel can request a variety of persons (eg affected persons, government officials, representatives of non-governmental organizations) to attend meetings and
submit written or oral submissions on specific issues.[63] Persons who provide the
Panel or Inspector with sufficient evidence indicating that they have an interest,
apart from an interest in common with the public, may submit information and
evidence relevant to the investigation.[64] Any member of the public may provide
the Panel or Inspector (via the Executive Secretary) with a written document not
exceeding ten pages (including a one-page summary), containing information
that they believe is relevant to the investigation.[65]

The borrowing state, the Executive Director representing that state (or the
guaranteeing state), the legal department of the Bank, and certain officials of the
Bank will also be consulted by the Panel during the inspection proceedings.[66]

Representation of parties

17.24 As noted above, a duly appointed local representative acting on explicit instruc-
tion as the agent of adversely affected people may present the request to the
Inspection Panel.[67] In exceptional circumstances, where there is clear evidence
that there is no adequate or appropriate local representation, a foreign representative acting as agent of the adversely affected people may submit a request, subject to the approval of the Executive Directors.[68] Proof of authority to represent
the affected party must be provided.[69]

Decision

17.25 The final conclusion of the Panel's inspection is prepared in the form of a report,
which is to contain the following information: summary discussion of relevant
facts and steps taken to conduct the investigation; conclusions on the degree of
compliance on the part of the Bank with its policies and procedures; and a list of
supporting documents (which will be available on request from the office of the
Inspection Panel).[70] If a Panel report was adopted by a majority vote, the minority view shall also be stated.[71] The Panel's report is to focus on whether there is a

---

[63] Ibid, para 45(a), (d).
[64] Operating Procedures, preamble ('Participants').
[65] Ibid, paras 50–51. Supporting documentation may be attached, and the Inspector(s) may
request more details if necessary.
[66] Panel Resolution, paras 15, 21; Operating Procedures, paras 60–62.
[67] Operating Procedures, para 4(b).
[68] Ibid, paras 4(c), 11.
[69] Ibid, para 10.
[70] Operating Procedures, para 52.
[71] Panel Resolution, para 24.

serious Bank failure to observe operational policies and procedures with respect to the project.[72] The mandate of the Panel does not extend to making specific recommendations for action that should be taken to remedy the situation.

The report is then submitted to the Executive Directors and the President. Within six weeks, the Bank's Management must submit a written report indicating its recommendations in response to the Panel's findings.[73] The Management's response will normally include an action plan to bring the project into compliance with the relevant policies and procedures. In practice, this action plan should be developed in consultation with the requester and other affected parties, and agreed with the borrowing state.[74]

The Executive Directors then decide what action to take, if any, to give effect to the Panel's recommendations.

Revision of report

A request may be resubmitted to the Panel if new evidence or circumstances not known at the time of the initial request so justify.[75] **17.26**

Appeal

There is no right of appeal over Panel reports. **17.27**

Costs

Proceedings before the Inspection Panel are free of charge, but the requesting party will incur its own legal or other costs. **17.28**

Enforcement of reports

The Bank's Executive Directors decide what follow-up action, if any, to take in response to Panel recommendations.[76] The Bank must inform the requester of the results of the investigation and any action decided by the Executive Directors.[77] The Panel has established a practice of making a return site visit to the project location to explain the findings of the Panel's investigation and the follow-up action agreed by Management.[78] **17.29**

Under the instruments that govern the inspection process, the Panel has no formal role in monitoring implementation of recommendations or the

---

[72] 1999 Clarification, para 13.
[73] Panel Resolution, paras 22, 23; Operating Procedures, paras 53, 54.
[74] 1999 Clarification, para 15; *The Inspection Panel at 15, supra* note 3, at 55–57.
[75] Panel Resolution, para 14(d); Operating Procedures, para 25.
[76] Panel Resolution, para 23.
[77] Operating Procedures, para 55.
[78] *The Inspection Panel at 15, supra* note 3, at 45.

Management's compliance action plan.[79] In practice, in a few cases, the Executive Directors have asked the Panel to play some role in follow-up to an investigation.[80] There have been cases in which a second request has been made where notwithstanding a Panel investigation and a follow-up action plan it is alleged that there remains non-compliance with Bank policies and procedures.[81]

Evaluation

The establishment of the Inspection Panel in 1993 was an innovation, providing a form of direct, if limited, recourse for affected persons to seek review of implementation of Bank-financed projects under certain circumstances. Given the nature and scope of the Bank's activities, the composition, mandate, and functioning of the Inspection Panel have been closely watched by governments and NGOs alike, as well as by other international and regional financial institutions.

It is perhaps surprising, in light of the scale of the Bank's activities, that over the 15 years of its operation, the Panel has received relatively few requests for inspection. This may reflect a lack of awareness of the availability of the procedure or understanding of its functioning, or, in some situations, perhaps concerns about potential consequences for potential requesters of seeking to initiate it. At the same time, it is quite possible that awareness of the Panel's function among Bank staff has served to promote enhanced compliance with applicable Bank policies and procedures.

The Panel is essentially a fact-finding mechanism. Its effectiveness as a recourse mechanism for affected persons might be considered limited by its rather restricted mandate, insofar as it is not intended to recommend specific actions to remedy non-compliance with Bank policies and procedures, nor to look into the substantive adequacy of those policies and procedures, or recommend their amendment. Further, as noted in the preceding section, without a specific request from the Executive Directors, the Panel has no formal role in monitoring compliance with follow-up measures after an investigation has found a case of non-compliance. Nonetheless, the role of the Panel has evolved over time. In some reports, the Panel has made certain observations on systemic issues, in particular as to possible

---

[79] The 1999 Clarification states that: 'The Board should not ask the Panel for its views on other aspects of the action plans not would it ask the Panel to monitor the implementation of the action plans', para 16.

[80] *The Inspection Panel at 15, supra* note 3, at 44–45.

[81] See eg *Argentina/Paraguay Yacyretá Hydroelectric Project* (1996), IPN Request RQ 96/2 and *Paraguay/Argentina Reform Project for the Water and Telecommunications Sector SEGBA V Power Distribution Project (Yacyretá)* (2002) IPN Request RQ02/1. See D Bradlow, 'Private Complainants and International Organizations: A Comparative Study of the Independent Inspection Mechanisms in International Financial Institutions' (2005) 36 *Georgetown Journal of International Law*, 403, at 419–20.

reasons for non-compliance with particular policies and procedures.[82] The Panel has also now been accorded some role after the inspection stage, in following up aspects of the action plans.[83] This is an area in relation to which further evolution might be desirable in the future, given the Panel's independence from the Bank's Management. To a large extent the credibility of the Panel depends upon positive results in terms of future compliance of the Bank's Management with its policies and procedures with respect to the project in question.

The Panel has faced certain challenges in terms of the perception of its role regarding the borrower state. The Panel reviews the Bank's conduct, not that of the borrower. Nonetheless, in some cases, there has been a degree of tension where states might consider that the Panel's activities constitute an unwarranted interference in their domestic affairs, and in some cases the Panel has in its reports drawn attention to some aspect of the situation in the borrower state.[84]

The Panel has taken a proactive approach in some respects, for example in efforts concerning the extent of its consultations with requesters and affected communities. As noted above, the Panel also has introduced elements of more recent 'problem-solving' approaches into its procedures in certain cases. Given the significant developments in this area in other international financial institutions, and given that a compliance adviser and ombudsman is already in place for IFC and MIGA, one might imagine that the establishment of similar alternative mechanisms might be considered in the World Bank, to sit alongside the Inspection Panel, in the future.

REFERENCE

CASE REPORTS

Information on requests for inspection, including panel reports, is available on the Inspection Panel website.

SELECT BIBLIOGRAPHY

International Bank for Reconstruction and Development, *Accountability at the World Bank: The Inspection Panel at 15 Years* (2009).

L Boisson de Chazournes, 'The World Bank Inspection Panel: About Public Participation and Dispute Settlement' in T Treves et al (eds), *Civil Society, International Courts and Compliance Bodies* (2005) 187–203.

D Clark, J Fox, and K Treakle (eds), *Demanding Accountability: Civil-Society Claims and the World Bank Inspection Panel* (2003).

G Alfredson and R Ring (eds), *The Inspection Panel of the World Bank: A Different Complaints Procedure* (2001).

I Shihata, *The World Bank Inspection Panel: In Practice* (2000).

I Shihata, *The World Bank Inspection Panel* (1994).

---

[82] *The Inspection Panel at 15, supra* note 3, at 64–65.
[83] Ibid, at 44–45.   [84] Ibid, at 16–17.

18

OTHER INSPECTION, REVIEW, AND COMPLIANCE MECHANISMS IN INTERNATIONAL FINANCIAL INSTITUTIONS

1. INTER-AMERICAN DEVELOPMENT BANK (IDB) INDEPENDENT INVESTIGATION MECHANISM

Name and seat of the body

18.1.1 The Independent Investigation Mechanism (IIM) of the Inter-American Development Bank was established in 1994, and reviewed in 2001. The IDB Mechanism was under review in 2009 with a view to the establishment of a new Independent Consultation and Investigation Mechanism. Its contact details are:

Independent Investigation Mechanism
Inter-American Development Bank
Stop E-1205
1300 New York Ave NW
Washington, DC 20577
USA
Tel: 202–623-2165

Fax: 202–312-4057
Email: sec-iim@iadb.org
Website: <http://www.iadb.org/mechanism>

General overview

The IIM may address complaints that the Bank has failed in the design, analysis, or **18.1.2**
implementation of proposed or ongoing operations to follow its established operational policies or norms formally adopted for the execution of those policies.[1]

The IIM is administered by a Coordinator who reports to the Board of
Executive Directors of the IDB through the Bank Secretary. Instead of a standing Inspection Panel, the IDB Mechanism establishes a roster of 15 investigators
of not less than ten different nationalities from IDB member countries, from
which panels may be drawn.[2] The roster is composed of individuals of integrity
and recognized competence in areas related to socio-economic development,
who are familiar with Latin America and the Caribbean, and who have indicated a willingness to serve on investigative panels or to advise the Bank on other
matters related to the Mechanism.[3] Former staff members of the Bank may not
be appointed to the roster until at least two years after their service with the Bank
has terminated.[4] Members of the roster may not be employed by the Bank for a
period of two years following termination of his or her appointment to the roster.[5] Appointment to the roster is for a five-year non-renewable term.[6] Members
are appointed to the roster by the Bank's Executive Directors.[7] A member of
the roster may not participate in the review of any request related to a matter in
which he or she has a personal interest or any significant personal involvement
in any capacity.[8]

The Bank receives requests for investigation presented to it by an affected
party in the territory of a borrower/recipient.[9] The request may be submitted
by a representative of an affected party in certain circumstances.[10] An 'affected
party' is a community of persons such as an organization, association, society, or
other grouping of individuals. The affected party must offer reasonable evidence
that its rights or interests have been or are likely to be directly and materially
affected by an action or omission of the Bank as a result of a failure by the Bank

---

[1] *The IDB Independent Investigation Mechanism*, para 1.1.
[2] *The IDB Independent Investigation Mechanism*, para 2.2.
[3] Ibid, para 2.2.
[4] Ibid, para 2.4.
[5] Ibid, para 2.7.
[6] Ibid, para 2.5.
[7] Ibid, para 2.3.
[8] Ibid, para 2.7.
[9] Ibid, paras 3.1–3.2.
[10] Ibid, para 3.3. If no local representative is available, the Executive Directors may agree in
exceptional cases that the request can be filed by another representative.

to follow its operational policies or norms. There is no mandatory format for the request which may be submitted in any of the IDB's official languages. The IIM will accept requests for confidentiality but will not accept anonymous requests. The complaint must state all relevant facts, and annex any evidence as to the validity of the allegations or indicate where such evidence may be obtained. It must also indicate what steps have already been taken to bring the allegations in question to the attention of the Bank's Management, and the response of the Management to those allegations.[11]

The Coordinator of the Investigation Mechanism,[12] in consultation with the Bank's Legal Department, determines whether the request is in compliance with the requirements for applicability of the Mechanism.[13] The review of the request and Management's response is conducted by a member of the roster, who makes a recommendation to the Board of Executive Directors, on the basis of which the Board determines whether an investigation should be conducted.[14] In the event of an investigation, the Board, in consultation with the President, names a panel of no less than three members from the individuals on the roster.[15] In exceptional circumstances, where a serious violation of the Bank's operational norms or policies may have occurred, a Director may request the Board to convene a panel to investigate a matter without a request having been made from outside the Bank.[16]

The panel submits the findings of its investigation to the Board of Executive Directors and to the President, addressing whether the Bank has complied with all relevant Bank operational policies and norms, as well as any recommendations that the panel wishes to make.[17] On the basis of the report and Management's response, the Board of Executive Directors determines what preventive or corrective action, if any, should be taken. Management must implement the decision of the Board and report to the Board on such implementation.[18]

According to the IDB website, by 2009, five cases had been processed under the IIM, and four investigation reports had been authorized.[19] There have, however, been a number of criticisms concerning the operation of the IIM. These

---

[11] Ibid, para 4.1.

[12] The creation of the Coordinator position followed a review of the policy in 2001 leading to a revision of the original Independent Investigation Mechanism procedure. Previously the screening at this stage was the responsibility of the President of the Bank.

[13] Ibid, para 4.3.

[14] Ibid, paras 4.5–4.7.

[15] Ibid, paras 5.1–5.2.

[16] Ibid, para 4.9.

[17] Ibid, para 6.2

[18] Ibid, paras 7.1–7.2.

[19] Termoelectrica Del Golfo project (Mexico), 2002; Yacyretá Hydroelectric project (Argentina/Paraguay), 1997; Cana Brava Hydroelectric project (Brazil), 2006; and Yacyretá Hydroelectric project (Argentina/Paraguay), 2004. The registry of cases and panel reports are available on the IIM website.

include, in particular, the lack of clear time limits within which the various stages of the procedure should be completed,[20] and arrangements for monitoring implementation of any recommendations arising out of investigations. Some consultations were commenced in 2004/05 regarding a review of the IIM. In 2009, the IDB initiated a process of consultations on the establishment of a new Independent Consultation and Investigation Mechanism.[21] The proposed new Mechanism would add a consultation phase to address community concerns through alternative dispute resolution methods. It would also introduce changes to the investigation process.

---

[20] See eg D Bradlow, 'Private Complainants and International Organization: A Comparative Study of the Independent Inspection Mechanisms in International Financial Institutions' (2005) 36 *Georgetown Journal of International Law* 403 at 422–23.

[21] IDB, *Proposed Independent Consultation and Investigation Mechanism, Invitation to Comment on draft of April 29, 2009*, available at <http://www.iadb.org/PublicConsultation/>.

2. ASIAN DEVELOPMENT BANK (ADB) INSPECTION FUNCTION

Name and seat of the body

18.2.1 In 2003, the ADB Accountability Mechanism replaced the Inspection Function established in 1995.[22] The Mechanism comprises a consultation phase and a compliance review phase. The contact details of the Accountability Mechanism are:

For the consultation phase:
Special Project Facilitator
Asian Development Bank
6 ADB Avenue, Mandaluyong City 1550
Metro Manila, Philippines
Tel: (63–2) 632–4825
Fax: (63–2) 636–2490
Email: spf@adb.org

For the compliance review phase:
Secretary, Compliance Review Panel
Asian Development Bank
6 ADB Avenue
Mandaluyong City 1550
Philippines
Tel: +632 632 4149
Fax: +632 636 2088
Email: crp@adb.org
Website:

---

[22] The Board of Directors of the Asian Development Bank initially approved the establishment of an Inspection Function in December 1995. Since 1996, the Bank received eight requests for inspection, relating to four projects. Of these, six were deemed ineligible by the Board Inspection Committee, and only one request went through a full inspection process. A review concluded that the first full inspection process revealed that 'the current inspection process and procedures are lengthy, confusing and complex for stakeholders inside and outside ADB'. ADB, Working Paper (for consideration of the Board on or about 17 March 2003), *Review of the Inspection Function: Establishment of a New Accountability Mechanism*, February 2003. The scope and procedures of the Accountability Mechanism are set out in the ADB *Operations Manual Bank Policies, OM Section L1/BP* and *Operations Manual Operational Procedures, OM Section L1/OP*, issued 19 November 2008.

General overview

The ADB Accountability Mechanism provides a procedure whereby people **18.2.2** adversely affected by ADB-assisted projects may file complaints. The consultation phase of the Accountability Mechanism consists of a special project facilitator (a senior staff member at the level of director-general, selected by and reporting to the President) to respond to specific problems and concerns of locally affected people through a range of informal and flexible methods. The compliance review phase comprises an independent three-member compliance review panel to investigate alleged violations of ADB's operational policies and procedures that have resulted in direct, adverse, and material impacts on project-affected people and to make recommendations for ensuring future compliance and reducing adverse impacts.

Consultation phase

Under the consultation phase, the Special Project Facilitator (SPF) is to seek con- **18.2.3** sensus and agreement among the parties as to the matters in dispute, the modality of problem solving, and its time frame.[23] The scope of the consultation phase is broader than that of compliance review, and is to focus on finding flexible, informal, and cost-effective ways to address issues identified in complaints made to the SPF.[24]

Complaints to the Office of the SPF may be filed only by: (i) any group of two or more people (such as an organization, association, society, or other grouping of individuals) in a borrowing country where the ADB-assisted project is located or a member country adjacent to the borrowing country; (ii) a local representative of the affected group; or (iii) a non-local representative in exceptional cases where local representation cannot be found and the SPF agrees.[25]

The complaint must specify, *inter alia*: (i) that the complainant is, or is likely to be, directly affected materially and adversely by an ADB-assisted project, irrespective of any allegation of non-compliance by the ADB of its operational policies and procedures; (ii) that the complainant claims that the direct and material harm is, or will be, the result of an act or omission of the ADB in the course of the formulation, processing, or implementation of the ADB-assisted project; (iii) a description of the direct and material harm, ie the rights and interests that have been, or are likely to be, directly affected materially and adversely by the ADB-assisted project; and (iv) the desired outcome or remedies that the affected people believe ADB should provide or help through the accountability

---

[23] *Operations Manual Bank Policies (BP), OM Section L1/BP*, issued 19 December 2008, para 8.
[24] *Operations Manual Operational Procedures, OM Section L1/OP*, issued 19 December 2008, para 9. Nonetheless, certain complaints, identified in para 10 of the Operational Procedures, are excluded from the consultation phase of the Accountability Mechanism.
[25] *Operations Manual Operational Policies (OP), OM Section L1/OP*, issued 19 December 2008, para 6.

mechanism.[26] The complaint must, *inter alia*, describe the complainant's good faith efforts to address the problems first to the relevant Operations Department concerned.[27] The identity of the complainant may be kept confidential.

At various stages of the consultation phase, the complainant may opt to request compliance review, including where the complaint is found by the SPF to be ineligible, where the complainant chooses not to continue the consultation phase, or while the course of action decided upon during the consultation phase is being implemented.[28] Any remedial actions that are adopted as a result of the consultation process will reflect an agreement among the relevant parties, subject to ADB's procedures. Remedial actions involving a major change in the project will require approval by Management or the Board according to ADB's procedures.[29]

Compliance review

18.2.4 With regard to compliance review, the Compliance Review Panel (CRP) consists of three members, two of whom are from regional countries and the third from a non-regional country.[30] The selection criteria for panel members include: (i) the ability to deal thoroughly and fairly with the request brought to them; (ii) integrity and independence from Management; (iii) exposure to developmental issues and living conditions in developing countries; and (iv) knowledge of and experience with the operations of ADB or comparable institutions, and/or private sector experience. Members are appointed by the Board for a non-renewable five-year term.[31]

The purpose of the compliance review is to investigate whether the ADB has complied with its operational policies and procedures in an ADB-assisted project that materially and adversely affects local people during the formulation, processing, or implementation of the project.[32] The conduct of other parties (such as the borrower, etc) is considered only to the extent directly relevant to an assessment of ADB's compliance. After carrying out its review, the CRP will issue to the Board its findings and recommendations, which may include recommendations, if appropriate, for any remedial changes in the scope or implementation of the project.[33]

The criteria for eligibility to file a request for compliance review mirror those for the consultation phase.[34] In addition, any one or more of the Board of Directors may make such a request, after raising their concerns first with Management of the ADB, in special cases involving allegations of serious

---

[26] *Operations Manual Operational Policies, OM Section L1/OP*, issued 19 December 2008, para 8.
[27] Ibid.
[28] Ibid, para 12.   [29] Ibid, para 31.
[30] In 2009, the current members are: Rusdian Lubis (Chair) (Indonesia); Antonio La Viña (Philippines); and Anne Deruyttere (Belgium).
[31] *Operations Manual Operational Policies (OP), OM Section L1/OP*, issued 19 December 2008, para 34.
[32] Ibid, para 37.   [33] Ibid.   [34] Ibid, para 41.

violations of ADB's operational policies and procedures relating to an ongoing ADB-assisted project that have or are likely to have a direct, material, and adverse effect on a community or other grouping of individuals residing in the country where the project is being implemented or residing in a member country adjacent to the borrowing country.

The request for compliance review must specify, *inter alia*: a description of the direct and material harm that is or will be the result of the ADB's alleged failure to comply with its operational policies and procedures in relation to the project; the desired outcome and remedies that the project-affected people believe the ADB should provide; and an explanation of the results of the requester's efforts to address the complaint first to the Office of the SPF, or, if the SPF has found the complaint ineligible, an explanation of why the request should nonetheless be eligible for compliance review.[35]

The CRP determines the eligibility of the request, and if it determines that it is eligible it will recommend to the Board that a compliance review is authorized. The Board authorizes the review on a no-objection basis.[36] The CRP then begins its compliance review, which is not time bound. The CRP will issue terms of reference and a methodology and estimated duration of the review within 14 days of the Board's authorization.[37] Once it has conducted its review, the CRP issues a draft report to the Bank Management and the requester for comment.[38] Having considered the responses, the CRP will finalize its report and submit it to the Board, with its findings and recommendations to ensure project compliance, including recommendations, if appropriate, for any remedial changes in the scope or implementation of the project.[39] The Board then considers the report and makes the final decision regarding any recommendations on how to bring the project into compliance and/or mitigate any harm, if appropriate.[40] In contrast to the World Bank Inspection Panel, the CRP has a formal role in monitoring implementation of remedial actions approved by the Board. The CRP is to report annually to the Board on the implementation of remedial actions, unless the Board specifies otherwise.[41]

By September 2009, 22 complaints had been received and registered by the Special Project Facilitator. Of these, 12 had been found ineligible, in most cases because the complainant had not yet raised the problems with the relevant Bank

---

[35] Ibid, para 45.   [36] Ibid, para 58.

[37] Ibid, para 59. The terms of reference and time frame must be cleared by the Board Compliance Review Committee, which, under the Accountability Mechanism, exercises an oversight function in relation to the CRP. See also *Operational Procedures for the Board Compliance Review Committee*, 29 March 2004.

[38] *Operations Manual Operational Policies (OP), OM Section L1/OP*, issued 19 December 2008, para 61.

[39] Ibid, para 63.   [40] Ibid, para 64.   [41] Ibid, para 70.

Operations Department. Three requests have been registered with the CRP.[42] In addition, in August 2004, the Bank approved the CRP to monitor implementation of a Board decision relating to an earlier inspection.[43]

---

[42] Fuzhou Environmental Improvement Project (China) (2009; compliance review pending); Melamchi Water Supply Project (Nepal) (2004, found ineligible); Southern Transport Development Project (Sri Lanka) (2004; compliance review conducted).

[43] Chashma Right Bank Irrigation Project (Stage III) (Pakistan).

3. THE OFFICE OF THE COMPLIANCE ADVISOR/ OMBUDSMAN (INTERNATIONAL FINANCE CORPORATION (IFC) AND THE MULTILATERAL INVESTMENT GUARANTEE AGENCY (MIGA))

Name and seat of the body

8.3.1 Although part of the World Bank Group, the IFC and MIGA are not presently covered by the World Bank Inspection Panel. However, in 1999, an Office of the Compliance Advisor/Ombudsman (CAO) was established for IFC and MIGA. The contact details of the CAO are:

> Office of the Compliance Advisor/Ombudsman (CAO)
> 2121 Pennsylvania Avenue, NW
> Washington, DC 20433, USA
> Tel: + 1 202 458 1973
> Fax: + 1 202 522 7400
> Email: cao-compliance@ifc.org
> Website: <http://www.cao-ombudsman.org/>

The Office is headed by the Compliance Adviser/Ombudsman and Vice-President.[44]

General overview

8.3.2 The Office of the CAO has three roles:[45]

(1) responding to complaints by persons who are affected by projects and attempting to resolve the issues raised using a flexible, problem-solving approach (the Ombudsman role);

(2) providing a source of independent advice to the President and management of IFC and MIGA in relation to particular projects and broader environmental and social policies (the Advisory role); and

(3) overseeing audits of IFC's and MIGA's social and environmental performance both overall and in relation to sensitive projects, to ensure compliance with policies, guidelines, procedures, and systems (the Compliance role).[46]

The Advisory role is not considered further in this Chapter.

---

[44] Currently Meg Taylor (Papua New Guinea).

[45] See CAO Terms of Reference, available at <http://www.cao-ombudsman.org/about/whoweare/documents/TOR_CAO.pdf>.

[46] CAO Operational Guidelines, April 2000, para 1.1.2, available at <http://www.cao-ombudsman.org>.

Ombudsman function

In relation to the Ombudsman function, any individual, group, community, **18.3.**
entity, or other party affected or likely to be affected by the social and/or environmental impacts of an IFC or MIGA project (or their representative) may make
a complaint to the CAO. The CAO examines the eligibility of the complaint.
In order to be eligible for assessment, the complaint must: pertain to a project
that IFC/MIGA is participating in or actively considering; raise issues pertaining to the CAO's mandate to examine environmental and social impacts; show
that the complainant may be affected if the environmental or social impacts
raised in the complaint occur.[47] If the complaint is found to be eligible, the
CAO Ombudsman notifies the complainants, IFC/MIGA, and the President
and Board of the World Bank Group.

The CAO undertakes a preliminary assessment to clarify the issues and
concerns raised by the complainant with a view to identifying a process for
addressing the issues raised. The assessment, to be completed within 120 days
of the determination of eligibility, results in a decision on whether to proceed to
seek a collaborative solution and an outline of the proposed process.[48] Methods
used to facilitate resolution of complaints may include a number of alternative
dispute resolution processes, such as informal consultations, mediation, fact-
finding, or conciliation. The complaint process is concluded when a settlement
agreement has been reached or when the CAO determines that further investigation or problem-solving efforts are unlikely to be productive. Where an
agreement is reached, the CAO Ombudsman will seek to ensure that it includes
arrangements for review and monitoring.[49] Where a collaborative solution is
not possible, the Ombudsman may transfer the case to the CAO Compliance
for appraisal.[50]

By mid-2009, 109 complaints had been made under the Ombudsman function, with more than 60 found eligible for assessment.[51] Some of these cases had
been transferred for consideration under the Compliance function.

Compliance function

The Operational Guidelines of the CAO provide that the compliance audit **18**
function of the CAO may be triggered by the Ombudsman process (above), by a
request by senior management of IFC or MIGA, or at the discretion of the CAO

---

[47] Ibid, para 2.3.1.
[48] Ibid, para 2.3.3.
[49] CAO Operational Guidelines, para 2.4.5.
[50] Ibid, para 2.4.4.
[51] <http://www.cao-ombudsman.org/cases/>. CAO-Office of the Compliance Advisor/
Ombudsman, *2008–09 Annual Report*, at 51–55, available at <http://www.cao-ombudsman.org/
publications/documents/CAO2008–9AnnualReportEnglish_low.pdf>.

Vice-President.[52] The purpose of CAO project-level auditing is to ensure compliance with policies, standards guidelines, and conditions for IFC and MIGA involvement.[53]

Prior to the commencement of a compliance audit, an appraisal is conducted to ascertain whether an audit is warranted.[54] A final decision to conduct an audit is taken by the CAO Vice-President.[55] If an audit is to take place, terms of reference for the audit are drawn up and submitted to the management of IFC/MIGA. These specify, *inter alia*, the object and scope of the audit, the approach and methods to be used, and the time frame.[56] Audit teams involve external experts, who must be competent, independent, and impartial.[57] Where the audit report finds that IFC/MIGA and/or project sponsors are in compliance, the audit will be closed. Where there is found to be non-compliance, the CAO Compliance office will keep the audit open and monitor the situation until they are satisfied that actions taken by IFC/MIGA will result in compliance.[58]

According to the 2008–9 report of the CAO, between 2000 and 2009 19 cases had been submitted to the CAO Compliance function (18 of which had been submitted since 2004). Compliance audit was found to be merited in seven cases, and the need for review had yet to be determined in three open cases.[59] Information on the status of Ombudsman and Compliance cases is available on the CAO website.

---

[52] CAO Operational Guidelines, para 3.3.1.

[53] Ibid, para 3.1. Compliance audits are conducted in relation to projects not programmes. Where there are more general concerns about policies, guidelines, or standards, these are to be addressed under the CAO's Advisory role. Ibid, para 3.3.2.

[54] Ibid, para 3.3.3. This should be conducted within 45 days from when the CAO Compliance office receives the case. The CAO Operational Guidelines set out a number of criteria to guide the appraisal process.

[55] Ibid, para 3.3.4.

[56] Ibid, para 3.3.5.

[57] Ibid, para 3.3.6.

[58] Ibid, para 3.4.3.

[59] CAO-Office of the Compliance Advisor/Ombudsman, *2008–09 Annual Report*, at 56–57, available at <http://www.cao-ombudsman.org/publications/documents/CAO2008–9AnnualReportEnglish_low.pdf>.

4. AFRICAN DEVELOPMENT BANK INDEPENDENT REVIEW MECHANISM

Name and seat of the body

The establishment of the Independent Review Mechanism of the African **18.4** Development Bank (AfDB IRM) was approved by the Bank's Board of Directors in June 2004.[60] In late 2009 a review of the IRM commenced. The contact details of the Mechanism are:

> Compliance Review and Mediation Unit (CRMU)
> PO Box 323–1002
> 10th Floor, EPI-C, African Development Bank Group
> Tunis-Belvedere,
> Tunisia
> Tel: +216 71 10 20 56, +216 71 10 29 56
> Fax: +216 71 10 37 27
> Email: crmuinfor@afdb.org
> Website: <http://www.afdb.org/en/about-us/structure/independent-review-mechanism/>

General overview

The purpose of the AfDB IRM is to provide people adversely affected by bank- **18.** financed projects a mechanism through which they can seek to ensure that the Bank Group complies with its own policies and procedures.

The Mechanism comprises a Compliance Review and Mediation Unit (CRMU) and a roster of experts. It comprises both problem-solving/mediation and compliance review functions. The CRMU is an organizational unit of the Bank. The Director of the CRMU is appointed by the Bank President in consultation with the Boards. The Director may not have worked for the Bank for two years prior to appointment, and may not work for the Bank in any capacity after serving as CRMU Director.[61] The roster of experts comprises three individuals who must be nationals of Bank member states or state participants in

---

[60] African Development Bank, African Development Fund, Board of Directors, *Resolution B/BD/2004/9-F/BD/2004/7, Independent Review Mechanism*, 30 June 2004 ('2004 Resolution'). Operating Rules and Procedures for the AfDB IRM were approved by the Boards of Directors in July 2006.

[61] Operating Rules and Procedures, para 60. The current CRMU Director is Per Eldar Sovik.

the African Development Fund. They are selected for a non-renewable five-year term, and on the basis of their knowledge and experience of Bank operations. Staff members of the Bank Group may not serve as experts on the roster until two years after termination of their Bank Group service.[62]

The IRM may receive requests from persons adversely affected by a project financed by a Bank Group entity. These must be presented to the CMRU by two or more persons (which may be a community of persons, an organization, association, society, or other grouping of individuals), or by a qualified representative of such persons.[63] The request must demonstrate that the affected persons' rights and interests are or are likely to be directly affected by failure of a Bank Group entity to comply with operational policies or procedures, or in the case of private sector guaranteed projects by failure to comply with certain policies and safeguards.[64] No specific form of request is mandated. People or entities seeking advice on how to submit a request may contact the CRMU for information.[65]

The Director of the CRMU conducts a preliminary review of the eligibility of the request. Having received the response of the Bank Management, the Director may determine whether the request should be addressed through a problem-solving exercise or may recommend compliance review. If the Director determines that the request should be addressed through a problem-solving exercise, all relevant parties are to be invited to participate. The exercise may involve a variety of techniques, including mediation, conciliation, facilitation, investigation, and reporting. At the end of the problem-solving exercise, the Director is to produce a problem-solving report, including conclusions and recommendations.[66] If the exercise is not successful within three months (or with the consent of the parties), the Director may recommend to the President or the Board such remedial action as he or she deems appropriate. This may include a recommendation for compliance review.[67] If the problem-solving exercise is successful, the problem-solving report is to include the agreed solution, the implementation of which will be monitored by the CRMU.[68] The Director's problem-solving report may include a recommendation, for consideration by the Boards or the President, that the project undergo compliance review.[69]

---

[62] 2004 Resolution, paras 4–6. The current members of the roster are: Madiodio Niasse (Chair); Maartje van Putten; and Daniel Bradlow.

[63] Operating Rules and Procedures, para 4. In the case of non-local representation, the CRMU requires clear evidence that there is no adequate or appropriate representative in the country in which the project is located, Operating Rules and Procedures, para 13.

[64] 2004 Resolution, para 11; Operating Rules and Procedures, para 2.

[65] Operating Rules and Procedures, para 17.

[66] Operating Rules and Procedures, para 38.

[67] 2004 Resolution, para 21; Operating Rules and Procedures, paras 41–43.

[68] Operating Rules and Procedures, paras 39–40.

[69] Ibid, paras 43, 46.

Where the Director determines that there is prima-facie evidence that the affected parties have been harmed or threatened with harm by a Bank Group-financed project due to the failure to follow relevant policies and procedures, he or she shall submit a report recommending compliance review, with draft terms of reference.[70] In such case, the Director of CRMU will also make recommendations as to the terms of reference and identify two experts to constitute the review panel with the Director.[71] When the panel conducts its compliance review, the Director may vote but only in the event of a deadlock in the deliberations between the other members of the panel.[72]

The panel reports its findings and recommendations to the Bank Boards (or, in certain circumstances, to the President), and they decide whether to accept them.[73] Where the panel finds a failure to observe Bank policies, it may recommend remedial changes to the systems or procedures within the Bank Group to avoid recurrence of similar violations. It may also recommend remedial changes in the scope or implementation of the project, as well as steps to monitor implementation of any changes proposed.[74] However, the panel may not recommend the award of compensation beyond that which may be expressly contemplated in a relevant Bank Group policy.[75]

By 2009, the AfDB IRM had registered four requests. One request had gone to compliance review,[76] and three were registered in 2009.[77] The register of requests is available on the IRM website.

---

[70] 2004 Resolution, para 22; Operating Rules and Procedures, para 44.
[71] Operating Rules and Procedures, para 24.
[72] 2004 Resolution, para 25; Operating Rules and Procedures, para 51.
[73] Operating Rules and Procedures, paras 55–57.
[74] Ibid, para 52.
[75] Ibid, para 53.
[76] Uganda: Bujagali Hydropower Project and Bujagali Interconnection Project.
[77] Ethiopia: Gibe III Hydroelectric Power Project (two requests); and Egypt: Nuweiba Combined Cycle Power Project.

5. EUROPEAN BANK FOR RECONSTRUCTION AND DEVELOPMENT (EBRD) INDEPENDENT RECOURSE MECHANISM

Name and seat of the body

8.5.1 On 29 April 2003, the Board of Directors of EBRD approved an Independent Recourse Mechanism (EBRD/IRM),[78] for local groups directly and adversely affected by a Bank-financed project to raise complaints with an independent arm of the Bank. Its contact details are:

Chief Compliance Officer
EBRD
One Exchange Square
London EC2A 2JN
UK
Tel: 44 (0)20 7338 6000
Fax: 44 (0)20 7338 7633
Email: irm@ebrd.com
Website: <http://www.ebrd.com/irm>

In May 2009, the Board approved a new Project Complaint Mechanism, which is due to come into effect when the requisite staff and experts have been appointed. Complaints received prior to the entry into force of the PCM Rules will generally be dealt with in accordance with the Rules of Procedure for the IRM.

General overview

8.5.2 In common with other similar mechanisms, the Independent Recourse Mechanism comprises both a 'problem-solving' function and a mechanism for reviewing compliance with the specified EBRD policies. The former may incorporate techniques such as fact finding, mediation, conciliation, dialogue facilitation, investigation, and reporting.[79]

---

[78] Document of the European Bank for Reconstruction and Development, *Independent Recourse Mechanism*, as approved by the Board of Directors on 29 April 2003, available at <http://www.ebrd.org/irm>. The EBRD/IRM is administered by the Chief Compliance Officer (CCO). The current CCO is Enery Quinones.

[79] *Independent Recourse Mechanism*, para 4.

Compliance review

18.5.3 Any group of two or more individuals with a common interest that is, or is likely to be, directly and adversely affected by a Bank-financed project, or a duly appointed agent of such group, may file a complaint.[80] The complaint must identify the project and the harm or potential harm resulting from it, and must indicate what steps the complainants have taken to resolve the matter with the EBRD, or the government or sponsor concerned.[81]

Upon registration of the complaint,[82] the Bank's Chief Compliance Officer (CCO) will appoint one of the independent experts from a roster to assist in assessing the eligibility of the complaint. This assessment is based on a desk review where possible, but where required an additional investigation may be conducted, including a site visit or consultations with some or all stakeholders.[83]

The roster of experts comprises 3–10 individuals appointed by the Board for a renewable term of three years. The experts must have expertise in areas relevant to the EBRD/IRM, including the workings of EBRD, exposure to transition issues and living conditions in the Bank's countries of operations, familiarity with responsible corporate practices, and the need to maintain confidentiality of commercially sensitive information. They must also have the ability to act thoroughly, fairly, independently, efficiently, and with integrity.[84] Roster members must not have worked for the Bank for at least two years prior to appointment, and, if they are called upon while on the roster, they shall not be entitled to work for the Bank in the future.

If the CCO and independent expert determine that the request is ineligible, they make a reasoned recommendation to that effect available to the complainants, the sponsor/government concerned, and the relevant Bank department.[85]

The President (if the project has not yet been approved by the Board) or the Board (if the project has been so approved) will consider the eligibility and compliance review assessment report. If the CCO and the expert are of the opinion that there was a possible material policy violation which warrants compliance review, the CCO report will recommend the appointment of a named expert from the roster and include specific terms of reference for the compliance review.

---

[80] Ibid, para 7. The EBRD/IRM will make all reasonable efforts to maintain the identity of complainants confidential where requested. It will not accept anonymous complaints.

[81] Ibid, para 8.

[82] The complaint will not be registered if it is manifestly frivolous or malicious or where the complainants have made no good faith efforts to resolve the issue with the relevant Bank department. *Independent Recourse Mechanism*, para 11.

[83] Ibid, para 15.   [84] Ibid, para 6.   [85] Ibid, para 14.

If following the eligibility assessment, or during the compliance review, the CCO or the expert is of the opinion that serious or irreparable harm will be caused by the continued processing of the operation or implementation of the project, they may recommend to the President the suspension of further work or disbursement relating to the project.[86]

The EBRD/IRM states that it will not have the effect of automatically suspending processing of, or disbursements to, the project pending investigation or review or have the power to suspend or cancel a Bank operation following an investigation. The latter decision may only be made by the President or the Board in exercise of their respective powers and if the Bank has the right to suspend or cancel in accordance with the terms of any applicable credit and/ or investment agreement. The CCO will not be able to recommend the award of compensation or any other benefits to complainants beyond what may be expressly contemplated in the relevant Bank policy.[87]

The compliance review is undertaken by an independent expert, which will report findings as to whether there has been a material policy violation and recommendations to the President or the Board depending upon the status of the project. It is noteworthy that recommendations may be made relating to systemic, prospective, internal changes within the EBRD to ensure future compliance with policies as well as remedial changes in the scope or implementation of the operation or project.[88] The President or the Board, as the case may be, will decide whether or not to accept the expert's findings and recommendations. Where recommendations have been made and approved by the President or by the Board, the CCO will monitor the implementation of the recommendations on a regular basis.[89]

Problem-solving initiatives

8.5.4 When making the eligibility and compliance review assessment of the complaint, the CCO is to consider whether other problem-solving techniques might be usefully employed to resolve the issues underlying the complaint. These may incorporate a range of processes. The CCO may recommend these whether or not the eligibility and compliance review report recommends a compliance review.[90]

By the end of 2008, five complaints had been found eligible under the EBRD/ IRM procedures. One had proceeded to compliance review,[91] and one to a problem-solving initiative.[92]

---

[86] Ibid, para 22. However, if the Bank is under a contractual obligation and there are no other grounds to suspend processing or disbursement, the contractual obligations will be honoured.

[87] Ibid, para 30.   [88] Ibid, para 24.   [89] Ibid, para 26.

[90] Ibid, paras 27–29.

[91] Vlore Thermal Power Generation Project (Albania), IRM, *Annual Report for 2008, Report of the Chief Compliance* Officer, at 1–2.

[92] Main Baku-Tblisi-Ceyhan (BTC) Oil Pipeline project (Atskuri Village, Georgia), ibid, at 2–3.

Project Complaint Mechanism

18.5.5 The new Project Complaint Mechanism (PCM) retains the problem-solving and compliance review functions, and sets out procedures that are broadly similar to those already applicable under the EBRD/IRM. The PCM will be located in the office of the Chief Compliance Officer. The PCM is designed to provide an opportunity for an independent review of complaints from one or more individual(s) or 'organizations'[93] concerning a Bank project which has allegedly caused or is likely to cause harm. An 'organization' is defined in the PCM Rules of Procedure as 'any entity, association or group around which civil society voluntarily organises itself which represents a range of specific interests. Organisations may include community-based organisations, indigenous peoples' organisations and non-governmental organisations.' Thus the new PCM gives NGOs standing to submit a complaint for compliance review where there is an allegation of harm, or likely harm, due to a Bank project.

Complaints under the new procedure must be delivered to the PCM Officer at the Bank.[94] Under the Mechanism, once a complaint is received and registered, an eligibility assessment will be conducted by the PCM Officer and a PCM Expert.[95] Where a complaint is eligible it may qualify for problem-solving initiatives as well as compliance review.[96] Where a compliance review is conducted, and the compliance review expert concludes that the Bank was not in compliance with the relevant EBRD policy, the PCM Officer will monitor the implementation of any recommendations in the Compliance Review Report and will issue biannual monitoring reports.[97]

Evaluation

There have been significant and rather rapid developments in the design of Bank inspection mechanisms since the World Bank Inspection Panel was established in 1993. This evolution is ongoing as evidenced by the reviews pending in 2009 of the mechanisms in the Inter-American Development Bank, African Development Bank, and European Bank for Reconstruction and Development. Development banks continue to face demands for greater transparency and

---

[93] *Project Complaint Mechanism: Rules of Procedure*, Introduction and Purpose, available at <http://www.ebrd.com/about/integrity/irm/about/pcm.pdf>.

[94] The contact details are as set out in para 18.5.1 above. The email address for the PCM is pcm@ebrd.com.

[95] Up to ten PCM experts will be appointed. Candidates will require experience in eg the economic, legal, social, environmental, and related fields, as well as demonstrating appropriate personal qualities. *PCM Rules of Procedure*, para 47.

[96] Ibid, para 29.   [97] Ibid, paras 40, 44.

accountability, and for the expansion of the inspection and review procedures that have thus far been put in place.

The various mechanisms established by the various banks mostly share several common features. They are established within the bank concerned, but key components of the process are meant to function independently of the bank. They are generally restricted to receiving complaints about whether or not, in relation to a particular project, the bank in question has followed its own operational policies, for example relating to environmental assessment, indigenous peoples, and/or resettlement policies. Requests for inspection can be submitted by, or on behalf of, persons directly affected (or likely to be affected) by the project in question. After a preliminary review of eligibility, a recommendation is made as to whether an investigation is required. The decision as to whether or not to hold an investigation is made, formally at least, by the Board of Directors of the bank itself. Typically, those who serve on the review panels are appointed by the Boards of Directors of the bank in question.

The establishment of such mechanisms has generally been welcomed as a valuable and necessary step towards improving the accountability of international financial institutions. However, over the first few years of experience of these inspection mechanisms, a number of common concerns were expressed. These have related, *inter alia*, to the complexity and transparency of the inspection procedures; the level of awareness of the procedures in recipient countries; the independence of the mechanism from the bank concerned; the impact of inspection on the disbursement of project funds (the question of interim protection); and the remedies that may, or may not, be available through the mechanism. Some of these types of concerns are addressed in more recent developments in relation to some of the mechanisms briefly surveyed in this Chapter. In particular, there appears to be growing recognition, at least in relation to some of the mechanisms, that panels should be able to make recommendations or observations of a more systematic nature, and also that there is a need to provide for review and monitoring of implementation of findings and recommendations.

The other notable development has been the evolution of alternative dispute resolution or problem-solving processes to assuage concerns about projects and seek to reach agreed solutions. This evolution can be seen in each of the mechanisms reviewed here, apart from the Inter-American Development Bank, which is currently considering the introduction of a revised process to incorporate such procedures.

Finally, it is striking that some of the mechanisms reviewed in this Chapter have been very sparsely utilized. This must raise questions about the degree of public awareness of their existence and mandates, and highlight the need for further outreach and awareness-raising activities as well as the need to ensure confidentiality for complainants where necessary.

REFERENCE

SELECT BIBLIOGRAPHY

D Bradlow, 'Private Complainants and International Organizations: A Comparative Study of the Independent Inspection Mechanisms in International Financial Institutions' (2005) 36 *Georgetown Journal of International Law*, 403.

PART VII

COMPLIANCE PROCEDURES IN
MULTILATERAL ENVIRONMENTAL
AGREEMENTS

19

COMPLIANCE PROCEDURES IN MULTILATERAL ENVIRONMENTAL AGREEMENTS

The first edition of this Manual addressed what was then 'the only example of a treaty-specific non-compliance procedure adopted under a multilateral environmental agreement'. The procedure concerned was that established under the Montreal Protocol on Substances that Deplete the Ozone Layer. It was noted that while the Montreal Protocol procedure was the only one of its type then in operation, the development of similar mechanisms for other environmental agreements was in progress. This has now come to pass, and there are numerous such mechanisms in existence.[1] It has been common for multilateral environmental agreements (MEAs) adopted since the early 1990s to contain 'enabling' provisions providing for the establishment of procedures and mechanisms on compliance by the treaty's governing body (generally termed the 'Conference of the Parties' or 'Meeting of the Parties') once they have entered into force.[2]

The mechanisms reviewed in this Chapter are not courts or tribunals and do not comprise dispute resolution mechanisms as such. As with the Montreal Protocol procedure, such procedures and mechanisms are stated to be without prejudice to other dispute settlement procedures contained in the agreement. Indeed their function is in most respects quite different: in general terms it is to promote compliance with the provisions of the agreement in question, including through the provision of assistance to parties where required. Their focus is on the review of compliance with treaty obligations. Their design generally

---

[1] For a more comprehensive review of such mechanisms, see, for example, T Treves et al (eds), *Non-Compliance Procedures and Mechanisms and the Effectiveness of International Environmental Agreements* (2009); United Nations Environment Programme, *Compliance Mechanisms under Selected Multilateral Environmental Agreements* (2007).

[2] See eg art 8, 1987 Montreal Protocol on Substances that Deplete the Ozone Layer; art 18, 1997 Kyoto Protocol to the UN Framework Convention on Climate Change; art 15, 1998 Aarhus Convention on Access to Information, Public Participation in Decision-Making and Access to Justice in Environmental Matters; art 34, 2000 Cartagena Protocol on Biosafety.

recognizes that a state may fail to comply with its obligations under a treaty as a result of factors beyond its control—for example, for reason of a lack of resources or capacity. To address such circumstances, compliance procedures provide that one response to non-compliance may be financial or technical assistance to the non-complying party.

This Chapter briefly surveys three of the mechanisms that have been established under different MEAs: the Montreal Protocol on Substances that Deplete the Ozone Layer, the Kyoto Protocol to the United Nations Framework Convention on Climate Change, and the UNECE Aarhus Convention on Access to Information, Public Participation in Decision-Making and Access to Justice in Environmental Matters. These have been selected as illustrations, as they exhibit some similar elements and general characteristics, but with some significant variations as to, for example, who can trigger and otherwise be involved in the procedure, and the possible responses to findings of non-compliance. Such questions tend to be among the most controversial elements when it comes to negotiating non-compliance rules and procedures under multilateral environmental agreements.

1. NON-COMPLIANCE PROCEDURE UNDER THE 1987 MONTREAL PROTOCOL ON SUBSTANCES THAT DEPLETE THE OZONE LAYER

Background

The 1987 Montreal Protocol, which was adopted pursuant to the 1985 Vienna Convention on Protection of the Ozone Layer, provides for the reduction and phase-out of the production and consumption of substances that deplete the ozone layer, such as chlorofluorocarbons (CFCs). By 2009, there were 196 parties to the Montreal Protocol. The Secretariat of the Vienna Convention and Montreal Protocol is located at:

19.1.1

> Ozone Secretariat
> United Nations Environment Programme
> United Nations Avenue, Gigiri
> PO Box 30552
> Nairobi 00100
> Kenya
> Telephone: (254 20) 762 3851/3611
> Facsimile: (254–20) 762 46 91/92/93
> Email: ozoneinfo@unep.org
> Website: <http://www.ozone.unep.org>

General overview

Article 8 of the Montreal Protocol required the parties, at their first meeting, to consider and approve procedures and institutional mechanisms for determining non-compliance with the provisions of the Protocol and for treatment of parties found to be in non-compliance. The groundwork for the non-compliance procedure was laid by a decision of the Meeting of the Parties to the Montreal Protocol in 1990. The present procedure was established in 1992 (and subsequently revised in 1998).[3]

19.1.2

---

[3] Decision II/5, Report of the Second Meeting of the Parties to the Montreal Protocol on Substances that Deplete the Ozone Layer, Annex IV, UN Doc UNEP/Oz L Pro 2/3, 29 June 1990; revised by UN Doc UNEP/Oz L Pro 2/3, 25 November 1992; and revised by Decision X/10, Annex II, Report of the Tenth Meeting of the Parties, UNEP/Oz L Pro 10/9, 3 December 1998. See now *Handbook on the Montreal Protocol on Substances that Deplete the Ozone Layer* (7th edn, 2006), Non-Compliance Procedure (1998) (Hereinafter '1998 Non-Compliance Procedure'). A detailed outline of the non-compliance procedure is contained in the Ozone Secretariat publication, *Implementation Committee under the Non-Compliance Procedure of the Montreal Protocol on Substances that Deplete the Ozone Layer: Primer for Members*, October 2007.

The Implementation Committee comprises ten parties elected by the Meeting of the Parties for two years, based on equitable geographical distribution.[4] In contrast to certain compliance mechanisms under other MEAs, membership in the Committee is accorded to state representatives, not to individuals. The Committee members serve a two-year term, and may be re-elected for a second term of the same duration. The Implementation Committee meets twice a year unless it decides otherwise.

Any party to the Protocol may submit to the Secretariat its reservations regarding the implementation of the Protocol by another state party.[5] The Secretariat then invites that party to respond. The complaint, the reply, and any supporting information are then referred to the Implementation Committee. A case can also be referred to the Implementation Committee by the Secretariat, acting on its own initiative, after giving the party concerned an opportunity to respond.[6] A party may also submit a matter to the Implementation Committee in relation to its own compliance with its obligations under the Protocol.[7]

The Implementation Committee considers information brought before it. In so doing, it may request further information and undertake, with the consent of the party concerned, on-site information gathering.[8] The procedure before the Implementation Committee is governed by the Rules of Procedure for the Meeting of the Parties to the Protocol, applied *mutatis mutandis.* The state party whose compliance is called into question is entitled to participate in the proceedings before the Committee.[9]

The Implementation Committee is required to seek to find an amicable solution to the matter, on the basis of respect for provisions of the Protocol.[10] The Committee submits its recommendations, which may include the identification of facts and causes relating to individual cases of non-compliance and steps that the party concerned should take in order to bring itself into compliance. These findings and recommendations are contained in a report to the Meeting of the Parties,[11] which has the authority to decide to take steps to bring about compliance with the Protocol.[12] According to the Indicative List of Measures in Decision II/5 of the Meeting of the Parties (on the establishment of the non-compliance procedure), such steps could include the provision of special assistance to the non-complying state, issuing of cautions, and suspension of rights and privileges under the Protocol. In practice, most actions have been aimed at facilitating compliance with the Protocol and monitoring measures to restore compliance, through, for example, the submission of action plans by the party concerned.

There have now been numerous decisions adopted by the Meeting of the Parties on the basis of findings of non-compliance by the Implementation Committee.[13]

---

[4] 1998 Non-Compliance Procedure, para 5.
[5] Ibid, para 1.   [6] Ibid, para 3.   [7] Ibid, para 4   [8] Ibid, para 7(c)–(e).
[9] Ibid, para 10.   [10] Ibid, para 8.   [11] Ibid, para 9.   [12] Ibid, para 9.
[13] The Decisions of the Meeting of the Parties on non-compliance can be found at <http://ozone.unep.org/Publications/MP_Handbook/Section_2_Decisions/Article_8/decs-non-compliance/>,

2. PROCEDURES AND MECHANISMS RELATING TO COMPLIANCE UNDER THE 1997 KYOTO PROTOCOL TO THE 1992 UNITED NATIONS FRAMEWORK CONVENTION ON CLIMATE CHANGE

Background

The 1997 Kyoto Protocol was adopted under the auspices of the 1992 UN Framework **19.2.1**
Convention on Climate Change (UNFCCC). Under the Protocol, developed country parties (referred to as Parties included in Annex I) are committed to quantified greenhouse gas emission limitation and reduction commitments for the period to 2012, as set out in Annex B to the Protocol. A significant portion of these reductions are meant to be achieved by the parties concerned at the domestic level. However, the Protocol also establishes certain 'flexibility' mechanisms, under articles 6, 12, and 17, to help parties cut the cost of meeting their emissions targets by taking advantage of opportunities to reduce emissions, or increase greenhouse gas removals from the atmosphere, that cost less to achieve in other countries than at home.

Article 18 of the Protocol provides that, at its first session, the Conference of the Parties serving as the Meeting of the Parties to the Kyoto Protocol (CMP) should approve appropriate and effective procedures and mechanisms on non-compliance.[14] The Protocol entered into force on 16 February 2005. The procedures and mechanisms relating to compliance under the Kyoto Protocol were adopted by Decision 27/CMP.1[15] of the CMP to the Kyoto Protocol in 2005. At the time of writing, the future of the Kyoto Protocol, and its compliance mechanism, remains uncertain as states seek to negotiate the framework for long-term cooperative action to mitigate climate change. Negotiations are being conducted under both the 1992 UNFCCC

where decisions in respect of some 51 parties are recorded. Romanin Jacur notes that decisions relating to findings of non-compliance have increased in number since 1999 when the 'grace period' for developing countries under art 5 of the Montreal Protocol ended and they became subject to control and phase-out obligations with respect to regulated ozone depleting substances. F Romanin Jacur, 'The Non-Compliance Procedure of the 1987 Montreal Protocol to the 1985 Vienna Convention on Substances that Deplete the Ozone Layer', in T Treves et al (eds), *Non-Compliance Procedures and Mechanisms and the Effectiveness of International Environmental Agreements* (2009) 11, at 31.

[14] Article 18 further provides that: 'Any procedures and mechanisms under this Article entailing binding consequences shall be adopted by means of an amendment to this Protocol.'

[15] *Procedures and mechanism relating to compliance under the Kyoto Protocol*, Decision 27/CMP.1, Doc FCCC/KP/CMP/2005/8/Add 3, at 92. The Committee's Rules of Procedure were adopted in Decision 4/CMP.2, Doc FCCC/KP/CMP/2006/10/Add 1, at 17, and amended by Decision 4/CMP.4, Doc FCCC/KP/CMP/2008/11/Add 1, at 14.

and the 1997 Kyoto Protocol. While parties to the Kyoto Protocol are obliged under its terms[16] to negotiate further commitments for the post-2012 period, it is by no means certain at the time of writing that the Kyoto Protocol or its procedures will survive in their present form.[17] The Secretariat to the Climate Change Convention and Kyoto Protocol (UNFCCC Secretariat) is located at:

Haus Carstanjen
Martin-Luther-King-Strasse 8
53175 Bonn
Germany

PO Box 260124
D-53153 Bonn
Germany
Tel: (49–228) 815–1000
Fax: (49–228) 815–1999
Website: <http://unfccc.int>

General overview

19.2.2 Decision 27/CMP.1 established a Compliance Committee composed of 20 members. The Committee is to function through a plenary, a bureau, and two branches: the facilitative branch and the enforcement branch.[18] Ten members of the Committee are elected to serve in each branch. Members of the Committee serve in their individual capacities, and must have recognized competence related to climate change in relevant fields such as the scientific, technical, socio-economic, or legal fields.[19] Members of the enforcement branch must have legal experience.[20] Special rules apply as to composition of each branch in terms of geographic representation, and representation of members from developing and developed country parties.[21] Members generally serve four-year terms and may not serve more than two consecutive terms.[22]

The adoption of decisions by the Committee requires a quorum of three-fourths of the members to be present. The Committee is to seek to reach decisions by consensus, but, where it is unable to do so, decisions may be made by three-fourths majority vote of the members present and voting. A special rule applies to decisions of the enforcement branch, whereby decisions must be adopted by a majority of members from parties in Annex I present and voting, as well as a majority of members from parties not in Annex I (ie in general terms, a majority of members from both developed and developing country parties).

---

[16] Kyoto Protocol, art 3(9).
[17] Further information on the progress and outcome of these negotiations will be made available on the UNFCCC website.
[18] Decision 27/CMP.1, Annex, para. II.3.
[19] Ibid, para II.6.   [20] Ibid, para V.3.   [21] Ibid, paras IV.1 and V.1.
[22] Ibid, paras. IV.2 and V.2.

Mandates of the facilitative and enforcement branches

.2.3 The facilitative branch of the Compliance Committee is responsible for providing advice and facilitation to the parties in implementing the Protocol and for promoting compliance by parties with their obligations under the Protocol.[23] Decision 27/CMP.1 sets out the types of compliance issues which fall within the mandate of the facilitative branch.[24]

The enforcement branch is responsible, *inter alia*, for determining whether a party in Annex I (a developed country party) is not in compliance with: its quantified limitation or emission reduction commitments under the Protocol; methodological and reporting requirements; or eligibility requirements in respect of the Protocol's so-called flexibility mechanisms, in articles 6, 12, and 17 of the Protocol.[25]

Submissions may be made to the Committee through the Secretariat by a party with respect to its own compliance or by any party with respect to another party, with corroborating information. Questions of implementation in reports of expert review teams under article 8 of the Protocol may also be submitted to the Committee through the Secretariat.[26]

The bureau of the Committee[27] allocates questions of implementation to the relevant branch in accordance with the mandates set out in Decision 27/CMP.1. The relevant branch then makes a preliminary examination of the question within three weeks of the date of receipt of the question by the branch. The preliminary examination is intended to ensure that, except in relation to communications made by a party in relation to itself, the question is supported by sufficient information, that it is not *de minimis* or ill-founded, and that it is based on the requirements of the Protocol.[28]

General procedures before the Committee

If, after the preliminary examination, a decision is taken to proceed, the party concerned is informed and given an opportunity to comment in writing.[29] In further proceedings before the Committee, the party is entitled to designate one or more persons to represent it during the consideration of the implementation question by the relevant branch. The party may not be present during the elaboration and adoption of the decision of the branch.[30] **19.2.4**

Each branch is to base its deliberations on relevant information provided by: expert review team reports under article 8 of the Protocol; the party concerned; any party that has submitted a question of implementation concerning another

---

[23] Ibid, para IV.4.   [24] Ibid, paras IV.5 and IV.6.
[25] Ibid, paras V.4–6.   [26] Ibid, para VI.1.
[27] Each branch of the Committee elects a chair and vice-chair from among its members (one from Annex I parties and the other from non-Annex I parties). The chairs and vice-chairs of each branch thus elected comprise the bureau of the Committee. Decision 27/CMP.1, Annex, para II.4.
[28] Ibid, para VII.2.   [29] Ibid, paras VII.4 and VII.7.
[30] Ibid, para VIII.2.

party; reports of bodies of the UNFCCC and Kyoto Protocol; and the other branch.[31] In addition, each branch may seek expert advice, and competent intergovernmental and non-governmental organizations may submit relevant factual and technical data.

The decision taken by the branch must include conclusions and reasons, and the party concerned must be informed and given an opportunity to comment in writing. Final decisions are made available to other parties and to the public.[32] Parties may request that decisions are translated into one of the six official languages of the United Nations.

Additional procedures before the enforcement branch

19.2.5 Decision 27/CMP.1 sets out certain specific procedures for proceedings before the enforcement branch. The party concerned is entitled to make a written submission to the enforcement branch, and to request a hearing at which it will have an opportunity to present its views. At the hearing, the party concerned may present expert testimony or opinion.[33] The enforcement branch may also put questions to and seek clarification from the party concerned at the hearing or in writing.

Subject to time limits established in Decision 27/CMP.1, the enforcement branch must either decide not to proceed further with the question, or adopt a preliminary finding of non-compliance.[34] In either case conclusions and reasons must be provided, and the party concerned must be informed. That party then has ten weeks to provide a further written submission regarding the preliminary finding of the enforcement branch. At the latest within four weeks of receipt of the party's submission, the enforcement branch is to adopt its final decision.[35] Time limits may be extended by the enforcement branch where the circumstances so warrant. Additional expedited procedures apply where the question relates to the eligibility requirements relating to the flexibility mechanisms under articles 6, 12, and 17 of the Protocol.[36]

The compliance mechanism provides for a right of appeal to the CMP to the Kyoto Protocol from a final decision of the enforcement branch relating to article 3(1) of the Kyoto Protocol,[37] if the party concerned believes it has been denied due process.[38] In such a case, the CMP may by three-fourths majority of parties present and voting decide to override the decision of the enforcement branch, and refer the matter back to that branch. Appeals must be lodged with the Secretariat within 45 days after the party concerned has been informed of the decision by the enforcement branch.

---

[31] Ibid, paras VIII.3–VIII.5
[32] Ibid, para VIII.7. Such decisions can be found on the website of the UNFCCC Secretariat.
[33] Ibid, paras IX.1, IX.2.   [34] Ibid, para IX.4.
[35] Ibid, para IX.8   [36] Ibid, section X.
[37] ie where the emissions of a party have exceeded its assigned amount under article 3 and Annex B to the Protocol.
[38] Ibid, section XI.

Consequences applied by the Compliance Committee

9.2.6 The compliance mechanism sets out the consequences of non-compliance which may be applied by the facilitative branch and the enforcement branch.

The facilitative branch remedies include the provision of advice and facilitation of assistance, including financial and technical assistance, technology transfer, and capacity building. The facilitative branch may also formulate recommendations to the party concerned.[39]

The enforcement branch may apply a range of consequences depending upon the obligation with which the party concerned is found to be in non-compliance. Where a party is found not to have complied with methodological and reporting requirements, under article 5(1) and (2) of the Protocol, the enforcement branch may issue a declaration of non-compliance and require the development of a plan to analyse causes of non-compliance and set out measures to remedy it, including a timetable.[40] The party concerned will then be required to submit regular progress reports on implementation of the plan.

Where the enforcement branch concludes that a party does not meet eligibility requirements under the flexibility mechanisms, it is to suspend the eligibility of that party.[41]

If the enforcement branch has determined that the emissions of a party have exceeded its assigned amount under Annex B to the Protocol, it shall declare the party not in compliance with its obligations under article 3(1) of the Protocol. The party concerned will be required to develop a compliance plan,[42] and to submit progress reports on an annual basis. The enforcement branch can suspend the party's eligibility to make transfers under article 17 of the Protocol (emissions trading).[43] Finally, the procedure provides that non-compliance under article 3(1) may have consequences in terms of a 'penalty' in respect of the party's assigned amount of emissions in the second commitment period (after 2012).[44]

By September 2009, according to information available on the UNFCCC website, the enforcement branch had considered three questions of implementation.[45] The facilitative branch had received 15 submissions by one state on behalf of the Group of 77 and China in relation to certain Annex I parties.

---

[39] Ibid, section XIV.
[40] Ibid, paras XV.1–2.
[41] Ibid, para XV.4.
[42] Ibid, paras XV.5–7
[43] Ibid, para XV.5(c).
[44] Ibid, para XV.5(a).
[45] In one case, the enforcement branch made a finding of non-compliance (subsequently resolved); in a second, it issued a decision not to proceed further with the question of implementation; and in a third, ongoing, matter it adopted a preliminary finding of non-compliance in October 2009. Further information and documentation relating to these cases can be located on the UNFCCC website at <http://unfccc.int/kyoto_protocol/compliance/enforcement_branch/items/3785.php>.

3. PROCEDURES FOR THE REVIEW OF COMPLIANCE UNDER THE AARHUS CONVENTION ON ACCESS TO INFORMATION, PUBLIC PARTICIPATION IN DECISION-MAKING AND ACCESS TO JUSTICE IN ENVIRONMENTAL MATTERS

Background

19.3.1 The Aarhus Convention was adopted under the auspices of the UN Economic Commission for Europe.[46] The Convention requires parties to guarantee rights of access to information, public participation in decision making, and access to justice in environmental matters. Minimum standards for the extent and implementation of these rights are set out in the Convention. The Secretariat of the Convention is at:

Aarhus Convention Secretariat
Environment, Housing and Land Management Division
United Nations Economic Commission for Europe
Palais des Nations, Av. de la Paix 10
1211 Geneva 10
Switzerland
Tel: + 41 22 917 2682 / 917 1502
Fax: + 41 22 917 0634
Email: public.participation@unece.org
Website: <http://www.unece.org/env/pp>

General overview

19.3.2 Article 35 of the Aarhus Convention requires the Meeting of the Parties to establish optional arrangements of a non-confrontational, non-judicial, and consultative nature for reviewing compliance with the provisions of the Convention. At its first meeting, the Meeting of the Parties to the Aarhus Convention adopted Decision I/7 on Review of Compliance. The decision established the Compliance Committee and set out its structure and functions as well as procedures for the review of compliance.[47]

---

[46] As at September 2009, there were 43 parties to the Aarhus Convention.

[47] ECE/MP.PP/2/Add 8, 2 April 2004, Report of the First Meeting of the Parties, Addendum, Decision I/7. In 2005, an amendment was introduced as regards the composition of the Committee, ECE/MP.PP/2005/2/Add 6, Report of the Second Meeting of the Parties, Addendum, Decision II/5.

The Compliance Committee consists of nine members, who serve in their personal capacity.[48] Members must be nationals of parties and signatories to the Convention and must be of high moral character and recognized competence in the fields to which the Convention relates. The Committee must include some persons with legal experience.[49] It may not include more than one national from the same state. Candidates may be nominated by parties and signatories to the Convention, and by certain types of non-governmental organization. Members are elected by the Meeting of the Parties by consensus (or failing that, may be elected by secret ballot). In the election of members, consideration should be given to geographical distribution of membership and diversity of expertise.[50]

The Committee meets once a year, unless it decides otherwise. In practice, the Committee has also adopted a practice of communicating by electronic means as necessary in dealing with certain preliminary communications as to admissibility of complaints.[51]

Among the functions of the Committee, it must consider submissions, referrals, or communications made under the terms of Decision I/7 by parties to the Convention,[52] by the Aarhus Convention Secretariat,[53] and from the public.[54] The possibility of receiving communications directly from the public is unusual in environmental compliance procedures, and reflects the particular subject matter of the Aarhus Convention.[55]

Submission by parties to the Convention may be brought before Committee: (i) by a party that concludes that despite its best endeavours it will be unable to comply fully with its own obligations under the Convention; or (ii) by one or more parties that have reservations about another party's compliance with its obligations under the Convention.

When the Committee receives a communication from the public, it will bring it to the attention of the party alleged to be in non-compliance as soon as possible, and the party must submit written explanations or statements to the Committee clarifying the matter or describing its response.

---

[48] As at September 2009, the members are: Mr Veit Koester (Chair) (Denmark); Ms Svitlana Kravchenko (Vice-Chair) (Ukraine); Mr Jerzy Jendroska (Poland); Mr Jonas Ebbesson (Sweden); Mr Merab Barbakadze (Georgia); Mr Alexander Kodjabashev (Bulgaria); Mr Vadim Nee (Kazakhstan); Mr Gerhard Loibl (Austria); and Ms Ellen Hey (Netherlands).

[49] Decision I/7, para 2.

[50] Ibid, para 8.

[51] *Guidance Document on Aarhus Convention Compliance Mechanism* (setting out the Committee's modus operandi), available at <http://www.unece.org/env/pp/compliance.htm#Documents>.

[52] Decision I/7, paras 15–16.

[53] Ibid, para 17.

[54] Ibid, paras 18–22.

[55] Under the terms of Decision I/7, para 18, parties were able to notify the Convention depositary that they were unable to accept, for a period of no more than four years, consideration by the Committee of communications from the public.

The Committee may seek the advice of experts in considering communications; it may request further information; or it may, with the consent of the party concerned, undertake information gathering in that party's territory.[56]

When the Committee considers the submission, referral, or communication, the party in respect of which it was made is entitled to participate in the discussions of the Committee, as is a member of the public who has submitted a communication. The Committee sends its draft findings to the party, and the member of the public if relevant, and takes their comments into account in finalization of its findings, measures, and recommendations. The Meeting of the Parties considers the Compliance Committee's report and may decide upon any measures to bring about full compliance with the Convention. Pending consideration of the report by the Meeting of the Parties, with a view to addressing compliance issues without delay, the Compliance Committee is entitled, in consultation with the party concerned, to provide advice and facilitate assistance to the party regarding implementation of the Convention. It may also, with the agreement of the party concerned, make recommendations to it, request it to submit a strategy, including a time schedule to achieve compliance, and make recommendations regarding specific measures to address matters raised by a member of the public.[57] The additional responses available to the Meeting of the Parties are to issue declarations of non-compliance; to issue cautions; to suspend the rights and privileges of the party under the Convention (in accordance with rules of treaty law); and to take other appropriate non-confrontational, non-judicial, and consultative measures.[58]

Unsurprisingly, given that it can receive communications from the public, the Compliance Committee of the Aarhus Convention has been one of the busiest such committees. By 2009, it had received 41 communications from the public, relating to complaints against 21 different parties to the Convention. It has also received one submission by a party regarding another party's compliance with its obligations.[59]

Evaluation

The three examples outlined in this Chapter demonstrate that compliance procedures vary greatly in their mandate, design, and functioning. While the Montreal Protocol procedure may be regarded as a 'prototype', there have been significant developments tailored to specific treaty regimes. It is unusual to find, as in the Aarhus Convention, that parties to a multilateral environmental

---

[56] Decision I/7, para 25.
[57] Ibid, para 37(a)–(d).   [58] Ibid, para 37(e)–(h).
[59] From Romania concerning compliance by Ukraine (2005).

agreement will agree to the submission of complaints directly by members of the public, for example. Similarly, the Kyoto Protocol enforcement branch may impose much harder consequences than those likely to be acceptable or available under other compliance procedures. Neither development then may necessarily be taken to indicate that compliance mechanisms established in the future, or under negotiation now, will adopt similar innovations. Differences still arise among parties to the multilateral environmental agreements as to the most basic elements of the compliance procedure: who should be entitled to trigger the mechanism, who should participate in it, and what consequences are appropriate to a finding of non-compliance? A number of non-compliance procedures remain under negotiation, and in others that have been established some basic decision-making rules remain controversial.[60] Nonetheless, the compliance procedures offer a valuable alternative to more conventional dispute resolution procedures in the context of MEAs.

REFERENCE

SELECT BIBLIOGRAPHY

T Treves et al (eds), *Non-Compliance Procedures and Mechanisms and the Effectiveness of International Environmental Agreements* (2009).

J Klabbers, 'Compliance Procedures' in D Bodansky, J Brunnée, and E Hey (eds), *Oxford Handbook of International Environmental Law* (2007) 996–1009.

United Nations Environment Programme, *Compliance Mechanisms under Selected Multilateral Environmental Agreements* (2007).

U Beyerlin, P-T Stoll, and R Wolfrum (eds), *Ensuring Compliance with Multilateral Environmental Agreements* (2006).

X Wang and G Wiser, 'The Implementation and Compliance Regimes under the Climate Change Convention and its Kyoto Protocol' (2002) 11 *Review of European Community and International Environmental Law* 181.

M Fitzmaurice and C Redgwell, 'Environmental Non-compliance Procedures and International Law' (2000) 31 *Netherlands Yearbook of International Law* 35.

M Koskenniemi, 'Breach of Treaty or Non-Compliance? Reflections on the Enforcement of the Montreal Protocol' (1992) 3 *Yearbook of International Environmental Law* 123.

---

[60] For example, in the procedures and mechanisms on compliance adopted under the 2000 Cartagena Protocol on Biosafety, parties to that agreement have been unable to agree if the rules of procedure of the Compliance Committee should enable it to take decisions by majority vote if there is no consensus. Decision BS-II/1, Rules of Procedure for meetings of the Compliance Committee, UNEP/CBD/BS/COP-MOP/2/15, 6 June 2005, Annex I.

Index

References in this index are to paragraph numbers, except where the text is not so divided, when they are to page numbers.

Index

Printed and bound by CPI Group (UK) Ltd, Croydon, CR0 4YY